THE SEPHARDIC JOURNEY: 1492–1992

THE SEPHARDIC JOURNEY
1492-1992

YESHIVA UNIVERSITY MUSEUM

NEW YORK 5752

This catalogue accompanies the Yeshiva University Museum
exhibition *The Sephardic Journey: 1492–1992*, November 13,
1990–December 31, 1992. Both the exhibition and the
catalogue commemorate the Quincentenary of the Expulsion
of the Jews from Spain and Columbus' arrival in America.

This catalogue contains sacred texts and should be handled with
appropriate respect.

LIBRARY OF CONGRESS CATALOGING-IN-PUBLICATION DATA

The Sephardic Journey, 1492–1992.
    p.   cm.
Includes bibliographical references and index.
ISBN 0–945447–04–3 (alk. paper)
ISBN 0–945447–03–5 (pbk.: alk. paper)
  1. Sephardim — Exhibitions.   2. Judaism — Liturgical objects —
Exhibitions.   3. Jews — Spain — Exhibitions.   4. Spain — Ethnic
relations — Exhibitions. I. Yeshiva University. Museum.
DS134.S38 1992   92–9948
909'.04924 — dc20   CIP

International Religious and Educational Advisor
Haham Solomon Gaon

Director of Exhibition   *Sylvia A. Herskowitz*

Guest Curators

History	Dr. Marc Angel
Manuscripts and Printed Books	Dr. Shalom Sabar
Ceremonial Objects	Chaya Benjamin

Museum Curatorial Staff

Assistant Curators	Gabriel M. Goldstein
	Bonni-Dara Michaels
Registrar	Ellin M. Burke
Research Volunteers	Vera Brodsky
	Haya Ettinger
	Jean Moldovan
Intern	Jodi Rubinstein

Museum Staff

Director	Sylvia A. Herskowitz
Administrator	Randi R. Glickberg
Executive Secretary	Eleanor M. Chiger
Secretaries	Eve Liss
	Judith Hoff
Contemporary Programs Coordinator	Susan Parkoff
Special Events Coordinator	June Aranoff
Education Curators	Jeannette Ornstein
	Robin Foreman
	Peggy Sunshine

Adjunct Exhibition Staff

Design	Robert Becker
Costume	June Bové
Appraisal	Aviva Jacobs Hoch
Object Mounts	Elizabeth McKean
Installation	Jeffrey Serwatien
	Hal Hirshorn
	Sibony Contracting Corp.
	J. Romeo Scenery Studio
Photography	Allen Rokach
Exhibit Assistant	Peggy Elliot

THIS CATALOGUE IS DEDICATED IN MEMORY OF
JACOB E. AND ESTHER SAFRA
BY THE SAFRA FAMILY

This volume was made possible through the generosity of
Ludwig and Erica Jesselson, the Safra family and Peter J. Cohn.
Additional funding was provided by the New York City
Department of Cultural Affairs, the Lucius N. Littauer
Foundation and the Jacob Burns Foundation.

CONTENTS

Map of the Sephardic Diaspora

Ceremonial *bindalli* dress and chemise, Ottoman empire, 19th century. Cat. no. 114; Veil, Ottoman empire, 19th–20th century. Cat. no. 121.

INTRODUCTION

In 1986 the Yeshiva University Museum inaugurated its first exhibition on the history of a discrete cultural group—*Ashkenaz: The German Jewish Heritage*. The spirited public response to this exhibition and its exhaustive catalogue emphasized the validity of our mission to educate the public in the cultural history of the Jewish people.

During the two years of the *Ashkenaz* exhibition, we were frequently asked when the Museum would organize a similar exhibition on the other major segment of world Jewry—Sepharad.

Three years ago, with 1992 looming in the distance, it seemed the time was right for such an ambitious project. World attention would soon focus on the Columbus Quincentenary, and American Jewry's attention, accordingly, would be drawn to the Expulsion from Spain and its consequences for the Iberian Jewish community, which, 1400 years after the Roman exile, found itself adrift again.

As in most exhibitions we produce, we knew we could count on the help of our colleagues on the University faculty. For the Sepharad project we had an added advantage—that of being able to consult, almost on a moment's notice, with a formidable triad of specialists, the scholars of the Sephardic Studies Department: Haham Dr. Solomon Gaon, Director of the Jacob E. Safra Institute of Sephardic Studies; Dr. Herbert Dobrinsky, Vice President for University Affairs; and Dr. Mitchell Serels, Director of Sephardic Communal Programs. These gentle men, whose learning, charm and graciousness guided us throughout the preparation of the exhibition, were the cicerones for our journey.

Additionally, we would also be able to draw on the students themselves—close to 300 Sephardic undergraduate and graduate students studying at the University, some of whom would provide us with personal links to collections, and others who would help us in translations, performances, and public programs.

Our next step was to assemble a curatorial team. We were fortunate to be able to enlist two world famous scholars from Israel—Chaya Benjamin, curator of the Steiglitz collection at the Israel Museum, and Dr. Shalom Sabar of Hebrew University. Despite the obvious hardships involved in leaving their families and delaying other professional commitments, both of them came to New York several times to research collections and work with our staff on planning and organizing the exhibition.

Even when they returned home, we were able to keep in touch with them on a daily, often hourly basis, thanks to our fax machine. Incidentally, this marvel of late 20th century technology provided us with an immediate link to each of the 10 countries from which we drew our exhibition: Holland, Yugoslavia, Greece, Spain, Bulgaria, Germany, Canada, England, Israel, and the United States, literally condensing months of effort into a few days of correspondence.

For the historical narrative of the exhibition, we asked Dr. Marc Angel, leader of the first Jewish congregation in North America, New York's Congregation Shearith Israel, The Spanish and Portuguese Synagogue. It was Dr. Angel who guided us in defining the term Sephardic to mean the descendants of those Jews expelled from the Iberian peninsula.

The exhibition opens with a few precious pre-Expulsion objects from Spain and Portugal and a 14 minute original video offering a concise history of Jewish settlement in Spain up to 1492. It then unfolds to reveal the five main areas of the Sephardic diaspora: Turkey and the Balkans, the Middle East, North Africa, Western Europe and the New World.

Each gallery in turn displays objects and environments from synagogue, home, and community: ceremonial pieces, costumes, illuminated manuscripts and documents, rare books, synagogue models, folk art and domestic items.

These historic articles, culled from numerous private and public collections, mirror the esthetic tastes, lifestyles and traditions of Iberian Jews and the communities to which they fled. In their collection, research and presentation, our staff members witnessed a not unfamiliar phenomenon: An exhibition in progress takes on a personality of its own. When the details are put in place, the spirit comes to rest.

Here we must acknowledge the work of our Museum curatorial staff: Bonni-Dara Michaels, Gabriel M. Goldstein and Ellin M. Burke. Their round-the-clock diligence, their love for the objects, and their painstaking precision, are evident in the quality of the exhibition and in this formidable catalogue — a gigantic labor of love for such a small team.

Finally, a word about Erica and Ludwig Jesselson, our patrons. It was Erica Jesselson, a staunch Ashkenazic Jew, who first urged us to undertake this exhibition, and who continued her loyal and unflagging support and enthusiasm through the preparation of this volume. Both the exhibition and this publication would not have been realized without their beneficence.

The Safra family deserve special recognition for their generosity in dedicating this book in memory of Jacob E. and Esther Safra.

Peter J. Cohn, a good friend of the Museum, contributed funds to enable us to complete publication. Our profound gratitude is extended to him for helping us produce a volume of quality.

The New York City Department of Cultural Affairs generously supported the development and implementation of the exhibition as well as the catalogue publication. Additional funding was provided by the Lucius N. Littauer Foundation and the Jacob Burns Foundation. We are grateful to the Maurice Amado Foundation for making possible the Museum's education and public programs related to *The Sephardic Journey* exhibition and the creation of the Sephardic Puppet Theatre for young audiences.

In acknowledging our appreciation to those who helped us with this exhibition, I find it appropriate to quote from the response of an eminent Sephardic rabbi of the 13th century, Rabbi Yonah of Gerona.

To the question posed in Ethics of The Fathers 2:1: "What is the upright path that a man should choose for himself? One that is an honor to him that does it and brings him honor from other men."

Rabbi Yonah comments that "Honor to him that does it" implies pride in the performance of a mitzvah. For example, if you are to don a tallit, choose a beautiful tallit; if you are to hold a lulav, pick an attractive lulav. In that way, the community will take pride in you.

It is our hope that this exhibition and catalogue not only help us fulfill our mission— to convey and interpret the Jewish experience—but do so in the most beautiful way possible.

SYLVIA AXELROD HERSKOWITZ
Director of the Exhibition

ACKNOWLEDGMENTS

In the preparation of this exhibition and catalogue, we were fortunate in being able to draw upon the talents and resources of the Yeshiva University family. We would like to express our thanks to the following departments and individuals: Yeshiva University Libraries: Dean Pearl Berger, Leah Adler, Zalman Alpert, Shulamith Berger, Zvi Erenyi, Haya Gordin, Rabbi Berish Mandelbaum, Marie Center and John Moryl; Graphic Arts: Sam Rockmaker, Judy Tucker, Pamela Weiman and Eileen Celli; Photography Services: Norman Goldberg, Mark Mellett and Roman Royzengurt; Publicity/Media Relations: Debra Rubin; Natural Science & Mathematics: Director of Laboratories Leonard Brandwein and technician William Muldro; and the members of the Security, Housekeeping and Maintenance divisions.

The design of the exhibition galleries and their environments are the inspired work of architect Robert Becker, a Museum board member, who abundantly contributes both his time and talent.

A host of professional colleagues generously extended their help whenver called upon. These include Dr. Shlomo Eidelberg, D. David Cohen, Dr. Judith Guedalia, Vicky Greenwald, Seth Haberman, Rachel Hasson, Dr. Sima Ingberman, Professor Israel Katz, Sharon Lieberman Mintz, Dr. Janice Ovadiah, Diane Saltzman, Ami Sibony and Rabbi Alberto Somekh.

Our erudite editorial consultant and author of the Chronology, Gertrude Hirschler, deserves a special word of gratitude. She edited the essays by Angel, Benjamin, Cohen-Sarano, Gaon and Sabar, and contributed significantly to the accuracy of the catalogue entries.

The introductory video for the exhibition was based on a script written by Ann Millman. Our thanks to her and to Ann and John Stapsky of Aerial Image for their excellent production.

This exhibition displays hundreds of fascinating and beautiful objects, for which we are greatly indebted to our many private and public lenders, listed on pages 16–17. Their enthusiastic participation was crucial to our success. Thanks are also due to the many communal leaders, private collectors and museum colleagues who provided assistance in locating and researching objects and in facilitating loan and shipping arrangements.

The Pre-Expulsion segment features a number of manuscript fragments recently unearthed in Spain. The loan of these pieces and their travel arrangements were facilitated by the Consul-General of Spain in New York City, Ambassador Miguel de Aldasoro; the Tourist Office of Spain: Francisco Giron and Pilar Vico; Iberia Airlines:

Alvaro Ureña; the Municipal Government of Gerona: Mayor Joaquin Nadal; the Tourist Office of Costa Brava Gerona: Joan Ferrer.

Young audiences were entertained by interpretive educational programs featuring puppets created by Virginia Conover and Marjorie Robbins.

We are grateful to Benjamin Bernard Zucker for sponsoring the lecture by Shalom Sabar and making possible Dr. Sabar's trip to New York. Additional research trips were made possible by a grant from the National Endowment for the Humanities.

Since the exhibition opened in November 1990, many thousands of visitors have seen it, and thousands of adults and children have participated in Sephardic workshops and programs. It is our hope that the serious contribution this exhibition and catalogue make to increasing public knowledge will become a landmark for the history of Sephardic Jewry in the Old World and the New.

SAH

Visitors admiring the majesty of Turkish cermonial objects.

LENDERS TO THE EXHIBITION

Mrs. Ita Aber, Yonkers, New York

Ms. Gloria Abrams, New York

Joseph and Devorah Alcabes, West Hempstead, New York

Sarah Alevy-Hirsch and Herbert Hirsch, Lakewood, New Jersey

Mr. and Mrs. Manfred Anson, Bergenfield, New Jersey

Ajuntament de Girona Arxiu Historic de la Ciutat (Civic Archives), Gerona, Spain

Arxiu capitular de Girona (Cathedral Archives), Gerona, Spain

Selma and Stanley I. Batkin, New Rochelle, New York

Dr. and Mrs. Raymond Behar, New Port Richey, Florida

Mr. Yossi Benyaminoff, Jerusalem, Israel

Mrs. Adina Bernstein, New York

Bibliotheca Rosenthaliana, Amsterdam, The Netherlands

Rev. and Mrs. Abraham Lopes Cardozo, New York

Cathedral of Seville, Seville, Spain

Mrs. Tulane Chartock, Cincinnati, Ohio

Civic Museum, Sarajevo, Yugoslavia

The Civil War Library and Museum, Philadelphia, Pennsylvania

Congregation Emanu-El, New York

Congregation K. K. Mikveh Israel, Philadelphia, Pennsylvania

Congregation Shearith Israel in the City of New York, The Spanish and Portuguese Synagogue

Mr. Derek J. Content, Houlton, Maine

Ernest and Maisie Corcos, Casablanca, Morocco

Mr. Yitzhak Einhorn, Tel Aviv, Israel

Mr. and Mrs. Max Eis, Oakland, California

Mrs. J. R. Elyachar, New York

Ets Haim Library/Livraria Montezinos of the Portugees Israëlietisch Seminarium Ets Haim, Amsterdam, The Netherlands

Prof. and Mrs. Solomon Feffer, New York

Mrs. Denise Gang, New York

Haham Dr. Solomon Gaon, New York

Mr. and Mrs. David Goldman, Fort Lee, New Jersey

Mr. and Mrs. William Gross, Tel Aviv, Israel

Mr. and Mrs. Abraham Halpern, New York

Mrs. Juliette Halioua, New York

Mrs. Linda Harary, New York

Hebrew Union College Library, Cincinnati, Ohio

Mrs. Sylvia A. Herskowitz, Yonkers, New York

Abigail Kursheedt Hoffman

Mrs. Esther Ben Oliel Ifrah, Buffalo, New York

The Israel Museum, Jerusalem, Israel

Mr. and Mrs. Ludwig Jesselson, New York

Mr. and Mrs. Michael Jesselson, New York

The Jewish Museum, New York

Jewish Historical Museum, Belgrade, Yugoslavia

Jewish Museum of Greece, Athens, Greece

Jewish National and University Library, Jerusalem, Israel

Jewish Religious Community of Sofia, Bulgaria

Judah L. Magnes Museum, Berkeley, California

Abraham J. and Deborah B. Karp, Riverdale, New York

Dr. Isak Kohenak, New York

Mr. and Mrs. Irving Kroopnick, New Haven, Connecticut

Rachel Rose Langnas, Rego Park, New York

Dr. and Mrs. Manfred R. Lehmann, Miami Beach, Florida

Mrs. Stella Levi, New York

Mr. William Loewy, Monsey, New York

Dr. and Mrs. Alfred Moldovan, New York

Museum of Jewish Heritage, New York

Jane Mushabac, New York

Bea Myones, Bayside, New York

Nahon Synagogue Restoration, New York

Florence Abravaya Newman and Joseph Newman, Massapequa, New York

Mrs. Coty Nussbaum, Kew Garden Hills, New York

Mona Hirsch Oppenheim

Rabbi Joshua Plaut, Weathersfield, Connecticut

Mr. and Mrs. Isaac Pollak, New York

Portuguees Israëlietische Gemeente, Amsterdam, The Netherlands

Mr. and Mrs. Peter Rava, St. Louis, Missouri

Mr. and Mrs. Norman Rosen, Cherry Hill, New Jersey

Cantor and Mrs. Jacob Rosenbaum, Monsey, New York

Mrs. Fortuna Calvo Roth, New York

Dr. Viviane A. Ryan and Tomás L. Ryan

Reuben and Helene Dennis Museum, Beth Tzedec Synagogue, Toronto, Canada

Santa Companhia de Dotar Orphas y Donzellas, Amsterdam, The Netherlands

Dr. Norman P. Schenker, Munich, Germany

Sephardic Reference Room, Safra Institute of Sephardic Studies, Yeshiva University, New York

Mr. and Mrs. Ivan Schick, New York

Rabbi and Mrs. Mitchell Serels, New Rochelle, New York

Mrs. Linda Shamah, Belle Harbor, New York

Mr. and Mrs. Ami Sibony, New York

Mr. and Mrs. Benjamin Simons, Delray Beach, Florida

Vida and Fred Simons, Jerusalem, Israel

Sir Isaac and Lady Edith Wolfson Museum, Hechal Shlomo, Jerusalem, Israel

Mrs. Regina Slovin, New York

Joan Sturhahn, Sarasota, Florida

Temple Judea Museum of Keneseth Israel, Elkins Park, Pennsylvania

Dr. and Mrs. Henry Toledano, New York

Mr. and Mrs. Victor H. Topper, Toronto, Canada

Mrs. Mathilde Turiel, New York

United States Museum of Natural History, Smithsonian Institution, Washington, D.C.

Dr. and Mrs. Carl Urbont, Larchmont, New York

Westchester Historical Society, Elmsford, New York

Mr. and Mrs. Benjamin Zucker, New York

THE SEPHARDIC JOURNEY
1492-1992

Costume and decorations of the *Haham Bashi* (Chief rabbi), Istanbul, ca. 1920. Cat. no. 66.

ASPECTS OF THE SEPHARDIC SPIRIT
Marc D. Angel

After centuries of material and spiritual flowering, the Jews of Spain and Portugal were driven into exile. The process began in 1391, when widespread anti-Jewish riots in Spain led to the death, forced conversion or flight of thousands of Jews and ended in the year 1492, when the Jews were expelled from Spain. In 1496/7 all manifestations of Jewish life were outlawed in Portugal as well. The expulsion of the Jews from the Iberian peninsula resulted in the growth of a far-flung, variegated Sephardic diaspora.

Large numbers of Sephardim found haven in the domains of the Ottoman empire. Others settled in Eretz Israel and elsewhere in the Middle East. North Africa also received an influx of Sephardic refugees. Thus, initially, the bulk of Sephardim came to live under Muslim rule.

Some Sephardic exiles sought safety in West European cities, especially in Italy, but conditions for Jews in Christian countries were generally not as good as they were in Muslim lands.

By the end of the sixteenth century, however, Amsterdam had become a center for ex-*conversos* who now wished to return to the Jewish fold. Greater tolerance toward Jews became manifest in Western Europe, resulting in the emergence of Sephardic communities in such cities as Bordeaux, Bayonne, Paris, Hamburg and London. During the seventeenth century some western Sephardim came to the New World and settled in the European colonies of the Americas.

Thus scattered in far-flung parts of the world, Sephardim were subjected to many diverse cultural, intellectual, linguistic and political influences. Over the centuries, the various Sephardic communities developed their own particular characteristics. The rich diversity among the Sephardim is well known to students of Sephardic history. But despite all this diversity, certain common threads can be seen in the tapestry of the Sephardic diaspora—or at least through large segments of Sephardic Jewry.

Halakhah

Sephardic communities were traditionally governed by the discipline of halakhah, the corpus of Jewish ceremonial and ethical law. The generations following the Expulsion from Spain and Portugal witnessed a veritable explosion of halakhic creativity in the Sephardic diaspora. This was the era of R. Yosef Caro (1488–1575), compiler of the *Shulhan Arukh*, the standard Code of Jewish Law; he was a native of Toledo who eventually settled in Eretz Israel, in the city of Safed. It also produced responsa masters such as R. David ben Solomon Ibn Abi Zimra (1479–1573), a native of Spain who became the official head of Egyptian Jewry, and R. Shemuel ben Moses de Medina of

Salonika (1506–1589). This period further saw the rise of authors and teachers such as R. Yaakov Berav (Berab) of Safed (c. 1474–1541), who was born in Toledo and later assumed roles of leadership in the Jewish communities of Eretz Israel, Egypt and Syria; R. Levi ben Habib (c. 1483–1545), a native of Zamora, Spain, who came to Jerusalem by way of Portugal and Salonika; and R. Yosef Taitatzak of Salonika (c. 1487/88–1545), the son of exiles from Spain.

Professor H. J. Zimmels has commented that it was "amazing that soon after the Expulsion in the year 1492 the contributions to the responsa literature by the rabbis who had come from Spain and settled in Turkey reached a height never witnessed before."[1]

Sephardic yeshivot followed the pattern of study developed in Spain, which emphasized practical halakhah. The goal was to arrive at proper halakhic conclusions rather than to engage in strictly abstract intellectual discussions of the texts.[2]

Halakhic creativity has continued to manifest itself throughout the Sephardic world to this day. Thousands of manuscripts and published works, covering every aspect of halakhic literature, amply demonstrate commitment to Torah scholarship on the highest level.

Rabbi Hayyim Yosef David Azulai (HIDA; 1724–1806), one of the great figures of eighteenth-century Jewish life, noted that in matters of halakhah, Sephardim inclined to the quality of *hessed*, compassion; they tended to be lenient as opposed to Ashkenazim who stressed *gevurah*, strength, and therefore tended to greater strictness in the interpretation of the Law.[3] Regardless of whether this view corresponds to objective fact, it does reflect the self-image of many Sephardic sages and has therefore influenced their approach to halakhah.

In describing the religious life of the Jews of North Africa, André Chouraqui, a native of Algeria who settled in Israel, noted that "the Judaism of the most conservative of the Maghreb's Jews was marked by a flexibility, a hospitality, a tolerance," a "touching generosity of spirit and a profound respect for meditation."[4] Rabbi Michael Molho, in his study of the Jews of Salonika, remarked that the members of that community generally eschewed extremism and were characterized by optimism, tolerance, graciousness and hospitality.[5] While both these descriptions may be somewhat romanticized, they do reflect the general sense of religious life among Sephardim.

A word should be said about the role of the rabbinate among Sephardim. Since halakhah was so central to Sephardim, rabbinical scholars were of paramount importance as teachers of halakhah. However, they were expected not only to be experts on halakhah but also saintly as human beings. They were prized and revered not only for their intellectual acumen but also for their spiritual qualities.[6] The members of the community looked to the rabbi not only for halakhic rulings but also for personal guidance and counseling.

It was the practice of many Sephardic communities to appoint a chief rabbi. His responsibilities included serving as the ultimate halakhic authority for the community, teaching Torah to advanced students as well as to the community at large, initiating or approving communal ordinances and acting as head of the rabbinical court (*bet din*). Sometimes the chief rabbi served as the Jewish community's spokesman before the government.

Kabbalah

The expulsion of the Jews from the Iberian peninsula was followed by a remarkable flowering of Kabbalah. Sixteenth-century Safed became the hub of the kabbalist world. It was home to such figures as R. Yosef Caro; R. Isaac ben Shelomo Luria (ARI; 1534–1572), the founder of practical Kabbalah; R. Moshe ben Hayyim Alshekh (1507– c. 1600); R. Moshe ben Yaakov Cordovero (1522–1570) and R. Shelomo ben Moshe Alkabetz (c. 1505–1584), the composer of the hymn *Lekha Dodi* ("Come, My Beloved"), with which Jews the world over welcome the Sabbath. The teachings of these personages and other kabbalists inspired Jewish spiritual life for generations to come.

Rabbi Yosef Garson, writing in Salonika shortly after the Expulsion, articulated the position that both the Talmud and the Kabbalah were basic elements in Jewish education.[7] Garson, who himself had studied at yeshivot in Castile, was apparently reflecting an attitude widely held in the Sephardic world. Most rabbinic scholars among the Sephardim were well-versed in kabbalist lore. The Sephardic masses also valued kabbalist ideas and texts.

R. Hayyim Yosef David Azulai strongly encouraged the reading of the Zohar, the basic work of Kabbalah, even by people who did not understand the sublime implications of the text. He wrote: "The study of the Zohar is above any other study, even if one does not understand what it says, and even if he errs in his reading. It is a great corrective for the soul."[8] Even a reader who cannot grasp the Zohar's teachings intellectually will find himself engaged emotionally in a profound religious experience.

The stress on Kabbalah was, in a certain sense, a counterpoise to halakhic erudition. Total devotion of intellectual energies to the details of the Law might produce narrow legalists. The study of Kabbalah was seen as a means of expanding one's intellectual horizon, of developing the poetic, mystical and spiritual aspects of one's personality.

Professor Joseph Dan has observed that the study of Kabbalah and halakhah led to the emergence of "kabbalistic ethics." He noted that ethics in Lurianic Kabbalah was not an attempt at achieving personal perfection alone. "It is a set of instructions directing the individual how to participate in the common struggle of the Jewish people."[9] Kabbalah infused halakhah with special meaning; it created new rituals and enhanced old ones. By observing halakhah with the proper kabbalist *kavvanah* (intention), one helped to purify the world and make it holy. The performance of *mitzvot* (religious acts) was not merely a personal obligation; every Jew was duty bound to help other Jews observe the *mitzvot* themselves. Each Jew was spiritually responsible for every other Jew.

Sephardic Pietists

A number of kabbalists wrote lists of pious practices to which a person should accustom himself.[10] Thus, the disciples of R. Isaac ben Shelomo Luria compiled a book of practices observed by their illustrious master. Among the influential books of kabbalist ethics were *Sefer Haredim* (Book of the Pious; Venice, 1601) by R. Eleazar ben Moshe Azikri of Safed (1533–1600), and *Reshit Hokhmah* (Beginning of Wisdom; completed 1575) by R. Eliyahu ben Moshe de Vidas.

Sephardic Jewry produced outstanding individuals who were steeped in both halakhah and Kabbalah. If the sixteenth century was a golden age for *musar* (works of moral guidance), so was the eighteenth century. Among the profound spiritual teachers in Morocco were R. Hayyim ben Moshe Benattar (Attar; 1696–1743), who later settled in Eretz Israel, and R. Raphael Berdugo (1747–1821). From Eretz Israel came R. Hayyim Yosef David Azulai and R. Moshe Hagiz (1672–c. 1751), a noted opponent of the Shabbetai Zvi movement. In Turkey, Rabbi Eliyahu HaKohen Ittamari wrote the classic *Shevet Musar* (Staff of Ethics; 1712). In Italy, R. Moshe Hayyim Luzatto (1707–1746) produced a number of *musar* works, including *Mesillat Yesharim* (The Path of the Upright), probably the most influential *musar* volume of the past two centuries. R. Eliezer Papo of Sarajevo, whose activity spanned the first quarter of the nineteenth century, also produced highly important ethical works, the most significant being his *Pele Yoetz* (Wondrous Counselor).[11]

The *musar* writers stressed the need for the individual to serve God selflessly and to deal compassionately and honestly with his fellow men. They emphasized that this world was only a temporary dwelling place; the world to come was of far greater significance. One had to live righteously in this world in order to be blessed in the world to come. *Musar* teachers also provided advice on ways in which a person could improve himself. Some of these suggestions included keeping a spiritual diary and regularly reviewing one's thoughts and actions; spending time alone in quiet meditation; discussing one's thoughts and deeds with trusted friends who could offer criticism and advice for correction. In short, the *musarists* sought to inspire their readers and disciples to strive constantly for self-perfection.

Other Literary Genres

The Sephardic world was blessed with gifted individuals who expressed themselves in various literary genres. During the generation following the Expulsion, philosophy still enjoyed popularity among some individuals. R. Yehuda Abrabanel (also called Leone Ebreo or Leo Hebraeus; c. 1460–after 1523), a philosopher, physician and poet who was born in Lisbon and settled in Italy, wrote, in Italian, *Dialoghi di Amore* (Dialogues of Love; Rome, 1535), a significant neo-Platonic work. Another physician-philosopher, R. Abraham Ibn Migash of Turkey (first half of sixteenth century) wrote: "One must know that the ultimate human achievement is attained in the most honorable human power—the power of reason."[12] He was an avid proponent of philosophical inquiry.

True, within one generation, Kabbalah had certainly eclipsed philosophy in most of the Sephardic world. But following the Shabbetai Zvi debacle in the latter part of the seventeenth century, western Sephardim tended to turn away from Kabbalah and to become increasingly interested in philosophy once more.

Religious Texts and Apologetics

Conversos who returned to Judaism during the sixteenth and seventeenth centuries needed religious instruction. A variety of books was published in the vernacular to explain the principal teachings and practices of Judaism. Rabbi Menasseh ben Israel of Amsterdam played a leading role in the writing and publication of such works. Among the major works written to convince the former converts of the Divine origin of the Oral Law were *Nomalogia* by R. Immanuel Aboab of Venice (c. 1555–1628) and *Matteh Dan* by Haham David Nieto (1654–1728).

Professor Yosef Hayyim Yerushalmi has noted that it was the ex-*conversos* who wrote books refuting Christian arguments against Judaism. A classic example of this genre was *Las Excelencias y calumnias de los Hebreos* (The Excellencies and Calumnies of the Hebrews; Amsterdam, 1679) by the physician, scientist and philosopher Isaac Cardoso (1604–1681), in which the author discusses ten virtues of the Jews and refutes ten common anti-Jewish calumnies.[13] Jewish apologetic literature was important not only as a defense against Christian antagonists but also as a means of strengthening the Jewish faith among the *conversos* who were just returning to Judaism. Since they had been raised and educated as Christians, they had to be taught the Jewish answers to Christian arguments against the Jewish religion.

A word should be said about the continued creativity of Sephardim in poetry, both in Hebrew and in the vernacular. Sephardic authors composed a considerable body of *piyyutim*, liturgical poems for various religious occasions.

Rabbinic scholarship flourished in the Sephardic world; Sephardic sages have produced significant Rabbinic works—Talmudic commentaries, halakhic treatises, sermons, Biblical commentaries, ethical literature, etc.—down to our own day.

During the nineteenth and twentieth centuries, various Sephardic authors confronted the challenges of modernity. In Italy, R. Eliyahu ben Abraham Benamozegh (1822–1900) wrote books demonstrating the ethical greatness of Judaism and its universal message to mankind. In London, Grace Aguilar (1816–1847) produced several works interpreting the teachings of Judaism for enlightened Jews. She was particularly anxious that suitable Jewish publications should be available for Jewish youth, especially girls and young women. R. Yehuda Shelomo Hai Alkalai of Sarajevo (1798–1878), a prolific author and lecturer, called on the Jewish people to return to the Land of Israel; the Messianic redemption, he asserted, must be preceded by the resettlement of the Jews in their homeland. Alkalai was a forerunner of modern Zionism; his writings reflect a spirit of Jewish activism and nationalism far ahead of his time.

The Judeo-Spanish Tradition

Judeo-Spanish was the mother tongue of most of the Sephardim living in Turkey, the Balkan countries, Eretz Israel and the north of Morocco. Much of the earlier literature in Ladino (the literary form of Judeo-Spanish) consisted of translations of Jewish classics from the Hebrew. However, original works were also produced in Ladino for the benefit of the Jewish masses who were not well-versed in Hebrew.

The major work in Ladino was unquestionably *Me'am Lo'ez*, and encyclopedic project originated by R. Yaakov Huli (c. 1689–1732). *Me'am Lo'ez* was conceived in the form of a commentary on the Bible; however, it also included halakhah, midrash and ethical guidance, and teachings from many Rabbinic sources. The author wrote in a lucid style, with stories and parables, so much so that he became concerned lest people would read *Me'am Lo'ez* purely for enjoyment rather than for uplift.

The first volume of the series appeared in Istanbul in 1730. R. Huli completed the section on Genesis and much of Exodus. After his untimely death, other authors continued the work along the lines of his approach. Ultimately, volumes were published on each of the Five Books of Moses, some of the Prophets, and the Book of Esther. *Me'am Lo'ez* was received enthusiastically and was printed in many editions.*

Among the recurrent themes in *Me'am Lo'ez* are respect for the common man, humility and other virtues, the value of Torah study, and the need for sincere, genuine piety.[14] The work reflects a blend of intellectual and folk wisdom and had a significant impact on the religious lives of many thousands of Sephardim.

During the nineteenth century the Sephardic world witnessed the emergence of a dynamic, modern Judeo-Spanish literature that was primarily secular. From the middle of the nineteenth century, over 300 Judeo-Spanish newspapers were published throughout the Sephardic diaspora. These publications not only provided news but also featured editorials, opinion essays, poetry, satire and humor. They were an important communications medium among the Sephardic communities and attracted contributions from leading intellectuals.

During that same period there was a burgeoning interest in Judeo-Spanish drama. Hundreds of plays were written and produced in that language, while many others were

---

*This work has been translated into English in part by the late R. Aryeh Kaplan, under the title *The Torah Anthology: Me'am Lo'ez* (New York and Jerusalem, 1977).

translated into Judeo-Spanish from other languages, mainly French. This era also saw the creation of novels and short stories in Judeo-Spanish.[15]

Along with this remarkable burst of creativity in Judeo-Spanish, there was also a renewed interest in collecting traditional Judeo-Spanish folklore—proverbs, ballads and stories. Scholars such as Abraham Galanté (1873–1961) and Mair José Benardete (c. 1895–1990) should be mentioned in this connection.

The Judeo-Spanish folk traditions were rich in references to love and other human emotions. Sephardim tended to view life in a "holistic" fashion, not drawing a sharp demarcation between religion and other aspects of life. Sephardic folk tradition reflects a generally optimistic spirit.

Customs and Values

A brief outline of some Sephardic customs will help show ideals and values typical of Sephardim.[16]

A fairly widespread custom among Sephardim has been to name children after grandparents even when the grandparents are still living. The normal pattern is for the first son and daughter to be named after the father's father and mother, and the second son and daughter to be given the names of the mother's parents. Subsequent children are named for other relatives, alternating from the father's to the mother's side of the family.

The observance of this custom reflects a number of significant concepts. First, it stresses the respect that children owe their parents. It reinforces the sense of family solidarity, of the living ties that unite the generations. It allows grandparents the joy of seeing themselves and their traditions projected into the next generation and at the same time gives the grandchildren living role models in the people after whom they are named.

Some of these values are manifested also in other Sephardic customs. Younger relatives rise when an older relative receives an *aliyah* to the Torah. Thus, when a man is called to the Torah, his younger relatives all rise in respect and remain standing until their elder's Torah portion has been read and he has recited the closing blessing.

This practice underscores the value placed upon respect for the elders of one's famliy. It ties the whole family together in a bond of unity. When one man is given an *aliyah* in the synagogue, it is not just an honor for him; his entire family shares in the distinction.

Sephardic synagogue customs reflect Sephardic attitudes toward public worship. For example, most of the synagogue service is chanted aloud by the *hazzan* as the congregation chants along. Though the *hazzan* is expected to have a pleasant voice, he is not supposed to be a "performer." His responsibility is to lead the community in prayer; very rarely does he have an opportunity to sing an "aria" on his own. Both the *hazzan* and the rabbi are expected to be expert readers of the Torah. Since reading from the

Torah is such a signal honor and responsibility, this function is generally assigned either to the rabbi or to the *hazzan* rather than to laymen.

In general, Sephardim placed a high value on esthetics. They enjoyed beautiful things—tapestries, needlework and jewelry. Even the simplest and poorest Sephardic homes were not without things of beauty.

Sephardic cooking was characterized not just by tasty foods but by the manner in which these foods were served. Sephardic women were concerned that the foods they prepared not only tasted good but also looked good. They were sensitive to shapes, colors and fragrances.

Sephardic society had its own customs which demonstrated concern for grace, good manners and consideration for others. Women would meet from time to time for *visitas* or social gatherings. The hostess would, of course, prepare special baked goods herself and serve them on her best china. The guests would dress as though they were going to meet a very important person. It was considered an honor to invite guests and just as great an honor to be invited. Thus, even a relatively simple event such as a get-together for coffee and cake assumed great social significance.

Another important custom related to the home observance of the anniversary of the death of a loved one. Known as *meldado* ("reading"), this observance normally took place at the home of a close relative of the deceased. Family members and friends would gather for prayer services in the evening. The rabbi would give a brief learned discourse. Those in attendance would read sections from the Mishnah that began with the letters in the name of the person whose death anniversary was being commemorated.

Following the prayers and studying, the guests would be served a light collation prepared by the hostess. This would generally include hard-boiled eggs, Greek olives, raisins, fried fish, home-baked sweet rolls and other baked goods. Raki and whiskey would also be offered. The evening thus became a social gathering, an occasion for family and friends to come together, to remember the past and to renew family ties.

Five hundred years after their expulsion from the Iberian peninsula, Sephardim still constitute a vital, creative part of the Jewish people. The largest concentration of Sephardim is now in the State of Israel, with other important communities in France, the United States, Canada, England, South America and elsewhere. Traditional patterns of Sephardic life are undergoing transformations; Sephardic culture in another 50 years will be considerably different from the cultural patterns which were dominant through the early twentieth century. Yet, there is little doubt that the Sephardic spirit will continue to have a profound influence on Jewish life for generations to come.

1. Hirsch Jakob Zimmels, "The Contributions of the Sephardim to the Responsa Literature Till the Beginning of the 16th Century," *The Sephardi Heritage*, ed. Richard Barnett, New York, 1971, p. 394.

2. Yitzhak Confanton, *Darkhei haTalmud*, Jerusalem, 5741 (1980/81). See also Hayyim Bentov, "Shitat Limud haTalmud bi-Yeshivot Saloniki ve-Turkiyah," *Sefunot*, 13, 5731 (1970/71), pp. 5–102.

3. Meir Benayahu, *Rabbi H.Y.D. Azulai* (Hebrew), Jerusalem, 1959, p. 165.

4. André Chouraqui, *Between East and West*, Philadelphia, 1968, p. 63.

5. Michael Molho, *Usos y costumbes de los Sephardies de Salonica*, Madrid, 1950, p. 155.

6. Marc D. Angel, *The Rhythms of Jewish Living: A Sephardic Approach*, New York, 1986, pp. 79–85.

7. Yosef Hacker, "Lidmutam haRuhanit shel Yehudei Sefarad be-Sof ha-Meah heHamesh Esrei," *Sefunot*, 17, 5743 (1982/83), pp. 47 f.

8. Hayyim Yosef David Azulai, *Avodat haKodesh*, Warsaw, 1879, p. 6.

9. Joseph Dan, *Jewish Mysticism and Jewish Ethics*, Seattle, 1986, pp. 100–01.

10. See Solomon Schechter, "Safed in the 16th Century," *Studies in Judaism*, Second Series, Philadelphia, 1908, pp. 292 f.

11. See Marc D. Angel, *Voices in Exile: A Study in Sephardic Intellectual History*, Hoboken, 1991, chapter 8.

12. Abraham Ibn Migash, *Kevod Elohim*, Jerusalem, 5737 (1976/77), p. 51b.

13. For a biography of Cardoso see Yosef Hayyim Yerushalmi, *From Spanish Court to Italian Ghetto: Isaac Cardoso, a Study in Seventeenth Century Marranism and Jewish Apologetics*, New York and London, 1971.

14. Marc D. Angel, *Voices in Exile*, chapter 7.

15. Ibid., chapter 11.

16. For a listing of customs of various Sephardic groups, see Herbert C. Dobrinsky, *A Treasury of Sephardic Laws and Customs*, Hoboken, 1988.

THE JEWS IN SPAIN: FROM THEIR ORIGINS TO THEIR EXPULSION IN 1492

Haim Beinart

The Early Years

A fundamental characteristic of Sephardic, or more accurately, Hispano-Portuguese Jewry, is the length of its settlement in one territory, the Iberian peninsula. It was an organic growth of expansion, which started, to the best of our knowledge, approximately around the first century of our modern counting, before or shortly after the destruction of the Second Temple. The beginnings were modest in some coastal settlements, like Tarragona and Tortosa, followed by a penetration inland and ending with settlement in hundreds of cities, towns, and villages all over the peninsula. All this came to an abrupt end in the united kingdoms of Castile and Aragón in 1492, and in Portugal in 1497, through the expulsion of the Jews from Spain and the forced mass conversion of 1497 in Portugal. But neither the Expulsion of 1492, nor the conversion of 1497, brought an end to the creative powers and vitality of this Jewry, either in the Iberian Peninsula, or outside it. We shall try here to describe some of the cornerstones on which this Jewry based its life and creative activity, how they were influenced by, and how they influenced in turn, their Christian neighbors, despite living in periods of strife with them or at times enjoying full harmony with their surroundings.

Let us ask: How can we characterize fifteen centuries of Jewish life in one place? It should be borne in mind that the first Jewish settlers in Iberia, or Hesperia, came from the Holy Land, whether directly or via Rome. They brought with them a Palestinian tradition which was their heritage during the late Roman period. This tradition was later reinforced and drew its sustenance from the Jewish national center in Babylonia as long as it flourished.

It is from those days that we possess a Jewish ossuary from Tarragona with a trilingual inscription of which the Hebrew inscription is: "Peace be upon Israel and upon us and our children, Amen."—a unique remains and inscription outside Eretz Israel. Another trilingual tombstone inscription, this one in Tortosa, tells us of a deceased girl named Meliosa, the daughter of Rabbi Yehuda, while in Elche, a mosaic inscription in Greek in a synagogue mentions an "Archisynagogus." These inscriptions are only a fragment of the material remains from the eastern coast of the peninsula, and this enables us to see how communities were founded at the end of the world of those days.[1] So does the blessing expressed in the Tractate Yevamot (63a): "All the nations of the world, even the ships that go from Gaul to Spain are blessed only for the sake of Israel." If this is not sufficient to indicate their way of life, we may learn about it from the deliberations of the Church Synod, held at the beginning of the fourth century at Elvira (Illiberis), near Granada. This Synod was very concerned about the Jewish influence on maintaining relations between Jews and Christian women; clause 49 of the Synod's decisions forbids Jews to bless the fields of Christians; a Christian who would permit this was liable to the penalty of excommunication. A Jewish farmer's blessing (and no doubt a Jewish blessing) of a field, cultivated by a Christian, was considered highly, perhaps not only because of the power of the blessing but as well for some advice given to the farmer. Another clause (No. 50) forbade Christians and their priests from partaking in meals with Jews. Another ban put a barrier preventing Jews and Christians from communicating socially. Let us remember that these restrictions were to serve as an indication of days to come.[2]

The Visigothic Period

The Visigoths ruled in Spain for about 300 years (412–711), but persecutions started when King Reccared left his Arian creed and converted to Catholicism (586). Three years after that the first anti-Jewish laws were issued. Church and State united from then on in forging an anti-Jewish policy, which became more severe from one Church Synod to the other. In 613, Sisebut, in full compliance with the Church Synod, decreed that Jews of his kingdom should either accept Christianity or leave. Many Jews crossed the Straits of Gibraltar to North Africa, and those who stayed behind formed the first *converso* community in Spain. Another Synod, the Fourth, held in Toledo in 633 under the reign of Sisenand, proclaimed a new series of restrictions, the most important of which was that those "who are from the Jews" (*hii qui ex Iudaeis sunt*), thus meaning the *conversos* and their descendants, were forbidden to hold any public office which might contain some jurisdiction over Christians of pure Christian origin. This was an expression of mistrust and a measure to prevent Jews from entering public life, even though we do not know to what extent Jews held public office at all.[3] The importance of this order is for later days when it became a bone of contention: in the fifteenth century it was publicly debated whether *conversos* should hold public office in Christian society at all. In short, Catholic Spain under the Visigoths is one long period of persecution, where it may have seemed unlikely that any Jewish creativity could have taken place. The last 200 years under Visigothic rule were years of terror and extreme persecution. Jews faced three choices: expulsion, conversion, or death. Their children were converted by force and given to Christian families to receive a Christian education. Christians saw in this deeds to be exalted. It was a period in which the State complied with the Church in the idea of founding a purely Christian state and society, in which there would be no place for Jews at all.

The Visigothic state came to an abrupt end with the Arab invasion of 711, when the whole peninsula fell into the hands of the invader like a ripe fruit. Fifteenth century Spanish historiography accused Jews of having abetted the invader, although we are in doubt as to whether the Jews were those who invited Mussa and Tarik to cross the straits and invade Spain.

As we shall learn later on, the Visigothic lesson did not serve Christian society when it tried again to forge a Christian state of one faith and one nationality.

We can use here Montesquieu's words (Esprit de Louis XXVIII:1) on the totalitarian Visigothic state, to say that such a regime could doubtless expect a persecuted population to oppose an invader and conqueror who had hope to offer and an end to persecution.

Christian Nuclei in the North

The Muslim invasion created new conditions for reestablishing Jewish life in the Iberian peninsula. But we lack any essential knowledge about the emigrational trends to Andalusia of those days. Nevertheless we do find remaining Jews in Northern Spain in the Christian pockets, which started to consolidate themselves, and in the Marca Hispanica, established by Charlemagne on the slopes of the Pyrenées, as a barrier to Muslim expansion. Documents of that period show that Jews were owners of arable land and vineyards, which they bought and sold, acquired by lease for themselves, or rented to others. We learn that the land was held in absolute ownership (*allodium*) or on lease, and that they worked on their land. Plots of land were exchanged with Church bodies, convents and churches, bishops and vicars of parishes; sometimes deeds were drawn up in Hebrew by the Jewish buyer or seller.[4] It was in many ways a peacefully conducted, neighborly life. We can already point out here that in many cases a Jewish oath given in Hebrew, or a deed signed in Hebrew, would be accepted by the Christian authorities up to the time of the Expulsion.

Although we do not know how Jews came to acquire land, we know for certain how their life was involved in that of their surroundings. Already at an early date Jews were among the pioneer settlers of Christian Spain, through its *reconquista*; and by virtue of this they were granted land in full ownership. This was their primary source of livelihood, though in the Muslim part of Spain, Jews were rapidly excluded from holding land through prohibitive taxation, and they increasingly became city dwellers.

Under Muslim Rule

A great upsurge in Jewish life occurred in tenth-century Al-Andalus of the days of Abd-a-Rahman III (912–961) and his son Hakam II (961–976).[5] Córdoba (c. 500,000 inhabitants) became a center of learning and of Jewish life under the leadership of R. Hasdai Ibn Shaprut (915–970), a famous physician and a man of learning; a diplomat who negotiated with a Byzantine mission which arrived in Al-Andalus, and with another mission headed by the abbot Johannes of Goerz (Gorizia) in 953, sent by Emperor Otto I. Ibn Shaprût cured Sancho, King of Navarre, of his obesity, and as an honor received ten fortresses for his ruler. He was deeply concerned about the fate of his brethren in Byzantium, intervening with Helene, daughter of Romanos I Lekapenos (919–944), on behalf of a Jewish community in southern Italy. R. Hasdai is to be seen as one of those Jewish *nesiim* or world leaders who bore the responsibility to lead world Jewry of his day. At his court in Córdoba gathered Jewish scholars who, under his guidance, undertook to work for a revival of Hebrew and Jewish learning. In his court the pulse of Jewish life in Andalusia was felt, and as *nasi* he wrote to Yosef, King of the Khazars, expressing his readiness to go through mountain and valley in order to visit this Jewish kingdom in whose revival he saw a sign of the advent of the Messiah.

R. Hisdai was the first Court Jew in Muslim Spain. Another great personality (in the eleventh century) was R. Shmuel ha-Naguid, poet, scholar, and statesman, who rose from humble origins to be the Vizier of the Emir of Granada. A personality who considered himself a tool in the hands of Providence, sent by God to fight for his people. Persecution of neighboring emirates, such as Almería and Seville, and of the Jews living there, was a casus belli for the emir of Granada, himself at the head of the army, leading it in battle to rescue his brethren. Those were great days of Jewish pride, of flourishing yeshivot and centers of learning like Alisana (Lucena of today), and not for nothing was Granada called by the population "Granata-al-Yahud." Another center of Jewish learning and scholarship was Saragossa of Abu Isaac (Yekutiel ben Isaac), Ibn Hassan, the Jewish counselor of Mundir II, the last of the Tujjib Dynasty. R. Yekutiel was a man of great learning versed both in Jewish and general studies. But his fate—he was decapitated in 1039—may indicate the fate of many court Jews in Christian Spain as well.[6] In places like these the cornerstone of Hebrew studies was laid and there it flourished, as Shelomo Ibn Gabirol wrote: "Know then that the Hebrew language is superior to that of all nations." And see further on.

Perhaps it would be most appropriate to sum up with a few lines of poetry by the same author, lines of hope for a people in the grips between Edom and Ismael, the one depicted as a Lion, the other a Crocodile trying to devour it:

> Root of our savior,
> The scion of Jesse,
> Till when wilt thou linger,
> Invisible, buried?
> Bring forth a flower,
> For winter is over!
>
> Why should a slave rule
> The lineage of princes,
> A hairy barbarian
> Replace our young sov'ran?
>
> The years are a thousand
> Since, broken and scattered,
> We wander in exile,

Like waterfowl lost in
The depths of the desert.

No man in white linen
Reveals at our asking
The end of our Exile.
God sealed up the matter,
And closed up the knowledge.*

That period was also one of Jewish settlement in the Christian North, where the transfer of the remains of St. James to Compostela opened a pilgrimage route and new settlements were founded there. Jews formed part of these settlements and there they were granted privileges from the ruler. Mention should be made here of the type of privileges granted: for killing or injuring a Jew a ransom (caloña) was to be paid to the local count (comes), who represented the king. In some instances, the sum was the same as the ransom for killing a knight (infanzon) or a priest, whereas the inhabitants in some places (like Castrojeriz) tried to lower it to that for a Christian farmer (villanus). Each district had its rights and privileges, but we must point out here that the Jewish population had a means for its defense granted by the King in a society whose customs and criteria of public welfare should not be judged by modern standards. Another privilege worth mentioning is that of Navarre, where the ruler, in cases of dispute between Jews and Christians, obliged himself to name a *bastonarius*, or champion, to fight on behalf of the Jews and thus settle the difference between the parties in strife.[7]

The Christian Reconquest (Reconquista)

The second half of the eleventh century, especially the reign of Alfonso VI, was a period of great impetus to Jewish settlement in the Reconquista regions of Northern Spain, which continued later in the United Kingdoms of Aragón and Cataluña in the twelfth century.

Toledo was conquered by Alfonso VI in 1085. The Jews of Toledo remained in their quarter in the southwestern corner of the town, where the Jewish fortress stood. In general it was customary in Christian Spain for Jews to have a wing in the fortress of the developing town. The conquest of Toledo encouraged Jews to settle in it, and it soon became the foremost settlement of Jewish Spain. A great Jewish personality was then in the service of Alfonso VI: Yosef Ha-Nasi ben Ferrizuel, better known by the name of Cidellus. Born in Cabra, near Granada, he was Alfonso's personal physician, who appointed him *nasi* of the Jews of his realm. It was Cidellus who stood by the Jews of Guadalajara, when it was taken by Alfonso; he also helped Jews who emigrated from

---

*English translation from the Hebrew taken from *Selected Religious Poems of Solomon Ibn Gabirol, Translated into English verse by Israel Zangwill from a critical text edited by Israel Davidson, Ph.D.*, Philadelphia, The Jewish Publication Society of America, 1923.

Muslim Spain to settle in the Christian North. R. Yehuda ha-Levi wrote in his praise in Romance:

Des' cuand meu Cidelo venid,	(Since my Cidellus came
tan buona albixara!	What a good breeze
Com' rayo del sol exid	Like a sun's ray
en Wadalachyara.	In Guadalajara).

This is considered to be one of the first poetic pieces, a *muwashaha*, in the Castilian language (known then as the Romance), and by whom: R. Yehuda ha-Levi![8]

Cidellus also worked for Jewish unity in Spain, excluding the Karaites from centers of Jewish settlement. As one of the first persons appointed by the king to act as head of the Jewish community under Christian rule, he showed how such an appointment should benefit his own people. He was a forerunner to the many *nesiim*, who later became known by the title *Rab de la Corte*. The *nasi* was virtually the administrative leader of the Jewish community and its official representative to the Royal Court in matters of taxation and as chief judge for appeals on Jewish matters. This office functioned in Castile till the last days before the expulsion of Spanish Jewry. Needless to stress that not every *nasi* or *Rab de la Corte* met the qualifications necessary for such an exalted office, nor was every *Rab de la Corte* sufficiently versed to deserve either the title of Rabbi or to head the Jewish community of Castile.[9]

These leaders of Judaism were a unifying force in Spanish Jewry. Many could unite their moral authority with learning. It is true that RaSHbA in Aragón-Cataluña and R. Hisdai Crescas after him had in their time been appointed by royalty to serve as supreme judges to Jews in certain defined fields. But in Castile a special appointment was made of a leader to serve as *Rab de la Corte*, whose duty it was to represent the Jews before the Court. He also served as chief justice for appeals among Jewish litigants and was responsible for the tax division among Jewish communities. This *Rab de la Corte* (in Portugal *Arrabi môr*) did not necessarily have to be an ordained rabbi to teach and judge. The holder of the post might equally well be some public figure in favor with the king, sufficiently trustworthy to be put in charge of the farming of Royal taxes and their collection. RaSHbA had noted (Responsa attributed to RaMBaM, No. 248) the necessity of drawing a line between such persons and the traditional rabbis:

> But he who is no Rabbi but a royal appointee is not of this status; we only punish anyone who puts him to shame for what he is; and this only if he shames him in deed, but not in word.

It should be emphasized that the *Rab de la Corte* was not the chief rabbi of the Jews in Castile nor did he serve as head of all the other rabbis. The rabbi played a unique role in forming the character of the Jewish community in Spain; he was the leader in his generation. Many generations were blessed with leaders and rabbis such as R. Moshe ben Nachman (Nachmanides; RaMbaN); R. Shelomo ben Adret (RaSHbA); R. Aharon

Halevi Na Clara, R. Yom Tov Ash'ili (RITbA); R. Yitzhak bar Sheshet Berfet (RIbaSH); R. Hisdai Crescas (RaHaK) in Aragón; R. Ahser ben Yehiel (ROSH) and his sons R. Yehuda and R. Yaakov; R. Abraham Ibn Shoshan, R. Meir Alguades in Castile, to name only a few. Their sphere of duty and leadership are beacons of light in Jewry to all ages.

Urban Jewish settlements in Spain (and Portugal) had a unique legal status in the code of relations laid down already in ancient days by *fueros*—a corpus of laws and local customs which set out to define the relations between local inhabitants and the Crown. *Fueros* should not be regarded as a legal relationship reversing privileges given to the Jewish population, but as a local phenomenon recognized by the Crown. In their uniqueness they are particularly important for the understanding of the conditions of Jewish existence. Their essence lies in the organic growth, over many centuries, giving clues to the problems of Jewish settlement in different parts of Spain (and Portugal). This accounts for the haphazard distribution of paragraphs dealing with Jews throughout the *fuero*, without any necessary connection between them. What is important here is the absolute equality in the definition of relations between the Jews and the local population. The burden of proof by witnesses falls equally on both the litigating parties; the Jewish oath is recognized in its traditional form; market activities are fixed on a basis of equality—to point out only some of the paragraphs of the *fueros*. Spain's uniqueness should be recognized here.

The Jewish Contribution to Literature and Culture

During the twelfth and thirteenth centuries, Toledo was witness to exceptional achievement. A translation center was founded in that city. True, it had already started in the days of Alfonso VI, but it reached its peak during the reign of Alfonso VII (1126–1157), when Archbishop Don Raimundo and a group of learned Jews and Christian clerics founded a college of translators in Toledo, which immediately gained renown. The chief acting personality was the abbot Dominicus Gundisalvus, himself an author of various philosophical works, some of which he copied from Ibn Gabirol's *Fons Vitae*. Gundisalvus surrounded himself with able translators, one of them a Jewish convert to Christianity by the name of Juan de Sevilla.[10] He was a mathematician who translated works from Arabic into Latin; Ibn Gabirol's *Fons Vitae*, works on medicine, philosophy, astronomy, etc., thus bringing to the knowledge of the West the great works of Plato and Aristotle. Another group of translators, which included the Jew Maestre Pedro of Toledo, translated the entire Koran in the course of one year (1143). This continued well into the fourteenth century, the Hebrew language serving as an intermediary language. Maimonides' great work, *A Guide to the Perplexed*, became known through its Hebrew translation and only then received its Latin version. We do not know who the translator into Latin was, but its impact on Christian scholasticism was enormous,

influencing Albertus Magnus and Thomas Aquinas in particular. In those days the poet
Fernán Pérez de Guzmán wrote:

. . . Si del sabio egipciano	If the wise Egyptian
Rabi Moysen	Rabbi Moshe
Se recuerda el reino hispano	Is remembered in the Spanish Kingdom
Bien vera que non en vano	Well be it seen that not in vain
Otra Atenas llame	Córdoba was called another Athens
A Córdoba.[11]	

Castile became a bridgehead for Western civilization. But Toledo was not alone in
this effort: Barcelona was another center where R. Abraham bar-Hiyya wrote his
famous works on mathematics.[12] To the list of translators we may add such names as:
Rabbi Zag, Moseh ha-Cohen, Abraham Alfaquim (Abraham de Toledo), and some
conversos as well. The Jewish contribution to the founding of the Studium generale in
Western Europe was vital indeed.

Another contribution to Spanish culture was made by R. Shemtov b. Isaac Ibn
Ardutiel, better known as Santob de Carrion, during the reign of King Alfonso XI of
Castile (1312–1350), who wrote not only in Hebrew (his *Vidduy* (Confession of sins)
has become part of the Mussaf service of Yom Kippur according to the Sephardic rite)
but in Spanish as well. His literary work *Proverbios Morales* shows the influence of
Hebrew ethics; the author seeks to apply morality and reason to man's daily life. This
work can be seen as one of the early foundations of Spanish literature and language and
it is a most important document with regard to the Jewish influence in medieval
literature. Through this book Jewish ideas penetrated into many literary and philosophical works in Spanish.[13]

Let us add here the contribution made by Jewish cartographers in fourteenth-century
Mallorca (a subject which deserves a study in its own right). Abraham Cresques (d.
1387) and his son Yehuda Cresques, both "magistri mapamundorum et buxolarum,"
and R. Abraham Zacuto in Salamanca and his *Almanach perpetuum* helped Christopher
Columbus at the end of the fifteenth century in charting his astronomical calculations
for his great voyage.

Jewish Social and Communal Structure

Is it in fact possible to ascribe a particular social personality to the Jewish presence in
Spain?

The characteristics of Spanish Jewry were, after all, shared by Jews in other countries.
They were city-dwellers, small-town inhabitants and villagers. All social relations,
public and social tensions, existed both above and below the surface. Spanish Jewish
society included rich men, middle-class men and poor men (the latter supported by the
community), scholars, students, religious dignitaries renowned for their learning,

physicians, merchants, artisans of the widest variety of crafts, and peasants, leaseholders and freeholders. Socially they were no more exempt from the stress of relations than any other society or community. This seems to have been true for Hispano-Jewish public life throughout the centuries of its existence. Yet, neither the political nor the social situation of the Jewish communities of Spain was the same at all times and in all its regions. It was affected by changing political conditions, such as the challenges of new settlements and new centers and new communities. These were especially demanding tasks, since in conquered cities, townships and villages there were old communities which now had to fit into the conquering Christian State. This was the case for many centuries, but not in the last phase of the *Reconquista*: the last war against Granada, in the 1480s, when the Catholic monarchs did not have the slightest intention of calling on the Jewish element to take part in settling conquered Granada. Jewish communal life in Spain was in full decline, and the rulers of United Spain had already decided on their total expulsion. This was the outcome of a social evolutionary process that had been going on since 1391, starting with a wave of massacres, of forced conversions and of voluntary abandoning of creed and nation. This fifteenth-century crisis carried in its wake a profound change in Jewish life, whose influence was apt to be felt for hundreds of years to come.[14]

Let us now examine Jewish communal life. Since we already mentioned some of the Court Jews, some remarks on this subject are in order. As a matter of fact, there was no king, either in the Kingdom of Castile-León or Aragón-Cataluña-Valencia, etc., who did not have a Jewish courtier. On the other hand, it should be stressed that in each reign in Spain, Jews had access to the Crown and direct connections were maintained between the parties concerned. True, this was a direct outcome of the old privileges, but also a recognition of the part the Jews played in the fiscal system of the realm as a provider of funds, directly and indirectly. For hundreds of years, Jews farmed the income of the Crown in taxes and organized the tax collections. The Crown thus became dependent in many ways on the flow of income which Jews were always supposed to deliver; for instance: the money needed for the daily upkeep of the Crown and its entourage; to keep the purse of a spendthrift queen or crown prince full at all times, etc. It was not only a question of the yearly tax, imposed through negotiations each year anew, which was farmed and collected by Jews; it was the whole tax system of the State that was in their hands. The Jews thus became identified with Crown impositions and unjust demands, in which cruel methods were a daily habit. It was a cause for anti-Jewish riots on the one hand and, as late as December, 1491, or a short while before the Expulsion, new regulations had to be issued ousting Jews from tax farming and tax collecting in order to assure the United Kingdom of Castile and Aragón of the necessary income after the Jews were expelled. The architect of this move of great foresight was Tomás de Torquemada.[15]

In many ways these great financiers were spokesmen for their Jewish brethren. Some of them were great personalities in Jewish life, true and devoted protectors of Judaism. A generation that had leaders like R. Moshe ben Nahman Nahmanides (the bailiff of King Jaime I in Gerona) or R. Shelomo ben Adret in Barcelona, was blessed through its leaders. For only a personality like Nahmanides could have withstood the pressure of the Barcelona disputation in 1263 against the convert Pablo Christiani, although even he had to flee Spain afterward. This man, who was held in the highest esteem by King and commoner alike, was a rebuilder of the Yishuv in the Holy Land upon his arrival there in 1267. Among the financiers were great personalities who joined forces with outstanding rabbis to keep Jewry within its boundaries of law and Torah. Just to name a few: the Ibn Wakkar brothers in Castile at the end of the thirteenth century; some members of the Caballeria family in Saragossa during the thirteenth and fourteenth centuries; R. Hisdai Crescas during the 1391 riots; R. Meir Aliguades of Segovia; R. Abraham Bienveniste of Soria, Don Isaac Abravanel—to name only a few.

But there was also another type of Court Jew. We find among them men of a bullying character, who oppressed their own and who imitated gentile ways. If not they, then their offspring, led lives of wealthy decadence. Among them we find those who easily crossed the border of conversion. We do not have to wonder why a personality like R. Menahem ben Zorah wrote his "Zeda la-Derekh" (Provisions for the wayfarer) in which he tried to explain the basic mitzvot of *kashruth*. The person to whom this book was dedicated, Don Samuel Abrabanel of Seville shortly afterwards became Don Juan Sánchez de Sevilla. He was not alone at the end of the fourteenth century. Such individuals set the tone of Jewish public life and in many ways the crisis of Spanish Jewry in those days should be laid at their doorstep. From over-involvement in affairs of state and Christian society, it was one mere step to conversion.

During that entire period, Jews played an important role in resettling the reconquered areas. We even have information on Jews participating as *jinetes* with the conquering armies in driving out the Muslims. Jews were given plots of land and shops in the newly conquered lands and towns. A condition was laid down that they had to settle on those lands with their families. They became frontier settlers and even took part in the plans of military orders who were granted great regions of land and fortresses in areas like Murcia, Valencia, La Mancha, Andalusia, Extremadura and the Balearic Islands. Spanish Jewry was an integral part in plans for the resettlement of Spain.

Jewish communal organization was unique in Spain, as in all the diaspora. The community was the basic unit of organized Jewish life. It was set within the communal bounds, as were the institutions of which Jews stood in need: the Synagogue, the Court of Jewish Law, kosher food supply, the mikvah, the cemetery, mutual aid—all aspects of Jewish organized life. Special privileges were granted by the king for all these needs. However, not all public and social aspects of Jewish life were defined by, or dependent on, official privileges. Jewish education in all its spheres was an internal affair rooted in a living organism. The organized Jewish community was a lighthouse of security for each Jew, the communal institutions were the ship, and the leaders of the community of each generation were, as the saying goes; "Jephtah in his generation like Samuel in his." Yet changing political conditions were a decisive factor in the life of all Jewish communities in the kingdoms of Castile-León as of Aragón-Cataluña. The Jewish communities adapted themselves to the political trends in those kingdoms as regarded local government, as Rabbi Shelomo ben Adret (RaSHbA) wrote in 1264:

> Local custom in these matters is not everywhere the same, as there are places where affairs are run entirely by the advice of the elders and councillors and there are places where even the majority has no right to do anything unless they consult all the people and obtain their consent, and there are places where they set people in authority to do as the see fit in all general affairs, and they are as wardens there (Responsa [ed. Leghorn 1778] III, No. 394).

This was perhaps the reason that prevented the creation of an overall national organization in Castile or in Aragón. However attempts to that end were made in Aragón in 1354 and in Castile in 1432. Self-organization on a smaller scale can be seen in the *collecta*, under which term tax-districts of a group of communities were organized. Although it was created by order of the king it reflected a special relationship between communities; as the RaSHbA expressed it, writing from Barcelona: (Responsa III, No. 411):

> Know that we and the community of Villafranca and the community of Tarragona and Montblanch have one coffer and one pocket between us in paying the taxes and property dues and all that the king imposes upon us. And whenever they wish to make new agreements in fixing taxes or giving reminders or obtaining what we seek from our lord the king, we never impose anything upon them, even though we be the greater number, and the head of all matters; for if we act without their advice they will not heed our voices. Sometimes we send people to them and sometimes delegates come from them to us with their consent. And if they do not heed us, to do any of these things, we force them by the arm of the government to come to us or to resolve and enforce in their local community, as we have done. But in other places the chief community may decree that the lesser ones must come, even against their will; for in all these matters the customs of places differ. This is and has always been the law and custom with us.

The privileges granted by various kings made possible an internal development along broad lines. Special mention should be made of communities such as Barcelona, whose organization comprised a "Council of Thirty," composed of three classes: the upper, the middle, the low (*ma mayor, ma mitchana, ma menor*), or Saragossa, Gerona, Perpignan, Mallorca, etc. (to name only a few), with an executive committee of *neemanim* (fideles or *secretarii* or *mukaddamin*), whose duty it was to carry out the local policy laid down by the Council. They had to be men of particular distinction, since all public affairs depended upon them and they were chosen for their public and private rectitude. But in practice the greatest influence was exerted by those "great men" who formed the Jewish aristocracy of the town. Perhaps it would be more accurate to call it an oligarchy with certain democratic trends. Special officers acted as *Berurei Averot* (as they are also called in Spanish documents) or as we may translate the term as "sin magistrates," whose duty it was to bring to court those who transgressed against Jewish law and the Jewish way of life. After the Expulsion this typically Catalan institution was transferred to the Jewish communities of the Ottoman empire. And of course there were *dayanim*, chosen to serve a certain term or to act for life, who judged according to Jewish law and custom, even sitting in judgment in cases of mixed Jewish-Christian litigations. So Castile, too, had its "Boards of Elders" which received their mandate from a "Closed Council" (*Consejo cerrado*), composed solely of members of distinguished families. They had complete control of communal affairs, and were supported by Castilian monarchs, who considered them an important force in maintaining order in the Jewish community and a moderating force as well in Christian society.[16]

Social order found detailed expression in the statutes of the Jewish communities of Spain, laid down for the management of their affairs and the determination of their way of life. This was a public that knew what it had to face and how to adapt a Jewish way of life to surrounding conditions. These statutes dealt not only with problems of internal jurisdiction; they also set limits to personal relations, to the duties of the individual to society and community. They were in force for generations, and the Jews who left with the Expulsion transplanted them to their new communities in North Africa, the Ottoman empire and wherever else they settled and built a new life. But each community had its own statutes, as Rabbi Isaac Berfet (RIbaSH) said: "Every community in the Kingdom makes by royal patent and enforces its Statutes" (Responsa No. 272). These regulations determined religious and social discipline within the framework of the Jewish community. It was a voluntary element in which each individual accepted the yoke of national responsibility and public duty. This gave Spanish Jewry one of its unique characteristics. It was this voluntary tradition that founded associations of mutual help and charity. Even fellowships of craftsmen who joined together for communal work specialized in mutual aid. Thus we may find in Saragossa a fellowship of *Osey Hesed* (Doers of Mercy), another of *Rodfei Zedek* (Pursuers of Righteousness), a third of *Leiley Ashmorot* (Nights of Vigil), for intercession through prayer on the woes of *galut*. Special mention should be made of the "Gravediggers" of Huesca, whose ordinances and statutes were promulgated by the king. (But Jewish Spain had no associations for the "Redemption of Captives.") Nevertheless they were at times incapable of uniting to face dangers (except for forming a *collecta* or tax district by Royal writ) or forming a national organization, such as was proposed, for instance, in the Kingdom of Aragón after the Black Death massacres, or in Castile in the 1430s.

In all, it was a closely woven web of public life, which suffered at times from inner crisis and yet would be capable of coping with the main problems of Jewish existence in the Diaspora.

Cultural Activity

The cultural activity of the Jews in Spain was exceptional. As is well known, Spanish Jewry received its cultural inspiration at its beginning from the great *yeshivot* in Babylonia. It also was Zion-oriented and Hebrew poetry and prose in Spain expressed these yearnings for Zion abundantly. Spanish Jewry supported the centers of learning in Babylonia and in the Holy Land. The love for Zion, its glory of the past, and the hope for the Messiah were expressed in all their profundity. Shelomo Ibn Gabirol, Shmuel ha-Naguid, R. Yehuda ha-Levi, and Ibn Ezra are only a few of the illustrious names in the list of poets and authors of the highest rank.

Hebrew poetry was not the only field where Jewish talent in Spain found ways of expressing itself. R. Isaac Alfasi (1103–1165), a Moroccan Jew who settled in Muslim Spain, is considered one of the foremost codifiers of Halakha. But though Maimonides (1135–1204) wrote his treatises in Fostat (near Cairo), yet his spiritual adherence, Sephardic in its basis, expressed itself not only in legal codifying, but in a gigantic philosophical, literary, historical and spiritual creative activity. In the field of Halakha we have to give a place of honor to R. Yaakov ben Asher (d. 1340), who together with his father and family, came as a refugee from the German lands in the 1290s, and created in Toledo, where his father R. Asher served as Rabbi, the great compendium *Arba Turim*, an exceptional synthesis between Ashkenazic and Sephardic learning. Ashkenazic tradition, though known in Spain through the Tosaphists, ascetic views on life and the *kiddush ha-Shem* ideology found their way into Spain in the early fourteenth century, thus giving a new sense to their meaning.[17] This found its expression in the days of trial during the massacres of 1348–49 and 1391 and the Expulsion of 1492. Finally, to round up this field of Halakhic creation we have to add the work of R. Yosef Caro of Zamora, who in sixteenth-century Safed laid down the foundations for that *magnum opus*, the *Shulhan Arukh*, to which (in the words of the late Zalman Shazar), R. Moshe Isserles of Cracow could only add a tablecloth (*mappah le Shulhan Arukh*).

Perhaps the greatest contribution to Jewry is to be found in the field of the *kabbalah* whose value to learning, to the human spirit in general and to Judaism in particular was so majestically described and evaluated by Gershom Scholem. Spain was the cradle of Jewish mysticism and from there it spread to all corners of the earth where Jews lived in dispersion.[18]

All this represented a vast creation in philosophy, science, medicine and a Responsa literature that tried to answer the needs of a community in those days of trial which Spanish Jewry was called to endure.

The Church becomes Militant

At that time, the Church was the main factor in pressing Crown and society towards an anti-Jewish attitude and calling for a great variety of restrictions, most of which became anti-Jewish rules and laws. This pressure was fomented by Pope Innocent III and continued by Pope Gregory IX. If this task was easy in Christian Europe it took more time to put into force in Spain and allow the attitude of the Church towards Judaism dominate there. Local political considerations and necessities in a land in the process of a *Reconquista* are to be seen as major features in the moderation of Church demands, although at times the government acceded to those demands to lead an anti-Jewish policy in one realm or another, be it Castile or Aragón. The attitude towards Jews was often a criterion of obedience to Church and Pope. Church pressure was one of the main causes of stagnation that set in among Spanish Jewry. The fourteenth and fifteenth centuries were not centuries of continued pressure against the Muslims, whose holdings had dwindled to the region of Granada only. To this we must add the repercussions of the Black Death and the massacres that followed them and left very deep marks in Spanish Jewry. Castile started at that time to outweigh Aragón. Another blow for the Jewish communities of Castile was the war between King Pedro, called the Cruel (1350–1369) and his bastard brother Enrique (Henry) II (1369–1379) Trastámara. For the first time, anti-Jewish propaganda became a major issue in the civil war. Enrique used anti-Jewish slogans against Pedro, accusing him of being a captive in Jewish hands. An anti-Jewish public ambience was created. But although Enrique later revised his anti-Jewish policy, after killing his brother and having seized power, the anti-Jewish seed found fertile ground. Seville was witness to local disturbances and anti-Jewish riots in the late 1370s. This was a forerunner to the crisis of 1391, the year that was named in our literature as Gezerat Ka'Na.[19]

Massacre, Martyrdom and Conversion

From a Jewish point of view there was a state of spiritual disintegration, both communally and socially, which prepared the ground for the movement of mass conversion following the terrible wave of massacres that engulfed the kingdom. Among wealthy and powerful Jews, Jewish life had lost most of its inner content, according to an anonymous writer of that time in his book *Ha Kaneh veha Pelia*. Another book, already mentioned, *Zedah la-Derekh*, tells much about the atmosphere of the time. There is little doubt that the crisis which overtook Spanish Jewry toward the end of the fourteenth century is rooted in an earlier period. From an external point of view, conditions were ripe for a physical attack on Jews, while at the same time within the communities themselves a rejection of Jewish values was taking place. Both these conditions brought about the heavy blow sustained by Spanish Jewry and led to the crisis of the fifteenth century, which ended with the establishment of the Inquisition in the early 1480s and the expulsion of the Jews from Spain in 1492.

Riots started in Seville on June 4, 1391, and spread all over Spain like wildfire. Many communities were razed to the ground and their members died as martyrs, while others, in order to save their lives, converted to Christianity. This mass conversion of about 200,000 people created one of the gravest social and religious problems of Spain (and later also of Portugal) and its possessions overseas, and also in Judaism.

For many communities it spelled their total end: the Jewish center of Barcelona was never reestablished. R. Hisdai Crescas succeeded only partially in reestablishing some communities, like Valencia and Burriana. In 1394, Mallorca accepted a settlement of 150 families from Portugal. This community was again destroyed and dispersed in 1435. Many fled to North Africa and a certain wave of emigration started towards Eretz Israel. With this, the foundations were laid for Sephardic nuclei outside Spain.

Immediately after this mass conversion, Church and Crown made efforts to create a barrier between the recent converts to Christianity and their former Jewish brethren. Jews and converts were ordered to live in separate quarters, an order which was to be repeated even as late as 1490. As a matter of fact, the order of Expulsion was the only order that finally succeeded in separating brothers. Pressure was put on Spanish Jewry to force the remaining Jews to convert. In 1412 the so-called Laws of Valladolid were issued, the convert Pablo de Santa María, chancellor of Castile, being their instigator; in Aragon, the anti-Pope Benedict XIII, after being advised by Jerónimo de Santa Fe (formerly Yehoshua haLorki), ordered and carried out, in 1413–1414, the notorious Tortosa disputation, which wrought havoc among Jews all over Spain. Jews, singly and in groups, went to Tortosa in despair to be converted there, and it seemed as if this meant the end of Spanish Jewry. A ship stood waiting in Valencia to go to Mallorca and bring Vicente Ferrer to the Spanish main, so that he would be honored with the completion of the task of baptizing the last Jews of Spain, and thus solve, once and for all, the problem of this Jewry. But, as is well known, it did not work out as this Pope and his henchmen wished.

The Search for a New Modus Vivendi

Great inner forces called for a new appraisal of Jewish life in Spain. R. Yosef Albo published his *Sefer haIkkarim*, in which the tenets of Judaism were evaluated anew. R. Shlomo Alami wrote his *Iggeret Musar* and tried to look for reasons for all that had overtaken Spanish Jewry, stressing that the crisis was the result of inner disintegration. Another author, R. Shemtov Ibn Shemtov, in his book entitled *Sefer haEmunot*, stressed that philosophical "enlightenment" was the main cause of this destruction. If *Sefer haIkkarim* was an analysis of the foundations of faith, giving answers to those who cast doubts upon it, the works of the other two were an investigation into the roots of the evils which had befallen Spanish Jewry. This introspection continued for generations to come—a question for which Spanish Jewry was hard pressed to find an appropriate answer.[20]

Spanish Jewry had great inner powers for recovery. In 1422, R. Moshe Arragel began his Spanish translation of the Bible and his Biblical commentary at the suggestion of Don Luis de Guzmán, head of the Order of Calatrava. This work was completed in 1430. R. Moshe was aided in his exegetical work by two monks, a Franciscan and a Dominican, Arias de Encinas and Don Vasco de Guzmán. This unique work of translation shows how, despite the prevailing official attitude toward Jewry and the looming of the *converso* problem, personal initiative was still a great force in Judeo-Christian relations. This work was carried out in a small town in Castile, Maqueda, and illuminated by a Christian illuminator after R. Moshe had completed his work of translating and commenting. It furnishes us with a living picture of Castilian Jewry in those days.

Another great accomplishment was the meeting of representatives of Castilian Jewry in Valladolid in 1432, called by R. Abraham Bienveniste of Soria. Here, an attempt was made to create a new constitution for the Jewish communities in a constructive attempt to organize Jewish education, renew the Jewish legal system and public taxation, form a basis for actions against those who harmed the Jewish community from within, and fix standards of modesty in dress and behavior for the Jewish community. This constitution, written in Hebrew letters in a mixture of Hebrew and Castilian, is not only a cultural heritage of exceptional value in the evolution of the vernacular of Spanish Jewry, but also an attempt to found a national organization under the leadership of the *Rab de la Corte*, R. Abraham Bienveniste. In this constructive effort the Jewish communal leaders sought to lay foundations upon which Jewish communal life could be reestablished. Herein lies the additional historical value of this meeting. Unfortunately it came late and could not revive Jewish life along those lines it laid down as a basis for Jewish existence. No aid from the government was forthcoming. Castile as well as Aragón were then passing through grave crises of their own.

The Road to Expulsion and a New Diaspora

The inability of Christian society to cope with the *converso* problem was laid at the threshold of those Jews who remained loyal to their faith and past. In the 1460s, Alonso de Espina, a Franciscan, suggested the total expulsion of the Jews from Spain along the same lines as the expulsion from England in 1290 and from France in 1306. If these kingdoms managed to survive without Jews for so many years, de Espina argued, so could Spain. This idea achieved substance when the Catholic monarchs, Ferdinand and Isabella, succeeded in uniting the kingdoms of Aragón and Castile as a Christian State with "one flock and one shepherd" (unum ovile et unus pastor). The idea was to create a state of one faith under one united throne. This goal could only be achieved by first solving the problems of the *conversos* and their adherence to Judaism, second by conquering Granada, the last stronghold of Islam in Europe, and third by solving the Jewish problem—a minority of a different faith and way of life. The most important ally in these aims was to be found in ecclesiastical circles, the militant group headed by the Dominican monk Tomás de Torquemada, prior of the Santa Cruz monastery in Segovia and father confessor to Queen Isabella from the days she was exiled to Segovia by her brother Enrique IV. Another ally was the Santa Hermandad, an organized police force active in many towns, which strove to attain peace in the kingdom by fighting rebellious gangs and marauding nobles. But there were also noblemen who wholeheartedly supported the Crown's efforts.[21]

To discuss here in full the *converso* problems of fifteenth-century Spain would be a task outside the scope of our description. As is well known, the Spanish Inquisition started to function in Seville in 1481; in 1483 the first attempt was made to expel the Jews from Andalusia, an attempt considered by Church and Crown as a failure in the effort to segregate Jews from their *converso* brethren. We have no exact information as to where the refugees turned. The Jewish population was called upon to make a heavy financial contribution to the war against Muslim Granada. The whole burden fell on the shoulders of the much reduced communities year after year until the fall of Granada. Anti-Jewish propaganda reached its peak with the so-called blood libel in 1490–1492 of the "Santo Niño de la Guardia," in which Jews and *conversos* were accused of having killed a Christian child whose body was never found. The matter was a complete fabrication: the Inquisition, in staging this trial, intended to prove that Jews and *conversos* were conspiring to bring about the destruction of Christendom. There was even an attempt to implicate Abraham Senior of Segovia, last *Rab de la Corte* and one of the most trusted counselors of Queen Isabella, in the conspiracy. Although the Crown put an end to these insinuations, a group of Jews and *conversos* were burned at the stake.[22]

On January 2, 1492, Ferdinand and Isabella took possession of Granada in a triumphal procession. On March 31, they signed the order of Expulsion; yet a month passed in negotiations to annul this order in which perhaps R. Isaac Abravanel and Abraham Senior but surely Micer Alfonso de la Caballería took part. But they were confronted by the forceful opposition of Tomás de Torquemada and his followers. The die was cast.

The Expulsion Order explicitly stated that the Jews themselves were responsible for their expulsion; as long as Jews would remain in Spain, there could be no hope for the *conversos* to cut themselves away from their Jewish past. The Jews were blocking *converso* assimilation in Christian society. Thus a religious policy became responsible for determining a matter which concerned the secular authorities. Only in this light can the significance of the Expulsion Order be understood. It should not be attributed to economic causes. On the contrary, the expulsion emptied whole areas of their Jewish inhabitants, leaving these places without the authorities to replace the exiled Jews and fulfill the social, public and economic functions the Jews had held in state, society, economy and community as a whole, although it may have been thought that the *converso* community would replace them.

The Expulsion Order dealt with all the arrangements for the departure of the Jews, by what routes they should leave, how guards should be hired, and what they were allowed to take out. Those who formulated the order assumed that most Jews would leave and some would convert. And so it was. About 200,000 Jews left Spain. Spanish Jewry saw their expulsion as a second "Exodus from Egypt," the beginning of the *geulah*, and miracles were expected to happen.

Private individuals started to sell their property and prices fell so low that a vineyard was sold for a donkey or a piece of cloth. They were not allowed to take out precious metals and stones. Measures were taken for the transfer of communal property such as synagogues and cemeteries turned officially into common pasture land. Jews found ways and means to save part of what they had by having access to clandestine border transfers (in the case of those who went to Portugal).

Here the greatness of a people is to be seen. They left disillusioned, leaving behind a heritage of fifteen centuries of life and creativity. A Royal decree put an end to all this upon Church insistence. It should be noted that immediately upon the publication of the Order of Expulsion, whole families started their preparations for the road. Negotiations started, and finally 120,000 Jews crossed the border to Portugal; about 50,000 went to North Africa; some went to Navarre, the remainder went to Papal Avignon, Italy and towards the Ottoman territories in the Balkans and Asia Minor. In all, about 200,000 Jews left Spain, by land routes and by ship. Their last day on Spanish soil was the seventh day of the month of Av, 5252 (July 31, 1492). Thus the Expulsion was easily associated with the tradition of the Destruction of the Temple. Indeed, it was considered a third *hurban*.

The blow fell when the state was ready for it after the conquest of Granada, after the state had been unified and Spanish territory freed from Muslim rule. Spanish Jewry had been lulled into believing that with Ferdinand and Isabella a new period of Jewish renaissance would begin. The blow was perhaps against all logic, but Spanish Jewry was not taken by surprise. Undaunted in spirit the Jews of Spain started their preparations to leave the land to which tradition had bound them for about 1500 years. With such a spirit, three months were enough for them to take leave of their past. Not for nothing did the chronicler-priest Andrés Bernáldez marvel—and he had no sympathy for Jews—about the deep faith of the exiles marching joyously accompanied by timbrels, on their way to an unknown future. Only a few years later, a similar fate was in store for the Sephardi settlers in Portugal and Portuguese Jewry.[23]

The departure of the Jews marked the foundation of the Sephardic Diaspora, a diaspora within a diaspora. It grew to encompass first the Mediterranean, but in the sixteenth and seventeenth centuries it spread to new lands, and new horizons for Jewry in general opened up. The history of Spanish Jewry until their expulsion is a unique page in Jewish life. It has saga-like dimensions, where courage and enterprise, undaunted spiritual values and down-to-earth realism, together with a deep sense of Jewish responsibility and mission, unite in one great chapter of Jewish historical experience.

1. On additional inscriptions, see Haim Beinart, "Cuando llegaron los judios a España?" *Estudios 2* (1962), pp. 1–32.

2. See James Parkes, *The Conflict of the Church and the Synagogue*, Cleveland, New York, and Philadelphia, 1961, pp. 345–70.

3. See J. Vives, *Concilios visigóticos*, Barcelona and Madrid, 1963, p. 186–225.

4. See J. Ma. Millás Vallicrosa, *Documents hebraics de jueus catalans*, Barcelona, 1927.

5. See E. Ashtor, *The Jews of Moselm Spain, Volume 1*, Philadelphia, 1973.

6. See Hayyim Schirman, *HaShirah haIvrit beSepharad u-be-Province*, Jerusalem and Tel Aviv, 5615 (1954–55) pp. 196 ff.

7. See Yitzhak Baer, *A History of the Jews in Christian Spain, Volume 1*, Philadelphia, 1961, 39–77, *et passim*.

8. A. Vilanova, *Antología literaria de Autores españoles*, Barcelona, 1964, p. 2.

9. Haim Beinart, "Demutha shel haHatzranut biSepharad haNotzrit," in *Kvutzot Elite veShikhvot Manhiguot*, Jerusalem, 5727 (1966/67), pp. 55–71.

10. He was also known as Juan Avendat or Avendar, or Ibn David, or Ben David, David Judaeus, Joannes Israelita, Philosophus, Johannes Judaeus Hispalensis, Juan de Luna.

11. See J. Vernet, *Historia de la ciencia española*, Madrid, 1975, pp. 66–67.

12. Also called Savasorda or Abraham Judaeius or ha-Nasi. Died in 1136.

13. See Santob de Carrion, *Proverbios Morales*, edited with an Introduction by Ig. Gonzalez Llubera, Cambridge, 1947; A. Garcia Calco, *Don Sem Tob Glosas de Sabiduría*, Madrid, 1974.

14. Baer, ibid., pp. 186–242.

15. See note 9.

16. Haim Beinart, "The Hispano-Jewish Society," *Cahier d'Histoire Mondiale XI*, 1–2 (1968), pp. 220–38.

17. See Baer, ibid., p. 243.

18. See Gershom Scholem, *Major Trends in Jewish Mysticism*, New York, 1941.

19. See Yitzhak Baer, *A History of the Jews in Christian Spain, Volume 2*, Philadelphia, 1966, pp. 95–237.

20. Baer, ibid., pp. 239–43.

21. Baer, ibid., pp. 300–23.

22. Baer, ibid., pp. 424–43.

23. Haim Beinart, *Gerush Sepharad*, Jerusalem (in press).

THE MAJESTY OF MINHAG:
THE SANCTITY OF CUSTOM IN
THE SPANISH AND PORTUGUESE SYNAGOGUES

Haham Dr. Solomon Gaon

Over nearly 1,000 years of prestige and prosperity the Sephardim on the Iberian peninsula accumulated a rich treasure of custom and ceremonial that still survives, largely
intact, in the Spanish and Portuguese congregations of London, New York, Philadelphia, Amsterdam and other parts of the Western world today. Unlike Ashkenazic Jewry,
the Sephardim have never become fragmented into Orthodox, Conservative, Reform
or Reconstructionist movements. Though not all Sephardic Jews maintain the same
level of personal observance, their general attitude toward Judaism is one of profound
reverence for tradition.[1] Jews of Spanish and Portuguese descent have been described
by some observers as "synagogue Jews." Their desire to identify with a religious
discipline founded on ancient tradition is expressed prominently in the strict adherence
to time-honored customs and practices (*minhagim*; sing.: *minhag*) which characterizes
their synagogue and communal life and which, according to Rabbinic dictum, may in
some cases even claim precedence over explicitly stated *halakhah*.

Thus, most Sephardim cling to the custom of not putting on their tefillin during the
intermediate days (*hol ha-moed*) of Pesah and Sukkot, even though, according to the
Shulhan Arukh, the standard Code of Jewish Law accepted by all Orthodox Jews
(including the Sephardim), tefillin should be worn during morning services on those
half-holidays. It is interesting that this particular Sephardic deviation from the *Shulhan
Arukh* should have been adopted also by Spanish and Portuguese congregations. For
the custom of not wearing tefillin during *hol ha-moed* was inspired by the Zohar, the
classic work of Kabbalah, which is favored by Oriental Sephardim but not by the less
mystically-inclined Sephardim of the Spanish and Portuguese lineage.

For the rest, the order of the ancient Castilian liturgy has survived virtually unchanged
in the prayer books used in Spanish and Portuguese congregations today. This can be
easily verified by comparing the present-day Spanish and Portuguese prayer book with
its counterpart of the Spanish rite printed in Venice in the year 1546, about 50 years
after the expulsion of the Jews from the Iberian peninsula, or with the Spanish translation
of that same prayer book, published in Ferrara, Italy, in 1552.

The determined resistance of Spanish and Portuguese Jews to any suggested change
in the order of their prayers is strikingly illustrated by a dispute involving Haham
Raphael Meldola,[2] the spiritual leader of the Spanish and Portuguese Jews of London
(Bevis Marks Synagogue), in the year 1827. It seems that Meldola had proposed that
the Prayer for Dew on the first day of Pesah and the Prayer for Rain on the final day of

Sukkot should no longer be inserted into the *mussaf* (additional, or late morning) service but should be recited just before *mussaf*, immediately after the return of the Torah scrolls to the Ark. This rearrangement, the Haham explained, would obviate a lengthy repetition of the *mussaf* prayers and prevent the festival service from becoming unduly long. He pointed out that this change was not an arbitrary directive on his part but should be accepted as a point of Jewish religious law because it was already followed as a matter of course by all the then-existing Sephardic congregations except the Spanish and Portuguese congregations of London, Amsterdam and New York. He believed that the failure of these three congregations to observe this sequence was due simply to an error which had somehow crept into the order of the festival service and which should be corrected.

There is no doubt that Meldola was right in his assertion that the sequence he wished to introduce was already used by most Sephardic congregations. However, he apparently overlooked the fact that the manner in which the prayers for dew and rain were offered in the three Spanish and Portuguese congregations was based on an ancient tradition dating back to Spain. The prayer books of Venice and Ferrara place them in the same order as that followed by the Spanish and Portuguese congregations. It must therefore be assumed that, as opposed to Meldola, the rabbis in Spain did not consider the old order an error running counter to the intent of Jewish law.

In any event, the lay officials of the community accepted Meldola's proposal for that Pesah, but revoked their approval immediately after the holiday. The original order was reintroduced despite indignant letters addressed by the Haham to the *mahamad* (lay board of directors) of his congregation. It is interesting to note that the same suggestion was repeated in London in 1946, and rejected again by the members of the congregation.

Note the power wielded by the *mahamad* (more correctly *maa'mad*)[3] in this dispute between the Haham and his congregation. The *mahamad*, an essential component of each Spanish and Portuguese congregation, was an elitist governing body that appointed its own successors.[4] Presiding over its congregation with a firm hand, the *mahamad* respected the Haham of the congregation as a guide to consult because of his Jewish erudition but did not defer to him as a final arbiter or authority in religious or communal matters. The *mahamad* claimed that prerogative as its own. Traumatized by what had happened to the Jews of Spain and Portugal after centuries of what had seemed like complete freedom, the *mahamad* assumed virtual police powers over the public and private lives of its constituents. Its stern rules, sometimes involving such petty details as where a congregant should be assigned his seat in the synagogue, or whether an Ashkenazi should be permitted to worship there when space was at a premium, were backed up by such disciplinary measures as fines, loss of synagogue honors, forfeiture of the right to vote and, in extreme cases, excommunication. In this manner the *mahamad* hoped to keep its constituents docile, well-mannered and unlikely to do anything that might bring the congregation into difficulties with the Gentiles. Baruch Spinoza and Uriel d'Acosta were not excommunicated by a Haham or other rabbinical authority but by the *mahamad* of Amsterdam.

On a less dramatic level, the *mahamad* and its constituents were greatly concerned about preserving the dignity and decorum of the synagogue service. The custom of stamping one's feet or using noisemakers when Haman's name is read from the Book of Esther on Purim is of ancient origin. It is already mentioned by the Talmudic scholar David ben Joseph Abudarham of Seville, who was active in Spain during the fifteenth century. But the Spanish and Portuguese Jews seem to have viewed this practice with distaste. In 1783 the officers of the Spanish and Portuguese Congregation of London decreed that no person "shall beat, or make a noise in the synagogue" while the Megillah was read. This ruling has become the *minhag* also in the Spanish and Portuguese congregations of Amsterdam and New York City.[5]

The joyous procession with the Torah scrolls (*hakafot*) on Simhat Torah was observed by many Sephardic congregations in the Orient, but it was not part of the Simhat Torah service at Spanish and Portuguese congregations until comparatively recent times. The Venice and Ferrara prayer books make no reference to it. In his famous diary, Samuel Pepys describes a visit he paid to the Spanish and Portuguese Congregation in London on the afternoon of October 14, 1693, which happened to be Simhat Torah. He writes that he was not very edified by the spectacle because on that day the Jews, as he put it, allowed themselves some license by singing and dancing in honor of the Law. Since we know that *hakafot* were not part of the "official" Simhat Torah service at Spanish and Portuguese synagogues, we must assume that the "spectacle" viewed by Pepys was an "unofficial" *hakafot* ceremony held by a private society whose members wanted to "rejoice in the Law" after the manner of their Oriental and Ashkenazic fellow Jews. In Amsterdam, a study circle held such a procession on Simhat Torah afternoon at a hired hall. In London, probably a similar society used the synagogue itself for the same purpose, also in the afternoon. Since Pepys tells us that his visit to the synagogue took place in the afternoon, he must have come to the synagogue just in time for such an "underground" Simhat Torah celebration. It seems that even these "unofficial" festivities were stopped in London early in the history of the Bevis Marks Synagogue, probably not too long after Pepys' visit there. *Hakafot* were incorporated into the "official" Simhat Torah service in London only after World War II. The Spanish and Portuguese Congregation in New York followed suit, but not the Spanish and Portuguese Congregation of Amsterdam.

But formal and ceremonious though the Spanish and Portuguese Jews may have been, they were not dour or insensitive to the beauties and pleasures of life. The Sephardic ritual was enriched by the lyrical hymns of Ibn Gabirol, Yehuda ha-Levi and other celebrated Hebrew poets. Special melodies were composed for some of these liturgical poems. In other instances, popular melodies were adapted for them and were soon generally accepted. On occasion, the melodies were drawn from the tunes of love songs whose original Spanish words left little to the imagination. The poet and kabbalist Menahem ben Judah of Lonzano (1550–before 1624), who lived variously in Eretz Israel, Turkey and Italy (finally returning to Jerusalem), noted that many rabbis and sages considered these tunes unfit for prayer, but he saw no harm in chanting prayers to popular, catchy melodies. Similar views were expressed by the poet Israel ben Moshe Najara (1555?–1625?), who himself collected and composed many of the hymns chanted in the Spanish congregations. He prefaced many of these liturgical poems with notes indicating the Arabic and Spanish melodies to which they were sung. He explains, somewhat naively, that if a person is given holy, inspiring words to sing to a pretty melody, he will not want to think of the prurient lyrics for which the melody might originally have been composed. Moreover, Najara adds, the sacred songs, chanted to these tunes, will live on long after the words originally associated with the tunes have been forgotten. This rather tolerant view of popular music in connection with worship in the synagogue was quoted in 1857 by the Rev. David Aaron de Sola (1796–1860),[6] senior minister of the Spanish and Portuguese Congregation of London and son-in-law of Raphael Meldola, the Haham whose suggested minor change in the order of the prayers for dew and rain brought him to grief with the *mahamad* of the congregation 30 years earlier.

The customs and ceremonial of the Spanish and Portuguese congregations made a profound impression on non-Sephardic Jews. Thus, many Ashkenazic Jews who settled in North America during the years prior and immediately following the Revolutionary War joined the Sephardic congregations they found in the New World. Today the membership lists of the Spanish and Portuguese Congregation of New York and its sister congregation in Montreal, Canada (both bear the Hebrew name Shearith Israel) show a large number, if not a majority, of Ashkenazic surnames. But in neither case have the Ashkenazim thought of taking over the congregation and changing its customs. The present rabbi of the New York congregation proudly aserts that "some of our best Sephardim are Ashkenazim" and adds an anecdote dating back over a century to show how the Ashkenazic majority in his synagogue at the time bent over backward to preserve the Sephardic character of the congregation. The Sephardim do not have *Yizkor*, the memorial service held by Ashkenazim on the major festivals. In an effort to accommodate the Ashkenazim, the *parnas* (president) of the Spanish and Portuguese Congregation appointed a committee composed of three Ashkenazim and two Sephardim to discuss whether or not *Yizkor* should be introduced into the synagogue. The two Sephardim gallantly voted in favor; the three Ashkenazim, against.[7]

1. Marc D. Angel, *Voices in Exile: A Study in Sephardic Intellectual History*, Hoboken, New Jersey and New York, N.Y., 1991, p. 162.

2. Raphael Meldola (1754–1828), a native of Livorno, Italy, combined traditional rabbinic training with a university education. He was elected Haham of the Spanish and Portuguese Jews of London in 1804/5. One of his great-grandsons, Rabbi Henry Pereira Mendes (1852–1937), became rabbi and *hazzan* of New York's Spanish and Portuguese Congregation, Shearith Israel, and was a founder of the Union of Orthodox Jewish Congregations of America, the Federation of American Zionists and (with Sabato Morais) of the original Jewish Theological Seminary of America before the advent of Solomon Schechter and the Conservative movement.

3. The term was originally used in the Talmud (Taanit 15b) for the representatives of the people, who had to be present at the Temple service on a rotation basis.

4. The *mahamad* had the authority to impose heavy fines on anyone refusing such an appointment. Sometimes, when a congregation was in dire need of funds, its *mahamad* might purposely nominate a wealthy man who could be expected to turn down the nomination. In 1813 the *mahamad* of London applied this fund-raising stratagem in the case of one Isaac D'Israeli, who was known to be rather indifferent to religious and communal life. Furious at what he considered an imposition (he claimed he would have made a donation if the *mahamad* had not used this trick to extract money from him), D'Israeli broke his connections with the congregation and subsequently with Judaism. Several years later, D'Israeli had his teenage son, Benjamin, converted to Christianity. This was young Benjamin Disraeli's first step toward a career in British politics.

5. Solomon Gaon, *Minhath Shelomo: A Commentary on the Book of Prayer of the Spanish and Portuguese Jews*, New York, 1990, p. 185.

6. David Aaron de Sola, *The Ancient Melodies of the Liturgy of the Spanish and Portuguese Jews*, London, 1867.

7. Marc D. Angel, "The Planting of Sephardic Culture in North America," in Joshua Stampfer, ed., *The Sephardim: A Cultural Journey from Spain to the Pacific Coast*, Portland, Oregon, 1987, pp. 99–100.

MANUSCRIPT AND BOOK ILLUSTRATION AMONG THE SEPHARDIM BEFORE AND AFTER THE EXPULSION

Shalom Sabar

BEFORE THE EXPULSION

Manuscript and Book Illustration

Manuscript illumination was practiced by the Sephardim long before the expulsion of the Jews from the Iberian peninsula. In medieval Spain and Portugal, numerous attractive Hebrew manuscripts were commissioned by wealthy Jewish patrons. Some of these costly codices rank amongst the richest and most captivating extant Jewish works of art, issued today in luxurious facsimile editions.[1] There were Spanish rabbis who even found good reasons for, and encouraged the use of, Hebrew books with illustrations. A noted example is the physician and scholar Profiat Duran (d. 1414), who wrote in his influential grammatical work *Maaseh Efod*:

> The contemplation and study of pleasing forms, beautiful images, and drawings broadens and stimulates the mind and strengthens its faculties . . . As with God, who wanted to beautify His Holy Place with gold, silver, jewels and precious stones, so it should be with His Holy Books.[2]

Extant illuminated Hebrew manuscripts from Spain, dating from the middle thirteenth century, are known to us today. However, scholars generally agree that this artistic tradition must have started earlier, possibly during the Golden Age of the tenth and eleventh centuries, when Spain was under Islamic rule.[3] In fact, Muslim patterns of book decoration are clearly found in the earliest extant Hebrew-Spanish illuminated codices, a group of Bibles with carpet pages produced in thirteenth-century Christian Spain. The leading centers of Hebrew manuscript illumination at the time were the cities of Toledo and Burgos. Toledo in particular was an important cultural center, attracting Muslim, Christian and Jewish intellectuals.

The mixture of the three cultures in Spain contributed significantly to the development of Hebrew manuscript illumination. The Jewish aristocracy that arose in the thirteenth and fourteenth centuries readily availed itself of the achievements of the Mudéjar (Islamic) and Gothic (Christian) styles in book illumination. While the former is especially characteristic of the early phase, the influence of the motifs, designs and compositional schemes that were current in Latin manuscripts became more and more prominent in the fourteenth and fifteenth centuries. The local styles were, however, used to create a new colorful and exuberant world of Jewish imagery, fitting the religious needs and refined artistic tastes of the upper-class Jewish society.[4]

Among the creative contributions of Spanish Jews to Hebrew book illumination one should mention at least two characteristic categories: Bibles and Passover Haggadot. Spanish-Hebrew Bibles from the late thirteenth to the fifteenth centuries were commonly introduced with two facing pages illustrated with the gold and silver implements of the Temple. The various implements are carefully arranged in panels next to each other so that each object is clearly visible and often accompanied by an identifying inscription. The unusual location of these folios (i.e., not as narrative illustrations to the corresponding Biblical passages), and the importance given to detailed and accurate depictions of each object, alludes to the strong Messianic hopes of contemporary Spanish Jews.[5] These hopes were raised particularly by Maimonides' influential work *Mishneh Torah*, in which the author provided a manual for the service in the Temple, its rituals and the implements that would be required in the Messianic future. The particular appellation of the Bible in Spain, *Mikdashyah* ("Sanctuary of God"), fits this innovative iconography.

Spanish Haggadot are important for different reasons. A group of particularly extravagant manuscripts is characterized by series of full-page miniatures which depict the stories of the Bible as well as illuminating episodes in the life of Spanish Jews. In the Sarajevo Haggadah, for example, no fewer than 34 folios which precede the text of the Haggadah proper are fully illuminated with a total of 69 miniatures.[6] The miniatures, set against alternating blue and red backgrounds, are painted only on the flesh side of the vellum, while the hair side is left blank. The first 31 folios are devoted to an elaborate Biblical cycle, beginning with the Creation of the World, through the Exodus story, and ending with Moses giving the charge to Joshua. Subsequent miniatures depict the Messianic Temple, the preparations for the Seder night, and a telling episode of Spanish Jews leaving the synagogue, the open doors of which provide a rare view of an early Sephardic Holy Ark (*heikhal*), fully equipped with "dressed" Torah scrolls.

During the last generation of Jewish life in Spain and Portugal a new form of book production was born: the printed book. The new invention had a far-reaching influence on the development of Sephardic art after the Expulsion and thus deserves more attention. Printing came relatively late to the Iberian peninsula; the first book known to be printed in Spain did not appear until 1473.[7] Despite the short and extremely difficult period which elapsed between that year and the expulsions in 1492 and 1497, Hebrew presses with a significant output were established in both Spain and Portugal.[8] It is for this reason that these two countries occupy a major place in the early history of Hebrew printing. Together with Italy and Turkey, they count as the only four countries in which Hebrew books were printed prior to 1500.[9] As an ironic result of the Expulsion, the books printed by Jews on Iberian soil before the modern era fall under the prestigious category of incunabula or "cradle books." It should also be noted that the Jewish printers in Spain and Portugal played a significant role in the introduction and dissemination of printing among the general society as well,[10] publishing books in Latin and vernacular languages.[11] Certainly, were it not for the Expulsion, Hebrew printing in the Iberian peninsula might have developed to occupy as important a place as Italy in the sixteenth century.

The first known printed Hebrew books were apparently issued in Rome around 1469–1473.[12] A year later, in 1474, Solomon ben Moses ibn Alkabetz established a Hebrew press in Guadalajara, Spain. In 1476 he published his first book, Rashi's commentary on the Pentateuch. Solomon's press was active until 1482, publishing various tractates of the Talmud, commentaries on the Bible, parts of Jacob ben Asher's *Arbaah Turim*, and the earliest known edition of the Haggadah (1482).[13] Another important early printer is the *converso* Juan de Lucena who, during the 1470s, in his small village of Montalbán (near Toledo), published prayer books in Spanish (apparently for the marranos who did not know Hebrew), and possibly also in Hebrew.[14] Subsequently, Hebrew print shops were founded in Zamora (by Samuel ben Musa and Immanuel; active ca. 1484–1492), and in Hijar (by the noted physician and printer Eliezer ben Abraham Alantansi, active ca. 1485–1488). In Portugal Hebrew presses were set up in Faro (established by Don Samuel Porteira with the support of Don Samuel Gacon, ca. 1486 to 1494 or 1496), Lisbon (Eliezer Toledano, 1488–1492), and Leiria (Samuel d'Ortas and his three sons, 1492–1496).[15]

The Hebrew presses of Spain and Portugal were closely connected. The press at Leiria was apparently founded by exiles from Spain, while that of Lisbon—the leading Hebrew press in Portugal—used the type, initial letters and decorated borders used previously at Hijar.[16] From the typographical-artistic point of view, the books printed in these three cities (i.e., Hijar, Leiria and Lisbon) are the most successful. Despite the persecutions of the Inquisition, by the late 1480s and early 1490s, when these books were published, the printers were far better equipped and more experienced in the art of mechanical reproduction. Side by side with growing attention to sharp, elegant types, the printers introduced attractive designs in selected sections of their books, particularly borders for initial letters and title pages.

The decorations in the early books are closely associated with the traditions, designs and motifs of contemporary illuminated Hebrew manuscripts. The most influential school of manuscript illumination which flourished in this period is the so-called Lisbon school.[17] Characteristic of this school are frontispieces surrounded with wide borders filled with delicate filigree designs, rich vegetation interspersed with colorful birds, lions, dragons, peacocks and other animals. Also typical are the initial letters written in gold in wide panels with filigree background. Almost all these elements were faithfully transferred into the printed books. The remarkable frame which appears first in Hijar and later in Lisbon (fig. no. 1) has been called in the art historical literature the "most delicate of all Iberian borders."[18] It is a metal engraving designed by Alfonso Fernandez de Cordoba, a noted silversmith, type-cutter and engraver, who skillfully used the black background to create balanced and pleasing forms of tendrils, scrolls, animals and grotesques.[19] As mentioned above, this delicate frame was later used in Lisbon as well. It should be noted, finally, that Eliezer Alantansi, in whose press de Cordoba worked, was also the first Hebrew printer to use a pictorial printer's device.[20]

FIG. NO. 1 Ornamental border from *Hidushei ha-Torah*, Nahmanides, Lisbon, 1489. Printer: Eliezer Toledano. Collection of the Jewish Division, New York Public Library, Astor, Lenox and Tilden Foundations.

Ketubbah Decoration

Until a few years ago very little was known about the physical appearance of the ketubbah in pre-Expulsion Spain. Unlike the precious manuscripts that were carried by the exiles to their new homes, or the printed books that were issued in many copies, there was no particular reason for preserving marriage contracts. As is the case with other small objects and ceremonial artifacts, the vicissitudes of exile caused the loss of such remnants. However, in recent years a number of ketubbot, whether complete or in a fragmentary form, have turned up in archives and libraries in Spain. Studies of this material have demonstrated the importance of the ketubbah and its artistic embellishment in the life of medieval Spanish Jews.

While in medieval Ashkenaz the rabbis introduced several *takkanot* (statutes) which actually standardized the text of the ketubbah and made its monetary clause fixed,[21] the marriage contract in Spain varied from one example to another and the value of the dowry (*nedunyah*) and the bridegroom's voluntary increment (*tosephet nedunyah*) were always expressed in actual amounts of money. In addition, the Spanish ketubbah often included a detailed and lengthy list of special provisions (*tenaim*) which discuss various

FIG. NO. 2 Ketubbah fragment, Majorca, ca. 1428, Barcelona, Biblioteca de Catalunya, manuscript no. 254.

personal and financial issues pertaining to the new marriage.[22] Furthermore, the bride and bridegroom are not presented merely by their first names and the first name of the fathers (as is the case with Ashkenazic ketubbot), but the lineage of the family as well as last names are commonly indicated, especially when affluent families were involved. Since the text of the ketubbah was read aloud at the wedding, these details served as an excellent indicator of the wealth and social status of the families. On some of the early contracts we notice signatures of more witnesses than the two required by Jewish Law. Evidently this practice reflects the custom of inviting important community figures to sign the contract as a sign of honor and respect to the families about to be united in marriage.

The festivities associated with the display of the bride's dowry and the reading of the text containing the special conditions and personal clauses naturally invited attempts to make the contract look more attractive. This was done by two methods which are attested to not only in preserved ketubbot but also in responsa literature.[23] The first method was to inscribe on the parchment appropriate Biblical verses and wishes for good luck in large square Hebrew letters; the second was to frame the text with decorative, colorful designs. Unfortunately, no pre-Expulsion example combining verses and decorations has been preserved. A fragment from Segura (148?) includes verses,[24] while a few other examples have only simple decorations. The latter are from the region of Navarre (dated 1300, 1309 and 1324); two fragments are from the island of Majorca (ca. early fifteenth century).[25] Their decoration is far removed from the sumptuous illuminations in the manuscripts or even the decorative frames in the printed books mentioned earlier. In the three Navarrese examples the text is set within a simple frame filled with geometrical patterns. The earliest example (Tudela, 1300) also contains two birds.[26] The outline of the designs is drawn in the same brown (faded) ink used for the text, with little additions of color. More colorful are the Majorcan fragments, featuring heart-shaped floral patterns in green and red while the narrow framing panels are in yellow (fig. no. 2).[27] Despite their relative simplicity, the extant ketubbot provide important clues for the later development of this art form among the exiled Sephardic communities.

AFTER THE EXPULSION

Illustrated Printed Books and Manuscripts

Most of the extant material pertaining to "Sephardic art" dates from the last three centuries. It chiefly originates from the many urban centers of the "Sephardic diaspora" in Italy, Holland, the Ottoman empire, North Africa and America. In addition to the expected wear and loss, and the general paucity of Judaica from the sixteenth century, one may conjecture that it took the Sephardim some time until they were firmly and safely settled and could resume their patronage of costly artistic objects. The curious question that arises is whether one can discern any characteristic, unifying elements which would point at common artistic sources in works created in distant and culturally distinct centers. The problem is more acute in these lands from which very little or no tangible evidence exists until several hundred years after the Expulsion (e.g., Morocco, Eretz Israel).

In the field of book and manuscript decoration, the best and most widely-spread medium for examining this phenomenon is the illuminated ketubbah. After the invention of printing, other types of manuscript illumination were, in general, on the decline. Although there was a revival of Hebrew manuscript illumination in the eighteenth century, especially of Haggadot in Bohemia and Moravia, the European Sephardim did not, by and large, take part in this phenomenon.[28] This is especially surprising in the light of the popularity and quality of pre-Expulsion Hebrew book illumination. Moreover, some of the sumptuous medieval manuscripts were carried by the exiled families and preserved in the hands of their descendants centuries later. The fact, however, is that the illustrated printed book or even single-page engravings and engraved Esther scrolls were much more popular (especially among Dutch Sephardim). Naturally there were various socio-cultural reasons which determined this development, and contributed, on the other hand, to the unusual popularity of the handmade illustrated ketubbah. Thus, for example, in North Africa, where printing could not develop as in Europe, numerous illuminated manuscripts and Esther scrolls continued to be produced down to the twentieth century.

The earliest preserved examples of material culture following the Expulsion from

Spain in 1492 and Portugal in 1497 are printed books. Among the exiles there were a number of printers who actually took with them their most valuable possessions, the tools of their craft. Within a short period, Hebrew presses were founded in three central locations in which the Sephardim established major communities: Istanbul and Salonika in Turkey and Fez in Morocco. In fact, the Hebrew presses in these towns printed the first known books on Turkish and African soil.

The press in Istanbul was established by members of the ibn Nahmias family, possibly as early as 1493.[29] The first book they printed, Jacob ben Asher's *Arbaah Turim*, bears a printer's mark: a six pointed star surrounded by flowers and leaves.[30] The use of a personal device in a book is clearly a continuation of the tradition we encountered earlier in the Iberian peninsula. Other European Hebrew printers started to use such devices only in the sixteenth century. Ibn Nahmias also used in his books the delicate frame of de Cordoba, previously used in Hijar and Lisbon (see above) (fig. no. 3).[31] Also connected with the Lisbon press was Don Judah Gedaliah, who started to publish books in Salonika in 1513, using the typographical material of Eliezer Toledano's Lisbon press, which he managed before the Expulsion.[32] Similarly, the founders of the Fez press, Samuel ben Isaac Nedivot and his son Isaac, must have learned the art of printing in Lisbon. Their press was apparently set up in 1516 and the first dated book issued was *Sefer Abudarham*.[33] Remarkably, this book is identical in almost every way with the edition of the same title printed in Lisbon in 1489 (cat. no. 16; fig. no. 4).

FIG. NO. 3 Ornamental border from *Zevah Pesah*, Yitzhak Abrabanel, Constantinople, 1505. Printers: David and Samuel ibn Nahmias. Rare Books and Manuscripts Collection, Mendel Gottesman Library, Yeshiva University, New York.

FIG. NO. 4 Calendrical chart from *Peirush ha-Berakhot ve-ha-Tefillot*, David ben Yosef Abudarham (14th century), Lisbon, 1489. Printer: Eliezer Toledano. Cat. no. 16.

The similarity between the books which the exiled printers published in the new diaspora, on the one hand, and imprints from Spain and Portugal, on the other, is so astounding that scholars and collectors alike have long been misled to believe that some of these sixteenth-century books are incunabula from the Iberian peninsula.[34] But it was in this way that the early printers disseminated the attainments of their art in the Jewish world. Moreover, thanks to their pioneering efforts, the new craft was introduced to communities that otherwise would not have had access to printing tools until long after the early sixteenth century.[35]

In the subsequent period it is more difficult to speak of a particularly Sephardic book art in the Ottoman empire. Rather than building on the imported tradition or creating a new one (as was the case with ketubbah decoration—see below), the Ottoman Hebrew printers often preferred to utilize ready-made designs from elsewhere. The Hebrew printing presses of Venice seem to have played a crucial role in this process. During the sixteenth century, Venice dominated the world of the Hebrew book, and the influence of its imprints reached Hebrew presses throughout Europe. The Venetian Hebrew printing shops were controlled at the time by prominent Christian printers, including Daniel Bomberg, Marco Antonio Giustiniani, Alvise Bragadini and Giovanni di Gara.[36] These printers introduced into the Hebrew books new designs and motifs that were often inspired by or taken directly from local, non-Hebrew books.

In some cases, the Jews who worked under the Christian printers attempted to give Jewish meaning to the borrowed elements. Perhaps the most characteristic example is the significant image of the gateway as a framing device on the title page. This design first appears in a Hebrew Bible printed by Daniel Bomberg in 1515–17.[37] Bomberg must have derived the idea to set the information on the title page in an architectural framework from contemporary Italian books.[38] The image, however, quickly acquired Jewish meaning as "the gateway to the Lord,"[39] and, in the vein of the curious Jewish tradition of attaching architectural metaphors to book terminology,[40] the title page acquired the Hebrew appellation *shaar* (lit. "gate"). As a result, and due to the great renown of Bomberg's press, the actual image appearing in his books was copied in numerous Hebrew books, first in Italy and then elsewhere. Thus, the Sephardic printers in Istanbul copied Bomberg's image, as did Hebrew printers in Germany and Poland. In fact, the motif appears in Hebrew books from Istanbul centuries after it was first introduced by Bomberg in Venice.[41]

The case of Bomberg is, nonetheless, just one typical example of the trend to imitate Venetian (and other Italian) designs in the Ottoman Hebrew (Sephardic) presses.[42] Furthermore, Italian printers actually settled in Turkey, bringing with them their Italian typographical material and decorations. Most noteworthy is the celebrated Italian-Ashkenazic printer Gershom Soncino, who was forced to leave Venice and Italy. In 1527 he arrived in Salonika and three years later settled in Istanbul. Together with his son,

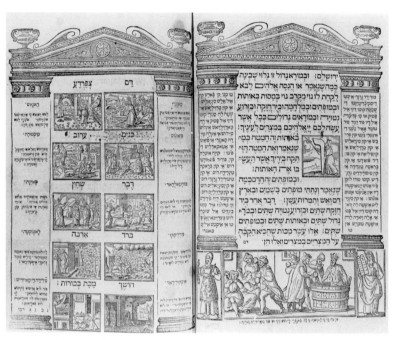

FIG. NO. 5 "Ten Plagues" from Haggadah—Ladino Edition, Venice, 1609. Printer: Giovanni da Gara. Cat. no. 580.

Eliezer, he printed attractive books in these cities,[43] using the decorative borders designed for him in Italy. The exquisite black and white frames and elaborate devices that were designed for him in Italy now adorned the books printed in Turkey.[44] Thus, the best examples of Ottoman Hebrew book decoration in the sixteenth century were imported designs with no particular local alterations.[45]

In Venice itself it is equally difficult to pinpoint a particular Sephardic tradition in book illustration. By 1589, when the Sephardim (*ponentini*) were permitted to settle permanently in the city (see below), the craft of Hebrew printing in Venice came of age, involving many experienced persons.[46] The decorations in the books printed for the newcomers did not differ significantly from those printed for the rest of the local Jewish community. This point is best demonstrated by the edition of the so-called Venice Haggadah of 1609. The printing of the Haggadah (conceived by the Italian-Jewish printer Israel ha-Zifroni and printed at the press of di Gara) set a new, remarkable standard in the history of the illustrated Hebrew book in general and the Haggadah in particular.[47] Unlike previous Haggadot, the unknown designer(s) of this one carefully planned every page to create a pleasant, harmonious balance between text and image. It is not surprising that this edition continued to serve as a model for imitation throughout the Jewish world for centuries to come. The example in this exhibition has a Ladino translation in the side columns flanking the main Hebrew text (cat. no. 580; fig. no. 5).

Obviously, this edition was intended for the Venetian and other Sephardim. But this does not mean it was specifically designed for them: in fact, Zifroni simultaneously issued three editions of the Haggadah, each in one of the Jewish dialects spoken in the ghetto of Venice: Judeo-Italian, Yiddish and Ladino.[48] Save for this difference in language, the three editions are identical.

Sephardic creativity in book art was given a fresh impetus and in fact reached its height with the foundation of the Hebrew press in Amsterdam. Early in the seventeenth century prayer books in Spanish were printed for the refugee marranos who arrived in that city and established the first Portuguese community there. Later, Hebrew and Ladino books were imported from the sister community in Venice. As the knowledge of Hebrew increased steadily, the first Hebrew press in Amsterdam was set up in 1626 by the noted scholar and rabbi Menasseh ben Israel (1604–1657).[49] Instead of relying heavily on Venetian types and designs, Menasseh preferred to cast his own type and have new decorations made in the spirit of the time. In so doing he opened—unknowingly, of course—a new period in the history of the Hebrew book. Amsterdam during this period became a leading center of printing in general, and with the success of Menasseh ben Israel many Hebrew printers were attracted to the city, enjoying the economic opportunities which it offered and the tolerant attitude of the authorities. In a relatively short period, Amsterdam dominated the Hebrew book market, taking the place of the declining Hebrew presses of Venice.[50]

FIG. NO. 6 Frontispiece of Bible prepared by Menasseh ben Israel, Amsterdam, 1635. Collection of the Jewish Division, New York Public Library, Astor, Lenox and Tilden Foundations.

FIG. NO. 7 Salom d'Italia, Portrait of Menasseh ben Israel, Amsterdam, ca. 1636, engraving.

FIG. NO. 8 Rembrandt van Rijn, "Jacob's Dream," engraved for Menasseh ben Israel's *Piedra gloriosa de la estatua de Nebuchadnesar*, Amsterdam, 1655.

FIG. NO. 9 Rembrandt van Rijn, "David and Goliath," engraved for Menasseh ben Israel's *Piedra gloriosa de la estatua de Nebuchadnesar*, Amsterdam, 1655.

FIG. NO. 10 Cornelius Janssens van Ceulen, "Portrait of G. Boudaan." Boudaan is depicted holding Menasseh ben Israel's Bible of 1635.

The title border in Menasseh's books consisted of an arch supported by two columns with entwined tendrils, and a typical Baroque broken gable above (fig. no. 6). This relatively simple architectural design was copied time and again by many presses, as well as by scribes and artists producing small Hebrew manuscripts.[51] As was the custom in Dutch books of the period, Menasseh introduced a new type of illustration: the portrait of the author. His own portrait, engraved by the renowned Jewish etcher Salom Italia (ca. 1619–ca. 1655), appears, for example, in his book *Nishmat Hayyim* (Amsterdam, 1652).[52] The dignified rabbi is shown within an oval medallion: in the custom of Dutch Sephardic rabbis, he has a short beard and mustache and wears a skullcap and a black coat buttoned to the neck (fig. no. 7). Menasseh's careful attention to the appearance of his books also led him to commission none other than Rembrandt himself to engrave four illustrations for his Messianic Spanish work *Piedra Gloriosa* (Amsterdam, 1655) (fig. nos. 8–9).[53] For some reason not entirely clear, Rembrandt's etchings do not appear in all the copies of the book; some are illustrated with inferior imitations produced by Italia.[54]

Menasseh ben Israel's close contacts with Rembrandt are indicative of a trend among the Dutch Sephardic upper class to associate with wealthy and intellectual Protestants. Dutch theologians and intellectuals, in their turn, were attracted to Jewish culture, seeking to understand the teachings of Judaism and its interpretation of the Bible.[55] The Calvinist emphasis on the Word of God induced many Protestants to study Hebrew and read the Bible in the original tongue. Taking advantage of the situation, the open-minded Sephardic printers, including Menasseh himself, issued special editions of the Hebrew Bible (and other books) for the Protestant readers. In a painting by the English-born Dutch master Cornelius Janssens van Ceulen (1593–ca. 1662), we see the Dutch preacher Boudaan pointing at the first page of a large Hebrew book which he holds in his left hand (fig. no. 10).[56] The open book is obviously Menasseh ben Israel's Hebrew Bible of 1635, the title page of which is decorated with the familiar architectural border mentioned above.

Besides Menasseh ben Israel, there were in seventeenth-century Amsterdam other prominent and influential Sephardic printers. Mention should be made of Joseph Athias, who, like Menasseh, associated with Dutch men of learning, most notably Holland's famous poet Joost van den Vondel.[57] The young Athias set up his press in 1658 and commissioned Christoffel van Dijk to cast elegant type for him. Athias engaged in publishing, advertising and selling books, in Hebrew and other languages, to a large clientele, Jewish and non-Jewish. In 1661 he was the first Jew to join the Amsterdam booksellers' guild—a right previously denied to Menasseh ben Israel.[58] Moreover, the Dutch States General granted him the monopoly on printing and selling Bibles in English. The success of Athias in this business is attested by his own words: "For several years I myself printed more than a million Bibles for England and Scotland. There is no plowboy or servant girl there without one."[59] In recognition of his services and for issuing a Bible that is "the most correct and exact edition that had ever been published," the States General presented Athias with a gold medal.

Joseph Athias, and later his son Immanuel, made a point of providing their books with attractive title pages that would be appropriate for their high-quality editions. The title page of the Bible printed in several languages was prepared from a copper engraving by an unknown artist (fig. no. 11). The design is divided into three sections: the upper depicts a detailed picture of the Giving of the Law, with a multitude of people watching Moses on the top of Mount Sinai as he receives the Tablets descending from a fiery heaven filled with sounding trumpets; the center section has a large coat of arms flanked by the figures of Moses holding the Tablets and his staff, and David with his harp; at the bottom, another crowded scene depicts the meeting between Joseph and Jacob on the road to Egypt (Genesis 46:29). The selection of these themes is hardly accidental. The upper two panels obviously refer to the origin and meaning of the Bible and two of its most prominent figures, while the bottom alludes to the printer by depicting an event in the life of a Biblical figure (Joseph) bearing the same name.[60]

Athias' title page reflects a new trend in Hebrew book illustration which became more and more popular among the Jewish printers (Sephardic and Ashkenazic) in Amsterdam

FIG. NO. 11 Title page of German Bible, Amsterdam, 1687. Printer: Joseph Athias.

FIG. NO. 12 Frontispiece of *Orden de Beniciones Mea Berachoth*, Amsterdam, 1675, engraving by Benjamin Godines.

FIG. NO. 13 Frontispiece of *Tikkun Keriah*, Amsterdam, 1666, with depiction of Shabbetai Zevi enthroned.

beginning with the second half of the seventeenth century. Instead of featuring the same ready-made designs over and over again, the illustrations of new title pages referred to the contents of the book, its writer, and more often to the printer himself. Moreover, in a number of cases the linkage was formed in a sophisticated manner by talented engravers, both Jewish and Christian. A noteworthy example is the title page designed in 1687 by the little-known Sephardic artist of Amsterdam, Benjamin Senior Godines, for the book *Orden de Beniciones Mea Berachoth* (fig. no. 12).[61] This curious little book is a special prayer book containing one hundred blessings in Hebrew with Spanish translations for the Marranos. Godines' engraving is composed of symmetrically arranged episodes referring to the five senses—a theme popular in contemporary Dutch art, but here adapted to correspond to the various types of blessings. A sixth episode, at the bottom of the page, refers both to the contents and the title of the book by showing a sowing scene and the verse: "And Isaac sowed in that land . . . a hundredfold (*meah shearim*) and the Lord blessed him" (Genesis 26:12).

The linkage to the author's or printer's name was done in a traditional Jewish manner. As we saw in the case of Athias, the engraver would select an episode in the life of a Biblical hero with the same first name as that of the contemporary figure.[62] The Biblical heroes are shown in their finest and most pious hours, serving as an ideal model for contemporaries. In a like manner such episodes adorned other categories of personal documents and objects, notably ketubbot and tombstones. In fact, the Biblical episodes on the title pages of the book served at times as the direct source for the attractive sculpted episodes on the tombstones of the Sephardim in the cemetery at Ouderkerk near Amsterdam.[63] In rare cases no Biblical episode was shown to honor a person of the period, but rather a narrative episode referring to a living person (as distinct from an author's portrait). The hero of such daring representations was, in most instances, the pseudo-Messiah Shabbetai Zevi (1626–1676). In one of the prayer books issued by his followers at the height of the Sabbatean movement, Shabbetai is shown seated on Solomon's majestic throne as four angels crown him (*Tikkun Keriah*, Amsterdam, 1666) (fig. no. 13).[64]

In the same vein, some of the illustrations in the Amsterdam books commemorated an event rather than a person. The most memorable festive event in the life of Amsterdam's Sephardic community was the dedication of the new Portuguese synagogue in 1675.[65] Much effort, careful planning, and enormous amounts of money were invested by the community to erect the largest and most extravagant Jewish building in Europe of the time.[66] The construction of the synagogue was entrusted to the Dutch master Elias Bouman (1636–1686), who studied his subject carefully before preparing a model.[67] The four cornerstones were laid in an impressive ceremony in 1671 by four leaders of the community who contributed large sums for the building fund. As construction progressed, the new structure rose high above the surrounding houses, standing out in the skyline of the city.[68] The huge interior (about 85 by 125 ft.) could seat close to 2,000 worshippers. It was furnished with a monumental *bimah* and an enormous Holy Ark (*heikhal*) made of costly wood imported from Brazil.

When the synagogue was finally ready for services (August 2, 1675), the community naturally wished to celebrate the event with much pomp and festivity. The dedication, attended by many notables and accompanied by an orchestra and choir, lasted a whole week. The sermons delivered during that week, first by the illustrious rabbi of the community, Haham Isaac Aboab da Fonseca, and then by his disciples, were printed in the book *Sermões que pregaraõ os Doctos Ingenios do K. K. de Talmud Torah desta Cidade de Amsterdam* (Amsterdam, 1675). *Sermões* was published by David ben Abraham de Castro Tartas, who appended to it a series of illustrations depicting in great detail the elevation of the imposing synagogue, its floor plan, the dedication ceremony, the *heikhal* and the *bimah* (cat. no. 582; fig. no. 14). The engravings were prepared by the well-known Dutch artist Romeyn de Hooghe, who was closely familiar with the Amsterdam Sephardic community and produced a number of works depicting its life.[69] De Hooghe also designed the official broadside for the dedication of the synagogue, accompanied by a praiseworthy poem composed by himself, in which he called the new synagogue "Bouman's masterpiece."[70]

FIG. NO. 14 *Sermoes que pregarao os Doctos Ingenios do K. K. de Talmud Torah desta Cidade de Amsterdam*, Amsterdam, 1675. Printer: David Castro Tartaz, engravings by Romeyn de Hooghe. Cat. no. 582.

The high quality of the illustrations of the Amsterdam imprints induced numerous printers in Europe and even in the East to imitate these designs. The term *be-otiot Amsterdam* (lit. "in Amsterdam letters," but usually understood in a wider typographical context) became the hallmark for a high standard in Hebrew printing. But the dissemination of Amsterdam typography and book design was not limited to printed books.

FIG. NO. 15 Frontispiece of *Sefer Heshek Shlomo*, Shlomo son of Yitzhak Saruco, The Hague, 1767–1773. Cat. no. 575.

FIG. NO. 16 Frontispiece of *Keter Shem Tov*, Shlomo ben Yitzhak Curiel Abaz, Amsterdam, 1725–1761. Cat. no. 574.

FIG. NO. 17 "Plague of Frogs" from Haggadah, Bordeaux, France, 1813. Scribe: Isaac Zoreph; Illustrator: Jacob Zoreph. Cat. no. 576.

While in the early stages of printing the layout of the page was modeled after, and the designs borrowed from, illuminated manuscripts, the reverse now became the norm. The printed Amsterdam books which arrived in almost every corner of the Jewish world provided an easily accessible, popular and inexpensive source of inspiration for many illuminators of Hebrew codices. In fact, the influence of the illustrations can be seen also in other media, such as pewter Seder plates and illuminated ketubbot.

In Holland itself the hand-illuminated manuscript was not very popular. In general, the Dutch Sephardic scribes preferred to limit the art work, as in most of the printed books, to the title page alone. Moreover, the decoration of the title page was mostly carried out not in colors but with the same ink as the written text; e.g., *Sefer Heshek Shelomo*, The Hague, 1767–1773 (cat. no. 575; fig. no. 15).[71] The imagery was either derived directly from the printed title page, or inspired by its shape, design, and selection of motifs. An example of the latter is the manuscript *Keter Shem Tov*, a register of the circumcisions performed by Solomon ben Isaac Curiel Abaz in Amsterdam, 1724–1760 (cat. no. 574; fig. no. 16).[72] The general layout of the page is familiar from a number of seventeenth-century printed title pages, but the selection of motifs is peculiar to this manuscript. As in the printed book, here, too, the episodes relate to the subject of the manuscript and its author. Since his name was Solomon, the selected episodes show the merits of King Solomon. At bottom center is Solomon's Judgment, flanked by a scene depicting the birth of the king (left) and a contemporary circumcision scene (right). Paralleling these episodes at top center are two semi-nude heraldic nymphs flanking the inscription "And the kingdom was established in the hands of Solomon" (I Kings 2:46). The central side niches symbolically represent the covenant between God and Israel through the implements and furnishings (Chair of Elijah) of the circumcision ceremony, accompanied by carefully chosen, appropriate verses.

The most influential illustrations in an Amsterdam Hebrew book were undoubtedly those of the famous Amsterdam Haggadah of 1695 and 1712.[73] These illustrations were copied countless times by Ashkenazic scribes and artists who produced attractive manuscript Haggadot in eighteenth-century Europe.[74] As noted earlier, the Sephardim did not generally share in this revival and the printed illustrated Haggadah continued to be the popular medium. An interesting exception to this rule is, however, a Sephardic manuscript Haggadah written and decorated by Isaac and Jacob Soreph at Bordeaux, France, as late as 1813 (cat. no. 576; fig. no. 17).[75] Although the instructions in the Hebrew text are given in Ladino, the entire text is translated into modern French, attesting to the assimilative tendencies of the Sephardim in Bordeaux.[76] The Soreph brothers, descendants of a Portuguese marrano family, created a manuscript reflecting the neo-classical spirit of contemporary French art, but they relied heavily on the Amsterdam Haggadah. Thus the classical architectural and decorative elements on the title page are combined with almost slavish imitations of the Haggadah printed about 100 years earlier.

By the time the Bordeaux Haggadah was produced, Amsterdam was no longer the dominant center of Sephardic printing that it had been in previous centuries. It was gradually being replaced by the city of Livorno (Leghorn), Italy, the last important European center of Hebrew book publishing for Sephardic use. The leading printer in Livorno was Solomon Belforte, an able scholar and businessman, who established his press in 1834.[77] In the course of the nineteenth and early twentieth centuries, Belforte's publishing house became more and more prominent, employing 100 workers in 1926. The books printed in Livorno were sent to Jewish communities in Islamic lands and North Africa, contributing to the standardization of Sephardic liturgy in these regions. Artistically speaking, however, Belforte's and other Livornese Hebrew books are of secondary interest.[78] The press was active until World War II. With the establishment of Israel, its equipment was transferred to the new Jewish state.

Ketubbah Decoration

The most characteristic form of Sephardic manuscript decoration from the seventeenth to the nineteenth centuries, and in some places also in the early twentieth, is undoubtedly ketubbah decoration. Decorated ketubbot have survived from virtually every major center and many small towns in which the Sephardim settled after the Expulsion. Local styles of writing and decorating the ketubbah developed in almost every center. At the same time the ketubbot of the various centers, no matter how distant from one another, show significant features in common.

Extant post-Expulsion ketubbot can be roughly divided into three larger cultural groups: Western Europe, North Africa, and the Ottoman empire. The first group includes the Sephardic communities of Italy (chiefly Venice and Livorno), Holland (Amsterdam and Rotterdam), Germany (Hamburg), the city-state of Ragusa (Dubrovnik), some Mediterranean islands (mainly Corfu, but also Malta and Minorca), and, to a lesser extent, also France (Bayonne and Bordeaux), England (London), and colonial America (New York and Curaçao). Grouped under the second heading are all the Sephardic communities in North Africa, including Morocco (Tetuan, Mogador and Tangier), Tunisia (Tunis), Algeria (Algiers and Oran), as well as Gibraltar, Portugal (Lisbon), the Azores and Brazil (Para). The third major group is the vast Ottoman empire, with major centers in Turkey and Greece (Istanbul, Izmir, Salonika and Rhodes). Two distinct sub-groups in this last category are: a) the European Ottoman communities in Austria (Vienna), Yugoslavia (Belgrade, Zemun, Monastir and Sarajevo), Bulgaria (Sofia and Shumen), Rumania (Bucharest and Timisoara) and b) Eastern Ottoman communities in Eretz Israel (Jerusalem, Jaffa, Hebron, Tiberias and Safed), Syria (Aleppo and Damascus) and Egypt (Alexandria and Cairo). Naturally these groups are not so clear-cut and there is some overlapping as well as reciprocal influences. We will attempt to outline the main characteristics of the ketubbot in each group, noting basic similarities and differences between them.[79]

The earliest evidence known to us that the Sephardim continued to commission decorated ketubbot after their expulsion from the Iberian peninsula is documented not by an actual contract but in the responsa literature. Rabbi Abraham di Boton (1545?– 1588), a descendant of exiles from the peninsula, who was born and lived in Salonika, mentions in his book *Lehem Rav* a ketubbah with pictures of the bridegroom and the bride and the sun and the moon.[80] And although Rabbi Boton does not recommend the use of such a document, these designs must have been very popular because they are later found on Sephardic ketubbot emanating from a number of major communities in our first group (e.g., Venice, Amsterdam and Hamburg), as well as a rare example from Salonika itself (see below).

Another early piece of rabbinical evidence attesting to the importance of the physical appearance of the ketubbah after the Expulsion comes from Fez, Morocco. In the series of early *takkanot* (statutes) issued by Sephardic rabbis for the exiled communities (*megorashim*), there is a complaint that members of their community rubbed out the original text of the contract and wrote their own instead.[81] This story is certainly indicative of the economic difficulties in which the new immigrants found themselves. However, in 1545, when the situation apparently improved, the Sephardic rabbis issued the following *takkanah*: "From this day on, ketubbot shall not be written on anything but parchment."[82] This statute fully agrees with the practice in medieval Spain, where parchment ketubbot were the norm. Based on Rabbi Boton and the Fez *takkanah*, we may thus safely conclude that at least in some of the well-established communities the Sephardim of the second generation after the Expulsion, after one generation of adjustment, reverted to the ketubbah traditions of their forefathers.

Notwithstanding the early written testimonies, extant post-Expulsion ketubbot date from a later period. The gap is especially serious in our second and third groups, since no illustrated examples have come down to us from North Africa and the Ottoman empire prior to the late eighteenth century, that is, almost three centuries after the Expulsion. The situation is much better in the case of the first group. Seventeenth-century Sephardic ketubbot have survived in relatively large numbers from Italy and Holland, as have isolated examples from other localities.

Western Europe

The earliest group of decorated Sephardic ketubbot dates from the opening years of the seventeenth century, and they are all from Venice.[83] Exiles from the Iberian peninsula tried to settle in the Republic of Venice at an early date, but not until 1589 did the Venetian government officially invite them to settle in the city itself and participate in the international trade of the Republic. Within a short time, as the Venetian *ponentini* prospered, they began to commission decorated ketubbot. Both the text and decorations of these marriage contracts can be characterized as typically Sephardic. The text is divided into two sections, the ketubbah text proper and the *tenaim* or special provisions. The latter are usually set down in a separate column, to the left of the standard text, or below it. They usually are written in minuscule cursive Sephardic script, while the main text is in elegant square Hebrew characters, familiar from medieval Spanish manuscripts. The clauses contained in the set of provisions are standardized to a certain degree, but also include particular, personal stipulations which shed light on the social standing of the families. Additional information on their economic status is contained in the dowry clause, which at times is very elaborate.

The decoration of these documents consists of an architectural setting embedded with geometric and floral motifs and verses.[84] An arcade comprised of two horseshoe arches frames the two sections of the text. This shape of an arch is perhaps the most typical visual design "imported" by the newcomers from the Iberian peninsula. It is familiar from Spanish synagogue architecture and art (e.g., the synagogues in Toledo) as well as ceremonial objects (e.g., the pair of *rimmonim* in Majorca), and manuscript illumination (e.g., the Kennicott Bible). It is therefore clear that only Sephardic craftsmen could have introduced this motif into the Venetian ghetto.

The calligraphic verses that surround the text are also significant. In Rabbi Duran's responsum mentioned earlier, we read his recommendation that the text of the ketubbah be framed by rhyming verses. And although he considers this practice as merely complying with a halakhic need, it is clear that it also served to enhance the appearance of the document. However, the connection with medieval Spain goes further than the mere inclusion of verses. The verses most often quoted on the Venetian ketubbot, namely, the passage from Ruth 4:11–12, is prominently inscribed on the borders of the pre-Expulsion Segura ketubbah mentioned earlier. The importance of this passage, which refers to the marriage of Ruth and Boaz before the elders at the city gate, is evident in the context of the marriage contract. But in Venetian and later Sephardic ketubbot it acquired additional meaning: its frequent occurrence with an architectural background closely connects it with a city gate and the building of a new house in Israel, both of which are mentioned in the passage.[85]

The Venetian ketubbot are not only the earliest extant post-Expulsion Sephardic examples, but also the first fully decorated ketubbot produced in Italy. As I have shown elsewhere,[86] the Sephardim in fact introduced and helped disseminate this art form in Italy, where the most attractive ketubbot were executed in the seventeenth and eighteenth centuries. However, from about 1650, though they continued their significant contribution to the development of ketubbah art in Italy, the Sephardim simply joined other creative sources among Italian Jewry in designing marriage contracts. No particular Sephardic motifs that would distinguish Sephardic ketubbot from those of other Jews living in Italy at the time can be noticed. In fact, only some details in the text, such as the names of the two parties and the list of stipulations entered into the *tenaim* columns, would tell us whether the wedding was Sephardic, Ashkenazic or Italian (*italiani*). By the second half of the seventeenth century, certain attractive designs gained widespread popularity and were copied time and again on numerous ketubbot.[87] Such designs were used by all sections of Italian Jewry, who wished to emulate the new decorations which reflected the spirit of the time and the place. Thus, one may speak of the style and designs which developed in, and are characteristic of, ketubbot in such major centers as Rome, Venice, Ancona and Ferrara, but not of distinctive denominational features within these cities.[88]

The situation is slightly different in Italian towns where the Sephardim constituted a majority of the local Jewish population. Especially in Livorno and Pisa the wealthy Sephardim in the eighteenth century commissioned elaborate ketubbot, which are closely related. Yet it is not always possible to speak of specifically Livornese or Pisan styles, for the influence of the major centers, particularly Venice and Ancona, predominates. In order to make their ketubbot even more attractive, the Sephardi patrons in both cities also employed local non-Jewish artists.[89] These ketubbot do not usually have any Jewish elements or Hebrew inscriptions along their borders. In one instance a semi-nude Venus is shown with Cupid at the top of the large parchment.[90] However, the text of these documents always includes a set of typical Sephardic *tenaim*.[91] The latter may appear in a separate column to the left (as in Venice), or below the main text (especially in the undecorated nineteenth-century examples).

Strong Venetian influences also prevail in the Sephardic ketubbot of Corfu, Greece and Ragusa (now Dubrovnik, Yugoslavia). Both cities were politically and economically tied to the Republic of Venice, and Jewish merchants frequently traveled between these ports. The ketubbot of Corfu and Ragusa can be divided into three groups: a) pre-decorated parchments, which were executed and purchased in Venice (or Ancona) and then filled in with appropriate text; b) decorations executed locally but copied from, or inspired by, Venetian borders; c) simple decorations with no relation to Venice but closer to designs found on typical Greek (Romaniot) or Yugoslav ketubbot (see below). The example from Corfu (1781) (cat. no. 562) in this exhibit belongs to the second group. It uses a simplified version of a popular Venetian border, comprised of the symbolic labyrinth or "lovers' knot" on top, and an arcade surrounded by cartouches containing the allegories of the four seasons in the four corners, the twelve signs of the zodiac, and, in the center of each band, a depiction of a Biblical hero or episode: David with his harp, Moses holding the Tablets, the Binding of Isaac, and Jacob's Dream. These Biblical representations, though familiar from Italian ketubbot, do not appear in the standard Venetian borders of this type and seem to be local inventions.[92]

FIG. NO. 18 Ketubbah, Amsterdam, 1617. Cat. no. 559.

As with printing, the growing community of Amsterdam was second only to Venice in the dissemination of pictorial ideas among Sephardic communities. The art of the ketubbah flourished in Amsterdam at an early date. Our example from 1617 (cat. no. 559; fig. no. 18)[93] was created only a few years after the Portuguese community was organized there. Despite its early date it shows a well-developed decorative program with a careful balance between a minuscule text and a delicate architectural background. It is interesting to note that the connection with the Iberian peninsula is conveyed here by the text rather than by the decorations. Since the families seem to have arrived from Portugal shortly before this contract was drawn up, the dowry clause includes lands in Portugal, implying that the refugees still hoped to regain the possessions they had left behind. Here again the overall image of an open gateway with two classic columns and other architectural details is enhanced by verses associating the wedding and the "woman of valor" with the gate (Ruth 14:11, Prov. 31:33).[94]

Italian motifs and designs in Dutch ketubbot were disseminated not only by close contacts between the Sephardim of Venice and Amsterdam but also by traveling artists. We have already mentioned the Mantuan etcher Salom Italia, who worked in Amsterdam during the 1640s and 1650s. Italia etched for the Amsterdam community two copperplates from which ketubbah borders were printed. The best-known one is preserved on two ketubbot.[95] It depicts a series of cartouches with Biblical couples, culminating with a Sephardic wedding scene. The second border, with the text from Amsterdam (1648), turned up recently in Amsterdam's Municipal Archives.[96] Although this border is much simpler, it is of the utmost significance in the development of Sephardic ketubbot. Italia's border served as the source for the most popular Sephardic ketubbah border, designed by an unknown artist during the late 1650s. The example from 1663 (cat. no. 560; fig. no. 19) in our exhibition is one of the earliest examples with this engraving. The typical gateway image here is flanked on top with marital symbols: a loving couple and the allegory of Caritas ("Charity"); on the sides are large urns filled with flowers in bloom and nesting birds. As is usually the case in Dutch Sephardic ketubbot, the *tenaim* appear below the main text, within a special large cartouche at bottom center.

This design gained widespread popularity among the Sephardim of Holland, England, France, Germany, and even the New World.[97] It continued to adorn Sephardic ketubbot until the second half of the nineteenth century. The print itself was copied and "updated" several times in this process. In some cases the black and white print was colored in by hand, and examples of ketubbot in which the entire border was copied and colored by hand are also known.[98] In fact, the influence of this border was so widespread that Sephardic craftsmen repeated its basic designs without always being aware of its origin. One example is the ketubbah of Bayonne (1757) (cat. no. 561; fig. no. 20) in our exhibition. The ketubbot of Bayonne are usually decorated with floral

FIG. NO. 19 Ketubbah, Amsterdam, 1663. Cat. no. 560.

FIG. NO. 20 Ketubbah, Bayonne, 1758. Cat. no. 561.

frames, surrounding a single column of text (*tenaim* are not included). Here the artist organized the flowers in two vases in a manner similar to the popular print. Additionally, he imitated the shape of the lettering in the words *be-siman tov* ("with a good omen") and the opening word "on the fourth day of the week;" i.e., Wednesday. Perhaps the death of Amsterdam's revered Haham Isaac Aboab da Fonseca in 1693 contributed to the increasing popularity of this print. The bereaved community added his name and the date of his death to the engraving, making it a lasting memorial. In this manner, the bride and groom and the guests at the wedding were reminded of their painful loss in much the same way the mention of Jerusalem is always made at such joyous events.

North Africa[99]

Sephardic traditions in the visual arts have been best preserved in the modern era among the communities in North Africa. The refugees from the Iberian peninsula settled at an early date in the major cities along the coast, a region which was always strongly influenced by Spanish culture. As early as 1497 the Sephardic rabbis spelled out in their *takkanot* certain differences between themselves, the *megorashim* ("exiles"), and the local Jews, whom they called *toshavim* ("natives"). The purpose of the new marriage regulations in these *takkanot* was to perpetuate the relative cultural and economic superiority of the exiles over the local Jewish population. It should be noted that the new attitude of the Sephardic rabbis on the personal status of women was by far more advanced than that of the "locals" and ultimately helped improve also the position of married Jewish women in North Africa.[100] A set of provisions included in the ketubbot of the *megorashim* prohibited the husband from marrying a second wife (which he legally could do) unless he gave the first wife an unconditional *get* (bill of divorce) and returned to her the full amount of money specified in the ketubbah for such an eventuality. This and other enactments inevitably led the *megorashim* to accept monogamous marriages as the preferred norm.

The North African ketubbot that have survived date from a later period. Except for a single example dated 1669 that was actually issued to a Moroccan couple in France,[101] surviving North African ketubbot date mostly from the nineteenth and early twentieth centuries. Throughout this period the *megorashim* continued to commission richly-decorated ketubbot executed on pieces of costly parchment (the *toshavim* generally used paper). The writing on the parchments, whether decorated or not, is mostly in tiny cursive Sephardic script, and only one column of text is used. The set of *tenaim* mentioned above is incorporated into this text in an abbreviated form. In Tunis, however, the scribes often wrote the ketubbot in square Sephardic script, and did incorporate a separate column for the terms. Indeed, the Sephardic ketubbot from Tunis very much resemble their West European counterparts, especially from Venice. Two other features in the text of North African ketubbot further emphasize the "Sephardi connection." The first is the custom to insert into the ketubbah an unusually long list of the bridegroom's and the bride's ancestors, supposedly to prove their Spanish origin. In addition, ketubbot of the *megorashim* ended with a prayer that the Lord might preserve, protect and help the communities that had been exiled from Castile.[102]

The most dominant motif of decoration in North African Sephardic ketubbot in cities such as Tetuan, Fez and Mogador is the framing device of a horseshoe arch (e.g., Tetuan, 1852, cat. no. 378; fig. no. 21; Meknes, 1855, cat. no. 379; fig. no. 22). The shape of the inner side of the arch is variously either circular or multifoil (round or pointed). It rests on two slender, flat columns; there is no attempt to create an illusion of space. Moreover, the arch is highly ornamental, painted in bright colors, and is usually surrounded by a profusion of flowers, with or without vases. In other instances the background is crowded with colorful, intricate geometrical designs that often recall ornamented Spanish tiles (*azulejos*). In the example from Meknes (1855) in our exhibition these richly and exquisitely drawn motifs create a pleasant and symmetrical rhythm of color and shape.

Similar decorative arches are found not only in ketubbot but also in other manuscripts of North African provenance. Esther scrolls, kabbalistic, liturgical and poetic works

FIG. NO. 21 Ketubbah, Tetuan, 1852. Cat. no. 378.

FIG. NO. 22 Ketubbah, Meknes, 1855. Cat. no. 379.

FIG. NO. 23 Frontispiece of *Zhahir Shel Pesah*, Morocco, 19th century. Cat. no. 401.

continued to be copied by hand in Morocco until recent times and the decorations in them are basically the same as in the ketubbot (see cat. nos. 373–376). Thus, in the scrolls each column of text is set in a decorative arch, so that a rhythmic arcade of horseshoe arches is formed. In the manuscripts the design is generally limited to the title page or other important pages in the book (fig. no. 23). The result in both cases is, in effect, a reduced picture of the large parchment ketubbah. Most of these scrolls and manuscripts lack specific indications of the date and place of origin, but this striking similarity should serve the serious scholar as the best source for the missing information.

The horseshoe arch is, as we have seen, the most typical Sephardic motif. In Tunisian ketubbot, where two columns of text were used, a double Moorish arch frames the text; this increases even further the affinity of these documents to the early Venetian examples, certainly pointing to a common source in medieval Spain.[103] Similarly, the primary colors that decorate the ketubbot in Tetuan, Mogador and other cities are reddish-yellow and green, colors typical of early Spanish art. These colors appear also on the medieval Majorca ketubbah mentioned earlier. Although representations of the human figure are generally avoided, faunal motifs, particularly birds, are used. In the Tetuan example (fig. no. 21), a pair of colorful birds is depicted at the sides of the arch. Such birds are in fact typical of many Jewish ceremonial objects such as Hanukkah lamps, and some scholars claim that this motif, too, had its origin in medieval Spain.[104]

While North African ketubbot are replete with Spanish designs, specifically Jewish motifs or symbols are, surprisingly, not as common. The early ketubbah from France mentioned earlier does depict a menorah, and in the case of Tetuan, we see the hands of the kohanim (priests) raised in blessing[105]—but these are isolated exceptions. Thus it is interesting to examine the attractive lithograph border in green and gold which was executed by an unknown Moroccan artist in the early twentieth century (see our example from Rabat, 1909) (cat. no. 380). The print incorporates hands inscribed with the Priestly Blessing, and wedding symbols: a gilt goblet marked "The Cup of the Seven [Marriage] Benedictions" and a pitcher marked "Wine Decanter." Curiously enough, another print of this lithograph records a marriage that took place in Pará, Brazil, in 1911.[106]

The Pará example is indicative of the spread of Moroccan-Sephardic designs outside North Africa. A "third diaspora" (following that of Spain and Morocco) was created when, in the course of the nineteenth century, Moroccan Jews settled in Gibraltar, Portugal, the Azores, Eretz Israel and Brazil. The ketubbot created in the new centers are frequently modeled on types that were popular in the former homes of the emigrés.[107] Sometimes, however, local elements were added, and in some instances new conventions and styles were created. In addition, the ketubbot produced in Morocco itself were, in turn, influenced by motifs used in the Jewish communities where the Moroccan emigrants settled. A typical example is the strong influence exerted

FIG. NO. 24 Ketubbah, Salonika, 1836. Cat. no. 100.

FIG. NO. 25 Ketubbah, Salonika, 1880. Cat. no. 104.

by the distinctive format of the Gibraltar ketubbot (see cat. no. 564) on Tangier and Mogador.[108] This whole complicated issue deserves a separate study.

The Ottoman Empire

The third and last group is comprised of a large geographical area: the Ottoman empire, which had active centers of Jewish population in the West[109] as well as the East. Here again we have extant examples only from recent generations. Unlike North Africa, many of the original designs which the Sephardim had brought with them had been lost by the nineteenth century. Even the time-honored custom of writing the ketubbah on parchment had gradually fallen into disuse. Thus, while the few extant late eighteenth- and early nineteenth-century Ottoman examples are still executed on parchment, the later ketubbot are all on paper. In addition, a certain decline in the art work can be noted in the course of the century. Yet, in the major centers of decoration (e.g., Istanbul and Rhodes), a few extravagant examples were still produced toward the end of the nineteenth century. Under Islamic influence, the Sephardim of the Ottoman empire generally avoided figural representations in the ketubbot. However, we may assume that this phenomenon was only a late development and that the early documents very likely included human figures. This hypothesis is clearly supported not only by the sixteenth-century responsum of Rabbi di Boton mentioned earlier in this study, but also by a relatively early ketubbah from Salonika (1790), featuring naive representations of a bride and bridegroom.[110]

Faunal motifs, particularly birds, are found in the Ottoman ketubbot of Izmir, Istanbul and Salonika, especially from the early nineteenth century. The Salonikan fragment from ca. 1836 in our exhibit (cat. no. 100; fig. no. 24) has a pair of lovebirds in the colorful floral wreaths at top center. The same arrangement of these elements appears in ketubbot from Izmir implying a common source for both cities.[111] It should be noted that two birds also appear in one pre-Expulsion Spanish ketubbah. In later Salonikan ketubbot (cat. nos. 101–104) the format and palette are simpler. The characteristic double arch and the flowers above it remain, but they are delineated in a schematic, almost abstract, manner, and are less colorful. In some instances the entire decoration is executed in one color (e.g., Salonika, 1880, cat. no. 104; fig. no. 25), and no decorative verses are included. With the transition to printed ketubbot in the 1880s, Salonikan craftsmen tried to revive the wealth of decorations from earlier days. In an example designed by or for the scribe David Yitzhak Amarillo (Salonika, 1897, cat. no. 106B; fig. no. 26),[112] the text is set in a magnificent arcade, resting on classic columns; there

FIG. NO. 26 Ketubbah, Salonika, 1891. Cat. no. 106B.

FIG. NO. 27 Ketubbah, Sofia, 1936. Cat. no. 111.

is a large amphora filled with flowers, and in the background there are rays of light.

Similar motifs and designs dominate the ketubbot of the Sephardim in other parts of the Ottoman empire in Europe. In countries such as Rumania, Austria, Bulgaria and Yugoslavia, the ketubbot are usually written, as in Salonika, in two parallel columns, set in a double arch decorated with floral designs.[113] In some cases a pair of fish, symbols of fertility, are added at the top. While some of these documents were executed by skilled craftsmen who paid attention to every detail, others are rather simplified versions. The latter category includes our examples from Monastir, Yugoslavia and Shumen (now Kolarovgrad), Bulgaria (cat. nos. 105, 109). In these two documents the designs are drawn directly on the page without outlines. However, the list of provisions is typical of numerous Sephardic ketubbot. With the change to printed ketubbot an attempt was made to create—again as in Amsterdam and Salonika—attractive borders that would be duplicated again and again. A noted example is the border which was designed in Sofia and gained popularity among Sephardim throughout Bulgaria (cat. no. 111; fig. no. 27). This multicolored lithograph incorporates such Jewish symbols as the Star of David, the seven-branched menorah, and fruit and vegetation, possibly the Biblical "seven species"—all set against a decorative architectural background. Printed in the center background is the official seal of the "Chief Council of Bulgarian Jewry."[114]

The second sub-group of Ottoman ketubbot, which comprises Middle Eastern communities, is more distinct in character. The local styles that developed in Eretz Israel, Syria and Egypt are, by and large, independent of west Ottoman examples.[115] Here again we may only conjecture that in the centuries that followed the Expulsion the picture was different. But by the nineteenth century, the period from which most of the extant material originates, the influence of local visual traditions had become considerable and most of the original "Sephardic" designs had been forgotten or lost. Still, the framing device of an arch—and only a single arch is used—supported by two columns, persists. Furthermore, although a single column of text is used, it incorporates an abbreviated version of typical Sephardic *tenaim*.

In Egypt at least the tradition of ketubbah decoration is known since the Middle Ages. In fact, the earliest known decorated ketubbot come from the Cairo Genizah, and are dated from the tenth to the eleventh–twelfth centuries.[116] However, these early fragments reflect local Islamic and Jewish traditions. Sephardic influence in shaping Egyptian ketubbot is from a much later period. It is best reflected in a ketubbah from Cairo dated 1821, which features the zodiac signs and highly unusual figures of a bride and bridegroom.[117] We have already noted the appearance of these same motifs in the Salonikan responsum and ketubbah of 1790. But it is more likely that the connection was formed here through Italian Sephardim, many of whom settled in Cairo and Alexandria in the nineteenth century.[118] Most Egyptian ketubbot of that period, as well

FIG. NO. 28 Ketubbah, Jerusalem, 1854. Cat. no. 272.

FIG. NO. 29 Ketubbah, Jerusalem, 1866. Cat. no. 274.

as those from Syria, are predominantly decorated with rich, vibrant floral patterns. At times, protective magical symbols, such as the *hamsa*, are incorporated into the design. In Damascus it became common from the eighteenth century to cut decorative gold paper and paste it along the borders of the ketubbah. This technique is reminiscent of the gold cutouts found in a Sephardic ketubbah from Vienna, and perhaps also of the multilayered colorful papercuts that profusely decorate Istanbul ketubbot.[119]

The most distinct group in the last category are the ketubbot from Eretz Israel. The center of the old Sephardic Yishuv in the Holy Land was undoubtedly Jerusalem. According to the testimony of the noted Jerusalem writer Abraham Moses Luncz (1854–1918), the ketubbah of Jerusalem's wealthy Sephardim "would be decorated along the borders with various designs and verses which praise the wise and industrious woman."[120] Indeed, the most attractive and extravagant ketubbot that were produced in nineteenth-century Eretz Israel were those of the Jerusalem Sephardim. The influence of these documents spread from Jerusalem to other cities in the Eretz Israel-Syria region.[121]

As is the case elsewhere in the Ottoman empire, the few Jerusalem ketubbot preserved from the eighteenth century are on parchment. In the nineteenth century, paper became the standard medium. The Jerusalem paper ketubbot are usually larger and wider than those used in most Sephardic communities. The shape of the text column follows the format of the page, usually occupying a few wide lines, with the writing in minuscule Sephardic script in the lower section of the page, leaving much empty space below. Often two simply drawn, narrow columns and an arch frame the wide, short column (fig. nos. 28–29). Most of the decorations, however, are concentrated in the upper part of the page, distinctly separated from the lower part by a decorative floral frame. This section is given a decorative contour, crowned by a large knop with bursting petals; below, there are large flowers in bright colors, ornamental vases and small palm and cypress trees. The latter in particular have been the subject of scholarly debate regarding their origin and significance.[122] Whether or not we accept the suggestion that these are the cypress trees that grow on the Temple Mount or the trees from which Solomon's Temple was built (I Kings 5:22, 24), it is clear that these trees symbolize the Temple of Jerusalem and perhaps the hope for its restoration.

The Sephardic Jerusalem ketubbah gained widespread popularity; it was imitated in Hebron and Jaffa (cat. no. 273), and is also known from Damascus ketubbot. But despite this success, toward the end of the nineteenth century the printed ketubbah was widely used also in Jerusalem (cat. no. 271; fig. no. 30). The new ketubbot were printed with small pictures of holy places in Jerusalem and other cities.[123] At the top of the page, two rampant lions hold the crowned official imprimatur of the community, inscribed in three languages: "Comité Central des Israélites Sephardim à Jerusalem."

FIG. NO. 30 Ketubbah, Jerusalem, 1913.
Printer: Avraham Moshe Luntz. Cat. no. 271.

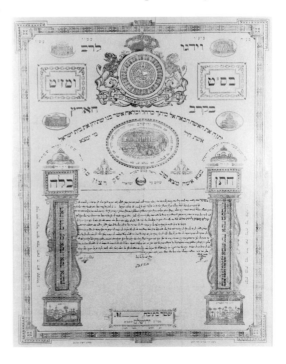

Whether handmade or printed, these Sephardic ketubbot included a version of Sephardic *tenaim*, with some clauses particular to Jerusalem. Thus, together with the symbolic cypress trees and the printed decorations of the Temple Mount, the bridegroom is exhorted not to leave his wife or to travel beyond Aleppo or Alexandria. The settlement in the historic Land of Israel symbolized, for the Sephardim, the end of their long journey.

1. The first monograph in the field of Jewish art was, in fact, devoted to a Spanish Haggadah manuscript: D. H. Müller, J. v. Schlosser, and D. Kaufmann, *Die Haggadah von Sarajevo* (facsimile), Vienna, 1898 (2 vols.). The Sarajevo Haggadah was subsequently issued in two additional facsimile editions with introductions by Cecil Roth (London, 1963) and Eugen Werber (Belgrade, 1985). Other important Hebrew manuscripts from medieval Spain which have appeared in facsimile editions are: *The Kaufmann Haggadah*, introduction by A. Scheiber (Budapest, 1957), and recently by G. Sed-Rajna, (Budapest, 1990); *The Golden Haggadah*, introduction by B. Narkiss (London, 1970; 2 vols.); *The Kennicott Bible*, introduction by B. Narkiss and A. Cohen-Mushlin (London, 1985; 2 vols.); *The Rylands Haggadah: A Medieval Sephardi Masterpiece in Facsimile*, introduction by R. Loewe (London, 1988). From Portugal: *Lisbon Bible, 1482. British Library Or. 2626*, introduction by G. Sed-Rajna (Tel-Aviv and London, 1988).

2. Quoted after J. Gutmann, *Hebrew Manuscript Painting*, New York, 1978, p. 9. See there for the negative opinion of the 13th-century Ashkenazic rabbi, Meir of Rothenburg, on the same issue.

3. *Ibid.*, p. 17; B. Narkiss, *Hebrew Illuminated Manuscripts*, Jerusalem, 1969, pp. 21f.; G. Sed-Rajna, "Toledo or Burgos?," *Journal of Jewish Art*, II, 1975, pp. 6–21 (esp. 18f.).

4. For a selection of annotated examples and a general introduction to the subject, see Narkiss, *Hebrew Illuminated Manuscripts*, pp. 21–28 and pls. 5–21 (cf. the updated Hebrew version, Jerusalem, 1984, pp. 28–40); Gutmann, *Hebrew Manuscript Painting*, pp. 17–21, pls. 5–16. See also B. Narkiss with A. Cohen-Mushlin and A. Tcherikover, *Hebrew Illuminated Manuscripts in the British Isles. A Catalogue Raisonné*, Vol. I, *The Spanish and Portuguese Manuscripts*, Jerusalem and London, 1982.

5. Cf. J. Gutmann, "The Messianic Temple in Spanish Medieval Hebrew Manuscripts," in *The Temple of Solomon. Archaeological Fact and Medieval Tradition in Christian, Islamic and Jewish Art*, ed., Gutmann, Missoula, 1976, pp. 125–45.

6. For a detailed description of the miniatures see the introductions to the facsimilies of the Sarajevo Hagaddah by Roth and Werber (as in note 1).

7. Cf. D. C. McMurtrie, *The Book: The Story of Printing and Bookmaking*, 1943 (reprinted New York, 1989), pp. 192–93.

8. For a detailed account of Hebrew book printing in the Iberian peninsula, see J. Bloch, "Early Hebrew Printing in Spain and Portugal," *Bulletin of the New York Public Library*, XLII, 1938, 371–420; reprinted in Ch. Berlin, ed. *Hebrew Printing and Bibliography*, New York, 1976, pp. 2–56 (following references are to this edition).

9. It should be noted that the only known Hebrew incunabulum from Turkey, as well as the other early books from there, were printed by Sephardic exiles (see below). In addition, the earliest Hebrew book that bears a date, Rashi's commentary to the Pentateuch, was printed in 1475 at Reggio di Calabria (southern Italy) by Abraham ben Garton—in all likelihood an immigrant from Spain. Cf. R. Posner and I. Ta-Shema, eds., *The Hebrew Book: An Historical Survey*, Jerusalem, 1975, p. 94.

10. The first book printed in Portugal was a Hebrew book (a Pentateuch printed in Faro in 1487). Moreover, the only press active in Lisbon in the 15th century was a Hebrew press. Cf. Bloch, "Early Hebrew Printing," pp. 29f., 36f.

11. A noteworthy example is the translation (into Latin and Spanish) of Abraham Zacuto's astronomical tables, which are said to have guided Columbus and Vasco de Gama in their voyages. The translations were printed by Abraham d'Ortas in Leiria, 1496 (see below). Cf. J. Bloch, "Zacuto and His *Almanach Perpetuum*," *Bulletin of the New York Public Library*, LVII, 1953, pp. 314–18 (reprinted in Berlin [as in note 8], pp. 58–62).

12. See on them P. Tishby, "Hebrew Incunabula," *Kiryat Sefer*, LVIII, 1983, pp. 808–46.

13. Only one copy of this Haggadah is known, preserved at the Jewish National and University Library. A facsimile of this copy is appended to A. Yaari, *Bibliography of the Passover Haggadah from the Earliest Printed Edition to 1960*, Jerusalem, 1960, p. 1, no. 1 (in Hebrew).

14. On the vicissitudes of Juan de Lucena's life, see Bloch, "Early Hebrew Printing," pp. 11–18.

15. Names of other Jewish printers who printed books in unidentified localities in Spain and Portugal are known. (Cf. Posner and Ta-Shema, *Hebrew Book* [as in note 9], p. 96). The editors list (*ibid.*, pp. 90–93) 175 Hebrew incunabula, of which 67 were printed in the Iberian peninsula.

16. Some scholars suggest that Eliezer Alantansi, who printed the books in Hijar, is identical with Eliezer Toledano of Lisbon. Cf. Posner and Ta-Shema, *Hebrew Book*, p. 96.

17. For the manuscripts of this school, see G. Sed-Rajna, *Manuscrits hébreux de Lisbonne: Un atelier de copistes et d'enlumineurs au XVe siècle*, Paris, 1970; Th. Metzger, *Les manuscrits hébreux copiés et decorés à Lisbonne dans les dernières décennies du XVe siècle*, Paris, 1977.

18. By Arthur M. Hind, late Keeper of Prints and Drawings at the British Museum. See his *An Introduction to a History of Woodcut*, New York, 1963, Vol. II, p. 744.

19. De Cordoba's frame actually first appears in a Latin work, *Manuele Caesar Augustanum*, printed by him in Hijar, 1487 (on his career there, see Bloch, "Early Hebrew Printing," pp. 23f.). However, scholars have deduced that it had been designed for Hebrew books. Futhermore, as noted above, the designs derive from the Lisbon school of Hebrew manuscripts (Cf. Sed-Rajna's introduction to *Lisbon Bible* [as in note 1], p. 21).

20. The emblem consists of a rampant lion in a red or black shield. Cf. A. Yaari, *Hebrew Printers' Marks from the Beginning of Hebrew Printing to the End of the 19th Century*, Jerusalem, 1943 (in Hebrew), items 1 and 2 (analyzed p. 123).

21. See the chapter on Ashkenazi ketubbot in S. Sabar, *Ketubbah: Jewish Marriage Contracts of the Hebrew Union College Skirball Museum and Klau Library*, Philadelphia and New York, 1990, esp. pp. 289–91 (with additional literature).

22. On the provisions in the early Spanish ketubbot, see I. Epstein, *The "Responsa" of Rabbi Solomon Ben Adreth of Barcelona (1235–1310) as a Source of the History of Spain*, London, 1925 (reprinted by Ktav, New York, 1968), pp. 85–87. And cf. the detailed provisions in the ketubbot from the 15th-century Tudela analyzed in J. L. Lacave, "Importante hallazgo de documentos hebreos en Tudela," *Sefarad*, XLIII, 1983, pp. 169–79.

23. In the responsa of Rabbi Simeon ben Ẓemaḥ Duran of Majorca (1361–1444), *Sefer Tashbeẓ*, Amsterdam, 1738, Vol. 1, responsum 6. Cf. I. Epstein, *The Responsa of Rabbi Simon b. Ẓemaḥ Duran*, London, 1930 (reprinted New York, 1968), pp. 83–84; H. J. Zimmels, *Ashkenazim and Sephardim. Their Relations, Differences and Problems as Reflected in Rabbinical Responsa*, London, 1976, p. 180.

24. Preserved at the Jewish National and University Library, Ketubbah no. 36. Reproduced in D. Davido-vitch, *The Ketuba: Jewish Marriage Contracts through the Ages*, Tel Aviv, 1968, p. 15.

25. On the Navarrese contracts see F. Cantera Burgos, "La *Ketuba* de D. Davidovitch y la ketubbot españolas," *Sefarad*, XXXIII, 1973, pp. 375–86. And cf. S. Sabar, "The Beginnings of Ketubbah Decoration in Italy: Venice in the Late 16th to the Early 17th Centuries," *Jewish Art*, XII/XIII, 1986/87, pp. 102–103.

26. Reproduced in color, *ibid.*, p. 103, fig. 6.

27. *Ibid.*, p. 103, fig. 5.

28. For a general survey of this revival, see E. Naményi, "La miniature juive au XVIIe et au XVIIIe siècle," *Revue des Études Juives*, CXVI, 1957, pp. 27–71.

29. On the ibn Nahmias family and for a list of the books they printed, see A. Yaari, *Hebrew Printing at Constantinople. Its History and Bibliography*, Jerusalem, 1967, pp. 17–21, and 59ff. (in Hebrew). Yaari accepts M. Steinschneider's suggestion that the first book printed by David and Samuel ibn Nahmias should be dated 1503 and not 1493 (as the period of merely 16 months after the Expulsion could not have been sufficient to set up a press and issue a large volume). Modern research, however, accepts the earlier date (cf. Posner and Ta-Shema, *Hebrew Book* [as in note 9], pp. 96–97).

30. Yaari, *Printers' Marks* (as in note 20), item 4 (described p. 123).

31. See the examples reproduced in Yaari, *Hebrew Printing at Constantinople*, p. 65; Y. H. Yerushalmi, *Haggadah and History. A Panorama in Facsimile of Five Centuries of the Printed Haggadah*, Philadelphia, 1975, pl. 5.

32. H. D. Friedberg, *History of Hebrew Typography in Italy, Spain-Portugal and Turkey*, 1956, pp. 130–42 (in Hebrew).

33. On their press, see E. R. Murciano, *Sefer Benei Melakhim: History of the Hebrew Book in Morocco from 1517 until 1989*, Jerusalem, 1989, pp. 11–14, (in Hebrew). Very few titles are known from this press (see the list *ibid.*, p. 35), which was forced to close down ca. 1522–25 due to difficulties in obtaining paper from Spain.

34. Cf. Bloch, "Early Hebrew Printing" (as in note 8), pp. 52ff.; also L. Goldschmidt, *Hebrew Incunables. A Bibliographical Essay*, Oxford, 1948, pp. 63ff.

35. In Turkey, for example, the first Turkish press was established as late as 1728, 224 years after the Hebrew press of the Sephardim. Cf. Yaari, *Hebrew Printing at Constantinople*, p. 11. In Morocco, the first publication in Hebrew letters printed following the activity of Samuel Nedivot (cf. note 33, above), is from the year 1891, which means that during the period of 369 years no Hebrew book was printed there.

36. On these printers, see the summary article: Joshua Bloch, "Venetian Printers of Hebrew Books," in Berlin, *Hebrew Bibliography and Booklore* (as in note 8), pp. 63–88.

37. Cf. A. M. Haberman, *The Printer Daniel Bomberg and the List of Books Published by his Press*, Safed, 1978, p. 29 (in Hebrew).

38. In the spirit of the Renaissance, classical architectural elements began to appear in title pages of Italian books as early as the 1490s. Cf. M. Corbett and R. Lightbown, *The Comely Frontispiece. The Emblematic Title-Page in England 1550–1660*, London, 1979, p. 4; E. P. Goldschmidt, *The Printed Book of the Renaissance. Three Lectures on Type, Illustration, Ornament*, Amsterdam, 1966, pp. 66ff.

39. This verse (Psalms 118:20) occasionally appears already in Bomberg's title pages (see the aforementioned Bible, reproduced by Haberman [as in note 37], between pp. 32–33). However, in other Bomberg editions the gateway image bears a few other verses in which the word "gate(s)" appears (e.g., "open the gates" from Isaiah 26:2—in the title page of *Talmud Yerushalmi*, 1523/4, reproduced *ibid.*, between pp. 56–57). It was only later that this verse from Psalms became the dominant one on Hebrew title pages, and was subsequently borrowed to architectural decorations in other media of Jewish art.

40. Cf. L. Avrin, "Architectural Decoration and Hebrew Manuscripts," *Manuscripta*, XXII, 1978, pp. 67–74 (esp. p. 73).

41. See, for example, the title page of *Sefer Meirat Enayim*, printed in Istanbul in 1666 (no. 258 in Yaari, *Hebrew Printing at Constantinople* [as in note 29]—the title page is reproduced on the facing page of Yaari's frontispiece). For an example of Bomberg's gate on a title page from Cracow 1640, see M. M. Kaplan, *Panorama of Ancient Letters: Four and a Half Centuries of Hebraica and Judaica*, New York, 1942, no. 144, p. 87.

42. Another example that is reproduced in Yaari (*Hebrew Printing at Constantinople*, facing p. 11) is the gateway

with twisted columns appearing on numerous Turkish Hebrew books—which is also borrowed from Venetian Hebrew imprints (e.g., Bragadini's press).

43. Cf. *ibid.*, pp. 21–24, and pp. 87ff.

44. See the examples of 1533, 1539, and 1549, reproduced *ibid.*, pp. 91, 97, 105, respectively. The third example was printed by Moses ben Eleazar Parnas, who inherited the Soncino types and decorations after Eliezer Soncino died in 1548. Another noted Italian family who printed books in Turkey is the Bat-Sheva (Basevi) family, who set up their press in Salonika in about 1590. Cf. Friedberg, *Hebrew Typography* (as in note 32), pp. 136–38.

45. Two interesting architectural title pages were created, however, in 18th-century Izmir. Although not copied fully from imported examples, the two designs are adaptations of popular Italian and Dutch types. See A. Yaari, "Hebrew Printing at Izmir," in *Aresheth: An Annual of Hebrew Booklore*, I, Jerusalem, 1958, pp. 97–222 (in Hebrew); reproductions of the two pages on pp. 138, 141. It should be noted that the first Hebrew printer in Izmir, Abraham ben Jedidiah Gabbai (active ca. 1657–75), used on the title pages the printer's device of the Venetian printer Bragadini (*ibid.*, pp. 119–25), while his followers used Bragadini's architectural frame (reproduced *ibid.*, p. 124).

46. As opposed, for example, to ketubbah decoration which was not practiced in the Venetian ghetto before the arrival of the Sephardim (see below).

47. Cf. the introduction by Bezalel Narkiss to the facsimile edition *The Passover Haggadah. Venice 1609*, Jerusalem, 1974 (in Hebrew); Cecil Roth, "The Illustrated Haggadah," *Studies in Bibliography and Booklore*, VII, 1965, pp. 45ff.

48. Cf. Yerushalmi, *Haggadah and History* (as in note 31), commentary to pl. 44. Yerushalmi's examples (pls. 44–48) are of the Judaeo-Italian issue.

49. See L. Fuks and R. G. Fuks-Mansfeld, *Hebrew Typography in the Netherlands, 1585–1815. Historical Evaluation and Descriptive Bibliography*, 2 vols., Leyden, 1984 and 1987 (for Menasseh ben Israel's press and the list of books printed there, see Vol. 1, pp. 99–135). It should be noted, however, that a few Hebrew books had been printed previously in the Netherlands by Christian printers.

50. Cf. H. I. Bloom, *The Economic Activities of the Jews of Amsterdam in the Seventeenth and Eighteenth Centuries*, Williamsport, Penn., 1937, pp. 44–60.

51. A rare example of this image in a manuscript is a *mahzor* according to the Provençal rite, from Avignon, France, dated 1721 (the manuscript is preserved at Columbia University, New York; unpublished).

52. Cf. M. Narkiss, "The Oeuvre of the Jewish Engraver Salom Italia," *Tarbiz*, XXV, 1956, item no. 8, pp. 449–50 (in Hebrew). For a description of a copy of the book with the portrait, see I. Yudlov, *The Israel Mehlman Collection in the Jewish National and University Library*, Jerusalem, 1984, item 1211, pp. 195–96 (in Hebrew).

53. Cf. H. van de Waal, "Rembrandts Radierungen zur *Piedra Gloriosa* des Menasseh Ben Israel," *Imprimatur: Ein Jahrbuch für Bücherfreunde*, XII, 1954/55, pp. 52–61.

54. Scholars have suggested that Menasseh ben Israel rejected Rembrandt's etchings because one of them shows the image of God. Cf. F. Landsberger, *Rembrandt, the Jews and the Bible*, Philadelphia, 1961, pp. 98–99. The author states that "when these [Rembrandt's] etchings appeared . . . they must have shocked prospective purchasers." However, the Amsterdam Sephardim were more inclined to admit such motifs than is generally assumed. The image of God in a monumental form appears on a tombstone in the Sephardic cemetery at Ouderkerk near Amsterdam. Cf. E. S. Saltman, "The 'Forbidden Image' in Jewish Art," *Journal of Jewish Art*, VIII, 1981, p. 52, fig. 17.

55. Cf. A. L. Katchen, *Christian Hebraists and Dutch Rabbis: Seventeenth-Century Apologetics and the Study of Maimonides' Mishneh Torah*, Cambridge, Mass. 1984, *passim*.

56. Reproduced in M. H. Gans, *Memorbook: History of Dutch Jewry from the Renaissance to 1940*, Baarn, 1977, p. 79.

57. On Athias and for a list of his books, see Fuks and Fuks-Mansfeld, *Hebrew Typography* (as in note 49), Vol. 2, pp. 286–339.

58. Cf. Bloom, *Economic Activities* (as in note 50), pp. 47 and 49.

59. Quoted *ibid.*, p. 49.

60. The meeting between Joseph and Jacob is depicted also on other title pages from Athias' press. The most common image is a gateway supported by two spiral columns, below which there is a large eagle containing the episode. See Yaari, *Printers' Marks* (as in note 20), no. 73. Yaari suggests (p. 149) that the eagle may also be associated with Athias, possibly alluding to his flight from oppression in Spain to freedom in Holland (in accordance with God's words "You have seen what I did unto the Egyptians, and how I bore you on *eagles' wings* and brought you unto Myself" [Exodus 19:4]).

61. A number of other works by Godines are preserved, including some interesting *memento mori* pictures. See A. Rubens, "Three Jewish Morality Pictures, 1679–81," *The Connoisseur*, August, 1954 (appeared as a separate reprint by the Jewish Museum, London; and see the color reproductions in R. D. Barnett, ed. *Catalogue of the Jewish Museum, London*, London 1974, p. 155).

62. In some cases not only one episode but a whole series of them appears on the title page. See, for example, the frontispiece to *Sifra di-Zeniuta de-Yaakov* by the kabbalist Rabbi Jacob b. Eliezer Temerls, which was published by David de Castro Tartas (Amsterdam, 1669; reproduced in Yaari, *Printers' Marks* [as in note 20], p. 43). Tartas did not dedicate even one episode to the writer, and the five pictures that surround the page are all to honor himself (i.e., scenes from the life of his namesake, King David).

63. Compare, for example, the title page of *Parafrasis comentado sobre el pentateuco . . .* (commentary on the Pentateuch by Haham Isaac Aboab, 1681), etched by J. van den Aveele (reproduced in Gans, *Memorbook* [as in note 56], p. 99), with the tombstone of Moses van Mordechai Senior, 1730 (*ibid.*, p. 127). On the Ouderkerk tombstones, see R. Weinstein, "Sepulchral Monuments of the Jews of Amsterdam in the Seventeenth and Eighteenth Centuries," unpublished Ph.D. dissertation, New York University, 1979.

64. Two other symbolic, praiseworthy title pages were prepared for the Sabbatean *Tikkun*. The three engravings are reproduced in A. M. Haberman, *Title Pages of Hebrew Books*, Safed, 1969, pp. 54–56 (in Hebrew with English summary). Significantly, the Hebrew date of the book is a chronogram of the Hebrew word *moshia* meaning "savior." For other Sabbatean images that were printed in Amsterdam, see Gans, *Memorbook* (as in note 56), pp. 94–97.

65. For the history and architectural evaluation of the synagogue, see R. Wischnitzer, *The Architecture of the European Synagogue*, Philadelphia, 1964, pp. 90–97; C. H. Krinsky, *Synagogues of Europe. Architecture, History, Meaning*, Cambridge, Mass. 1985, pp. 391–94.

66. The costs of the building and the interior furnishings have survived in manuscript pages appended to a copy of *Sermões que pregaraõ . . .* (see below). The book is now at the Jewish National and University Library, Jerusalem; see *Treasures from the Library Ets Haim/Livraria Montezinos of the Portugees Isräelietisch Seminarium Ets Haim, Amsterdam*, Exhibition Catalog, JNUL, Jerusalem, 1980, item no. 5, p. 17. The manuscript list is transliterated in D. H. De Castro, *De Synagoge der Portugees-Isräelietische Gemeente te Amsterdam*, new edition ed. J. Meijer, Amsterdam 1950, pp. 45–47. The total costs amounted to 186,060 florins.

67. In planning the synagogue Bouman combined architectural principles of Dutch Reformed churches with Jewish designs. His most influential Jewish source was the model of the Temple, prepared by the Amsterdam ex-marrano rabbi and teacher Jacob Judah Leon "Templo" (1603–75). The unusual buttresses of the synagogue were most probably inspired by the "Templo" model. Cf. Wischnitzer, *Architecture* (as in note 65), pp. 92–97.

68. Cf. the profile views and maps of Amsterdam issued in the late 17th and 18th centuries, in which the

Portuguese synagogue is featured. It is also prominently depicted in many works by noted Dutch artists. See the selection reproduced in S. W. Morgenstein and R. E. Levine, *The Jews in the Age of Rembrandt*, Exhibition Catalog, The Judaic Museum of the Jewish Community Center of Greater Washington, Rockville, Maryland, 1981.

69. On de Hooghe and for reproductions of his Sephardic illustrations, see J. Landwehr, *Romeyn de Hooghe as Book Illustrator*, Amsterdam, 1970, and *idem.*, *Romeyn de Hooghe the Etcher*, Leyden, 1972. For a study of a Jewish subject by the artist, see W. H. Wilson, "'The Circumcision,' A Drawing by Romeyn de Hooghe," *Master Drawings*, XIII, 1975, pp. 250–58.

70. This appellation is actually a pun on the architect's name ("architect" in Dutch is *bouwman*). Cf. Gans, *Memorbook* (as in note 56), pp. 102–03.

71. On this manuscript, see *Treasures* (as in note 66), item no. 57, pp. 39–40; L. Fuks and R. G. Fuks-Mansfeld, *Hebrew and Judaic Manuscripts in Amsterdam Public Collections*, Leyden, 1975, Vol. II, item 439, p. 8.

72. *Ibid.*, item no. 378, p. 125; *Treasures*, item 30, p. 26.

73. On the two editions of the Amsterdam Haggadah and their origins, see R. Wischnitzer, "Von der Holbeinbibel zur Amsterdamer Haggadah" (originally, 1931), now reprinted in the selection of her articles, *From Dura to Rembrandt: Studies in the History of Art*, Jerusalem, 1990, pp. 29–48. And cf. the plates of the Haggadah and its imitations in Yerushalmi, *Haggadah and History* (as in note 31), 59–62, 64, 66–69, 71–72, 86, 97–98 (from Bombay, India, 1846), etc.

74. See the exhibition catalogue H. Peled-Carmeli, *Illustrated Haggadot of the Eighteenth Century*, The Israel Museum, Jerusalem, 1983.

75. The Haggadah was issued in a facsimile edition by Nahar-Stavit, Paris, 1987, with an introduction by Alfred Moldovan.

76. Cf. F. Malino, *The Sephardic Community of Bordeaux. Assimilation and Emancipation in Revolutionary and Napoleonic France*, University of Alabama, 1978.

77. On Belforte, see Posner and Ta-Shema, *Hebrew Book* (as in note 9), p. 152.

78. The illustrations in the Livornese Haggadot, for example, were taken directly from the Venice Haggadot of 1609 and 1629. Cf. Yerushalmi, *Haggadah and History* (as in note 31), commentary to pl. 91 (Haggadah of 1837), and pls. 106 (1867), 111–13 (printed by Belforte for the Jews of Tunis in 1878).

79. No study of Sephardic ketubbot and their decorations as a coherent group has been published. A brief introduction to the subject is Cecil Roth, "The Sephardi Ketubah," *La Judisme Sephardi*, N.S. no. 6, 1955, pp. 257–60. For an analysis of specific examples, see the chapter "Sephardi Europe" in Sabar, *Ketubbah* (as in note 21), pp. 235–86 (with introductory entries to Albania, Austria, Bulgaria, England, France, Gibraltar, Greece, Holland, Turkey and Yugoslavia).

80. *Leḥem Rav*, Izmir, 1660, responsum no. 6. Cf. F. Landsberger, "Illuminated Marriage Contracts," *Hebrew Union College Annual*, XXVI, 1955, pp. 510–11.

81. See S. Bar-Asher, ed., *The Takkanot of the Jews of Morocco: A Collection of Communal Ordinances from the 16th to the 18th Century . . .* , Jerusalem, 1977, *takkanah* 12, pp. 22–3 (in Hebrew and Ladino).

82. *Ibid.*, *takkanah* 18, p. 24.

83. On these ketubbot see Sabar, "The Beginnings" (as in note 25), pp. 96–110 (esp. 103ff.).

84. Reproduced *ibid.*, figs. 3, 7, 10 (pp. 100, 104, 106, respectively).

85. For more on the meaning of architectural elements in ketubbah decoration, see the chapter "Praise Her in the Gates" in the forthcoming catalogue of the Israel Museum ketubbah catalogue by this author.

86. Sabar, "The Beginnings," pp. 106–10.

87. Cf. the examples reproduced in *Ketubbot italiane. Antichi contratti nuziali ebraici miniati*, Milan, 1984.

88. See the introductory entries to the various Italian cities in Sabar, *Ketubbah* (as in note 21), pp. 43–234.

89. E.g., a ketubbah from Livorno (1782), signed in abbreviations by N.D.M., who was apparently a non-Jewish artist; cf. *ibid.*, pp. 109–11.

90. A ketubbah from Pisa (1790); see *ibid.*, pp. 134–37.

91. For an English translation of the Sephardic *tenaim* in Livorno ketubbot, see *ibid.*, p. 108.

92. For typical Italian examples of this type, see *Ketubbot italiane* (as in note 87), pls. 11, 13, 16, 21. For an example of this type that was actually executed in Venice and the text filled in (Corfu, 1714), see Sabar, *Ketubbah*, pp. 259–60. The "Corfu elements" in our ketubbah (cat. no. 562) are more obvious in a Corfu contract dated 1819, now at the Israel Museum; see C. Benjamin, *The Stieglitz Collection: Masterpieces of Jewish Art*, Jerusalem, 1987, p. 331.

93. On this document, see *ibid.*, pp. 318–19. On the relationship of this and other Amsterdam contracts to Venetian ketubbot, see Shalom Sabar, "The Golden Age of *Ketubah* Decoration in Venice and Amsterdam," in *The Ghetto in Venice: Ponentini, Levantini e Tedeschi 1516–1797*, Exhibition Catalog, Joods Historisch Museum, Amsterdam ('s-Gravenhage 1990), pp. 86–105.

94. Despite the dominant Italian influence in western Sephardic ketubbot, some artists used the "imported" designs and motifs to create decorative borders that outdo their Italian counterparts. The most important example of this is a rare ketubbah from Hamburg (1690), commemorating the union by marriage of two distinguished Sephardic families, Teixeira and de Mattos. The extravagant contract depicts, *inter alia*, an elaborate marriage ceremony, with all the participants dressed in the highest fashion of the time. See color reproduction in *The Image of the Word: Jewish Tradition in Manuscripts and Printed Books*, Exhibition Catalogue, Amsterdam University Library and Jewish Historical Museum, Amsterdam, 1990, fig. 42.

95. One commemorates a wedding in Rotterdam in 1648 (Israel Museum, Jerusalem; reproduced in *Encyclopaedia Judaica*, Jerusalem, 1971, Vol. 10, pl. 4 following col. 940), and the second is from Amsterdam (1654) (Ets Haim Library, Amsterdam; reproduced in Fuks and Fuks-Mansfeld, *Judaic Manscripts* [as in note 71], Vol. II, color frontispiece). On these contracts, see also Sabar, "Golden Age" (as in note 93), pp. 96–97.

96. Cf. *ibid.*, p. 97 (reproduced on p. 99, fig. 9).

97. For examples from London (1861) and Bayonne (1705), see Sabar, *Ketubbah* (as in note 21), pp. 244–45 and 248–50, respectively. An example from Hamburg (1706) is at the Israel Museum (reproduced in H. Feuchtwanger, "Ketubot: jüdische Ehe-Urkunden aus Italien, Deutschland, Holland, Persien, Israel und der Türkei," *Du*, XXX, 1976, pl. following p. 556). Preserved examples from America are from New York (1751) (with some highly unusual variations in the two top pictures; in the collection of Yosef Goldman, New York), and Curaçao (1828) (YIVO, New York). Both examples are unpublished.

98. For example, the Bayonne (1705) contract referred to in the previous note.

99. This section is an abbreviated version of "The Illustrated *Ketubbah* in North Africa," by this author in *Recherches sur la culture des Juifs d'Afrique du Nord*, ed. I. Ben-Ami, Jerusalem, 1991, pp. 191–208 (in Hebrew).

100. Cf. A. N. Chouraqui, *Between East and West: A History of the Jews in North Africa*, New York, 1973, p. 97.

101. Preserved in the collection of Victor Klagsbald, Paris (on this contract see *La vie juive au Maroc*, Exhibition Catalog, Israel Museum, ed. A. Müller-Lancet, Jerusalem 1983, pp. 109–10; V. Klagsbald, "L'art cultuel juif au Maroc," *Revue des Études Juives*, CXXXIV, 1975, p. 148; Sabar, "North Africa" [as in note 99], pp. 194–96, reproduced p. 193, fig. 1 [pictures transposed]).

102. The same clause appears also in the ketubbot of the Gibraltar Sephardim (cf. *ibid.*, p. 208).

103. For reproductions of such Tunisian contracts (1822 and 1858), see *ibid.*, p. 195, fig. 4 (Israel Museum), and *idem*, "The Beginnings" (as in note 25), p. 109, fig. 15 (Jewish Theological Seminary of America, New York).

104. See in particular Y. K. Stillman, "Spanish Influences on the Material Culture of Moroccan Jews," in *The Sephardi and Oriental Jewish Heritage. Studies*, ed. I. Ben-Ami, Jerusalem, 1982, esp. pp. 364–66 (in Hebrew).

105. Examples dated 1887 and 1891 are preserved at the Israel Museum (unpublished).

106. Preserved at Hebrew Union College Skirball Museum, Los Angeles; see Sabar, *Ketubbah*, pp. 366–68.

107. For a large selection of examples from the above locales, see *Jewellery and Judaica: Books, Manuscripts and Works of Art*, Sotheby's Auction Catalog, Tel-Aviv, April, 1989, items 543–62, pp. 115–23.

108. The ketubbot of Gibraltar in the second half of the 19th century are characterized by two floral wreaths which frame the text in an oval shape and a bejeweled crown atop; in the middle of the cursive text appear the large square Hebrew letters *het* and *yud*, standing for "life" in Hebrew, and at the bottom the Latin initials of the bridal couple. Cf. Sabar, *Ketubbah*, pp. 254–56. For this program in a Mogador ketubbah see *ibid.*, pp. 352–53; in Tangier: R. Attal, *Ketoubot d'Afrique du Nord à Jerusalem*, Jerusalem, 1984, pls. V–VI.

109. For a detailed account of the ketubbah traditions in the centers of the western Ottoman empire (including Istanbul, Izmir, Salonika, Rhodes and Edirne), see S. Sabar, "Decorated *Ketubbot*," in *Sephardi Jews in the Ottoman Empire: Aspects of Material Culture*, Exhibition Catalog, ed. E. Juhasz, The Israel Museum, Jerusalem, 1990, pp. 218–37.

110. Preserved in the collection of Victor Klagsbald, Paris. See *ibid.*, p. 220 and pl. 54.

111. Cf. *ibid.*, esp. p. 224.

112. Many other prints of Amarillo's lithograph have survived from the 1880s and 1890s (e.g., *ibid.*, p. 228, fig. 9). Interestingly, one exhibited example (cat. no. 106A) is not a usual ketubbah but a replacement one (*ketubbah d'irkhesa*), which, according to halakhah, should be issued immediately if the original contract is lost.

113. For the ketubbah traditions in these lands, see Sabar, *Ketubbah* (as in note 21), pp. 238–42 (Austria and Bulgaria), 272–75 (Rumania), 282–86 (Yugoslavia).

114. Cf. *ibid.*, pp. 241–2.

115. On the ketubbot of Egypt and Eretz Israel, see *ibid.*, pp. 306–21.

116. On these, see S. D. Goitein, *A Mediterranean Society. The Jewish Communities of the Arab World as Portrayed in the Documents of the Cairo Geniza*, Berkeley, 1978, Vol. 3, pp. 109–13.

117. On this contract, see G. Weiss, "An Illuminated Marriage Contract from the Cairo Geniza from April 16, 1821," *Gratz College Annual of Jewish Studies*, VII, 1978, pp. 91–98.

118. Cf. A. Milano, *Storia degli ebrei italiani nel Levante*, Florence, 1949, esp. pp. 196–200.

119. For the Vienna contract (dated 1831), see Sabar, *Ketubbah*, pp. 238–9.

120. Luncz, "The Religious and Daily Customs of Our Brethren in the Holy Land," in *Yerushalayim*, Vol. 1, Vienna, 1882, p. 7 (in Hebrew).

121. For the development of the decorations in the Jerusalem-type ketubbot, see J. Benjamin, "Ketubah Ornamentation in Nineteenth-Century Eretz-Israel," *The Israel Museum News*, XII, 1977, pp. 129–37.

122. See *ibid.*, 134–35; I. Einhorn, "The Cypress Trees in the *Ketubbot*," in *Arts and Crafts in Nineteenth-Century Eretz-Israel*, Exhibition Catalog, The Israel Museum, Jerusalem, 1979, pp. 53–55 (in Hebrew).

123. Such pictures appear on numerous printed pages and other objects from 19th-century Eretz-Israel. See the many examples reproduced *ibid.*, *passim*.

THE SEPHARDIC JOURNEY—500 YEARS
OF JEWISH CEREMONIAL OBJECTS

Chaya Benjamin

A treasure of color, materials, and forms is revealed in "The Sephardic Journey: 1492–1992." In selecting the items for this exhibition, emphasis was placed on finding treasures that had not previously been displayed in a Sephardic cultural context. Most of the pieces had been preserved in synagogues and in private and public collections. They originate from lands around the Mediterranean: North Africa, Italy and areas once under Ottoman rule such as Romania, Yugoslavia, Bulgaria, Greece, Turkey and Eretz Israel, and from lands where the marranos of Portugal and Spain joined their brethren or established new communities, mainly in Europe; The Netherlands, several cities in Germany, such as Hamburg, Altona and Emden; and England, mainly London.

Most of the objects date from the late seventeenth century to the twentieth century. The scarcity of Sephardic ceremonial art from this and earlier periods is due in part to the devastating fires that swept away whole communities, with their synagogues and treasures, as for example in Edirne and Izmir;[1] also, historical and political circumstances forced Jews to sell their valuables as a ransom for their own lives or for immunity from expulsion. Many other objects disintegrated through the ravages of time, and in addition to all these vicissitudes stand the traumatic events of the Expulsion itself. Yet the paucity of surviving ceremonial objects dating from before the Expulsion and up to 200 years later is still a mystery. This and the scarcity of documentary material on these objects hinder conclusive research on the subject. For instance, in a relatively small and defined area such as northern Italy, where by the end of the fifteenth century the old Italian Jewish families had been joined by Spanish, Levantine and Ashkenazic Jews, and the great waves of migration were augmented by a steady influx of smaller groups of Jews throughout the Renaissance, silver ceremonial objects are identifiable by their style and hallmarks, but where there is no detailed dedication inscription, it is impossible to attribute them to a particular synagogue.[2]

While the process of acculturation in different locations generally tended to leave local traditions intact, the relationship between tradition and artistic innovation is not always clear. There are similarities in style from place to place, but this is true also of later, more settled periods, when such similarities could be attributed to contacts between established communities rather than their shared Iberian origin. Style was further influenced by the material culture of the host country. A complex chain of reciprocity is under study, including research citing Jewish and other documentary sources as well as historical and sociological data.

Documents dating before the Expulsion mention the names of Jewish silversmiths and craftsmen from Spain.[3] In Renaissance Italy many Jews were silversmiths and goldsmiths. The finest of these artists served also the Church, the rulers and the aristocracy. For centuries northern Italy, particularly Padua and Venice, was a leading center of bronze casting. During the period between the last decades of the fifteenth century and the seventeenth century some bronze founders were apparently of Jewish, and, in some cases, of Sephardic origin. Their wares included mortars bearing Jewish symbols, and Hanukkah lamps.[4] Silver ceremonial objects from later periods were usually produced by gentile silversmiths, though some were made by Jewish craftsmen, a number of whom are mentioned in the guild registers of cities such as Livorno and Florence (see e.g. the Torah shield by Pacifico Levi, cat. no. 534; fig. no. 31).[5] Here as in other locations the right to reside and work as silversmiths or in any other craft depended on their precarious position and privileges.

The Sephardic physicians, other professionals and presumably also artisans who settled in North Africa, continued to work in their occupations. The oldest Sephardic artifact extant from Morocco is a sixteenth-century mortar owned by a refugee physician and decorated with a Hebrew inscription (cat. no. 439; fig. no. 32). Since the Koran condemns the hoarding of gold and silver,[6] pious Muslims avoided working as gold- and silversmiths leaving these occupations largely to the Jews. From the early eighteenth century on, ample documentation testifies to the existence of whole communities of Jewish silversmiths in North Africa.[7]

FIG. NO. 32 Mortar, North Africa, second half of the 16th century. Cat. no. 439.

FIG. NO. 31 Torah shield, Turin, Italy, after 1832, Pacifico Levi. Cat. no. 534.

It was economic considerations that impelled the sultans to open the gates of the Ottoman empire to the Sephardic exiles. These Jews had engaged in international commerce for centuries; they were also astute financiers and well versed in the use of the most modern techniques. Moreover, unlike the large Christian minority in the empire, the Jews proved to be loyal subjects.

Economic life, and to a large extent social life as well, centered around the activities of the guilds. Between the sixteenth and eighteenth centuries guild members included Jews, Muslims (Turkish and Arab), and Christians (Greek and Armenian); other guilds were exclusively Jewish.[8] Ceremonial objects surviving from this period reflect the tolerance extended to the Jews over long periods, their social ties with their neighbors and the participation of members of different religions in the production of, and trade in, silver goods. Hallmarks on Jewish ritual objects from the late nineteenth to the early twentieth century name, alongside the identifying mark of the ruling sultan, Jewish, Armenian and Christian silversmiths; e.g. the Jews B. Bitton and Yehudah Kazaz; the Armenian, L. M. Karayan; and the Christian, Prosen.[9]

In England, Germany, and The Netherlands, most Jewish silver ceremonial objects were produced by non-Jewish craftsmen who were commissioned by synagogues. Some objects were made by Jewish craftsmen, such as Abraham de Oliveyra of London, who as a Jew had been unable to join a guild in his native Amsterdam. His earliest traceable piece is dated 1716.[10]

In London, Hamburg and Altona, but primarily in Amsterdam, where marranos began to arrive in the seventeenth century, many Jewish ceremonial objects were created by local silversmiths according to specifications from Portuguese patrons newly re-turned to the Jewish faith. The affluence of these patrons, the atmosphere of tolerance in which they now lived, and the fact that they did not feel bound to an earlier artistic tradition all signaled a new tendency to artistic freedom. The craftsmen depicted Scrip-tural stories on ceremonial artifacts according to their own interpretations, borrowing from the opulence of Italian ceremonial art and the folk exuberance of Moroccan Hanukkah lamp decoration; also, the Jewish refugees adapted the style of sumptuous local wares to their own community's ritual needs.

The Torah Scroll and its Decorations

Jewish ceremonial art is epitomized by the Torah scroll, resplendent in its mantle and fine ornamentation. Sometimes one Torah scroll will be decorated with a gilt crown over a mantle embroidered centuries earlier; a pointer, engraved with the name of a son who returned safely from battle, suspended beside a Torah shield in memory of a bride-to-be who died before her wedding; the Torah scroll itself wrapped in a textile embroidered with silver and gold thread executed in honor of an elder of the com-munity. On the other hand, it was not uncommon for complete sets of Torah ornaments to be ordered from the same silversmith; a few such sets are still extant.

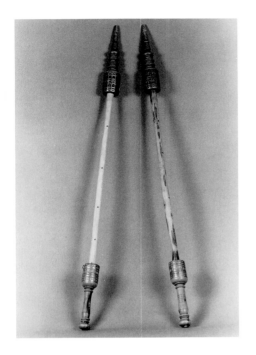

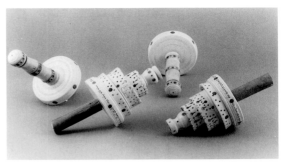

FIG. NO. 34 Torah staves, Izmir, 1823/4. Cat. no. 26.

FIG. NO. 33 Torah staves, Meknes, Morocco, 19th–20th century. Cat. no. 315.

When entire communities moved to the new State of Israel, many such ceremonial objects were brought along by the immigrants; others were left in their countries of origin or were carried by their owners from place to place and left somewhere on their journey. Each of these pieces is a world unto itself—its making, its embellishment, its metamorphosis, and especially the dedication inscription that tells the human story behind it.

Each Torah scroll, placed in the *heikhal* (Torah ark), rolled and bound, either in its *meil* (mantle) or its *tik* (case), has its *avnet* (binder), *mappah* (wrapper), *mitpahat* (cover), *rimmonim* (finials), *atarah* or *keter* (crown), *tas* (shield) and *yad* (pointer). These ornaments were kept in the Torah ark, and sometimes also in small arks which were placed in niches adjoining the ark proper. In many synagogues there are special stands for Torah ornaments; the finials are placed on brackets or on a bar affixed to the *bimah* railing or alongside the Torah ark. In some synagogues in Izmir, the Torah crowns and finials were displayed on festivals on a special stand near the *bimah*. The stand, made of cast brass, rests on a pedestal with looped and bracketed arms at either side, engraved with dedication inscriptions.[11]

Torah Staves—"Trees of Life"

The ends of the Torah scroll are attached to wooden rods with ornamental handles and circular rollers for winding the scroll. These are called *atzei hayyim* (trees of life), referring to the verse: "She [i.e. the Torah] is a tree of life to those who grasp her, and whoever holds on to her is happy" (Proverbs 3:18). In North Africa, particularly in Morocco, the circular disks that hold the scrolls in place take the form of wooden cylinders, which, like the ends of the rods, are sometimes decorated with metal strips and tiny rivets (cat. no. 315; fig. no. 33). Others are inlaid with ivory and mother-of-pearl, sometimes with dedicatory inscriptions. On some Torah staves from North Africa hands are carved holding the two rods, decorated with twisted silver thread.[12] In Italy, wooden "trees of life" carved with foliage are usually gilded,[13] and those of silver are embossed and chased. Rare examples from Izmir are made of ivory, engraved with a dedication inscription and carved in the form of three graded crowns, similar to Esther scroll holders created in the same region (cat. no. 26; fig. no. 34).

Torah Mantles and Cases

In Sephardic communities the Torah scroll is usually kept in a decorated textile mantle (*meil*), with occasional examples in Italy, North Africa, and the Ottoman empire where a Torah case (*tik*) is used alongside the textile mantles. In North African Torah mantles the embroidery is dense and couched with gilt thread on velvet.[14] The velvet or other textile is sewn and attached at the back to sheets of leather, parchment or cardboard. Dedicatory inscriptions are embroidered at the center or the borders of the mantle, or interlaced with the decoration—be it arabesque, floral, or symmetrical (e.g. cat. nos. 317, 318; fig. no. 35).

The Torah case (*tik*), used mainly in Algeria, Tunisia, and Libya, is made of wood, sometimes painted with floral designs but usually wrapped in a *mappah*, a cloth suspended from the top of the case. These cloths tend to be sparsely embroidered with symmetrical motifs, occasionally interlaced with the Tablets of the Law, the seven branched candelabrum (menorah), birds or fish, and a dedicatory inscription at the center (e.g. cat. no. 338; fig. no. 36). *Mezuzah* covers and tefillin and tallit bags are adorned with similar motifs and needlework (e.g. cat. nos. 387–390, 446; fig. no. 37).

In the Ottoman empire, too, Torah mantles are adorned with couched embroidery of metallic thread, couched velvet or other fabric, but without the hard backing. With their floral decoration, they boast sequined vases and rocailles. Dedicatory inscriptions are interlaced with the design, in a manner suggesting that the textiles had once served secular purposes. Many of the mantles combine embroidered fabrics of local origin with brocade and damask imported from France and Italy.[15]

The Sephardic communities in the cities of the central Ottoman empire, such as Istanbul, Edirne, Salonika and Izmir, as well as in Bosnia, Herzegovina, Serbia, Macedonia and Kosovo (now Yugoslavia and Bulgaria), are noted for combining fabric with metal plaques. Silver and brass plates, large and small, perforated at the borders and stitched to the fabric, are found principally in Torah ark curtains and mantles. Seventeenth- and early eighteenth-century church vestments from different parts of Serbia show similar decoration.[16] Two unusual Izmir Torah cases in particular exemplify

FIG. NO. 35 Left to right: Torah finials, North Africa, 18th–19th century; Torah mantle, Fez, Morocco, 1933; Torah finials, North Africa, 19th century; Torah mantle, Fez, Morocco, 1933. Cat. nos. 323, 318, 330 and 317.

FIG. NO. 36 Cover for a *Tik*, Algeria or Libya, 19th century. Cat. no. 338.

FIG. NO. 37 Left to right: Top row: Tefillin bag, North Africa, 19th–20th century; Tefillin bag, North Africa, 19th–20th century; Tefillin bag, North Africa, 19th–20th century; Bottom row: Tallit Bag, North Africa, 19th–20th century; Mezuzah Cover, North Africa, 19th–20th century. Cat. nos. 388, 390, 389, 387, 446.

FIG. NO. 38 Torah mantle, Ottoman empire, 1874. Cat. no. 27.

FIG. NO. 39 Torah mantle, Izmir, 1909. Cat. no. 30.

the combination of the two materials, both forming one unit of a cylindrical case and its accessories. One case is made of a metal plaque attached to velvet, in which silver adornments are combined, such as a circular gilt shield and a crown at the top of the case (cat. no. 27; fig. no. 38). The second case, of silver repoussé, imitates an embroidered textile (cat. no. 30; fig. no. 39). (In North Africa, the combination of textile and metal is different: pierced silver plaques are attached and sewn to a velvet textile, which serves as a colorful background for the "lace" pattern pierced into the metal. See, for example, mezuzah covers, fig. no. 61, and tefillin and tallit bags.)

From Italy there are a few cylindrical or faceted wooden Torah scroll cases, decorated with gilt gesso, their upper rim sometimes carved to form crowns.[17]

The Sephardic mantles of the late seventeenth century are among the few examples of this type that have survived. Similar mantles are in the possession of the Italian community and the Sephardic communities of Holland and England.

The mantles with their hard cape or soft top are made of vertical embroidered strips alternating with plain ones, and have an opening at the back. Frequently long fringes

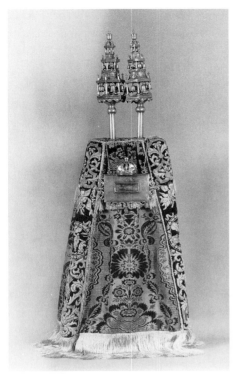

FIG. NO. 40 Torah finials, Amsterdam, 1770; Torah shield, Amsterdam, 1606; Torah mantle, Amsterdam, late 17th century. Cat. nos. 538, 533, 531.

FIG. NO. 41 Torah mantle, Amsterdam, late 17th century (detail). Cat. no. 531.

encircle their hems about one third of the way down. In addition to the heavy embroidery in gold, silver and silk threads of these Sephardic mantles in Italy, The Netherlands and England, gold fringes and tassels of the most elaborate and costly kind have been freely added (see cat. nos. 531, 532; fig. nos. 40, 53).

The textiles of the mantles are chosen from a wide range of fine fabrics: brocade, velvet, silk and satin. Brocade dating from the 16th century is incorporated in a mantle executed in the early eighteenth century; French woven fabrics were widely employed at a time when Lyons supplied the whole of Europe with its sumptuous weaving. Production of fine velvets, on the other hand, has always been the prerogative of Italy.[18] It seems that Jewish women's needlework in Italian cities, especially in Venice, was the central inspiration for ceremonial textiles and embroidery. Torah binders (*fascias* or *mappot*) from the sixteenth to the nineteenth century are embroidered with Sephardic or Ashkenazic script, giving the names of the Jewish women who made them, and occasionally also dates.[19]

Motifs and symbols adorning these mantles include the Torah ark, the Tablets of the

Law, Temple utensils, vines, olives, pomegranates, wheat, and family coats of arms. Torah mantles in the Portuguese Synagogue of Amsterdam are embroidered with depictions of angels, the binding of Isaac, and Jacob's dream (cat. no. 531; fig. nos. 40, 41).

In synagogues in Livorno, Rome and other Italian cities rectangular textiles wrap the entire width of the Torah scroll. The central section of the cloth is usually embroidered with a family coat of arms in couched embroidery.[20] This cloth, like the tallit, is used by one called for an *aliyah* for the ritual of touching the scroll and kissing the cloth. In some places, such as Livorno, cloth bands were added to tie the *mappah* around the Torah scroll. According to custom, after this cloth is removed from the Torah scroll it is brought by children to the women's gallery. There, by turns, beginning with the rabbi's wife, the women fold it.[21]

Torah Finials

Fitting over the two upper handles of the staves are Torah finials, *rimmonim*, or *tappuhim*. Though of diverse design, nearly all finials are topped by a bud, a tiny flower, a bouquet, or a fruit—perhaps to identify the Torah as the "Tree of Life." The two predominant forms are the "pomegranate" or fruit, and the tower. Usually, finials are tower-shaped, echoing local architecture. One such pair, among the few surviving ceremonial objects from the fifteenth century, was made in Camerata, Sicily, and features Moorish arches.[22] Most similar to these finials are examples from North Africa, particularly Algiers and Djerba. These stand tall and slender on a cylindrical shaft, and are surmounted by hollow spheres supporting a hexagonal tower with pointed roof and conical finial. Their surface is decorated with circles and a symmetrically patterned scrolling foliage. As in the Camerata pair, some are decorated with filigree work; the scrolled silver thread is attached and soldered to the plate and the dedication is inscribed on the facets of the tower.[23] Other examples, decorated with repoussé, engraved and chased, are often embellished with colored enamelwork.

Architectural Torah finials from Morocco are occasionally decorated with arabesques and symmetrical vegetal motifs. Most have arched windows, sometimes hung with bells. Through the glass window panes a dedicatory inscription is visible, sometimes including the name of the maker. In several finials of this kind, instead of windows, carnelians inlaid at the center of each facet are engraved with inscriptions. Moroccan Torah finials may be linked by a chain, attached by tiny rings on the head of the finial or at the base of each foot (e.g. cat. no. 332; fig. no. 42).

North African Torah finials are outstanding for their rich palette, with their blue and green enamelwork (cat. no. 325; fig. no. 43), multicolored glass beads suspended from short chains, and polychrome textiles peeping through pierced openwork (e.g. cat. nos. 323, 325, 326). Carved wooden Torah finials painted in gold, red and green, in the form of tall towers or fruit, come mainly from Morocco and Libya (cat. no. 327; fig. no. 44).

FIG. NO. 42 Torah finials, Asrir, Morocco, 19th–20th century. Cat. no. 332.

FIG. NO. 43 Torah finials, North Africa, 19th century. Cat. no. 325.

FIG. NO. 44 Torah finial, Libya, 19th century. Cat. no. 327.

The metalwork and decoration of Torah finials in North Africa recall local jewelry worn by Jewish women.[24] Examples of the jewelry forms used in finials are the flat brass plaques cast to form the symmetrical petals of a rosette, gilded diamond shapes inlaid with semiprecious stones (e.g. cat. no. 332; fig. no. 42), or the elongated cones in *ajouré* work that recall the tall headdresses worn by Algerian women. Naturally, all the Torah finials are hollow, cylindrical or multifaceted, to fit over the Torah staves. Strikingly tall silver Torah finials from Constantine, Algeria, dated 1877, echo multistoreyed towers with balustrades, reflecting an Italian influence (cat. no. 329).

Italian, particularly Venetian, Torah finials from the end of the seventeenth century and early eighteenth century are of a tall multistoreyed tower-form with balustrades, and are ornamented with bells on long chains. Many have added small gilt plaques depicting Tablets of the Law; Temple utensils; High Priest's vestments; hands posed for the priestly benediction; a Levite's ewer; and vegetal decoration. In Italy, finials, like Torah crowns, book covers and amulet cases, are embellished with baroque and rococo ornamental patterns. High-relief repoussé, chiseling and punching emphasize the play of light and shade, sculptural quality and movement. Gilding and the blush of coral bead inlay impart an opulence typical of Italian Jewish ritual art. The style and design of Torah finials and of ritual objects in general in Italy vary from city to city. Unique styles evolved in some cities, such as Rome and Turin, or Vercelli, where Torah finials were created in the shape of two small crowns. Styles of decoration changed over time, with the baroque and rococo remaining dominant also in later periods. It was, however, the early Venetian tower that served as a prototype for centuries not only in Europe but in North Africa and parts of the Ottoman empire.

Torah finials and other ceremonial artifacts closely resembling Italian Torah ornaments are found in Sephardic communities along the Adriatic coast that were once under Ottoman and Venetian rule.[25] In Rijeka (Fiume), Sibenik, Split (Spalato) and Dubrovnik (Ragusa), all now in Yugoslavia, close ties were maintained with Venice and the cities of north Italy. Yet, despite formal and stylistic affinities with the Italian model, local craftsmen have left their clear imprint on these wares (fig. no. 45).

In other cities of the Ottoman empire, particularly Istanbul, Izmir, Ankara and smaller communities, Torah finials were designed in a wide range of forms. Most are monumental in size, mounted on a long shaft. As in other locations, *rimmonim* are topped by bud finials, blossoms, tiny Stars of David, stars, or crescents. The forms fall into five basic groups (see fig. no. 46):

1) Cup above cup, each with a convex lid, the base a flattened bulb, usually covered with a uniformly engraved pattern (cat. nos. 47, 49; fig. no. 47).

2) Faceted (polygonal), architectural, with a hemispheric top or base, resembling multistorey towers, each facet decorated with a vegetal design.

3) Pear-shaped, some with stepped convex circles; repoussé with gadroons, or hooped at the center, usually decorated with geometric motifs (e.g. cat. no. 45).

4) Ovoid or spherical, in varying sizes, occasionally engraved with parallel lines or single flowers.

5) Multi-domed, ovoid, hollow, delicately engraved with branches and leaves, usually matched to a crown which stands on a plain base. Like the finials, the crown too is

FIG. NO. 46 Types of Ottoman Torah finials: 1. Cup above cup; 2. Faceted (polygonal); 3. Pear-shaped; 4. Ovoid or spherical; 5. Multi-domed, usually matched to a crown.

FIG. NO. 45 View of the Ark in the synagogue of Split, now Yugoslavia. Photograph: Aavija, Split. The Israel Museum Archives, no. 1097–11–42.

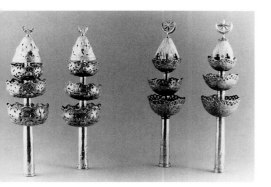

FIG. NO. 47 Left to right: Torah finials, Istanbul, 19th century; Torah finials, Turkey, 1861–77. Cat. nos. 47A, 49.

FIG. NO. 48 Torah finials, Holland, 18th century. Cat. no. 539.

convex and multi–domed. The straight shafts of the finials are fitted into holes drilled in the crown (cat. no. 44; fig. no. 53).

The large, pear-shaped finials recall *bimah* ornaments depicted in pre-Expulsion Spanish manuscripts, which may explain the large proportions of the finials in general.[26] Torah finials from the Ottoman empire bear a striking resemblance in their proportions to seventeenth-century Serbian church utensils.[27] It is difficult to ascertain what is the common origin of their design.[28]

In England and The Netherlands, Torah finials are surmounted by crowns. Finials are made of gilt silver and shaped like turreted towers with openwork galleries set with bells, sometimes with family coats of arms or initials (cat. nos. 538, 539; fig. nos. 40, 48). That most of the silversmiths were master craftsmen, is demonstrated in the excellence of their workmanship.

To this day it is customary in the Portuguese Synagogue in Amsterdam to assign special types of Torah finials to specific occasions; thus, the fine, lacy filigree finials are used chiefly during the High Holidays (cat. no. 540; fig. no. 49). Relatively small Torah finials topped with crowns and adorned with tendrils and rows of gilt bells were used during *levantar* (*hagbahah*, the raising of the Torah scroll before the congregation preceding the Torah reading) (cat. no. 537; fig. no. 50). Special Torah finials for the same purpose in the Amsterdam synagogue date from the end of the seventeenth or early eighteenth century. Their entire surface, including the shaft, is covered with interlaced acanthus leaves. Around the middle of the fruit shape, bells are suspended from tendrils (cat. no. 536; fig. no. 51).[29]

FIG. NO. 49 Torah finials, Holland, 18th century. Cat. no. 540.

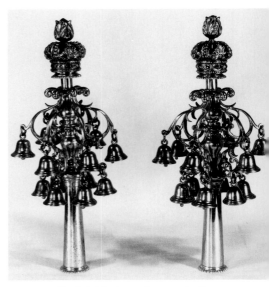

FIG. NO. 50 Torah finials, Amsterdam, 1703/4. Cat. no. 537.

FIG. NO. 51 Torah finials, Amsterdam, ca. 1690–1715; Torah mantle, Amsterdam, 17th century. Cat. nos. 536, 532.

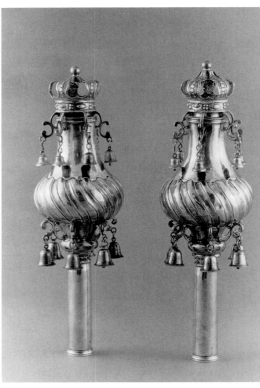

FIG. NO. 52 Torah finials, New York, ca. 1772, Myer Myers. Cat. no. 652.

Dutch finial types were also used by the Spanish and Portuguese congregations founded in the New World, revealing their connections to the Amsterdam community. In Curaçao, finials and other ritual silver made by master Dutch craftsmen such as Pieter van Hoven (1658–1735), were imported from The Netherlands or were brought by Dutch immigrants. The early American congregations in New York, Newport and Philadelphia used finials (called "bells" in these communities) made by the Jewish American silversmith Myer Myers (1725–1795). These finials combine Dutch forms, such as gilt crowns and bells, with neo-classical elements, such as urn shapes (cat. no. 652; fig. no. 52). Neo-classicism was popular in the late eighteenth century, particularly in Revolutionary-era America, as it evoked the spirit of ancient democracy which served as a role model for the newly established United States.[30]

Torah Crowns

The use of Torah crowns in medieval Spain can be seen in their depiction on page 34 of the Sarajevo Haggadah, a manuscript produced in Barcelona during the second half of the fourteenth century. Torah crowns were made in Italy, in the Ottoman empire and to a lesser degree in the Portuguese community of Amsterdam. The Dutch crowns, influenced by European models, are noted for their splendor and opulence. The typical Italian crowns are cylindrical and have metalwork and ornamentation similar to that found on finials, with motifs such as rocailles, foliage, Temple utensils, Tablets of the Law, and accessories of the High Priest.[31]

Torah crowns in the Ottoman empire are also cylindrical, with more varied proportions and rich ornamentation, some cut with scalloped or foliate rims, others shaped as convex or ribbed hoops; domed (e.g. cat. no. 44; fig. no. 53; see section on Torah finials above), and more. Surfaces are engraved and chased, with dedicatory inscriptions, geometric designs, rocailles, flowers and vases, cypress trees, leaves, ships and sailboats (e.g. cat. nos. 38–41, 44; fig. no. 54). Similar crowns and *atarot* made of plaques (e.g. cat. no. 340), in smaller numbers, were created in Algeria (e.g. cat. no. 321; Plate 14).

Torah Shields

The Torah shield is draped over the "trees of life" (staves) of the Torah scroll. In the Ashkenazic and Eastern European communities, the shield in addition to its decorative function, was used to indicate the portion to be read in the synagogue from that scroll. For this purpose the shield had a rectangular frame into which plaques were inserted. In Italy the inscription may appear on the shield itself. Generally in Italy and throughout the Ottoman empire the function of the shield was purely ornamental, usually with a dedicatory inscription. In Italy, where there are relatively few examples, the Torah shield was usually a silver plate cut in the shape of a crown, sometimes bearing the inscription *Keter Torah* (Torah crown). This may be the source of the term *atarah* (lit. crown) coined by Leone da Modena in *Historia de Riti Hebraici* to describe a Torah shield. These crown-shaped plaques are characteristic mainly of Italy and the areas of Dalmatia (Yugoslavia) bordering on northern Italy (see above, fig. no. 45).[32] Other Italian Torah shields combine the shield with heraldic forms or architectural structures reflecting an Ashkenazic influence. Especially noteworthy is the art of Pacifico Levi of Turin, who began working in 1817 and is one of twelve Jewish silversmiths listed in the city guild register (see above, note 5; cat. no. 534; fig. no. 31).

In cities at the center of the Ottoman empire, such as Istanbul, Edirne, Salonika, Izmir and Ankara, Torah shields have their own unique forms, primarily round, oval or triangular, with high relief repoussé depictions of flower filled vases. Dedicatory inscriptions appear in cartouches along the upper section or circle the center (e.g. cat. no. 35; fig. no. 55). Other forms include the Star of David, shield or crescent. Many of the shields are made of plaques which originally served as mirror holders and frames, to which were affixed crescent-shaped plaques bearing dedicatory inscriptions (cat. no. 37; fig. no. 56). Torah shield decoration in this area is executed in repoussé, filigree, cutting and piercing, and sometimes combinations of these techniques. Dedicatory inscriptions are either engraved or embossed, often with chasing or niello. The wide range of forms in ritual objects, and particularly the unhesitating secondary use of objects from the Muslim world, testify to the relationship of reciprocity and tolerance that prevailed between Jews and their neighbors in the central Ottoman empire.

Particularly in Izmir, Istanbul and Edirne, exceptional plaques adorn Torah crowns, in the form of the Star of David, *hamsa* (hand),[33] or crown. The plaques stand on a narrow, flat plate attached with hooks to the inside of the crown (cat. nos. 42, 43; fig. no. 57).

FIG. NO. 53 Torah crown and finials, Istanbul or Bulgaria, 1840. Cat. no. 44.

FIG. NO. 54 Torah crown, Ankara, 1865. Cat. no. 40.

FIG. NO. 55 Torah shield, Ankara, 1865. Cat. no. 35.   FIG. NO. 56 Torah shield, Izmir, 1923. Cat. no. 37.

In Syria and Eretz Israel dedicatory plaques were made of silver, and were often attached to the Torah ark curtain, Torah case or mantle. A dedicatory plaque of this type from Aleppo, Syria, bears the date "Tammuz, 1693." Like many other dedicatory inscriptions, this one tells a tragic human story: this Torah scroll and finials were dedicated to the benevolent society of the Sephardic community by a father in memory of his only son, Yaakov Laniado, who died at the age of twenty. The Torah scroll and other items were created from the son's legacy, and the scroll was to be known as *Nahlat Yaakov* (Jacob's Portion) in the deceased's name (cat. no. 250). Short benedictions or protective acronyms are invariably added to the names of the donors and communities that appear on these plaques, investing the plaques with amuletic significance.[34] See for example a dedication plaque for a Torah ark curtain donated to the Damascus Community Synagogue in Jerusalem by Regina Farhi (cat. no. 252).

Among the Spanish-Portuguese Jews who settled in the cities of Germany and The Netherlands, the Torah shield is a rare phenomenon. The oldest example extant among several shields from Hamburg from the end of the seventeenth century is made by a master silversmith, Tobias Folsch, who worked in the city from 1690–1707 (fig. no. 58).[35] Apparently, such a costly piece could only be commissioned by Jews as affluent as those of Spanish and Portuguese origins. The Hamburg Sephardic community, marranos who had returned to Judaism with the aid of the local rabbis, probably first learned about Torah shields from Ashkenazic practice. Most of the marranos came to

Hamburg directly from the Iberian peninsula, or via Antwerp or northern Italy, where they probably first beheld the beauty and profusion of ritual ornament.

The colorful Hamburg shield does indeed recall Italian ceremonial prototypes, with its inlaid coral and other semiprecious stones,[36] vine shoots and clusters of grapes winding around the pillars, and high relief rocailles and flowers. In the *Pinkas Kehillah* (communal register) of the Portuguese community of Hamburg in 1652 one of the beneficiaries listed is a Jewish silversmith from Italy, ". . . who is now departing for Poland." It is impossible to tell whether this silversmith created ceremonial objects in Hamburg, but it could be that he advised a client or brought samples with him.[37] The inscription appearing on the suspended plaques is dissimilar to that found on the Ashkenazic prototype, thus suggesting that the Sephardic patron chose Biblical verses according to his personal preference and integrated the Hebrew date in a chronogram. Characteristic of the Hamburg group of Torah shields are the three and sometimes four convex crowns rising from their upper section. These represent the crown of Torah, the crown of priesthood, and the crown of royalty (Avot 4:13).[38]

Of special interest is the story of the only Torah shield in the Portuguese Synagogue of Amsterdam (cat. no. 533; fig. no. 40). Made of silver in Amsterdam in 1606, it is the oldest Torah shield extant.[39] It bears the engraved Hebrew inscriptions "Crown of Torah" next to the convex crown in its upper section and "for the New Moon" at the center, where Ashkenazic shields usually affix the frame for interchangeable plaques;

FIG. NO. 57 Left to right: Torah crown ornament, Gallipoli, 1862/3; Torah crown ornament, Gallipoli, mid-19th century. Cat. nos. 42, 43.

FIG. NO. 58 Torah shield, Hamburg, late 17th century, Tobias Folsch, Collection of the Israel Museum, Jerusalem, 148/30.

on the back are engraved the names of the donors, "Yaakov Tirado Rachel Tiradah." At the close of the sixteenth century a number of marrano families from Spain and Portugal arrived in the German city of Emden. A local townsman, Uri Feibisch ben Yosef ha-Levi, helped them continue on to Amsterdam, where they were able to undergo ritual conversion under more congenial conditions than those prevailing in Emden at the time.[40] Among these marranos was the family of Yaakov Tirado, who first learned Jewish customs in the German city and then when he arrived in Amsterdam commissioned the Torah shield and dedicated it to the Amsterdam congregation. The shield was made by the silversmith Leendert Claesz, who came to Amsterdam via Emden, where he was apprenticed to a local silversmith and thus may have been inspired by similar types of shields crafted in Emden.[41] Yaakov Tirado was one of the founders and elders of the Amsterdam Jewish community. He emigrated to Eretz Israel with his family in 1616.

A small group of Torah shields comes from Constantine, Algeria, mainly from the late nineteenth and early twentieth century. These shields are unique: they follow the Ashkenazic model but with their own distinct Islamic-influenced silverwork and decoration. All bear dedicatory inscriptions, but unlike the Ashkenazic shields, they are engraved on most of the central section (cat. no. 320).

Torah Pointers

To follow the text, the Torah reader uses a pointer, called a *yad* (hand), *etzba* (finger), or *moreh* (guide). Usually the silver pointer is hand-shaped, on a long plaque shaft with a pointing finger at one end and a ring for a chain at the other. The dedication inscription is engraved or cast along the shaft.

In Italy and The Netherlands most of the pointers are made of silver, the shaft decorated at the center and end with knops and circlets. Some are lavishly decorated with vegetal patterns applied in various techniques. Gold or carved coral are also used, sometimes in combination.

Pointers in the Ottoman empire are marked by their own distinctive style: narrow and long—sometimes with a shaft exceeding 19 inches—they consist of a narrow, flat stave, with the palm of the hand flat, a long, pointing finger, and a twisted shaft. The chains, too, are very long and often decorated with small crescent plaques.

In North Africa, especially Morocco, the pointer is short and the finger long, or all the fingers of the hand are the same size, aligned as in a *hamsa*. The flat shaft is engraved with arabesques, flowers and foliage, sometimes centered or topped by an interlaced flower or rosette bearing the ring and suspension chain. These are made of silver or brass, with engraved inscriptions, niello, and occasionally even painting.

Striking examples display a rectangular stave centered by a hollow, three-dimensional rosette. Tunisian pointers are flat and leaf-form, terminating in the palm of a hand, with pointing finger, the other end a short, narrow stave with suspension chain. In some pointers, a cloth tassel or wick replaces the chain.

Synagogue and Memorial Lamps

Among the synagogue lights are the memorial lamps which are hung in front of the Torah ark. In Italy and the Ottoman empire these usually consist of a silver vessel containing a glass oil cup and fitted with tiny arms or rings for long suspension chains. Dedicatory inscriptions often appear on the silver vessel. These lamps based on the contemporary style of lamps used in churches and mosques, probably stem from an early source such as seventeenth-century mosque lamps.[42] The hanging lamp motif occurs in embroideries and carpets, especially in Ottoman ark curtains of all periods[43] (e.g. cat. no. 61; fig. no. 59). Memorial lamps in North Africa, particularly Morocco, are made mainly of brass, but sometimes of silver, with the hook in the shape of a *hamsa*.

Outstanding among these lamps are the *ghoch*, *hoch*, or *helya* lamps, suspended in the synagogue over the head of someone celebrating a special occasion, such as a bar mitzvah or wedding. These are in the form of a miniature canopy bearing a Star of David on chains. At its center, suspended from a chain, is a large glass bowl surrounded

FIG. NO. 59 Synagogue rug, Istanbul or Cairo, 17th century. Cat. no. 61.

FIG. NO. 60 *Qendil*, Morocco, 18th–19th century. Cat. no. 344.

FIG. NO. 61 Left to right: Hanukkah Lamp, North Africa, 19th century; Mezuzah cover, North Africa, 19th–20th century; Tallit bag, Morocco, 19th century; Mezuzah cover, North Africa, 19th–20th century. Cat. nos. 366, 444, 386, 452.

by hoops supporting smaller bowls. A decorated *hamsa* hangs from each corner and from the center of the small plate supporting the central bowl.

The use of oil lamps, especially in Morocco, is not entirely clear; it probably varied according to local custom. The hanging *kas* was a memorial lamp for men, and the *qendil* for women. The *qendil* was usually attached to the wall, and consisted mainly of a square tin container with truncated corners for storing the wicks, over a similarly shaped drip pan. The backplate, oilpan and the sides of the container are all decorated with vegetal motifs, arabesques, and birds (cat. no. 344; fig. no. 60). These two types of lamps were hung in the home and lit mainly on the Sabbath and festivals. At the end of the one year mourning period, the lamps were transferred to the synagogue. Often they are inscribed with the name of the deceased or with references to the Sabbath and festivals. Other wall lamps have two arms, each holding a glass oil vessel; one vessel, according to tradition, is dedicated to Rabbi Meir Baal ha-Nes, and the other to Rabbi Shimon Bar Yohai. Their backplates are similar to those of cast brass Hanukkah lamps.[44]

An unusual *qendil* type is represented by an example with pierced silver backplate, with vegetal patterns and roosters. Identical workmanship and designs appear on mezuzah covers bearing the name of the mistress of the house; on tallit bags presented to a bar mitzvah boy or bridegroom; and on Hanukkah lamps (e.g. cat. nos. 366, 386, 444, 452; fig. no. 61).

Almsboxes

The oldest known extant almsbox is from Spain, dating from 1319, almost two centuries before the Expulsion.[45] With its inscription referring to Purim, it appears to have been connected to the custom of *maot Purim*, the half-shekel coins (or their equivalents) collected at the synagogue as charity before the reading of the Esther scroll on Purim.[46]

Four gilt silver shallow-footed bowls, called tazzas, were donated to the Portuguese Synagogue in Amsterdam on Adar 14 5444 (1684). According to tradition, they were dedicated for use as collection plates for the coins collected on Purim. The tazzas are small, flat plates, each standing on a foot and small base. Created by master silversmiths of that period, they are engraved with dedicatory inscriptions (cat. no. 544; fig. no. 62). This type of tazza, found in Europe in small numbers, occasionally includes depictions of Biblical or mythological scenes. The original use of dishes of this type is unclear; certainly, such bowls must have been purely ornamental, especially during the late Renaissance, as was the case with many other silver vessels.[47]

Almsboxes varied in shape and material; they were made of simple tin or silver, mobile or fixed. A seventeenth-century set of alms boxes from the *Matir Asurim* Synagogue in Florence consists of a row of attached boxes fronted by a colonnade of hewn marble. Each opening is sealed with a tiny wooden door secured by an iron latch, and over each door is a coin opening and an inscription indicating the respective beneficiaries: "Hospital" "Charity" "[Synagogue] Building Repairs" "Old Age Home" "Lighting" "Jerusalem" and "Rabbi Meir [Baal ha-Nes]" (fig. no. 63).

In the Ottoman empire, particularly Turkey and the Balkans, almsboxes are bulbous silver containers, slotted, and usually with a curved handle, engraved with vegetal motifs and dedicatory inscriptions (cat. no. 71; fig. no. 64).[48] A rare charity plate, made

FIG. NO. 62 Tazza, Holland, 1684. Cat. no. 544.

FIG. NO. 63 Alms boxes, *Matir Asurim* Synagogue, Florence, 17th century, Collection of the Nahon Museum of Italian Jewish Art, Jerusalem.

in Istanbul, has in its center a gondola-shaped boat with a bird on its prow, covered by a canopy with a crescent at each corner. Around the base are engraved the names of the donors (*mishtadlim*), and the Hebrew date 5626 (1866) (cat. no. 70; fig. no. 65). Ships and sailboats adorn a variety of objects and documents such as marriage contracts, carpets and Torah crowns (see above, cat. no. 321; Plate 14), boxes and incense utensils. Yet the unusual design of the plate, the boat, and the list of donors suggest that this plate belonged to one of the charitable societies founded independently by the Jewish guilds that rebelled against the rabbinical establishment.[49] One of these, the "Bosphorus Boat Owners Guild," had a special box "to which every man may contribute generously one *prutah* [small coin] a week . . . for the welfare of the poor and needy . . ."[50]

Silver objects reveal the history and traditions of the Sephardic communities of London and Amsterdam. One group of silver vessels belongs to the Society *Santa*

FIG. NO. 65 Alms plate, Ottoman empire, 1863/4. Cat. no. 70.

FIG. NO. 64 Alms box, Turkey, 1903/4. Cat. no. 71.

FIG. NO. 66 Container for dowry lottery tickets, Amsterdam, 1781/2. Cat. no. 548.

FIG. NO. 67 Lord Mayor's dish, London, 1737, Jos. Sanders. Cat. no. 546.

Companhia de Dotar Orphas e Donzellas, usually referred to as *Dotar*, which was founded
in 1615 by some twenty members of the Portuguese-Jewish congregations in Amsterdam to supply dowries for needy and deserving brides. Some donations to the society,
such as the bequests made by Joseph Henriques Sequeira (1718), Moseh and Jeudith
Teixeira de Mattos (1781), and Nathan of Salomon Dias Brandon (1872), stipulate that
dowries be distributed by lottery. Drawing takes place on the *theba*, the pulpit, in the
Portuguese Synagogue in Amsterdam on Shushan Purim, a day traditionally associated
with lotteries.[51] Before the lots are drawn, the reader recites prayers for the repose of
the souls of the founders and members that have died during the current year; he also
pronounces a blessing on the members of the committee. The *mahamad* (trustees) bear
silver vessels containing the lottery tickets (see cat. no. 548; fig. no. 66). The actual
drawing of the lots is carried out with much ceremony; each canister is shaken by each
member of the committee in turn. A small boy draws a ticket from a canister and the
Haham (chief rabbi of the community) then unfolds the ticket and hands it to the
president, who reads out the name of the lucky candidate.[52]

The second group of silver wares relates to the history of the London Spanish and
Portuguese community. Between 1679 and 1778 an annual gift was presented to the
Lord Mayor of London by the Sephardic community. Silver vessels, such as the tray
presented in 1737 (cat. no. 546; fig. no. 67), were accompanied by a purse of £50, or
sweetmeats.[53] Engraved in the center of the 1737 plate is the emblem of the Spanish
and Portuguese Congregation of London and a dedicatory inscription. The style of
uniform of the figure representing the Guardian of Israel in the Bevis Marks Synagogue
emblem was altered as fashion changed. In this example the figure is shown wearing a
uniform closely resembling a British grenadier early in the reign of George II. Following
the presentation of the Lord Mayor's plate in 1778, the *mahamad* (trustees) of the Spanish
and Portuguese Congregation of London decided to write a letter to the Lord Mayor
explaining that "the expense being now too great," they were obliged to discontinue
this custom.[54]

Esther Scroll Cases and Book Bindings

Esther scroll cases, book bindings and boxes are intended to keep and protect the written
parchment or paper. They were typical engagement gifts; those presented to brides and
bridegrooms were generally wrought from precious materials. In Italian silver book
bindings both sides are engraved with the initials of the bridal pair or with their family
crests; in many Balkan Esther scroll cases a dedicatory inscription to the bridegroom
runs along the narrow opening.[55] Enameled filigree cases inlaid with semiprecious
stones from the region of the Ottoman empire that now comprises Yugoslavia recall
traditional jewelry from the same area and Jewish wedding rings from Venice in their
design and decoration.[56]

In Morocco, Esther scrolls are usually rolled around one wooden handle embellished

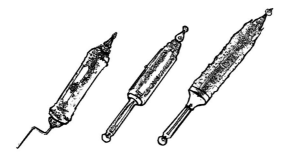

FIG. NO. 68 Types of Ottoman Esther scroll cases: 1. Cylindrical with *lamed*-shaped handle; 2. Polygonal; 3. Filigree.

with narrow silver bands, similar in form and decoration to Torah staves. Some Moroccan and Italian wooden cases enclose the scroll completely. A slit along the cylinder facilitates unrolling the scroll during the reading (cat. no. 374).

In the Ottoman empire Esther scrolls are often rolled on a wooden rod inlaid with ivory at either end. The finials are three graded crowns, pierced or punched, surmounted by a knop and crescent. The ends of the scroll are triangular or wavy, with a band for tying (e.g. cat. no. 81). The Esther scroll cases in the central Ottoman empire are usually of three types (see fig. nos. 68, 69):

1) Cylindrical, plain or gilt silver, domed at both ends. The opening is covered by a long, narrow, ringed strip. At the upper end of the case, a tiny finial rises from the dome: a bird with outspread wings and a suspension ring on its back, a bouquet or vase of flowers; a crescent, or a Star of David. The dome may be encircled by a crown motif. The handle is usually in the form of the Hebrew letter *lamed* with a knop terminal. The cylinder is decorated with light repoussé, chased with outlines and punched with vegetal and geometric motifs.

FIG. NO. 69 Left to right: Esther scroll, roller and cover, Izmir, 19th century; Esther scroll and case, Ottoman empire, 19th–20th century; Esther scroll, roller and cover, Turkey, mid-19th century; Esther scroll, roller and cover, Ottoman empire, 19th century. Cat. nos. 83, 86, 84, 82.

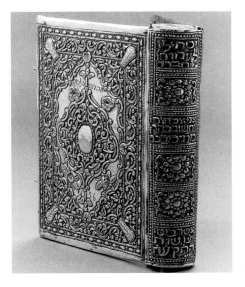

FIG. NO. 71 Esther scroll and roller, Holland, 1673, Salom d'Italia. Cat. no. 559.

FIG. NO. 70 Book cover, Ottoman empire, 1817/18. Cat. no. 136.

2) Polygonal, similar to North African Esther scroll cases, and also recalling North African and Italian Torah cases. The ribs are decorated with scrolled foliage. One rib opens at the rim, usually with a ring handle. At both ends a faceted dome, encircled by a hoop, is surmounted by a bud, knop, flower or bird and suspension ring (cat. no. 82).
3) Cases of gold or gilt filigree and granulation, inlaid with coral or pearls. These are usually cylindrical, with three-tiered crown finials terminating in a cone, knop, and bead (often carnelian). The case opens on a hinge and closes with a latch. Sometimes the central cylinder is replaced by an embroidered textile encircling the scroll (cat. nos. 83–85).

In scroll cases of the first two types the workmanship and decoration often recall the silverwork of rifle and pistol butts.[57] Ottoman book covers and cases, almsboxes and amulet cases are identical in design and ornamentation to those for storing books of the Koran and firman documents, as well as gunpowder boxes (e.g. cat. no. 136; fig. no. 70).[58] These cases and boxes were created mainly in the Balkans. When gunpowder was supplanted by bullets, the production of boxes and cases used by Jews also ceased.

Exquisite cases from Italy are made of gold and decorated with depictions of Temple utensils;[59] from Ancona, made of silver pierced with foliate scrollwork imitating the cut-out decoration of the parchment scroll;[60] silver handles with plates decorated with repoussé scenes from the Purim story;[61] or ivory carved in the shape of a queen and king, like those created for the scroll illustrated by the Jewish artist Salom d'Italia (cat. no. 559; fig. no. 71).

Hanukkah Lamps

Little is known about Hanukkah lamps (*hanukkiot*) before the Expulsion in 1492. In his book *The Hanukkah Lamp*, Mordecai Narkiss links their fate with that of ceremonial

FIG. NO. 72 Synagogue Hanukkah lamp, Damascus, early 20th century. Cat. no. 255.

FIG. NO. 73 Hanukkah lamp, North Africa, 19th century. Cat. no. 367.

art in general: "As with all Jewish ceremonial objects, the Hanukkah lamp was subject to the same adventures experienced by its owners. Together with them it disappears, and together with them it resurfaces. Like its owners, the Hanukkah lamp is a product of a time and a place, borrowing from its surroundings whatever enhances its form and traditional function, integrating the foreign into the Jewish."[62] The Hanukkah lamp is one of the most widespread of all Jewish ritual artifacts, found in almost every Jewish home. Yet hardly any Hanukkah lamps have survived from the central Ottoman empire, principally the Sephardic communities of Turkey.[63] Few lamps dating from the eighteeenth or nineteenth century are attributed to this region. Two of them are inspired by Hanukkah lamps brought from Jerusalem.[64]

Syrian Hanukkah lamps, dating largely from the end of the nineteenth century, are more lavish in decoration, fashioned from inlaid damascene work (e.g. cat. no. 255; fig. no. 72) or more simply from sheet brass, usually engraved with the candlelighting blessings. Facing birds or lions frequently surmount the backplates of lamps from this region.

Hanukkah lamps in Jerusalem, since earliest times, have been as varied in design and material as the communities that have entered the city's gates throughout its long history. In the nineteenth century Hanukkah lamps were crafted and sold by the poor of the Jewish community of Jerusalem. Made of colored glass beads, these were sold as souvenirs'to pilgrims.[65] Special fundraising emissaries (*shadarim*) were sent out from Jerusalem to solicit contributions for yeshiva scholars and their families (see the letter of accreditation for rabbinical emissary, cat. no. 257 and appeal for charity, cat. no. 258). Traveling from one community to another, from country to country, the emissaries were absent from home for long periods. For them, travel Hanukkah lamps were made with arched backplates, fixed with a bar and hook, supporting a hinged folding plaque. On the plaque are openings or hoops for the glass oil fonts. Stars, cypresses, and sometimes the name of the owner decorate the backplate (cat. no. 265; Plate 9).[66]

The oldest known extant Hanukkah lamp was probably made either in Spain or Provence during the fourteenth century. A triangle with a trefoil apex, its backplate features a rosette window and a row of Moorish arched gates. This lamp, which may have served as a prototype for all those that followed, is discussed by Mordecai Narkiss, as is a fifteenth-century Sicilian lamp, also triangular, with a pattern of interlaced tendrils and a palmette finial. In his study Narkiss sets out to trace the changes and developments in their design to the migrations of the Sephardic Jews north to Italy and south to North Africa. A fifteenth-century Hanukkah lamp, apparently inspired by the prototype and with the same architectural motif, bears an inscription cast in elongated rectangular letters in Sephardic script.[67]

In the earliest extant Hanukkah lamps the architectural form is already established as a standard pattern for the backplate, symbolizing the festival of the rededication of the Temple. A building facade or architectural elements, such as arches, gates, windows, columns, balconies and towers, usually reflects local architectural styles. In North Africa, especially in Morocco, these are interwoven with arabesques and birds (e.g. cat. no. 367; fig. no. 73).

Hanukkah lamps from Morocco were also made of carved stone, with three large depressions for gathering oil and slits for wicks. These were carved with circles, hatching, and inscriptions (cat. no. 368; fig. no. 74).[68] Jerusalem stone lamps are carved in

FIG. NO. 74 Hanukkah lamp, Morocco, 19th century. Cat. no. 368.

FIG. NO. 75 Hanukkah lamp, Jerusalem. Cat. no. 262.

the form of buildings, or imitate metal prototypes (cat. no. 262; fig. no. 75. Mainly in Djerba and Tunis, green glazed pottery lamps were fashioned as a row of truncated oil fonts on an elongated basin, without any architectural elements (cat. no. 369; fig. no. 76).[69]

In Italy, architectural motifs in Hanukkah lamps reflect Renaissance elements such as church cupolas, cathedral windows, grillwork, tiled roofs and masonry. Some of the lamps resemble depictions of pilgrimage sites in the Holy Land and its environs as executed by an Italian pilgrim in the sixteenth century.[70] Family coats of arms were occasionally added to the decoration. Heraldic family emblems already appear in manuscripts from Spain hundreds of years before the Expulsion. Family coats of arms were popular among Italian Jews and the Spanish-Portuguese Jews who reached The Netherlands and England. They adorned their ceremonial objects and synagogue textiles,

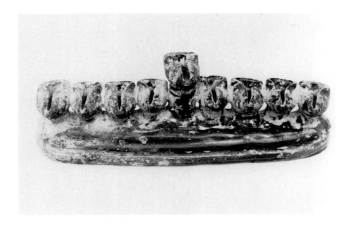

FIG. NO. 76 Hanukkah lamp, Tunisia, 19th century. Cat. no. 369.

amulet cases, books, book covers, marriage contracts and documents with these heraldic emblems.

A further Italian Renaissance influence is apparent in the inclusion of mythical creatures, angels, mermaids, seahorses and centaurs on Hanukkah lamps. During the Renaissance these figures were transformed from pagan religious symbols to purely decorative elements, and thus the appearance of seemingly "inappropriate" motifs on Jewish ceremonial objects. The popular mermaid or siren motif, which appears also in Dutch and Moroccan Hanukkah lamps was already widespread in pre-Expulsion manuscripts and Jewish literature in the sixteenth and seventeenth centuries.[71] A seventeenth-century brass Hanukkah lamp engraved and pierced with "nondescript animals" (mythical creatures), signed by its Spanish Jewish maker, David Lopez Pereira, is described in *The Catalogue of the Anglo-Jewish Historical Exhibition* of 1887.[72]

Most Italian and North African Hanukkah lamps are made of bronze or brass. The Moroccan sheet brass lamps are similar to those of The Netherlands. In cast lamps from Italy the backplates are usually in high, almost sculptural relief, while the Moroccan lamps tend to be flat, with chased decoration. Most backplates of Moroccan Hanukkah lamps incorporate Islamic architectural compositions, ornament and arabesque decoration as found in Spain and Morocco, motifs used also to adorn books, scrolls, documents, and amulets.

Decorative elements include birds, roosters, crescents, the *hamsa*, vegetation, and geometric forms, virtually all of which have magical significance, mainly in the Islamic world.[73] In Hanukkah lamps or other Jewish ceremonial objects, extreme stylization and schematization may turn a magical-charged symbol, such as a sun, star, *hamsa*, and Star of David motif, into a purely ornamental design. Colors and semiprecious stones, also invested with magical meaning, adorn ceremonial objects such as Torah finials (see above) and synagogue textiles. Hanukkah lamps were crafted with colorful woven cloth behind glass or gold-painted metal. Many motifs frequently used in Islamic art assumed magical significance among Jews as well, who used them as amulets and symbols. Birds, alone or integrated in a larger design, spread their wings on the lids of scroll cases or serve as the thumb on a *hamsa*. According to Victor Klagsbald, bird motifs on Hanukkah lamps symbolize the lost bird looking for its nest, like the wandering Jew in search of the restored Tabernacle of the Lord (Psalms 68, 84).[74]

In The Netherlands the earliest known brass Hanukkah lamp is dated 1629 and was donated to the Portuguese Synagogue in Amsterdam. The owner, Abraham Farar the Younger, was a Lisbon physician born in Porto who fled to Amsterdam, where he published in 1627 a book in Portuguese setting out all the commandments and prohibitions of Jewish law. He died in 1663.[75] The lamp's backplate is cast with the Hebrew inscription: "For the Commandment is a lamp and the Torah is Light," and the Hebrew date, while the lower part, in Portuguese, gives the name of the owners and the term *hanukkiya*, as is current today. Large in size, and standing on a large drip basin, the lamp is decorated with lily petals and ogee arches. It is the prototype for many later lamps. Most sheet brass Hanukkah lamps date from the eighteenth century, when the devastating wars of the seventeenth century had left the Dutch economy in shambles and fluctuations in the European metal market in general had lowered the economic status of the Jewish communities of The Netherlands, inducing the use of cheaper metals.[76]

Moroccan and Dutch Hanukkah lamps of brass, particularly brass sheet, are strikingly similar, with their pierced, punched and engraved decoration. High-relief roundels, hearts, rosettes, seven-branched candelabra, tendrils, leaves, vases, figures and other motifs were added as light reflectors. According to Mordecai Narkiss, the marranos brought with them from Portugal to Amsterdam "oriental style motifs, a kind of enlarged arabesque."[77] Yet in fact it is the Moroccan and Dutch brass lamps that are almost interchangeable, attesting to the close ties between these two Jewish communities at the time. Both work in a folk style, occasionally borrowing motifs from one another, and executing them with similar tools (cat. nos 361, 553; fig. nos. 77, 78). In the Moroccan sheet brass Hanukkah lamps, but not the Dutch, cast pillars were sometimes added, as were engraved oil pitchers, seven-branched candelabra, and pierced Stars of David.

Pewter Hanukkah lamps from England and The Netherlands imitate or resemble silver artifacts. Most of the lamps have smooth backplates decorated at their rim with rocailles or foliate scrollwork.[78] The engraving is delicate and intricate, as in silver, in contrast to the German Hanukkah lamps, for example, which are engraved with folk motifs and zigzagging.[79]

An unusual pewter Hanukkah lamp has a row of oil fonts, each with a small lid, the backplate decorated with the emblem of the city of Amsterdam. On the front of the drip basin are engraved two family crests and clasped hands, usually signifying a marriage. An interval of more than 100 years separates the date engraved on the Hanukkah lamp, "Anno 1674," and the date of the hallmark on its back. The earlier date may have marked an unknown event or marriage in the annals of two distinguished families in the Portuguese community (fig. no. 79).[80]

Silver Hanukkah lamps were less frequently used than those of bronze or brass. In Morocco, silver lamps consisted of plaques, pierced like mezuzah covers, Sabbath lamps and tallit bags (e.g. cat. no. 366; fig. no. 61). The Italian lamps have opaque backplates, decorated with repoussé rocailles, foliage and flowers, or family coats of arms.[81] Occasionally, the oil fonts along the lower section have short arms (as in eighteenth-century brass lamps).[82]

Silver Hanukkah lamps in The Netherlands and England, made at the end of the seventeenth and beginning of the eighteenth century, refer closely to the Italian lamps, with their opaque backplates and repoussé and chased decoration. The lower section

FIG. NO. 77 Hanukkah lamp, Meknes, Morocco, 19th century. Cat. no. 361.

FIG. NO. 78 Hanukah lamp, Holland, 18th century. Cat. no. 553.

FIG. NO. 79 Hanukkah lamp, Holland, 1785, Collection of the Israel Museum, 118/568. Gift of Rudolf Herz Collection, London, 1966.

terminates in a kind of basin with two spouts at the sides, and the oil fonts are almond shaped, with the *shammash* (servitor) at the center above. The decoration is often late baroque.[83] On an 18th century silver Hanukkah lamp donated by the de Castro family to the Portuguese Synagogue in Amsterdam in 1877, a figure attired in the fashion of the period holds a book as he kindles the lights on an eight-branched candelabrum. He is surrounded by pillars with flowers and cornices, an arch, a shell, and potted plants, recalling late baroque chambers (cat. no. 555; Plate 16; fig. no. 80).

Scriptural Scenes on Ceremonial Objects

Jewish ceremonial metalware from England and The Netherlands is distinguished by its depiction of Biblical scenes, an uncommon trait in other Sephardic communities. A Hanukkah lamp made in London in 1712 depicts the prophet Elisha and the widow, illustrating the miracle of the cruse of oil in II Kings 4:1–6. The choice of this biblical scene may have been due to the fact that the marranos erroneously believed in a biblical source for the Hanukkah story and were unaware of the true sources in the Apocrypha and the Talmud.[84] In a silver Hanukkah lamp of 1709, the prophet Elijah is fed by the ravens, perhaps a reference to the name of the patron, probably Elias Lindo.[85] The backplate of this lamp is identical to the carved, sculptural tombstones of Portuguese Jews.[86] The Portuguese Jews of The Netherlands and England were apparently influenced by the proliferation of Bible illustration in Europe. They did not hesitate to

FIG. NO. 80 Hanukkah lamp, Amsterdam, 1795 (detail). Cat. no. 555.

FIG. NO. 81 Medal commemorating the birth of a son, Amsterdam, 1665 (reverse—David dancing before the Ark of the Covenant). Cat. no. 612.

FIG. NO. 82 Medal commemorating the birth of a son, Amsterdam, 1665 (obverse—Samuel Annointing David). Cat. no. 612.

adopt Christian iconography, mainly that of Protestant artists who depicted Old Testament stories in paintings, illustrated printed books, and printed broadsides. These themes were popular also on silver and gold artifacts such as plates, tazzas, plaques and medallions.[87] A unique Jewish gold medallion from Amsterdam (1665) commemorates the birth and circumcision of a boy named David. One side shows the anointment of King David; on the other, King David dances in front of the Ark of the Covenant. The borders quote the relevant Biblical passages and note the Hebrew date. Both scenes are of sculptural repoussé, with a play of varying depths and delicate engraving. Beside the main figures stand soldiers, priests and Saul's daughter Michal mocking David from the window, while in the background, behind Samuel and David, stand a throne, scepter and harp (cat. no. 612; fig. nos. 81, 82).[88]

A large, sumptuous German laver, donated to the Portuguese Synagogue in Amsterdam, was crafted by an Augsburg master in the middle of the eighteenth century, with a chromatic interplay between gilt and silver, high and low relief, repoussé, and delicate engraving. Hunting dogs race around the border of the plate, which is centered by what was apparently the donor's chosen subject, King Solomon on a splendid throne, receiving the Queen of Sheba surrounded by handmaidens bearing gifts. This subject is a general favorite in European art, in innumerable variations related to the prevailing political or religious conditions (cat. no. 543; fig. no. 83).[89]

A rare spice container, made in 1712, is in the Portuguese Synagogue in Amsterdam.

As with the adoption of the use of Torah shields in Amsterdam and Hamburg, the marrano Elias Gabai Henriques, who returned to Judaism, adopted the Ashkenazic custom of using a special utensil for spices for havdalah, and commissioned one from a silversmith according to his specifications: a hexagonal apple rising from a tree trunk entwined by a serpent, each facet depicting a different scene as follows:

(1) Adam and Eve, with a figure in the background holding a ring.   (2) *Visia* (sight), a lighted candle in a candlestick standing on a table.   (3) *Tacto* (touch), Elisha departing from Elijah, who rises heavenward in a horse-drawn chariot, an angel pulling the reins.   (4) *Ouvir* (hearing), an angel blowing a ram's horn, holding a trumpet in his hand, against a background landscape.   (5) *Gosto* (taste), a hand holding a goblet, curtain, and a table standing on a tiled floor.   (6) *Cheiro* (smell), flowers in a vase standing on a hill.

On the lid an inscription refers to Elijah, mentioned in liturgical poems (*piyyutim*) sung at the end of the Sabbath (Malachi 3:24) (cat. no. 551; fig. nos. 84, 85). The five senses as depicted in this spicebox are unique, although this subject was popular, especially in Italian marriage contracts.

The Abraham de Herrera Laver

Like the other objects in the exhibition, a unique laver, identified with one of the important figures in the annals of Spanish and Portuguese Jewry, joins artistic value with a human story reflecting the fate of the Jews of Spain after the Expulsion. Its inspiration endures to this day.

The laver, of partly gilt silver, is large, some 49 centimeters in diameter, and was

Jewish Ceremonial Objects   129

FIG. NO. 84 Spice Container, Amsterdam, 1711/12. Cat. no. 551.

FIG. NO. 85 Spice Container, Amsterdam, 1711/12 (detail). Cat. no. 551.

probably made in Lisbon in the second half of the sixteenth century (cat. no. 542; fig. no. 86). The dish is designed with concentric circles, the narrow outer rim repoussé and chased with hunting scenes including beasts and monsters, gazelles, deer and hounds, eagles and rabbits, wild boar and warriors. The inner, concave and wide circle is embossed with spiral teardrops, alternating with gilt-engraved areas. The raised round center within a plaited wreath frame is engraved and repoussé with eight teardrops, alternating with scrolls, eagle, angel and running rabbit; the teardrops filled with depictions of: (1) a dog in the claws of a lion; (2) a lion devouring a deer; (3) an eagle devouring a stork; (4) a bear devouring a gazelle.

The style and decoration of the piece recall Lisbon dishes, some set with coats of arms, from the sixteenth century.[90] The laver is not marked; like Spanish silver, Portuguese silver is rare for that period, and is not always marked.[91] The center is set with a plaque framed with a wreath identical to the one in the central boss. The round plaque-cartouche engraved with hands poised for the Priestly Benediction bears a Hebrew dedication inscription: "Gift of Avraham and Sarah Kohen de Herrera." This valuable piece was probably included in the property of the family since the time they were in Portugal, and the inscription with the priestly symbol was engraved after de Herrera converted to Judaism, close to his arrival in Amsterdam, around 1605. The laver was dedicated to one of the three small Sephardic synagogues in the city: *Neve Shalom*, built in 1612; *Bet Yaakov*, in 1614; or *Bet Israel*, in 1615 and 1630.

Abraham Kohen (Alonso Nunez de) Herrera (1570 [?]–1635), also called "Irira" or "Ferreira," was a religious philosopher and a kabbalist. He was descended from a noble marrano family and probably emigrated to Portugal and later, perhaps, to Italy. From Florence, Herrera went to Morocco, where he served with his uncle as a trading agent of the Sultan. In the British conquest of Cadiz, in southern Spain (1596), he was captured and taken to England, where he was freed in a diplomatic exchange between the Moroccan sultan and Queen Elizabeth I of England. Later Herrera lived in Ragusa (now Dubrovnik), where he apparently converted to Judaism and, according to his testimony, studied Isaac Luria's Kabbalah. Herrera arrived in The Netherlands around 1605 and lived there for 30 years. His opinions strongly influenced the Jewish community of Amsterdam, and the esteem in which he was held is demonstrated by the eight approbations (*haskamot*) he was asked to write, the first of which was written to Menasseh Ben Israel's *Conciliador*, reconciling apparently discordant Biblical passages (September 6, 1632).

Herrera's two known works are in Spanish, one completing the other: *Casa de Dios* (*Beit Elohim*, or House of God) (see cat. no. 571), which deals mainly with theories about angels and spiritual phenomena; and *Puerta del Cielo* (*Shaarei Shamayim*, or Gates of Heaven), expounding kabbalistic doctrine about God and the cosmos, related to the Neo-platonic school. Herrera's works were translated and abridged in several languages. The first two works were translated into Hebrew by R. Isaac Aboab da Fonseca (Amsterdam, 1665). The importance of his work, from the historical and research aspects of kabbalah, are still evident in our time. In 1974 Gershom Scholem published a study of Herrera's life, work and influence.[92]

There is no way of following the history of the Herrera plate, or of knowing whether it was the property of the marrano family before they left Portugal, whether the central cartouche bore their "Catholic" coat of arms until it was altered when the family reached Amsterdam. Or, they may have acquired or commissioned the plate through an agent, or directly in Portugal, after they had settled in Amsterdam as Jews.

Whatever the answer, the plate—like many other items—is a means for telling the story of the status and customs of a specific community, especially as it introduces the figure of Herrera and a Jewish family whose destiny was dictated by the decrees of expulsion from the Iberian peninsula—traumatic events which determined the fate of the Jewish people for five hundred years.

Translated from the Hebrew by Malka Jagendorf

<small>FIG. NO. 86</small> Laver used by *Kohanim* before Priestly Blessing, Portugal, 16th century. Cat. no. 542.

1. See M. Benayahu, "The Great Fires in Izmir and Adrianople," *Reshumot*, 2 n.s. (1946), pp. 144–54 (in Hebrew).

2. See D. L. Bemporad, "Jewish Ceremonial Art in the Era of the City State and Ghettos" in NYJM, *Gardens*, p. 130.

3. See C. Roth, *The Jews in the Renaissance*, Jerusalem, 1962, pp. 176–78, (in Hebrew).

4. See C. Avery, "Giuseppe de Levis of Verona, Bronze Founder and Sculptor," in *Studies in European Sculpture*, London, 1981, pp. 45–78; IM, *Stieglitz*, cat. nos. 279, 279.1, 113, 114, 117–131; Grossman, *Temple*, no. 154; NYJM, *Gardens*, cat. nos. 170–176.

5. On Jewish goldsmiths in Italy, see: Bemporad, "Jewish Ceremonial Art" in NYJM, *Gardens*, pp. 115–63; Gaglia, "L'arredo in argento" in *Ebrei a Torino*, pp. 115–59; on Pacifico Levi, see: Gaglia, "L'arredo in argento," pp. 140–43, no. 9.

6. Koran, 3:14, 9:34, 18:31, 22:23, 43:35, 76:15.

7. See: P. Shinar, "Magic and Symbolism in North African Jewellery and Personal Adornment," in N. Brosh, ed., *Jewellery and Goldsmithing in the Islamic World*, Jerusalem, 1987, p. 146, note 77.

8. See: J. Barnai, "Jewish Guilds in Turkey in the Sixteenth to Nineteenth Centuries" in *Jews in Economic Life: Collected Essays in Memory of Arkadius Kahan (1920–1982)*, ed. N. Gross, Jerusalem, 1985 (in Hebrew), pp. 135–37.

9. For example: Torah finials made by L. M. Karayan, Israel Museum Coll. no. 879.82, 147/286; by B. Bitton, 1910, Israel Museum Coll. no. 768.74. According to the silversmith Ben-Zion Bitton of Izmir, who emigrated to Israel, most of the filigree work was done by Armenian silversmiths. He and other Jewish silversmiths learned their craft at the workshop of the Christian silversmith named Prosen.

10. See Barnett, p. xxv, nos. 112, 114, 115, 117, 119, 120, 163, 373. (See also note 72).

11. A Torah decoration stand, 1.5 meters high and one meter in diameter, from a synagogue in Izmir, is now in the Israel Museum collection, Jerusalem, 197/8.

12. Examples of staves of this type are in the collection of the Israel Museum, Jerusalem, 153/10.

13. Examples of staves of this type are in the collection of the U. Nahon Museum of Italian Jewish Art, Jerusalem, ON 31, 36.

14. In couched embroidery the thread is coiled around leather or thick paper strips cut to the desired shape and affixed to the cloth.

15. See: E. Juhasz, "Textiles for Home and Synagogue," in IM, *Ottoman*, pp. 36–51.

16. For metal appliqué decoration see IM, *Ottoman*, p. 90, figs. 32–37. For Serbian church vestments see B. Radojkovic, "Srpsko zlatarstvo XVI:XVII veka," in *Matica Srpska Odeljne za Likorne umethnati (Studije za istorijie srpske umetnosti.3.)* ("Serbian Goldsmith's Art in the 16th and 17th centuries" in *Studies in Serbian Art History.3.*), Novi Sad, 1966 (in Serbian), cat. nos. 183, 184, 184A.

17. See for example NYJM, *Gardens*, cat. no. 121 and V. Klagsbald, *Catalogue raisonné de la collection juive de la musée de Cluny*, Paris, 1981, no. 122.

18. On the textiles used in mantles see A. F. Kendrick and R. D. Barnett, "The Mantles, Introduction and Catalogue" in Grimwade, pp. 57–59.

19. See C. Grossman, "Womanly Arts: A Study of Italian Torah Binders in the New York Jewish Museum Collection," *JA*, 7 (1980), 35–43. On the Jewish role in the making of textiles and embroideries, see Kendrick and Barnett, "The Mantles" in Grimwade, pp. 52–54, and Bemporad, "Jewish Ceremonial Art" in NYJM, *Gardens*, pp. 124–127.

20. See for example NYJM, *Gardens*, cat. no. 152.

21. As related by Prof. Renzo Toaff and Mrs. Gioia Perugia in Jerusalem.

22. On these finials from Sicily, 15th century, Cathedral Treasury of Palma de Majorca, see F. Cantera and J. M. Millás, *Las inscripciones hebraicas de Espana*, Madrid, 1956, pp. 389–93. Also illustrated in NYJM, *Treasures*, p. 88.

23. For examples of this type see IM, *Maroc*, fig. no. 62.

24. Cf. IM, *Maroc*, pp. 22–40; Shinar, "Magic and Symbolism" in Brosh, *Jewellery and Goldsmithing*.

25. For the universal distribution of Venetian types of ceremonial objects, especially among Levantine Jews see D. L. Bemporad, "Venetian Ceremonial Art" in Joods-Historisch, *The Ghetto*, pp. 81–83; cf. Torah ornaments from Dubrovnik, *Jugoslavije*, pp. 42–43.

26. The large finials which decorate the *bimah* columns recall pomegranate or pear shapes in the illustrated manuscript, "Sister to the Golden Haggadah," from Barcelona, Spain, middle of the 14th century, in the British Museum collection, London, no. OR.MS.2884. Folio 17V. See J. Gutmann, "The Illuminated Medieval Passover Haggadah—Investigations and Research Problems," *Studies in Bibliography and Booklore*, VII (1965), nos. 26, 33.

27. For 17th century church utensils in the collection of the Serbian-Pruvoslavian Museum in Belgrade, Yugoslavia, see Radojkovic, "Srpsko zlatarstvo," cat. nos. 150, 170–172.

28. Their common origin may stem from long established metalwork traditions in these areas. In Bulgaria, for example, metal mounts and mechanisms for closing doors and closets had their traditional forms in remote antiquity, with two main influences noticeable in their form and ornamentation: the medieval Byzantine tradition, crossed with late baroque influences which reached Bulgaria through Constantinople. See T. Gerassimov, *Metal Work, Wrought Iron, Weapons and Pewter Vessels*, Sofia, 1983 (in Bulgarian, with Russian and English summaries), p. 178.

29. For almost identical finials, from Amsterdam, 1690 or 1714, with unidentified mark (H), in the Franklin Collection, see: Barnett, cat. no. 107.

30. On Curaçao see J. B. Maslin, *An Analysis of Jewish Ceremonial Objects of Congregation Mikve Israel-Emanuel, Curaçao, Netherlands Antilles; Dutch Silver: 1700–1800*, unpub. thesis, University of Chicago, 1980; on New York, Philadelphia and Newport, see Schoenberger, "Myer Myers"; cf. Torah finials from the British

Colonies, probably North America or the West Indies, ca. 1800, with decorative elements typical of late 18th-century English silver, NYJM, *Personal Vision: The Furman Collection of Jewish Ceremonial Art*, exhibition catalogue by S. L. Braunstein, 1985, no. 9; NYJM, *Treasures*, pp. 136–137.

31. For examples of Italian crowns of this type, see Gaglia, *Ebrei a Torino*, cat. nos. 2–4, 9, NYJM, *Gardens*, cat. nos. 205–208 and IM, *Stieglitz*, cat. no. 8.

32. For crown-shaped Italian Torah shields see Ferrara, Palazzo dei Diamanti, Palazzo Paradisio, *Arte e Cultura Ebraiche in Emilia-Romagna*, exhibition catalogue, 1988–89, cat. nos. 44–57.

33. *Hamsa* in Arabic, known as "Hand of Fatima" to Europeans, was regarded as an amulet; the motif was widespread in North Africa and the Middle East, among Muslims as well as Jews, in varying degrees of stylization. See D. Champault and A. R. Verbrugge, *La main ses figurations au Maghreb et au Levant*, Paris, 1965.

34. A large number of amuletic-dedicatory plaques festoon Torah Arks in the synagogues of Ioannina, Greece, whose Jews are considered to be a Romaniot congregation who lived in this area before the Expulsion. See Israel Museum Coll. single amulets—nos. 103/808–840; 928–931, 933; belts with attached amulets—nos. 103/942–944; cf. dedication plaque from Bosnia, 1716, Zagreb, Museum Gallery Centre, *Jews in Yugoslavia*, 1989, p. 46.

35. Torah shield, Israel Museum Coll. no. 148/30. On the silversmith Tobias Folsch, see: E. Schliemann, *Die Goldschmiede Hamburgs*, Hamburg, 1985, no. 307. Three Torah shields from Hamburg, which were inspired by the earliest one, were made by three silversmiths: (1) F. Wagner (1709–18), who was an apprentice of Folsch and continued to work in his workshop after his death in the year 1707; (2) Johann Wiese (ca. 1740); (3) Johann Wilhelm Henmann (1728–32). See: Schliemann, fig. nos. 841–843.

36. In Livorno, Jews held a monopoly over the coral trade. They caught the coral in the seas of Sicily and cut and worked it in Livorno. This is perhaps why so much Italian Judaica is embellished with this material. See Bemporad, "Jewish Ceremonial Art" in NYJM, *Gardens*, p. 123.

37. See M. Grunwald, *Portugiesengräber auf Deutscher Erde, Beiträge zur Kultur und Kunstgeschichte*, Hamburg, 1902, p. 112, note 3.

38. Three convex crowns also grace a Torah shield made in Frankfurt in 1700, see IM, *Paris*, no. 145, and other Torah shields from later periods. The motif of three or four crowns is primarily found on embroidered Torah ark curtains and valances in synagogues in Bohemia, Moravia, and Germany. It is interesting to note that in the city of Emden, where Portuguese Jews also settled, there was a marriage-stone (*Giebelsteine*), dated 1629, fixed to the outside wall of a house, carved with three crowns and a Hebrew inscription. See Siebern, "Stadt Emden" in *Die Kunstdenkmäler der Provinc Hannover*, VI, no. 1, 2, Hanover, 1927, p. 207, fig. no. 6.

39. For a Torah shield from the Middle Ages, see V. Klagsbald, "Un plaque de Torah antique," *JA*, VI (1979), pp. 127–132.

40. See B. Brilling, "Die Estehung der jüdischen Gemeinde in Emden (1570–1613)," *Westfallen Hefte für Geschichte, Kunst, und Volkskunde*, 51. Band, Heft 1–4 (1973), 210–214.

41. The silversmith Leendert Claesz was registered in 1587 as an apprentice of Peter Mylemann in Emden. In 1603 he became a master in Amsterdam, where he lived for twelve years. His marked works which are still extant are dated from the years 1606–1609. It is interesting to note that there are no church objects done by him or by his teacher. See E. Voet, *Merken van Amsterdamsche Goud- en Zilversmeden*, The Hague, 1912 (in Dutch), no. 25, p. 21; G. Müller Jürgens, *Vasa Sacra: Altargeräte in Ostfriesland*, Aurich, 1960, p. 32, note 20.

42. See J. Furman, "A Glass Synagogue Lamp from Damascus," *JA*, 12–13 (1986/87), pp. 279–284.

43. See: E. Juhasz, "Textiles for the Home and Synagogue," in IM, *Ottoman*, pp. 103–113, fig. nos. 28, 41, 42, 45–48, 53–54, pl. 17; 18b; 19; 20a.

44. See IM, *Maroc*, figs. 40, 42–45, 48–50, 96, 121.

45. See IM, *Paris*, cat. no. 87.

46. The donation of the half-shekel on Purim symbolizes the ancient practice from the days of the Temple, when coins to pay for public offerings were donated during the month of Adar. In synagogues after the destruction of the Temple these coins went mainly to charity but also to the cantor, musicians, and other participants in the synagogue service and to aid members of the community emigrating to Eretz Israel.

47. See: C. Hernmarck, *The Art of the European Silversmith, 1430–1830*, London, 1977, vol. I, p. 125.

48. Cf. Barnett, no. 578, plate CLVIII; Mann, "Tale," no. 210.

49. See: Barnai, "Jewish Guilds in Turkey," pp. 139–43.

50. See: Y. Rophe, "Benevolent Society of the Boat-Owners in Constantinople," *Sefunot* X (1966) (in Hebrew), p. 625.

51. Purim literally means "lots," referring to the lots chosen by Haman to determine the day for his planned, and later thwarted, massacre of the Jews.

52. See W. C. Pieterse, *350 jaar Dotar, Santa Companhia de Dotar Orphas e Donzellas*, Amsterdam, 1965 (in Dutch; English summary).

53. This practice of an annual *douceur* to the Lord Mayor was observed also by the French and Dutch Protestant churches in London. See "The Ritual Silver," in Grimwade, p. 15. A silver salver was presented by Menasseh ben Israel to Oliver Cromwell, and later came into the possession of the first Earl of Argyll. The main body of this salver is Dutch work from about the middle of the 17th century. The border and handles, which were added later, bear the Queen Anne mark. See *The Catalogue of the Anglo-Jewish Historical Exhibition* London, 1887, no. 616; for Lord Mayor's dishes see C. Roth, "The Lord Mayor's Salvers" *The Connoisseur*, 96 (May, 1935), 246–99; Barnett, nos. 656–658; NYJM, *Treasures*, p. 78.

54. See: Barnett, p. 134, no. 658.

55. See: M. Narkiss, "Oriental Esther Scroll Cases" in *Sefer Hamoadim*, VI, Tel Aviv, 1956, (in Hebrew), pp. 67–68.

56. For enameled filigree Esther scroll cases and marriage rings see Barnett, nos. 280, 462, 463.

57. Cf. chased silver plates mounted on both sides of the barrels of *boiliga* rifles, mid 19th century, in the District Historical Museum, Turgorishte, Bulgaria, see Gerassimov, *Metal Work*, no. 86 a–c.

58. Cf. B. Radojkovic, *Phylaktarien Enamluks Patrontaschen*, Belgrade, 1947 (in Serbian; German summary).

59. Israel Museum collection no. 140/72.

60. Israel Museum collection no. 182/131.

61. Israel Museum collection no. 182/6.

62. See: M. Narkiss, *The Hanukkah Lamp*, Jerusalem, 1939 (in Hebrew; English summary), p. xv.

63. According to Mrs. Miriam Russo-Katz of Jerusalem, the Sephardic Jews in Turkey used Hanukkah lamps made of very simple sheet metal which were discarded after use.

64. One dates from the 18th century, and is made of cast brass with openwork backplate featuring scrolled branches. It is attributed to Salonika or Corfu, see Bialer, p. 159. Two others, from the 19th century, are made of silver and are inspired by the Hanukkah lamps brought by *shadarim*, fundraising emissaries from Jerusalem. See: Barnett, Plate LXXXIII, no. 265; and a Hanukkah lamp from the Israel Museum Coll., depicting Judith and the head of Holofernes, no. 118/924.

65. IM, *Feuchtwanger*, cat. no. 393 (Israel Museum Coll. no. 118/659).

66. See IM, *Amanut*, p. 29, fig. nos. 13, 14, 15.

67. See IM, *Stieglitz*, cat. nos. 113, 114.

68. On the earliest stone lamps, see B. Narkiss, "The Gerona Hanukkah Lamp—Fact and Fiction," *JA*, 14 (1988), 6–15.

69. Single, separate, green-glazed standing lamps recalling those Moroccan Hanukkah lamps, were made for the Sabbath. See Grossman, *Temple*, cat. no. 91. In Morocco, they were made for the Passover seder table, see IM, *Maroc*, fig. no. 138.

70. See *The Casale Pilgrim, a Sixteenth-Century Illustrated Guide to the Holy Places*, facsimile, intro., trans. and notes by C. Roth, London, 1929; IM, *Stieglitz*, cat. nos. 118, 122, 127, 128, 131, 132.

71. See: M. Narkiss, *The Hanukkah Lamp*, p. 55, notes 88–90.

72. For description of this lamp (17th century?!) and other works of the silversmith named David Lopez Pereira, 5520 (1760?!) see *Catalogue of the Anglo-Jewish Historical Exhibition*, nos. 1717, 2040.

73. See: Shinar, "Magic and Symbolism" in Brosh, *Jewellery and Goldsmithing*, pp. 124–140.

74. See: V. Klagsbald, "Lampes de Hanukkah," in IM, *Maroc*, p. 72.

75. See: Gans, *Memorbook*, p. 31.

76. See IM, *Stielglitz*, nos. 167–170.

77. See: M. Narkiss, *The Hanukkah Lamp*, p. 54, note 81.

78. See Barnett, no. 260; M. Narkiss, *The Hanukkah Lamp*, nos. 131, 132; H. H. Cotterel, A. Riff, R. M. Vetter, *National Types of Old Pewter*, New York, 1972, no. 312; Israel Museum collection no. 118/175; cf. Grimwade, plate XIII, no. 72.

79. Cf. IM, *Stieglitz*, nos. 140, 141.

80. Hanukkah lamp, Israel Museum Coll. no. 118/568, see: *Stieglitz*, no. 167.1. For the association of Hanukkah lamps with weddings, see a silver lamp, made in Amsterdam in 1699, Gans, *Memorbook*, p. 162 and two other lamps from London, one from the year 1712, the second from 1755, see Grimwade, p. 14, note 57; plate XIII, no. 72. The monograms of two families which appear on the same object probably indicate that they were united in marriage; found also in Torah finials from Amsterdam, dated 1717, with the monograms of the da Fonseca and Mendez families, see Grossman, *Temple*, no. 19.

81. See M. Narkiss, *The Hanukkah Lamp*, no. 54; NYJM, *Gardens*, cat. nos. 190–91.

82. Cf. M. Narkiss, *The Hanukkah Lamp*, nos. 135, 136.

83. Cf. Gans, *Memorbook*, p. 162; NYJM, *Treasures*, pp. 100–01.

84. Hanukkah lamp with the scene of Elisha and the widow, probably by Richard Edwards, 1712, London. See Grimwade, no. 73, p. 46, pl. X; M. Narkiss, *The Hanukkah Lamp*, p. 32, fig. 61; *The Catalogue of the Anglo-Jewish Historical Exhibition*, no. 1720.

85. Hanukkah lamp with the scene of Elijah and the Ravens, made by John Ruslen, 1709, see Grimwade, p. 14; *Catalogue of the Anglo-Jewish Historical Exhibition*, no. 1737; Barnett, no. 230; M. Narkiss, *The Hanukkah Lamp*, no. 62.

86. See D. de Castro, *Keur van Graafsteenen op de nederl.-Portug. Israel. Begraafsplaats te Ouderkerk aan den Amstel*, Leyden, 1883; R. Weinstein, *Sepulchral Monuments of the Jews of Amsterdam in the Seventeenth and Eighteenth Centuries*, PhD diss., New York University, 1979.

87. See R. Weinstein, "Art in historical context, sculptural programs determined by use: religious, secular, civic, private; sources of motifs in graphics, painting, sculpture," in Weinstein, *Sepulchral Monuments*, chapter 4, pp. 66–75.

88. See: Freidenberg, *Medals*, pp. 65–67.

89. See: R. Beyer, *Die Königin von Saba, Engel un Damon Der Mythos einer Frau*, Cologne, 1978, pp. 249–262.

90. Cf. C. Oman, *The Golden Age of Hispanic Silver, 1400–1665*, London, 1968, cat. nos. 81, 82, 84, 87, fig. nos. 156, 160, 162, 169.

91. See: C. Oman, *The Golden Age*, p. xxxiv; J. Hayward, *Virtuoso Goldsmiths, 1540–1620*, London, 1976, pp. 189–99.

92. See G. Scholem, *Abraham Koen Herrera's "Puerta del Cielo," His Life, His Work, and Its Influence*, Tel Aviv, 1974 (in Hebrew).

THE FORMATION OF
THE WESTERN SEPHARDIC DIASPORA
Yosef Kaplan

The settlement of marranos in the "Lands of Freedom" in Western Europe and the New World and their open affiliation with Judaism are part of a long and complex process which began in the sixteenth century and in fact continued until the middle of the eighteenth century. The transition from Christianity to Judaism involved many difficulties, for these "New Christians" had lived for generations utterly cut off from the rest of Jewry, and they were forced, for fear of the vigilant eyes of the Inquisition in Spain and Portugal, to minimize and restrict expressions of their attachment to the faith of their forefathers. Unlike the *conversos* of Spain before the Expulsion, whose Judaism was nourished by daily contact with a supportive and helpful Jewish population, the crypto-Jews of Spain and Portugal in the sixteenth and seventeenth centuries were forced to preserve the embers of their Judaism without any outside assistance, while the censorship of the Inquisition deprived them of all direct contact with the sources of Judaism.

When they returned openly to Judaism outside the Iberian peninsula, they established new communities, mainly in places in Western Europe where there had not been any Jewish settlement before their arrival. Often the first Jewish community which they encountered was the one they themselves had established. Although they were assisted by rabbis who came to them from the Sephardic centers in the Ottoman empire and also from the communities of Italy and North Africa, the main burden of construction and rehabilitation fell upon their shoulders. Naturally, the community they established was not an imitation of any existing traditional, characteristic Jewish community of the time. Unlike the Sephardic diaspora in the East and in Islamic countries, where the exiles from Spain and their descendants established communities and Jewish centers soon after the expulsions from Spain and Portugal, the centers of the western Sephardic diaspora were established by former "New Christians" who had lived in isolation from the sources of Judaism for four generations or more. Once they openly rejoined the Jewish people, they had to redefine their Jewish identity for themselves and to establish the boundaries of their affiliation with the collective. That task was not at all a simple one, since those returning to their origins found it difficult to accept the discipline of Torah, and quite a few of them rebelled against the dominion of Jewish tradition. In the course of the seventeenth and eighteenth centuries the new communities occasionally became embroiled in struggle against various sorts of heretics who challenged the world of the halakhah and the authority of the Rabbis.

The people of this diaspora viewed themselves as members of the "nation" (*"membros da nação"*) or "members of the Spanish-Portuguese Nation." Consequently they intended to accentuate their particularity and lineage. The term *nación* or *nação* mainly referred not only to the Sephardic Jewish diaspora, but also to the "New Christians" who had remained in the "Lands of Apostasy," whether or not they identified with Judaism.[1]

The world of the "Spanish and Portuguese Nation" was marvelously well organized: not only did its members manage to establish a broad network of settlement centers and communities which straddled important routes of international commerce, but they also established institutions and organizations whose goal was to foster the mutual bonds within the diaspora, to encourage crypto-Jews to return openly to Judaism, to struggle against heterodox tendencies which had gained a foothold in their world, and to solve the problems of poverty which weighed heavily upon their associations. These communities were interconnected by bonds of a shared fate, and one cannot comprehend the history of a given community without seeing it within the overall context of the entire western Sephardic diaspora.

Settlement in Western Europe in the Sixteenth Century

During the sixteenth century "New Christians" had already arrived in Western Europe from Spain and especially from Portugal. In most Western countries they were forbidden to settle as Jews. Hence they continued living as Christians, at least outwardly, but in many cases it is known that they secretly preserved the embers of Judaism and even maintained contacts with the centers of the Sephardic Jewish diaspora in the Ottoman empire and elsewhere. In The Netherlands, which were under Spanish dominion, there was an important settlement of Portuguese merchants, most of whom were "New Christians" of Jewish extraction; their principal center was Antwerp.[2]

In 1549–50, under Charles V, the expulsion of all "New Christians" from The Netherlands was proclaimed because they were suspected of converting to Judaism and of observing the Torah of Moses. However, this decree of expulsion did not put an end to the presence of "New Christians" throughout The Netherlands; they provided the vital kernel of the incipient centers of Spanish and Portuguese Jews in northwestern Europe towards the end of the sixteenth century and the start of the seventeenth. In France, from which the Jews had been expelled in 1394, many "New Christians" had gathered by the first half of the sixteenth century. That country naturally served as the first place of refuge for those fleeing the Spanish and Portuguese Inquisition, for even those who intended to proceed towards other lands of freedom had virtually no choice but to take the route leading to France. However, not until 1550 did Henry II of France grant "Lettres Patentes" to Portuguese merchants of Jewish extraction who had been accepted in France as "New Christians," granting them the full protection of the central authorities and even permitting them to settle undisturbed throughout the kingdom. After that time, it became part of the policy of the "New Christians" from Portugal in France to renegotiate with the central authorities for renewal of the "Lettres Patentes," and at the start of each new reign they sought to assure the continuation of the charter which had been granted to them by making a monetary payment. Since the middle of the sixteenth century and throughout the seventeenth century, settlements by Portuguese merchants, that is, marranos, who continued to live as "New Christians," were established in Bordeaux, Bayonne, Bidache, Peyrehorade, Labastide-Clairence and other localities. Abundant documentation shows that despite their Christian cover, they managed to preserve Jewish ceremonies and customs and to maintain close ties with Sephardic Jewish centers outside France. There are also many indications that the authorities and the Church in France also knew of the true identity of the Portuguese "New Christians," but that they intentionally ignored it. In the second half of the seventeenth century, especially after 1660, the Jewish expressions of the "New Christians" in France became increasingly open. They maintained separate cemeteries, where they began to indicate the year according to the Jewish rather than the Christian calendar on the tombstones. In the early eighteenth century the authorities began to acknowledge these Portuguese people as Jews, permitting them to practice Judaism openly. In June, 1723, Louis XV granted them a special deed of privilege which was issued at Meudon, officially confirming their right to maintain the Jewish religion. Then, too, however, the Spanish and Portuguese Jews of France, who were mainly termed by the appellation, "Nations juives portugaises," continued to depend upon the Sephardic Jewish centers which had been established in Western Europe during the seventeenth century, and especially upon the large and prosperous community of Amsterdam. Nevertheless, the Portuguese Jews in France succeeded in developing an independent culture during the eighteenth century, especially in the centers of Bayonne and Bordeaux. While the Jewish community of Bayonne was outstanding for the intense Jewish life that developed there, the Portuguese Jews of Bordeaux were prominent on account of their economic activity and their secular intellectual and literary creativity.[3]

In some of the Italian states where marranos arrived from the Iberian peninsula, especially during the 1630s, Jewish communities had existed before their arrival. The Jewish population of Italy in the sixteenth century was sparse demographically and scattered geographically; only in a few places (such as Rome and Ferrara) did groups of Jews who had been expelled from Spain manage to strike root during the first generation after the Expulsion of 1492; however, from the third decade of the sixteenth century, Levantine Jews (that is, Jews from the Near East, who were subjects of the Ottoman empire, and some of whom were descendants of those who had been expelled from Spain) began to stream into other areas of Italy. These were joined by "New Christians" fleeing from the Iberian peninsula, especially from Portugal after the establishment of the Inquisition there. Some of these *conversos* continued to live as Christians even in Italy; others threw off the veil of Christianity and openly reverted to Judaism. In Italy they were known as "ponentines." These immigrants, both the Levantine Jews and the

"New Christians" from Portugal, played economic roles of the first order and belonged to an extensive network of commercial houses and financial firms that were established by the Spanish and Portuguese exiles, reaching from The Netherlands to the Ottoman empire. They were outstanding economic entrepreneurs, they managed banks with extensive capital, and they played an important role in international commerce, especially that between Italy and the Ottoman empire. It was their economic importance which brought the rulers of the Italian States, including the popes themselves, to ignore the fact that many of the new Jewish settlers, in fact all of those who arrived directly from the Iberian peninsula, were baptized Christians who had betrayed Christianity and joined the Jewish religion. As a result of this policy, a Sephardic Jewish community developed in Ancona, which was in the Papal States, and the duchies of Ferrara and Florence also opened their gates to the Spanish Jewish immigrants.[4] Ancona became a major port, especially for the transfer of merchandise to Ragusa, across the Adriatic Sea, and from there to Vallona, Salonika, and Istanbul. However, Pope Paul IV changed the policy towards the Jews, rescinding the promises given by his predecessors to the "New Christians" who had settled in Ancona, and 25 of their number were burned at the stake in 1555. In response, Jews from various places, especially from the Ottoman empire, at the initiative of Dona Gracia Mendes, exerted heavy pressure upon the pope and organized an economic boycott of Ancona. They attempted to divert ties with the Levant to the port of Pesaro. However, despite the interest first displayed by the Duke of Pesaro, this effort failed within a relatively short time.[5]

In Venice, too, the marranos, especially those who sought to identify openly with Judaism, did not fare well at first. In the middle of the sixteenth century they were expelled from the Venetian Republic under the pressure of its merchants. However, in the course of time this policy changed, when it became clear that the Venetian merchants were not inclined to risk voyages to the Orient, whereas the Jewish merchants, both those from the Levant and also those from Iberia, showed willingness to take their places. In 1589 the Venetian Republic granted extensive privileges for the settlement of "Ebrei Levantini e viandanti" (Levantine and transient Hebrews). A few years earlier, in 1577, a Jew named Daniel Rodriga had proposed the construction of a port in Spalato to the Venetian Senate. This port was to replace Ragusa and thus link Italy and the West with the Ottoman empire.[6]

Several years earlier the Duke of Savoy, Emmanuel Philibert, had failed in an attempt to develop the port of Nice as a competitor of Venice. In 1572 he offered attractive terms, but, under pressure from the Spanish crown and the Papal throne, he was unable to attract "New Christians" to settle in his duchy.[7]

One of the most impressive efforts to attract *conversos* to the Italian region was made by the Duke of Tuscany, Ferdinand I. In a document dated June 10, 1593, he invited the Jewish merchants—in fact he especially meant the "New Christians" from Portugal—to come and settle in Livorno (Leghorn) and Pisa. He hoped to turn the port of Livorno into an international center for the distribution of merchandise imported both from the Orient and from the West throughout Europe and also to breathe life into the textile industry there. This effort was highly successful, and Livorno became a most important center in the Sephardic Jewish diaspora. The Spanish-Portuguese congregation flourished there during the seventeenth and eighteenth centuries, even after the Jewish community of Venice had lost its momentum.[8]

The Communities in Northwest Europe

While the foundations were being laid for the Sephardic Jewish settlement in Tuscany and Italy, conditions also became propitious for the establishment of new centers of the Sephardic diaspora in northwest Europe. These new communities were consolidated during the seventeenth century, and they were distinct from the other communities of the western Sephardic diaspora. In contrast with the Sephardic communities which had been founded in the Italian States during the sixteenth century near long-established Jewish communities by Jews expelled from the Iberian peninsula or by "New Christians," the communities of Amsterdam, Hamburg and London were created in an environment where Judaism had been completely forbidden until their establishment. Unlike the Portuguese communities of France, which did not openly revert to Judaism until the early eighteenth century, after Portuguese "New Christians" had been present there for more than 150 years, during which they had been forced to preserve the spark of Judaism in secret, the northwestern Jewish communities were founded after a relatively short period of embryonic existence as centers of "New Christians."

The origin of the northwest European Jewish community in the early modern period is doubtless connected with the outcome of the rebellion of the seven northern provinces of The Netherlands against the Spanish Crown. The alliance formed by these provinces in 1579 created a new reality with possibilities for true Jewish settlement in the northern Netherlands, which had hitherto been closed to Jews. The fall of Antwerp to the Spanish army in 1585 brought a large wave of Calvinist immigrants to the northern provinces. With these refugees came quite a few Portuguese "New Christians," some of whom were crypto-Jews with a spiritual attachment to Judaism. For around 1570 about 80 families of Portuguese "New Christians" were living in Antwerp, numbering close to 400 souls. The development following the revolt against Spain and especially the blockade imposed on Antwerp by the Dutch rebels in 1595 dealt a mortal blow to the commercial power of that city, which had been a central port in northwest Europe and had played a vital role in the international trade routes of the Portuguese "New Christians" during the sixteenth century.

The decline of Antwerp from the status of a major center for "New Christians" and the transfer of the preponderance of their activity to other port cities in the Protestant states ultimately brought about the creation of new Spanish-Portuguese communities, whose founders were former "New Christians."

Between 1585 and 1595 the marrano merchants showed clear preference for Hamburg over Amsterdam: at that time Hamburg became the major center in northern Europe for trade in sugar, spices and other colonial commodities. By the late 1570s a number of isolated "New Christians" were already living in Hamburg, and in 1595 about a dozen marrano families were permitted to settle in the city. It was they who laid the foundations for the Sephardic community there. Their number gradually increased, and in 1612 they numbered 125 adults. A year previously they had bought a plot of land in Altona, where they gave their dead a Jewish burial. In Altona itself, which was under the Danish crown, a sparse Portuguese community existed; it began to grow slightly only in the early eighteenth century. At first it was called "Beth Yaakov Ha-Katan;" later it was known as "Neveh Shalom." A small community was also established in Glückstadt in 1622, three years after Christian IV of Denmark had formulated the royal writ of privilege which granted the Jews rather extensive rights. In nearby Emden, Portuguese merchants arrived in the course of the seventeenth century and laid the first foundations of community life.

The charter granted in 1612 gave the first official approval for Jewish life in Hamburg, although the Jews' ability to give public expression to their Judaism was limited (they were forbidden to worship publicly or to perform circumcisions within the bounds of the city). At first the Jews held services in three places of worship which formed the basis for three separate communities. In 1650, a year after the Ashkenazic Jews of Hamburg had been expelled, the Senate finally permitted the Portuguese Jews to worship in public. Following this decision, the three communities united in 1652 to form a single congregation which was called "Beth Israel." Among the main sponsors of this merger was Diego Teixeira de Sampayo, who changed his name to Abraham Senior after reaching Hamburg in 1646 and openly joining the Jewish community. Teixeira founded a family-owned bank known as Teixeira de Mattos. In 1654 he was the host of Queen Christina of Sweden; his house became a kind of hostelry for Catholic rulers who passed through the city.

In 1697, when the total tax upon the Jews of Hamburg was raised to 6,000 marks, many wealthy members of the Portuguese community abandoned the city and settled in Altona and Amsterdam. This was, perhaps, the first sign of the decline of the Sephardic Jewish community of Hamburg, whose glory was dimmed during the eighteenth century.[9]

From the mid-1590s, when Amsterdam began to assume a central place in colonial trade, an increasing number of Portuguese merchants began to settle there, most of whom were "New Christians" who retained the outward guise of Catholicism, but within a short time their Jewish identity was made public. Some of them came from

Antwerp, but most came directly from Portugal or after staying in Spain for some time.

It could be that the dizzying ascent of Amsterdam, at a time when the war against Spain was still in progress, brought the municipal authorities to give favorable consideration to the advantages of the presence of refugees from the Iberian Inquisition in the city. It seems likely that between 1602 and 1604 the foundations were laid for the establishment of the first community in the city, which was named "Beth Yaakov," after Jacob Tirado, one of the important magnates of the Portuguese community in the city.

At that time the Portuguese Jews in Amsterdam had not yet succeeded in attaining official recognition as Jews, and therefore some of them tried their luck elsewhere. In 1604 the city council of Alkmaar signed a declaration of privilege which accorded the Jews rather good conditions, and this was the first document given to the Jews in Holland granting them protection *qua* Jews. A year and a half later, in the city of Haarlem, for the first time an extensive grant of privilege was made with generous conditions, promising the Jews the right to worship openly in a synagogue and to bury their dead in their own cemetery. In Rotterdam, too, the Jews were given a grant of privileges in 1610, promising them the right to enjoy "freedom and liberty of conscience" and to practice Judaism both privately and publicly. Here for the first time in the history of the Dutch Republic, they were explicitly permitted to establish a synagogue. This agreement was rescinded two years later, and several Portuguese families left that city for Amsterdam. Only in 1647 did the real growth of the community in Rotterdam begin, when a new wave of "New Christian" immigrants arrived from Antwerp. The new arrivals were led by Gil Lopes de Pinto and his brother Rodrigo Alvares. These extremely wealthy men founded a society for the study of Torah known as "Jesiba de los Pintos," which was transferred to Amsterdam in 1669.

Meanwhile, however, the Spanish-Portuguese community grew progressively stronger in Amsterdam, though it had not yet explicitly been granted rights beyond de facto recognition. In 1608 the Portuguese Jews established another congregation, known as "Neveh Shalom." A third community, called "Beth Israel," was founded after a quarrel broke out within the "Beth Yaakov" congregation in 1618, leading to the split.

In 1612 nearly 500 Jews were present in Amsterdam, the vast majority of whom were of Portuguese origin, while only a handful of Ashkenazic Jews lived by their side. By 1620 their number had increased to more than 1,000 souls, following the great migration to the city during the armistice between Spain and Holland from 1609 to 1620.

In 1622 the three Jewish congregations of Amsterdam established the "Imposta," an umbrella organization designed to collect taxes on imports and exports, and thus to overcome the problems of poverty and distress that weighed heavily upon the life of the community. It must be remembered that many of the marranos arriving in Amsterdam and other centers of settlement in the Sephardic diaspora were indigent and became a heavy social burden upon the community leadership. This poverty increased progressively following the economic crisis which struck the Portuguese merchants of Amsterdam when the war with Spain was resumed.[10]

In 1639 representatives of the three congregations decided to unite into a single community known as "Talmud Torah." The years that followed saw the beginning of the greatest growth of the Sephardic community in Amsterdam. When Portugal became independent in 1640, it became possible once more for the Portuguese merchants in Amsterdam to gain access to its ports, bringing the community an impressive economic recovery. This process reached a peak with the signing of the Peace Treaty with Spain in 1648, opening up new possibilities for the Jews of Amsterdam. The waves of immigration of marranos from the Iberian peninsula and elsewhere grew stronger at the end of the 1640s and throughout the 1650s. Many "New Christians" came to Holland in general and to Amsterdam in particular, fleeing from Spain and Antwerp following the fall of Olivares and the great economic crisis which struck the kingdom of Philip IV.

The Jews of Amsterdam received official recognition, with certain restrictions, on November 8, 1616, and, in 1657, together with all the Jews of the Dutch Republic, they were recognized as subjects of the state with all the conditions and rights to which the other subjects were entitled when abroad.

In 1672 the Jews of Amsterdam numbered nearly 2,500 souls. Together with the German Jews (around 2,000 souls), and the Polish Jews (around 500, most of whom were from Lithuania), who had reached Amsterdam mainly after the Swedish invasion, there were close to 5,000 Jews in Amsterdam, out of a total population of 200,000.[11]

The Great Synagogue was dedicated in 1675, one of the most splendid synagogues in all of Western Europe. The "Talmud Torah" community overcame the spiritual crises which afflicted it at the time of the excommunications of Baruch Spinoza and Juan de Prado in 1656 and 1658 respectively, and during the messianic fervor associated with the Sabbatean movement which swept the Jewish world in 1665–66. The French invasion in the early 1670s and the economic crises which broke out in its wake provoked the temporary flight of several Portuguese merchants from Amsterdam to Hamburg, Antwerp and other places and caused a certain economic stagnation within the community. However, all of these factors could not dim the glorious life of the leading class of the community. In their way of life, in their outward appearance, and in their habits of consumption they resembled the European gentry which they emulated.

During the last quarter of the seventeenth century the community of Amsterdam reached hitherto unknown heights. Under the leadership of the *Hahamim* Rabbi Isaac

Aboab da Fonseca and Rabbi Jacob Sasportas, the status of the rabbinate and the power of the religious court were strengthened within the community. Alongside many societies for Torah study and charity, several literary academies flourished, in which the artistic talents of members of the community from various social classes found expression. In this period several of the important authors and poets who arose within the community were active: Daniel Levi de Barrios, Joseph Penso de la Vega, as well as the most prominent intellectual of the community, Isaac Orobio de Castro. In addition to his apologetic writings against Christianity, the latter also composed a series of works combatting the heterodox trends which emerged among the former marranos, directed especially against Spinoza and Prado.[12]

New breezes began to blow in seventeenth-century England with the strengthening of Puritanism and the rise of millenarian hopes among many thinkers within English society. The question of the return of the Jews, who had been driven from England in 1290, began to assume a prominent place in English millenarian thought, and voices were increasingly heard advocating freedom of religion for Jews within the kingdom of England. These tendencies gained momentum in the middle of the seventeenth century after the overthrow of the monarchy and its replacement by the Commonwealth. Rabbi Menasseh ben Israel, who maintained contacts with millenarian circles in Holland and England at that time, tried to bridge the gap between their expectations and the messianic hopes of the Jews, giving expression to this effort in *The Hope of Israel*, which was published in Latin and Spanish in 1650 and in an English translation immediately afterwards.[13]

Practical contacts for the purpose of permitting the Jews to return to England began, however, towards the end of 1654, after the fall to Portugal of the Dutch colony in northeast Brazil and the dissolution of the important Jewish center there. The Portuguese Jewish merchants who had been involved in colonial trade with the colony of Recife now sought to create an avenue of commerce between northwest Europe and the New World by means of an alternative colonial power, which would have a foothold in the Caribbean region. It is against this background that we are to understand the petitions presented by Manuel Martínez Dormido, who was actually David Abarbanel, to Cromwell on November 3, 1654.[14]

Menasseh ben Israel arrived in London in 1655 and presented to Cromwell a detailed treatise in English in which he raised the principal economic and political grounds for the idea of the return of the Jews to England. He hoped that the new regime would permit the Jews to come and settle in England and grant them full freedom of religion.

At that time 27 Portuguese men, members of the "Nation" (including Menasseh ben Israel), were living in London, and it seems likely that, with their households, their number came to 100 souls. They were the first seed of the Portuguese Jewish center which was established there. Most of them were "New Christians" who had not yet savored the taste of open Jewish life. Antonio Fernández Carvajal, the central figure within this group, seems to have been of completely Christian origin. He became the leader of the Portuguese "New Christian" group in London, which gathered in his house on Sabbaths and holidays, though outwardly they all maintained the appearance of being Catholics and were in the habit of attending mass in the chapel of the Spanish embassy.

In early 1656, following the war between Spain and England, when it was decided to confiscate the property of one Antonio Rodrigues Robles, a member of the "New Christian" society in London, the members of the Portuguese colony in London decided to declare their origins and their religion openly.* The authorities were not quick to respond positively to their requests for recognition as Jews, but Cromwell apparently promised them, on his own initiative, or perhaps upon consultation with the Council of State, that they could open a synagogue for worship and also purchase a plot of land outside of London and establish their cemetery. Within a short time they bought a building in Creechurch Lane and converted it for use as a house of worship; this building served the congregation until 1701, when they inaugurated their new synagogue in Bevis Marks. In early 1657 the new synagogue, called "Shaar Ha-Shamayim," was opened, and at that time land was purchased in Mile End for the cemetery.

Not only did the London community sustain no damage with the restoration of the monarchy, when Charles II returned from exile in 1660, but it also became more firmly ensconced and began to expand. According to a list compiled in the early 1680s, the community then numbered 414 souls.

The elders of the community in London struggled vigorously against blurring the distinction between those who maintained a Jewish way of life and those who preferred to continue living as crypto-Jews, whose Judaism was only a matter of inner identification, without open obligation. The leaders of the community forbade the burial of uncircumcised males in the congregation's cemetery; only in certain exceptional cases did they agree to bury them in a special section beyond the fence.

As in other places within the western Sephardic diaspora, so in London, too, the "Members of the Nation" were careful to keep themselves apart from the Ashkenazic brethren, most of whom were penniless. As the number of Ashkenazic Jews grew, relations between them and the Sephardic community became strained, so that around 1692 they established a separate community with its own synagogue.[15]

However, despite the internal difficulties, the Spanish-Portuguese community in London continued to expand during the first 40 years until it became a significant factor in the Sephardic Jewish world. Although the paths to assimilation were open to it from the start, it preserved its vitality during the entire eighteenth century and took the place

*In this landmark case, Robles claimed, and won, exemption from having his property confiscated as an enemy alien on the grounds that he was not a Spaniard but a "Portuguese of the Hebrew nation."

of Hamburg as the second community within the western Sephardic diaspora, behind Amsterdam, which maintained its predominance.

Sephardic Jews in the New World

During the 1640s the first Jewish community in the New World was established: the community of Recife in northeastern Brazil, in an area which had been conquered by the Dutch. In 1645 it contained about 1,400 souls, most of them Spanish and Portuguese Jews, who constituted about half of the white population of the place and enjoyed rights equal to those of the local Dutch population. When the colony fell to the Portuguese, most of the Jews fled back to Holland.[16] Only a minority was dispersed around the Caribbean region (23 of whom eventually reached New Amsterdam and became the nucleus of New York's Jewish community). Thereafter the Jewish presence in the Caribbean grew ever more solidly based, especially in the Dutch and English colonies. The Spanish and Portuguese Jews looked attractive to these colonial powers, who had established a foothold in the New World. Holland and England greatly valued the widespread connections of these Jews, their experience in colonial trade, and their expertise in international commerce. These merchants, who knew Spanish and Portuguese, could serve as intermediaries between the colonial authorities and the local population of the American continent, which also included "New Christians," who were scattered throughout the New World as early as the beginning of the sixteenth century. For that reason, and in order to attract them there, tempting conditions were promised to the Sephardic Jews, usually better than those offered to the Jews from Western Europe, including Holland itself.

The Dutch West India Company was an accelerating factor in exploiting Sephardic Jews for colonial purposes in the Caribbean. In Curaçao a Jewish community was established in 1659. Although the intention of the Dutch West India Company was to direct the Jewish immigrants to work in agriculture, commerce became their main occupation. Many Jews among the inhabitants of the island were involved in shipping; some of them became merchant ship captains. The Jews of the island also speeded the manufacture and marketing of sugar.[17] A short time before the foundations were laid for the "Mikve Israel" community in Curaçao, the infrastructure was created for a Jewish settlement in Essequibo, Dutch Guiana, and in 1658 Jews who were willing to come there were offered rights equal to those of the other settlers, most of whom were Calvinists from Zeeland who had emigrated at that time. David Nassy, who handled the negotiations on behalf of the Jews, received a promise from the directorate of the Dutch West India Company that the Jewish settlers would be supplied with slaves. The Jewish immigrants from Holland were joined by Portuguese Jews from Livorno. These immigrants established two centers, one in Essequibo and the other on the banks of the Pomaroon River, where they became the owners of sugar plantations.[18]

In New Amsterdam, the governor, Peter Stuyvesant, did try to prevent the refugees from Recife from remaining there, but there, too, the Dutch West India Company intervened in their favor and ordered that the Jews there be given the same rights as those enjoyed by the Jews of Holland. When the English conquered New Amsterdam in 1664, they extended the rights of the Jews and, among other things, granted them the right to establish a synagogue and permitted them to be elected to public office.[19] Jews had arrived relatively early in Surinam as well. Under British rule they received an area within the city, on the banks of the Surinam River; to this day that area is called Joden Savanne. They prepared the land for agriculture and grew sugar there. In the privilege granted to the Jewish settlers by the British in 1665, they were given all the liberties and rights enjoyed by the other inhabitants of the colony. When Surinam fell under the rule of the Dutch Republic in 1667, the rights granted by the previous rulers were reconfirmed. Towards the end of the seventeenth century more than 90 Portuguese Jewish families lived there as well as about a dozen Ashkenazic families; together they numbered nearly 570 souls. In their possession were a total of 40 sugar plantations and 9,000 slaves. By 1730, the number of plantations owned by Jews had increased to 115, out of 400 plantations in the entire colony.[20]

As we have seen, the Jews gained recognition and extensive rights in British colonies as well, often before receiving such rights in England itself. This was the case in Barbados, where nearly 300 Sephardic Jews were living in 1679, and also in Jamaica, where Sephardic Jews became a social and economic factor of the first order.[21] In the French colonies the picture was different, for the French adopted a stiff and conservative attitude, not deviating from the policy towards the Jews then in force in France itself. It should be mentioned that marrano merchants from Bayonne and Bordeaux reached Martinique and Saint Domingue. They owned plantations, and some of them engaged in commerce, but they were not allowed to worship publicly as Jews. In the wake of pressure from the Jesuits, a few Jews were driven from Martinique in 1684. A year later the French forbade the entry of Jews to all their colonies. Nevertheless it is known that crypto-Jews from southern France still continued to arrive there at the end of the seventeenth century.[22]

Organization and Leadership

When the Sephardic communities in the West began to form patterns of autonomous organizations, they took the Sephardic community of Venice as their primary model. It was natural that these new communities, most of whose members were former "New Christians," should depend on the organizational pattern of the most important community in the western Sephardic world at the end of the sixteenth century, which stood at a central crossroads between the East and the West, where cultural traditions from many lands encountered each other. However, by the middle of the seventeenth century, once the Amsterdam community had become established, it became the leading community in the western Sephardic diaspora.[23]

At the head of every community stood the *maamad* or *mahamad*, a ruling body generally chosen annually, in whose hands was placed absolute rule of community affairs. The members of the community were called *yehidim*, and only the person who had paid the regular taxes was counted as a *yahid* and permitted to enjoy all the rights attending that status. It must be noted that many of the members of the Sephardic community in the centers of the western Sephardic diaspora were poor and lived on charity. They did not pay taxes, and therefore were not full members of the community. Except for the regulations of the "Zur Israel" and "Magen Abraham" communities in northeast Brazil, which made no explicit distinction between Sephardim and Ashkenazim, ethnic distinctions were prominent throughout the communities of the *nación*, and it was emphasized that only Jews of Spanish and Portuguese nationality were permitted to join the congregation. It should be noted that in most of the places where the western Sephardic diaspora established itself, Sephardic Jews had arrived before their Ashkenazic brethren ever set foot there. When the latter began to arrive, the social and cultural differences between them and the long established Sephardic Jews were evident. As long as it was a question of only isolated Ashkenazic immigrants, the Sephardim permitted them to join the periphery of their community. Although they were not accepted as members with full rights, they did enjoy basic religious services, they could pray in Sephardic synagogues and even be buried in their cemeteries. However, when the flow of Ashkenazic immigrants increased following the Thirty Years' War and the Swedish invasion of the German lands, the leaders of the Sephardic community became increasingly apprehensive at the increase in the number of beggars and mendicants. They therefore invested considerable effort in directing them to other countries. At the same time, Jewish solidarity among the "Members of the Nation" was not impaired, and they contributed generously to the rehabilitation of communities in Poland which had been afflicted by the pogroms of 1648–49, and they also ransomed prisoners from the communities of Eastern Europe.[24]

In the Sephardic communities it was customary to choose the leadership by co-optation: the members of each *maamad* chose their own successors. Some members of the community of Hamburg attempted to institute a democratic system, but this effort failed once they realized that the democratic system "was not practiced anywhere" in the Sephardic diaspora.

Use of the threat of excommunication was widespread in most of the western Sephardic communities; it was commonly imposed for transgressions which, in most Jewish communities, would have been punishable by less severe measures. The severe punishment customary in the Sephardic communities was meant to define the collective identity of these communities, which were initially composed of former "New Christians," who had been distant from Jewish values and for whom communal discipline was alien.

It is no coincidence that the most dramatic cases of excommunication known in the seventeenth-century Jewish world, those imposed against heretics and heterodox Jews who challenged the Jewish tradition, should have taken place within the western Sephardic diaspora. Uriel da Costa was excommunicated by the communities of Venice, Hamburg and Amsterdam, and the Amsterdam community excommunicated Spinoza, Prado, and three Sephardic Jews who claimed to be Karaites in the early eighteenth century.[25]

Spiritual Creativity

In the process of returning to the faith of their fathers, and out of an existential need to define the substance of their Judaism for themselves, the Sephardic Jews of the West created a rich literature, the main purpose of which was to translate the principles of the Jewish religion and the elements of the Jewish way of life into Spanish and Portuguese and into the language of the philosophical and theological concepts familiar to them. They wrote most of their original works in Spanish and Portuguese, the two languages which they took with them from the Iberian peninsula and which they generally handled with full mastery. However, most of their intellectuals also knew other languages. Those who had studied at Iberian universities while living in Spain and Portugal knew Latin perfectly; this permitted them to engage in discourse with the Christian intellectuals of their new countries of residence, who were manifesting increasing interest in Jewish creativity. One man who was particularly outstanding in developing relations with Christian intellectuals from several countries and of various inclinations was Rabbi Menasseh ben Israel. There were others, however, especially in Amsterdam, who showed initiative and talent in forging intellectual bonds with Christian intellectuals.[26]

Jews and Christians cooperated with each other on various levels against their common enemies who, at the time, were the deists, the skeptics, the libertines and the Spinozists, who threatened the stability and solidity of both the Jewish and the Christian establishments. Isaac Orobio de Castro did indeed engage in an intense theological disputation, though a friendly one, with the Christian theologian Ph. van Limborch, but he also cooperated with Limborch in their common struggle against the philosophy of Spinoza. The brothers Jacob and Isaac Abendana cooperated with Christian Hebraists in England; Isaac Abendana also taught Hebrew at the universities of Oxford and Cambridge.[27]

Many of the intellectual elite of the *nación* were physicians. Some of them arrived with medical degrees from prestigious Iberian universities in Salamanca, Alcalá, Valladolid and Coimbra. In the sixteenth and seventeenth centuries many marranos in the Iberian peninsula were prominent in medicine, so much so that it was considered a Jewish profession there. When they rejoined Judaism, many of these physicians became the heads of their new communities, and in all the centers of the western Sephardic diaspora, in various periods, there were many leaders with the degree of Doctor of Medicine.

Characteristically, in the Sephardic communities in Western Europe a special effort was devoted to teaching children Hebrew from an early age. In so doing these communities doubtless were clinging to an ancient tradition rooted in the culture of Islamic Spain. The children learned grammar and composition according to the best tradition of Spanish Jewry, and, with the completion of their studies, the most talented among them were capable of writing verses in Hebrew and even complex works. When he was but a seventeen-year-old youth, Joseph Penso de la Vega, who later gained fame as an important author in the Spanish language, especially because of his satirical work on the activities of the stock exchange, *Confusión de Confusiones*, wrote a drama in Hebrew called "Asirei Hatikvah" (Prisoners of Hope), which was printed in Amsterdam in 1658.[28]

The graduated course of study instituted in these communities did not produce the erudition in Torah or the mastery of the Talmud which was found in the rest of the traditional Jewish world. Nevertheless, halakhic works of considerable merit were written in the western Sephardic diaspora. When Rabbis David Israel Atias and Isaac Abendana de Britto were appointed in Amsterdam in 1728, the Etz Hayim seminary began to publish responsa in a regular and systematic fashion, written by the senior, authoritative scholars, in volumes which were called *Peri Etz Hayim* (The Fruit of the Tree of Life). At approximately the same time the writings of R. Raphael ben Elazar Meldola were published. He had come from Pisa to Bayonne, where he served as rabbi and ushered Bayonne and the kingdom of France into the world of the halakhah. In 1734 in Amsterdam a long halakhic responsum of his was published in Hebrew: *Pareshat Ha-'Ibbur asher be-Bayonne she-be-Malkhut Zarfat* (The Matter of the Boundaries in Bayonne in the Kingdom of France). In 1737 this book was included in a collection of responsa called *Sefer Mayyim Rabbim* (The Book of Many Waters).

Lexicons and grammar texts written in Hebrew show the great interest taken by members of the Sephardic diaspora in the study of that language. Dr. Benjamin Mussafia, who was active in Hamburg during the first half of the seventeenth century and later moved to Amsterdam, wrote a supplement to the *'Arukh* of Rabbi Nathan ben Yehiel of Rome, which he called *Mussaf Ha-'Arukh*. In 1633, in Hamburg, Moses Gideon Abudiente published a Hebrew grammar in Spanish, and in Leyden, in 1660, R. Moses Raphael D'Aguilar published a short work which he wrote in that field. Among his many works, R. Solomon de Oliveyra of Amsterdam wrote books in Portuguese about the Hebrew language, as well as a book of Aramaic grammar and a dictionary of Portuguese in Hebrew. Moreover, years after he was excommunicated, Spinoza also wrote a book on Hebrew grammar.[29]

The Spanish and Portuguese Jewish printing houses in Western Europe played a prime role in the dissemination of fundamental works of Judaism both in Hebrew and in other languages, and also in the distribution of various kinds of works written in the Iberian languages. In Ferrara, the seat of the most important center of Portuguese marranos who had openly returned to Judaism during the first half of the sixteenth century, in addition to the well-known Spanish translation of the Bible, known as the *Biblia de Ferrara*, prayer books and other works were also printed, among them the masterpiece of Samuel Usque, *Consolaçam das Tribulações de Israel* (Consolation of the Tribulations of Israel), which is regarded not only as one of the most interesting Jewish books of historiography of the sixteenth century but also as a classical work of Portuguese Renaissance literature.[30] In the sixteenth and seventeenth centuries Venice and Amsterdam played central roles in the printing industry of the Sephardic Jewish world. The Hebrew language flourished in the numerous printing houses, which were owned by Sephardic Jews in Amsterdam during the seventeenth and eighteenth centuries. Many dozens of Hebrew books were printed by Menasseh ben Israel, who owned the first Jewish printing house in Amsterdam. The printing house of Immanuel Benveniste produced the well-known Amsterdam edition of the Babylonian Talmud. The first Spanish-language Jewish newspaper, the *Gazeta de Amsterdam*, was designed to provide political and economic information to merchants; it was printed by David de Castro Tartas.[31]

The principal original works of the western Sephardic diaspora were written in Spanish, especially philosophical books, translations of the prayers, and literary works, and in Portuguese, which was generally regarded as a vernacular language for daily life, used also for announcements in the synagogue and for communal ordinances. One must also stress the special effort invested by the leadership class of Sephardic Jewry in Western Europe in translating the basic and venerable works of the Jewish tradition into Spanish and Portuguese; these became prized cultural possessions of the Hispanic Jewish diaspora. *Sefer Hovat ha-Levavot* (The Duties of the Heart) by Bahya Ibn Pakuda was translated into Spanish by David Pardo and printed in Amsterdam in 1610; Samuel Abas translated this work into Portuguese (Amsterdam, 1670). Rabbi Jacob Abendana translated the *Kuzari* of Rabbi Yehuda Ha-Levi into Spanish (Amsterdam, 1663). Meir de León produced a Spanish translation of *Shebet Yehudah* (Amsterdam, 1640; a revised edition was printed in 1744). Works by Maimonides and Rabbi Jonah Gerondi were also translated into Spanish and Portuguese. Not only daily prayer books, holiday prayer books, books of penitential prayers, and the like were translated into the Iberian languages, but also books of religious law. A good number of responsa written in Spanish and Portuguese by several Sephardic rabbis are preserved in manuscript. Several decisions made by the rabbinical courts which were written in Portuguese have also come down to us. Menasseh ben Israel published the *Thesouro dos Dinim* in Portuguese, in two parts (1645–1646). This is a compilation summarizing ordinances and customs.

Many apologetic works, most of them arguments against the various trends and sects of Christianity, which were written by the spokesmen of Sephardic Jewry, have remained in manuscript. These works were not originally intended for publication, for the Jews in all of these states were forbidden to print material condemning the Christian religion. However, some of these works were copied often, and dozens of copies of the writings of Dr. Eliahu Montalto, Saul Levi Mortera, Moses Raphael D'Aguilar and Dr. Isaac Orobio de Castro have been preserved in many manuscript collections. Similarly fascinating works have been preserved in manuscript which reflect the intellectual ferment that agitated the world of the marranos who had returned to Judaism. These works were written by many writers from various backgrounds; here we shall merely mention the names of Abraham Gómez Silveyra and Joseph López, among many others.[32] These writings are a treasure trove of knowledge about the heterodox views which were common among the former "New Christians" who had returned to Judaism. In addition to these polemical works which have remained in manuscript, one must also mention the works which were printed, including the *Tratado da Immortalidade de alma* (Treatise on the Immortality of the Soul, Amsterdam, 1623) by Dr. Samuel da Silva of Hamburg, written against Da Costa; the *Nomologia* by Immanuel Aboab of Venice (Amsterdam, 1629); the *Conciliador* by Rabbi Menasseh ben Israel (Amsterdam, 1632–1651); and *Matteh Dan* by David Nieto, printed in Hebrew and Spanish (London, 1714).

The works of the magnate Abraham Israel Pereyra, *La Certeza del Camino* (Certitude of the Path) and *Espejo de la Vanidad del Mundo* (Mirror of the World's Vanity), which were printed in Amsterdam in 1666 and 1671, shed light on the intellectual and religious views of a Jewish international merchant of the age of mercantilism, a former "New Christian" who had returned to Judaism. They show his deep cultural and ideological affinity with the Christian tradition of Iberia, which was the patrimony of these Jews.[33]

The contents and forms of the secular Spanish tradition also found expression in the literary academies established by these Jews in Amsterdam and Livorno at the end of the seventeenth century, which were faithful copies of the literary and artistic associations that were active in Spain during the baroque period.

The new syntheses created by the Spanish and Portuguese Jews in the West grew directly out of their social and spiritual experience. Being close to the Jewish sources, on the one hand, and familiar with the Christian culture of Europe on the other, brought them to reevaluate the Jewish tradition. In their creativity and cultural activity they were forerunners of the beginnings of modernization in Jewish society.[34] In the course of the seventeenth century this colorful branch of Jewry reached great heights both in economic and spiritual terms. However, the economic stagnation which overcame the world of the international traders of the "Spanish and Portuguese Jewish Nation" in the eighteenth century greatly diminished the weight of the western Sephardic diaspora.

Also the great decline in the numbers of "New Christians" leaving the Iberian peninsula after the 1730s dealt a serious blow to the demographic development of the Spanish and Portuguese communities. Moreover, the relatively easy terms which prevailed in the states where these Jews had settled and their integration within the surrounding society ultimately led many of them to depart from the framework of Judaism. However, even during the modern period, with its shocks and upheavals, this branch of Jewry still maintained the proud memory of its glorious past.

Translated from the Hebrew by Jeffrey M. Green

1. On the process of the marranos' return to Judaism during the sixteenth and seventeenth centuries, see Yosef Hayyim Yerushalmi, *From Spanish Court to Italian Ghetto: Isaac Cardoso, a Study in Seventeenth-Century Marranism and Jewish Apologetics* (New York and London, 1971). Basic problems in this area are examined in I. S. Révah, "Les marranes," *Revue des Études Juives* 118 (1959–1960), pp. 29–77. See also Yosef Kaplan, *From Christianity to Judaism: The Story of Isaac Orobio de Castro* (Oxford, 1989).

2. On "New Christians" in Antwerp, see H. Pohl, *Die Portugiesen in Antwerpen (1567–1648). Zur Geschichte einer Minderheit* (Wiesbaden, 1977).

3. A rich literature exists on the "Portuguese Jewish Nation" in France. Among others, see Th. Malvézin, *Histoire des Juifs à Bordeaux* (Bordeaux, 1875; rpt. Marseilles, 1967); H. Léon, *Histoire des Juifs de Bayonne* (Paris, 1893; rpt. Marseilles, 1976); G. Cirot, *Recherches sur les Juifs espagnols et portugais à Bordeaux*, Part I (Bordeaux, 1908); G. Nahon, *Les "Nations" juifs portugaises du Sud-Ouest de la France (1648–1791). Documents* (Paris, 1981); idem, "The Sephardim of France," in R. D. Barnett and W. M. Schwab (eds.), *The Sephardi Heritage*, Vol. II (Grendon, Northants, 1989), pp. 46–74; S. Schwarzfuchs (ed.), *Le Registre des Délibérations de la Nation Juive Portugaise de Bordeaux (1711–1787)* (Paris, 1981).

4. On the settlement of Spanish and Portuguese marranos in Ancona see A. Toaff, "L'Universitas Hebraeorum Portugallensium' di Ancona del Cinquecento; Interessi economici e ambiguita religiosa," *Mercati, Mercanti denaro nelle Marche (secoli xiv–xix)*, [= *Atti e Memorie della Deputazione di Storia Patria per le Marche* 87] (1982), pp. 115–45. On Ferrara see L. Modona, "Les exilés d'Espagne à Ferrare en 1493," *Revue des Études Juives* 15 (1887), pp. 117–21; A. Balleti, *Gli Ebrei e gli Estensi* (Reggio Emilia, 1920; rpt. Bologna, 1969); A. DiLeone Leoni, "Gli ebrei sefarditi a Ferrara da Ercole I a Ercole II; nuove ricerche e interpretazione," *La Rassegna Mensile di Israel* 52 (1986), pp. 406–43; on Florence see M. D. Cassuto, *The Jews of Florence in the Renaissance* (Hebrew, Jerusalem, 1967), pp. 56, 69, 71, 133–37.

5. On the burning of the former "New Christians" in Ancona and its ramifications, see I. Sonne, "Une source nouvelle pour l'histoire des martyrs d'Ancone," *Revue des Études Juives* 89 (1930), pp. 360–80; M. Saperstein, "Martyrs, Merchants and Rabbis: Jewish Communal Conflict as Reflected in the Responsa on the Boycott of Ancona," *Jewish Social Studies* 43 (1981), pp. 215–28; A. Toaff, "Nuova luce sui Marani di Ancona (1556)," in *Studi sull'Ebraismo Italiano in memoria de Cecil Roth* (Rome, 1974), pp. 261–80; R. Segre, "Nuovi documenti sui marrani d'Ancona (1555–1559)," *Michael* 9 (1985), pp. 130–233.

6. On the Sephardic Jews and the marranos in Venice, see Cecil Roth, *The History of the Jews in Venice* (Philadelphia, 1930; rpt. N.Y. 1975); B. Pullan, *The Jews of Europe and the Inquisition of Venice, 1550–1670* (Oxford, 1983); B. Ravid, "The Religious, Economic and Social Background and Context of the Establishment of the Ghetti of Venice," in *Gli Ebrei a Venezia secoli xiv–xvii* (Milano, 1987), pp. 727–70; idem, *Economics and Toleration in Seventeenth-Century Venice* (Jerusalem, 1978); idem, "The First Charter of the Jewish Merchants of Venice, 1589," *American Jewish Studies Review* 1 (1976), pp. 187–222.

7. On this affair see Haim Beinart, "Sephardic Settlement in Savoy," in D. Carpi et al. (eds.), *Scritti in Memori di Leone Carpi* (Hebrew, Jerusalem, 1967), pp. 72–118.

8. On this matter see mainly B. D. Cooperman, *Trade and Settlement: The Establishment and Early Development*

of the Jewish Communities in Leghorn and Pisa (1591–1626), Harvard University Doctoral Dissertation, October, 1976; A. Toaff, "Cenni storici sulla communitá ebraica e sulla sinagoga di Livorno," *La Rassegna Mensile di Israel* 21 (1955), pp. 356–59; R. Toaff, "Statuti e Leggi della 'Nazione Ebrea' di Livorno—I. Gli Statuti del 1655," *La Rassegna Mensile di Israel*, 34 (1968), supl. pp. 1–51; idem, "II. La Legislazione dal 1655 al 1677," *ibid.* 38 (1972), supl., pp. 1–68.

9. On the Portuguese community in Hamburg see mainly H. Kellenbenz, *Sephardim an der unteren Elbe* (Wiesbaden, 1958); on the Sephardic Jews in Altona see G. Marwedel, *Die Privilegien der Juden in Altona* (Hamburg, 1976); on the settlement in Glückstadt see A. Cassuto, "Die portugiesischen Juden in Glückstadt," *Jahrbuch der jüdisch-literarischen Gesellschaft* 21 (1930), pp. 287–317.

10. On the first Portuguese Jews in Amsterdam see E. M. Koen, "The Earliest Sources Relating to the Portuguese Jews in the Municipal Archives of Amsterdam up to 1620," *Studia Rosenthaliana* 5 (1970), pp. 25–42; Koen has been publishing an abstract of the notarial documents from Amsterdam touching upon the Portuguese Jews there in chronological order in *Studia Rosenthalia* starting from the first issue, in 1967; cf. H. P. Salomon, *Os primeiros portugueses de Amesterdão* (Braga, 1982). On the history of the Spanish and Portuguese Jews of Amsterdam during the seventeenth century there exists a very rich body of literature, see mainly: I. S. da Silva Rosa, *Geschiedenis der Portugeesche Joden te Amsterdam 1593–1925* (Amsterdam, 1925); D. M. Swetschinski, *The Portuguese Jewish Merchants of Seventeenth-Century Amsterdam: A Social Profile*, doctoral dissertation, Brandeis University, 1979; J. I. Israel, "Spain and the Dutch Sephardim, 1609–1660," *Studia Rosenthaliana* 12 (1978), pp. 1–61; idem, "The Economic Contribution of Dutch Sephardi Jewry to Holland's Golden Age, 1595–1713," *Tijdschrift voor Geschiedenis* 96 (1983), pp. 505–35.

11. See J. I. Israel, "Sephardic Immigration into the Dutch Republic," *Studia Rosenthaliana*, special issue published together with volume 23(2), Fall, 1989.

12. On the spiritual ferment within the Portuguese community of Amsterdam, see, among others: I. S. Révah, *Spinoza et le Dr. Juan de Prado* (Paris and The Hague, 1959); Herman P. Salomon, *Saul Levi Mortera en zijn "Traktaat betreffende de Waarheid van de Wet van Mozes"* (Braga, 1988); Y. Kaplan, *From Christianity to Judaism. The Story of Isaac Orobio de Castro* (Oxford, 1989).

13. See D. S. Katz, *Philo-Semitism and the Readmission of the Jews to England 1603–1655* (Oxford, 1982).

14. J. I. Israel, "Menasseh Ben Israel and the Dutch Sephardic Colonization Movement of the Mid-Seventeenth Century (1645–1657)" in Yosef Kaplan et al. (eds.), *Menasseh Ben Israel and his World* (Leyden, 1989), pp. 139–63.

15. On the Sephardic community in London there exists a rich literature. See, among others: L. D. Barnett, *Bevis Marks Records*, I (Oxford, 1940); A. M. Hyamson, *The Sephardim of England* (London, 1951); W. S. Samuel, "The First London Synagogue of the Re-Settlement," *Transactions of the Jewish Historical Society in England* 10 (1924), pp. 1–147; E. R. Samuel, "The First Fifty Years," in Vivian D. Lipman (ed.), *Three Centuries of Anglo-Jewish History* (Cambridge, 1961), pp. 27–44; A. S. Diamond, "The Community of the Resettlement, 1656–1684; A Social Survey," *Transactions of the Jewish Historical Society* 24 (1974), pp. 134–50; Haim Beinart, "The Jews in the Canary Islands: A Re-evaluation," *ibid.* 25 (1977), pp. 48–86; and see also the interesting studies of Lucien Wolf on the crypto-Jews of London before the establishment of the Sephardic community there: "Crypto-Jews under the Commonwealth," *Transactions of the Jewish Historical Society in England* 1 (1893–94), pp. 55–99; "The First English Jew," *ibid.* 2 (1894–95), pp. 14–46.

16. See A. Wiznitzer, *The Records of the Earliest Jewish Community in the New World* (New York, 1954); idem, *Jews in Colonial Brazil* (New York, 1960).

17. See I. S. and S. A. Emmanuel, *History of the Netherlands Antilles*, I–II (Cincinnati, 1970); I. S. Emmanuel, *Precious Stones of the Jews of Curaçao: Curaçaoan Jewry 1656–1975* (New York, 1975).

18. See S. Oppenheim, "An Early Jewish Colony in Western Guiana, 1658–1666, and its Relation to the Jews in Surinam, Cayenne and Tobago," *Proceedings of the American Jewish Historical Society* 16 (1907), pp. 95–186; 17 (1908), pp. 53–70.

19. On the beginning of the Jewish settlement in New York see S. Oppenheim, "The Early History of the Jews in New York, 1654–1664. Some New Matter on the Subject," *Proceedings of the American Jewish Historical Society* 18 (1909), pp. 1–91; A. Wiznitzer, "The Exodus from Brazil and Arrival in New Amsterdam of the Jewish Pilgrim Fathers 1654," *ibid.* 44 (1954–55), pp. 80–97; E. and F. Wolff, "The Problem of the First Jewish Settlers in New Amsterdam 1654," *Studia Rosenthaliana* 15 (1981), pp. 169–77.

20. A book by Robert Cohen on the Jews in Surinam will be published shortly. Meanwhile, see R. Cohen (ed.), *The Jewish Nation in Surinam—Historical Essays* (Amsterdam, 1982).

21. On the Jews of Barbados, see: W. S. Samuel, "A Review of the Jewish Colonists in Barbados in the Year 1680," *Transactions of the Jewish Historical Society in England* 13 (1932–35), pp. i–iii; J.A.P.M. Andrada, *A Record of the Jews in Jamaica from the English Conquest to the Present Time* (Kingston, 1941).

22. On the Jewish settlements in French colonies, see A. Cahen, "Les Juifs de la Martinique au xviié siècle," *Revue des Etudes Juives* 3 (1881), pp. 93–122; on Cayenne, see the Hebrew article by Z. Loker in *Zion* 48 (1983).

23. On the influence of the community of Venice on the Sephardic Jewry of Amsterdam see Julie-Marthen Cohen (ed.), *The Ghetto in Venice. Ponentini, Levantini e Tedeschi 1516–1797*, (The Hague, 1990).

24. See, for example, regarding Amsterdam, my article on the migration of Ashkenazim to Amsterdam, published in *Studia Rosenthalia*, special issue published together with volume 23(2), Fall, 1989.

25. See Yosef Kaplan, "The Social Functions of the 'Herem' in the Portuguese Jewish Community of Amsterdam in the Seventeenth Century," in J. Michman (ed.), *Dutch Jewish History* (Jerusalem, 1984), pp. 111–55; idem, "'Karaites' in Early Eighteenth-Century Amsterdam," in D. S. Katz and J. I. Israel (eds.), *Sceptics, Millenarians and Jews* (Leyden, 1990), pp. 196–236.

26. See J. van den Berg, *Joden en Christenen in Nederland gedurende de zeventiende eeuw* (Kampen, 1962); Yosef Kaplan et al. (eds.), *Menasseh Ben Israel and his World* (Leyden, 1989); R. H. Popkin, "Menasseh ben Israel and Isaac La Peyrè," *Studia Rosenthalia* 8 (1974), pp. 59–63.

27. See D. S. Katz, "The Abendana Brothers and the Christian Hebraists of Seventeenth-Century England," *Journal of Ecclesiastical History* 40 (1989), pp. 28–52.

28. The pedagogical methods of the Sephardic Jews of Amsterdam were treated in detail by Bass in *Siftei Yeshenim* (Amsterdam, 1680), fol. 8a–b.

29. A list of the Spanish and Portuguese Jewish writers and their works can be found, among other places, in M. Kayserling, *Biblioteca Española Portugueza Judaica* (Strasbourg, 1890); M. dos Remedios, *Os Judeus Portugueses em Amsterdam* (Coimbra, 1911), pp. 57–148; J. S. da Silva Rosa, *Die Spanischen und Portugiesischen Gedruckten Judaica in der Bibliothek des Jüd. Portug. Seminars 'Ets Haim' in Amsterdam* (Amsterdam, 1933); on poetry in Hebrew, especially in Amsterdam, see the recent study: A. van der Heide, "Dutch Hebrew Poetry of the 17th Century," in J. Michman (ed.), *Dutch Jewish History* II (Jerusalem, 1989); J. A. Brombacher, "Poetry on Gravestones—Poetry by the 17th-Century Portuguese Rabbi Solomon de Oliveyra found in the Jewish Cemetery at Ouderkerk aan de Amstel," *ibid.*, pp. 153–65.

30. The book was printed in 1553. See the splendid recent two-volume edition, published in Lisbon in 1990, with comprehensive articles on the work by Yosef Hayyim Yerushalmi and J. V. de Pina Martins.

31. On Hebrew printing in Amsterdam see L. Fuks and R. G. Fuks-Mansfeld, *Hebrew Typography in the Northern Netherlands 1585–1815*, I–II (Leyden, 1984–1987).

32. See, for example, in L. Fuks and R. G. Fuks-Mansfeld, *Hebrew Typography in the Northern Netherlands 1585–1815*, I–II (Leyden, 1984–1987), indices.

33. On Pereyra and his work see: H. Méchoulan, *Hispanidad y Judaísmo en Tiempos de Espinoza. Edición de 'La Certeza del Camino' de Abraham Pereyra* (Salamanca, 1987).

34. On this subject see Yosef Kaplan, "The Portuguese Community in Amsterdam in the Seventeenth Century, between Tradition and Change" (Hebrew), *Proceedings of the Israel Academy of Science and Humanities*, Vol. 7 (1988).

JEWISH THEMES AND THOUGHTS IN THE JUDEO-SPANISH *REFRÁN*

Matilda Cohen Sarano

"Polished and repolished over the years, decades and centuries, *refránes* are a faithful mirror of the [ethnic] groups that use them," Professor Haim Vidal Sephiha writes in his preface to Saporta y Beja's book, *Refránes de los Judios Sefardis* (Barcelona, 1978). This description is applicable to the Judeo-Spanish *refránes* as, indeed, it is to all folk proverbs.

Let me note at the outset that, for reasons I shall explain shortly, I will, in these observations, spell *refrán* as *reflán*, as I heard it pronounced among the older generation of my family.

What is a *refrán* (or *reflán*) and what is the origin of the term? Isaac Jack Levy, another scholar who has written on the Sephardic *refrán*, takes his definition from the Corominas dictionary of the Spanish language. Considering the vast amount of oral material gathered from dozens of informants, we find ourselves wondering whether a *reflán* is only that which is commonly understood today by the word "proverb" or "maxim," a lapidary phrase which can describe a situation, underscore analogies, enunciate or criticize an idea, breathe life into that idea, poke fun at it, or refute it in order to modify or change it. Or could the term, perhaps, have broader connotations? Could it be not merely a phrase but a single word, an interjection that, with the passing of time, has acquired the authority of tradition and is used in everday conversation to obtain a specific effect or give added weight to the speaker's words? This, in fact, is the definition given by Corominas.

In tracing the origin of the term *refrán*, Jack Levy gives us a wide selection of etymologies. For instance, he suggests, "It is also conceivable that the term *refrán* is derived from the French *refrain*. In any case, it indicates frequent repetition" (Levy, p. 16).

The difference in pronunciation—*refrán* versus *reflán*— does not present a problem because in Spanish the *r* and *l* are phonetically interchangeable. This leads us to my own theory about the etymology of *refrán*. It seems to me that *reflán*, as I have learned to pronounce it, has an association with the Latin *refló* (*refláre*, *reflávi*, *reflátus*) (D'Arbela-

Names or titles in parentheses following various *refránes* refer to the bibliography at the end of this essay, or to individual informants. Names followed by an asterisk refer to my own unpublished collection (Koleksión Cohen-Sarano).

I have transcribed all the Ladino *refránes* in a unified homogenous transliteration. [M.C.S.]

Translator's Note: I have included the original texts of the proverbs so that the reader may savor them in the original. About one fourth of the proverbs cited rhyme, and I have attempted to rhyme part of these in English. I wish to thank Estelle Mushabac, Victor Mushabac and Raul Ramos for their gracious help with challenging words and phrases. [J.M.]

Annaratone-Cammelli, *Vocabolario Latino-Italiano, Italiano-Latino*), literally, "to blow;" i.e., to blow out, or to breathe out (Judeo-Spanish: "respiro"). The implication would be that a *reflán* consists of a minimum of words; it summarizes in the tersest manner possible—in one breath, as it were—the idea the speaker seeks to convey.

The fact that the Judeo-Spanish *reflán* truly mirrors the life and thought of the Judeo-Spanish ethnic group in all the regions to which this group has been dispersed is clear from both the language and content of the *reflán*. The language is the Judeo-Spanish spoken by the Jews who, following their expulsion from Spain in 1492, settled in the Ottoman empire, in Italy (particularly Livorno [Leghorn]) and in what later became Spanish Morocco. This language remained crystallized in the phonetic forms of fifteenth-century Spanish, to which Turkish, Greek, Arabic, Slavic, French and Italian forms and terms were added over a period of nearly five centuries, depending on the locality in which the language was spoken.

In time, there evolved two distinct Judeo-Spanish variants: (1) The Judeo-Spanish spoken in the Ottoman empire, which is known as "Ladino" in Israel, "Espagnol" in Turkey and Greece, and as "Judezmo" in Bulgaria and Yugoslavia, and which scholars have come to call "Oriental Judeo-Spanish;" and (2) "Hakitia," which was the Judeo-Spanish spoken in Spanish Morocco and which today is known to scholars as "Occidental Judeo-Spanish."

The influence of Hebrew in this connection merits separate consideration, because Hebrew infiltrated into the Spanish language at various stages before and after the expulsion of the Jews from Spain, and the influence of Hebrew on Judeo-Spanish varies even in our own day, depending on the locality where the language is spoken, the age of the person speaking it, and his or her personal association with the modern State of Israel.

The second factor that characterizes the Judeo-Spanish *reflán* is the complexity of the subject matter treated therein. The effect of this complexity is not always uniform because the *reflán* deals with such a variety of matters as life and death, family and children, God and fate, good and evil, and friendship and love. We find identical *reflánes* on the same subject even in localities separated by considerable geographic distance. The same *reflánes*, with only minor linguistic differences, crop up in the variants of Judeo-Spanish spoken in Turkey and Bulgaria, in Yugoslavia and Greece. The differences between the *reflánes* occurring in the Ottoman empire and in Spanish Morocco are more pronounced, but even where the *reflánes* are not identical, there are close analogies.

We see, therefore, that the Judeo-Spanish *reflán* is based on the *reflán* of the Spanish language, as Isaac Jack Levy also notes: "The *refrán*, which the Sephardim still use in everyday discourse, had its source in the oral tradition—principally that of Spain and to a lesser degree that of Turkey and Greece" (Levy, p. 84). However, the framework of this essay is not the place for a detailed discussion of the origins of the *reflánes*. The purpose of the present study is to point out the uniquely Jewish character of the Judeo-Spanish *reflán*. This is not at all difficult to do.

The main themes characteristic of the Judeo-Spanish *reflán* are: the Jew as seen by himself and others; the figure of the *haham*, the Sephardic spiritual leader who stands out above all the other Jewish figures; the Sabbath and the Jewish holidays; Jewish names derived from the Bible; and the behavior of the Jew in this world and his conceptions of the world to come. Any one of these themes can be of interest to all Jews, no matter what their provenance. But the *reflánes* of the Judeo-Spanish languages are deserving of special attention because of the particular manner in which they reflect the essence of Sephardic Judaism and its philosophy of life.

Before we cite specific examples, it is important to note the didactic function of the *reflán* which, as already indicated earlier, reflects the life experience of many generations, is repeated over and over again and which, without its sententious tone and, in many instances, its rhyme, would not carry the same weight.

In order to attract the listener's attention, the *reflán* uses a tone of irony, or sometimes even mordant sarcasm, which may startle anyone not familiar with the circumstances that gave rise to that particular *reflán*. It is therefore a good idea to explain the background of a *reflán* to the non-initiate who hears or reads it for the first time.

The Essence of the Sephardic Jew

While the *reflán* never explicitly states that the Jew to whom it refers is Sephardic, we know this to be true from the context of the localities where the *reflán* is used and from the terms in which it is couched.

Basically, the *reflán* sets a high tone. For instance: *Asigún es el Djudió, ansina le ayuda el Dio* (God will help you according to what you are as a Jew) *(Proverbs and Sayings of the Sephardi Jews of Bosnia and Herzegovina)*, or, from another vantage point, *Sigún va el Djidió ansi le ayuda el Dio* (God will help you according to what you do as a Jew) (Moscona, *Pniné Sfarad*). The first *reflán* states that you will receive from God whatever you deserve by virtue of your character, while the second explains that God will give you whatever you deserve by virtue of your actions.

If we want to know more precisely what God regards as good and ethical, we can learn it from this *reflán*: *Dos kozas valen mas ke Israel: Adonay i la Torá. Ken eyas toma bien pasará* (There are two things that matter more than Israel: *Adonay* [God] and the Torah. Whosoever respects both of these will do well) (Levy). Everything else is a consequence of this thought, as is, for instance, this *reflán*, which is a little humorous: *Por una magajika semos Djidiós* (Because of just one little knife, we are Jews) (Saporta y Beja)—a clear, if not very elegant allusion to the *brit milah*. Another *reflán* states: *Shabbat i Yomtov es sólo al Djidió* (The Sabbath and the holidays are [intended] only for the Jew) *(Bosnia and*

Herzegovina); they are the two treasures God gave to the Jews because they keep His Law.

Next, we will examine the light in which the *reflán* sees the Jew. Two *reflánes*: *Djidio bovo no hay* (There is no such thing as a Jewish fool) (Kolonomós, *Proverbs, Sayings and Tales of the Sephardi Jews of Macaedonia*) and *Djudió savi lo ke otros no tienin ni la idea* (The Jew knows things of which others don't even have an inkling) (Levy), imply that the Jew is supposedly of superior intelligence. A third *reflán* points to the prudent behavior resulting from such superior intelligence: *El Djudió no mete pie en tavle rote* (A Jew won't set his foot on a broken board) (Kolonomós).

The following *reflán* expresses the proverbial solidarity for which Jews are known: *Djudió ki no ayuda a otro djudió no ay* (There is no such thing as a Jew who does not help another Jew) (Levy). On the other hand, we see that the opposite may sometimes be true, but with one noteworthy reservation: *Ken es enemigo del Djudió? Otro Djudió, ma no en la ora di angustia* (Who is the enemy of the Jew? Another Jew—but never in the hour of affliction) (Levy). When all goes well for them, Jews are always ready to engage in polemics and to pick fights with one another: *Dos Djidiós en tres killot* (Two Jews, three congregations) (Diana Sarano, Izmir*). But as soon as things begin to go badly for the Jews, their solidarity comes to the fore and helps them to survive.

Jews are found all over the world. *Kada país tiene sus Djidiós* (Every country has its Jews) (Moscona), with their particular qualities and peculiarities. But sometimes *Toparás el Djudio ande no lo ensembras* (You may find a Jew where you least expect him) (Levy), or *De adientro de un frandjola salió un Djudió*) (A Jew came forth from inside a loaf of fancy French bread) (Saporta y Beja).

What of the virtues and shortcomings of the Jews? One area in which Jews do not enjoy the best of reputations is money, and it seems that it is not so much the others as the Jews themselves that point to this unpleasant reality. As one *reflán* has it, *Espántate de Djudió riko, de Grego boracho i de Turko prove* (Beware of a rich Jew, a drunk Greek and a poor Turk) (Arié Alkalay, *Dichos i Refránes Sefaradies*); as soon as a Jew gets rich, he sets his sights too high. Or: *Kuando se enrekese un Djidió la mujer se le vee fea i la kaza estrecha* (When a Jew gets rich his wife sees herself as ugly and her house as miserable) (Moscana; Alkalay). Even worse: *Si keres quadrar parás no se las des al Djidió* (If you want to keep your pennies, don't give them to a Jew) (Saporta y Beja). This last *reflán* in particular reflects an embarrassing lack of self-esteem on the part of the Jew.

Other *reflánes* depict the Jew as a contrary breed: *El Djidió bive riko i se muere prove* (The Jew lives rich and dies poor) (Moscana). *El Djidió kunado kevra se asavienta* (When a Jew loses, he gets smart) (Levy). And when we want to criticize a Jew for his miserliness, we sadly say, *Gana komo el Djudió i gasta komo el kristiano* (He earns like a Jew but spends like a Christian) (Levy).

The quasi-clairvoyant intelligence of the Jew, as well as his vitality and "busyness," are duly acknowledged: *El ijo del Judió al mes anda i al año gatea* (The son of the Jew walks at the age of one month and climbs at the age of one year) (Raphael Benazeraf, *Refranero, Recueil de Proverbe Judeo-Espagnols du Maroc*), and *Ija del Djudió, no keda sin kazar* (No daughter of a Jew ever remains unmarried) (Moscona) because the Jews, with their proverbial solidarity, will do everything to find her a husband.

As for the relationship between Jews and non-Jews, we find many *reflánes* that allude to the wanderings of the speaker, or his ancestors, following the expulsion of the Jews from Spain. *Mas vale murir Djidió i no murir Turko* (It is better to die as a Jew than not to die as a Turk) (Alkalay) is not only a trenchant admonition against assimilation but also recalls the Ottoman empire as the land in which Sephardic Jews resided for nearly 500 years. *Turko no aharva Djidió. I si aharvo?* (A Turk never beats up a Jew. But what if he *does* beat him up?) (Itzhak Sarfaty, Izmir*) reflects the basic friendship that existed between Turks and Jews; yet, the apprehensive, "but what if . . ." was ever present. The Jew must always be prepared for the eventuality that even the friendliest of Gentiles may suddenly turn against him.

A *reflán* that occurs in many versions warns the Jew against following a double standard for his relationships with Jews on the one hand and Gentiles on the other: *Ken peka kon Ismael, peka kon Israel* (He that sins against Ishmael will also sin against Israel) (Moscona). This proverb is a warning to those who think they can be dishonest in their dealings with "the *goyim*" and still remain honest in their dealings with their fellow Jews.

The *reflánes* do not describe Gentiles exclusively as Turks or Muslims. The proverb *Djidió ke kazaliko medio kristianiko* (A small-town Jew is half a Christian) (Ester Levy, Jerusalem*) deplores the gradual assimilatory trend among Jews living in places far away from larger centers of Jewish life.

The belief that the Jew is always doomed to suffer is stated in two very significant *reflánes*, both originating from the Jews of Greece: *El Djidio es de vidro. Si aharva la piedra al vidro, qual del vidro; i.si aharva el vidro a la pieda, quay del vidro* (The Jew is made of glass. If a rock hits the glass, woe to the glass; if the glass hits a rock, woe to the glass) (Saporta y Beja). No matter what the Jew does, it is his destiny to suffer, not only in this world but even in the next. As the second *reflán* has it: *En este mundo sufrimos porké somos Djidiós. En el otro sufriremos porké no fuemos Djidiós* (In this world we suffer because we are Jews. In the next we will suffer because we were not Jewish [enough]) (Saporta y Beja). It seems that the Jew is never allowed to forget who he is and what is expected of him. If he ever forgets, there are always those who will remind him, and at what a price! And as if this were not enough, when he arrives in the other world, he will be asked what kind of a Jew he was. If he was not Jewish enough, he will have to suffer some more.

But though our lot as a people may be difficult, our position as individuals is a little more encouraging because we are not burdened by original sin as the Christians consider themselves to be, nor are we like pagans who believe that no matter what they do, they are helplessly at the mercy of the gods. We are born free of sin, and we can influence our fate by the way in which we conduct ourselves. We always have an opportunity to save ourselves by choosing the path of repentance.

Shabbat and the Jewish Holidays

The most prominent institution that sets the Jew apart from all others is the Shabbat. This subject alone is the theme of dozens of *reflánes* in Judeo-Spanish folklore.

The Jew prepares for the Shabbat all week long, but the final hours of Friday afternoon are the most difficult. Hence, if you wish to describe someone who is very busy and does not have even one free moment, you say, *Apinado asigún va el Djudió tadri di viernes* (In a rush like a Jew on Friday afternoon) (Levy). A busy person who is annoyed with what someone else, perhaps a child, has done but is unable or unwilling to do something about it, may say: *Vate a lavar k'es tadre de viernes* (Go wash up—it's Friday afternoon) (Alfredo Sarano, Rhodes*). In other words: You're lucky that I'm busy with other things now and I don't have time to deal with you, so you can get away with it this time.

Shabbat is not the time to talk or even think about the workday week. *No tokes lumbre en Shabbat* (Don't touch fire on the Shabbat) is a *reflán* known in approximately the same form in Bosnia, Greece, Turkey and Bulgaria. When people talk on the Sabbath about their plans for the coming week, they add: *Sin dicho Shabbat* (Not speaking on the Shabbat) (Alfredo Sarano, Rhodes*). One who wants to curse another person without actually expressing the curse may say: *El Dio no paga en Shabbat* (God doesn't settle His accounts on the Sabbath) (Alfredo Sarano, Rhodes*)—a hint about the watchfulness of Divine justice, which ultimately rewards the righteous and punishes the sinners.

When a person does something out of the ordinary, even if the act is objectionable, one might say to him, *No Sabá ni Rosh Hodes* ([Why now of all days?] It's neither the Sabbath nor Rosh Hodesh) (Saporta y Beja), or, all in Hebrew, *Lo hodesh ve-lo Shabbat* (It's neither Rosh Hodesh nor Shabbat) (Alfredo Sarano, Rhodes*). Or, to express the same idea more vividly: *Si vistió Djohá vestido de Sabá en diá de semana o de rikeza o de provedá* (Joha dressed for the Sabbath on a weekday either because he is so rich or because he is so poor) (Saporta y Beja). Joha, a character adopted by Sephardic Jews from Turkish folklore, is a clever fool from whom all kinds of crazy actions can be expected.

An explanation for conspicuously inappropriate behavior can be found in the *reflán*: *El prove ke lo vesh vestido de diá de Sabá, o so kayó al kanyo o está parido* (When you see a poor man in Sabbath clothes, [it means that] he has either fallen into a ditch [and ruined his weekday clothes] or else his wife has just given birth to a child) (Saporta y Beja). The Jew puts on festive clothing only on Shabbat or on special (or unusual) occasions.

The prohibition against doing any kind of work on the Shabbat is very strict, but there are circumstances when there might be an excuse for stretching a point: *Ken tiene ija de kazar i en Shabbat tenía de lavrar* (Bosnia) or *lavar* (Alkalay) (One who has a daughter to marry off has to work and carry even on the Sabbath). The message conveyed by this *reflán* is not that the Sabbath laws are unimportant but that the task of marrying off a daughter is of such vital importance that it may take precedence even over Shabbat.

In a similar vein, there is a *reflán* which, like many others, tells a complete story, albeit in verbal shorthand: *El azniko kayó al pozo. Di ken es? Di el haham! Kitaldo!* (A donkey fell into a well. To whom does the donkey belong? It belongs to the *haham*! Pull it out, then!) (Renée Arochas, Jerusalem*). It would be necessary, of course, to explain that the accident befell the donkey on Shabbat. It is argued that under Jewish law the animal must be left in the well because pulling him out is regarded as labor forbidden on Shabbat. But there are circumstances under which the animal might be pulled out, even on the Day of Rest—for instance, if the donkey happens to belong to an important figure, such as the rabbi. The intent of this *reflán* is to tell us that everything is relative. That which people consider as a violation of the Shabbat when it is done to help someone else might be justified as "breaking the Shabbat in order to save a life" when the act is performed to save your own property. Especially, people are inclined to bend the law if the problem involves a person of authority who is in a position to adapt the law to his needs. The irony here is obvious.

So, some Jews know how to circumvent the law according to the situation in which they find themselves. *Ni Shabbat es, ni el dukado no está en basho* (It's not Shabbat and the coin isn't on the ground) (Stella Afumado, Istanbul*), a *reflán* quoted with a note of irony to imply that someone is "beating around the bush" or not talking to the point, alludes to the story of a Jew who had his own way of getting around the Shabbat. Walking in the street one Shabbat, he saw a coin lying on the ground. He could not pick it up because it is forbidden to touch money on Shabbat. So, in order that no one else should be able to pick it up, he stepped on the coin and remained standing there, with his foot on the coin, waiting until the stars would appear in the sky, a sign that the Shabbat was over. But after only a short while someone passed by and gave him a swift kick so that the unfortunate Jew "saw the stars." The Jew persuaded himself that if he saw stars, Shabbat must be over, so he could pick up the coin and put it into his pocket.

The festive atmosphere of Shabbat is produced not only by complete rest but also by the good Shabbat meals: *Buen Djudió kome en Shabbat pastel de kezo i quevo de baba* (On Shabbat, a good Jew eats an egg, cheese *boreka* and other delicacies) (Alkalay). But this atmosphere must be preserved by good behavior; it must not be spoiled by fights and arguments because *Shabbat kon pletos es dezrepozado, aunke de muncha karne i peshe artado* (Shabbat with fights can never be sweet, even if it's stuffed with fish and meat) (Bosnia).

Reflánes about the *moadim*, the Jewish holidays, are numerous. Some are used as analogies for situations unrelated to the holiday as such. For instance, if something comes, or is done, too late, there is the famous saying, *Después de Purim platikos* (Platters of sweets received after Purim). This *reflán* is known and used wherever Sephardic Jews reside. It is equivalent to the Hebrew *Avar zmano batel korbano* (An offering has no value if it is made after its season). The same idea is conveyed by the *reflán*: *Después de Sukot los etrogim* (Etrogim after Sukkot) (Moshé David Gaón, *Spices from Spain*).

Of course we cannot quote in this study all the *refláes* that have to do with the Jewish holidays. We will therefore limit ourselves to a discussion of only the most significant ones. The holidays most popular in the Judeo-Spanish *reflán* are Purim and Pesah. *Kada día no es Purim* (Every day isn't Purim) (Alkalay; Kolonomós) is a direct translation from the Hebrew *Lo kol yom Purim*, reminding us that miracles and celebrations are not everyday occurrences.

A father happy with something good or clever his son has said or done might say: *Ke darse (o ke riya) mi ijo, ke sea en Purim* (When my son makes a speech (or laughs), let it be on Purim) (Diana Sarano, Izmir*). If someone is not known for his sense of humor and goes about with a stern look on his face, people say of him, *Ya riyó Purim* (Even he laughed on Purim) (Stella Afumado, Istanbul*). In another context, when you tell someone exactly what you think of him, you *kanta la de Purim* (you sing him the Purim song) (Saporta y Beja).

One whose expectations are unrealistic or impossible to satisfy is told ironically: *Empréstame la Megilla por Purim* (Lend me the Megillah on Purim) (Edith Hasson, Istanbul*). As everyone knows, it is difficult to find a Megillah to borrow on Purim because everybody needs his own scroll for reading the story of Esther. A Purim *reflán* can be serious and sententious, as in *El día de Purim no se serra puerta* (The door isn't closed on Purim day) (Renée Arochas, Jerusalem*). The tone of this *reflán* is reminiscent of the *refláes* associated with Jerusalem. Since the Jews of Jerusalem were known for their generosity, this *reflán* is a hint for others to give charity as well.

It is only a short step from Purim to Pesah. This reminds of a *reflán* that is half Hebrew, half Judeo-Spanish: *Purim Purim lanu, Pésah en la mano* (With Purim in our land, Pesah is at hand) (Diana Sarano, Izmir;* Moscona; Kolonomós). A *reflán* alluding to the elaborate preparations, special meals and great expense involved in the observance of Pesah is: *Pésah, parás sin heshbón* (Pesah, money without accounting) (Bosnia; Moshe Elazar, Jerusalem*). On the other hand, *Bendicha sea la limpieza de noche de Pésah* (Blessed be the cleanliness [that prevails] on the eve of Passover) (Saporta y Beja; Alkalay) because our homes would never be scrubbed so clean if we did not have to search for every bit of *hametz* and sweep it away before Pesah.

The frantic preparations for Passover somehow never get finished until just before the deadline set by the law. One *reflán* compares the last-minute rush to get ready for Passover with the work and worry of parents whose daughter is about to get married: *La fija i el Pésah no se eskapan asta la noche de Pésah* (Neither the daughter nor Pesah are ever ready before the [very] eve of Pesah) (Saporta y Beja). On the other hand, we are advised not to worry because in the end we always manage to be ready on time: *Ni Pésah sin masá ni ija* (or *ijos*) *sin kazar* (No Pesah ever comes without matzot nor is there any daughter [or are there any sons] who fails to get married) (Moscona has *ija*; Alkalay, *ijos*).

Two interesting *reflánes* are similar in wording but different in meaning. The most popular form is *Al Shefoh sintirésh (o oyiremos, o se sienten) las bozes* (In the prayer "Shefo" you will feel or "we will hear," or "are felt" the voices) (Saporta y Beja, Alkalay and Moscona, respectively). Here, the "voices" are interpreted as referring to the wails and screams of the sinners who will be punished by God at the hour of *redde rationem* (judgment and accounting). A similar *reflán* occurs in another, more original form: *Al Shofar oyerésh las bozes* (Stella Afumado, Istanbul*). This *reflán* can be rendered as, "In the shofar you will hear the voices," but the interpretation is not the same. This version alludes to the final blasts of the shofar at the end of Yom Kippur, and the "voices" are the cries of the Jews who avail themselves of this final opportunity to ask God's forgiveness for their sins. When a person is plagued by many worries, the *reflán*: *La nochada mal pasada i Selihot a la madrugada* (Spend a bad night, *selihot* at first light) (Saporta y Beja) advises him to rise up early the next morning and recite *selihot*, the special prayers for Divine forgiveness.

The holiday of Shavuot marks the end of the winter season for the Sephardim. *Si no viene Shavuot no te kites samarrón* (If Shavuot hasn't come, don't take off your furs) (Diana Sarano, Izmir;* Saporta y Beja), or *Si no viene el kante no te kites el mante* (If you are not yet singing *Ketuba a la ley,* keep your winter coat on for at least another day) (Yaakov Elazar, Jerusalem*). *Ketuba a la ley,* or *Kante,* is a hymn sung by Sephardim on Shavuot in honor of the Torah; it is a synecdoche symbolizing the holiday.

The fast of Tisha beAv, which commemorates the destruction of the Temple in Jerusalem, is the subject of abundant *reflán* material wherever Judeo-Spanish is spoken. Its use is ironic, as in *Ke darse mi ijo, ke sea en Tesá-Beav* (If my son makes a speech, let it be on Tisha beAv), obviously meaning that the father is displeased with his son's performance (Mosco Galimir, *Proverbios*; Bosnia), or *Nunka kaminó mi fijo, ke sea en noche de Tesabeá* (My son hasn't walked yet; may it be on the eve of Tisha beAv) (Saporta y Beja). Or, in even stronger terms, *Ke riyga mi kijo, ke sea en Nahamu* (May my son laugh, and let it be on Shabbat Nahamú) (Diana Sarano, Jerusalem*). Shabbat Nahamu is the "Sabbath of Consolation" immediately following Tisha beAv.

An expression used with reference to rare happenings is *A la Shemitá una vez* (Once in a *shemitah* period) (Julide Avzaradel, Milás*). *Shemitah* is the Sabbatical year, the "seventh year" during which fields in the Holy Land must be allowed to lie fallow.

The Jewish holiday cycle ends with Sukkot. The *reflán*: *Ken metió a Djohá en mi suká?* (Who put Joha into my *sukkah*?) (Diana Sarano, Izmir*) means that you don't want to have anything to do, or to become involved, with something or someone. Joha, the legendary fool already mentioned earlier, was not even a Jew; what business, then, does he have in my life?

The Haham

In the Judeo–Spanish world the *haham*, as rabbi of his community, is not only the official expounder of the Jewish faith, who is familiar with Jewish law, recites the prayers and acts as judge and arbitrator. He is also considered the wisest, most intelligent man in the whole community. (Hence the title *haham*, literally "wise man" or "sage," for rabbis in the Sephardic world to this day.) Nevertheless, the authority of the *haham* is derived from his community: *Haham sin keilá no vale* (A *haham* without a community counts for nothing) (Levy), and *Bueno darse el sinyor haham komo ay ken lo sienta* (The *haham*'s sermon is [only] as good as the people who listen to it) (Moscona).

The functions of the *haham* as a teacher are duly acknowledged: *Ambeza il haham lo ke no kere el talmid* (The *haham* can teach the student what the student doesn't want to learn) (Levy). This *reflán* and the one quoted in the preceding paragraph have a slightly ironic ring.

The *haham* is expected to be an impartial judge: *El Rav no djuzga si ne oye las dos partes* (A rabbi doesn't judge before he has heard both sides of the story) (Saporta y Beja). Note that this *reflán* refers to the *haham* as *rav*, "rabbi."

Reflánes about the *haham* sometimes contain a snide element: *El haham abolta lo oja por ande la kere* (The *haham* turns the page whenever he wishes) (Julia Shrem, Jerusalem*); this *reflán*, which is current among Sephardim in Jerusalem, suggests the possibility that a *haham* may know how to adapt religious requirements to suit his own needs, for the *haham* is not only wise but perhaps also a little shrewd. A downright negative *reflán*: *Haham i no de mi kal* ([He plays the] *haham* [even though] he isn't even from my my community) (Gaón), is used with reference to one who meddles in things that are none of his business.

When a Sephardic Jew wants to apologize for an error he has made, he does not say: *Errare humanum est* (To err is human) but: *I el haham se yerre en la Tevá* (Even a *haham* can make an error at the reader's stand) (Saporta y Beja; Galimir), or, as in Spanish Morocco, *en la Teba* (Benazeraf).

On a more serious note: *Mas vale rabino sin barva, ke barva sin rabino* (A rabbi without a beard is worth more than a beard without a rabbi) (Moscona); i.e., outward appearances do not always count.

In the olden days, the profession of *haham* seems to have had its material rewards, at least judging from the *reflán*: *Haham i merkader aligría para la mujer* (If a *haham* is also a businessman, his wife will be happy) (Diana Sarano, Jerusalem;* Levy; Saporta y Beja; Moscona; Galimir; *Bosnia*). If the *haham* spent a great deal of time away from home, his wife was happy because she could then attend to her housewifely chores without interference from her husband. The same thought is conveyed by *Los fijos al Rubí, el marido a charshi* (The sons are [away from home] with the rabbi; the husband is [also away] downtown) (Saporta y Beja; Alkalay); this last *reflán* also alludes to the role of the *haham* as a teacher of the young.

Biblical and Historical Figures

The proper names used in the Judeo-Spanish *reflán* are mostly Jewish names derived from Biblical or Jewish historical figures, or variants or corruptions of such names. The names employed are those that eventually became popular among Jews and became associated with certain ideas or character traits.

Reflánes and similes derived from Biblical literature are numerous and hardly require detailed explanation. *Azerse del Mordehay* (Act like Mordecai) (Diana Sarano, Jerusalem;* Moscona; Alkalay; Kolonomós) means: Listen carefully but pretend not to hear or understand. *Pensada de Amán* (Alkalay) or *de Paró* (Diana Sarano, Jerusalem*) (Thoughts of Haman, or of Pharaoh) are evil thoughts. *Males de Paró* (the troubles of Pharaoh) (Saporta y Beja) are the Ten Plagues of Egypt. *Anyos de Metushélah* (years of Methuselah) (Alkalay) are a great many years; *De Antiohós zmaní* (The days of Antiochus) (Moscona) implies great antiquity. *Kórah, ermano de Amalek* (Korah, brother of Amalek) (Diana Sarano, Jerusalem*) refers to a person or thing so evil that he or it can be compared only to the rebel Korah and the vile nation of Amalek. *Yermiá el marido, Yermiá la mujer* (A Jeremiah husband, a Jeremiah wife) (Saporta y Beja): a husband and wife who are both chronic complainers. *La mula de Pinhás ke no va ni adelantre ni atrás* is the mule of Pinhas, which moves neither forward nor backward (Saporta y Beja). A hospitable home is characterized as *kaza de Eliau Anavi* (the house of the Prophet Elijah) (Julide Avzaradel, Milás*), *kaza de Avram Avinu* (the house of our Father Abraham) (Itshak Nahum, Izmir*) or *kaza de Moshé Rabenu* (the house of Moses, our Teacher) (Edith Hasson, Istanbul*).

Todos vinimos d'Adam (We all come from Adam) (Kolonomós) reminds us that we are all made of flesh and blood; hence no man is better than anyone else. *Todos pekan, Moshé lo izo)* (Everyone sins, even Moses did) (Levy). So we can take comfort from the thought that even Moses, who was considered virtually perfect, fell victim to sin.

More about Moses: *Akontentose Moshé kon la parte ke le dio el Dio* (Moses was content with the portion God gave him) (Saporta y Beja); he did not complain even though he was denied his heart's desire; i.e., to enter the Promised Land. One should never despair, no matter what befalls: *Si Moshé murió, Adonay kedó* (Moses died, but God has remained) (Moscona; Levy; Kolonomós; Galimar). Moses was only human and therefore, like all men, had to die, but God lives forever and will always be ready to come to our aid.

When we suffer, we are not alone. Great figures in Jewish history, too, have suffered. Some *reflánes* put the blame for these sufferings on women. *Kon la mujer ni el Arambam salió abásh* (Not even RaMBaM* was able to prevail over his wife) (Alkalay) and *Aun Shimshón por su mujer kayó* (Even Samson fell on account of his wife) (Levy). Samson was regarded not only as a symbol of superhuman strength but also as a rescuer in the hour of peril (Judges 16:30): *En ora de peligro el ombre es Shimshón* (In the hour of danger Samson is the man) (Levy). Samson was also a man of vengeance; the very mention of his name suggested a person ready to take revenge even at the cost of his own life, causing countless others to perish with him: *Muera Shimshón kon kuantos son i no son* (Let Samson die along with some who are guilty and some who are not) (Diana Sarano, Jerusalem;* Saporta y Beja; *Bosnia*). Jephthah's daughter (Judges 11:35) symbolizes an irrevocable sacrifice made in vain: *Ben kah uven kah quay de la ija de Iftah* (In any event, woe to Jephthah's daughter) (*Bosnia*), or *Ben kah uben kah, boló la ija de Yivtah* (In any event, Jephthah's daughter is gone) (Moscona). These two *reflános* are often used as analogies to describe real-life situations.

To imply that someone was given a promise and discovers, too late, that he received something different from what he had been promised, there is the *reflán*: *Le aprometieron a Rahel, le dieron a Leá* (They promised him Rachel but they gave him Leah) (Alkalay), from the Biblical account of Jacob finding himself married to Leah when he had been promised Rachel, the woman he really loved (Genesis 29:25).

We will cite only a few *reflánes* in which popular Jewish names are used. *Si riyó Yusé, no savi purke* (If Joseph laughed, he didn't know why) (Kolonomós). *Estírate Issahar, si keres despozar* (If you want to get married, Issakhar, you have to make some effort) (Saporta y Beja). *Todo tiene Shimshón, solo le manka sarna i sarampión* (Samson has everything; all he needs now is the mange and the measles) (Levy; Saporta y Beja; Moscona; Kolonomós; *Bosnia*).

In some instances, it is clear that the name has no particular significance in the *reflán* but is used only for rhyming purposes; for instance, *Shimshón* (Samson) rhymes with *sarampión* (measles). In other cases, as already indicated earlier, the name of a Biblical figure is used in similes or *reflánes* to denote a personality trait; e.g., *Hana, la pensadera* (Hannah [I Samuel 1 and 2] in a pensive mood) (*Bosnia*) or *Yermiá, el yoroń* (Jeremiah the whiner). We do not know why Menahem is not portrayed as a likable character in the *reflán*. The *reflán* known to us makes him an ugly, devious individual: *Menahem el korkovado, echa la piedra i eskonde la mano* (Menahem, the hunchback, throws a rock and then hides his hand [so that no one should see who threw the rock]) (Menashe Hadjes, Izmir;* Saporta y Beja).

The classic sobriquet for a Sephardic Jew is Moses, which often takes the form of Moshiko, Moshon or Mushon. Many *reflánes* have Moshiko as the protagonist. In speaking of an idler, one may say, *En ke se la va al tiyo Moshé el día? En kitar i sakudir la*

---

*I.e., R. Moses ben Maimon (Maimonides), considered the greatest Jewish philosopher and sage of his era.

barva (How does Uncle Moshe spend his day? Shaving and shaking off the hair from his beard) (Moscona). Of one so evil that he seems beyond redemption it is said that *Moshiko se fue a Safed, mas negro vino de lo ke se fue* (Moshiko went [on a pilgrimage] to Safed but came back even more evil than he was when he left) (Saporta y Beja; Diana Sarano, Izmir*); i.e., not even a pilgrimage to a holy shrine could make him a better person. If we suspect that a friend has been guilty of making slightly exaggerated statements, we may say, *De tanto ke te kero bien, Moshiko, ke te kito el ojiko* (Much as I love you, little Moe, though I don't know why, I'm going to take out your little eye) (Diana Sarano, Izmir*).

The Judeo-Spanish Philosophy of Life

The corpus of Judeo-Spanish *reflánes* on Jewish themes reflects a particular philosophy of life, sometimes simple, sometimes a little more sophisticated.

El Bet Amigdásh se destruyó, la keilá kedó (The Holy Temple was destroyed, but the community has remained) (Levy) conveys a message similar to that of *Si Moshé murió, Adonay kedó*: Even when we have suffered a cruel loss, we still have something left to which to cling. Another *reflán* urging acceptance of a blow of fate is *Es lo k'es: boré peri aetz* (Things must be as they must be; [blessed be He] Who created the fruit of the tree) (Diana Sarano, Izmir*). When you cannot change things, you must accept them and bless God, giving thanks to Him that nothing worse befell.

A Sephardic Jew never leaves his home without kissing the *mezuzah* on his doorpost. As the *reflán* puts it, *Beza la mizuza i metité a kaminar* (Kiss the mezuzah and get going) (Levy). The mezuzah contains a parchment scroll with the *Shema*, the Jewish declaration of faith, inscribed upon it. The *Shema* and the mezuzah protect the Jew from all evil: *Dí la Shemá i fuité del Satán* (Recite the *Shema* and run from Satan) (Levy). God sends His blessings to any home where sincere faith and piety abide: *Onde ay Baruhú ay berahá* (Blessings come [to any place] where God is blessed) (Renée Arochas, Jerusalem*).

However, piety based on the letter of the Law is not enough. You must be genuinely honest and good and not be among those who *beza mezuzás i arrova pitas* (kiss mezuzot but steal *pitas*) (Diana Sarano, Izmir* et al. in various forms). Another *reflán* condemns those who recite their prayers punctiliously but whose heart is not pure: *Arvi i minha i korason trefá* (Evening prayers and afternoon prayers but a heart that is *trefe*) (Diana Sarano, Izmir*). One *reflán* pokes fun at people given to excessive praying: *Tanto dizimos amén ke mos kaye el talet* (We said "Amen" so many times that our prayer shawl fell off our shoulders) (Ester Levy, Jerusalem;* Saporta y Beja; Alkalay; *Bosnia*). Sephardim generally believe that anything carried to extremes is ludicrous and can be harmful.

How should a Jew conduct himself in his daily life? Above all, he should never forget that *La para se auadá (avodá) zará* (Money worship is idol worship) (Renée Arochas,

Jerusalem*). A Jew must be able to defend himself against his enemies: *Piedra i Pasuk* ([You need] a rock and a verse [from Scripture]) (Benazeraf; Saporta y Beja). Prayer alone is not enough to save you from the hands of an enemy.

On a more humorous note, we are advised not to commit petty sins that bring no gain to anyone: *Para comer hazir, comerlo gordo* (If you must eat pork, make it a really fat pig) (Benazeraf).

On a higher level of Jewish philosophy, the tone of the *reflán* may be light and satirical, too, but sometimes it becomes serious and didactic.

Man is endowed with a free will; he can change his fate by the manner in which he conducts himself. *La sedaká abalda la gezerá* (Charity nullifies the evil decree) (A. Sarano). Charity is a virtue which, along with prayer and penitence, can cancel preordained calamity. As already noted earlier, the Jew does not consider himself a victim of blind fate; he can influence his destiny by his actions.

Charity is not merely a matter of private concern; it can have a positive influence on the entire community. *Sedaká i bienfezensia enaltesen la nasión* (Charity and good deeds ennoble the entire nation) (B., D.D., S.P.; *Bosnia*) because every Jew is responsible for all the other Jews in whose midst he lives. But never give charity if it does not come from your heart: *El dar i la sedaká ke vengan de buena voluntá* (Giving and charity should come from good will) (Saporta y Beja). Nor need you fear that you will become poor from giving too much charity: *Azer sedaká nunka amengua la bolsa* (Giving charity never shrinks your purse) (D.D., S.P.; *Bosnia*). On the other hand, *Sedaká sin hohmá es komo una muchacha siega* (Charity unwisely given is like a girl who is blind) (David Benvenisti, *Hebrew Words in Judeo-Spanish*; D.D., S.P.; *Bosnia*).

A poor person should not be too proud to ask for help. *Ken demanda sedaká no se echa sin senar* (One who asks for charity will not go without supper) (Ester Levy, Jerusalem*). However, it is not right to rely completely on charity. *Vende bamia, vende halvá i no asperes a nedavá* (Sell okra, sell halvah but don't hope for a handout) (D.D.; *Bosnia*). Any work, no matter how menial, is preferable to relying on charity.

Charity without true penitence will not work to change a person's fate. *Pur azer tanit no se salva l'alma* (Fasting alone won't save your soul) (Levy).

Replacing a Torah scroll into the Ark during services is considered one of the most important *mitzvot* (religious acts). The expression *meter Sefer en el Kal* (putting the Scroll back into the Ark) (Stella Afumado, Istanbul*) is used with reference to any exceptionally good deed. Speaking of *mitzvot*, and in a more humorous vein, *Arovar del ladrón es mitsva* (It's a mitzvah to rob a thief) (Moscona). This last *reflán* is quoted with a smile.

The most cherished wish of every Jew is to go to Jerusalem—in the olden days in order to die there, today in order to be able to live there. *Ken muncho pensa no se va a Yerushaláyim* (He who thinks too much will never make it to Jerusalem) (Stella Afumado, Istanbul;* Saporta y Beja; Moscona; Alkalay) is a *reflán* urging a person not to have too many second thoughts when he has an opportunity to carry out a plan or fulfill a long-cherished desire, for else he may miss the opportunity.

The Jew believes that after death he will be sent either to heaven or to hell. *Si el Ganeden está serrado, el Ginnam está siempre avierto!* (If the Garden of Eden [Paradise] is closed, *Gehinnam* [hell] is always open!) (Alkalay). It may be difficult to get to heaven, but there is never a lack of sinners bound for hell. If a person says, *El paliko salió de Ganeden* (This little stick left Paradise (i.e., heaven]) (Moscona) because it was intended to punish sinners on earth, he should be told, *El paliko salió de Ginnam para enderechar al benadam* (The little stick left *Gehinnam* [hell] to set man straight and make him well) (A. Sarano). It is not pleasant to be disciplined by a stick, but it has its uses when it makes the victim a better person. So even hell has its positive aspects.

The Jew yearns for the coming of the Messiah. The Sephardim say, *Ke venga el Mashiah, ke sea en nuestros dias* (May the Messiah come in our lifetime) (Diana Sarano, Izmir*). At the same time, the advent of the Messiah is anticipated with some trepidation because of the wars and catastrophes which, according to tradition, must precede the Messianic era. Hence the *reflán*: *Ke venga el Mashiah, ke no sea en nuestros dias* (May the Messiah come, but *not* in our lifetime) (Diana Sarano, Izmir*).

Yet the Jew never ceases to hope for peace and final deliverance from evil, as expressed in the following two *refláns*: *Sol i llobiendo, Mashiah biniendo* (Rain and sun, the Messiah will come) (Benazeraf), and *Luvia i sol, rihmisión para los Djidiós* (Sun and rain, the Jews will be delivered from pain) (Diana Sarano, Izmir*). Each time the Jew beholds a rainbow in the sky, he sees it as the symbol of eternal hope.

In studying the Jewish themes in the Judeo-Spanish *reflán* we obtain many insights into the essence of the Sephardic world, from east to west. We see the Sephardic Jew trusting in God, obeying the religious laws of Judaism and cherishing tradition with profound love and respect. But he does all this with sound moderation, free of all extremism. Furthermore, he is blessed with a healthy measure of self-criticism based on wisdom and on a remarkable sense of humor.

Basically, then, the watchword of Sephardic Judaism is *Bive i desha bivir*, "Live and let live," reflecting a mentality of genuine tolerance and love for all mankind.

Translated from the Ladino by Jane Mushabac

BIBLIOGRAPHY

Arié Alkalay, *Dichos i refránes sefaradies*, Edition of the Comunidad Sefardita de Jerusalen y el Centro de Intercalar el Patrimonio Judeo-Sefardita, Ministry of Education and Culture, Jerusalem, 1984.

Raphael Benazeraf, *Refranero, Recueil de Proverbes Judeo-Espanols du Maroc*, Paris, 1975.

David Benvenisti, *Hebrew Words in Judeo-Spanish* (Hebrew), Jerusalem, 1984.

D'Arbela-Annaratone-Cammelli, *Vocabolario Latino-Italiano, Italiano-Latino*, Milan, Signorelli, 1950.

Mosco Galimir, *Proverbios*, Albert Martin, Inc., USA, 1951.

Moshé David Gaón, *Spices from Spain* (Hebrew), Jerusalem, Keter, 1989.

Źamila Kolonomós, *Proverbs, Sayings and Tales of the Sephardi Jews of Macaedonia*, Belgrade, Federation of Jewish Communities in Yugoslavia, 1978.

Isaac Jack Levy, prologue to *The Study of the Refranero Sefardi*, New York, Las Americas Publishing, 1969.

Itshak Moscona, *Pniné Sfarad*, Tel Aviv, Sifriat Maariv, 1981.

Enrique Saporta y Beja, *Refránes de los Judios Sefardis*, Barcelona, Ameller Ediciones, 1978.

Proverbs and Sayings of the Sephardi Jews of Bosnia and Herzegovina, Belgrade, Federation of Jewish Communities in Yugoslavia, 1976.

PLATE I Long view of the Ottoman empire gallery, showing the Moorish archway outlining the Turkish Rabbi's study. The color-coded ceiling stripes define the five areas of the exhibition.

PLATE 2 Long view of the Western Europe gallery, leading to the Portuguese Synagogue environment.

PLATE 3 Long view of the New World gallery. The model of Newport's Touro Synagogue is on the left; Amsterdam's Portuguese Synagogue is on the right.

PLATE 4 Long view of the West corridor linking all five areas.

PLATE 5 Our alert photographer captured this surreal scene during installation: the Balkan brides seem to be encountering the exhibition.

PLATE 6 Lectern cover, Turkey, 18th–19th century (detail). Cat. no. 69.

PLATE 7 View of the Dowry room environment. Ottoman empire, 19th–20th century. The lavish display of the bridal trousseau (*asugar*) was a major component of Ottoman Jewish pre-nuptial celebrations.

PLATE 8 Lira Society banner, Sarajevo, Yugoslavia, 1921 (obverse and reverse). Cat. no. 73.

PLATE 9 Hanukkah lamp for a Rabbinical emissary, Syria, 1901/2. Cat. no. 265.

PLATE 10 View of the "Women and Home" vitrine in the North Africa gallery. Above are Hanukkah lamps.

PLATE 11 Long view of the North Africa gallery showing the manuscript vitrine in the foreground against a painted mural of the Nahon synagogue interior.

PLATE 12 View of the Moroccan wedding environment, 19th–20th century. The bride and groom wear traditional ceremonial costumes.

PLATE 13 The Ben Oliel Family, Tangier, ca. 1940s. Cat. no. 525.

PLATE 14 Torah crown, Algeria, 19th century. Cat. no. 321.

PLATE 15 View of the Portuguese Synagogue environment, Amsterdam, 16th–18th century. Torah ornaments and ceremonial objects from Amsterdam's Portugees-Israëlietische Gemeente. The majestic Augsburg laver is in the foreground.

PLATE 16 Hanukkah lamp of the Portugees-Israëlietische Gemeente, Amsterdam, 1795. Cat. no. 555.

PLATE 17 View of the 19th century America environment. Furnishings and costumes from the Civil War era belonging to a Sephardic family which emigrated to America in the 17th century.

PLATE 18 Portrait miniature of Charity Hays Solis, America, early 19th century. Cat. no. 733.

PLATE 19 View of the Turkish Rabbi environment, Ottoman empire, 19th–20th century. In the Ottoman empire, rabbis were appointed by the Sultan and wore official uniforms and decorations.

CATALOGUE
OF THE EXHIBITION

NOTE TO THE READER

Bibliographical references in the catalogue entries lead the reader to additional specialized information and comparisons. The term "References" is used for publications of the specific object and general discussions; "Cf." notes comparisons of similar artifacts and specific types. Abbreviated references are explained in full in the bibliography on pages 395–403. Maximum dimensions are listed in inches in the following order: length or height, width, depth or diameter. Omissions, such as standard honorifics, within the translations of inscriptions are indicated by ellipses.

Transliterations of Hebrew and the spelling of terms and proper names follow the *Encyclopaedia Judaica*, with the following exceptions: (1) no diacritical marks are used and some spellings have been altered to clarify the Hebrew character employed; (2) names are transliterated according to Hebrew pronunciation, except when an individual was best known by a particular Latin form; (3) terms follow the *Style Book of Yeshiva University*, New York, 1980. Transliterated terms in languages other than Hebrew follow common usage.

Biblical translations primarily follow the new Jewish Publication Society of America editions (1974, 1978, 1982), with some emendations. Authors of catalogue essays, at times, chose particular translations, spellings or bibliographical methods specific to their topics.

An asterisk next to a catalogue entry indicates that a photograph of this object appears in the Catalogue of the Exhibition.

GOLDEN AGE, EXPULSION
& INQUISITION

SPAIN · PORTUGAL

. . .
Hear O earth and heaven
And I will weep many tears
For the destruction of thousands
From the day I left Jerusalem

There will be an especially great wail
For the year 1391 of the destruction
For the community of Seville was destroyed
And many communities in Castile

And the communities of the people of Andalusia and Provincia
Were struck by evil
Catalonia was disgraced
Together with Aragon

Judah and the people of Israel
Depart from evil
Perhaps the Almighty will have compassion
And send the Redeemer to you

The Son of David will come to you
He will build the sanctuary of the Lord
There you will all praise him
Blessed be He who spoke and the world came to be

YEHUDAH BEN DAVID (David ibn Yahya, 14th c.)

I

SPAIN AND PORTUGAL:
GOLDEN AGE, EXPULSION AND INQUISITION

I LA BLANCA SYNAGOGUE MODEL*

Toledo, Spain, ca. 1200. Architect unknown. 36 x 48 x 19 in. Collection of Yeshiva University Museum, New York, endowed by Erica and Ludwig Jesselson, 89.85.

The La Blanca Synagogue is an outstanding example of both the style and the tragic fate of Spain's Mudéjar synagogues. It was one of many Jewish houses of worship built during the 13th century under the sympathetic rule of the Christian kings of Castile who conquered the land from the Muslim Moors. By the 14th century that era of optimism had come to an end, and subsequent centuries brought waves of persecution in which many of these synagogues were destroyed or taken over by the Catholic Church. La Blanca, among the grandest to survive the purges, was stripped of its Judaic elements in the early 15th century and subsequently converted into the convent and church of Santa Maria La Blanca.

Architecturally, the surviving building exemplifies the Mudéjar tradition—a combination of Moorish elements and Romanesque prototypes favored by the Christian conquerors. La Blanca's stark unadorned facades recall Romanesque sources, while the richly embellished interior indicates a strong Moorish influence. Though hardly grand spatially (85' x 62'), the interior's five-aisle plan nonetheless projects a sense of grandeur. The aisles are separated by 24 octagonal piers which support 28 horseshoe arches whose capitals are lavishly ornamented with pine-cone motifs. This powerful display of structure is further enhanced by a detailed frieze and an upper-story gallery over the central three aisles which may have housed a women's gallery. Scholars cannot ascertain the original synagogue seating plan nor the forms of its *bimah* and Ark.

In 1851 the La Blanca Synagogue was declared a national monument by the Spanish government.

REFERENCE: Krinsky, pp. 331–38.

2 IMPRESSION OF THE PERSONAL SEAL OF R. MOSHE BEN NAHMAN

(Known as Nahmanides or by the Hebrew acronym RaMBaN)

Eretz Israel, 1267–1270(?). Polymer impression of cast copper seal. Hebrew inscription: Moshe s[on of] R[abbi] Nahman r[estful] s[oul of] Gerona [be] strong. Seal: 11/16 x 7/8 in. diam. Collection of the Israel Museum, Jerusalem, 105/215.

The seal was found in 1972 at Tell Kisan in the Acre plain. The Hebrew script of the seal, in a typical Spanish hand, is similar to 13th- and 14th-century Hebrew inscriptions discovered in Catalonia, the Spanish province where Nahmanides was born, in Barcelona and Gerona (his native town) and environs.

The seal differs from most medieval Spanish and West European Hebrew seals in its lack of ornamentation or depiction. The handle resembles other contemporaneous seals in its simplicity.

Nahmanides fled to Eretz Israel following the increased pressure upon King Jaime I of Aragon to punish him for having published his arguments in his well-known disputation at Barcelona (1263), in which he successfully defended the Jewish faith from attacks by the convert Pablo Christiani. Nahmanides arrived at Acre in the year 1267. Later he arrived in Jerusalem and found the city in ruins and almost without Jews. A year later he returned to settle in Acre, which during the 13th century had the largest and most important Jewish community in the country.

3 KEYS TO THE CITY OF SEVILLE*

Spain, mid-13th century (19th century facsimile). Bronze: cast. 7 1/3 x 6 1/16 in. Hebrew, Arabic and Latin inscription: The King of Kings shall open, the King of all the land shall come. Collection of the Cathedral of Seville.

When Alfonso X (1252–1284) captured the city of Seville, the Jewish community presented him with symbolic keys to the city, of which these are 19th-century copies. Known as Alfonso the Wise, this ruler was a patron of Jewish scholars and scientists. The code known as the *Siete Partidas* was produced under his auspices. Though it guaranteed the Jews physical security and freedom of worship, this code ordered the strict enforcement of the usual anti-Jewish restrictions, including the wearing of the Jewish badge, and authorized ritual murder trials. Toward the end of his reign, Alfonso's attitude toward the Jews changed for the worse. In 1279 he ordered the imprisonment of all Jewish tax farmers and, two years later, a mass arrest of Jews in return for an exorbitant ransom.

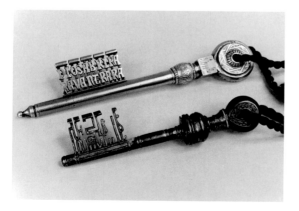

3

MEDIEVAL SPANISH MANUSCRIPT FRAGMENTS

(cat. nos. 4–13)

These manuscript fragments were chosen from a significant group of documents recently discovered in Spanish archival collections, and are being exhibited for the first time. They survived because they were used as binding material for other books, and in this manner were preserved.

The variety of texts found in these fragments reveals the nature of the scholarly and communal activities of medieval Spanish Jewry. The heir of the Babylonian tradition, Spain was a great center for Talmudic study. Iberian rabbinic scholarship is famed for codes, exegesis, grammatical analysis and mysticism. The symbiosis of Islamic and Jewish cultures produced great works of philosophy, medicine and poetry. The Jewish community was highly organized, and individual Jews were deeply involved in science, finance and statesmanship. The scholarship and creativity of medieval Spanish Jewry created the "Golden Age" and provided the basis for the continuity of Sephardic literary and scholastic tradition after 1492.

4 FRAGMENT OF A CODEX

(Exodus 9)*

Spain, 14th century. Ink on parchment. Collection of the Arxiu capitular de Girona (Cathedral Archives), Gerona, Spain.

This manuscript is typical of Spanish Bible texts with Masora Magna and Parva. This type of text was used to follow and check the reading from the Torah.

5 FRAGMENT FROM PIRKEI AVOT (Ethics of the Fathers)

Spain, 14th century. Ink on paper. Collection of the Arxiu capitular de Girona (Cathedral Archives), Gerona, Spain.

6 FRAGMENT OF BABYLONIAN TALMUD, TRACTATE AVODAH ZARAH, 62a–65b

Spain, 14th century. Ink on parchment. Collection of the Arxiu capitular de Girona (Cathedral Archives), Gerona, Spain.

This manuscript text includes all of the mishnayot for the chapter *Ha-sokher et ha-poel* preceding the Talmudic discussion, and not the more usual arrangement of each mishnah immediately followed by the Talmudic text.

7 FRAGMENT OF PEIRUSH RASHI AL MASEKHET SOTAH

(Rashi's commentary on Babylonian Talmud, Tractate *Sotah*, 9b–10b)

R. Shlomo Yitzhaki (acronym RaSHI; 1040–1105). Spain, 14th century. Ink on paper. Collection of the Arxiu capitular de Girona (Cathedral Archives), Gerona, Spain.

Rashi lived in Troyes, France, but his commentary circulated very quickly, so that by the early 13th century it was used by almost every Talmudic scholar.

8 FRAGMENT OF PEIRUSH RASHI AL MASEKHET GITTIN

(Rashi's commentary on Babylonian Talmud, Tractate *Gittin*, 38a–39a)

Spain, 14th century. Ink on paper. Collection of the Arxiu capitular de Girona (Cathedral Archives), Gerona, Spain.

9 FRAGMENT OF MISHNEH TORAH, HILKHOT ISSUREI BIAH (14, 15, 18)

Maimonides (R. Moshe ben Maimon; acronym RaMBaM; 1135–1204). Spain, 14th century. Ink on paper. *Collection of the Arxiu capitular de Girona (Cathedral Archives), Gerona, Spain.*

Mishneh Torah, also known as *Yad Hazakah* (see also cat. no. 14), is the Hebrew compendium of Jewish law written by Maimonides, the Cordoba-born physician, philosopher and halakhist. Maimonides lived briefly in Eretz Israel, but spent most of his active years in Egypt.

10 FRAGMENT OF HIDDUSHEI HA-RAMBAN AL MASEKHET SHEVUOT

(Nahmanides' novellae on Babylonian Talmud, Tractate *Shevuot*, 41b–42a)

Nahmanides (R. Moshe ben Nahman; acronym RaMBaN; 1194–1270). Spain, 14th century. Ink on paper. Collection of the Arxiu capitular de Girona (Cathedral Archives), Gerona, Spain.

Nahmanides' works of biblical exegesis, Talmudic scholarship, poetry, responsa and philosophy are masterpieces of rabbinic literature. In the mid-13th century, Gerona became the first center of kabbalism in Spain. Nahmanides is renowned as both a halakhist and kabbalist (see also cat. nos. 2 and 11).

11 FRAGMENT OF HIDDUSHEI HA-RAMBAN AL MASEKHET AVODAH ZARAH

(Nahmanides' novellae on Babylonian Talmud, Tractate *Avodah Zarah*, 13b–15a)

Nahmanides (R. Moshe ben Nahman; acronym RaMBaN; 1194–1270). Spain, 14th century. Ink on paper. Collection of the Ajuntament de Girona Arxiu Historic de la Ciutat (Civic Archives), Gerona, Spain.

Prior to 1492, Nahmanides' novellaes occupied a prime role in Talmud study (alongside Rashi's commentary, see cat. no. 7), similar to the importance of the *tosafot* in the post-Expulsion period.

12 FRAGMENT OF SEFER MIVHAR HA-PENINIM

(Shaar ha-Hokhma, Shaar Bikur ha-Ohavim, Shaar Bikur Holim, Shaar ha-Hanaah)

Spain, 14th century. Ink on paper. Collection of the Arxiu capitular de Girona (Cathedral Archives), Gerona, Spain.

This Hebrew manuscript of *Mivhar ha-Peninim* ("A Choice of Pearls") contains a collection of epigrams and wise sayings with slight variations from the more usual known text. The original Arabic text has been attributed to R. Shlomo ben Yehuda ibn Gabirol (ca. 1021–ca. 1056) and was probably translated by R. Yehuda ben R. Shaul ibn Tibbon (ca. 1120–after 1190), the translator of Yehuda ha-Levi's *Kuzari* and Saadiah's *Emunot ve-De ot*.

13 FRAGMENT OF A SYNAGOGUE PINKAS

(Record book)

Spain, 14th century. Ink on paper. Collection of the Arxiu capitular de Girona (Cathedral Archives), Gerona, Spain.

Various communal expenditures and donations are recorded in the page from a record book.

14 MISHNEH TORAH

Maimonides (1135–1204). Spain, 15th century. Ink on parchment. Collection of the Jewish National and University Library, Jerusalem, Yah. Ms. Heb. 8/1.

This manuscript contains *Sefer Avodah* ("Book of Worship") and *Sefer Korbanot* ("Book of Offerings") of Maimonides' important Hebrew compendium of Jewish law (see cat. no. 9). The square gold script and delicate blue filigree background seen in the displayed opening (*Sefer Avodah* IX) illustrate the artistry of Spanish medieval Hebrew illuminated manuscripts.

15 IBN MUSA BIBLE

Lisbon, 1475. Scribe: Shmuel ben Shmuel ibn Musa. Ink and paint on vellum; leather binding. Collection of the Klau Library, Hebrew Union College–Jewish Institute of Religion, Cincinnati, Ohio, Ms. 2.

This manuscript contains the Pentateuch, *haftarot*, megillot and *Megillat Antiochus*, a text which was read on Hanukkah in some synagogues. The text is decorated with elegant arabesques and is an example of the greatness of medieval Iberian Jewish artistry. The Spanish-style Mudéjar (Hispano-Moresque) box binding is an unusual feature. Similar bindings are found on four other Hebrew manuscripts from Portugal and suggest that a binder trained in Toledo worked exclusively for Jewish patrons in Lisbon between 1475 and 1492, before the worst anti-Jewish outbreaks.

The scribe has been identified as Shmuel ben Musa, who established a printing press in Zamora, Spain, in 1484 or 1487. Few Hebrew scribes were able to become printers, due to the great expense involved in establishing a press. However, they probably worked with the newly developed technology, as seen from the scribal practices carried over into the setting of type in Hebrew incunabula.

REFERENCES: L. Avrin, "The Box Binding in the Klau Library Hebrew Union College," *Studies in Bibliography and Booklore* 17 (1989), 27–35; L. Avrin, "The Sephardi Box Binding," *Scripta Hierosolymitana 29* (1989), 27–43.

16 PEIRUSH HA-BERAKHOT VE-HA-TEFILLOT

(Commentary on the Blessings and the Prayers)

David ben Yosef Abudarham (14th century). Lisbon, November 25, 1489. Printer: Eliezer Toledano. Ink on paper: printed. Private Collection.

This liturgical commentary, also known as *Sefer Abudarham*, includes calendrical and astronomical tables. Astronomy was a subject of special interest to Portuguese Jewry. A Jewish printer issued a Latin edition of Avraham Zacuto's astronomical tables at Leiria, a work which Columbus took with him on his voyage to the New World.

Printing was first introduced to Portugal in 1487 by Jews at Faro. The Hebrew press at Lisbon was the first printing press to be established in the Portuguese capital. The materials of the Lisbon Hebrew press continued to be used after the expulsion of the Jews from Portugal in 1497. Don Yehudah Guedaliah, foreman or typesetter of the Lisbon press, used some of Toledano's materials in a press at Salonika, ca. 1512. Refugee Jewish printers from Lisbon established a press at Fez, Morocco. A line-by-line reprint of this Lisbon *Abudarham* printed there in 1516 is the earliest dated book from the first printing press in Africa. The promise of modern Jewish life in Spain and Portugal can be seen in Iberian Hebrew incunabula (15th-century printed books), a future of development encouraged by technology and cross-fertilization that was destroyed by the decrees of 1492 and 1497. *(fig. 4)*

REFERENCE: New York, Pierpont Morgan Library, *Hebraica from the Valmadonna Trust*, exhibition catalogue, by B. Sabin Hill, 1989, cat. no. 12.

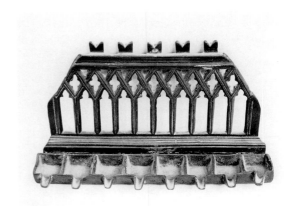

17

17 HANUKKAH LAMP*

Spain (?), 15th century. Bronze: cast. Einhorn Collection, Tel Aviv.

This lamp is based on Gothic architecture, with an arcade of elongated trefoil arches topped by windows and battlements.

REFERENCE: *EJ*, 7, col. 1305, fig. 24.

18 PORTOLAN CHART

Alexandria, Egypt, 1500. Judah Abenzara. Ink and paint on parchment. Italian inscription: I, Judah Abenzara, [made this map] in Alexandria in the year 1500. 22 x 31½ in. Collection of Hebrew Union College Library, Cincinnati, Ohio.

A portolan is a chart of the coastlines of oceans designed for the use of navigators. This chart includes most of the regions covered in "The Sephardic Journey" from Spain north to the Black Sea; east to the Red Sea; south to the Atlas Mountains, and west to the British Isles. Important harbors are painted in red and show Christian and Muslim coats of arms. The three fortified cities are Venice, Genoa and the islands of the Danube, a common feature of contemporary Catalan portolans.

The island of Majorca was a center of maritime trade, drawing on both Muslim and Latin culture and science. A school of Jewish cartographers and mapmakers considered unsurpassed for their knowledge of the arts of navigation, geography and cartography, flourished there during the 14th and 15th centuries.

The artist, Juda Abenzara (Ibn Zara), probably lived in Egypt from ca. 1497, when he signed and dated a portolan now in the Vatican Library, Rome (Borgiana vii). Another map by Abenzara, no longer extant, was executed in Safed. He probably came from the region of Catalonia or Majorca in Spain, and learned mapmaking and illumination there. Leaving Spain ca. 1492, he may have traveled to Italy and thence to Cairo and Safed. Cecil Roth regards this as evidence that cultured Spanish exiles came to Eretz Israel within a decade after the expulsion of the Jews from Spain.

REFERENCES: C. Roth, "Judah Abenzara's Map of the Mediterranean World, 1500," *Studies in Bibliography and Booklore*, IX, no. 2–3, 1970, pp. 116–120; Montreal, Canada, The Jewish Public Library, *Planets, Potions and Parchments*, exhibition catalogue, B. Levy, 1990.

19 AUTOS DE FEE [sic]

Palma de Majorca, 1691. Ink on paper. 8⅞ x 5¾ in. Collection of Yeshiva University Museum, New York, gift of Herbert M. Honig in memory of Alexander and Esther Honig, 87.55.

An *auto da fé* (roughly "religious act") was the ceremony at which the Inquisition pronounced the sentence on persons found guilty of its charges. This ceremony was generally held with great pomp at a prominent church or central square (see cat. no. 20). Contrary to popular notions, the burning of the condemned was not an official part of the ceremony. Since the Church did not wish to be formally associated with the shedding of blood, the condemned were subsequently turned over to secular authorities for execution.

These handwritten pages contain a moving account of four *autos da fé* held in Majorca on March 1, May 1, May 6 and June 2, 1691, with a list of specific charges against the condemned. Although the Jewish community had officially ceased to exist after massacres and forced conversions in 1391, an "underground" Jewish community had survived. As the result of these *autos da fé* thirty-seven people were burned at the stake; three of them were burned alive having chosen to die *al kiddush ha-Shem* (for the sanctification of God's name) rather than confessing guilt and repentance to the Inquisitors for having remained Jews.

The last recorded *auto da fé* took place in Valencia, Spain, as recently as 1826.

REFERENCES: C. Roth, *A History of the Marranos*, Philadelphia, 1932, pp. 93–96; J. M. Markham, "After 300 Years, Inquisition Still Taints Some Majorcans," *The New York Times*, April 25, 1978; G. Levenson, "Mallorca's 'Lost' Jews," *The Jewish Week & The American Examiner Inc.*, September 2, 1983, p. 34.

20 IUGEMENT DE L'INQUISITION DANS LA GRANDE PLACE DE MADRID

(The Inquisitors pronounce sentence in the Great Square of Madrid)

[and] LA PROCESSION DE L'INQUISITION À GOA

(Procession of the Inquisition at Goa)

London, 1733. Artist: Bernard Picart (1673–1733). "Historical Memoirs Relating to the Inquisition," The Ceremonies and Religious Customs of the Various Nations of the Known World, vol. 2, no. 30. Black and white engravings. Impression: 13⅛ x 8½ in. Einhorn Collection, Tel Aviv.

Among the tribunals of the Spanish Inquisition were those located in Madrid, Barcelona, Cordova, Seville, Toledo and Palma de Majorca (see cat. no. 19). Goa, India, was the site of a branch of the Portuguese Inquisition.

REFERENCES: Rubens, *Iconography*, 1981, nos. 2071, 2072.

21 LA SALLE DE L'INQUISITION

(Great Hall of the Inquisition)

[and] DIVERSES MANIÈRES DONT LE ST OFICE FAIT DONNER LA QUESTION

(Various methods of torture inflicted by the Holy Office)

London, 1733. Artist: Bernard Picart (1673–1733). Engraver: C. du Bosc. "Historical Memoirs Relating to the Inquisition," The Ceremonies and Religious Customs of the Various Nations of the Known World, vol. 2, No. 29. Black and white engravings. Impression: 13½ x 8½ in. Einhorn Collection, Tel Aviv.

It is often forgotten that the methods used by the Inquisition were those in everyday use by the secular legal powers throughout Europe.

REFERENCES: Rubens, *Iconography*, 1981, nos. 2069, 2070; Held, *Inquisition*.

22 L'AUTO-DA FÉ OU L'ACTE DE FOI

(The *Auto da Fé* or Religious Act)

[and] SUPLICE DES CONDAMNEZ

(Punishment of the Condemned)

London, 1733. Artist: Bernard Picart (1673–1733). "Historical Memoirs Relating to the Inquisition," The Ceremonies and Religious Customs of the Various Nations of the Known World, vol. 2, no. 31. Black and white engravings. Impression: 13⅛ x 8½ in. Einhorn Collection, Tel Aviv.

This series was originally engraved by Picart during 1722–1723.

REFERENCE: Rubens, *Iconography*, 1981, no. 2073.

23 HOMME CONDAMNÉ AU FEU, MAIS QUI L'A ÉVITÉ PAR SA CONFESSION

(A man condemned to the flames, but who has avoided them by confessing his guilt)

[and] FILLE QUI A ÉVITÉ LE FEU EN AVOUANT APRES SON JUGEMENT

(A maiden who has escaped the flames by confessing after her sentence)

[and] FEMME CONDAMNÉE PAR L'INQUISITION Á ÊTRE BRULÉE VIVE

(A woman sentenced by the Inquisition to be burned alive)

[and] HOMME QUI VA ÊTRE BRULÉ PAR ARREST DE L'INQUISITION

(A man who will be burned by decree of the Inquisition)

London, 1733. Artist: Bernard Picart (1673–1733). "Historical Memoirs Relating to the Inquisition," The Ceremonies and Religious Customs of the Various Nations of the Known World, vol. 2, no. 32. Black and white engravings. Impression: 13¼ x 8½ in. Einhorn Collection, Tel Aviv.

REFERENCES: Rubens, *Iconography*, 1981, nos. 2075–2078; Held, *Inquisition*, fig. 59.

24 DEPUTATION OF JEWS BEFORE FERDINAND & ISABELLA

New York, 1869. Black and white engraving. Image: 5¼ x 7½ in. The Moldovan Family Collection, New York.

The court of King Ferdinand and Queen Isabella of Spain included Jews who had remained true to their religion. Among them was Don Abraham Seneor (ca. 1412–ca. 1493), Chief Rabbi of Castile, assessor of Jewish taxes thoughout the unified kingdom of Spain and treasurer of the Hermandad, a military organization that insured security and order in the kingdom. There were also respected scientists, such as the astronomer Avraham Zacuto (1452–ca. 1515) whose patron was Gonzalo de Vivero, Bishop of Sala-manca, and Don Juan de Zuñiga, grand master of the Order of Knights of Alcátara, whose work was used by Christopher Columbus and Vasco da Gama.

History painting, considered the most important genre of painting, was favored for its educational impact. This print, probably based on a contemporary (19th-century) painting, is an imaginative rendering of a deputation of important Jews pleading with Ferdinand and Isabella to end the travails of the Jews of Spain.

25 FLAG OF THE KINGDOM OF ARAGON

Spain, 20th century. Cotton: printed. Collection of Yeshiva University Museum, New York, gift of Enrique Calvo, Minister of Culture of Aragon.

Ferdinand, prince of Aragon and Léon (1474–1504) married Isabella the Catholic (1451–1504), heiress to the crown of Castile. With the accession of Ferdinand to the throne of Aragon in 1479, the two kingdoms were united. Although their marriage had been arranged by a Jew, Abraham Seneor (see cat. no. 24), and many of the luminaries of their court were Jewish, the couple, who were known for their religious zeal, soon turned against the Jews. The Spanish Inquisition was set up in 1480, and the Jews expelled from Spain 12 years later.

TURKEY AND THE BALKANS

TURKEY · BULGARIA · GREECE
ROMANIA · YUGOSLAVIA

"Do they call this Ferdinand a wise prince, who can thus impoverish his own kingdom and thereby enrich ours?"

SULTAN BAYAZID II (ca. 1447–1512)

28, 45

TURKEY AND THE BALKANS

SYNAGOGUE

26 ATZEI HAYYIM (Torah staves)

Izmir, 1823/4. Ivory: pierced, engraved and inlaid with gold thread and semiprecious stones. Hebrew inscription: The le[aders] of the h[oly] c[ongregation] the Society . . . by . . . Yaakov Palombo . . . and . . . Yitzhak the Kohen . . . and . . . Shabbetai Dinar . . . t[he year] 5584. Top handles: 7⅜ in.; 8½ in.; bottom handles: 7¼ in.; 5½ in. Gross Family Collection, Tel Aviv, 54.9.1.

The ivory work, a design of three graduated crowns with refined decorations, is similar to the typical Esther scroll handles of this area. (*fig. 34*)

27 MEIL (Torah mantle)

Ottoman empire, 1874. Nickel silver sheet covered with velvet; silver: engraved, punched, stamped and parcel-gilt. 33⅝ x 8⅞ in. diam. Collection of the Israel Museum, Jerusalem, 145/23.

The rigid *meil* emulates the form of a soft textile mantle adorned with a Torah crown and shields. The silver plaques on the front were probably refashioned from secular objects, such as mirror covers (cf. cat. no. 37). (*fig. 38*)

REFERENCE: IM, *Ottoman*, pl. 21b.

28 MEIL (Torah mantle)*

Shumen, Bulgaria, 1877/8. Velvet: embroidered with metallic threads. Hebrew inscription: C[rown of the] T[orah] granted to the h[oly] c[ongregation] of Shumen by Yeudah s[on of] Yisrael 5638. 34½ x 9¼ in. diam. Collection of the Jewish Religious Community of Sofia, Bulgaria.

This tall, cylindrical mantle is the shape common in the Ottoman empire. The embroidered velvet from which it was made may originally have been a *bindalli* wedding dress (see cat. nos. 114, 116–118).

29 MEIL (Torah mantle)

Timisoara (Temesvár), Romania, 1877/8. Velvet: embroidered with metallic threads. Hebrew inscrip-tion: To the h[oly] c[ongregation] of Timisoara b[uild the] c[ity of the] L[ord] by . . . Shmuel Haim and . . . Yitzhak Ezriel . . . t[he year] 5638. 29½ x 10½ in. Collection of Abraham J. and Deborah B. Karp, New York.

Although the oval shape of the mantle is modeled after East European Ashkenazic examples, the metallic embroidery and turban-shaped crown are evidence of Ottoman influence.

30 MEIL (Torah mantle)

Izmir, 1909. Silver: repoussé, punched and stamped. 30½ x 10¼ in. diam. Collection of the Israel Museum, Jerusalem, 145/121.

Rigid Torah mantles made of silver and open in the back were typically found in Izmir and Rhodes. These cylindrical mantles were used in the same fashion as textile mantles. (*fig. 39*)

REFERENCE: IM, *Ottoman*, p. 54, fig. 29.

31 FASHA (Torah binder)

Ottoman empire, 19th century. Silk: embroidered with metallic threads. 6½ x 43 in. Collection of Gloria Abrams, New York.

This binder is made from remnants of worn Italian brocades.

32 FASHA (Torah binder)

Izmir, late 19th–early 20th century. Linen: embroidered with silk and metallic threads. 7 x 33⅞ in. Collection of the Israel Museum, Jerusalem, 150/213.

This binder is made of sections of embroidered towels that have been recut and attached together. After domestic textiles became worn, the precious embroidered components were often used to make ritual textiles that were donated to the synagogue. Elaborately embroidered towels of this type were usually found in bridal trousseaus (see cat. nos. 203–212).

REFERENCE: IM, *Ottoman*, pl. 17.

33   TORAH COVER

Ottoman empire, dedicated 1917. Silk: embroidered with silk and metallic threads; sequins. Hebrew inscription: For the repose of the youth Yitzhak Kohen h[is resting place in] E[den] on the 17th day of Adar I in the year "I shall call" [Chronogram = (5)677] m[ay his] s[oul] b[e bound in the] b[onds of] l[ife]. 18¼ x 38⅞ in. Collection of Mr. and Mrs. Abraham Halpern, New York.

This cover was made from a pre-existing embroidery to which a Hebrew inscription was added. The decoration is based on depictions of archways with hanging lamps, and probably stems from imagery of the mosque lamp hanging in the *mihrab* (prayer niche).

REFERENCE: New York, Christie's, *Fine Judaica*, June 26, 1984, lot no. 61.

34   MINIATURE TORAH SHIELD*

Rhodes, 18th century. Silver: repoussé and chased. Hebrew inscription: . . . Yaakov Franco H[oly] C[ommunity] Shalom. 5½ x 9 in. Collection of the Jewish Museum of Greece, Athens, gift of Maurice Sorianos.

This shield and a miniature crown (cat. no. 38) were part of a set of ornaments for a very small Torah. Ottoman shields were frequently circular and typically were decorated with chains and hanging ornaments.

35   TORAH SHIELD

Ankara, 1865. Silver: repoussé and punched. 10¼ x 14½ in. Collection of the Israel Museum, Jerusalem, 148/202.

Triangular shields were typically found in the region surrounding Ankara. The ornaments hanging on chains are an element common to many Ottoman ritual objects.*(fig. 55)*

REFERENCE: IM, *Ottoman*, p. 55, fig. 32.

36   TORAH SHIELD*

Izmir, 1921. Silver: engraved. 10 x 10½ in. Collection of the Israel Museum, Jerusalem, 148/229.

Shields in crescent form became popular in Turkey following the rise of nationalistic movements, such as the Young Turks, and after the establishment of the Republic in 1923.

Cf. Magnes, *Embellished*, p. 12.

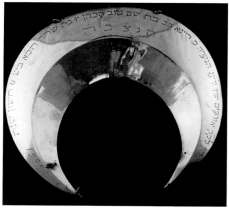

36

37   TORAH SHIELD

Izmir, 1923. Silver: repoussé, punched and engraved. Hebrew inscription: Dedicated to the H[oly] C[ongregation] Portugal . . . i[n] m[emory of] Bekhor Moshe ha-Levi son of Gioia(?) p[assed] o[n] 16 Sivan [5]683. 14 x 11½ in. Collection of the Israel Museum, Jerusalem, 148/249.

34

This shield is made from a mirror-back. In Turkey mirrors were considered symbols of vanity and were thought to be unlucky. Mirror-backs were often beautifully ornamented, so that the mirror could be hung on the wall with the decorated back facing out. The mirror could then be reversed when needed for use. Ottoman domestic silver was frequently made into ritual objects.

The reference to Portugal, in the congregation's name inscribed on this shield, indicates the pride in Iberian heritage maintained by Ottoman Sephardim through the 20th century. (*fig. 56*)

REFERENCE: IM, *Secular*, cat. no. 18.

38 MINIATURE TORAH CROWN

Rhodes or Izmir, 19th century. Silver: stamped, repoussé and engraved. 4 x 4¾ in. diam. Collection of the Jewish Museum of Greece, Athens.

This crown for a miniature Torah is typical of full-size Ottoman crowns (for a similarly shaped, large cylindrical crown, see cat. no. 39).

39 TORAH CROWN

Ottoman empire, 1838, repaired 1899/1900. Silver: stamped, chased, cut and parcel-gilt. Hebrew inscriptions: F[rom the] H[oly] C[ongregation] . . . according to the treasurers the gentleman Raphael Moshe Yisrael and R[abbi] Eliau Zurnami and H[aham] Eliau Makfoi . . . completed in Shevat 5598; Repaired from the treasury of Shemen le-Meor [the organization "Oil for the Lamp"] b[y] the treasurer Hai[m] Shmuel Soriano . . . t[he year] "Secret" [Chronogram = (5)660]. 6⁹⁄₁₆ x 8½ x 9⅜ in. Collection of Mr. and Mrs. Abraham Halpern, New York.

The large cylindrical form of this crown is typical of Ottoman crowns based on Italian models. The initial gilt dedicatory inscription runs around the band at the base of the crown. A lower strut to support and balance the crown atop the Torah staves bears the later inscription, and was probably added at the time of the repair.

40 TORAH CROWN

Ankara, 1865. Silver: repoussé, engraved and punched. 8 x 10 in. diam. Collection of the Israel Museum, Jerusalem, 146/59. (fig. 54)

41 TORAH CROWN

Izmir, early 20th century. Silver: repoussé, punched, pierced and cast. Collection of the Israel Museum, Jerusalem, gift of Alan Flacks of Monte Carlo, in memory of his uncle Samuel Angel of London, 146/52.

This Torah crown is unusually large and was used with a pair of finials. The use of matched sets of crowns and finials was probably adopted by Ottoman Jews after the Italian custom.

42 TORAH CROWN ORNAMENT

Gallipoli, 1862/3. Silver: cut and engraved. Hebrew inscriptions: Num. 6:24–27; the 42 letter name of God; Avot 4:13; Ecclesiastes Rabbah 7:2; Avot de Rabbi Nathan 41:1; dedicated from the charity box of Shuva la—Asot [the organization "return to do"] this crown is f[rom the] h[oly] c[ommunity] Gallipoli t[he] g[ood] c[ommunity] 5623. 10⁷⁄₁₆ x 3⁹⁄₁₆ in. Collection of Mr. and Mrs. Abraham Halpern, New York.

Ornaments of this type (see also cat. no. 43) were inserted into notches on the sides of cylindrical Torah crowns. The *hamsa* (hand) shape of the ornament, the central six-pointed star with magical hexagram inscription and the various Biblical and rabbinic texts are characteristics typical of protective amulets. This ornament features very primitive engraved floral and triangle patterns. (*fig. 57*)

REFERENCE: Weinstein, fig. nos. 101–102. Cf. IM, *Ottoman*, p. 59.

43 TORAH CROWN ORNAMENT

Gallipoli, mid-19th century. Silver: cut and engraved. Hebrew inscriptions: Num. 6:24–27; the 42 letter name of God; Avot 4:13; Ecclesiastes Rabbah 7:2; Avot de Rabbi Nathan 41:1; dedicated from the charity box o[f the] h[oly] c[ommunity] Gallipoli b[uild the] c[ity] o[f the Lord]. 9½ x 3⅜ in. Collection of Mr. and Mrs. Abraham Halpern, New York.

The engraving on this ornament is of a fine quality. Such ornaments were placed individually on the inner edge of Torah crowns, and were not used in pairs in the fashion of

Torah finials. The use of ornaments of this type (see also cat. no. 42) may be based on the Biblical description of God's covenant with Israel: ". . . I never forget you. See, I have engraved you on the palms of My hands . . ." (Is. 49:15–16). *(fig. 57)*

REFERENCE: Weinstein, fig. nos. 101–102. *Cf.* IM, *Ottoman*, p. 59.

44 TORAH CROWN AND FINIALS

Istanbul or Bulgaria, 1840. Silver: repoussé, engraved and cast. 8½ x 8¾ in. diam.; 12 x 3¾ in. Collection of the Israel Museum, Jerusalem, 146/33; 147/271.

Cone-shaped Torah crowns were used in Istanbul and Bulgaria. *(fig. 53)*

45 RIMMONIM (Torah finials)*

Sofia, Bulgaria, 1794. Silver: repoussé, chased, engraved and parcel-gilt. Hebrew inscription: The brothers Yaakov and Yitzhak, s[ons of] Mordekhai, may God protect their names, donated finials for the Torah staves for the repose of their mother w[ho passed away] . . . on the first of the m[onth of] Av t[he year] and they called Rivka (Genesis 24:58) [Chronogram = (5)554]. 13¾ x 4¾ in. diam. Collection of the Jewish Religious Community of Sofia, Bulgaria.

The bulbous acorn shape of these finials is common in examples throughout the Ottoman empire. These finials are unusual due to their early date. The date is recorded in a chronogram, a Biblical verse with individual letters marked so that the numerical values of the Hebrew characters can be added to equal the year in the Hebrew calendar. The choice of verse suggests that the mother of the donors was named Rivka.

46 RIMMONIM (Torah finials)

Yugoslavia, 18th–19th century. Iron: hammered, pierced and parcel-gilt. 22 in. Collection of the Jewish Museum, New York, F5010 a,b.

The use of iron for Torah ornaments is generally uncommon, but was prevalent in Yugoslavia. These finials were probably originally plated with silver and decorated with gilding.

47A RIMMONIM (Torah finials)

Istanbul, 19th century. Silver: punched, pierced and parcel-gilt. 15⅝ x 4 in. Collection of the Israel Museum, Jerusalem, 147/214. (fig. 47)

REFERENCE: IM, *Ottoman*, p. 55, fig. 30.

47B RIMMON (Torah finial)

Ottoman empire, 19th century. Silver: repoussé and parcel-gilt. Hebrew inscriptions: "The treasurers of the holy alms box . . . Shmuel Yerushalmi . . . Kaver Bashi . . . David Sevillia . . . Moshe Albíhar . . . Barukh . . ." 13¾ x 3⅞ in. Collection of the Jewish Museum, New York, F3175.

This finial is modeled after a pine cone with naturalistically rendered scales, a popular form in Ottoman silver (see cat no. 183), and is topped by a crescent and star.

48 FRAGMENT OF A TORAH FINIAL

Bezarjik, Yugoslavia, 1837/8. Silver: stamped, chased and cast. Hebrew inscriptions: Through the dedicated efforts of . . . Yosef Hananel Ligehi and . . . Binyamin Ligehi may God bestow upon them life for days and years; to the H[oly] C[ommunity] Bezarjik m[ay the] c[ity of the] L[ord be built], the silver from the treasury of the large study hall the earnings of the artisan were covered and appointed, given in the year [5]598. 3⅜ x 3½ x 3⅞ in. Collection of the Jewish Historical Museum, Belgrade.

The holes for hanging chains and bells indicate the original use of this fragment. The use of mechanical stamping and naturalistic tulip motifs are common elements of Ottoman metalwork. Tulips were first cultivated in the Ottoman empire, and were later exported to the Netherlands (for the use of this motif in Dutch Judaica, see cat. nos. 552–553).

The dedicatory inscriptions suggest that the silver for the finials came from the actual coins collected in the charity box of the study hall, while funds to cover the expense of the silversmith's labor were donated by the Ligehi family.

49 RIMMONIM (Torah finials)

Turkey, 1861–1877. Silver: cast and engraved.

14¹³⁄₁₆ x 3¹⁵⁄₁₆ in. Hebrew inscription: Belongs to the betrothed. Collection of the Jewish Museum, New York, F3141 a,b.

The arrangement of multi-tiered baskets seen in these finials is frequently found in Ottoman ceremonial objects. It can be seen in Torah finials, staves, *megillah* cases and rollers (see cat. nos. 26, 81 and 83). *(fig. 47)*

REFERENCES: Schoenberger, "Myer Myers," p. 75; NYJM, *Tale*, cat. no. 205; Magnes, *Embellished*, p. 12.

50 RIMMON (Torah finial)

Turkey, late 19th century. Silver: engraved and stamped. 15³⁄₈ x 4¹⁄₂ in. Collection of the Jewish Museum, New York, F1956.

The decorative stamped lines on the finial are frequently found on Ottoman domestic silver, such as sweet dishes and cutlery (see cat. no. 175). The crescent form at the top was popular throughout the Ottoman empire, particularly with the spread of nationalism at the end of the 19th century.

REFERENCE: NYJM, *Tale*, cat. no. 204.

51 RIMMONIM (Torah finials)

Ottoman empire, before 1923. Silver: repoussé, engraved and cast. 14¹⁄₂ x 3³⁄₄ in. Moldovan Family Collection, New York.

Ottoman Torah finials are typically bulbous and fruit shaped.

52 RIMMONIM (Torah finials)

Skopje, Yugoslavia, 1927. Silver: hammered, engraved and cast. Hebrew inscription: Dedicated by o[ur teacher] t[he Rabbi] o[ur Rabbi] Nissim A. Suri and his wife Nira(?), Skopje, 1 Tishrei, 5688. 8¹⁄₂ x 3³⁄₄ in. Collection of the Reuben and Helene Dennis Museum, Beth Tzedec Synagogue, Toronto, CR 47.

According to the dedicatory inscription these finials were donated on the first day of Rosh Hashanah, as was the exhibited Ark curtain from Skopje (see cat. no. 63).

Their bulbous form is common in Ottoman examples. The somewhat primitive modeling and engraving suggest that they may have belonged to a small congregation.

53 YAD (Torah pointer)

Ottoman empire, 1885. Silver: hammered, chiseled and engraved; tassel of metallic threads. 17⁵⁄₈ in. Collection of Mr. and Mrs. Abraham Halpern, New York.

Decorative tassels were frequently attached to Ottoman Torah pointers.

54 YAD (Torah pointer)

Ottoman empire, 19th–20th century. Silver: cast and engraved. 11¹⁄₂ in. Hebrew inscription: Avraham Cavaleiro. The Abraham J. and Deborah B. Karp Collection, New York.

55 YAD (Torah pointer)

Ottoman empire, 19th–20th century. Silver: cast and engraved. 12¹⁄₂ in. Hebrew inscription: And this is the pointer of the d[eceased] Prahia daughter of Rahel h[er resting place in] E[den]. Moldovan Family Collection, New York.

56 YAD (Torah pointer)

Ottoman empire, 19th–20th century. Silver: cast and engraved. 10 in. Hebrew inscription: Dedicated by the wife of the r[ighteous] K[ohen] Sultana di Zarfatti b[lessed among] w[omen]. Moldovan Family Collection, New York.

57 YAD (Torah pointer)

Ottoman empire, late 19th–early 20th century. Silver: engraved. 14¹⁄₂ in. Collection of the Israel Museum, Jerusalem, 149/243.

58 YAD (Torah pointer)

Ottoman empire, late 19th–early 20th century. Silver: engraved, parcel-gilt. 15¹⁄₂ in. Collection of the Israel Museum, Jerusalem, 149/222.

59 YAD (Torah pointer)

Ottoman empire, late 19th–early 20th century. Silver: engraved and cast. Hebrew inscription: Zion. 15 in. Collection of the Israel Museum, Jerusalem, 149/221.

The cast finial at the top of this pointer with the word "Zion" in a Star of David may suggest early interest in Zionism.

60   YAD (Torah pointer)

Ottoman empire, 1919/20. Silver: cast and engraved. Hebrew inscription: To t[he holy] c[ongregation] Eliyahu ha-Navi . . . from the woman Zul di Boton Waladha 7th of the month of Tevet t[he year] [5]680. 13½ in. The Abraham J. and Deborah B. Karp Collection, New York.

61   SYNAGOGUE RUG

Istanbul or Cairo, 17th century. Wool: knotted. Hebrew inscription: This is the gateway to the Lord, . . . (Ps. 118:20). 75 x 54 in. Collection of the Sir Isaac and Lady Edith Wolfson Museum, Hechal Shlomo, Jerusalem.

Few Hebrew inscribed rugs of this type are known. The composition is based on mosque rugs with a portal suggesting the *mihrab* (prayer niche) and hanging lamps. The inscription relates to the imagery of the gateway. Compositions of this type may have been based on gate-shaped frontispieces in Hebrew books published in Italy or the Ottoman empire. It has been suggested that this rug and other similar examples were made in a court atelier in Istanbul or in a well-known workshop in Cairo. It is unclear if rugs of this type were used as Ark curtains, reader's desk covers or synagogue wall hangings.[1] It has been suggested that this rug may be a 19th-century copy based on a 17th-century model. *(fig. 59)*

REFERENCE: Bialer, p. 104; B. Yaniv, "The Origin of the 'Two-Column Motif' in European *Parokhot*," *JA* 15 (1989), p. 32. *Cf.* IM, *Ottoman*, pp. 100–03; NYJM, *Gardens*, cat. no. 141.

62   PAROKHET (Ark curtain)*

Ottoman empire, 19th century. Satin: appliquéed with velvet and embroidered with silk and metallic threads. 73 x 44 in. Collection of Yossi Benyaminoff, Jerusalem.

This curtain features a central archway with floral motifs suggesting a hanging lamp. Compositions of this type are found both in Islamic rugs, where the *mihrab* (prayer niche) and hanging mosque lamp are depicted, and in synagogue textiles, where the imagery relates to the *Ner Tamid* (eternal lamp) hanging before the Torah Ark.

Cf. IM, *Ottoman*, p. 106, fig. 47.

---

1. See IM, *Ottoman*, pp. 97–113.

63   PAROKHET (Ark curtain)*

Skopje, Yugoslavia, 1933. Silk: decorated with gold paint, crystal beads and metal sequins. Ladino inscription: Dedicated by Señor Shlomo and his wife Clara Adroki as a memorial to his departed father the Rabbi . . . Moshe Adroki h[is resting place is in] E[den] the first of Tishrei 5694. 85½ x 71 in. Collection of the Jewish Historical Museum, Belgrade, gift of the Jewish Community of Skopje, 415.

The elaborate painted and beaded decoration on this curtain is most unusual. This curtain follows a standard composition, a central mirror panel containing a dedicatory inscription surmounted by a crown and flanking lions, which is frequently found in Central European Ashkenazic embroidered Ark curtains. However, the Ladino dedicatory inscription clearly reflects the Sephardic heritage of the Skopje community. Ottoman influence can be seen in the turban form of the crown.

REFERENCE: *Jugoslavije*, cat. no. 6/15.

62

63

64

64 SYNAGOGUE AMULETIC DEDICATION PLAQUE*

Istanbul, 1827/8. Silver: engraved and chased. Hebrew inscriptions: The 42 letter name of God, this silver was dedicated by . . . David Elisha the Kohen . . . to the H[oly] C[ongregation of] Kastoria . . . today the 14th of t[he month of] Mercy [Elul] t[he year] 5588. 6⅝ x 4 in. Collection of the Israel Museum, Jerusalem, 148/262.

This plaque was dedicated to the congregation of Kastoria, a wooden synagogue in the Bulat quarter of Istanbul, which is in virtual ruins today. This type of amuletic dedication plaque was usually fixed or hung, among other plaques, on the Torah mantle or the Ark curtain.

65 SYNAGOGUE WALL SCONCE*

Venice, 18th century. Silver: repoussé, chased, engraved and parcel-gilt over a wood core. Hebrew inscription: The Macchiero brothers. 28½ x 21¼ in. Collection of the Jewish Historical Museum, Belgrade, 64.

This sconce is one of a pair that hung beside the Torah Ark of the synagogue in Split, Yugoslavia. Split (Spalato) was under Vene-

tian rule from 1420 to 1797, and thus adopted Italianate stylistic approaches, as seen in the rich, baroque character of this sconce. Split was a major port and a center for trade with Venice. It is therefore not surprising that Venetian silver was imported for the synagogue, especially since many Jewish families in Split were of Venetian origin.

REFERENCE: *Jugoslavije*, cat. no. 6/1k, pp. 40, 66.

65

COMMUNITY

Haham bashi was the official title of the chief rabbi in the Ottoman empire. This personage, whose title was composed of the Hebrew word *haham* (sage) and the Turkish *bashi* (head or chief), was appointed by the sultan. The first to hold this office was R. Avraham ha-Levi, who was appointed by Sultan Mahmud II (1808–1838) in 1836 as *haham bashi* in Istanbul (Contantinople). This confirmation signified official recognition of the Jewish community, placing it on a par with the Armenian and Greek Orthodox communities within the Ottoman empire. *Hahamei bashi* were subsequently appointed also in Adrianople, Salonika, Izmir and Bursa in 1836; in Iraq, Yemen and other provinces in 1839; and in Jerusalem in 1841.

66 COSTUME AND DECORATIONS OF THE HAHAM BASHI

(Chief Rabbi)

Istanbul, ca. 1920. Robe: wool, silk, silver thread washed in gold, wrapped around cardboard. L: 54 in. (IM 1140.77). Hat: wool felt, silk. (IM 1141.77). Decorations: Buckle: silver, gold (plate?) and enamel. D: 4¼ in. (IM 1142.77 A1). Sash: taffeta. 33 x 8 in. (diam. of bow) (IM 1142.77 A2). Star: white metal, yellow metal, enamel. 2½ x 2½ in. (IM 1143.77). Medal: metal, enamel, silk ribbon. 3⅞ x 1¼ in. (IM 1144.77 a,b). Medal: bronze with portrait and crest of King of Rumania (on reverse), silk. 3⁵⁄₁₆ x 1¼ in. (IM 1148.77 a,b). Medals: rosette with 2 pendant silk grosgrain ribbons, metal fibula, red enamel. 16½ x 2½ in. (IM 1150.77). Collection of the Israel Museum, Jerusalem.

In the Ottoman empire, Turkish rabbis wore robes similar to those of non-Jewish dignitaries. The fine cloth of the *djubba* (overcoat) with its embroidered trim composed of metal thread sewn over cardboard in characteristic Turkish arabesque and foliate patterns (*rumi*) would have been worn over an *entari* of silk. The shape of the collar is modeled on those of European military uniforms of the time.

This costume was worn by Rabbi Bekhor Hayyim Moshe Bejerano (1850–1931), Chief Rabbi of Istanbul from 1920 to 1931. Like other religious functionaries, he received it from the government along with his official insignia of office and a written certificate of appointment.

A native of Bulgaria, Rabbi Bejerano was active as a religious educator and functionary in Bucharest, Rumania, before being appointed chief rabbi of Istanbul. He was the author of numerous Hebrew scholarly articles and a corresponding member of the Spanish and French academies.

A similar costume is worn by Moïse Halevy (1826–1910), acting *haham bashi* in Istanbul from 1874 to 1908 (cat. no. 221). A prominent rabbinical scholar and Talmudist, he was held in high esteem by Sultan Abdülhamid II (1876–1909) and was buried with great pomp at the expense of Abdülhamid's successor, Sultan Mehmed V (1909–1918). The hat is similar to that worn by David, son of Rabbi Samuel Majha, Chief Rabbi of Jerusalem (cat. no. 309). The embroidery on the mantle of the *Rishon le-Zion* (Sephardic Chief Rabbi of Israel) is modeled on the Ottoman type. *(See illustration on p. 20)*

REFERENCE: Juhasz, "Costume," IM, *Ottoman*, p. 133, fig. 19.

67 RABBI'S HAT

Istanbul, 19th century. Wool: satin; silk tassel. Diam: 10 in. Collection of the United States Museum of Natural History, Smithsonian Institution, Washington D.C., 26818; 154761.

REFERENCES: Casanowicz, no. 64; NYJM, *Tale*, cat. no. 188.

68 RABBI'S SHOES

*Istanbul, 19th century. Maker: T. Papazran. L:
11¾ in. Collection of the United States Museum
of Natural History, Smithsonian Institution,
Washington D.C., 26818; 154761.*

REFERENCES: Casanowicz, no. 64; NYJM, *Tale*, cat.
no. 188.

69 LECTERN COVER*

*Turkey, 18th–19th century. Velvet: gold-washed
silver threads wrapped around cardboard; embroidered with silver strips washed with gold wrapped
around thread; seed pearls. Diam: 36⁹/₁₆ in. Collection of Yeshiva University Museum, New York,
gift of Victor Alhadef, 77.162.*

Floral sprays and tulips were popular Ottoman decorative elements. Here we see them
on a piece commonly used in Turkey as a cover
for the coffee table, adapted for Jewish use as
a lectern cover. It was used by the last Chief
Rabbi of Izmir (Smyrna). In view of the high
quality of the piece, some scholars believe that
it was made at a workshop patronized by the
Sultan's court. Fine pieces of this type were
produced in provincial centers as well. Applied metal thread embroidery was used for
sashes, clothing, wrappers, sheets, cradle textiles, cushion covers, wall hangings and prayer
mats as well as pieces for the service of coffee.
Several sumptuous examples exist in the Topkapi Saray collection. Such pieces illustrate the
taste for luxurious textiles that survived in the
Ottoman empire from its heyday in the 16th
century through its decline.

Sometimes various craftsmen participated
in the elaborate work for one such piece. One
drew the pattern on the ground fabric, while
others executed the embroidery. Men appear
to have been primarily responsible for gold
embroidery, while women executed silk embroidery, even that produced on commission
for the Sultan's harem.

Heavy embroidery on satin or velvet could
be ordered from professionals, or from Venetian merchants in Galata who purchased
ready-made pieces (bolsters, covers, etc.) for
resale. *(Plate 6)*

REFERENCE: NYJM, *Tale*, cat. no. 208. *Cf.* Tezcan
and Delibas, cat. nos. 110, 111, 115.

70 ALMS PLATE

*Ottoman empire, 1863/4. Silver: repoussé, en-
graved and cut. Hebrew inscription: Avraham Nis-
sim Haim Yisrael Shabbetai . . . Moshe Nissim
Aloraki . . . Zaccaro . . . 5624. 12½ in. diam.
Collection of the Israel Museum, Jerusalem, gift of
Eliezer Burshtein Collection, Lugano, 163/31.*

This charity plate illustrates the communal
involvement of the Jewish guilds. In the
late 18th and early 19th centuries the Jewish
guilds took on social and organizational functions in addition to their professional ones.
They established charitable organizations,
synagogues and houses of study, and gradually became a key factor in the social life of
Jewish communities.

The canopied boat at the center of this plate
suggests that this plate belonged to the Charitable Society of the Boat Owners Guild (*Hu
Kayikjit*). This guild, founded in Istanbul at
the beginning of the 19th century by the
"Charitable Society of Boat-Owners in Constantinople," and also known as the "Society
of Boat-Owners on the Bosphorus," established a special fund to which each member
gave "what his heart moved him to give" one
pruta per week . . . "to give joy and happiness
to the needy and impoverished. . . ." *(fig. 65)*

REFERENCE: IM, *Ottoman*, p. 58, fig. 37.

71 ALMS BOX

*Turkey, 1903/4. Silver: hammered, engraved and
cast. Hebrew inscription: Rabbi Haim son of Attar
. . . Shmuel s[on of] Yitzhak the Burial Society
. . . of Hasköy Aharon Albuha for the hands of
Shabbetai first-born of Moshe the treasurers Yisrael
s[on of] Mordekhai . . . Yitzhak Alahu . . . 5664.
3¹/₁₆ x 4¾ in. Collection of the Jewish Museum,
New York, S1502.*

This barrel-shaped box was used to collect
funds for the Burial Society of Hasköy, a
Jewish neighborhood in Istanbul located along
the Bosphorus Straits. *(fig. 64)*

REFERENCE: NYJM, *Tale*, cat. no. 210. *Cf.* Barnett,
cat. no. 578; IM, *Paris*, cat. no. 59; Magnes, *Embellished*, p. 12.

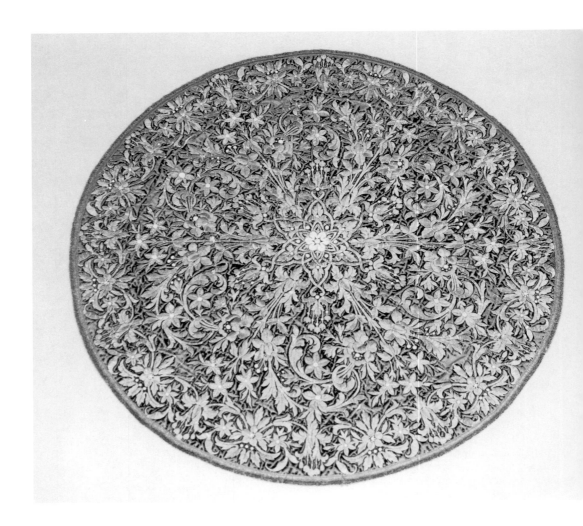

72 PROGRES CLUB BANNER

Izmir, 19th–20th century. Velvet: embroidered with metallic threads. Turkish, Ladino and French inscriptions: Progress Club Izmir Salhane. Collection of the Israel Museum, Jerusalem, 909.82.

The inscriptions on this banner in Turkish, Ladino and French indicate the linguistic and cultural mix of Ottoman Sephardic life.

73 LIRA SOCIETY BANNER

Sarajevo, Yugoslavia, 1921. Silk: embroidered with silk threads. Hebrew inscriptions: The Jewish Choral Association Lira; Zion. Serbo-Croatian inscriptions: The Jewish Choral Association Lira; Our life into sounds streams and of the Song of Songs dreams. 50 x 62 in. Collection of the Civic Museum, Sarajevo.

The Lira society was a Jewish musical organization founded in Sarajevo in 1901. This banner, featuring extremely fine multi-colored embroidery, was made in celebration of the society's twentieth anniversary. The banner is two-sided; one side features an inscription in Hebrew, and the reverse bears a text in Serbo-Croatian. The banner includes depictions of a lyre, of the symbols of the Twelve Tribes, and of a *Magen David* with the Hebrew word for Zion, an indication of early Zionist spirit. The Serbo-Croatian inscription is written in a combination of Latin and Cyrillic script indicating the Jewish association's involvement in the newly united Yugoslavia. *(Plate 8)*

SABBATH AND FESTIVALS

74 SABBATH KIDDUSH CUP

Turkey, late 19th century. Silver: cast and engraved. Hebrew inscription: Kiddush for the Sabbath day Ovadia[h] son of Yaakov ha-Kohen. 2³/₁₆ x 2 in. Collection of the Jewish Museum, New York, F1125.

Elaborate kiddush cups from Islamic countries are rare. Due to the Islamic prohibition against the consumption of alcohol, no indigenous tradition of sumptuous wine vessels existed in these regions. When silver kiddush cups were crafted in areas under Islamic rule, they were often modeled after Western examples, as seen in the scrolled handle of this cup.

REFERENCE: NYJM, *Cups*, no. 7.

75 HALLAH COVER

Turkey, 20th century. Velvet: embroidered with silk thread; satin appliqué. Collection of the Judah L. Magnes Museum, Berkeley, California, 82.38.5.

Delicate floral motifs enliven this hallah cover executed in a late Victorian style. The raised flower petals resemble Turkish *memento mori* made with shaped whole cocoons applied to velvet. This one was used by Sultana Barouk (Ades), sister of the donor.

REFERENCE: Magnes, *Embellished*, p. 14.

76 KIDDUSH AND HAV-DALAH CUP FOR FESTIVALS

Turkey, 19th century. Silver: repoussé and chased. Hebrew inscription: W[ine] k[iddush] c[andle] h[avdalah] s[eason]. 4³/₈ x 4³/₄ in. diam. Private collection.

This beautifully crafted beaker features the abbreviated order (*YKNHZ*) for kiddush when a festival occurs on a Saturday night. The order of the blessings is first the wine (*y[ayyin]*), then the festival (*k[iddush]*), the candle (*n[er]*), the separation between the Sabbath and the weekday (*h[avdalah]*), and finally the *she-hehiyanu*, thanking God for enabling us to reach this time (*z[eman]*).

77 ROSH HASHANAH KIDDUSH PRINT

Sarajevo, Yugoslavia, 20th century. Lithograph on paper. 20 x 9¹/₈ in. Collection of the Jewish Historical Museum, Belgrade, 5524.

This broadside is interesting for its linguistic mix. Ladino instructions and the Hebrew text of the kiddush and blessings over special foods for the eve of Rosh Hashanah are transliterated into Serbo-Croatian. It is a prevalent custom among Sephardim to eat symbolic foods such as fish, pomegranates and leeks on Rosh Hashanah, as omens for prosperity and fertility.

78 ETROG CONTAINER

Turkey, 19th century. Silver: cast and hammered. Hebrew inscription: On the first day you shall take the product of hadar (beautiful) trees (Lev. 23:40). 5⁷⁄₁₆ x 3 in. Collection of the Jewish Museum, New York, S108.

The urn shape of this container suggests the influence of Western silversmiths on Turkish craftsmen. This container is inscribed with the Biblical verse which is the source for the commandment to bless the *etrog* on Sukkot.

REFERENCE: NYJM, *Tale*, cat. no. 22.

79 SHIVVITI PLAQUE
(Sukkah decoration)

Yosef ha-Levi, known as Bahor, son of Yitzhak. Izmir, 1893/4. Papercut; ink on paper; embossed metallic foil. 16 x 22½ in. Collection of Mr. and Mrs. Abraham Halpern, New York.

This elaborate papercut is typical of Ottoman examples, with its monochromatic decoration and gold background foil. The various Hebrew inscriptions combine a variety of amuletic texts and include the *ushpizin*, the invitation to Abraham, Isaac, Jacob, Joseph, Moses, Aaron and David to be guests in the *sukkah*. This papercut is signed by the artist, who was well-known, and is a typical example of his work.

REFERENCE: Y. and J. Shadur, "Three Papercuts from Jerusalem," *JA* 16/17 (1990/1), p. 11. *Cf.* G. Frankel, *Migzeirot Niyyar*, pp. 96–99; IM, *Ottoman*, p. 246, fig. 8.

80 HANUKKAH LAMP

Salonika(?), 18th–19th century. Brass: cast. Hebrew inscription: For the light is a commandment and the Torah light (Prov. 6:23). Collection of the Jewish Museum, New York, F4708.

Hanukkah lamps from the Ottoman empire are very rare. Inexpensive and fragile lamps made of ceramic or glass were frequently used, but examples of these have not survived. Lamps of this type have often been associated with Salonika, but examples are known from Corfu, Cairo and probably Venice.[1]

---

1. See Bialer, p. 159; Magnes, *Hanukkah Lamps*, cat. nos. 6 and 54; Toronto, Royal Ontario Museum acc. no. 909.75.5.

81 ESTHER SCROLL AND ROLLER

Ottoman empire, early 19th century. Ink and gouache on parchment; ivory: carved. 12¾ in. Gross Family Collection, Tel Aviv, 81.12.32.

The ivory work, a design of three graduated crowns with refined decorations, is similar to the design of metalwork Esther scroll handles and Torah staves typical of this area. A small crescent-shaped finial (now broken) tops the roller.

82 ESTHER SCROLL, ROLLER AND COVER

Ottoman empire, 19th century. Ink on parchment; silver: repoussé, chased and gilt; coral. 14¼ x 2 in. Private collection.

The cover on this case is a totally separable hinged piece, a characteristic element in Ottoman *megillot*. Coral may have been chosen as a decorative component because it was seen to protect the owner from evil. *(fig. 69)*

83 ESTHER SCROLL, ROLLER, COVER AND SHEET OF BLESSINGS

Izmir, 19th century. Ink on parchment; silver: filigree, granulation and gilt; coral; ink, gouache, watercolor and paper collage on parchment. 17³⁄₈ x 2 in. diam.; 5¼ x 6⁷⁄₈ in. Gross Family Collection, Tel Aviv, 80.1.6; 80.1.6a.

This scroll was presented to a bridegroom named Yeoshua Amado. Paper collage was frequently used for the decoration of manuscripts and amulets in a variety of Sephardic communities (see cat. nos. 85, 131, 277 and 577). *(fig. 69)*

REFERENCES: *Gross*, pp. 221–26; IM, *Ottoman*, p. 199.

84 ESTHER SCROLL, ROLLER AND COVER

Turkey, mid-19th century. Ink on parchment; silver: filigree, gilt; velvet: embroidered with metallic threads; sequins. 15½ x 1¾ in. Collection of Mr. and Mrs. Victor Topper, Toronto.

Precious domestic embroideries were often used to make synagogue textiles, but objects used for ritual purpose could not be adapted for mundane use. Even small pieces of embroidery were treasured, and were made into covers for *megillot*, as in this example, or were pieced together to compose large synagogue textiles. (*fig. 69*)

REFERENCES: New York, Sotheby's, *Important Judaica, Books, Manuscripts, and Works of Art*, December 12, 1988, lot no. 167; Geneva, Habsburg, Feldman, *Judaica*, June 19, 1989, lot no. 51/182.

85 ESTHER SCROLL, ROLLER AND SHEET OF BLESSINGS

Turkey, 1862. Ink on parchment; gold: filigree and granulation; pearl; ink and gouache on parchment; printed paper collage. 9⅜ x 1⅛ in. diam. Gross Family Collection, Tel Aviv.

Ottoman Jews frequently presented Esther scrolls and decorative cases as gifts to bridegrooms. In the wealthiest of families, gold cases or rollers were commissioned, but very few examples of this type have survived. Accompanying this scroll is a separate sheet of parchment, with the blessings recited before reading the *megillah* and a dedication and blessings for the groom, Señor David Leon.

REFERENCE: IM, *Ottoman*, plate 41.

86 ESTHER SCROLL AND CASE

Ottoman empire, 19th–20th century. Ink on parchment; silver: filigree, parcel-gilt. 13¼ x 2⅝ in. Moldovan Family Collection, New York.

The stacked filigree tiers at the top of this scroll case are characteristic of Ottoman examples. The case is topped by a naturalistic flower rendered with great precision, including a stylized suggestion of stamens. (*fig. 69*)

87 CHILD'S PURIM COSTUME

Bulgaria, early 20th century. Velvet: embroidered with silver thread washed with gold. Collection of the Israel Museum, Jerusalem, 413.75 a,b,c,d.

Bulgarian children over the age of three were dressed in elaborately embroidered costumes when they were brought to the synagogue on Purim. Note the elaborate, open sleeves similar to those on the ceremonial dress from Sarajevo, Yugoslavia (cat. no. 115).

LIFE CYCLE

88 AMULETIC KERCHIEF

Ottoman empire, 19th century. Silk gauze: embroidered with gold metallic thread, gold beads, sequins. 45½ x 14½ in. Collection of the Israel Museum, Jerusalem, 170/76.

Among the amulets used for protection during and after childbirth are amuletic kerchiefs such as this. The inscription would be visible over the woman's forehead when the kerchief was placed on her head.

REFERENCE: M. Russo-Katz, "Childbirth," IM, *Ottoman*, pp. 260–261; plate 45b.

89 BIRTH CERTIFICATE

Ottoman empire, 1895. Ink and gouache on paper. 20 x 15¾ in. Collection of Bea Myones, New York.

It was customary in Ottoman Jewish families to prepare amuletic birth certificates for children. This certificate records the birth and naming of Avraham, son of Calev Eliya Yitzhak Attas. The certificate includes the text of the *shema*, the names of angels and menorot.

90 SHIVVITI FOR NEWBORN CHILD

Ottoman empire, 1906. Ink and watercolor on paper. 21½ x 16⅝ in. Collection of Yeshiva University Museum, New York, 73.6.

91 CIRCUMCISION KNIFE*

Ottoman empire, 19th century. Silver: cut and chiseled. Hebrew inscription: David Azulai of p[ure] S[ephardic lineage]. 3⅛ x 1¾ in. Collection of Mr. and Mrs. Abraham Halpern, New York.

91

The depiction of a swaddled infant on the handle of this knife is unusual. Representations of the human form are uncommon in Jewish ceremonial objects, particularly in objects crafted in Islamic countries, where figural representation was frowned upon.

92   CIRCUMCISION KNIFE*

Ottoman empire, 19th century. Silver: cut and chiseled. Hebrew inscription: S[ervant of] G[od] Shlomo Zarfati of p[ure] S[ephardic lineage]. 1 x 3½ in. Collection of Mr. and Mrs. Abraham Halpern, New York.

The leaf shape of this knife and the floral decoration indicate Turkish interest in stylized naturalistic motifs.

92

93   CIRCUMCISION OUTFIT*

Salonika, late 19th century. Cotton: machine lace trim. Collection of the Jewish Museum of Greece, Athens, 89.27.

This charming set, consisting of a bonnet, jacket, lap robe and bunting, shows European influence. It is similar to the *kamiza lárga*, a long gown symbolizing the wish of a long life for the child.

Infants' clothes, like those of their mothers, could be purchased ready-made, or fashioned

from bolts of cloth and trimming. Fabrics for infants' clothes often formed part of a bride's trousseau. In parts of the Ottoman empire, long gowns such as this would be used for a boy's circumcision, a girl's naming or a baby's first outing. A cloth from Yeshiva University Museum's collection used for *las fádas* (the naming of a girl) is also included in this exhibition (cat. no. 121).

REFERENCES: M. Russo-Katz, "Childbirth," IM, *Ottoman*, p. 256; Rose, pp. 55–66; 103–108.

94   CIRCUMCISION CLOTH

Ottoman empire, probably Rhodes, 19th century. Silk: embroidered with silver thread washed with gold over cardboard; beads; cotton backing. 41 x 27¼ in. Collection of Stella Levi, New York.

The birth of a son was a joyous occasion that sparked a week of festivities. The evening before the *brit*, *leil ha-shemira* (vigil night) took place during which one or two women sat up guarding the infant until the circumcision. At the *brit*, performed in the synagogue or at the home of the infant's parents, *el kubár* (the godfather or *sandak*) sat in the Chair of Elijah; he received the baby from *la kubára* (the godmother), and held him on his knees during the actual circumcision.

Rhodes was one of the centers of production of high-quality metal embroidery. This piece was used for the circumcision ceremony in the lender's family. Similar pieces were used as wrapping cloths.

REFERENCE: Russo-Katz, "Childbirth."

95   CIRCUMCISION CLOTH

Monastir, 19th century. Silk: embroidered with strips of silver washed with gold, wrapped around yellow silk (?) thread; metal sequins. 40½ x 38½ in. Collection of Sarah Alevy-Hirsch and Herbert Hirsch, Lakewood, New Jersey.

A traditional Ottoman cloth in red and green, embroidered with lively floral motifs.

96   CIRCUMCISION CLOTH

Monastir, 19th–20th century. Linen; lace. 49½ x 47¾. Collection of Sarah Alevy-Hirsch and Herbert Hirsch, Lakewood, New Jersey.

Leil ha-Shemirah (vigil night before circumcision) installation. On the night preceding a baby's circumcision, scholars and rabbis studied and prayed in the home of the new mother and child. In later generations, this became an occasion for festivities. In order to protect the newborn child, the infant was held throughout the night by his mother or by family members.

Entari (outer robe) and *sayo* (underdress), Salonika, late 19th century. Cat. nos. 138–139; Woman's bodice and skirt, Ottoman empire, 1875, remade ca. 1890. Cat. no. 119; Circumcision outfit, Salonika, late 19th century. Cat. no. 93.

This fine, lace-trimmed cloth was used during the circumcision ceremony in addition to the more traditional Ottoman embroidered silk cloth (cat. no. 95).

97 CIRCUMCISION CLOTH*

Ottoman empire, 19th–20th century. Silk: embroidered with silver thread washed with gold. 6⅝ x 4¼ in. Collection of Joseph and Devorah Alcabes, West Hempstead, New York.

Characteristic Turkish *bohğa* (wrapping cloth), used by a Jewish family for the circumcision ceremony.

98 QUILT FOR BRIT MILAH

Ottoman empire, 19th century. Satin: quilted ("Bursa work"), dival work; cotton, buttons. 30 x 27 in. Collection of the Jewish Museum of Greece, Athens, 89.88.

99 COVERLET FOR A BABY

Istanbul, early 20th century. Satin; embroidered with silk thread. 37½ x 37½ in. French inscription: Bébé (baby). Collection of Yeshiva University Museum, New York, gift of Mrs. Emma Adatto Schlesinger, Monroeville, Pennsylvania, 79.50.

This coverlet was used by the family to cover male babies at the circumcision ceremony; most recently at the *brit* of the donor's brother, Albert, in 1911. It was also used for female babies during the *zeved ha-bat* (naming ceremony). A drawstring forms a cap for the baby's head. This drawstring, the scalloped edges and the inscription differentiate this coverlet from the more traditional pieces in the exhibition used for Jewish ceremonial purposes—the Turkish *bohğas* (wrapping cloths) that were used for the circumcision ceremony (cat. nos. 94, 95, 97), and the embroidered towel used for *zeved ha-bat* (naming of an infant girl) (cat. no. 121). This piece is another example of the adoption of European forms in Turkish textiles, although the color and embroidery are Turkish rather than European.

97

100 KETUBBAH (Marriage contract)

Salonika, 1836 (?). Ink and watercolor on paper. 26½ x 17½ in. Collection of Yeshiva University Museum, New York, 78.5.

The motif of two birds is characteristic of Salonika *ketubbot*. This document was later used as the binding for a book, but the illustrations faced inward and were not damaged by the glue. Many texts and documents have survived only because they were considered unimportant and used as binding material for books (see cat. nos. 4–13). *(fig. 24)*

Cf. Sabar, "Decorated Ketubbot," pp. 227–30.

101 KETUBBAH (Marriage contract)

Salonika, 1862. Ink and watercolor on paper. 19¼ x 13⅜ in. Einhorn Collection, Tel Aviv.

Groom: Yeuda [*sic*] son of Mikhael
Bride: Miriam daughter of Mordekhai Krispin
The double arch is common in many Sephardic communities; the right arch encloses the text of the ketubbah proper, while the left arch encloses the special provisions (*tenaim*) of the contract.

Cf. Sabar, "Decorated *Ketubbot*," pp. 227–30.

102 KETUBBAH (Marriage contract)

Salonika, 1866. Ink and watercolor on paper. 16½ x 13¼ in. Collection of the Jewish National and University Library, Jerusalem, 25.

Groom: Shlomo son of Aharon, called Bekhor Moshe
Bride: Rahel daughter of Pinhas Meshulam
Three basic colors are used here to draw the familiar Salonika elements: orange double arch, yellow flowers and blue petals. The designs are drawn directly on the page without outlining.

Cf. Sabar, "Decorated *Ketubbot*," pp. 227–30.

103 KETUBBAH (Marriage contract)

Salonika, 1872. Ink and watercolor on paper. Einhorn Collection, Tel Aviv.

Groom: Aharon son of Shlomo Khalfon (?)
Bride: Esther daughter of Shlomo Avraham Khalfon (?)

Cf. Sabar, "Decorated *Ketubbot*," pp. 227–30.

104 KETUBBAH (Marriage contract)

Salonika, 1880. Ink and watercolor on paper. 21¾ x 16 in. Collection of the Jewish National and University Library, Jerusalem, 29.

Groom: Moshe son of Yaakov Dasa
Bride: Benvenida daughter of Yaakov the Kohen
This contract shows the decline of ketubbah decoration among Salonika Sephardim. Toward the end of the 19th century, less and less attractive ketubbot were produced locally. In this case only the basic elements appear, almost in abstract form and simply delineated in a single color. *(fig. 25)*

Cf. Sabar, "Decorated *Ketubbot*," pp. 227–30.

105 KETUBBAH (Marriage contract)

Monastir, Yugoslavia, 1889. Ink and watercolor on paper. 20 x 14⅜ in. Einhorn Collection, Tel Aviv.

Groom: Yizhak son of Mordekhai
Bride: Miriam daughter of Aharon Calaveron (?)
The text and special provisions (*tenaim*) are arranged in two arches, as in the ketubbot of Salonika and other Sephardic communities.

106A KETUBBAH

(Marriage contract)

Salonika, 1890. Lithograph on paper with hand-written text. 25½ x 19 in. Collection of the Jewish National and University Library, Jerusalem, 471.

Groom: Haim son of David Franco
Bride: Havah called Vida daughter of Avraham the Kohen
At the top of the page is the large inscription: "The scribe is David Yitzhak Amarillo." Amarillo was apparently a qualified scribe who made his living writing ketubbot and other documents for members of his community. He used a printed border designed for him by a local artist. Interestingly, the contract itself is not the usual ketubbah but a duplicate (*ketubbah d'irkhesa*), which according to Jewish law should be issued immediately if the original contract is lost.

Cf. IM, *Ottoman*, p. 228, fig. 9.

106B KETUBBAH

(Marriage contract)

Salonika, 1897. Lithograph on paper with hand-written text. 24¾ x 17⅝ in. Collection of Yeshiva University Museum, New York, gift of Grace Grant, 91.128.

Groom: . . . Yitzhak son of Moshe(?) Binyamin
Bride: Palomba daughter of Shulimah(?) ha-Levi
This printed ketubbah is similar to the previous example and bears the same inscription across its top, indicating that it too was printed for the scribe David Yitzhak Amarillo (see cat. no. 106A). This printed border was executed in blue ink, while the example from the collection of the Jewish National and University Library is in gold.

The name of the bride reflects an interesting folkloric practice. Prior to Mercada's birth, her mother had a number of miscarriages. Hoping to avert misfortune when she became pregnant with Mercada, she "sold" her unborn child to another woman who had many children, a common practice in such circumstances. Therefore, although her given name was Palomba, she was called Mercada, which means "bought." (*fig. 26*)

Cf. IM, *Ottoman*, p. 228, fig. 9.

107 KETUBBAH (Marriage contract)

Ottoman empire, 1897. Ink and graphite on paper. 21¼ x 16 in. Collection of Yeshiva University Museum, New York, gift of Mrs. Esther Confino, 73.5.

Groom: Yitzhak Coffina
Bride: Rivka Samuel

108 KETUBBAH (Marriage contract)

Izmir, 1912. Lithograph on paper with handwritten text. 25½ x 17¼ in. Collection of the Jewish National and University Library, Jerusalem, 557.

Groom: Nissim of Trani son of Barzilai of Trani, known as Bekhor
Bride: Victoria daughter of Ben Zion Pesahiahu ibn Haviv
Toward the end of the 19th century, Izmir's Sephardim started to use printed ketubbot, replacing the hand-decorated contracts of previous periods. However, the new borders were printed with decorations. This example, curiously printed by an Armenian press in Izmir, is a typical example, incorporating both standard and new designs and motifs. The wedding itself did not take place in Izmir but in a nearby village.

Cf. Sabar, "Decorated *Ketubbot*," pp. 224–27.

109 KETUBBAH (Marriage contract)

Shumen, 1914. Ink and watercolor on paper. 21¼ x 14⅝ in. Einhorn Collection, Tel Aviv.

Groom: Yitzhak son of Mordekhai
Bride: Sarah daughter of Avraham David
Shumen, or in the Hebrew sources "Shumla," is now part of northwest Bulgaria and is known as Kolarovgrad. The Sephardim in this town were the strongest Jewish element and virtually absorbed the indigenous Bulgarian Jews, who followed the distinctive Romaniot (Byzantine) rite.

110 KETUBBAH (Marriage contract)

Novi Bazar, Yugoslavia, 1928. Lithograph on paper with handwritten text. Artist: M. Altarae. Printer: Sarajevska Jiskaraj Lijografija. 19¾ x 13⅝ in. Collection of the Jewish Historical Museum, Belgrade.

Groom: Shmuel son of Moshe Bahor
Bride: Sarah daughter of Binyamin Barukh

The lithographed border of this ketubbah, an arched portal with flanking columns topped by Biblical verses relating to marriage, was printed in Sarajevo.

I I I KETUBBAH (Marriage contract)

Sofia, Bulgaria, 1936. Lithograph on paper with handwritten text. 22½ x 16¾ in. Collection of the Jewish National and University Library, Jerusalem, 87.

Groom: Avraham son of Yaakov Alfanadri
Bride: Sophie daughter of David Ben Avraham
The Sephardic community of Sofia and other Bulgarian cities used this colorfully printed border for the marriages of its sons and daughters in the period preceding World War II. The page incorporates typical Jewish motifs, such as the Star of David, the seven-branched menorah, and possibly the Biblical Seven Species—all set in the decorative architectural background. In the center background is the printed official seal of the "Chief Council of Bulgarian Jewry" (inscription in Hebrew and Bulgarian). *(fig. 27)*

Cf. Sabar, Ketubbah, no. 153.

I I 2 WEDDING POEM

Yeniköy (New Village), Istanbul, 1867. Ink on silk: printed; silk and metallic banding. Collection of the Judah L. Magnes Museum, Berkeley, California, in memory of Simcha Stern, 82.57.

From the 17th to the 19th century, Hebrew, Italian or Judeo-Italian wedding poems, epithalamia patterned after Renaissance models, were frequently composed to celebrate the marriage of Italian Jews (see also cat nos. 565–566). This silk sheet printed with sonnets in Italian and Hebrew was published to mark the wedding of Clarina Contessa de Camondo to Leone Alfassa. The spread of this Italian custom to Istanbul reveals the migration of Sephardic Jewry between various international centers. A community of *Levantini*, Ottoman Jews, was established in Venice, and many Italian Jews, particularly merchants and traders, lived in Istanbul and other Ottoman ports. Wedding broadsides were most usually printed on paper; the use of silk in this example is unusual. The name printed at the bottom of the sheet "E. F. Veneziani" identifies either the printer or poet.

REFERENCE: Magnes, *Embellished*, p. 13. *Cf.* NYJM, *Fabric*, cat. no. 133.

I I 3 RECEIPT FOR PAYMENT OF WEDDING TAX

Sarajevo, 1907. Ink on paper. 10⅝ x 14¼ in. Collection of the Jewish Historical Museum, Belgrade, 12/4.

This Ladino document records the payment to the community treasury of a wedding tax. The tax was calculated as 3 percent of a certain amount, probably the total value of the bridal dowry.

I I 4 CEREMONIAL BINDALLI DRESS AND CHEMISE

Ottoman empire, 19th century. Dress: velvet: silver thread washed with gold, sewn over cardboard; silver thread washed with gold wrapped around yellow silk (?) thread; silver thread twisted into coils; metal sequins. Chemise: silk; embroidered with silver thread washed with gold. L: 51½ in. Collection of Yeshiva University Museum, New York, gift of Mr. and Mrs. Nahman Yohai, 76.23.

Mrs. Buka Yohai, the donor, wore this dress during her ceremonial walk to the *mikvah*, witnessed by the community, before her marriage to Nahman Yohai in Gallipoli in 1910 (see cat. no. 122). The dress was worn by her mother, Naomi Ben Ezra, and grandmother before her. Although dresses of this type were generally worn for the prenuptial henna ceremony, or for the reception following the marriage ceremony, Western-style costumes were worn for the wedding.

This type of dress is called *bindalli*; the word means 1,000 branches. The decoration is executed in elegant radiating scrolling stems and sprays in a "tree of life" pattern. The grape clusters and sheaves of wheat are unusual decorative elements and could symbolize fertility. The style became popular with urban dwellers in Turkey during the 19th century. The triangular pieces inserted at the sides impart freedom of movement to a garment that would otherwise be narrow.

The *gömlek* (chemise) is embroidered at the neck and sleeves where the decoration would be visible. The *camisa morisca* (Moorish chemise) was a popular fashion in Spain around the time of the Expulsion; neck and sleeve ends were frequently embroidered with floral motifs or Arabic letters; even Queen Isabella's wardrobe included such items.

The style of embroidery—gold-washed metal thread wrapped around pasteboard—is called *dival* work or *kaveséra*. (*See illustration on p. 10*)

REFERENCES: Juhasz, "Marriage," IM, *Ottoman*, pp. 206; 210–213 (cf. p. 212, fig. 17; p. 213, fig. 18); NYJM, *Tale*, cat. no. 186; Micklewright, "Transformations," pp. 33–43. Micklewright, "Costumes," pp. 161–74; Anderson, pp. 189, 215. Cf. Tezcan and Delibas, cat. nos. 110, 111.

115 CEREMONIAL DRESS

Sarajevo, Yugoslavia, ca. 1890. Velvet: embroidered with strips of silver thread washed with gold, wrapped around silk (?) thread; coral beads. L: 67½ in. Collection of Yeshiva University Museum, gift of Joseph Levi, preserved by Lotti and Isidor Sumbulovic of Buenos Aires, Argentina, 75.53.

Worn by Safira Danon for her marriage to Samuel Sumbulovic in Sarajevo (then part of the Habsburg monarchy) in 1890. The embroidered ornamentation of this dress, called an *antiríya*, was created by a craftsman known as *terziya*. This is the traditional style worn on ceremonial occasions by Sephardic women in Sarajevo. It would be worn over a chemise. On her head the woman wore a *tokádo*.

The wide false sleeves resemble those fashionable in Europe during the 15th and 16th centuries, and can also be seen in the child's Purim costume from the Israel Museum (cat. no. 87).

REFERENCES: YUM, *Wedding*, cat. no. 68A; Juhasz, "Costume," IM, *Ottoman*, pp. 162–66. Cf. Rubens, *Costume*, 1967, fig. 66; Anderson, fig. 419; *Vezene*, cat. no. 74.

116 CEREMONIAL BINDALLI DRESS

Gallipoli, Turkey, 1893. Velvet: embroidered with silver threads washed with gold, sewn over cardboard; silver thread washed with gold wrapped around silk (?) thread; metal sequins. L: 86 in. Collection of Yeshiva University Museum, New York, gift of Mr. and Mrs. Sam Levine, 85.31.

These dresses, embroidered with symmetrically arranged branches, sometimes growing upwards from a vase or resembling a "tree of life," were called *bindalli* dresses. The literal translation of *bindalli* is "a thousand branches." Such dresses were popular among 19th-century urban Ottoman Moslems, Christians and Jews. This example has had material added at the waist with gathers to give it added width for ease of movement.

REFERENCE: Micklewright, "Costumes," pp. 161–74.

117 CEREMONIAL BINDALLI DRESS

Turkey, 19th–20th century. Velvet: embroidered with silver threads washed with gold, sewn over cardboard; silver thread washed with gold wrapped around silk (?) thread. L: 52 in. Collection of Yeshiva University Museum, New York, gift of Emily Caffin, 83.85.

After being used as bridal dresses, *bindalli* dresses such as this were worn on festivals, used for the *talamó* (booth-like wedding canopy used by Ottoman Jews), or donated to synagogues and converted into Torah Ark curtains. A similar custom existed in pre-Expulsion Spain, where a noblewoman's *brial* (an elegant dress) would frequently be donated to the Church and used for vestments, altar cloths or clothing for statues of the Virgin Mary.

REFERENCE: Anderson, p. 200.

118 CEREMONIAL BINDALLI DRESS

Turkey, 19th–20th century. Velvet: silver threads washed with gold, sewn over cardboard; embroidered with silver thread washed with gold wrapped around silk (?) thread; metal sequins. L: 51½ in. Collection of Mr. and Mrs. Max Eis, Oakland, California.

These elaborate dresses were popular in Turkish cities from around 1850 and could be worn by bridesmaids and relatives of the bride as well as by the bride herself during various phases of the marriage festivities. Many were subsequently donated to synagogues and converted into ceremonial textiles (see cat. no. 28).

119 WOMAN'S BODICE AND SKIRT*

Ottoman empire, 1875, remade ca. 1890. Moiré: stamped floral print. Bodice: 19½ in. long; skirt: 39 in. long. Collection of Sarah Alevy-Hirsch and Herbert Hirsch, Lakewood, New Jersey.

According to family tradition, this dress was worn by Sarah Fernandez (b. ca. 1856) of Salonika, who married Moshon Alevy of Monastir (b. ca. 1850) in 1875. The dress and lining were carefully altered in the 1890s to form a day or promenade dress in the close-fitting princess shape consisting of a basque with frill at the front, shaped to the figure, closing down the front with buttons and buttonholes, with leg-of-mutton sleeves (full in the upper part of the arm), and a flaring skirt.

The fashionable European styling demonstrates the influence and predominance of foreign fashions over local tradition as early as the 1870s when the original dress was made, and the Ottoman tailor's ability to construct European-style garments.

REFERENCES: Cunnington, pp. 368, 370; *American Dress Pattern Catalogs*, ill. 2145; pp. 78–79; Scarce, pp. 82–85; *In Style*, pp. 44–5.

120 WEDDING COSTUME

Turkey, ca. 1890. Blouse: lace. Skirt: damask. Shoes: leather, damask, embroidery. Collection of Yeshiva University Museum, New York, gift of Emily Caffin, 77.159.

The bride wore the ecru lace blouse, damask skirt and shoes for the marriage ceremony. The adoption of the European-style wedding costume, made with hooks and buttons in the Western manner instead of traditional Turkish dress, attests to the widespread Westernization prevalent in cities during the final decades of the Ottoman empire. Traditional Ottoman-style costume was loose-fitting, not tailored, and was held together with drawstrings or sashes, not with buttons. Although it could be decorated with elaborate embroidery like the *bindalli* dresses (see cat. nos. 114, 116–118), there were no ruffles or flounces.

REFERENCES: Micklewright, "Transformations," pp. 33–43; Micklewright, "Costumes," pp. 161–174.

121 VEIL

Ottoman empire, 19th–20th century. Silk: embroidered with strips of silver thread washed with gold; lace trim: silver thread, washed with gold, wrapped around silk (?) thread. 37½ x 44¾ in. Collection of Yeshiva University Museum, New York, gift of Rabbi Mitchell Serels, 79.43.

This cloth was used in the family for the *las fádas* ceremony (or *zeved ha-bat*), the naming of a baby girl. The veil is placed over the head of the mother and baby. The rabbi names the child and then lifts the veil from the baby's head. The veil is kept by the mother and eventually given to the daughter to wear at her wedding. The infant would usually be clothed in a lavish dress, often of silk. The cloth is characteristic of Turkish embroidered cloths used as headcoverings, handkerchiefs and napkins (see cat. nos. 203–212). *(See illustration on p. 10)*

REFERENCES: Juhasz, "Costume," IM, *Ottoman*, p. 143; Russo-Katz, "Childbirth," IM, *Ottoman*, p. 267.

123

122 TALLIT KATAN*

Gallipoli, 19th century. Silk batiste; embroidered with strips of silver thread washed with gold, wrapped around silk (?) thread; drawn work; wool fringes. 38 x 21½ in. Hebrew inscription: Ben Porat Yosef. Collection of Yeshiva University Museum, New York, gift of Mr. and Mrs. Nahman Yohai, 77.157.

Jewish males wear *tzitzit* (fringes) at the corners of their garments to remind them to follow the commandments in compliance with the Law as set forth in Numbers 15:37: "And you shall look upon them and remember all the commandments of the Lord and do them. . . ." This is an elaborate version of the fringed garments, worn by Nahman Yohai in Gallipoli in 1910 at his marriage to Buka (see cat. no. 114). The embroidery around the neck would be visible under his caftan.

A chemise decorated at the neck (where it would be visible) with an Arabic inscription was a popular man's garment in 15th-century Spain.

REFERENCE: Anderson, pp. 65–67.

123 BURIAL SOCIETY BOWL*

Gallipoli, 16th century. Silver: cast. Hebrew inscription: This is the vessel that was presented by the R[abbi] Mordekhai h[onored] s[on of] Yaakov Mori of b[lessed] m[emory] to the burial society of graves from the holy community of Gallipoli. M[ay it] b[e righteous] a[nd blessed] so that his memory should not be forgotten from this world for the members m[ay they] b[e righteous] a[nd blessed] and may it go up as willed. 5½ in. diam. The Pollack Collection, New York.*

This bowl may have been used for the ritual washing of the corpse by the *lavadores* (members of the burial society who performed the washing) or for collecting donations for funeral expenses.

REFERENCE: New York, Sotheby's, *Highly Important Judaica*, June 23, 1983, lot 383 (ill.).

124 MORTEJA SET (Shrouds)

Larissa, 19th century. Bembizari (raw) silk. Collection of the Jewish Museum of Greece, Athens, 85.105.

This set includes a *gömlek* (shirt), *šalvár* (bloomers), pants and tunic. *Bembizari* silk is woven on a narrow loom. Two kinds of warp threads are used—single or double strands of silk and three- or four-ply strands.

REFERENCE: Stavroulakis, pp. 13–14.

PERSONAL AND MISCELLANEOUS JUDAICA

125 TALLIT AND BAG

Yugoslavia, early 20th century. Bag: velvet, gold embroidery. Tallit: silk. Bag: 23 x 24½ x 3 in. Collection of Yeshiva University Museum, New York, gift of Haham Dr. Solomon Gaon, 86.10.

Typical tallit and bag used by upper middle class Jews in Bosnia. This tallit and bag belonged to David Finzi of Sarajevo, Yugoslavia. Finzi was the first Jew to be shot by the Nazis in Sarajevo on August 1, 1941, along with five other Jews and three Serbs.

Cf. Vezene, cat. no. 64.

126 TALLIT CORNER

Bosnia, 1888/9. Silk velvet: embroidered with silk and gilt silver threads over cardboard. Hebrew inscription: S[on of] G[oodness] Moshe Yosef Confortiah [5]649. 6 x 6½ in. Collection of the Jewish Historical Museum, Belgrade, 359.

Embroidered tallit corners are typical of Ottoman ceremonial textiles in their use of dark-colored velvets decorated with metallic threads. Due to the preciousness of the materials used in such embroideries, it was usual, as in the examples in this exhibition (cat. nos. 127–128), to wash silver threads with gold, to twist the metallic threads around a core of orange or yellow silk thread, and then to couch the twisted threads over cardboard cutouts, so as to create the impression of an expansive use of high-relief gold embroidery. Such corners were frequently made for a boy for his bar mitzvah or for a bridegroom.

REFERENCES: *Vezene,* cat. no. 55; *Jugoslavije,* cat. no. 7/15.

127 TALLIT CORNER

Godine, Bosnia, 1891/2. Silk velvet: embroidered with silk and gilt silver threads over cardboard; sequins. Hebrew incription: Yosef David Barukh [May] G[od] s[ustain him] a[nd protect him] [5]652. 6³/₁₆ x 6 in. Collection of the Jewish Historical Museum, Belgrade, 366.

REFERENCES: *Vezene,* cat. no. 51; *Jugoslavije,* cat. no. 7/22.

128 TALLIT CORNER

Godine, Bosnia, 1903/4. Silk velvet: embroidered with silk and gilt silver threads over cardboard; silver braided cord. Hebrew inscription: Avraham Shlomo Gaon t[he honorable (?)] 5664. 7³/₁₆ x 7⅜ in. Collection of the Jewish Historical Museum, Belgrade, 364.

REFERENCES: *Vezene,* cat. no. 60; *Jugoslavije,* cat. no. 7/17.

129 AMULET INDICATING UNLUCKY DAYS

Ottoman empire, 19th century. Ink, gouache and tempera(?) on paper. 14½ x 9¼ in. Collection of the Israel Museum, Jerusalem, 103/152.

This calendar marks certain days which were considered unlucky according to Sephardic folklore.

130 MULTILAYERED PAPER-CUT SHIVVITI PLAQUE

Ottoman empire, 1858/9. Ink and gouache on paper; embossed gold paper. 28 x 17 in. Collection of the Israel Museum, Jerusalem, 168/54.

Papercuts composed of many colors and textures of overlapping pieces of paper were a specialty of Ottoman craftsmen.

REFERENCE: IM, *Ottoman,* pl. 64.

131

131 AMULETIC PLAQUE*

Ottoman empire, 19th–20th century. Ink on paper; foil cutouts. 15 x 10½ in. Collection of Gloria Abrams, New York.

Cutouts were frequently used as decoration in Ottoman Judaica, and are found on a marriage contract, Esther scrolls and a manuscript in this exhibition (see cat. nos. 83, 85, 277 and 577).

MANUSCRIPTS, PRINTED BOOKS AND BINDINGS

132 ZIVHEI SHELAMIM

Istanbul, 1825. Scribe: Mordekhai Aboab. Ink and watercolor on paper. 7¼ x 4⅞ in. Gross Family Collection, Tel Aviv, Ms. OT.11.1.

This manuscript of ritual slaughter laws was copied from a printed compilation by Yehudah Divan, first published in Istanbul in 1728. The delicately decorated title page is highly unusual in Ottoman Sephardic manuscripts.

133 SHULHAN ARUKH

Constantinople, 1800/01. Ink on paper: printed; leather binding with gold tooling. Printer: Raphael Eliah Pardo. Hebrew inscription (on cover): Dedicated to G[od] by the d[eparted] . . . Eliyahu Avraham Shalom . . . 6³⁄₁₆ x 4¼ in. Gross Family Collection, Tel Aviv.

This text of the standard code of Jewish law abridged for schoolchildren includes a Ladino title page and a curious labyrinth-like illustration of the seven walls of Jericho.

134 ALEF BET EN LINGUA EBRAICA LASHON HA-KODESH

(Hebrew Alphabet)

Raphael Coria Irgat Bazar. Izmir, 1895/6. Printer: G. Tatikan. Ink on paper: printed. 6¾ x 4¾ x ⅛ in. Moldovan Family Collection, New York.

This Hebrew primer for children includes instructions in Ladino.

135 AGADA DE PESAH

(Passover Haggadah)

Ed. Eliya Gayus. Istanbul, 20th century. Ink on paper: printed. 8 x 5¾ x ¼ in. Moldovan Family Collection, New York.

This Haggadah was printed for a bookdealer, and the back cover shows an advertisement for Ladino romance novels.

136 BOOK COVER

Ottoman empire, 1817/18. Silver: chiseled, chased and engraved. Hebrew inscriptions: spine: It was merited to me for the worship of the Blessed, I . . . Mordekhai s[on of] . . . Asher Biti the year 5578; covers: Avraham Shlomo Leon . . . 6⅞ x 5⅛ x ¼ in. Gross Family Collection, Tel Aviv, 25.1.9.

This cover is exceptionally finely crafted, and was most probably presented as a gift to a prospective bridegroom from his fiancée's family. The engraved inscription on the covers is of inferior quality and was probably added by a later owner. *(fig. 70)*

137

137 BINDING FOR MAHZOR LE-ROSH HASHANAH*

(Rosh Hashanah Prayer Book)

Ottoman empire, 1890. Silver: chiseled, chased and engraved; leather: tooled. Hebrew inscription: Menahem s[on of] Mordekhai Alkalai . . . today the 14th of Nisan t[he year] (5)650. 7¾ x 5¼ x 1⅜ in. Gross Family Collection, Tel Aviv, 25.1.18.

Decorative bindings were frequently presented as gifts to bridegrooms. Although this binding is Ottoman, the prayer book was printed in Vienna, testifying to the close connections between the Habsburg and Ottoman empires (see cat. no. 541).

COSTUME

The clothing worn by Jewish women in the Ottoman empire reflected local urban styles, with the difference that married Jewish women traditionally covered their hair completely. By the mid–19th century, many Turkish women had abandoned the traditional *salvár* (baggy pants), chemise and outer robe, and replaced their traditional garb with Western styles. A velvet dress with traditional Turkish embroidery was often worn for the henna night; by the late 19th century the bride usually wore white Western-style dress and veil for the actual marriage ceremony (see cat. nos. 114–120).

138 ENTARI (Outer robe)*

Salonika, late 19th century. Silk. L: 64½ in. Collection of the Jewish Museum of Greece, Athens, 81.436.

While Jewish women in Istanbul (Constantinople) adopted elements of Western dress, Jewish women in Salonika wore clothes fashionable in Istanbul a century or two earlier. The names of the elements of womens' costume in Salonika are primarily Turkish, and the pieces were adapted from Ottoman dress.

This *entari* (outer robe) is of violet mauve graded striped silk, with a larger stripe worked in moiré. It was worn gathered with one section tucked into the pocket of the *sáyo* (underdress). On very formal occasions, a *gögüslük* (bib/plastron) would cover the upper portion of the woman's body. Over this a *devantál* (apron) would have been tied.

REFERENCES: Stavroulakis, pl. 11, pp. 17–20; Juhasz, "Costume," IM, *Ottoman*, pp. 143–52; *Cf.* p. 148, fig. 35.

139 SÁYO (Underdress)*

Salonika, late 19th century. Silk; velvet appliqué. L: 52 in. Collection of the Jewish Museum of Greece, Athens, 81.51.

This is a garment worn under the *entari* (outer robe) in Salonika over the *salvár* (baggy pants). It consists of a wrap-around skirt with an upper section having a back, cut to accommodate arm openings, and deeply scooped out over the bust. This *sáyo* is of cream silk with striped pattern in silk threads and a repeat appliquéd floral design.

REFERENCES: Stavroulakis, pl. 11, pp. 17–20; Juhasz, "Costume," IM, *Ottoman*, pp. 143–52; *Cf.* p. 149, fig. 36.

140 ENTARI (Outer robe)

Salonika, early 20th century. Silk. Collection of the Judah L. Magnes Museum, Berkeley, California, 78.26.1.

This long-sleeved dress would have been worn over a *sáyo* or *fálda* (underdress), a plain, undyed *kamíza* (chemise) with lace or embroidered decoration at the neck and wrists, *salvár* (pants) and possibly European-style underwear. The red stripes visible on the underside of the garment when it is folded as it was worn in Salonika were to ward off the *ayin ha-ra* (the evil eye).

REFERENCES: Juhasz, "Costume," IM, *Ottoman*, pp. 143–52; *Cf.* p. 148, fig. 35; Magnes, *Threads*, cat. no. 21.

141 BLOUSE

Turkey, ca. 1890. Taffeta: lace, brocade band, silk ribbon. Collection of Yeshiva University Museum, New York, gift of Emily Caffin, 77.159.

Women often wore the dress in which they had been married on subsequent occasions, rather than putting it in storage never to be worn again. According to family tradition, this blouse was sometimes worn with the ecru skirt (cat. no. 120) which was worn by Esther Ouriel Coffina (see cat. no. 142) at her wedding.

142 YACHTING/SAILOR DRESS

Turkey, ca. 1890. Silk taffeta: lace trim. L: 38 in. Collection of Yeshiva University Museum, New York, gift of Emily Caffin, 77.158.

This dress was made for the bridal trousseau of Esther Ouriel Coffina. Ottoman Jews prepared elaborate trousseaux for their brides. Dowries consisting of personal clothing, jewelry, housewares, heirloom trousseau artifacts and possibly a house or a business partnership, were traditionally arranged as part of the marital agreement. Several days before the wedding, the trousseau was displayed at the bride's home in a festivity known as *ašugar*.

Sailor costumes first became popular in England because of a portrait by Winterhalter of the future King Edward VII wearing a sailor suit. Their popularity continued because of the passion of this king and his family for yachting. This style spread through Europe and America. Western styles, such as this dress, became popular in the Ottoman empire in the 19th century and were widely accepted after World War I and the establishment of the modern Turkish state.

143 DRESS

Ottoman empire, 19th–20th century. Silk: embroidered with silver thread washed with gold wrapped around silk(?) thread. L: 51 in. Collection of Yossi Benyaminoff, Jerusalem.

This costume could have been worn by a woman living on the periphery of the Ottoman empire.

144 SKIRT

Turkey, 19th–20th century. Wool flannel. L: 39 in. Collection of Mr. and Mrs. Benjamin Simons, Delray Beach, Florida.

145 SKIRT

Turkey, 19th–20th century. Linen. L: 39 in. Collection of Mr. and Mrs. Benjamin Simons, Delray Beach, Florida.

146 MEST (Socks)

Canakkale, Turkey, late 19th/early 20th century. Cotton. 20¼ x 5¼ in. Collection of Yeshiva University Museum, New York, gift of Betty Pinto, 90.53.

Worn under slippers.

147 VEIL

Ottoman empire, possibly Egypt, 20th century. Cotton tulle: silver thread. 86 x 26 in. Collection of Yeshiva University Museum, New York, 90.51.

Veils of this type were popular during the early 20th century, both as head coverings and as shawls. Many were made in the Middle East.

Cf. Israel Museum, IM.115.77.

High wooden shoes (clogs) called *galéčas* or *kam kam* were sometimes worn in the street to protect shoes and the hems of clothing. They were also worn to the *mikvah* (ritual bath) and the *hammam* (public bath), in which the ritual bath was generally housed. Their design is highly functional: water would not ruin the wooden clogs and their elevated soles protected the wearer from slipping on the wet floor, burning her feet on the heated marble floor or being burned by residue from corrosive depilatories. Clogs also prevented delicately embroidered bath towels from becoming stained.

Clogs were sent as a gift before the wedding from the prospective bridegroom to his betrothed as a component of the *bógo de bányo* (bath bundle kerchief), a group of bath accessories to be used by the bride in preparation for her prenuptial immersion in the *mikvah* and at the party held at the bath house in her honor.

One version of this footwear was popular among ladies in 15th-century Spain for keeping the hems of their clothes clear of mud and sand. The Spanish *chapín* had cork soles covered with leather (often tooled) or metal, or covered with fabric; the vamps were often fabric. The shape of the Spanish *chapín* was oval, while the Italian version was narrower at the center, as are the Turkish examples (cat. nos. 148–150).

The bath houses were modeled on the Roman system: steaming, scrubbing, massaging, tepidarium (warm room) and caldarium (hot room). They were frequently built on Roman sites adapted by the Byzantines. Socialization was an important part of a visit to the bath, which frequently took up a great deal of time. The bath was also a place for exchanging gossip. Lady Mary Wortley Montagu (1689–1762) spent fifteen months in Adrianople and Constantinople with her husband, who served as English ambassador to the court of Sultan Ahmed III (1703–1730). Her published letters provide a vivid account of a visit to the bath house which Turkish ladies generally visited once a week. "In short, 'tis the women's coffee-house, where all the news of the town is told, scandal invented, etc."

REFERENCES: Juhasz, "Marriage," IM, *Ottoman*, pp. 205–6; Wilcox, p. 74; Lewis, pp. 112–14; Anderson, pp. 229–34; Pick, p. 97.

148 GALÉČAS (Bath clogs)

Ottoman empire, 19th–20th century. Sole: wood: applied silver plate; hammered, repoussé. Vamps: leather, fabric; embroidered with metal thread. 5¾ x 9⅜ x 3⅜ in. Collection of Yossi Benyaminoff, Jerusalem.

149 GALÉČAS (Bath clogs)

Ottoman empire, 19th–20th century. Sole: wood: lead; mother-of-pearl. Vamps: leather, velvet; embroidered with metal thread. 4¾ x 9¼ x 4½ in. Collection of Yossi Benyaminoff, Jerusalem.

150 GALÉČAS (Bath clogs)

Ottoman empire, 19th–20th century. Wood: carved. 5¼ x 9¾ x 3½ in. Collection of Yeshiva University Museum, New York, gift of Emily Caffin, 83.93a,b.

151 SHOES

Istanbul, 19th–20th century. Stamped: Yerlimamulati Mercan Terlikeles. Velvet: embroidered with silver thread washed with gold. 8½ x 2 in. Collection of the Sephardic Studies Department, Yeshiva University, New York, gift of Abraham Pinto, Yeshiva University Museum, 77.161 a,b.

Worn by the bride to the *mikvah* the night before her wedding.

CLOTHING FROM THE TROUSSEAU OF DJOYA HATTEM

(cat. nos. 152–156) *Canakkale, late 19th century Collection of Jane Mushabac, New York*

152 SUMMER SKIRT

Cotton: handmade lace. 84 x 77 in.

153 SKIRT

Wool: embroidered with silk thread. Monogram: D H. L: 39½ in.

These two skirts are cut in the silhouette fashionable in Europe in the 1830s and 1840s rather than contemporary late 19th-century style.

154 CHEMISE

Cotton: lace. L: 49½ in.

The chemise is a Western-style garment worn over the body, under the corset. The decorative lace could have been purchased ready-made, or copied from European fashion books.

REFERENCES: Wilcox, pp. 70, 229, 239; Kybalová, Herbenová and Lamarová, p. 450. Cf. Blum, fig. c, p. 146; figs. g and i, pp. 246–47.

155 DRAWERS

Cotton: embroidered, cut work; buttons. Monogram: D H. L: 50 in.

Few references to this form of women's undergarment exist before the early 19th century, when the revealing Empire style became popular. Both these pairs of drawers have ties to close them rather than drawstrings like the Turkish *salvár* (pants); this shows the influence of European methods of tailoring as well as style and fabric.

REFERENCES: Micklewright, "Transformations," pp. 33–43. *Cf.* Blum, figs. h–j, p. 207; fig. h, p. 246.

156 DRAWERS

Cotton: machine-made lace; silk ribbon trim. Monogram: D H. L: 31¾ in.

157

PERSONAL ARTIFACTS

The first public announcement of a marriage was made at the *shiddukhin* (betrothal) ceremony, at which time both families agreed on their respective economic obligations to the couple. In the Ottoman empire, it was customary for the groom or his father to purchase jewelry for the bride with the *medudim* (money received from the bride's father). This jewelry, and the jewelry the bride received from her father, included necklaces, bracelets and belts, and was included in the valuation of the dowry.

One of the Jewish prenuptial festivities in Turkey was the *ašugar*, at which the bride's dowry was displayed on the walls, tables, chairs and beds of her home for inspection by the community. At this time, the elders of the community assessed the value of the dowry and incorporated it into the marriage contract. The dowry would then be ceremonially carried to the groom's home by relatives of the bride. It included personal clothing (sometimes including shrouds), *shimmushei arsa* (bedclothes including a richly embroidered bedspread), home furnishings (especially a rug), jewelry, a sweet set, and other silver. Although embroidered items could be purchased, all girls learned to embroider, and many worked on articles for their own trousseaux. A Sephardic expression *la ija en la faša l'ašugar en la kaša* ("The girl is in diapers but her dowry is already in the chest") attests to the early stage in a girl's life at which the preparation of the dowry could begin. The bride's clothes were often embroidered (or purchased) during the interval between the betrothal and the wedding. Trousseau shops could provide the bride with all required linens, although during the 19th and 20th centuries many families who could afford to do so either purchased clothing and linens abroad or ordered them from Europe.

REFERENCES: Wilcox, 1969, p. 74; Juhasz, "Marriage," IM, *Ottoman*, pp. 197–205.

157 NECKLACE*

*Ottoman empire, 19th–20th century. Gold: cast.
L: 18½; w: 2¼ in. Collection of Mr. and Mrs.
Abraham Halpern, New York.*

Delicate necklace typical of Turkish jewelry
owned by urban women, frequently given to
brides as part of their dowry.

REFERENCE: Russo-Katz, "Jewelry," IM, *Ottoman*,
pp. 172–95.

158

158 PAIR OF BRACELETS*

*Ottoman empire, 19th–20th century. Gold: open-
work. Diam.: 2½ in.; w: ⅞ in. Collection of Mr.
and Mrs. Abraham Halpern, New York.*

Openwork bracelets with floral motifs characteristic of the jewelry worn by Jewish women
in urban areas.

159 MANÍA DE ČATÓN

(Bracelet)

*Ottoman empire, 19th–20th century. Silver: gold
wash. 2⅜ x 3½ in. Collection of Yossi Benyaminoff, Jerusalem.*

A matched pair of chain bracelets was a popular wedding gift to a bride from her father. She
would have worn one such trinket on each
wrist. Such bracelets are known as *manía de
čatón* or *manía de menteše* (hinged bracelets).

162

The chain is composed of geometric elements,
while the engraving on the terminal is foliate.

REFERENCE: Russo-Katz, "Jewelry," IM, *Ottoman*,
pp. 179–80.

160 MANÍA DE ČATÓN

(Bracelet)

*Ottoman empire, 19th–20th century. Silver: gold
wash. 3¼ x 3 in. Collection of Yossi Benyaminoff,
Jerusalem.*

Elizabeth Anne Finn (d. 1921), whose husband served as British consul in Jerusalem
from 1846 to 1862 (see also cat. nos. 305–
306), wrote a detailed description of the
clothes and jewels worn by women of a Jewish
family she visited, including bracelets similar
to these, ". . . composed of a multitude of
beautifully-wrought flexible chains. . . ."

REFERENCE: Rubens, *Costume*, 1973, p. 47.

161 BELT WITH BUCKLE

*Ottoman empire, probably Bulgaria, late 19th cen-
tury. Silver: filigree; gilt. 3¹¹⁄₁₆ x 30¾ in. Moldovan Family Collection, New York.*

Belts were popular elements of women's dress
in the Ottoman empire and were frequently
given as wedding gifts. This belt is composed
of rounded rectangular silver filigree plaques
joined together, fastened by a filigree buckle
in the form of a bow. Although belts composed of metal plates are known from 16th-
century Bulgaria, this type is not typical of
traditional (or folk) forms, and does not derive
from amuletic jewelry. The belt reflects Ottoman style and probably belonged to a wealthy
urban woman.

Cf. Dancheva-Blagoeva, fig. 74.

162 BELT AND BUCKLE*

*Ottoman empire, 19th–20th century. Buckle:
metal: filigree, gold wash; glass inlays. Belt:
leather. 4⅛ x 31 in. Collection of Yossi Benyaminoff, Jerusalem.*

Leather belt with metal buckle consisting of
three separate elements with foliate filigree
decoration, typical of Ottoman dress. Belts
similar to this can be seen in several prints in
this exhibition.

REFERENCE: Rosen-Ayalon, "Ashkelon," fig. 1.

163 BELT WITH BUCKLE

Ottoman empire, 19th–20th century. Silver: mesh and cast. 2 x 35 in. Collection of Yossi Benyaminoff, Jerusalem.

The motif of the hand holding flowers is popular in Ottoman decorative vocabulary; we see it also in a belt buckle from Morocco (cat. no. 423).

Cf. Russo-Katz, "Jewelry," IM, *Ottoman*, pp. 178–79; pl. 40 (IM 471.67).

164 BELT BUCKLE

Ottoman empire, 19th–20th century. Gold: filigree; turquoise. 2 x 1¾; 2 x 3 in. Collection of Yossi Benyaminoff, Jerusalem.

Delicate gold buckle, originally consisting of two separate elements, now joined on a gold backing. This may have been a bridegroom's wedding gift to his bride.

165 BELT BUCKLE

Ottoman empire, 19th–20th century. Silver: filigree, paste inlay. 6¾ x 6½ in. Collection of Yossi Benyaminoff, Jerusalem.

Elaborate buckle decorated with a six-pointed star. Similar pieces were used as lids for boxes. This piece may have been made in a locality near the Russian border.

166 BELT BUCKLE

Ottoman empire, 19th–20th century. Silver: filigree, embossed; coral. 3¾ x 2½; 2¼ x 4½ in. Collection of Yossi Benyaminoff, Jerusalem.

This buckle could have been attached to a belt of woven or embroidered cloth or leather. The six-pointed star is probably purely decorative, without specific Jewish reference.

Cf. Russo-Katz, "Jewelry," IM, *Ottoman*, pl. 39 (IM 522.75).

167 WORRY BEADS

Turkey, 19th–20th century. Celluloid (?). Collection of Fortuna Calvo Roth, New York.

Although Jews do not use beads for prayer as do their Christian neighbors, these beads were useful for tense and nervous hands, especially for the men on Shabbat when they could not smoke. This set belonged to the lender's father, Isaac Calvos.

168 AMULET CASE

Asia Minor, 19th century. Silver: repoussé and gilt. 1⅛ x 3½ in. diam. Collection of the Jewish Museum, New York, F4918.

169 ESKRIVANIÁ (Pencase)

Turkey, 19th–20th century. Silver: cast. 1¾ x 10¼ in. Collection of Mr. and Mrs. Abraham Halpern, New York.

A container for writing implements (quills or steel pens) and an inkwell are joined in this simple, utilitarian form, characteristic of the Ottoman empire. An *eskrivaniá* was frequently a wedding gift made to a bridegroom. A similar piece is worn by the *Jewish Scribe of Today in His Workroom* (cat. no. 314).

REFERENCES: Rubens, *Iconography*, 1981, fig. 176; Juhasz, "Marriage," IM, *Ottoman*, pp. 199–200.

170 STAR OF DAVID BUTTON

Sofia, Bulgaria, ca. 1941. Bakelite. Collection of Museum of Jewish Heritage, New York, gift of Rosette Bakish, 275.88.

Under Nazi rule, Bulgarian Jews were forced to wear bakelite buttons rather than the more familiar cloth stars imposed in other Central and East European countries. This button was worn by Rosette Bakish as a child in Sofia.

DOMESTIC OBJECTS

171 WATER JUG

Turkey, 19th–20th century. Copper: cast. 17 x 8 in. Collection of Fortuna Calvo Roth, New York.

This simple domestic item, with its elegant shape, is characteristic of the "plain tradition" of Turkish metalwork. The graceful shape, the structural elements (the hinged lid, the joints between body and handle) and the smooth expanse of metal are the only decorative elements.

REFERENCE: Allen, p. 27.

172

172 EWER AND BASIN*

Ottoman empire, 19th–20th century. Brass: cast. 13 x 11½ in.; 14 x 5¼ in. Collection of Rabbi Joshua Plaut, Weathersfield, Connecticut.

This pitcher and basin were used for the washing of hands by a *mohel* (ritual circumciser). The elegant proportions of these pieces are characteristic of Turkish metalwork. Such sets were used for domestic and ritual purposes also by Muslims.

Cf. NYJM, *Tale,* cat. no. 161; NYJM, *Treasures,* p. 46.

173 COFFEE GRINDER

Turkey, 19th–20th century. Brass: cast; engraved. H: 11¼ in. Collection of Fortuna Calvo Roth, New York.

Characteristic form of coffee grinder found in many parts of the Ottoman empire, including Turkey and Greece. This one is stamped "Murat Hasan / Demir / Uzuncarsi No. 59" on the base.

174 SHERBET POT

Turkey, 19th–20th century. Brass. 10½ x 8 in. Collection of Fortuna Calvo Roth, New York.

In Turkey, sherbet was served in liquid form as a cold drink.

175 FOUR SWEET SPOONS

Turkey, 19th–20th century. Silver: cast, chased. L: 6¾ in. Collection of Florence Abravaya Newman and Joseph Newman, Massapequa, New York.

The stamped pattern on the shaft of these spoons is characteristic of Ottoman metalwork and can be found on Jewish ritual objects as well (cat. no. 50). Special sweets were offered to guests on entering the home. A *tavlá de dúlse* (set for serving sweets) or pieces used for serving sweets were common wedding gifts. A complete sweet set is included in this exhibition (cat. no. 176).

176 TAVLÁ DE DÚLSE
(Set for serving sweets)*

*Turkey, 19th–20th century. platikos and forks:
Y[ehudah] Kazaz. platikos: 8¾ x 5¾ in.; forks:
L: 7 in. kuçarera: B[en-Zion] Bitton; 5¾ x 1¾ in.
spoons: A. Anesian; L: 6¾ in.; goblets: 5½ x 3¼
in.; tray: 22½ x 15 in. Silver: cast. Collection of
Mrs. Mathilde Turiel, New York.*

A bride's dowry frequently included a *tavlá de
dúlse* (serving set for sweets) consisting of the
platas (silver tray), the *kuçarera* (on which forks
and spoons hung), spoons and forks (six of
each), and two or more *platikos* (dishes for the
sweets). Cups of water would also be placed
on the tray. The sweets served were fruit pre-
serves and *sarope* (boiled white sugar containing almonds and nuts). A servant, a daughter
of the household, or the hostess herself would
greet the guest holding out the tray to him.
The guest would partake of the sweets, replace
the utensil in the *kuçarera*, and then take a sip
of water. Coffee would be served later. Serving sets for sweets were used in many parts of
the Ottoman empire, including Syria (cat. no.
291).

The hallmark "Y. Kazaz" is stamped in
Hebrew and Latin characters on several of
these pieces. Yehuda Kazaz was a merchant in
Izmir (Smyrna) who commissioned silver
from craftsmen for Jewish clients.

Ben-Zion Bitton is a Jewish silversmith
who worked in Izmir from the 1920s until
1976, when he settled in Israel. The *kuçarera* is
decorated with a classical scene of graces holding garlands.

REFERENCE: Juhasz, "Sweets," pp. 72–79. *Cf.* Juhasz, "Marriage," IM, *Ottoman*, p. 204, fig. 5.

177 BONBONNIÈRE

*Ottoman empire, 19th–20th century. Silver fili-
gree; glass insert. 5¾ x 7 in. Collection of Mrs.
Mathilde Turiel, New York.*

Filigree was popular throughout the Ottoman
empire; for a silver filigree sweet set used in
Syria, see cat. no. 291.

178 COFFEE SET

*Ottoman empire, 19th–20th century. Copper:
enamel. Collection of the Judah L. Magnes Museum, Berkeley, California, 85.35.2.*

Drinking small cups of very strong, sweet coffee was part of the ritual following the serving of sweets. However, during periods of
mourning, only coffee was served. Although
there were some early bronze pieces decorated
with enamel work, enamel was rarely used
on metal other than weapons in the Ottoman
empire.

REFERENCE: Kühnel, pp. 185–86.

179 BOWL

*Luneville, France, and Ottoman empire, 19th–
20th century. Earthenware: glazed. 2¾ x 4⅛ in.
diam. Collection of Prof. and Mrs. Solomon Feffer,
New York.*

This bowl was manufactured in France, but
the overglaze decoration was added in the Ottoman empire. The six-pointed star was a
popular Islamic motif; it does not necessarily
indicate any association with a Jewish owner
or craftsman.

180 TEA CUP, SAUCER AND SPOON

*Turkey, 20th century. Cup and saucer: glass.
Spoon: silver. Collection of Fortuna Calvo Roth,
New York.*

Pieces from a tea set used in Turkey; the
spoons are decorated with a crescent moon,
which became the official emblem of the
military in the early 19th century, and the
emblem on the flag of the Turkish Republic in
1923.

181 ROSE WATER CONTAINER*

*Turkey, mid-19th century. Silver: repoussé,
chased, engraved and parcel-gilt. Hebrew inscription: C[reator of the] s[pecies of] s[pices]. 7¼ x
2⅝ in. Collection of Mr. and Mrs. Victor Topper,
Toronto, Canada.*

Rose water was used in the home for welcom-
ing guests, and for creating an aromatic ambience. Ottoman Jews also used rosewater for
havdalah when a blessing over fragrance marks
the end of the Sabbath, and in the synagogue.
The Hebrew inscription on this example was
probably added by a Jewish owner; it is an

176

abbreviation referring to the blessing recited before inhaling fragrant spices or perfumes, either at *havdalah* or at any other time.

REFERENCE: Geneva, Habsburg, Feldman, *Judaica*, June 19, 1989, lot no. 51/173.

182 TÜTSÜLÜK
(Incense container and burner)*

Turkey, mid-19th century. Silver: repoussé, chased, engraved, cast and parcel-gilt. 5 x 5½ x 5¾ in. Collection of Mr. and Mrs. Victor Topper, Toronto, Canada.

Containers of this type are known to have been used in Jewish homes in Turkey and elsewhere in the Ottoman empire. The larger fruit shape held burning charcoal; the smaller one, incense which was sprinkled on the embers. These containers were not used for the blessing over spices at *havdalah*, when Ottoman Jews used rose water sprinklers or hand-held spices to mark the separation between the Sabbath and weekday.

REFERENCE: Geneva, Habsburg, Feldman, *Judaica*, June 19, 1989, lot no. 51/183.

183 TÜTSÜLÜK
(Incense container and burner)

Turkey, 19th century. Silver: cast, engraved and parcel-gilt. 5¼ x 5⁵⁄₁₆ x 4¹⁵⁄₁₆ in. Collection of the Jewish Museum, New York, F4072.

This container reflects the Turkish interest in naturalistic depiction. The pine cone–shaped fruits tilt as if blown by the wind. The pine cone was a popular form in Ottoman silver, and can be seen in a Torah finial in this exhibition (cat. no. 47B).

REFERENCE: NYJM, *Tale*, cat. no. 160.

184 TÁSA DE BÁNYO
(Bowl for use in bath)

Turkey, 20th century. Silver: repoussé. 2 x 7⅞ in. Collection of Mr. and Mrs. Ivan Schick, New York.

The baths had basins with running water, into which bowls were dipped and emptied over the bather to remove soap. Women visiting the *hammam* (public baths) brought their own bowls, soap, pumice and towels. The bowls could be simple or lavishly decorated, made of copper or of silver like this example based on a traditional form. A *tása* could form part of the *bógo de bányo* (bath bundle) of bath items given by a groom to his fiancée.

182

181

185 BOX

Turkey, 19th–20th century. Leather: velvet, embroidered with silver thread washed with gold. Collection of Yossi Benyaminoff, Jerusalem.

Such boxes could be used to hold treasures of any sort: books, jewels or documents. Note the similarity of the decorative embroidery to that on the *bindalli* dresses (cat. nos. 114, 116–118).

186 SEWING MACHINE

American, 19th–20th century. Singer Manufacturing Co. 11 x 9½. Collection of Jane Mushabac, New York.

A *mákina de kuzír* (sewing machine) was a major item on Turkish dowry lists. This one was used in Turkey by Djoya Hattem Crespi

to sew her trousseau, of which several items are included in this catalogue (cat. nos. 152–156). She brought this machine, a prized possession, to America with her when she emigrated.

187 DECORATIVE TEXTILE

Ottoman empire, 19th–20th century. Linen: embroidered with silk threads. Hebrew inscription: Zion. 35 in. diam. Moldovan Family Collection, New York.

Tambour chain-stitch embroideries of this type were very popular in the Ottoman empire. Textiles with distinctly Jewish imagery may have been made for domestic or ceremonial use, or sold as souvenirs.

REFERENCE: Weinstein, fig. no. 210. *Cf.* IM, *Ottoman*, pp. 86–90.

188

188 WALL HANGINGS MADE FROM PILLOWCASES*

Canakkale, Turkey, late 19th century. Silk: embroidered with silk thread; watercolor. 17¾ x 19¾. Collection of Florence Abravaya Newman and Joseph Newman, Massapequa, New York.

These wall hangings were probably made for the lender's grandmother, Rachel Cohen (Abravaya) when she came to America from Turkey in the early 20th century. One depicts a harbor scene with a boat which flies an American flag, symbolizing Rachel's new home.

On the second pillowcase, a young girl under her mother's watchful eye performs the *mitzvah* of charity by giving a coin to a beggar. The girl and her mother both wear stylish Edwardian clothes.

189 WALL HANGING DEPICTING PASTORAL SCENE*

Canakkale, Turkey, ca. 1902. Maker: Djoya Hattem Crespi. Silk: embroidered with silk threads. 41¼ x 25 in. Collection of Jane Mushabac, New York.

Charming pastoral embroidery depicting a shepherd with his flock. Canakkale is identified as the site of ancient Troy.

190 BEDSPREAD

Velvet: silver threads washed with gold, sewn over cardboard; embroidered with silver thread washed with gold wrapped around thread; metal sequins. Collection of Dr. and Mrs. Raymond Behar, New Port Richey, Florida.

189

An elaborate bedspread was an important item in a bride's trousseau. After the woman gave birth, it would be placed on her bed when she received visitors. Many such bedspreads were later inscribed and donated to a synagogue for use as ark curtains.

REFERENCES: Russo-Katz, "Childbirth," IM, *Ottoman*, pp. 259–60; *Cf.* p. 258, fig. 3; p. 259, fig. 4.

191 BEDCOVER

Turkey, 19th–20th century. Linen: drawn work. 79 x 88 in. Collection of Mr. and Mrs. Benjamin Simons, Delray Beach, Florida.

European-style textiles became popular in Turkey and gradually replaced the traditional elaborately embroidered velvet pieces. This bedspread was part of a trousseau (see cat. nos. 196–202 for other items from this trousseau).

192 PILLOWCASE

Ottoman empire, 19th–20th century. Velvet: silver threads washed with gold, sewn over cardboard; embroidered with silver threads washed with gold wrapped around silk(?) thread; metal sequins. 17 x 34½ in. Collection of Dr. and Mrs. Raymond Behar, New Port Richey, Florida.

This pillowcase was used on the bed when receiving guests after childbirth.

193 PILLOWCASE

Turkey, 19th–20th century. Silk: cotton net; silk embroidery. 20½ x 18½ in. Collection of Fortuna Calvo Roth, New York.

Pillowcases with net and floral embroidery were popular in the Ottoman empire in the late 19th–early 20th centuries. This one is appliquéd with a pattern of violets and reflects the influence of European taste and patterns.

194 BATH TOWELS

Turkey, 19th–20th century. Cotton: metal thread embroidery. Collection of Fortuna Calvo Roth, New York.

Pulled-thread cotton towels of the type known to us as "Turkish towels" are not known to have been used in Turkey until early in the 19th century. Used to dry the body, they are called *tuváža*.

REFERENCE: Berry, "Towels—II," p. 254.

195 RUG

Ottoman empire, 19th–20th century. Wool. Collection of Dr. and Mrs. Raymond Behar, New Port Richey, Florida.

TEXTILES FROM A TROUSSEAU

(cat. nos. 196–202) *Turkey, 19th–20th century*
Collection of Mr. and Mrs. Benjamin Simons, Delray Beach, Florida

196 TABLE COVER
31¾ x 15¾ in.

197 BEDCOVER
Cotton: crocheted. 90 x 102 in.

198 TABLE COVER
31¾ x 15¾ in.

199 TABLE COVER
Linen: lace. 37 x 39 in.

200 TABLE COVER
Linen. 27 x 40 in.

201 SHELF BORDER
Cotton: crocheted. 4½ x 82½ in.

202 RUG
Ottoman empire, late 19th–early 20th century. Wool, woven. 26¾ x 32½ in.

Rugs were often part of a woman's dowry.

In Turkey, gold and silver thread for embroidery was widely available. However, in times of financial trouble, sumptuary laws were enacted forbidding its manufacture. There was no governmental quality control, and foreigners were warned that gold and silver thread could be debased with copper. George I Rákóczy, Prince of Transylvania, returned one shipment in which the silver had been debased with copper. The manufacture of towels and handkerchiefs with gold or silver embroidery was a cottage industry in Istanbul. Women executed the silk embroidery, including commissions for the Sultan's harem.

Embroidered rectangles and squares were used for wrapping cloths (bohça), napkins (long rectangular textiles called yaglik), handkerchiefs, towels and head coverings and were often given as gifts. The lace-trimmed towel used to cover the hair after bathing at the hammam was sometimes called tokadór de bányo.

Virtually every woman who visited Turkey during the 18th and 19th centuries managed to visit a harem. Lady Mary Wortley Montagu (1689–1762), the wife of the English Ambassador to the Sultan's court, records that at the end of a visit to a harem in Adrianople (Edirne), she was given a basket of embroidered handkerchiefs by her hostess who requested that she ". . . wear the richest one for her sake, and [give] the others to my woman and interpretress." Another visitor, a Mrs. Harvey, remarked that a lady was expected to pat the tips of her fingers daintily rather than rub them when presented with an embroidered towel with which to dry her hands. But Lady Mary, in a letter written to her sister in 1718, mentions her regret at using such fine napkins ". . . all tiffany embroidered with silks and gold in the finest manner in natural flowers" to wipe her fingers during the meal, and later using fresh ones to dry her hands after washing them.

REFERENCES: Berry, "Towels—II," pp. 251–65; Tezcan and Delibas, p. 163; Lewis, p. 111; Johnstone, pp. 10–11; von Palotay, p. 3659; Juhasz, "Marriage," IM, Ottoman, p. 205; Pick, pp. 132, 164.

203 TOWEL

Bitolj, Macedonia, 19th century. Cotton: embroidered with silver thread washed with gold. 29½ x 62 in. Collection of the Jewish Historical Museum, Belgrade, 182/241.

REFERENCE: Vezene, cat. no. 85.

204 TOWEL

Macedonia, 19th century. Cotton: embroidered with silk and with silver thread washed with gold. 16 x 35½ in. Collection of the Jewish Historical Museum, Belgrade.

205 TOWEL

Ottoman empire, 19th–20th century. Linen: embroidered with silk and with silver thread washed with gold. Collection of Mrs. Mathilde Turiel, New York.

Sections of embroidered decoration from a towel have been sewn together to form a rectangle.

206 TOWEL

Turkey, 19th–20th century. Linen: embroidered with silk thread, and with silver strips washed with gold; drawn work. Collection of Fortuna Calvo Roth, New York.

A variety of flowers and sprays, with the addition of a grapevine motif. The pattern is the same on both sides.

207 TOWEL*

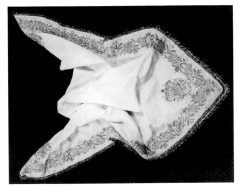

207

Ottoman empire, possibly Rhodes, 19th–20th century. Linen: embroidered with strips of silver washed with gold; and with silver strips washed with gold around silk(?); silk thread; pulled work. 35 x 35 in. Collection of Stella Levi, New York.

Used as a *tokadór de bányo* (head towel for the bath) by the leader's mother, Miriam Notrica Levi. Similar headdresses, called *yemeni*, are characterized by the *oya* (needle lace) with which they are trimmed, which would frame the forehead.

Cf. Juhasz, "Costume," *Ottoman*, p. 144; cat. no. 31.

208 TOWEL

Ottoman empire, possibly Rhodes, 19th–20th century. Linen: embroidered with strips of silver washed with gold; silver wire washed in gold wrapped around silk(?) thread; silk thread. 42 x 42 in. Collection of Stella Levi, New York.

The floral motifs include tulips (which are native to Asia [Russia/Armenia/Turkey]; they were brought from Constantinople and the Levant to the Netherlands, where they were widely cultivated in the 16th century) and carnations executed in pastel shades. The embroidery, in a stitch similar to satin stitch, is very fine, and looks the same on both sides. This piece was used as a *tokadór de bányo* (head towel for the bath).

210

212

209 TOWEL

Probably Ottoman empire, 19th–20th century. Linen: embroidered with silk thread and with silver thread washed with gold; drawn work. 49 x 22 in. Collection of Rabbi Mitchell Serels, New Rochelle, New York.

According to family tradition the hillocks with flowers embroidered on this towel were intended to recall a landscape at the banks of the Nile. The towel was used at the Passover Seder.

    This towel is a fine example of the Ottoman type used as napkins and head coverings in the bathhouse. The work is equally fine on both sides.

210 TOWEL*

Ottoman empire, late 19th century. Linen: embroidered with silk thread and with strips of silver. 54 x 18 in. Collection of Ita Aber, Yonkers, New York.

Stylized cypress trees and bowls of flowers in a finely-embroidered design appear the same on both sides of the towel. The pattern of the fabric alternates flat and tufted areas.

211 TOWEL

Ottoman empire, late 19th century. Linen: embroidered with silk thread and with strips of silver thread washed with gold. 54 x 18 in. Collection of Ita Aber, Yonkers, New York.

A lively pattern of floral sprays in pale shades of blue, green, cream and pink.

212 BORDER FROM A TOWEL*

Ottoman empire, 19th–20th century. Linen: embroidered with silk thread and strips of silver thread washed with gold; drawn work. Fringe: strips of silver thread wrapped around silk(?) thread; fringe is braided. 11 x 18¾ in. Collection of Yossi Ben-yaminoff, Jerusalem.

Garden scene consisting of cypress trees and of kiosks on small hills alongside a stream. The pattern is the same on both sides. Evidence of the continuity of certain elements of Ottoman culture from its heyday in the 16th and 17th centuries, including the passion for gardens and the ornamentation of textiles with brightly colored flowers.

REFERENCES: Tezcan and Delibas, p. 163; Lewis, p. 111; Johnstone, pp. 10–11; Berry, "Towels – II," pp. 251–65; Mackie, pp. 365–68; Cf. Mackie, fig. 219.

PRINTS

213 FEMME JUIVE COURTIÈRE QUI PORTE SES MARCHANDISES AUX JEUNES DAMES TURQUES QUI NE PEUVENT SORTIR*

(Jewish broker bringing her merchandise to young Turkish women unable to go out)

Paris, 1714. Jean-Baptiste Vanmour. Engraver: Philippe Simmoneau (1685–ca. 1753). M. de Ferriol, Ambasador du Roi à la Porte, Recueil de cent estampes représentant differentes Nations du Levant, #65. Colored engraving. 14¹/₁₆ x 9³/₄ in. Moldovan Family Collection, New York.

The woman wears a characteristic dark (blue) outdoors cloak, a white head shawl and yellow leather shoes. Charles, Marquis de Ferriol (1652?–1722), served as Ambassador of Louis XIV of France to the Sultan from 1699–1709; the Sultan in question would have been Mustafa II (reigned 1695–1703), followed by Ahmed III (reigned 1703–1730).

The figure of the Jewish woman with connections at the court of the Sultan captivated the imagination of several European travelers, perhaps because of the heights of power to which such a woman could rise.

Generally, the women who handled relations with the outside world for the Sultan's wives in the royal harem were Jewish; their official title was Kiera. The most notable of these was the 16th-century Esther Kiera (or Kyra), wife of the merchant Elijah Handali, who supplied jewelry to women of the harem and became the favorite of Safiyeh, favorite wife of Sultan Murad III and mother of Sultan Muhammad III. Esther was also of assistance to Catherine de Medici, and aided the settlement of a diplomatic conflict between the Ottomans and Venetians during the 1580s. She was charitable, and aided scholars and authors, including Shmuel Shullam and Yitzhak Akrish. She is credited with preventing Murad III's planned destruction of the Jewish communities of the Ottoman empire. Her execution resulted in part from a military move against the power of Safiyeh, and in part from economic problems including the devaluation of the Ottoman currency.

The peddler woman selling merchandise to harem women existed into the 20th century; some were known as "bundle women" since they carried their wares in fabric bundles. Their merchandise included exotic silks, cottons and lace, as well as combs and trinkets.

REFERENCES: *EJ* 10, col. 990–91; NYJM, *Tale,* cat. no. 142; Croutier, pp. 167–68; Rubens, *Iconography,* 1981, no. 2374.

214 FEMME JUIVE EN HABIT DE CEREMONIE

(Jewish woman in ceremonial dress)*

Paris, 1714. Jean-Baptiste Vanmour. Engraver: Philippe Simmoneau (1685–ca. 1753). M. de Ferriol, Ambasador du Roi à la Porte, Recueil de cent estampes représentant differentes Nations du Levant, #64. Colored engraving. 14¹/₁₆ x 9³/₄ in. Moldovan Family Collection, New York.

This elaborate costume includes a flat metal plate worn on the head, covered with elaborate cloths; an ermine-trimmed overgarment that would appear to reach to her hips; sheer *gömlek* (chemise); *entari* (robe); and *salvár* (pants); in addition, she wears a belt with a jeweled metal buckle similar to one in this exhibition.

REFERENCES: Rubens, *Iconography,* nos. 2372 and 2378; NYJM, *Tale,* cat. no. 143.

215 JUIVE DE CONSTANTINOPLE

(Jewish woman of Constantinople)*

Paris, 1842. Camille Rogier. Galerie Royale de Costumes. Colored lithograph. 13¹/₄ x 8¹/₄ in. Moldovan Family Collection, New York.

Camille Rogier was a painter and engraver who exhibited at the Paris Salon between 1833 and 1848. He is best known for his Orientalist works.

This woman wears the headdress called *hotoz* (also *halebi* or *chalebi*), a ball of linen rags wrapped in one or more shawls, the edges of which hang down the back. This completely covered the woman's hair. It is a distinctive item of Jewish woman's attire in Istanbul, Bursa and Jerusalem, the earliest evidence for which dates from the 18th century. At that time it was also worn by Muslim women although it did not conceal all their hair; the

headdress went out of fashion for Muslim women, but remained popular among Jews into the 19th century. The long sleeveless robe is called a *hyrka*.

REFERENCES: Rubens, *Iconography*, 1981, no. 2414; Cf. IM, *Ottoman*, p. 141, fig. 27.

216 JEWISH FAMILY IN THE RUINS OF CONSTANTINE'S PALACE*

Paris, 1847. Camille Rogier. La Turquie #5. Colored lithograph. 12¼ x 6¾ in. Moldovan Family Collection, New York.

The woman wearing the *hotoz*, and the young girl to her left, are richly attired in a *nimten* (fur-trimmed overgarment). The woman also wears a gold metal belt inlaid with jewels, similar to others in this exhibition. All have removed their slippers to sit on the couch.

Despite the romantic title of the work, the details of the image coincide with what we know to have been characteristic of Jewish dress in Izmir during the 19th century.

Cf. IM, *Ottoman*, pl. 48.

217 BRIDE'S DANCE: JEWISH WEDDING AT SMYRNA*

Paris, 1847. Camille Rogier. La Turquie #11. Colored lithograph. 12¼ x 6¾ in. Moldovan Family Collection, New York.

The dancer wears *salvár* (pants), an *entari* (outer robe) with a low v-necked opening revealing the chemise and necklaces, an *ogadéro* (multi-chained necklace) and *résta de dukádos* (coin necklace). Over this she wears a *nimten* (fur-trimmed overgarment). Her cloth belt with metal buckle is similar to one in this exhibition (cat. no. 162), and shows that it could be worn low on the hips or tight around the waist. Her hat is decorated with a *lelál* (head ornament).

The title of this print raises questions similar to those elicited by Delacroix's painting of a Jewish wedding in Morocco (a print after this painting is included in this exhibition, cat. no. 507) regarding the identity of the dancer.

Cf. IM, *Ottoman*, pl. 37.

218 JUIVES DE CONSTANTINOPLE

(Jewish women of Constantinople)

Paris, 1847. Camille Rogier. La Turquie #22. Colored lithograph. Moldovan Family Collection, New York.

The women wear white *hotoz* and dark robes over their clothes.

219 JEWISH MARRIAGE*

New York, 1862. H. S. Van Lennep. Engraver: C. Parsons. Colored engraving. 11¾ x 10¼ in. Moldovan Family Collection, New York.

The bride and groom stand under a *talamó* (canopy) made from textiles composing the bride's trousseau; more textiles and other parts of the dowry are in the chests behind the bridal couple. The bride's eyes would remain closed

215

217

219

throughout the ceremony, after which she could remove the cone-shaped headdress, open her eyes and mingle with the guests.

REFERENCES: Rubens, *Iconography*, fig. 2422; Rubens, *Costume*, 1973, pl. 43, p. 48; NYJM, *Tale*, cat. no. 184.

220 STAMBOUL: JUIFS

(Istanbul: Jews)*

Paris, 1865. Amadeo Preziosi (1816–1882). Stamboul, Souvenir d'Orient. Lithograph on paper, colored. 13⅛ x 10⅛ in. Moldovan Family Collection, New York.

Preziosi, a Maltese Count, studied art in Paris despite the objections of his family. Succumbing to the lure of the exotic, he moved to Constantinople in 1842 and remained there until his death from a hunting accident. His depictions of Ottoman life link him to a tradition of European artists going back to Bellini in the 15th century.

The two Jews in this lithograph have been identified as a rabbi/*haham* and a widow in the Jewish cemetery at Pera, Istanbul. In the background we see the Mosque of Sultan Beyazid II and the Tower of Mahmud II. The woman, wearing a *ferace* (concealing outdoor costume) and *makrama*, may be praying at the tomb of a revered rabbi rather than that of a relative, as the tomb behind her is characteristic of 16th- and 17th-century Sephardic sepulchers. The man recites the prayers as the woman, like many of her female peers, may not be able to read Hebrew.

REFERENCES: "Preziosi's Jews," *The Jewish Museum of Greece Newsletter*, 24, Spring 1988, p. 5; Rubens, *Iconography*, 1981, fig. 2425; Cf. IM, *Ottoman*, pl. 25.

221 MOÏS[E] HALEVY, GRAND-RABBIN DE CONSTANTINOPLE

(Moses Halevy, Chief Rabbi of Istanbul)

Turkey, ca. 1880. P. R: W.; BDJARSKI; BK. Engraving. 8¾ x 5¼ in. Collection of Yeshiva University Museum, New York, gift of Sylvia A. Herskowitz, 90.121.

Turkish rabbis wore contemporary Ottoman dress. The *haham bashi* (Chief Rabbi) was given this costume by the government, as well as insignia and a written certificate of appointment. A similar costume is worn by Rabbi Hayyim Moshe Bejerano, Chief Rabbi of Istanbul from 1922 to 1931 (cat. no. 66).

REFERENCE: Rubens, *Costume*, 1973, p. 177.

222 JÜDINNEN AUS DER TÜRKEI (Jewish Women of Turkey)

A. v. R. Henkel. Publisher: Lipperheide. Colored engraving. 7¼ x 6 in. Moldovan Family Collection, New York.

The women wear dark outdoor costumes. Their white shawls are wrapped around the *hotoz* and around the neck, hanging down in front. Over their backs are distinctive garments, resembling a medieval tabard. The brightly-colored *salvár* (pants) are tucked into the women's boots.

REFERENCES: Rubens, *Costume*, 1973, pl. 46; Rubens, *Iconography*, 1981, cat. no. 2429; *Cf.* IM, *Ottoman*, p. 140, fig. 26.

223 HAHAM SEPHARDI

Jerusalem, early 20th century. Shmuel Ben David (Davidov; 1884–1927; unsigned). Watercolor on paper. 19½ x 12½ in. Einhorn Collection, Tel Aviv.

Shmuel Ben David, a native of Sofia, Bulgaria, was a contemporary of Boris Schatz, founder of the Bezalel School, who was also from Sofia. Ben David studied at the Bezalel Academy in Jerusalem from 1906 on. In 1907 he became chairman of the school's first committee of students and workers, and later taught drafting and decorative art. This painting is from the artist's bequest.

PHOTOGRAPHS

224 S[ON] EM[INENCE] RÉBI JACOB MÉÏR GRAND RABBIN DE SALONIQUE

(H[is] Em[inence] Rabbi Jacob Meir, Chief Rabbi of Salonika)*

Early 20th century. Photographic postcard. Jacques Saul. 5¼ x 3⅝ in. Einhorn Collection, Tel Aviv.

Rabbi Meir (1856–1939), a native of Jerusalem, was Chief Rabbi of Salonika from 1908 until 1919. In 1921, when an official chief rabbinate was first established in Eretz Israel under the British mandate, Meir was elected Sephardic Chief Rabbi with the title of *Rishon le-Zion*. His Ashkenazic counterpart was Rabbi Abraham Isaac Kook.

This picture postcard shows Rabbi Meir as Chief Rabbi of Salonika, wearing a robe and medals similar to those of Rabbi Bejerano (cat. no. 66). The headpiece appears to consist of a turban wrapped around a fez, with a ribbon worn across it, topped by a finial. The inscription is written in Greek, French and Hebrew.

225 PORTRAIT OF ALLEGRA HATTEM

Canakkale, ca. 1870. Photograph; colored. 19 x 13 in. Collection of Jane Mushabac, New York.

226 ROSA SERKUS MIKLESKO*

Monastir, ca. 1890. Black and white photograph. 6¼ x 4³⁄₁₆ in. Collection of Mr. and Mrs. Ivan Schick, New York.

Rosa Serkus Miklesko (1870–1957) was the lender's maternal grandmother. She was an Ashkenazic woman, married to a Sephardic husband; her costume is characteristic of that worn by Sephardic women in her region. On her head she wears a beautifully embroidered rectangular textile, of the sort used also as towels and napkins. In her hand she holds a spindle.

227 CEMIL ABRAHAM SCHEMTOB*

Constantinople, ca. 1892. Abdullah Frères. Black and white photograph. 4⅛ x 2½ in. Collection of Mr. and Mrs. Ivan Schick, New York.

Cemil Abraham Schemtob (1888–1938) was the third son in the family. According to family tradition, he was dressed in girl's clothes until his sisters were born.

European styles were adopted for children's clothing as well as for their elders. For centuries, Europeans and Americans clothed their very young children of both sexes alike; boys sometimes wore skirts until they were six years old. However, their hair was usually cut short, as is this boy's, rather than worn long and tied with ribbons as was the fashion for girls.

228 TURKISH COUPLE

Late 19th–early 20th century. Black and white photograph (copy). 4 x 5 in. Collection of Bea Myones, Bayside, New York.

Elderly bearded man wearing traditional long dark robe.

229 TURKISH MAN

Late 19th–early 20th century. Black and white photograph (copy) 4 x 5 in. Collection of Bea Myones, Bayside, New York.

230 JEWISH SCHOOL

Adrianople, early 20th century. Black and white photograph (copy). 8 x 10 in. Collection of Yeshiva University Museum, New York, gift of Gladys S. Benbasat.

231 PORTRAIT OF JACQUES COHEN

Turkey, ca. 1910–1912. Black and white photograph. 13⅛ x 10¼ in. Collection of Dr. Isak Kohenak, New York.

Jacques Cohen, the father of Isak Kohenak, served in the Ottoman army during the Balkan War during the years preceding the outbreak of World War I. Jews and other non-Muslims were accepted into the military services beginning in 1856. If they wanted to be exempt from service they had to pay a fixed tax.

227

232 FAMILY PHOTOGRAPH

Larissa, Greece, ca. 1911. Black and white photograph. Collection of Regina Slovin, New York.

233 TWO YOUNG MEN

Istanbul, ca. 1911. Black and white photograph. 6⅝ x 4¼ in. Collection of Joseph and Devorah Alcabes, West Hempstead, New York.

234 FAMILY GROUP

Istanbul, ca. 1911. Black and white photograph. 4¹³/₁₆ x 6⅞ in. Collection of Joseph and Devorah Alcabes, West Hempstead, New York.

The grandfather is wearing traditional Ottoman dress, including a fur-trimmed robe and holds a string of worry beads. The other family members are dressed in contemporary Western styles.

235 SOUVENIR DE SALONIQUE – TYPES DE PORTEFAIX/SALONICA — TYPES OF PORTERS*

235

Paris, early 20th century. Photographic postcard.
5½ x 3½ in. Einhorn Collection, Tel Aviv.

Two of the men wear fez with cloth wrapped around them. They all wear work shirts with a vest over pantaloons. Their feet are bare. The photograph was taken against a backdrop depicting a wooded area by the side of a lake; one edge of the backdrop is visible in the foreground of the picture. The porters of Salonika were renowned for their physical strength, and they derided their brethren in Western Europe for submitting without a fight during the Holocaust. However, their strength did not help; the Jewish community of Salonika was wiped out by the Nazis.

236 SALONICA — JEWISH TYPES*

Italy, before 1918. Photographic postcard, colored.
5⅜ x 3½ in. Einhorn Collection, Tel Aviv.

Two elderly bearded men, each wearing a red fez, dark overrobe and striped *entari*. The man at left wears stout Western work shoes.

237 SALONICA — A JEWISH MERCHANT*

Italy, 1917. Photographic postcard, colored. 5½ x 3⅜ in. Einhorn Collection, Tel Aviv.

238 SOUVENIR DE SALONIQUE. LES SIECLES SE RENCONTRANT. JUIVES — LA MERE ET LA FILLE/TWO CENTURIES MEETING. JEWISH — MOTHER AND DAUGHTER*

Paris, before 1917. Photographic postcard. Baudinière. 5¼ x 3¼ in. Einhorn Collection, Tel Aviv.

The mother wears an *entari* (outer robe) draped in the traditional Salonika manner (see cat. nos. 138), and a *kófya* (characteristic fringed head covering). The daughter wears a European-style tailored skirt and blouse.

239 SOUVENIR DE SALONIQUE — COSTUME DE DAME ISRAÉLITE

(Souvenir of Salonika – costume of a Jewish woman)*

Salonika, early 20th century (before 1917). Photographic postcard, colored. Hananel Naar, 5½ x 3½ in. Einhorn Collection, Tel Aviv.

The woman is photographed in a romantic pose, leaning on a wooden fence against a backdrop of the setting sun. The headpiece is held to her head with a band running under the chin (a rear view of this type of headpiece is seen in cat. no. 238). She wears a fur-trimmed *entari* of deep red-brown, open to reveal the lacy plastron and her necklace of large pearls (known as *yadrán* in Salonika).

REFERENCE: Russo-Katz, "Jewelry," IM, *Ottoman*, p. 188.

238

240 KEHILLA SHALOM

Rhodes, late 1930s. Black and white photograph.
2⅞ x 4⅛ in. Collection of Stella Levi, New York.

The synagogue in Rhodes was photographed
by a non-Jewish visitor to the island. Misled
by the costumes of the men, the photographer
identified this picture as that of a mosque.

241 SARA, RENÉE AND STELLA LEVI

Rhodes, 1930s. Black and white photograph. 5¼
x 3⅞ in. Collection of Stella Levi, New York.

The youngest child, Stella, wears a necklace
with good-luck charms around her neck.

239

242 COLLEGIO RABBINICO ITALIANO

(Italian rabbinical seminary)*

Rhodes, 1934. Black and white photograph (copy). Emanuele Pacifici Archives. 7 x 9⅜ in. Collection of Stella Levi, New York.

The Rabbinical Seminary was founded in Rhodes in 1927 to serve the Italian Levant but was closed in 1938 when Benito Mussolini's government promulgated the Fascist racial laws. The island of Rhodes, formerly part of Greece, came under Italian rule in 1912, and portraits of Italian royalty hang prominently in this room.

243 EXTERIOR OF THE COLLEGIO RABBINICO ITALIANO

Rhodes, 1934. Black and white photograph (copy). Emanuele Pacifici Archives. 7 x 9⅜ in. Collection of Stella Levi, New York.

244 THE LEVI FAMILY SUKKAH*

Rhodes, ca. 1935. Black and white photograph. 2⅜ x 4⅛ in. Collection of Stella Levi, New York.

Notrica Levi with her daughter Sara and friend Rika Cohen in the Levi family's sukkah. In characteristic Turkish Jewish fashion, the sukkah is fashioned from textiles hung on a wooden frame with a roof of branches and leaves. While men used the sukkah for meals and study, and even slept in it in literal obedience to the Biblical commandment that the children of Israel should "dwell in booths" during the festival of Sukkot (Lev. 23:42), women often used it for socializing.

242

244

Parokhet (Ark curtain), Eretz Israel, ca. 1869. Cat. no. 249A.

MIDDLE EAST

ERETZ ISRAEL · SYRIA · EGYPT

My heart is in the east, and I in the uttermost west—
How can I find savor in food? How shall it be sweet to me?
How shall I render my vows and my bonds, while yet
Zion layeth beneath the fetter of Edom, and I in Arab chains?
A light thing would it seem to me to leave all the good things of Spain—
Seeing how precious in mine eyes it is to behold the dust of the desolate
    sanctuary

YEHUDAH HALEVI (before 1075–1141)

245

MIDDLE EAST

SYNAGOGUE

245 MODEL OF THE SEPHARDIC SYNAGOGUE OF THE ARI*

Safed, Israel, 16th–17th century. Architect unknown. 49 x 22 x 18 in. Collection of Yeshiva University Museum, New York, endowed by Erica and Ludwig Jesselson, 89.87.

After the Expulsion from Spain, 16th-century Safed became the center of Kabbalism, led by Rabbi Yitzhak Luria Ashkenazi (Ari; 1533–1572). His followers built over twenty synagogues, the oldest of which is the Sephardic synagogue in Safed. Named for Rabbi Luria, this building incorporates features specifically associated with kabbalistic tradition.

Kabbalistic studies were often conducted in the natural caves surrounding Safed. The Ari synagogue accordingly has a "cave," a rectilinear room entered through the east wall, that is said to have been the Ari's study. Since visual symbolism was also an important element of kabbalistic lore, multicolored symbols originally decorated the interior of the main room.

The synagogue, which was originally named after the Prophet Elijah, stylistically reflects the Safed community's multinational heritage. By the 16th century the Crusaders, the Ottoman empire and waves of Ashkenazic and Sephardic immigrations had already left their imprint on Eretz Israel's culture. The building's fortified nature and its unmistakable buttresses clearly recall Crusader construction methods. Typically Ottoman is the synagogue's plan of a long single hall with three vaulted bays, and an exterior courtyard. The striking contrast of brilliant polychrome decorative elements against whitewashed walls and seating banquettes lining the main rooms are further examples of the Ottoman approach. Ashkenazic custom can be seen in the central siting of the *bimah*. The tripartite Ark is specifically Sephardic in tradition.

The women's gallery in the outer chamber was added in the 18th century.

246 TIK (Torah case)

Egypt, 20th century. Velvet; silver: stamped and engraved. Hebrew inscription: Donation from the dear Señor Shlomo Tziyon Hadad m[ay] G[od] b[less him and] p[rotect him] to the h[oly] c[ongregation] Rabbi Natan Amram of b[lessed and] r[ighteous] m[emory] . . . 28 x 12 in. diam. Collection of Mr. and Mrs. Norman Rosen, Cherry Hill, New Jersey.

Large cylindrical Torah cases made of velvet and metal were frequently used by Egyptian communities.

247 RIMMONIM (Torah finials)

Egypt, 1929. Silver: stamped and cast. Hebrew inscription: Donation i[n memory of the] s[oul of] the daughter the virgin Djoya Danielle w[ho rests in] E[den]. 13 x 4½ in. Collection of Mr. and Norman Rosen, Cherry Hill, New Jersey.

These finials are modeled after an Italian form popular throughout North Africa (see cat. nos. 324 and 328).

248 YAD (Torah pointer)

Jerusalem, 1891/92. Silver: cast and engraved. Hebrew inscription: Dedicated to t[he holy] c[ommunity] by Shalom di Boaz Turiel . . . t[he year] [5]692 t[he] h[oly] c[ity] Jerusalem m[ay it be built] a[nd established]. 11¾ x ⅞ in. The Abraham J. and Deborah B. Karp Collection, New York.

The flat shape of this pointer is based on North African models. Although Jerusalem was a center for the production of Judaica, it is unusual to find locally crafted ceremonial objects which are known to have been used in Jerusalem itself. Many of the locally crafted wares were produced for export or as souvenir items (see cat. no. 267).

249A PAROKHET (Ark curtain)

Eretz Israel, ca. 1869. Wool; metallic thread, sequins. Hebrew inscription: C[rown of the] T[orah], Ark curtain dedicated by me the servant of G[od] Rafael Yeoshua Elyachar . . . i[n] m[emory] of my Lady . . . my mother the righteous woman . . . Esther Bulisa daughter of Dinah,

passed away a[fter] br[ief] d[ays] a[nd] y[ears] by
the decree of the One who dwells [in all] places on
the 23rd of Kisler, 5629 m[ay] h[er soul] b[e bound]
i[n the bonds of] l[ife] m[ay it] b[e his] w[ill]
A[men]. *Collection of Mrs. J. R. Elyachar, New
York.*

The curtain is decorated with crescent moons
in sunburst motifs resembling one of the medals of the Chief Rabbi (cat. no. 66). *(See illustration on p. 256)*

249B PAROKHET (Ark curtain)

*Egypt, 20th century. Velvet: embroidered with
metallic threads; sequins. Hebrew inscription: Donation to the h[oly] c[ongregation] Magen Avraham (Shield of Abraham) from Allegra Moko
Antivi . . . m[ay] h[er soul] b[e bound] i[n the
bonds of] l[ife]. 84 x 70 in. Collection of the Judah
L. Magnes Museum, Berkeley, California.*

This curtain was made of embroidery fabrics
originally intended for a secular purpose. The
vertical panels in the center were embroidered
for use as pillows, but were later adapted for
ceremonial use. The crescent motif seen on
this curtain was popular throughout the Ottoman empire.

250 TORAH PLAQUE

*Aleppo, Syria, 1693. Silver: engraved. Hebrew
inscription: The teaching of the Lord is perfect,
renewing life (Ps. 19:8) my cherished, my only son
. . . Yaakov Laniado . . . passed away at the age
of 20 on the 25th day of Tammuz [5]453. The
scroll, the case and the finials were made from his
bequest and will be called in Israel Sefer Nahlat
Yaakov (the Scroll of Yaakov's Inheritance), for
this is his inheritance, and it is dedicated to the
Society of the Performers of Righteous Deeds of the
Holy Congregation of Sephardim . . . 4½ x 3½
in. Einhorn Collection, Tel Aviv.*

According to this plaque's inscription, a Torah
scroll, case and finials were dedicated by a
father in memory of his only son Yaakov Laniado, who died at the age of 20. This plaque
is unusual due to its very early date, and because it documents the naming of a Torah
scroll and accompanying appurtenances.

251 MEMORIAL PLAQUE*

*Aleppo, Syria, 1915/16. Brass: inlaid with silver
and copper. Hebrew inscription: D[edicated] t[o
God] i[n memory of the] so[ul] of the charming*

and pleasant young man w[ho died] after brief years
. . . Yitzhak t[he] K[ohen] Soviya p[assed] o[n]
. . . in the yea[r] [5]676. 9⅜ x 9 in. Collection of
Selma and Stanley I. Batkin, New Rochelle, New
York.

Inlaid metalwork of this type was made in
various parts of the Ottoman empire. It is a
descendant of the spectacular metalwork created by the Mamluks, who ruled the Near East
from 1250. This plaque is shaped like the *luhot*
(Tablets of the Ten Commandments).

252 DEDICATION PLAQUE
FOR AN ARK CURTAIN

*Jerusalem, 1921. Silver: engraved and punched.
Hebrew inscription: And the Ark curtain was dedicated to Yeshivat Yagdil Torah of sons of Damascus
. . . in Jerusalem they were dedicated by the woman
Regina . . . wife of G. Yosef Farhi and may the
merit of the Torah protect her and her children and
grandchildren . . . Elul "Beautify" [Chronogram
= (5)681]. 10¼ x 17⅞ in. Einhorn Collection,
Tel Aviv.*

This plaque was placed on an Ark curtain in a
Jerusalem yeshiva established by immigrants
from Damascus. Ottoman Ark curtains were
frequently decorated with added metal plaques
and studs.

253 MEMORIAL PLAQUE

*Aleppo, Syria, 1928. Brass: inlaid with copper.
Hebrew inscription: D[edicated] to G[od] to t[he
holy] c[ommunity] in m[emory of the] soul of the
daughter the virgin Rahel Abboud . . . who passed
away . . . on the 18th day of Elul t[he year] 5688
. . . 7 x 6⅝ in. Collection of Selma and Stanley
I. Batkin, New Rochelle, New York.*

The heart shape of this plaque is unusual and reflects the adoption of Western folk-art motifs.

Cf. Bialer, p. 176.

254 MEMORIAL HANGING
LAMP

*Syria, 1904. Silver: repoussé. Hebrew inscription:
An eternal lamp in m[emory of] . . . David son of
Mazal the r[ighteous] K[ohen] . . . Zofe . . .
w[ho] p[assed on] to [his] e[ternal] h[ome] 17th
day of Tammuz, 5664. 22½ x 7 in. diam. The
Feuchtwanger Collection was purchased and donated to the Israel Museum, Jerusalem, by Baruch
and Ruth Rappaport of Geneva, 1969, 120/5.*

The silver hoop holds a glass oil-vessel. Both rim and bottom have floral bands and between them a seven-branched menorah, oil flask and Hebrew inscription.

REFERENCE: IM, *Feuchtwanger*, cat. no. 189.

255 SYNAGOGUE HANUKKAH LAMP

Damascus, early 20th century. Brass: inlaid with copper and silver. 33½ x 19 x 8½ in. Collection of the Sir Isaac and Lady Edith Wolfson Museum, Hechal Shlomo, Jerusalem.

This lamp is decorated with various scenes and motifs, including the Temple site, the Western Wall and the Ten Commandments. Large menorah-shaped lamps were frequently used in synagogues. *(fig. 72)*

REFERENCE: Bialer, p. 162.

256 TICKET FOR WOMAN'S SEAT IN SYNAGOGUE*

Stambouli Synagogue, Jerusalem, Eretz Israel, 19th–20th century. Letterpress and woodcut on paper. Hebrew inscriptions: H[oly] C[ongrega-tion] of Istanbulians; "O House of Jacob! Come, let us walk" (Is. 2:5); Women's section; The place of the honored woman . . . t[he] h[oly] c[ity] Jerusalem m[ay it be built] a[nd established]. 7¾ x 5½ in. The Feuchtwanger Collection, purchased and donated to the Israel Museum, Jerusalem, by Baruch and Ruth Rappaport of Geneva, 1969, 178/17.

This seat ticket for a Jerusalem congregation established by immigrants from Istanbul includes blank spaces for the woman's name, her husband's name, amount of her donation and date. In the center are depictions of the Western Wall, the Temple Mount and the Mount of Olives.

REFERENCE: IM, *Feuchtwanger*, cat. no. 498.

257 LETTER OF ACCREDITA-TION FOR RABBINICAL EMISSARY (SHADAR)

Jerusalem, 1891 (addition: Marrakesh, Morocco). Ink on parchment. 30⅛ x 22⅛ in. The Feuchtwanger Collection, purchased and donated to the Israel Museum, Jerusalem, by Baruch and Ruth Rappaport of Geneva, 1969, 178/24.

256

This letter was sent by the heads of the *Kollel Maarvim* in Jerusalem to the Jewish communities of Gibraltar, Portugal, Spain and Morocco, and shows both signatures and stamps.

It introduces Rabbi Avraham Pinto, mentioning his important ancestors. His mission is to collect funds for the purchase of land in Jerusalem on which to build homes. The text describes the plight of the many homeless people in Jerusalem: ". . . There are places not big enough even for a chicken coop . . . The poorhouse is full of the homeless—it overflows up unto the gate of the yard . . . Even 4–5 would be sufficient to build one house and their names will be written on each entrance. . . . "

REFERENCE: IM, *Feuchtwanger*, cat. no. 505.

258 APPEAL FOR CHARITY

Hebron, Eretz Israel, 1920–1929. Ink on paper: printed, handwritten and stamped. 11⅛ x 8¾ in. Collection of the Israel Museum, Jerusalem, gift of Baroness Alix de Rothschild and the Friends of the Israel Museum in Paris, 1972, 178/41.

Written on the stationery of the Chief Rabbi and Central Committee of *Adat Israel Sephardim* in Hebron. At the top of the letter is a depiction of the Cave of Machpelah. The letter, sent to Rabbi Yehuda ben Shimol, introduces Rabbi Gavriel Aharon Satthun. It shows the signatures and stamps of Chief Rabbi Hanokh Hassoun and the President of the Sephardic community, Meir Sh. Kastil.

259 ALMS BOWL

Damascus, 1904/5. Brass: inlaid with silver, copper and gold. Arabic inscriptions: Whoever is patient will achieve; deeds accord with intentions; according to a person's intentions, so will be done unto him. Hebrew inscriptions: "Send your bread forth upon the water; for after many days you will find it" (Eccl. 11:1), Damascus work, the year [5]665. 5⅜ x 11¹/₁₆ in. diam. Collection of the Jewish Museum, New York, F919.

The Hebrew inscriptions, which include a Biblical verse extolling the virtue of giving charity, contain many errors. This bowl is typical of metalwork produced during the Mamluk Revival (1878–1914), a stylistic period marked by the production of glass and metal artifacts which emulated those crafted during the Mamluk period (1250–1517).

REFERENCES: NYJM, *Mamluk*, cat. no. 8; NYJM, *Treasures*, pp. 50–51.

260 ALMS PLATE*

Syria, 20th century. Brass: inlaid with copper and silver. Hebrew inscription: "Wealth is of no avail on the day of wrath, but charity saves from death" (Prov. 11:4). Arabic inscriptions: quotations from the Hadis (sayings of the Prophet Mohammed).

12⅞ in. diam. Collection of Mr. and Mrs. Victor Topper, Toronto, Canada.

The Hebrew inscription suggests that this plate may have been used to collect funds for the Burial Society. The Arabic inscriptions seem to indicate that the Hebrew text was added to a pre-existing plate with Arabic calligraphy, and that the latter was viewed as a purely decorative element.

REFERENCE: Geneva, Habsburg, Feldman, *Judaica*, June 19, 1989, lot no. 51/97.

SABBATH AND FESTIVALS

261 KIDDUSH WINE BOTTLE

Syria, 19th century (?). Glass: etched. Hebrew inscriptions: The opening lines of the kiddush; Mordekhai. 8¼ x 5½ in. Collection of the Israel Museum, Jerusalem, gift of Sidney Lissauer, Los Angeles, 138/9.

The bottle surface is etched with the Hebrew text of the kiddush, the sanctification of wine which begins the Sabbath meal, and with the name of the owner of this bottle, "Mordekhai." The text contains some abbreviations and errors.

263

262 HANUKKAH LAMP

Jerusalem, 19th century. Stone: carved. 9½ x 9¾ x 2¾ in. Collection of the Israel Museum, Jerusalem, 118/117.

White or pink stone was used to create this type of massive, simply decorated Hanukkah lamp. (*fig. 75*)

263 HANUKKAH LAMP*

Syria, 19th–20th century. White metal: engraved. Hebrew inscription: We kindle these lights . . . 8½ x 9¾ x 2½ in. Collection of the Israel Museum, Jerusalem, 118/213.

The backplate of this lamp is engraved with the liturgy recited when kindling the Hanukkah lights.

264 HANUKKAH LAMP*

Egypt, 19th–20th century. Tin; glass; brass buttons; metallic paint. 20 x 17½ x 4¾ x in. Private collection.

This unusual lamp was used in a synagogue in Cairo. Oil and wicks were placed in glass vessels, which originally hung from the row of metal rings at the base of the lamp.

A most unusual feature of this lamp is its decorative use of brass buttons. Naive, folk-art Hanukkah lamps were often crafted in North Africa of found materials, such as existing cast brass elements (see cat. no. 371) or from metal used for commerical purposes, such as sardine and oil cans.[1]

---

1. See also IM, *Secular*, cat. no. 25.

264

265 HANUKKAH LAMP

Syria, 1901/2. Brass sheet: engraved and pierced; painted cardboard. Hebrew inscriptions: [May the] L[ord] g[uard him]; Ps. 30:2; the year [5]662; The commandment of the Hanukkah light. 8½ x 14¼ x 9⅝ in. (open). Collection of the Israel Museum, Jerusalem, 118/301.

This type of Hanukkah lamp is known as a *ShaDaR* lamp. *ShaDaR* is an abbreviation for *Shaliah de-Rabbanan* (emissary of the Rabbis). Rabbinical emissaries were sent abroad from Eretz Israel to collect funds for the support of the inhabitants of Jerusalem (see cat. no. 257).

This lamp is easy to transport on a long journey. It is hinged so it can be closed flat, and is topped by a carrying handle. *(Plate 9)*

Cf. IM, *Amanut*, pp. 34–35.

266 HANUKKAH LAMP*

Damascus, Syria, 1924/25. Maker: Morile Masslaton. Copper: inlaid with silver, engraved; cast brass oil fonts. Hebrew inscriptions: These lights are sacred; This Hanukkah lamp [is dedicated] to the synagogue in Damascus [by] Shemaya, t[he year] [5]685. 11⅜ x 13⅛ x 2½ in. Collection of the Israel Museum, Jerusalem.

In Damascus during the late 19th and early 20th centuries, the art of inlaying metal with gold, silver, copper and brass was practiced mainly by Jewish craftsmen. This kind of inlay, known as damascene, was based on Islamic techniques and decoration from the Mamluk period (1250–1517). The dedicatory inscription is engraved on the back of this lamp.

267 PASSOVER CUP

Jerusalem, 19th century. Stone: carved. Hebrew inscriptions: Cup for Passover in honor of . . . Yosef the Kohen . . .; the Western Wall; Cave of Machpelah; Rahel's grave; Jerusalem. 3¾ x 2¹¹/₁₆ in. diam. Moldovan Family Collection, New York.

Carved stone ceremonial objects were crafted in Jerusalem for use by the local Jewish population and as souvenirs for purchase by travelers. The inscription suggests that this cup may have been made as a presentation piece, perhaps for a patron of a Jerusalem-based institution. Ceremonial objects made of materials associated with the Holy Land, such as olive wood or stone, were frequently used for this purpose. Carved on this cup are depictions of holy places in Jerusalem, Hebron and Bethlehem.

268 PASSOVER PLATE

Eretz Israel, 19th century. Copper: engraved, pewter plated. Hebrew inscriptions: The order of the Passover seder; kiddush; Jerusalem m[ay it be built] a[nd established] q[uickly] i[n our days]. 13½ x 17⅞ in. Einhorn Collection, Tel Aviv.

The text of the kiddush (sanctification of wine for festivals) inscribed on this plate is according to the rite of the Maghrebi (North African) community of Jerusalem.

REFERENCE: IM, *Amanut*, p. 41, fig. 18.

LIFE CYCLE

269 AMULETIC PLAQUE PROTECTING MOTHER AND CHILD

Jerusalem, 19th century. Ink, watercolor and gold paint on paper. 21¾ x 14½. Einhorn Collection, Tel Aviv.

Colorful symbols against the evil eye and protective inscriptions, including the remembrance of Jerusalem and names of God and the angels, are featured on this plaque.

REFERENCE: IM, *Amanut*, p. 23, fig. 8.

270 AMULET FOR A CHILD

Eretz Israel, 19th century. Ink on paper; silver; glass. Hebrew inscriptions: Names of angels; names of God; magic square of Ps. 106:30 with repeated Tetragrammaton; Jerusalem Safed Hebron Tiberias shall be a protection and shield upon this child A[men] m[ay it] b[e] H[is will]. 1⅜ in. diam. The Feuchtwanger Collection, purchased and donated to the Israel Museum, Jerusalem, by Baruch and Ruth Rappaport of Geneva, 1969, 103/661.

REFERENCE: IM, *Feuchtwanger*, cat. no. 1028.

271 KETUBBAH (Marriage contract)

Jerusalem, 1913. Lithograph on paper with handwritten text. Printer: Avraham Moshe Luntz. 22¼ x 17 in. Zucker Family Collection (RZ), New York.

The frame of this ketubbah features the seal of the Sephardic community of Jerusalem and depictions of holy places. *(fig. 30)*

Cf. Sabar, *Ketubbah*, cat. no. 203.

272 KETUBBAH (Marriage contract)

Jerusalem, 1854. Ink and watercolor on paper. 25¼ x 18⅜ in. Einhorn Collection, Tel Aviv.

Groom: Nissim Yisrael Sasson.
Bride: Leah daughter of Avraham Hashuel
The two columns flanking the text, a common element in European Sephardic ketubbot, are rare in examples from Islamic Jewish communities. *(fig. 28)*

Cf. Benjamin, "Ketubah Ornamentation"; IM, *Amanut*, pp. 53–55.

273 KETUBBAH (Marriage contract)

Jaffa, 1865. Ink and watercolor on paper. 24½ x 18½ in. Einhorn Collection, Tel Aviv.

Groom: Reuven son of Moshe Yosef
Bride: Mazal-Tov daughter of Reuven
Since Jaffa Jewry in this period was under the jurisdiction of the Jerusalem Rabbinate, the designs show the strong influence of the Holy City (see cat. nos. 272 and 274).

Cf. Benjamin, "Ketubah Ornamentation"; IM, *Amanut*, pp. 53–55.

274 KETUBBAH (Marriage contract)

Jerusalem, 1866. Ink and watercolor on paper. 25¼ x 18¼ in. Einhorn Collection, Tel Aviv.

Groom: Hillel son of Yitzhak Alkaim
Bride: Esther daughter of Shalom Malka
The dominant columns in this example are accompanied by rich floral decorations. *(fig. 29)*

Cf. Benjamin, "Ketubah Ornamentation"; IM, *Amanut,* pp. 53–55.

275 KETUBBAH (Marriage contract)

Jerusalem, 1910. Colored inks on paper: printed and handwritten. Collection of the Judah L. Magnes Museum, Berkeley, California.

Groom: Joseph Ezoui
Bride: Devorah Barukh
The frame of this ketubbah is decorated with depictions of holy places.

Cf. IM, *Amanut,* fig. no. 30.

276 KETUBBAH (Marriage contract)

Tiberias, 1930. Ink and gouache on paper. 14½ x 13¾ in. Zucker Family Collection, (RZ), New York.

Groom: Yitzhak son of Sammon
Bride: Yokheved daughter of Avraham Hayyim
Fish, symbols of fertility, are used as an ornamental motif on this ketubbah.

REFERENCE: YUM, *Wedding,* cat. no. 225.

277 KETUBBAH (Marriage contract)

Damascus, 1930. Watercolor, cutouts, ink on paper. 16 x 22⅛ in. Einhorn Collection, Tel Aviv.

Groom: Nissim son of Shalom Aslan
Bride: Afifa daughter of Jacob ha-Levi
In Damascus, as in Istanbul, local craftsmen frequently used cutouts as decorative motifs (see cat. nos. 83, 85, 131). Here gold foil is cut in the shape of a vase, illustrated with flowers.

278 BRIDAL MIRROR

Syria, 20th century. Copper: inlaid with brass and silver; glass mirror. Hebrew inscriptions: Against
the Evil Eye; "The sound of mirth and gladness, the voice of bridegroom and bride" (Jer. 7:34); Zion. 18⅛ x 14⅜ in. Collection of Cantor and Mrs. Jacob Rosenbaum, Monsey, New York.

The frame of this mirror is shaped like a *hamsa,* a hand-shaped amulet used to ward off the evil eye. It is decorated with a Biblical passage describing the rejoicing of the bride and groom. This mirror was probably used in a bridal chamber.

MANUSCRIPTS AND PRINTED BOOKS

279 SEFER ZIKHRON LI–VNEI YISRAEL

Rashid (Rosetta), Egypt, 1700. Scribe: Aharon Tawil. Ink and watercolor on paper. 6⅞ x 4⅝ in. Gross Family Collection, Tel Aviv, Ms. no. OT.11.5.

This manuscript is a treatise on *shehitah* (kosher slaughter) regulations by Rabbi Avraham Mizrahi of Jerusalem. Title, author, date and the name of the scribe are enclosed in a decorative floral frame on the frontispiece—the only decorated page in this small manuscript.

280 SEFER ZEVAH HA–SHELAMIM

Rashid (Rosetta), Egypt, 1700. Scribe: Aharon Tawil. Ink and watercolor on paper. 6⅝ x 4½ in. Gross Family Collection, Tel Aviv, Ms. no. OT.11.4.

This manuscript deals with the laws of *shehitah* (kosher slaughter) from various points of view. It appears that Tawil, the scribe of the two exhibited manuscripts from Rashid (see also cat. no. 279), was himself a *shohet.*

281 MEGILLAT YUHASIN

(Letter of lineage)

Jerusalem, 1867. Ink on paper. 5½ x 4 x ½ in. Einhorn Collection, Tel Aviv.

282 SEFER SHIVHEI HA-ARI

(The Praises of the Ari)

Shaul ben Avraham Dayan. Aleppo, 1871/72. Printer: Eliyahu Sasson. 6 x 4 x ½ in. Collection of the Sephardic Reference Room, Yeshiva University, New York.

Abraham Sasson established a Hebrew printing press in Aleppo in 1865, after one of his sons had learned the craft in Livorno. This text is a collection of stories about R. Yitzhak Luria (1534–1572, known as *ha-Ari*) of Safed (see cat. no. 245).

283 LIBRO DI PASSETIEMPO

Jerusalem, 1899/1900. Ink on paper: printed. 4¾ x 3½ x ½ in. Einhorn Collection, Tel Aviv.

This Ladino newspaper was printed in Jerusalem and edited by Shlomo Yisrael Shirizli.

284 SEFER VE-YALKUT YOSEF U-BIRKAT SHAMAYIM

Yosef Stihon. Aleppo, 1914/15. Printer: Yishayah Dayan. Ex Libris: Hevrat Talmud Torah Ahava ve-Ahva, Egypt. 7¼ x 4¾ x ½ in. Collection of the Sephardic Reference Room, Yeshiva University, New York.

Although this book was printed in Syria, it was used by a congregation in Egypt, attesting to the close cultural links between Middle Eastern Sephardic communities.

PERSONAL ARTIFACTS

285 SNUFF BOX

Eretz Israel, 19th century. Silver: engraved. 1⅞ x 2¾ x ⅞ in. The Feuchtwanger Collection, purchased and donated to the Israel Museum, Jerusalem, by Baruch and Ruth Rappaport of Geneva, 1969, 131/39.

On the lid is a stylized depiction of the Western Wall, with gates and towers on the sides and five trees above. A domed building topped by a crescent is depicted on the base.

REFERENCE: IM, *Feuchtwanger*, cat. no. 155. *Cf.* IM, *Amanut*, pp. 84–85.

286 PENCASE

Middle East, 19th–20th century. Brass: cast. 8¹¹⁄₁₆ x 7⅛ in. Collection of Yeshiva University Museum, New York, gift of Mrs. A. R. Elyachar, 89.294.

This convenient combination of pen/quill holder and inkwell was common in the Ottoman empire. It could be made of brass, as this one is, or of silver as is the other exhibited example (cat. no. 169). A print showing a scribe with a similar pencase is described below (cat. no. 314).

DOMESTIC OBJECTS

287 MEZUZAH COVER*

Syria (?), 19th–20th century. Brass: inlaid with copper and silver. 7⅞ x 3⅞ in. Collection of Cantor and Mrs. Jacob Rosenbaum, Monsey, New York.

This mezuzah cover is decorated with two very common amuletic images: the *hamsa* (hand) which stops the evil eye, and the fish, a symbol of fertility.

288 MEZUZAH COVER*

Syria (?), 19th–20th century. Brass: inlaid with copper and silver. 4¾ x 2¼ in. Collection of Cantor and Mrs. Jacob Rosenbaum, Monsey, New York.

Artifacts made with this metal inlay technique, known as damascene wares, were popular throughout the Ottoman empire, but were a specialty of Jewish craftsmen in Damascus.

289 ROSE WATER CONTAINER*

Egypt, 19th century. Silver: repoussé, chased and cast. 8¼ x 2⅝ in. Moldovan Family Collection, New York.

The use of ornamental bird motifs, as seen on the neck and spout of this container, may have been adopted from either North African or Ottoman sources.

289

290 PLATE

Damascus, 19th century. Brass: hammered. Hebrew inscription: "Joseph is a fruitful bough, a fruitful bough by a spring . . ." (Gen. 49:22). 29¼ in. diam. Collection of the Jewish Museum, New York, F4586.

This Hebrew inscription is frequently found on Sephardic domestic and decorative items and is believed to provide amuletic protection.[1]

---

1. See Dobrinsky, pp. 44–45.

291 HALAWIYAT SET

Syria, ca. 1920s. Silver: filigree. Dishes: 6¼ x 6⅛ in. Holder: 6 x 4¹/₁₆ in. Water container: 3½ x 4¼ in. Forks and spoons: 5¾ x ¼ in; 5½ x 1 in. Collection of Linda Shamah, Belle Harbor, New York.

This *halawiyat* set consists of two dishes for *hilu* (sweetened and preserved fruits and vegetables), a holder for forks and spoons and the utensils themselves, and a piece to hold water for rinsing the serving pieces. The set was used for special occasions and receptions. Similar pieces were used in Turkey (cat. no. 176).

292 BASKET

Middle East, 20th century. Silver: filigree. 8½ x 6½ in. diam. Collection of Adina Bernstein, New York.

This filigree basket is part of a sweet service, a formal hospitality ritual of the Syrian Jewish community. Although filigree work was commonly used in Syria, most of it was made elsewhere. This piece was a gift to a Jewish serviceman stationed in Syria during World War II from a Jewish family with whom he spent Shabbat.

293 EWER AND BASIN

Syria, 19th–20th century. Brass: inlaid with silver and copper. Basin: 4 x 8⅞ x 6¹³⁄₁₆ in. Ewer: 9⅝ x 7⅝ x 2⅞ in. Tray: ½ x 7⅞ x 6½ in. Collection of Mr. and Mrs. Irving Kroopnick, New Haven, Connecticut.

The decoration consists of foliate forms, fish and Hebrew inscriptions. The ewer finial is missing.

REFERENCE: New York, Sotheby's, *Important Judaica*, December 18, 1986, lot no. 364.

294 BOX*

Syria (?), 19th–20th century. Brass: inlaid with copper and silver; wood: inlaid with bone and ivory. Hebrew inscriptions: The Exodus of the Children of Israel from Egypt; The Binding of Isaac; And he said from the water they shall drink Moses struck the rock. 3⅞ x 6 x 3¼ in. Collection of the Jewish Museum, New York, F2380.

This box is decorated with many scenes depicting Biblical events. The lid also features depictions of twelve men, a representation of the Twelve Tribes. The interior of the box is beautifully crafted wood inlay.

295 CHAIR

Syria (?), 19th–20th century. Wood: carved; mother-of-pearl and bone inlay, lead. 35 x 15¼ x 22 in. Collection of Yossi Benyaminoff, Jerusalem.

This folding chair resembles the *sgabelli* of the Western Renaissance. The technique of inlaid wood was popular throughout the Ottoman empire, and was used for many wood items. Pieces using this technique in the exhibition include a table, mirror and shelf (cat. nos. 297–299), and Turkish and Moroccan clogs (cat. nos. 149 and 414). This technique is known as "Damascus work," named after a major center of production.

296 WRITING DESK

Syria (?), 19th–20th century. Wood: carved; bone inlay. 17 x 29 x 50 in. Collection of Yossi Benyaminoff, Jerusalem.

297 TABLE

Syria (?), 19th–20th century. Wood: inlaid with bone and mother-of-pearl; lead. 15¼ x 13⅜ x 12⅞ in. Collection of Yossi Benyaminoff, Jerusalem.

This table is said to have come from the Damascus Synagogue.

298 MIRROR

Syria (?), 19th–20th century. Wood: inlaid with mother-of-pearl; glass mirror. 17¼ x 8¾ in. Collection of Yossi Benyaminoff, Jerusalem.

299 SHELF

Syria (?), 19th–20th century. Wood: inlaid with bone and mother-of-pearl. 36 x 13⅛ x 9⅞ in. Collection of Yossi Benyaminoff, Jerusalem.

Such shelves were used to display prized glass and ceramics.

300 MANGAL (Charcoal burner)

Syria (?), 19th–20th century. Brass: cast, inlaid with copper and silver, pierced. 34 x 21 in. Collection of Yossi Benyaminoff, Jerusalem.

One of the pieces used in sparsely furnished Turkish homes, this charcoal-burning brazier was used to heat the high-ceilinged rooms.

REFERENCE: Lewis, p. 109; fig. 38.

301 STANDING LAMP

Syria (?), early 20th century. Brass: silver and copper inlay; glass beads. 70 x 18 in. Collection of Yossi Benyaminoff, Jerusalem.

This lamp merges the decorative elements of several cultures: the damascene technique; the shape of Safavid pillar candlesticks; and an Edwardian beaded lampshade.

PRINTS AND
PHOTOGRAPHS

302 JEWISH WOMAN OF SYRIA

Vecellio. Engraving. 8⅝ x 6⁵⁄₁₆ in. Moldovan Family Collection, New York.

This engraving depicts a lady wearing a tall hat covered with an embroidered silk veil, held in place by a gold circlet set with gemstones. Her dress ends above her ankle, revealing her shoes. From Vecellio's "Hebrea in Soria," *Abiti Antici* (published in Venice in 1590).

REFERENCES: Rubens, *Iconography*, 1981, no. 2331; Rubens, *Costume*, 1973, pl. 55.

303 HABILLEMENS DES ARABES ET DES JUIFS QUI SONT AU CAIRE: HABITS DES JUIFS; FEMME JUIVE

(Costumes of Arabs and Jews in Cairo: clothes of Jews; Jewish woman)

Amsterdam, 1719. M. Guerdeville, Atlas Historique, p. 26. Engraving. 4⅛ x 5⅞ in. Moldovan Family Collection, New York.

The figures were copied from *Reizen van Cornelis de Bruyn*, Delft, 1698. De Bruyn (1652–1726/7) was a Dutch painter who traveled to Asia Minor and Egypt in the late 1670s. According to him, contemporary Jews were re-

quired to wear a blue striped turban and violet-colored clothing. The women wore tall black hats with white or brown kerchiefs striped with gold or silver. In this depiction the woman is smoking; the man is playing a stringed musical instrument.

REFERENCES: Rubens, *Iconography*, 1981, pp. 758–59; Rubens, *Costume*, 1973, fig. 74.

304 FEMMES JUIVES DE DAMAS (Jewish women of Damascus)*

France, 19th century. Colored engraving. 3⁵⁄₁₆ x 2½ in. Einhorn Collection, Tel Aviv.

The women wear *salvár* (pants) under a chemise, a long robe with a sash at the hips, and a sleeveless outer robe. They represent married women, as they both have scarves covering their hair under their hats. Both women wear wooden street clogs, similar in shape to an inlaid wooden pair in this exhibition (cat. no. 149) to keep their feet from the damp and to protect the hems of their clothes. Similar clogs were worn in Greece and the Middle East. One woman plays a four-stringed long-necked lute, resembling a Persian *tar* with a sound hole, rather than the *tanbur*, a traditional folk music instrument popular in Syria.

305 JEWISH FAMILY ON MOUNT ZION*

304

308

England, 19th century. Engraver: Cousen. W. H. Bartlett, Walks about Jerusalem. Engraving. 3 x 4 in. Moldovan Family Collection, New York.

Bartlett describes his visit in 1842 to the family of the wealthiest Jew in Jerusalem. There he met the women in the family as well as the men and expressed his surprise at the "equality" of the women with the males of the family, in contrast to the manner of "... the wives of oriental Christians." A later visitor, Elizabeth Anne Finn (see also cat. nos. 160 and 306), describes the profusion of gold jewelry worn by the women of this family.

REFERENCES: Rubens, *Iconography*, 1981, no. 1985; Rubens, *Costume*, 1973, fig. 59 and pp. 46–47.

306 JEWISH BRIDESMAIDS

19th century. Artist: M.K. Engraving. 6⁷⁄₁₆ x 5 in. Moldovan Family Collection, New York.

This print depicts Jewish girls of Jerusalem, dressed for a wedding in their best clothes and jewelry, holding oil lamps. Note the intrusion of European style in the short jacket of the girl in the right foreground, worn over a long striped *entari*, in contrast to the more traditional overdress of the girl facing us to the left.

309

This print accompanied an article written by Elizabeth Anne Finn (d. 1921; see also cat. nos. 160 and 305), wife of the British consul in Jerusalem (1845–1862), titled "Weddings in Jerusalem." The Finns attended a Sephardic wedding in Jerusalem, and Mrs. Finn describes the ceremony and the costumes of the young women. Their fingers were stained with henna, their eyelids and eyebrows accented with kohl (antimony). Those who were married hid their hair under turbans decorated with gold chains and flowers. Although Mrs. Finn describes the turbans as "moon shaped," the artist did not draw them as curved as the *hotoz* worn by the woman in *Costume and Likeness of a Native Jew and Jewess of Jerusalem* (cat. no. 310); its shape is more like that of the fez. Many of the dresses and jewels were heirlooms.

307   SYNAGOGUE OF THE JEWS, JERUSALEM

London, 1837. Artist: Jacques Pierre François Salmon (1781–1865). Engraver: J. Redaway. Syria, The Holy Land, Asia Minor, etc. Engraving. 14 x 10 in. Moldovan Family Collection, New York.

Salmon was a pupil of Bardin and Regnault. A history painter and lithographer, he served as professor at the College of Orléans.

The article accompanying this illustration describes the location of the synagogue as miserable, full of winding, crooked lanes, where one's nose is assailed by an unpleasant combination of odors ". . . from coffee-houses, eating-houses, mechanics' shops, and a thousand nameless domiciles. . . ." The author then contrasts the servile daily deportment of the Jews with the pride and wealth they display at the synagogue, where they dwell on their illustrious past.

REFERENCE: Rubens, *Iconography*, 1981, no. 1979.

308   HEBREW WOMEN READING THE SCRIPTURES AT JERUSALEM*

London, 1843. Sir David Wilkie (1785–1841). Sir David Wilkie's Sketches in Turkey, Syria &

Egypt 1840 & 1841, pl. 26. Lithograph. 9½ x 6⅜ in. Moldovan Family Collection, New York.

David Wilkie, the son of a minister in Scotland, studied painting in England, was elected to the Royal Academy and succeeded Sir Thomas Lawrence as Painter in Ordinary to the King in 1830. Wilkie traveled to the East in 1840. During his travels, he painted a portrait of Sultan Abdülmecid I in Istanbul and was the guest of Sir Moses Montefiore. Wilkie died during this trip, and was buried at sea off Gibraltar.

It is interesting that the artist chose to portray three women studying Torah; he probably thought that they would have more appeal for his audience back in England than a depiction of men, especially in view of the inclusion of the nursing mother. Despite the possibilities such a motif might suggest, Wilkie's depiction of the nursing mother is understated, almost casual.

REFERENCE: Rubens, *Iconography*, 1981, no. 1977.

309   DAVID, SON OF RABBI SAMUEL MAJHA, SECOND CHIEF RABBI OF JERUSALEM*

London, 1849. Artist: Rev. W. J. Woodcock. Engraver: M. & N. Hanhart. Colored engraving. Rev. W. J. Woodcock, Scripture Lands. 5½ x 3¼ in. Moldovan Family Collection, New York.

The author/artist, Rev. W. J. Woodcock, traveled through Eretz Israel in 1848 with the Rev. Moses Margoliouth (1818–1881), a Polish-born Jew who had converted to Christianity in England and become an Anglican clergyman. In 1858 Margoliouth published a book, *Pilgrimage to the Land of My Fathers*, on his journey to Eretz Israel. Woodcock records that he ". . . took, in Jerusalem, the likeness of a youth about fourteen years of age, the son of Rabbi D. S. Majahr, a lad of studious habits and considerable intelligence. . . ."

David wears a head covering typical of those worn by rabbis or students, the *kaveze*—a high crown of cardboard covered with black material around which is wrapped a piece of light-colored cotton (see also cat. no. 66 and 67).

REFERENCES: Rubens, *Iconography*, 1981, no. 1982; Rubens, *Costume*, 1973, fig. 60, p. 48.

310

311 THE FIRST WINDMILL AT JERUSALEM

December 18, 1858. Illustrated London News, p. 586. Engraving. 7 x 5¾ in. Moldovan Family Collection, New York.

Sir Moses Montefiore built this windmill outside the walls of Jerusalem to help farmers who were still grinding grain themselves. The parts were built by a firm in Canterbury, England, and carried by camel from Jaffa. The windmill, and the adjacent settlement built by Sir Moses, *Mishkenot Shaananim*, were the nucleus of the first new suburb outside Jerusalem.

Cf. For other items relating to Sir Moses Montefiore, see cat. nos. 600–603 and 615–616.

312 OLD JEWISH WOMAN OF CAIRO [AND] YOUNG JEWISH WOMAN OF CAIRO

London, 1882. The Illustrated London News, Nov. 18, 1882, p. 518. Artist: Montbaro (Charles Auguste Loye, 1841–1905). Engraver: W.B. Engraving. 8¹⁵⁄₁₆ x 5¹⁵⁄₁₆ each. Moldovan Family Collection, New York.

Charles Auguste Loye was called Montbaro after his homeland on the Gold Coast. A caricaturist and watercolorist, he drew the pictures on which these engravings were based during his visit to Cairo.

310 COSTUME AND LIKENESS OF A NATIVE JEW AND JEWESS OF JERUSALEM*

London, 1854. Jerusalem and Holy Land. Being a Collection of Lithographic Views and Native Costumes from drawings taken on the spot by Mrs. Ewald. Day & Son, Lithographers to the Queen. Colored lithograph. 11 x 7⅞ in. Inscription: Through your mercy they also may obtain mercy (Romans 11:31). Moldovan Family Collection, New York.

In the 19th century, Jews of Eretz Israel dressed in the same styles as other inhabitants of the Ottoman empire. The man wears the same head covering as young David (cat. no. 309), the *kaveze*—a high crown of cardboard covered with black material around which is wrapped a piece of light-colored cotton. His wife wears the half-moon-shaped headdress, the *hotoz* (see cat. no. 215). At her waist is a belt buckle composed of two large gold circles.

REFERENCES: Rubens, *Iconography*, 1979, London, 1981, no. 1987; Rubens, *Costume*, 1973, fig. 61.

313 DAMAS: COUR D'UNE MAISON JUIVE

(Damascus: courtyard of a Jewish home)*

Syria, ca. 1890. Photograph. 4½ x 6¾ in. Moldovan Family Collection, New York.

Homes in the Near East were usually built around a central courtyard. In contrast to the sedate exterior facing the street, the courtyard facade would be elaborately decorated. Trees and water fountains provided shade, cool air and pleasant sounds. Entrances to the home from the courtyard were often recessed to provide cool, shaded areas in which to sit. A lavish example of this type of Islamic architecture is the Courtyard of the Lions at the Alhambra.

The family here, for the most part, has

3 1

adopted European dress, which contrasts oddly with the decorative facade of their home.

Cf. A similar photograph of the interior of a Jewish home in Damascus taken before 1901, is illustrated in Sarah Graham-Brown, *Images of Women*, New York, 1988, p. 73; Rubens, *Iconography*, 1981, no. 2333 "Interior of Jewish House at Damascus," wood engraving, ca. 1860.

314 A JEWISH SCRIBE OF TODAY IN HIS WORKROOM

New York, January 10, 1917. Christian Herald, front cover. Colored photograph. Underwood and Underwood. 11¼ x 9 in. Moldovan Family Collection, New York.

The traditional implements of the scribe, the pose and the simple workroom evoke a timeless chain of Jewish scribes stretching back to ancient times. The image is a modern descendant of author portraits in illuminated manuscripts. A pencase like the one used by this scribe is described above (cat. no. 286).

NORTH AFRICA

ALGERIA · LIBYA · MOROCCO · TUNISIA

*"And in the year 1492 . . . we were exiled from all of the kingdoms of Ferdinand
. . . and all Israel was scattered to the East, West, North and South, and some
came to the kingdom of Fez . . . and after a time, God had mercy on his people
. . . and blessed us with His blessings, until we built spacious homes with
decorated walls; . . . academies and students, and extremely beautiful synagogues
and Torah scrolls dressed in fine linen, silk and embroidery, crowned in silver.
And so developed the nature of the Jewish neighborhoods in all of the lands of
Ishmael until this day . . ."*

RABBI HAIM GAGUINE (b. ca. 1460)

Keswa el kbira (ceremonial costume), Morocco, late 19th–early 20th century. Cat. no. 382; Bridal crown, Middle East/North Africa, 19th–20th century. Cat. No. 385.

מפה זו למנוחת האשה חנה עו'א [...] ואשית אברהם הלוי ✳

אנכי ה / לא תרצח
יהיה / לא תנאף
לא תשא / לא תגנב
זכור את / לא תענה
כבד את / לא תחמד

תורה

כתר

5717

היו שנפטר יהיוס ה'א'יר שנת התש'ט'ז לפק תנצב'ה ✳✳

319

NORTH AFRICA

SYNAGOGUE

315 ATZEI HAYYIM (Torah staves)

Meknes, Morocco, 19th–20th century. Wood; lead: cut. 43⅞ x 2¼ in. diam. Collection of Dr. and Mrs. Henry Toledano, New York.

The decoration on this pair of staves is based on an architectural motif: an arcade of Moorish arches. *(fig. 33)*

Cf. IM, *Maroc*, fig. no. 297.

316 MEIL (Torah mantle)

Fez, Morocco, 1892/93. Velvet: embroidered with metallic threads; woven bands. Hebrew inscriptions: T[he year] [5]553, May the merit of the Torah protect Shlomo son of Shmuel the Kohen . . . Fez . . . ; "She is a tree of life to those who grasp her, and whoever holds on to her is happy" (Prov. 3:18). 24⅜ x 10⅝ in. diam. Collection of
the Israel Museum, Jerusalem, anonymous gift, 151/85.

The interlace patterns embroidered on this mantle can also be found in ceremonial metalwork and manuscripts from this region.

REFERENCE: IM, *Maroc*, fig. no. 61.

317 MEIL (Torah mantle)

Fez, Morocco, 1933. Silk: embroidered with silk and metallic threads. Hebrew inscription: Donation of . . . "the royal princess" (Ps. 45:14) Sultana Zarfatti h[er] s[oul] i[s bound] i[n the bonds of] l[ife] . . . 28th of Sivan . . . "help" [Chronogram = (5)693]. 25⅞ x 13½ in. Collection of Yeshiva University Museum, New York, gift of Mark Samoil, 90.125.

Rigid cylindrical textile mantles were generally used in North African communities. A mantle made of cotton, linen or lace would be placed beneath mantles of this type. *(fig. 35)*

318   MEIL (Torah mantle)

Fez, Morocco, 1933. Silk: embroidered with silk and metallic threads. Hebrew inscription: Donation of the pure heart [from] the precious Hayyim Mammon m[ay] G[od] b[less him] a[nd guard him] that fulfills the commandment "Therefore write down this poem." (Deut. 31:19); Crown of the Torah; the Ten Commandments [with abbreviated text]; "You shall make a lampstand of pure gold" (Ex. 25:31); For the repose of his dear father Yedidiah Mammon h[is resting place in] E[den] the merit of the Torah should be a shield and command upon him and upon the members of his household; Sivan [5]693. 27¼ x 12⅛ in. diam. Collection of Yeshiva University Museum, New York, gift of Mark Samoil, 90.126. (fig. 35)

319   TORAH COVER*

North Africa, 1957. Velvet: embroidered with metallic threads. Hebrew inscriptions: Crown of the Torah; This cover [has been donated] for the woman Hannah Azran w[ho rests in] E[den], wife of Avraham the Levite . . . ; who passed away on the 5th of Iyar, the year 5717. M[ay her] s[oul] b[e bound] i[n the bonds of] l[ife]. 26 x 35½ in. Collection of Yossi Benyaminoff, Jerusalem.

On this cover the representation of the Temple in Jerusalem is modeled after a mosque. Many of the motifs frequently found on North African ceremonial objects, such as lions, roosters and the menorah, can be seen on this cover. The fact that this textile was dedicated in the second half of the 20th century indicates the preservation and continuity of traditional craftsmanship in North Africa.

Cf. IM, *Maroc,* fig. no. 35.

320   TORAH SHIELD

Constantine, Algeria, ca. 1925–1935. Silver: pierced and engraved. Collection of the Sir Isaac and Lady Edith Wolfson Museum, Hechal Shlomo, Jerusalem.

This shield is most unusual, as Torah shields were not generally used in North Africa. The shield combines an overall European format with Islamic decoration and workmanship.

321   TORAH CROWN

Algeria, 19th century. Silver: repoussé, pierced, engraved and parcel-gilt. 7½ x 9¼ in. diam. Collection of the Sir Isaac and Lady Edith Wolfson Museum, Hechal Shlomo, Jerusalem.

This crown is very similar in style and workmanship to examples made in the Ottoman empire, but includes small cast decoration typical of Italian ceremonial silver. The depiction of a ship on one side of this crown is unusual. (Plate 14)

REFERENCE: Bialer, p. 121.

322   MINIATURE TAPPUHIM
(Torah finials)

North Africa, 18th century. Silver: engraved. 7¼ x 2½ in. Einhorn Collection, Tel Aviv.

The term *tappuhim* (literally apples) is used in North African communities to describe Torah finials. The apple is seen as a symbol of revelation, and alludes to the mystic relationship between God and the Jewish nation. In the Biblical verse "Under the apple tree I roused you; It was there your mother conceived you, There she who bore you conceived you." (Cant. 8:5), the apple tree is traditionally interpreted symbolically as Mount Sinai (Rashi, ad loc.). Most other communities use the term *rimmonim* (literally pomegranates) to describe Torah finials. The pomegranate is seen as a symbol of the Torah since it is traditionally believed to hold 613 seeds, one seed for each commandment in the Torah. The use of fruit terminology to describe Torah finials relates to the fructiform shapes common in these ornaments.

323   TAPPUHIM (Torah finials)

North Africa, 18th–19th century. Silver: pierced and chased; velvet. Hebrew inscriptions: Shmuel Mattityahu . . . ; belonging to . . . Shmuel Mattityahu . . . son of Massoud . . . 13¾ x 3½ in. Collection of Mr. and Mrs. Abraham Halpern, New York.

These hexagonal finials are very finely crafted. The pierced ogival (pointed) archway resembles the architectural form of the *mihrab*, the prayer niche in a mosque. (fig. 35)

REFERENCES: New York, Sotheby's, *Fine Judaica: Printed Books, Manuscripts and Works of Art,* June 2–3, 1982, lot no. 500; Weinstein, fig. no. 98.

324 TAPPUHIM (Torah finials)

North Africa, 18th–19th century. Silver: repoussé, chased and cast. Hebrew inscriptions: Consecrated to G[od]; Made by the hands of the craftsman Arahon [sic]. 15½ x 4¼ in. Collection of the Reuben and Helene Dennis Museum, Beth Tzedec Synagogue, Toronto, Canada, CR 1169.

The overall shape of these finials and the scrollwork and floral motifs may be modeled on examples made in Livorno. There is a strong relationship between finely crafted North African Judaica and Italian examples (see also cat. nos. 321, 329–331 and 341). The abstraction and roundness of the vegetal and floral forms, and the use of a teardrop-shaped cast finial at the top of the domed roof of the tower-like structure, indicate a North African origin. The spelling error in the artisan's Hebrew signature suggests that while this Jewish silversmith was a masterful craftsman, he probably had little training in Hebrew reading and writing.

325 TAPPUHIM (Torah finials)

North Africa, 19th century. Silver: hammered, chased, enameled, pierced and cast; wood. 12½ x 3¼ in. Collection of Mr. and Mrs. Abraham Halpern, New York.

These finials are modeled after minarets and feature enamel decoration and ogee-shaped windows, elements frequently found in mosque towers. *(fig. 43)*

326 TAPPUHIM (Torah finials)*

Meknes, Morocco, 19th century. Silver: enameled. 13¼ x 3½ in. Collection of Dr. and Mrs. Henry Toledano, New York.

Multicolored enamel decoration in geometric patterns was a common feature of Islamic architectural ornament and decorative arts, and was also adopted for use in Jewish ceremonial objects.

327 TAPPUHIM (Torah finials)

Libya, 19th century. Wood: gessoed, painted and gilt. 14¾ x 3½ in. diam. Gross Family Collection, Tel Aviv, 50.8.1–2. (fig. 44)

The two finials are not identical, and prob-

326

ably were not originally intended for use as a matched pair.

REFERENCE: IJA, *Gross*, pp. 27–28.

328 TAPPUHIM (Torah finials)*

North Africa, 19th century. Silver: cast, pierced and chased. Hebrew inscriptions: Consecrated to G[od] by Suleiman son of Makka Attia; Made by the hands of the craftsman Anifa Partos. 14½ x 3¼ in. Collection of the Reuben and Helene Dennis Museum, Beth Tzedec Synagogue, Toronto, Canada, CR 711.

These finials are modeled on the Islamic architectural form of minarets. They are unusual due to the fish-scale pattern on the lower shaft and the finial at top, which is shaped like an animal's horns. There were many Jewish silversmiths in North Africa. The arrangement of inscriptions on this pair, with one finial bearing a dedicatory inscription naming the donor and the second finial inscribed with the

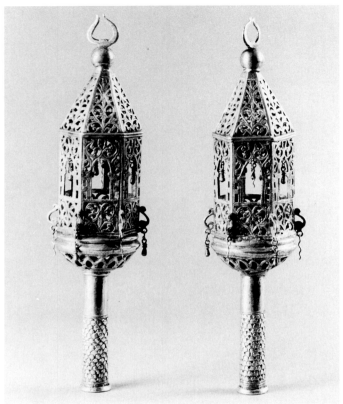

328

name of the craftsman, is frequently found on examples from this region (see also cat. no. 324).

329   TAPPUHIM (Torah finials)

Constantine, Algeria, dated 1877. Silver: pierced and engraved. 23 x 4⅞ in. Collection of the Sir Isaac and Lady Edith Wolfson Museum, Hechal Shlomo, Jerusalem.

These finials, unusual in their massive size, are modeled after an Italian type.

330   TAPPUHIM (Torah finials)

North Africa, 19th century. Silver: repoussé, chased, pierced and engraved over a wood core. 10⅜ x 3 in. Moldovan Family Collection.

This pair of delicately crafted finials features a melding of native North African traditions with stylistic characteristics modeled after Italian ceremonial objects. The overall shape of the finials, a domed tower with pierced pointed trefoil windows, is based on Islamic architecture and suggests the form of a minaret. The shafts of the finials are rope-twist columns embellished with scrolling vegetal motifs. Twisted columns frequently appear on Italian ceremonial silver, printed books, manuscripts, ketubbot and synagogue architecture, probably due to the association of this motif with Solomon's Temple. The twisted columns in the Capella della Pietà of St. Peter's, Rome, were popularly believed to have come from the Temple in Jerusalem.[1] The use of twisted columns in these finials indicates the North African tendency to adopt Italian symbolism and stylistic models. The inclusion of hanging bells attached to elongated chains also follows Italian custom. *(fig. 35)*

Cf. IM, *Maroc*, fig. no. 63.

1. See NYJM, *Gardens*, cat. no. 187.

331 TAPPUHIM (Torah finials)

Spanish Morocco, 1892. Silver: cast, pierced and engraved. Hebrew inscriptions: A dedication made in his lifetime by . . . Yihye the Kohen for the repose of his brother . . . Eliyahu, both sons of . . . Amram the Kohen . . . ; Dedicated by . . . Yihye the Kohen . . . son of Amram . . . on the 13th of the month of Adar, the year "and order" (Num. 20:8) [Chronogram = (5)652]. Gross Family Collection, Tel Aviv, 50.1.25.

These finials are very finely crafted, and are examples of the masterful piercing typical of North African ceremonial silver. The use of bells suspended on very long chains is probably modeled on Italian finials.

332 TAPPUHIM (Torah finials)

Asrir, Morocco, 19th–20th century. Silver: pierced and engraved; semiprecious stones. 9⅜ x 3¼ in. Collection of the Israel Museum, Jerusalem, anonymous gift, 147/151.

Pairs of Moroccan Torah finials are frequently joined by a chain, as in this example. *(fig. 42)*

REFERENCE: IM, *Maroc*, cat. no. 69.

333 YAD (Torah pointer)

Tunisia, 19th century. Silver: cast and engraved; tassel of metallic threads and sequins. Hebrew inscription: The youth Yaakov Palilos. Collection of the Judah L. Magnes Museum, Berkeley, California, 77.242.

334 YAD (Torah pointer)

North Africa, 19th–20th century. Silver: engraved and chiseled. Hebrew inscription: Dedicated to God and donation of the pleasant student Yitzhak son of Avraham Algazi . . . 10 x ⅞ in. Collection of Mr. and Mrs. Abraham Halpern, New York.

335 YAD (Torah pointer)*

North Africa, 19th–20th century. Silver: chased, chiseled and engraved. Hebrew inscription: Arturo Gora . . . 10¾ x 1¼ in. Moldovan Family Collection, New York.

This flat pointer bears a dedicatory inscription on one side and delicate arabesques on the reverse.

336 YAD (Torah pointer)

Fez, Morocco, 19th–20th century. Silver: engraved. Hebrew inscription: Yaakov ben Raphael Yitzhak Aben Sur . . . 6¾ x 1¹/₁₆ in. Gross Family Collection, Tel Aviv, 52.1.11.

The Aben Sur family was prominent in the rabbinic leadership of the Fez community.

337 TIK (Torah case)

North Africa, 19th century. Wood: inlaid with mother-of-pearl. Inscription: 3. Collection of the Jewish Museum, New York, 1984–70a.

This octagonal *tik* features cut-out scrollwork on its top, in the shape of an *atarah*, a crown placed atop a Torah case (see cat. nos. 340 and 341). The number carved on this case was probably used in order to differentiate between various Torah cases in the synagogue. Moroccan congregations primarily used textile mantles, while Torah cases were more often used in Algeria and Tunisia.[1]

338 COVER FOR A TIK
(Torah case cover)

Algeria or Libya, 19th century. Velvet: embroidered with metallic threads. Hebrew inscription: Azizo and his wife Tita Tikhmon . . . 20¼ x 39⅞ in. Einhorn Collection, Tel Aviv. (fig. 36)

1. See Dobrinsky, p. 179.

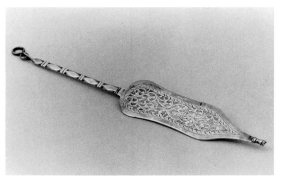

340

341

339 COVER FOR A TIK
(Torah case cover)

North Africa, 19th century. Velvet: embroidered with silk and metallic threads; silk banding. Hebrew inscription: For the r[epose of] Moshe di Shekhti Arviv h[is resting place in] E[den]. 19⅛ x 33½ in. Collection of Mr. and Mrs. Abraham Halpern, New York.

This finely embroidered textile was hung on the outside of a Torah case. The silk banding which frames the embroidery is woven with a pattern combining favorite motifs of Ottoman and North African culture, the crescent, star and amuletic hand (*hamsa*).

340 ATARAH (Crown for Torah case)*

Bou-Saâda, Algeria, before 1910. Silver: pierced and engraved. Hebrew inscription: This Torah crown was donated by Ephraim Sulam . . . It was damaged and had . . . to be repaired anew, and it is dedicated to God, made by the hands of . . . Shalom son of . . . Yaakov Monsonigo . . . French inscription: Made in Bou-Saâda on October 30, 1910. 5¼ x 8½ in. diam. Gross Family Collection, Tel Aviv, 53.1.6.

This crown is composed of eight square plaques, each surmounted by a scalloped dome. The inscriptions and decorations are arranged so as to imitate manuscript pages. A variety of decorative and symbolic motifs, such as the Tablets of the Law, a crescent with a flower in place of a star, hands outstretched for the priestly benediction, crowns, fish and a menorah, as well as Biblical, Mishnaic and amuletic texts, ornament this crown.

341 ATARAH (Crown for Torah case)*

Mazagan, Morocco, 1928. Silver: pierced, chased, engraved, cast and parcel-gilt; coral. Hebrew inscriptions: Deut. 33:4; Deut. 4:44; Prov. 3:17–18; Prov. 18:10; Prov. 9:11; Ps. 19:8; Deut. 31:8; Deut. 33:29; Deut. 33:9; Ruth 2:12; Is. 51:16; Ps. 118:5; A Torah Crown dedicated by . . . Amram Zarmon . . . son of . . . Kohen . . . [and] his mother the woman of valor . . . Ranina . . . made by the hands of the craftsman . . . Mihlof Aznanu . . . Mazagan . . . in the m[onth of] Sivan 5688 f[rom] c[reation]. 8½ x 9½ in. diam. Collection of Mr. and Mrs. Abraham Halpern, New York.

This crown consists of twelve panels, an allusion to the Twelve Tribes, and is constructed so that the top can be removed and the panels can be opened into a continuous strip. It was probably originally used on top of a twelve-sided *tik*, a rigid Torah case. It features unusually extensive Hebrew inscriptions extolling the virtues of the Torah.

This crown reflects a combination of Islamic and Italian influences. The arched panels and raised filigree ornament indicate Islamic models, but the delicate tracery is based on Italian rococo scrollwork. Both traditions attributed protective, amuletic powers to corals. Coral decoration is also found on an important set of mid-18th-century Venetian Torah crown and finials.[1] The piercing on the top of this crown suggests that it, too, may have been used with finials, an adoption of the Italian custom.

REFERENCE: Weinstein, fig. nos. 73–74.

342 ARK CURTAIN PLAQUE

North Africa, 1918. Silver: engraved. Hebrew inscription: D[edicated] to G[od] this is the holy Ark curtain that was dedicated by . . . Shmuel Firi . . . on behalf of the soul of the d[eparted] his mother Aziza m[other of] Shmuel Yitzhak Firi w[ho passed on to her] w[orld in] E[den] on the second day of the N[ew] M[oon] of Adar t[he year] 5678 that was dedicated on the e[ve of] R[osh] H[ashanah] 5679 m[ay her] s[oul] b[e bound] in [the bonds of] l[ife]. 7¾ x 5¾ in. The Abraham J. and Deborah B. Karp Collection, New York.

As the inscription indicates, the donor gave an Ark curtain in memory of his mother only a few months after her death; this may account for the somewhat uneven quality of the engraving and for an error in the text.

343 MEMORIAL PLAQUE

Algeria or French Morocco, 1945. Silver: repoussé and stamped. French inscription: MOISE ALLOUCHE DECEDE LE 22 DEC 1945 (Moise Allouche deceased on December 22, 1945). 6⁵⁄₁₆ x 5¾ in. Abraham J. and Deborah B. Karp Collection, New York.

---

1. See NYJM, *Gardens*, cat. nos. 197 and 205.

344 QENDIL (Wall sconce oil lamp)

Morocco, 18th–19th century. Brass: cast and chiseled; copper rivets. 15¾ x 6¼ in. Moldovan Family Collection, New York.

Lamps of this type were used for kindling lights on Sabbath and festivals in the home and as memorial lamps in the synagogue. All the surfaces of this lamp, even the underside of the oil pan, are decorated with ornamental motifs and patterns typical of North African metalwork, such as birds and vegetal and floral arabesques. (*fig. 60*)

Cf. IM, *Maroc,* fig. no. 53.

345 SYNAGOGUE MEMORIAL LAMP*

Sfax, Tunisia, 19th century. Silver: pierced and engraved. Hebrew inscription: This lamp was dedicated in memory of . . . Yehuda Kamos Berabi . . . 20½ x 4½ in. Collection of the Israel Museum, Jerusalem, anonymous gift, 117/134.

Memorial lamps of this type were used in synagogues. The suspended silver container held a glass vessel in which were placed water, oil and a wick.

346 SYNAGOGUE MEMORIAL LAMP

Meknes, Morocco, 20th century. Glass: gold paint; brass: cast. Hebrew inscription: "The lampstand for lighting" (Ex. 35:14; Num. 4:9) in memory of the departed m[ay] h[is soul] b[e bound] i[n the bonds of] l[ife]. 11¾ x 8¼ x 32 in. Collection of Dr. and Mrs. Henry Toledano, New York.

It was customary in Morocco to dedicate lamps to the synagogue in memory of deceased relatives. The glass containers were filled with water on which oil and a wick were floated. The survival, intact, of the original inscribed glass insert in this example is unusual.

347 SYNAGOGUE MEMORIAL LAMP

North Africa, 1949. Silver: pierced; glass. Hebrew inscription: The departed Yosef Bartilon passed on to his world on [the] e[ve of] 1 Tevet 5709. 13 x 11 in. diam. Collection of Mr. and Mrs. Norman Rosen, Cherry Hill, New Jersey.

345

This lamp is unusually elaborate. The use of inscribed pierced silver is distinctive. Most hanging memorial lamps were made of brass and were more simply fashioned (see cat. no. 346).

348 ARCHITECTURAL FRAGMENTS*

Tangier, Morocco, 19th century. Stucco: cast, carved and painted. Hebrew inscription: Know be-

fore [Whom you stand]. 12½ x 12½ in.; 8½ x 18⅛ in.; 18¹⁄₁₆ x 12¼ in. Collection of the Nahon Synagogue Restoration, New York.

These fragments are typical of architectural stucco work used to decorate North African synagogues. Similar cast and carved plaster can be found in Spanish Synagogues from before 1492, as seen in the model of the La Blanca synagogue in Toledo (cat. no. 1). These fragments were removed during the restoration of the Nahon synagogue, and have been re-cast, so as to provide complete stucco panels in the restored synagogue.

349 DEPICTION OF THE INTERIOR OF THE NAHON SYNAGOGUE

Tangier, Morocco, and New York, 1989. Adelaide Murphy. Oil on canvas. 119 x 164 in. Collection of the Nahon Synagogue Restoration, New York.

This canvas depicts the *trompe l'oeil* painting above the *heikhal* (Ark) of the Nahon Synagogue in Tangier. The Nahon Synagogue was founded in Tangier, Morocco in 1878 by Moses Nahon, a prominent banker and active member of the Jewish community. Nahon named the synagogue *Maasat Moshe* (Feats of Moshe). The name refers to the Moses of the Bible, and simultaneously suggests a tribute to Moses Nahon's own accomplishments.

The synagogue served as a central place of worship for 100 years before it fell into disuse. Over a century after its establishment, the Nahon Synagogue is now being restored to its original glory. The Nahon Synagogue Restoration is sponsored by the Lucius N. Littauer Foundation.

COMMUNITY

350 DJELLAK Y CAPA

(Rabbi's costume)

Tetuan, 19th century. Wool; braid trim. Collection of the Judah L. Magnes Museum, Berkeley, California, 78.4.17a,b.

Rabbi Samuel Barchilon Benzimra of Tetuan wore this outfit, consisting of a dark blue wool *zokha* (robe) with a three-quarter-length wool

bedaiya (overcoat). The sleeve is decorated with braid trim on the inside as well, so that it could be turned to face out. *Seroual* (trousers) would be worn underneath. This is part of the typical costume worn by urban males in Morocco.

REFERENCES: Magnes, *Threads*, cat. no. 5. Cf. IM, *Maroc*, p. 218, fig. no. 419.

351 SEAL

Fez, Morocco, 19th–20th century. Bronze: cast. Hebrew inscriptions: S[ervant of] G[od] Shlomo s[on of] . . . Raphael Aben Sur; "If I forget you O Jerusalem . . ." (Ps. 137:5); Fez; The Western

Wall. French inscription: *SALAMON ABEN
SUR FES (MAROC)*. 1 x 1¾ x ⅞ in. Gross
Family Collection, Tel Aviv, 41.2.1.

In the center of this seal is a depiction of
Jerusalem.

352 SEAL

*Fez, Morocco, 19th–20th century. Brass; wood.
Hebrew inscription: Shlomo [Abe]n Sur.* ⁷⁄₁₆ x ½
x 3 in. Gross Family Collection, Tel Aviv, 41.2.2.

SABBATH AND FESTIVALS

353 SABBATH WALL SCONCE

*North Africa, 18th century. Brass: engraved. He-
brew inscription: Lamp for the holy Sabbath Gracia
Ben Hayyim.* Collection of the Sir Isaac and Lady

Edith Wolfson Museum, Hechal Shlomo,
Jerusalem.

Sabbath lamps, like Hanukkah lamps, were
frequently hung on walls. Lamps similar to
this one were also used in Holland (see cat. no.
549).

354 KIDDUSH WINE BOTTLE

*North Africa, early 20th century. Silver: chased
and engraved. Hebrew inscription: Wine in honor
of the holy Sabbath.* 13¾ x 4¾ in. Einhorn Collection, Tel Aviv.

355 SHOFAR

*Meknes, Morocco, 19th–20th century. Horn:
carved.* 9¼ x 6¼ in. Collection of Dr. and Mrs.
Henry Toledano, New York.

NORTH AFRICAN HANUKKAH LAMPS

Hanukkah lamps crafted in North Africa reveal the blending of local characteristics with traditions established in Spain and Portugal. Hanukkah lamps are frequently modeled after architectural compositions. This probably stems from the association of these lamps with the Temple edifice in Jerusalem and from the halakhic requirement to publicize the miraculous victory of the Hasmoneans by displaying the lit lamps in doorways or windows.[1] North African lamps combine a variety of Islamic architectural motifs, such as the Moorish horseshoe arch typical of medieval Spain and the pointed ogival arch frequently found in Morocco. Sephardim were familiar with Islamic ornamental patterns found in both Iberian and North African architecture, such as interlace, stylized floral patterns and arabesques, and such motifs frequently decorate their Hanukkah lamps.

Birds, a popular folk motif in North African art which may have originated in medieval Spain,[2] are a common decorative element on Hanukkah lamps from this region. The use of bird motifs in Hanukkah lamps may stem from the Biblical association of birds with the Temple: "Even the sparrow has found a home, and the swallow a nest for herself in which to set her young, near Your altar, O Lord of hosts, my king and my God" (Ps. 84:4).

Silver lamps were crafted for the wealthy, but most surviving examples are made of brass. Found objects, jewelry and scrap metal, such as brass buttons, cast ornaments and even metal from oil and sardine cans, were used to construct and decorate lamps.[3]

In Tetuan, Morocco, a distinct local lamp tradition existed. Hanukkah lamps from Tetuan feature actual gates that swing open and shut. The lamps are inscribed with the Biblical verse "Blessed shall you be in your comings and blessed shall you be in your goings" (Deut. 28:6). When placed in a doorway or window, such lamps served to publicize the miraculous events associated with Hanukkah and at the same time to greet visitors and guests celebrating the holiday.

Cf. IM, *Maroc*, pp. 72–73.

---

1. See IM, *Architecture.*   2. See Stillman, "*Hashpaat,*" pp. 364–66.   3. See IM, *Secular,* cat. nos. 24–27.

356 HANUKKAH LAMP

North Africa, late 18th century. Brass sheet: engraved. 14½ x 9¾ x 2½ in. Einhorn Collection, Tel Aviv.

The overall shape of this lamp is based on the pointed ogival arch. The decorative use of a single bird, rather than a pair as in the other examples in this exhibition, is unusual.

357 HANUKKAH LAMP

North Africa, 18th–19th century. Brass: cast and chased. Moldovan Family Collection, New York.

The finely crafted, elaborate scrollwork on this lamp is reminiscent of Italian renaissance and baroque brass Hanukkah lamps. Italian ceremonial objects frequently served as models for North African artisans, as can be seen in many of the exhibited Torah finials and crowns (see cat. nos. 321–332).

358 HANUKKAH LAMP

North Africa, 19th century. Brass: cast. 8 x 8⅞ x 2½ in. Moldovan Family Collection, New York.

This lamp is modeled after an architectural composition, with an overall shape based on a triangular, gabled pediment with Moorish horseshoe arch apertures.

Cf. IM, *Architecture,* cat. no. 24.

359 HANUKKAH LAMP

Morocco, 19th century. Brass: cast. 6⅜ x 8⅝ x 2¾ in. Gross Family Collection, Tel Aviv, 10.2.8.

Ornamented gates surmounted by foliate finials, similar to those seen on this lamp, are found in illustrated manuscripts and decorated Esther scrolls from this region (see cat. nos. 398 and 375, respectively).

REFERENCE: IJA, *Gross,* pp. 175–77.

360 HANUKKAH LAMP

Tetuan, Morocco, 19th century. Brass: hammered and engraved. 12 x 9½ x 2½ in. Collection of Mr. and Mrs. Ami Sibony, New York.

Hanukkah lamps are frequently based on architectural models, as seen in the swinging gates found on lamps from Tetuan. This may be due to the halakhic requirement to display the lamp in windows or doorways in order to publicize the miracle of Hanukkah.

Cf. IM, *Architecture,* cat. no. 13.

361 HANUKKAH LAMP

Meknes, Morocco, 19th century. Brass sheet: hammered and chased. 11½ x 8½ x 3 in. Collection of the Israel Museum, Jerusalem, anonymous gift, 118/377.

This lamp is almost identical with a Dutch type popular in the 18th and 19th centuries (see cat. nos. 552–554 and 556), and testifies to the connections between the Sephardic communities of Western Europe and North Africa. *(fig. 77)*

362 HANUKKAH LAMP

North Africa, 19th century. Brass: cast. 7⅞ x 7 x 2 in. Moldovan Family Collection, New York.

This lamp is based on early Spanish models, testifying to the continuity of Iberian ceremonial art traditions among the North African Sephardim. It features design elements incorporated from Moorish and Gothic sources, such as horseshoe arches, rose window, arabesques and floral patterning.

363   HANUKKAH LAMP

Fez, Morocco, 19th century. Brass: cast. 7½ x 5½ x 2 in. Collection of Prof. and Mrs. Solomon Feffer, New York.

This lamp has many characteristics found in Moorish architecture, such as horseshoe arches and a triangular, gabled form. The lamp may have been modeled after local Moroccan buildings, or perhaps based on a tradition of earlier Hanukkah lamps from Spain.

Cf. IM, *Stieglitz*, cat. no. 173.

364   HANUKKAH LAMP MADE FROM A TALLIT BAG*

Morocco, 19th century. Silver: pierced and engraved. Hebrew inscription: S[ervant of] G[od] Shlomo son of Avraham [ib]n Ezra . . . 12⅝ x 9¾ x 3¼ in. Moldovan Family Collection, New York.

This lamp was made from the cut silver plates of a tallit bag (see cat. no. 386). North African Hanukkah lamps were frequently crafted from metal sheet or artifacts made for other uses (see cat. nos. 264 and 371).

365   HANUKKAH LAMP

Chechouan, Morocco, 19th century. Brass: hammered. 9¾ x 8½ x 2⅞ in. Collection of Mr. and Mrs. Ami Sibony, New York.

This lamp comes from a small rural Moroccan town, and reflects naive provincial craftsmanship. The pediment shape and heart motifs are frequently found on 18th- and 19th-century Dutch *hannukiyot* (see cat. nos. 552, 553 and 556), which probably served as the model for North African lamps of this type.

366   HANUKKAH LAMP

North Africa, 19th century. Silver: pierced and engraved. 13¼ x 7½ in. Collection of Prof. and Mrs. Solomon Feffer, New York.

Silver Hanukkah lamps were preferred in many North African communities, probably because of *hiddur mitzvah*, the desire to beautify the observance of the commandment.[1] Most surviving examples are crafted of brass and other base metals, as can be seen in the other exhibited lamps. Silver lamps would have been expensive, and beyond the means of many North African Jews. Objects crafted of precious metals were often melted down when outdated, while simpler objects may simply have been stored away. In many Moroccan communities a rooster was eaten on Hanukkah,[2] and the use of this motif may relate to this custom. *(fig. 61)*

Cf. Bialer, p. 157.

367   HANUKKAH LAMP

North Africa, 19th century. Brass: cast and engraved. 17 x 9½ x 2⅞ in. Moldovan Family Collection, New York.

This lamp follows the architectural format seen in early Spanish examples, with a rose window above two tiers of Moorish arch apertures. The spaces between the arches are filled with engraved menorot. Birds are frequently used as an ornamental motif in North African metalwork and textiles. *(fig. 73)*

Cf. IM, *Stieglitz*, cat. no. 175.

368   HANUKKAH LAMP

Morocco, 19th century. Marble: carved. 6½ x 1½ x 4⅛ in. Collection of the Israel Museum, Jerusalem, anonymous gift, 118/484.

Stone Hanukkah lamps of this type, used in the Anti-Atlas region of Morocco, resemble medieval Spanish examples. Similar lamps were also used in Yemen. A 4th-century oil lamp found in Jerusalem suggests that the prototype for lamps of this type of various origins stems from Talmudic Eretz Israel. *(fig. 74)*

---

1. Dobrinsky, p. 372.   2. *Ibid.*

Cf. E. Muchawsky-Schnapper, "Oil Sabbath-Lamps and Hanukkah-Lamps of Stone from the Yemen," *JA* 9 (1982), 80–81; B. Narkiss, "The Gerona Hanukkah Lamp: Fact and Fiction," *JA* 14 (1988), 12–13.

369 HANUKKAH LAMP

Tunisia, 19th century. Earthenware: glazed. 2¾ x 11⅞ in. Collection of the Israel Museum, anonymous gift, 118/463.

Each of the oil fonts is shaped like an ancient clay oil lamp. *(fig. 76)*

Cf. Grossman, *Temple*, cat. no. 91.

370 HANUKKAH LAMP

Tetuan, Morocco, 19th–20th century. Hebrew inscriptions: Deut. 28:6. Brass: cast and engraved. 13 x 10 x 2½ in. Collection of Mr. and Mrs. Norman Rosen, Cherry Hill, New Jersey.

The swinging gates on this lamp are a detail found on Hanukkah lamps from Tetuan. The architectural format of this lamp includes a six-pointed star positioned as a central rose window.

Cf. IM, *Architecture*, cat. no. 14.

371

371 HANUKKAH LAMP*

North Africa, 19th–20th century. Brass: cast. 11½ x 10 x 2¼ in. Collection of Mr. and Mrs. Abraham Halpern, New York.

372

This lamp is constructed from various cast brass elements. It combines many characteristic traits of North African lamps: decorative bird motifs; an architectural composition based on the pointed ogival arch; and the use of found objects and scrap metal.

REFERENCE: Weinstein, fig. no. 185.

372 HANUKKAH LAMP*

Tetuan, Morocco, 19th–20th century. Brass: cut, engraved and tinned; copper rivets; pressed tin oil pan and shelf. 11⅛ x 10⅛ x 2¼ in. Hebrew inscriptions: Deut. 28:6; Num. 8:2–3; Ps. 67. Moldovan Family Collection, New York.

This lamp is an example of a type unique to Tetuan, featuring a central seven-branch menorah. On the sides of this lamp hinged gates, now lost, were originally fastened. The gates were an allusion to the inscribed biblical verse, "Blessed shall you be in your comings and blessed shall you be in your goings" (Deut. 28:6). The arrangement of the unusually extensive inscriptions on this lamp are based on the composition of the amuletic prayer plaque known as a menorah or a *shivviti*.

373 ESTHER SCROLL

Morocco, 18th century. Ink and gouache on parchment. L: 13⅝ in. Gross Family Collection, Tel Aviv, 81.12.24.

In this unusually large scroll a variety of geometric patterns is used to decorate the columns flanking the text. The first opening is a later addition.

374 ESTHER SCROLL WITH WOODEN CASE

Morocco, 18th–19th century. Ink and watercolor on parchment; wood. L: 9½ in. Gross Family Collection, Tel Aviv, 81.12.16.

375 ESTHER SCROLL

Tetuan (?), Morocco, mid-19th century. Ink and watercolor on vellum. 5½ x 94⅞ in. Gross Family Collection, Tel Aviv, 81.12.13.

The orange and green paint and architectural, ornamental and faunal forms used in the decoration of this scroll are typical of Tetuan (see cat. no. 378). The text is written in an arcade of Moorish horseshoe arches. The pillars and spandrels are filled with floral and geometric patterns. Four colorful birds replace the patterning in one spandrel.

REFERENCE: IJA, *Gross*, pp. 361–67.

376 ESTHER SCROLL

North Africa, 19th century. Ink and watercolor on parchment. Moldovan Family Collection, New York.

This scroll is decorated with scrolling vegetal arabesques typical of North African ornament.

377 ESTHER SCROLL AND CASE

Meknes, Morocco, 19th century. Ink on parchment; silver: chiseled, pierced, chased and parcel-gilt. 6¾ x 1¼ in. Collection of Dr. and Mrs. Henry Toledano, New York.

The hexagonal shape of this case is modeled after tower forms common in Islamic architecture.

LIFE CYCLE

Marriages in Morocco are traditionally held on Wednesdays. The entire village is invited to the wedding: either a messenger goes from house to house to extend the invitation in person, or the *Bab el-ros* is painted on the entrance door of the groom's home, with the names of the bride and groom and the date of the marriage. The day before the wedding, the two families agree on the value of the property to be exchanged and the terms of the ketubbah. That evening the *lilt el-henna* (henna ceremony) is held. Women come to the bride's home in their festive costumes, a *keswa el kbira* (grand costume) if possible, and the palms of the bride's hands and the soles of her feet are stained with henna. Henna is one of the components of the gift sent by the fiancé on a silver platter three days before the wedding when the bride visits the *mikvah*. The marriage is held in the home of the bride. She sits on the *talamon* (canopied dais) while ritual chants are sung, the blessings are recited, and the ketubbah is read.

REFERENCE: IM, *Maroc*, pp. 106–7.

378 KETUBBAH (Marriage contract)

Tetuan, Morocco, 1852. Ink and tempera on parchment. 23 x 17¼ in. Gross Family Collection, Tel Aviv, 35.12.2.

Groom: Yitzhak son of Yaakov Bibas
Bride: Dona daughter of David Kasis
This is a fine and delicate example of typical Tetuan ketubbot. The motifs appearing here, such as the pair of birds, are commonly found in other Judaica objects from Tetuan (see cat. no. 375). *(fig. 21)*

REFERENCES: IM, *Maroc*, fig. no. 195; New York, Christie's, *An Important Collection of Judaica*, Oct. 9, 1980, lot no. 54; IJA, *Gross*, pp. 353–55.

379 KETUBBAH (Marriage contract)

Meknes, 1855. Ink, gouache and gold paint on paper. 22½ x 17¾ in. Gross Family Collection, Tel Aviv, 35.11.10.

Groom: Yehuda ha-Levi son of Moshe ha-Levi
Bride: Zahra daughter of Yitzhak Ben Hassin
A richly and exquisitely illuminated ketubbah with the text set in colorful Moorish arches, surrounded by delicate vegetal and floral motifs. Each of the bridal couple, particularly the groom, is introduced by many honorific titles extolling their merits. *(fig. 22)*

380 KETUBBAH (Marriage contract)

Rabat, 1909. Lithograph on paper with handwritten text. 23 x 17¼ in. Zucker Family Collection (RZ), New York.

The green and gold printed border of this document consists of a monumental arch and a rectangular exterior frame. To the sides of the arch are two hands inscribed with the Priestly Blessing. Below the text are depictions of a goblet labeled "Cup of the Seven Blessings" (i.e., the blessings of the marriage ceremony) and a pitcher labeled "wine decanter." This contract documents a levirate marriage, the required union of a childless man's widow to his brother. Inscribed in large square Hebrew letters are Biblical verses relating to *yibbum*, levirate marriage (Deut. 25:5–6).

REFERENCE: YUM, *Wedding*, cat. no. 231; Cf. Sabar, *Ketubbah*, cat. no. 246.

381 KESWA EL KBIRA
(Grand costume)

Morocco, 19th century. Skirt: velvet, metallic embroidery, L: 38½ in. Jacket: velvet, metallic embroidery, L: 24 in. Front: velvet, metallic embroidery, 16¾ x 16 in. Sleeves: muslin, 39 x 35 in. Headpiece: velvet, metallic embroidery, silk, 19½ x 14½ in. Shoes: leather, velvet, metallic embroidery, 2¾ x 10 x 3¾ in. Sash: brocade, 2¼ x 20 in. Collection of Mr. and Mrs. Abraham Halpern, New York.

This is the traditional festive dress of Moroccan Jewish women. In former times it was given to Sephardic Jewish brides for their wedding and they would subsequently wear it on other ceremonial occasions. By the 20th century, such outfits became so expensive that few women could order them. In consequence existing costumes were shared by brides in the family or community. Embroidered velvet caftans became the festive dress on other occasions.

The origin of the *keswa el kbira* is usually traced to the 15th-century Spanish *vertugada* (hoop skirt, called farthingale in England). This originated in Castile around 1470 as a bell-shaped underskirt supported with circular hoops of flexible wood. The tradition of elaborate decoration (*se'illi*, "Sicilian work") is maintained today in the embroidered costumes of contemporary Spanish matadors.

The fabrication of the *sqelli* (gold thread) is a Jewish craft, brought to Morocco by Spanish Jews. Jean Besancenot, an authority on Morrocan costume, uses the *keswa el kbira* to trace the migration of Jewish exiles from Spain through Tangier, Tetuan, Rabat, Meknes, Fez and Marrakech. In the south and east, where local culture subsumed the Sephardic tradition, the *keswa el kbira* was not widely used.

The *keswa el kbira* consists of the following articles of clothing:

ENGLISH	MOROCCAN	LADINO
skirt	*zeltita*	*giraldeta*
jacket	*gombayz*	*gasot*
front	*ktef*	*punta*
sleeves	*kmam*	*mangos*
sash	*hzam*	*cuchaca*

It is worn with slippers (*rihiyyat el kbar/babusat*) and a headpiece. The color of the dress was traditional and depended on the city of origin.

REFERENCES: Besancenot, *Costumes*, pp. 176–77. IM, *Maroc*, pp. 146, 150, 200–205; Müller-Lancet, "Costume and Jewellery," pp. 51–54; Stillman, "Costume," pp. 343–75; Stillman, "*Hashpaat*," pp. 361–66; Anderson, pp. 208–11; Cf. Besancenot, *Costumes*, pls. 51, F.

382   KESWA EL KBIRA
(Grand costume)

Morocco, late 19th–early 20th century. Skirt: velvet, embroidered with silver thread washed with gold. L: 42 in. Jacket: sleeve length 28¼ in. Front: velvet embroidered with silver thread washed with gold. Sleeves: synthetic. L: 28¼ in. Sash: silk. L: 90 in. Shoes: leather, velvet, metallic embroidery. 8½ x 2 in. Collection of the Sephardic Studies Department, Yeshiva University, New York, gift of Mr. Abraham Pinto, Yeshiva University Museum, 77.160a–h.

Moroccan costume worn for weddings and other festive occasions. Each region of Morocco has its own style of dress. This costume is in the style typical of Rabat. The outfit consists of a skirt (*zeltita*), bodice (*gombaz*), front (*punta* or *ktef*), sash (*hzam*) and sleeves. The shoes, called *babucha* or *srabli*, are decorated with traditional embroidery patterns. This pair of shoes is more closed than the style usually favored by Jewish women of Morocco. The decoration includes floral and *hamsa* motifs for good luck.

The sleeves are separate in this and the other example of the *keswa el kbira* (cat. no. 381). In pre-Expulsion Spain, detachable sleeves were sometimes given by ladies to knights as tokens. These sleeves are recent additions.

Sashes were popular in pre-Expulsion Spain; these could be decorated with gold embroidery, and fringes like the sash worn with the *keswa el kbira*. *(See illustration on p. 276)*

REFERENCES: Anderson, pp. 208–11; Stillman, "*Hashpaat*," pp. 361–66.

383   GROOM'S WEDDING COAT

Morocco, 19th century. Wool; braided trim and buttons. Collection of the Judah L. Magnes Museum, Berkeley, California, 78.4.39.

White *zokha* (robe) decorated with braid worn by a Moroccan groom. White was sometimes worn for festivals and Shabbat by rabbis and by some Jews of Tetuan.

REFERENCES: Magnes, *Threads*, no. 18; IM, *Maroc*, p. 218.

384   SFIFA (Wedding crown)

Tetuan or Tangier, late 19th century. Seed pearls, gold beads, semiprecious stones in gold settings; sewn on cotton, silk lined. 16¼ x 4⅛ in. Collection of Congregation Emanu-El, New York, bequest of Judge Irving Lehman, 1945.

Worn by Moroccan Jewish brides at their wedding and later on ceremonial occasions, this crown is held to the head with a scarf covering the hair. This could be topped with a *panwelo de manila* (shawl, see cat. no. 408).

REFERENCE: Grossman, *Temple*, cat. no. 132.

385   BRIDAL CROWN*

Middle East/North Africa, 19th–20th century. Copper: gold plated; glass inlay. Hebrew inscriptions: Jerusalem of gold; Finding a good wife is finding good; May he achieve God's approval and all good fortune. Amen. Aramaic inscription: If I forget thee, O Jerusalem. . . . 3½ x 10¼ in. Collection of Selma and Stanley I. Batkin, New Rochelle, New York.

The *twiyyiz* (little tiara) is a recent variation of the traditional *taj*, a diadem composed of plaques, believed to be modeled on European (particularly Byzantine) jewelry. It was worn with the *keswa el kbira* (grand costume) during the week-long marriage festivities, and sometimes also on later festive occasions by married women in the cities in northern Morocco. *(See illustration on p. 276)*

REFERENCES: Stillman, "Costume," pp. 343–75; Sijelmassi, pp. 148–49. Cf. Besancenot, *Bijoux*, p. 5, pl. X, no. 32; Stillman, "Costume," ill. 16; IM, *Maroc*, cat. no. 426.

PERSONAL AND MISCELLANEOUS JUDAICA

386 TALLIT BAG*

Morocco, 19th century. Silver: pierced and engraved; velvet. Hebrew inscription: Maimon son of Yitzhak the Kohen . . . 7¾ x 10½ x 1⅜ in. Moldovan Family Collection, New York.

Tallit bags of this type were frequently presented as a gift to a boy at the time of his bar mitzvah, when he would wear a tallit for the first time. The use of cut silver, rather than the embroidered decoration seen in other exhibited examples, indicates the wealth of the owner. *(fig. 61)*

Cf. Magnes, *Ornamented Bags*, no. 146.

387 TALLIT BAG

North Africa, 19th–20th century. Velvet: embroidered with metallic and silk threads. Hebrew inscriptions: Meir son of Reuven Kasos. 7 x 10⅛ x ½ in. Moldovan Family Collection, New York.

Roosters are a common motif in North African ceremonial art. This bag is frayed from use

and the orange threads over which the metallic threads are sewn can be clearly seen. *(fig. 37)*

Cf. Magnes, *Ornamented Bags*, nos. 137–38.

388 TEFILLIN BAG

North Africa, 19th–20th century. Velvet: embroidered with metallic threads; metallic braid; satin; silk cord. Hebrew inscription: S[ervant of] G[od] Avraham Halioua. 11 x 8 in. Moldovan Family Collection, New York.

The decoration on this bag includes the amuletic *hamsa* (hand) depicted as a flower atop scrolled branches and leaves. *(fig. 37)*

389 TEFILLIN BAG

North Africa, 19th–20th century. Velvet: embroidered with metallic threads; metallic braid; sequins; silk cord. Hebrew inscription: S[ervant of] G[od] Menahem Anhoriste. 10⅞ x 8 in. Moldovan Family Collection, New York.

The shield form of this bag is unique to North Africa. The owner's monogram in Latin letters is embroidered on one side of this bag. *(fig. 37)*

Cf. Magnes, *Ornamented Bags*, no. 140.

364 & 386

390 TEFILLIN BAG

North Africa, 19th–20th century. Velvet: embroidered with metallic threads. Hebrew inscription: S[ervant of] G[od] Eliezer son of Yaakov Elmaleh. 10½ x 6½ in. Collection of Abraham J. and Deborah B. Karp, New York. (fig. 37)

Cf. Magnes, *Ornamented Bags*, no. 140.

391 MENORAH (Shivviti)

North Africa (?), 1844. Artist: Yaakov G——. Papercut; ink on paper; metallic papers. 35¼ x 27¾ in. Gross Family Collection, Tel Aviv, 36.11.3.

Amuletic prayer plaques of this type are often found in synagogues. The name "menorah" derives from the central seven-branched arrangement of Biblical verses. This unusually large papercut is decorated with delicate designs of a menorah, Temple implements and floral motifs. Brightly colored metallic foil backgrounds are typical of North African papercuts.

392 MENORAH (Shivviti)

Tangier, Morocco, ca. 1860. Ink on parchment. 6⅛ x 4¼ in. Collection of Rabbi and Mrs. Mitchell Serels, New Rochelle, New York.

393 MENORAH (Shivviti)*

North Africa, 19th century. Ink and gouache on paper. 19½ x 13¼ in. Moldovan Family Collection, New York.

This amuletic plaque is decorated with ornamental motifs common to North African ceremonial art, such as pierced archways and scrolling floral arabesques.

394 MENORAH (Shivviti)

Meknes, Morocco, 20th century. Lithograph on paper; ink; gouache. 24½ x 17½ in. Collection of Dr. and Mrs. Henry Toledano, New York.

This plaque was written on a blank border printed in Vienna. This print depicts a pointed double archway. It was very popular among

North African and Ottoman Jews and was frequently used for marriage contracts.

Cf. Sabar, *Ketubbah*, cat. no. 254.

395 DEPICTION OF TEMPLE IMPLEMENTS*

North Africa, 19th–20th century. Ink on paper. 9½ x 7⅞ in. Collection of the Sephardic Reference Room, Yeshiva University, New York.

396 DEPICTION OF HOLY SITES IN JERUSALEM

North Africa, 19th–20th century. Ink and water-color on paper. 6¼ x 10⅛ in. Collection of the Sephardic Reference Room, Yeshiva University, New York.

397 RABBINICAL DOCUMENT

Fez, 19th–20th century. Ink on paper. 6¼ x 4¼ in. Gross Family Collection, Tel Aviv.

Moroccan rabbis signed their names on religious and commercial documents with uniquely decorative and complex flourishes. The complex patterns of these signatures probably relate to Islamic arabesques, interlace and decorative calligraphy. The signature of Raphael Aben Sur can be seen on this document.

393

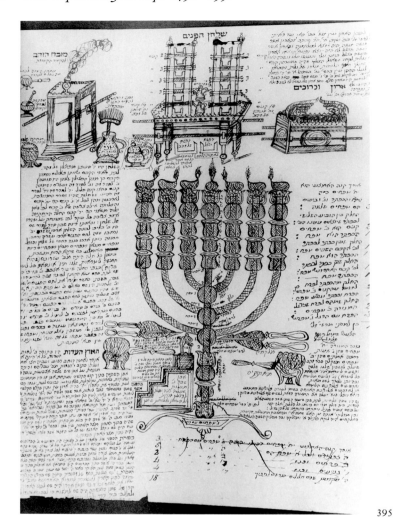

395

MANUSCRIPTS AND
PRINTED BOOKS

398 OTZEROT HAYYIM

Marrakech, Morocco, 1752. Rabbi Hayyim Vital (1542–1620) Scribe: Aharon ben Avraham Corcos. Ink, gouache and watercolor on paper. 8¾ x 6¾ in. Gross Family Collection, Tel Aviv, Ms. no. MO.11.17.

This is a typical kabbalistic work by the noted Safed Sephardic kabbalist. The only decorated page is the title page, which consists of a horse-shoe arch drawn delicately and symmetrically in a style typical of the Sephardic communities of Mogador and Marrakesh.

Rabbi Hayyim Vital was born in Safed and educated by Moshe Alsheikh. In 1570 he became the pupil of Yitzhak Luria. After Luria's death in an epidemic at the age of 38, Vital succeeded him as the leader of the kabbalists.

The scribe may be a member of the Corcos family, whose family tree is included in this exhibition (see cat. no. 758).

399 SEFER HA-LIKKUTIM
(Book of Selections)

Morocco, 1786. Rabbi Hayyim Vital (1542–1620). Scribe: Makhluf Ben Chetrit. Ink and watercolor on paper. Gross Family Collection, Tel Aviv, Ms. no. MO.11.18.

The most curious fact about this copy of Vital's kabbalistic work is the age of the scribe. As he himself notes in the colophon, he was only 13 years old when he finished copying this complicated work.

400 SEFER SHIUR KOMAH

Morocco (Fez?), 1789. Ink, gouache and watercolor on paper. Scribe: Yehuda Elbaz. 6⅜ x 4⅜ in. Gross Family Collection, Tel Aviv, Ms. no. MO.11.8.

This is an early kabbalistic work with commentaries derived from the Zohar. The only decorated page in this manuscript is the title page, where author, title, scribe and date are listed in a decorative window with a Moorish arch. An 18th-century rabbi in Fez by the name of Yehudah Elbaz may very well be identical with our scribe.

401 ZHAHIR SHEL PESAH*
(Passover miscellany)

Morocco (Sijilmasa?), 19th century. Ink and gouache on paper. 6¾ x 4¼ in. Gross Family Collection, Tel Aviv, Ms. no. MO.11.11.

This text contains readings for Passover and sections of the Haggadah in Hebrew and Judeo-Arabic. Several pages are richly decorated with typical Sephardic Moorish arches. *(fig. 23)*

402 PIYYUTIM

Morocco, second half of the 19th century. Scribe: Yosef ben Enan. Ink and gouache on paper. 7½ x 5 in. Gross Family Collection, Tel Aviv, Ms. no. MO.11.2.

This manuscript contains liturgical poems composed by several known North African rabbis. Four carpet pages are decorated with rectangular frames filled with floral designs and other motifs.

403 ZHAHIR SHEL PESAH
(Passover miscellany)

Outat, Morocco, second half of the 19th century. Scribe: Moshe ben Yitzhak Ben Maman. Ink on paper. 7½ x 5 in. Gross Family Collection, Tel Aviv, Ms. no. MO.11.9.

This manuscript consists of a Passover Haggadah (fols. 1r–22r), *piyyutim* and liturgical readings for Passover in Hebrew and Judeo-Arabic. The many delicate decorations throughout the book are all in black ink.

REFERENCE: Jerusalem, The Society of Judaica Collectors, *International Jewish Prints & Manuscripts*, Dec. 30, 1987, lot no. 567.

404 SEFER KOL YAAKOV

Fez, Morocco, ca. 1870s. Scribe: Yosef Hayyim ben Yisrael Yaakov Maimaran. Ink on paper. 7⅜ x 4⅞ in. Gross Family Collection, Tel Aviv, Ms. no. MO.11.7.

401

This manuscript has a curious story. The original text is by Rabbi Yaakov Koppel Margolioth, a 15th-century Polish rabbi. His book was printed twice (Venice, 1648; Amsterdam, 1708). One of the copies reached Fez, Morocco, where a local scribe copied it by hand, but with modifications fitting the time and place. The decorations on the title page are executed in the same ink used for the text and resemble the designs on Fez ketubbot.

405   MEGILLAT HITLER

P. Hassine. Casablanca, ca. 1943. Ink on paper: printed. Collection of Museum of Jewish Heritage, New York, anonymous gift.

This scroll celebrates the victory of the Allied forces and the liberation of Casablanca from Vichy French control. Published by its author, the scroll recounts the history of World War II and of Hitler's persecution of the Jews; the narrative is modeled on the story of Haman and Esther. On the first anniversary of Casablanca's liberation by American troops, the Jews of the city instituted a special Purim in accordance with similar local "Purim" celebrations held by other Jewish communities to commemorate their escape from destruction. Though Moroccan Jewry was never under direct German control, serious restrictions were imposed on Jews and mob violence caused great strife. Spanish Moroccan cities such as Tangier were major centers for the *Vaad Hatzala* and other organized efforts to save Jews trapped in Nazi-occupied Europe.[1]

The conclusion of this megillah is a variant on the traditional "Cursed be Haman, blessed be Mordekhai"; it reads: "Cursed be Hitler, cursed be Mussolini . . . Blessed be Roosevelt, blessed be Churchill, blessed be Stalin. . . ."

---

[1]. See M. Serels, *A history of the Jews in Tangier in the 19th and 20th centuries*, New York, 1991, chapter 9.

COSTUME

406   CAFTAN

Tangier, early 20th century. Velvet: embroidered with silver ribbon washed with gold, wrapped around silk(?) thread. L: 56 in. Collection of Yeshiva University Museum, New York, gift of Abraham Pinto, 78.22.

According to the donors, this woman's caftan was embroidered by a Jewish embroiderer. The decoration consists of foliage with bird and peacock designs, motifs which have been linked to medieval Spain.

Cf. Stillman, *Hashpaat*, pp. 364–66.

407   WOMAN'S CAFTAN, BELT AND SHOES

Morocco, 1940s. Dress: velvet: metal thread washed with gold. Belt: leather, velvet, metal thread.˙ Shoes: leather, velvet, metal thread. Collection of Juliette Halioua, New York.

Caftans like this one were worn by women in Morocco for ceremonial and formal occasions. This one was probably embroidered by a Jew since it has only floral rather than figural decoration, and for a Jew since the buttons are patterned with a six-pointed star. On very formal occasions, this garment might be worn with a gold and jeweled belt.

The caftan was a traditional dress of Muslim women in Morocco, and is common in other Islamic countries. It was originally adopted by Jewish women for the *Maimuna* festival when they disguised themselves in Muslim costume. *Maimuna* celebration is a traditional feast held by North African Jews at the end of the last day of Passover, which according to tradition is the anniversary of the death of Maimonides' father, Maimon ben Joseph, who lived for some time in Fez, Morocco. The *Maimuna* includes dairy and other meatless foods and drinks with symbolic significance. Gifts of food are exchanged.

While non-Jewish women wore a caftan over a chemise, Jewish women in urban areas often wore a contemporary evening slip under the caftan instead.

REFERENCES: Müller-Lancet, "Costume and Jewellery," p. 54; IM, *Maroc*, pp. 87–88. *Cf.* IM, *Maroc*, fig. no. 142; for buttons see fig. no. 313.

408 SHAWL

China and the Philippines, early 20th century. Cotton: silk embroidery. Collection of Juliette Halioua, New York.

This embroidered shawl was used by a Moroccan family to cover the *hallah* (Sabbath loaves) on Shabbat before and during the *kiddush*. The embroidery was done in China and the shawl fringed in the Philippines. Such shawls could also be used as headcoverings or worn over the shoulders.

Cf. Besancenot, *Costumes*, fig. no. 51; IM, *Maroc*, fig. no. 207.

409 MAN'S KERSIYYA (Sash)

Morocco, 19th–20th century. Silk. 15¾ x 120 in. Collection of the Sephardic Studies Department, Yeshiva University, New York, gift of Abraham Pinto, Yeshiva University Museum, 81.34.

Worn indoors over (sometimes under) the *zokha*, a blouse-like garment of variable length. It would be folded lengthwise four times, and wrapped two or three times around the waist. It is sometimes used to decorate the synagogue.

REFERENCE: IM, *Maroc*, p. 218.

410 MAN'S KERSIYYA (Sash)

Morocco, 19th–20th century. Silk. Collection of Dr. and Mrs. Henry Toledano, New York.

Provincial costumes still worn in Spain today include wide, bright sashes from which the Moroccan version might have evolved, and *toreros* (bullfighters) in Spain still wear brightly-colored sashes.

411 BEBRAS (Shoes)

Morocco, 20th century. Leather. Collection of Rabbi Mitchell Serels, New Rochelle, New York.

412 KIPPAH (Cap)

Morocco, 20th century. Cotton. Collection of Rabbi Mitchell Serels, New Rochelle, New York.

The *kippah* was sometimes called a *tarbush*.

REFERENCE: Besancenot, *Costumes*, p. 178.

413 MAN'S WALLET

Morocco, 19th–20th century. Leather: tooled; gold washed silver thread wrapped around cardboard; metal snaps. 4½ x 6 in. Collection of the Sephardic Studies Department, gift of Abraham Pinto, Yeshiva University Museum, New York, 81.35.

This wallet is decorated with floral and calligraphic motifs. An embroidered *hamsa* motif is used; this motif is also stamped on the metal snap.

414 BATH CLOGS*

Morocco, 19th–20th century. Wood: lead; mother-of-pearl inlay. 2⅝ x 9 x 2¾ in. Collection of Ita Aber, New York.

These special shoes were worn in the bath house because they prevented the wearer from slipping on wet floors and protected her feet from spilled depilatories. The warm, moist air of the bath house is the perfect climate to preserve the delicate inlay. These clogs are similar in design as well as function to those worn in the Ottoman empire (see cat. no. 149).

A similar pair with mother-of-pearl inlay in what is called the Turkish kub-kob style is in the collection of the Northampton Shoe Museum Collection.

REFERENCE: Yarwood, p. 351.

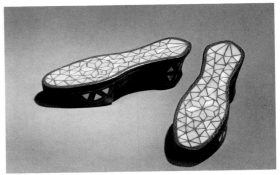

PERSONAL ARTIFACTS
JEWELRY

Jews were the primary craftsmen in the production of jewelry in Morocco. They worked in a variety of media and techniques, including gold set with pearls and gemstones as well as silver set with enamel. The forms could be birds (as in the pectoral worn by the woman in the postcard showing the Jewish woman from Tetuan), floral forms (such as the *lebba*), architectural or geometric forms. The latter are usually decorated with geometric ornament in enamel.

Most urban jewelry in Morocco is of gold, or gilded; much of it is decorated with rubies and emeralds. It can include a *twiyyiz* (little tiara) such as the one described above (cat. no. 385), worn on festive occasions, as well as earrings, necklaces and bracelets. The *lebba* is among the most notable of the traditional necklace types. While much of the gold jewelry of urban Morocco reflects current international fashion, or uses Moorish/Arab motifs such as arabesques, the silver pieces are frequently influenced by Berber forms. These are characterized by a preference for geometric forms and sharp contrast between unadorned and decorated surfaces.

Fibulae are the most common form of functional rural jewelry, used to maintain the drape of the costume. Moroccan craftsmen were inventive in the creation of diverse forms of fibulae and the necklace-like chains sometimes used to link them, each characteristic of a different region. Most silver pieces are decorated in cloisonné enamel—raised compartments in which applied enamel colors with a silicon base are melted. The basic enamel colors come from the application of powdered metal oxides—yellow (lead), blue (cobalt) and green (copper). Some regions add blue (made from frit). Besides being decorative, the colors have symbolic meanings connected with the elements: red (often coral rather than enamel) stands for fire (or blood); yellow for air and the sun; green for water and vegetation. All are intended to avert evil, or the evil eye.

Unfortunately, very little antique jewelry in gold or silver has survived. Most pieces have been reworked in "modern" styles or sold for the value of the metal and melted down. It is difficult to date pieces securely since few, if any, are marked.

REFERENCE: IM, *Maroc*, pp. 106–7.

415 TIJAJIN D'MAHDOUH
(Headdress)

Morocco, 19th–20th century. Silver thread: enamel, colored glass; cow or horse hair; coins; beads. 3½ x 10¼ in. Collection of Mr. and Mrs. Abraham Halpern, New York.

This is the characteristic headpiece worn by married Jewish women in the region of Tiznit, Morocco, to conceal their hair. The *tijajin d'mahdouh* was worn by married women at all times, as was most of the jewelry she owned, even in the performance of her daily chores.

Coins were frequently added to jewelry because the entire ensemble represented the woman's wealth. This headdress includes 20-kopek silver pieces (ranging in date from 1860 to 1905); lightweight brass Arabic coins; large silver Arabic coins; and Maria Theresa thalers from Austria. The latter were popular in many countries as a medium of exchange, and continued to be minted into the 20th century. The blue stones were added for good luck.

The exiles from Spain could have gone no further south; they settled in the villages of Tiznit, Talaint, Ifrane and Tahala. Jewish craftsmen were known for their fine silver and enamel jewelry. Muslims did not engage in making jewelry because it was believed that evil spirits dwelled in the metal or the forge.

REFERENCES: Besancenot, *Costumes*, p. 178; IM, *Maroc*, fig. nos. 405–7; Cf. Besancenot, *Costumes*, pl. 53.

416 NECKLACE

Morocco, 19th–20th century. Silver: cast, filigree; enamel and glass inlay; coins. 20 x 4 in. Collection of Mr. and Mrs. Abraham Halpern, New York.

A necklace of this type could have been used to link a pair of fibulae such as the elaborate triangular, enameled pair (cat. no. 422). The piece is called an *issersel*; its central element is the *taguemmout*, an elongated ball of silver filigree with enamel decoration.

REFERENCES: Rouach, fig. no. 279; Besancenot, *Bijoux*, pl. 38, fig. no. 158; Besancenot, *Costumes*, pl. 43; Hasson, *Jewellery*, no. 71.

417 LEBBA

Morocco, 19th–20th century. Silver: gold wash; glass inlay. 18 x 4 in. Collection of Yossi Ben-yaminoff, Jerusalem.

The *lebba* is part of a traditional set of wedding jewelry worn in Morocco. This necklace originated as a cosmopolitan style, but its popularity led to its being copied also in rural areas. It was worn by Muslim as well as Jewish women. Crescent moons and lobed fruit shapes, a pomegranate motif known as *rarnati*, are separated by almond-shaped beads called *grageb/kragueb*. The pomegranate, a fertility symbol, is appropriate for wedding jewelry.

The pomegranate was (and is) used on the shield of Granada and can be found in some Spanish jewelry. The use of this motif in Morocco may stem from Spain and Morocco's shared decorative vocabulary, or may be evidence of Spanish influence on Moroccan jewelry.

In contrast to the Yemenite *labba* worn under the chin, the Moroccan version was worn as a necklace.

REFERENCES: IM, *Maroc*, cat. no. 440a; Besancenot, *Bijoux*, pl. 8, fig. no. 25; Rouach, fig. no. 1; Sijelmassi, p. 147; Müller-Lancet, "Motifs," pp. 115–16.

418 KHLAL AFTAH

(Crescent fibulae)

North Africa, 19th–20th century. Silver: hammered; engraved. 4⅞ x 5 in. Collection of Mr. and Mrs. Abraham Halpern, New York.

It is likely that these fibulae were made by Jewish craftsmen, as Jews held a monopoly on the manufacture of jewelry in North Africa. These probably originated in Tunisia. While one side is decorated with leaves, the other has a central six-pointed star enclosing a rosette, confronting birds, and *houta* (fish). These elements appear to have been combined for their esthetic appearance and their general amuletic function.

The six-pointed star, a cosmic symbol, is both the Muslim *Khatem Souleiman* (Seal of Solomon) and the Jewish *Magen David* (Star of David). The bird frequently represents the human soul seeking eternal rest in the House of the Lord (Ps. 84). The fish is a Jewish and Muslim symbol of fertility, longevity and prosperity that protects the wearer from the evil eye (*Berakhot* 20a: "as the fish, who live in the water . . . escape . . . the evil eye, so let it be also for the descendants of Joseph.").

REFERENCES: Hasson, *Jewellery*, no. 70; Gargouri-Sethom, p. 66, nos. 4, 5; p. 86, pl. 2, lower left; Rouach, pp. 26–27, 31, 36–37; Champault, pp. 126–27, fig. no. 3.

419 FIBULAE

North Africa, 19th–20th century. Silver; hammered, chased; coral. 9½ x 1¼ in. (each). Collection of Yossi Benyaminoff, Jerusalem.

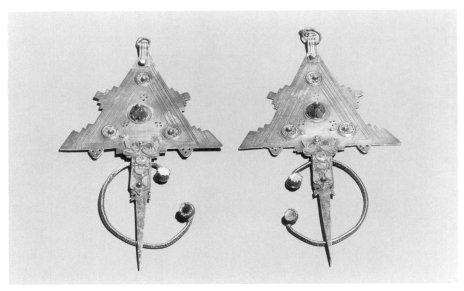

422

Characteristic of the Meknes region, the coral repels evil spirits. The horseshoe arches recall the early appearance of such elements on Sephardic ketubbot after the Expulsion, and the Spanish-Moorish origin of the Jewish craftsmen who probably created these pieces.

REFERENCE: Rouach, fig. nos. 45, 46.

420 ROUND FIBULA

Morocco or Algeria, 19th–20th century. Silver: enamel. Diam: 4 in. Collection of Yossi Benyaminoff, Jerusalem.

Usually the pin on ring-shaped brooches such as this is much longer in order to gather the bunched material that would be pulled through the center hole. Such pieces are characteristic of eastern Morocco or western Algeria. Among the people of Kabylia in northern Algeria, similar pieces are sometimes worn on the headdress. This piece has enamel decoration on the reverse as well as the front. The pieces which appear to be coral are actually a red paste applied over a wax core.

REFERENCES: Rouach, fig. no. 80; Hasson, *Jewellery*, no. 95, p. 72.

421 PECTORAL WITH FIBULAE

North Africa, 19th–20th century. Silver: cast, cut-out; coral inlay. 3¼ x 23½ in. Collection of Yossi Benyaminoff, Jerusalem.

The *luha* (central element), sometimes considered a *hamsa*, depicts a double *mihrab* (Muslim prayer niche).

REFERENCE: Rouach, fig. nos. 98, 441; p. 206.

422 TIZERZAI or TIKHOULLALIN (Fibulae)*

Morocco, 19th–20th century. Silver: cast, engraved; enamel inlay. 8¼ x 4¾ in. Collection of Yossi Benyaminoff, Jerusalem.

Pins have long been necessary accessories of clothing and were used by the Romans, Celts and Goths, among others in decorative, often elaborate forms. These Moroccan examples are highly elaborate, with stepped decoration on the arms of the triangle and enameled bosses (raised ornamentation). These are similar to a type characteristic of the Agadir-Tiznit-Tafraout region, and of the Issafène.

REFERENCES: Gotzmann, "Jewelry," pp. 15–16; Rouach, fig. no. 279; Sijelmassi, p. 153 bottom; Besancenot, *Bijoux*, pl. XXXV, fig. no. 145.

423 BELT

North Africa, 19th–20th century. Silver: hammered, cast, engraved, gilt; coral. L: 47½ in. The Moldovan Family Collection, New York.

The flat round links are characteristic of traditional Tunisian jewelry, while the hands holding flowers show Ottoman (see cat. no. 163) influence on North African metalwork.

REFERENCE: Gargouri-Sethom, pp. 26, 139, 147.

424 BRACELETS*

Morocco, 19th–20th century. Silver: cast, engraved. 1 x 2⅞ in.; ½ x 2¾ in. Moldovan Family Collection, New York.

These bracelets are the type known as *deblij* (bracelet) *sems ugmar* (sun and moon), named for the alternating silver and gold sections. They were worn by urbanites and wealthy inhabitants of rural districts.

REFERENCES: IM, *Maroc*, p. 238, cat. no. 451; Besancenot, *Bijoux*, pl. XII, fig. no. 43; Hasson, no. 88.

425 CUFF BRACELET*

Morocco, 19th–20th century. Silver: cast; enamel and coral inlay. 3 x 2½ in. Collection of Yossi Benyaminoff, Jerusalem.

This type of bracelet, called *nbala*, was made and worn by Jews. The enamel technique demonstrates the survival of Moorish techniques, imported by Jewish refugee craftsmen from Spain and Portugal. The red stones are for good luck.

REFERENCES: Besancenot, *Bijoux*, pl. 29, fig. no. 119; IM, *Maroc*, cat. nos. 457, 460; Sijelmassi, pp. 168 (bottom), 169; Muller, pp. 22–23.

426 CUFF BRACELET

Morocco, 19th–20th century. Silver: cast; enamel and coral inlay. 2¼ x 2 in. Collection of Yossi Benyaminoff, Jerusalem.

This type of bracelet, called *nbala*, was made and worn by Jews (see also cat. nos. 425 and 428).

REFERENCES: IM, *Maroc*, cat. nos. 457, 460. *Cf.* Besancenot, *Bijoux*, pl. 29, fig. no. 119.

427 BRACELET

Morocco, 19th–20th century. Silver: cast; niello; enamel. 2¼ x 2¾ in. Collection of Yossi Benyaminoff, Jerusalem.

Azbeg bracelet, typical of rural areas of Morocco, especially Tahala and Tiznit. The geometric decoration reflects Berber influence, as does the interplay between smooth, undecorated areas of silver and decorated areas.

REFERENCES: Gotzmann, "Jewelry," p. 19; IM, *Maroc*, cat. no. 455; Sijelmassi, p. 168 (top).

424, 425, 428

428 CUFF BRACELET*

Morocco, 19th–20th century. Silver: cast, enamel and glass inlay. 2½ x 2¼ in. Collection of Yossi Benyaminoff, Jerusalem.

Nbala type bracelets were made by Jews and are believed by Jean Besancenot to be worn primarily by Jews (see also cat. nos. 425–426).

REFERENCES: Besancenot, *Bijoux*, fig. no. 119; IM, *Maroc*, cat. nos. 457, 460.

429 HAMSA AMULET

Morocco, 19th–20th century. Silver: cast, engraved. 2¾ x 1½ in. Collection of Yossi Benyaminoff, Jerusalem.

All five fingers and the hand of the traditional *hamsa* are depicted in this amulet worn to ward off the evil eye. It is decorated with vine motifs, and represents a characteristic type of jewelry worn by city dwellers.

   The *hamsa* (literally, five, alluding to the number of fingers of the hand) protects the wearer against the evil eye. For Jews, the hand represents Divine protection and intervention.

It is represented several times in the earliest examples of Jewish figural art, the narrative Biblical paintings in the 3rd-century synagogue at Dura-Europos. Similar amulets depicting the open hand were used in Muslim Spain and subsequently in Christian Spain to avert the evil eye.

REFERENCES: Rouach, fig. nos. 451–52; IM, *Maroc*, p. 129; cat. no. 288; W. L. Hildburgh, "Images of the Human Hand as Amulets in Spain," *The Warburg and Courtauld Institutes Journal*, Vol. 18, 1955, pp. 67–89; Besancenot, *Bijoux*, pl. XXIII, fig. no. 92.

430 HAMSA AMULET

Morocco, 19th–20th century. Silver: cast, engraved. 6⅜ x 3½ in. Collection of Yossi Benyaminoff, Jerusalem.

The five elements characteristic of the *hamsa* are indistinct, possibly symbolized by the five semicircular elements at the bottom of the pendant. The main motifs consist of one complete rosette and two half-rosettes.

REFERENCE: Rouach, fig. nos. 415–17.

Amulet cases of a type used to contain a prayer parchment or soil from Eretz Israel, decorated with geometric motifs. Arabs used similar amulets to hold a verse from the Koran or a collection of prayers (*dalil al khayrat*).

REFERENCES: Rouach, p. 103, fig. nos. 130, 302; Sijelmassi, p. 167.

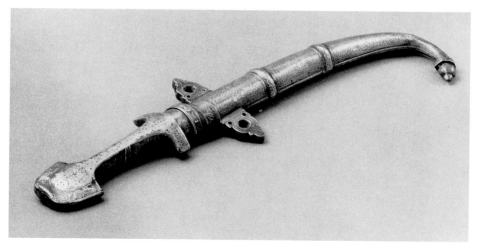

431 AMULET CASE

Morocco, 19th–20th century. Silver: cast, engraved. 3¾ x 4⅞ x ¾ in. Collection of Mr. and Mrs. Max Eis, Oakland, California.

432 AMULET CASE

Morocco, 19th–20th century. Silver: cast, engraved. 3¾ x 4⅞ x ¾ in. Collection of Mr. and Mrs. Max Eis, Oakland, California.

433 DAGGER AND SHEATH*

Morocco, 19th–20th century. Knife blade: steel. Knife handle and sheath: silver over wood core: cast, engraved; enamel inlay. Dagger: 15 x 2¼ in. Sheath: 10 x 3½ in. Collection of Yossi Benyaminoff, Jerusalem.

Although rarely worn in cities, weapons such as guns, sabers and knives formed part of the costume worn by Moroccan men in rural areas for ceremonies and festivities, almost like ceremonial jewelry. The curved form (rather than a straight knife) is the most frequent in Morocco and is known as *khenjar* or *koumiya*. Note the decorative geometric patterns, similar to those in women's silver jewelry from Morocco.

The dagger would be worn on a bandoleer—a brightly colored linen or silk cord—across the chest and over the right shoulder so that it falls on the left hip.

REFERENCE: Sijelmassi, pp. 176, 180, 182. Cf. Besancenot, *Costumes*, pl. C, nos. 16, 17.

434 SNUFF BOX

North Africa, 19th century. Silver: engraved. Hebrew inscription: S[ervant of] G[od] Avitvol Yaakov. ⅜ x 2¹/₁₆ x 1⅝ in. The Feuchtwanger Collection, purchased and donated to the Israel Museum by Baruch and Ruth Rappaport of Geneva, 1969, 131/35.

This box is in the form of a book with decorated cover and spine.

REFERENCE: IM, *Feuchtwanger*, cat. no. 151.

435 HEKK DI TABAQO

(Snuff container)

Morocco, 19th–20th century. Silver: cast, chiseled. 4¼ x 1¼ in. Collection of Yossi Benyaminoff, Jerusalem.

Teardrop-shaped container with chiseled decoration, and small wand/applicator forming part of the stopper.

Cf. IM, *Maroc*, cat. no. 190; Sijelmassi, p. 146.

436 HEKK DI TABAQO

(Snuff container)

Morocco, 19th–20th century. Silver: cast, engraved. 5⅜ x 3⅜ in. Collection of Rabbi Mitchell Serels, New Rochelle, New York.

Graceful floral patterns demonstrate the love of ornament and careful workmanship of Moroccan craftsmen.

437 SNUFF SPOON

North Africa, 19th–20th century. Silver, cast. 7⅛ x 5½ in. Collection of Rabbi Mitchell Serels, New Rochelle, New York.

This snuff spoon incorporates a *hamsa* (hand) with five fingers to ward off evil and a coin as decorative elements. Some considered snuff spoons to be a more refined way of taking snuff.

438 KOHL CONTAINER

North Africa, 20th century. Metal, glass. 3⅛ x 2 in. Collection of Sylvia A. Herskowitz, New York.

The combination of a mirror with a kohl container and applicator is evidence of the influence of Western forms on Moroccan crafts.

PERSONAL ARTIFACTS
PROFESSIONS AND CRAFTS

Jews in North Africa served as ambassadors, interpreters, doctors, lawyers, bankers, farmers, merchants, peddlers and craftsmen. The latter included metalworkers, leatherworkers, woodworkers, and those who produced the metal thread used for embroidered decorations. Craft tools such as those shown here were usually simple in form and based on ancient prototypes. Occasionally, as with the razors in this case, a tool was adapted for a use different from that for which it was originally developed.

Metalwork and trade in precious metals was practically a Jewish monopoly. Craftsmen produced ritual objects including *tappuhim* (Torah finials) as well as silver and gold jewelry.

Artisans frequently had their own synagogue, or met together to study Torah. The role of Jews in the Moroccan postal system is explained elsewhere (see cat. nos. 473–504). Rabbis, mystics, scholars and authors from such prominent families as the Toledanos (see cat. nos. 315, 326, 355 and 527–528) and the Aben Surs (cat. nos. 351, 352, 397 and 447) were leading figures in Jewish life in Morocco.

REFERENCE: IM, *Maroc*, p. 138.

439 MORTAR

North Africa, second half of the 16th century. Bronze: cast. Hebrew inscription: I am Yosef, son of Dan, son of the greatest physician among the exiles from Spain, Azaria, son of the holy Hushiel, physician. 5⅛ x 7⅟16 in. diam. Collection of the Israel Museum, Jerusalem, purchased through the Feuchtwanger Memorial Fund with the help of P. Mayer, New York, 192/5.

According to the inscription, this mortar, used in the preparation of medicine, was the property of a Jewish physician, a member of a family of physicians whose grandfather was among the exiles from Spain. *(fig. 32)*

REFERENCE: IM, *Maroc*, fig. no. 278.

440 SHEARS

Morocco, 19th century. Metal, cut. 13½ x 9½ in. Collection of the Judah L. Magnes Museum, Berkeley, California, 78.78.29.1.

The shoemaker would use shears of this type to cut the leather sole in the shape of the customer's foot for the elaborate *babouches* (shoes). The *tiyyal* (shoe embroiderer) would execute the decorative embroidery which was sewn to the leather sole.

441 RAZOR

Morocco, 20th century. Handle: enameled metal. Blade: steel. Jaguar. 9⅛ x ¾ in. Collection of Dr. and Mrs. Henry Toledano, New York.

442 RAZOR

Morocco, 20th century. Handle: plastic (bakelite?). Blade: steel. 9⅜ x ⅝ in. Collection of Dr. and Mrs. Henry Toledano, New York.

443 TWO WHETSTONES

Morocco, 20th century. 1³⁄16 x 4³⁄16 in.; 1 x 4¾ in. Collection of Dr. and Mrs. Henry Toledano, New York.

The above (cat. nos. 441–443) were used for the kosher slaughter of fowl. The concept underlying the rules for *shehitah* (the Jewish ritual slaughter of animals for food) is that the procedure be as quick, painless and humane as possible. The knife used for *shehitah* must not be pointed; it must be clean and smooth without a notch or dent, and must be at least twice as long as the width of the animal's throat.

DOMESTIC OBJECTS

The objects used and taken for granted in daily life can tell us much about the patterns and values of a culture. These include common domestic pieces such as teakettles, as well as articles such as glassware and silver used on social occasions. Just as the shapes of the water jug and the sherbet pot in the Turkish dowry room are uniquely Turkish and find no parallel in Morocco, the shape of the Moroccan teapot and the decoration of the Morroccan teakettle are uniquely Moroccan. Occasionally, there are pictorial records demonstrating the use of such objects and there are artists' representations of the manner in which costume and jewelry were worn so that we comprehend the role of these pieces visually and intellectually.

Though furnishings in a Moroccan home were sparse, walls and floors were covered by a variety of richly colored embroidered fabrics. Decorative objects were displayed on elaborate shelves (cat. no. 470).

444 MEZUZAH COVER

North Africa, 19th–20th century. Silver: pierced, chiseled and chased. Hebrew inscription: Yvette Coriat. 9 x 6⅛ in. Collection of Prof. and Mrs. Solomon Feffer, New York.

The use of French names such as Yvette among North African Jews reflects the influence of the French colonial rulers and of the Alliance Israélite Universelle. The Paris-based Alliance was the main educational institution for Ottoman and North African Jews and established schools and other institutions which encouraged the dissemination of French language and culture among its students. *(fig. 61)*

445 MEZUZAH COVER

North Africa, 19th–20th century. Silver: pierced, chiseled and chased. Hebrew inscription: Rahel Toledano. 8⁹/₁₆ x 6⅞ in. Collection of Mr. and Mrs. Max Eis, Oakland, California.

Mezuzah covers were frequently presented as gifts from a prospective bridegroom to his fiancée. The inclusion of the name of an individual on an object of this type allowed it to function simultaneously as a cover for a mezuzah scroll and as a personal amulet. This mezuzah cover is inscribed with the owner's name in Hebrew and her monogram in Latin characters.

446 MEZUZAH COVER

North Africa, 19th–20th century. Velvet: embroidered with metallic threads; sequins. Hebrew inscription: The righteous . . . the holy Rabbi Amram son of Diouane [of] b[lessed and] r[ighteous] m[emory]. 11½ x 10½ in. Collection of Cantor and Mrs. Jacob Rosenbaum, Monsey, New York.

This mezuzah cover invokes Divine protection for the home in the merit of Rabbi Diouane (see cat. no. 520), and may possibly be a souvenir of a pilgrimage to his grave. *(fig. 37)*

447 MEZUZAH COVER

Fez, Morocco 19th–20th century. Silver: pierced and engraved. 7 x 6¼ in. Hebrew inscriptions: "Inscribe them on the doorposts of your house and upon your gates" (Deut. 11:20); Mezuzah cover of the home of Raphael Aben Sur . . . Gross Family Collection, Tel Aviv, 40.1.1.

The Biblical commandment to place mezuzot on doorposts is inscribed on this cover.

448 MEZUZAH COVER

North Africa, 19th–20th century. Silver: repoussé; wood. 8¹¹/₁₆ x 6 in. Einhorn Collection, Tel Aviv.

The wooden core of this cover contains a carved niche into which the parchment was placed.

454

455

449   MEZUZAH COVER

North Africa, 19th–20th century. Silver: repoussé and chased. 5⅛ x 1½ in. Einhorn Collection, Tel Aviv.

450   MEZUZAH COVER

North Africa, 19th–20th century. Metal sheet; wood; paint. 5⅛ x 1¼ in. Einhorn Collection, Tel Aviv.

451   MEZUZAH COVER

North Africa, 19th–20th century. Silver: filigree. 4 x 1⅝ in. Einhorn Collection, Tel Aviv.

Fish, traditionally viewed as symbols of fertility, were widely used in domestic decoration.

452   MEZUZAH COVER

North Africa, 19th–20th century. Silver: cut and engraved; velvet. Hebrew inscription: Sul Adhan . . . 10¾ x 6¼ in. The Moldovan Family Collection, New York.

Affluent North African Jews purchased mezuzah covers made of silver rather than the common embroidered velvet examples. Birds are used as an ornamental motif on this cover, as they are on many North African ceremonial objects. *(fig. 61)*

453   AMULETS

North Africa, 19th century. Ink on paper; glass; iron. 4¼ x 2½ in.; 3½ x 2 in.; 2⅛ x 2 in.; 1¾ x 1⅞ in. The Moldovan Family Collection, New York.

Amulets mounted in this type of naively crafted iron frame are quite rare. These amulets and other similar examples were kept as a group in an embroidered bag.

454   FISH–SHAPED AMULETS*

Tunisia, 19th–20th century. Brass sheet: engraved. Hebrew inscription: "And God said to them: Be fertile and increase, fill the waters" (Gen. 1:22). 16⅛ x 8½ in.; 16⅛ x 8½ in. Einhorn Collection, Tel Aviv.

The use of fish as fertility symbols stems from the Biblical commandment inscribed on these amulets.

455   AMULET*

North Africa, 19th century. Cotton; sequins; stuffing. 4¼ x 9½ in. Einhorn Collection, Tel Aviv.

Fish motifs were frequently used as fertility symbols in North African homes (see cat. no. 454). In this amulet a large fish holds a baby fish in its mouth, stressing the fertility imagery.

In Morocco the ritual of serving tea is a gesture of hospitality shared by Jew and non-Jew alike.

The tray holds one or two teapots, glasses, metal containers for sugar, tea leaves and sometimes fresh mint (or orange or jasmine flowers) and a *deggaga* (sugar hammer) to break the sugar cone.

456 MARA (Tea tray)

Morocco, 19th–20th century. Silver: cast, engraved. 16 in. diam. Collection of Denise Gang, New York.

457 TEAPOT

North Africa, 19th–20th century. Silver: cast; engraved. 8½ x 8¾ in. Collection of Coty Nussbaum, New York.

This teapot has the characteristic shape of Moroccan teapots; the finial is a replacement.

Cf. Sijelmassi, p. 67; IM, *Maroc*, cat. no. 353.

458 FOUR TEA GLASSES

Morocco, 19th–20th century. Glass: painted. 4 x 2½ in.; 3⅞ x 2¼ in.; 3¾ x 2¼ in.; 3¾ x 2½ in. Collection of Mrs. Linda Harary, New York.

The decorative motifs include horseshoe-shaped arches with hanging lamps and vine scrolls, common motifs in other decorative media in North Africa.

Cf. IM, *Maroc*, cat. no. 357.

459 ZENBIL (Tea container)

North Africa, 19th–20th century. Tin: hammered, engraved. 7 x 6⅛ x 4¾ in. Collection of Sylvia A. Herskowitz, New York.

Although manufactured as a tea container, this container was used by a Jewish family for the *etrog* on Sukkot, just as Jewish families in America and England sometimes used silver sugar boxes for their *etrogim*.

REFERENCES: IM, *Maroc*, p. 177; *Cf.* IM, *Maroc*, cat. no. 361.

460 DEGGAGA (Sugar hammer)

Morocco, 19th–20th century. Brass: cast. Collection of the Judah L. Magnes Museum, Berkeley, California, 78.78.37a.

Tea, especially mint tea, is the favorite beverage of the Moroccans. A Moroccan tea set usually includes a tray, one or two silver or brass teapots, glasses, a metal box for the tea and another for the *galb des-sekkar* (sugar cone), which had to be broken with a *deggaga* (sugar hammer) or cut with a special sugar cutter (see cat. no. 461).

Cf. IM, *Maroc*, cat. nos. 353, 363.

461 SUGAR CUTTER

Morocco, 19th–20th century. Steel. Collection of the Judah L. Magnes Museum, Berkeley, California, 78.78.37b.

462 KETTLE

Morocco, 19th–20th century. Copper, brass: cast, hammered, engraved. 14¼ x 15¼ in. Collection of Yossi Benyaminoff, Jerusalem.

This teakettle would be heated over a brazier filled with coals. Although a simple domestic object, it demonstrates the Moroccan craftsman's concern for form and color.

Cf. Sijelmassi, p. 65.

463 MBEKHRA (Incense burner)

Morocco, 19th–20th century. Silver: cast. H: 9½ in. Collection of Denise Gang, New York.

Cf. IM, *Maroc*, cat. no. 356.

464 PAIR OF CANDLESTICKS

Morocco, 19th–20th century. Brass: cast. 9⅝ x 4 in. Collection of Rachel Rose Langnas, Rego Park, New York.

These simple geometric candlesticks were used for lighting candles on *Shabbat*.

One of the gestures of hospitality extended to guests in Morocco is to sprinkle their hands with rose water, which is also used for the *havdalah* ceremony. Most rose water sprinklers resemble the Turkish rose water sprinklers (see cat. no. 181).

REFERENCE: Allan, "Metalwork," figs. 13a,b. *Cf.* IM, *Maroc*, cat. no. 354.

465 ROSE WATER SPRINKLER

Morocco, 19th–20th century. Silver: cast. H: 5¾ in. Collection of Denise Gang, New York.

466 ROSE WATER SPRINKLER

Morocco, 19th–20th century. Silver: cast, repoussé. H: 10½ in. Collection of Coty Nussbaum, New York.

467 ROSE WATER SPRINKLER

Morocco, 19th–20th century. Silver: cast. Collection of Denise Gang, New York.

468 WALL HANGING

North Africa, 19th–20th century. Felt. 77 x 59 in. Collection of Yossi Benyaminoff, Jerusalem.

Furnishings in Moroccan Arab and Jewish homes were simple: they consisted of rugs, wall hangings, cushions, chests and wall shelves. In the *bet el kbira* (main room), the walls were covered with *hyati*, wall hangings decorated with arcades alternating a green and red background with appliqués or embroidered decoration.

REFERENCE: IM, *Maroc*, p. 166 *cf.* IM, *Maroc*, cat. no. 332.

469 WALL HANGING

North Africa, 19th–20th century. Silk: embroidered with silk and metallic threads; beads. 19½ x 63 in. Collection of Ita Aber, New York.

The buttons at the ends of the tassels are similar to sachets used for spices for the havdalah ceremony.

Cf. IM, *Maroc*, cat. no. 103.

470 SHELF

Morocco, 19th–20th century. Wood: carved and painted. 14½ x 37½ x 8 in. Collection of Ami Sibony, New York.

The open arches recall architectural forms characteristic of Morocco. Such shelves are used to display prized glass or other articles used for formal occasions.

REFERENCE: Sijelmassi, p. 60.

471 TABLE

North Africa, 19th–20th century. Wood: mother-of-pearl inlay, lead. 21 x 15 x 15¼ in. Collection of Yossi Benyaminoff, Jerusalem.

The elegant inlaid table with graceful open arches was popular in North Africa and the Middle East. A similar piece is illustrated in the print, *Juif et Juives à Tanger* (cat. no. 505).

472 PAIR OF VASES

Morocco, 19th–20th century. Brass: inlaid with copper and silver. 24⅛ x 10 in. Collection of Yossi Benyaminoff, Jerusalem.

Decorative metalwork objects such as these vases, executed in a technique known as damascene work, were common in the Ottoman empire (see cat. nos. 266, 268, 287, 288, 293, 300, 301). These vases are of characteristic Moroccan shape.

PHILATELY

JEWISH LOCAL POST IN MOROCCO

Described by William Gross, Gross Family Collection, Tel Aviv

By 1891 postal services existed in many countries of the world. However, in Morocco, divided into spheres of influence under rather chaotic conditions, the population had no official mail service. Since the need existed, almost 20 private services were established in the last decade of the 19th century. Of these, 15 services were initiated and managed by Jews.

The first of these "local posts" was established in January, 1891, by Isaac Brudo, the son of Joseph Brudo of Mazagan, who served as French consul in that city. The mail was carried by men who traveled the routes by foot.

Isaac Brudo's initial success came to the attention of the Sultan Moulay Hassan. The Sultan realized the potential revenue of this enterprise, and after failing to convince Brudo to sell to him the initial post service between Marrakech and Mazagan, he decided to establish his own network. This took place in November, 1892, and involved local mail with stations in Morocco's 13 largest communities. However, due to their superior organization, the private postal services continued to exist and proliferate.

The Sultan's mail, or *cherifien poste*, did not use printed stamps until 1913. Until then it used hand stamps, such as seen on the four exhibited covers (cat. nos. 501–504). It is astonishing that these covers, which were sent through the Sultan's *cherifien poste*, are addressed in Hebrew! It must have been a widely known and accepted fact that workers in the Sultan's mail, as well as in the private posts, were Jewish.

Cf. IM, *Maroc*, p. 136.

473 BLOCK OF SIX BLACK FIRST ISSUE STAMPS — SERVICE DE COURRIERS/ MAZAGAN A MAROC

Denomination: 25 centimes

Isaac Brudo printed stamps of 25 centimes for his service. The cancellation bore the name J. Brudo, the name of Isaac Brudo's firm.

474 FOUR SPECIAL CANCELLATION STAMPS — JACOB HAZAN MIRAKEZ SERVICE DE COURRIERS/MAZAGAN A MAROC

Denomination: 25 centimes.

Brudo's correspondent in Marrakech, Jacob Hazan, used a cancellation with his name in French and Hebrew.

475 SIX OVERPRINT STAMPS — SERVICE DE COURRIERS/MAZAGAN A MAROC

Denomination: 10 centimes overprint of 25 centimes.

Brudo's service was such a success that he soon reduced the postage from 25 to 10 centimes, as shown by the overprint on the stamps.

476 REGISTERED COVER

This envelope was mailed in Mazagan on September 12, 1892. The address is in Hebrew. J. Brudo's name appears in the cancellation.

477 SIX REGULAR ISSUE STAMPS — POSTE MAZAGAN MARAKECH

Denominations: 5, 10, 20, 25 and 50 centimos; 1 peseta.

In 1893 Isaac Brudo, in response to an expanding business, printed a new series of stamps. In the upper corners of these stamps are his initials I. B.

478 ONE OVERPRINT POSTE MAZAGAN MARAKECH STAMP

20 centimos overprint of a 5 centimos stamp.

479 ENVELOPE ADDRESSED TO MONSIEUR SAMUEL AZUELAS, FEZ

Letter mailed on September 11, 1899, at Brudo's station in Marrakech, received by Brudo's office in Mazagan on September 13 and handed to the French mail the same day. According to cancellations on the back, this letter arrived in Tangier on September 15 and in Fez on September 18. The address is written in Latin and Hebrew characters.

480 SEVEN STAMPS — MAZAGAN MARAKECH POSTE

Denominations: 5, 10, 20, 25, 50 and 75 centimos; 1 peseta.

In 1898 Brudo printed a third series, this time of 7 values. This stamp was pictured on an official Moroccan stamp in 1949 in honor of the local posts.

481 POSTCARD ADDRESSED TO JAMES SILVERSON (?), ESQ., GLASGOW

Postcard mailed by Brudo's local post at Marrakech on March 5, 1900. It arrived at Brudo's office in Mazagan on March 7. On March 8 it was forwarded by French mail to Glasgow.

482 SEVEN POSTAGE DUE (CHIFFRE TAXE) STAMPS, 1898

Denominations: 5, 10, 20, 30, 40 and 50 centimos; 1 peseta.

Brudo also printed a series of "postage due" stamps in 1898.

In November, 1900, Isaac Brudo signed an agreement with the French administration turning over to them control of Morocco's first local post service, Mazagan-Marrakech. The Brudo stamps remained in use until 1902.

483 FOUR STAMPS — SERVICE DE COURRIERS MOGADOR A MAROC

Denomination: 20 centimos.

The second local postal service to be attempted was the Mogador–Marrakech route of 205 km. It was established by Mayer Maimaran in August, 1892. This service was not well organized and by the end of the year was no longer functioning.

484 FIVE FIRST ISSUE STAMPS — MOGADOR MARRAKECH, 1893

Denominations: 5, 10, 15 and 50 centimos; 1 peseta.

On April 1, 1893, Marx & Co. of Mogador along with Nissian Coriat of Marrakech established a mail service between the two cities to replace that of Maimaran. It lasted until January, 1911.

485 FIVE SECOND ISSUE STAMPS — MOGADOR MARRAKECH, 1898

Denominations: 5, 10, 20, 30, 50 centimos.

These include an overprint as well.

486 REGISTERED COVER

This registered cover was either mailed or received in Marrakech on November 24, 1901; the address is written in Hebrew.

487 FIVE STAMPS — SERVICIO DE COURRIERS FEZ SEFROU

Denominations: 5, 10, 15 and 20 cents; 1 peseta.

In September, 1894 S. Aboudarham established a mail service between Fez and Sefrou, a distance of 28 km. taking 7 hours to traverse. This service continued until December, 1901.

488 LETTER TO AVRAHAM AZULAI, SEFROU

This cover was mailed at Fez on December 17, 1894, and according to the cancellation on the back, arrived in Sefrou on December 18.

**489 EIGHT STAMPS —
SERVICIO DE CORREOS
MARRUECOS**

Denominations: 5, 10, 20, 25 and 50 centimos; 1, 2 and 5 pesetas.

On December 1, 1895, Mr. Aaron Cohen established mail service between Tangier and Arzila, a distance of 50 km. The service closed in September, 1898. The stamps show a large six-pointed star at the center.

**490 ENVELOPE ADDRESSED
TO JUAN POZO, ARZILA**

This cover was mailed at Arzila on April 28, 1898.

**491 SIX STAMPS — CORREOS
MAZAGAN AZEMMOUR
MARRAKECH**

Denominations: 5, 10, 15, 20 and 50 centimos; 1 peseta.

In July, 1897, Messod Bensimon started a mail service between Mazagan-Azemmour-Marrakech, a distance of 205 km. taking 46 hours to traverse. This service was disbanded in 1899.

**492 ENVELOPE ADDRESSED
IN HEBREW**

This cover was mailed in Azemmour on June 28, 1898, and according to a cancellation on the back, received in Marrakech on June 30.

**493 ENVELOPE WITH EIGHT
STAMPS OF DIFFERENT
DENOMINATIONS — POSTES
FEZ MAQUINEZ**

Denominations: 5, 10, 15, 20, 25, 30 and 50 centimes; 1 franc.

The director of the Écoles de l'Alliance Israélite in Fez, Mr. Bensimon, began postal service between that city and Meknes, a distance of 56 km., in January of 1897. The post remained active until May, 1901. The envelope is addressed to J. C. North, Tangier.

**494 ENVELOPE WITH EIGHT
CHIFFRE TAXE A PERCEVOIR
(POSTAGE DUE) STAMPS**

Denominations: 5, 10, 20, 30, 40, 50 and 60 centimes; 1 franc.

In 1898 a postage due series was printed by Bensimon. This envelope is addressed to J. C. North, Tangier.

**495 SEVEN STAMPS — SAFFI
MARRAKECH**

Denominations: 5, 10, 20, 25, 50 and 75 centimos; 1 peseta.

In June, 1898, the dynamic Isaac Brudo founded another service, between Saffi and Marrakech, a distance of 160 km. requiring 42 hours of travel. This service was discontinued in January, 1901.

**496 ENVELOPE ADDRESSED
TO JUDA ABITBOL**

This cover was mailed in Saffi on October 18, 1900. The address is in English (Latin) and Hebrew characters.

**497 SEVEN STAMPS —
MAROC, ALCAZAR A OUAZ-
ZAN, SERVICE POSTAGE
BIHEBDOMADAIRE**

Denominations: 5, 10, 15, 20, 40 and 50 c.; 1 f.

A service between Algazar and Ouazzan, a distance of 42 km., was inaugurated on February 26, 1896, with Mr. Sirfaty in Algazar. The service continued until January, 1897.

**498 SEVEN STAMPS — MAROC
1896 TETOUAN CHECHOUAN**

Denominations: 5, 10, 20, 25, 40 and 50 c.; 1 f.

J. M. Benchimol organized the service between Tetuan and Chechouan, 70 km. distance, beginning March 1, 1896. The service ended in May, 1898.

**499 SEVEN STAMPS —
MOROCCO TANGIER
LARAICHE**

505

Denominations: 5, 10, 20, 25 and 50 centimos; 1 peseta; 1 peseta.

In February, 1898, a new postal service began between Tangier and Larache. Initiated by James Nahon, it covered the distance of 80 km. in 15 hours.

500   SEVEN STAMPS MOGADOR AGADIR

Denominations: 5, 10, 20, 25, 40 and 50 centimos; 1 peseta.

One of the last of the local posts organized was the route Mogador-Agadir, 130 km. This was started by El Maley David in September, 1899, and continued through the end of 1900.

501 ENVELOPE ADDRESSED IN HEBREW — SULTAN'S MAIL

Cancellation of Fez; first print.

502 ENVELOPE FROM BEN-SABAT & TOLEDANO, FEZ — SULTAN'S MAIL

Cancellation of Fez; violet color; address in Arabic and Hebrew.

503 ENVELOPE ADDRESSED IN HEBREW — SULTAN'S MAIL

Cancellation of Saffi.

504 ENVELOPE ADDRESSED IN HEBREW — SULTAN'S MAIL

Cancellation of Mogador.

PRINTS

North Africa and the Middle East captured the imagination of 19th-century Romantic artists such as Eugène Delacroix (1798–1863), who spent six months in Morocco in 1832. The Romantic movement in painting was characterized by artists who craved emotional experience and attempted to convey its intensity to the viewer in black and white lithographs and engravings as well as paintings.

505 JUIF ET JUIVES À TANGER

(Jewish man and Jewish women in Tangier)*

France, 19th century. Émile Antoine Bayard (1837–1891). Engraving. 15 x 11 in. Moldovan Family Collection, New York.

A man and two women drinking tea from bowl-like cups. The three are formally dressed: the women wear the *keswa el kbira* (see cat. nos. 381–382) and jewels; the man wears an embroidered *zokha* similar to the rabbi's costume (cat. no. 350). The inlaid table is similar to one described above (cat. no. 471). Bayard was a traveling correspondent for the *Journal des voyages* and the *Illustration*.

506 TUNESER JÜDEN

(Jews of Tunisia)

Germany, 19th century. Engraving. 7⅞ x 6 in. Moldovan Family Collection, New York.

A similar engraving in a contemporary French journal identifies this scene as a Saturday night social gathering in a Jewish home in Tunisia.

The woman plays a portable organ accordian with push-action bellows, developed in the mid-nineteenth century. Some models encompassed three octaves.

507 NOCE JUIVE DANS LE MAROC (Jewish wedding in Morocco)*

France, 19th century. Eugène Delacroix (1798–1863). Etching. 7 x 9 in. Moldovan Family Collection, New York.

Delacroix attended a Jewish wedding in Tangier while visiting Morocco with Count Charles de Mornay, who was there on a diplomatic mission for France. The wedding was that of the daughter of their interpreter, Abraham ben Chimol. In 1841, Delacroix exhibited a painting of a Jewish wedding in Morocco at the Paris Salon. The painting was composed from sketches made in 1832 while he was traveling in Morocco, and based on notes and letters he wrote at the time. In a recent article, Cissy Grossman has identified this scene as the entertainment of wedding guests on the night after the wedding ceremony.

REFERENCE: Grossman, "Delacroix," pp. 64–73.

508 JUIVE D'ALGER

(Algerian woman)*

Paris, 1833. Eugène Delacroix (1798–1863). De-larie. Etching. 8¼ x 7 in. Moldovan Family Collection, New York.

On February 12, 1832, Delacroix noted in his journal that he had sketched a Jewish woman by the name of Dititia in Algerian costume. Her dress, especially the wraparound skirt with the decorated panel, is similar to the festival dress of urban Moroccan Jewish women (see cat. nos. 381–382).

REFERENCES: Rubens, *Costume*, 1973, fig. no. 82; Rubens, *Iconography*, 1981, no. 40.

509 JUIFS TUNISIENS

(Tunisian Jews)*

Paris, ca. 1840. Artist: Rouergue. Engraver: Ed. Willman. Colored engraving. 4½ x 8¾ in. Moldovan Family Collection, New York.

A charming vignette of a family relaxing outdoors. The women wear the *kufia* or *çarma* (conical headpieces with hanging veils) resembling those worn by Algerian Jewish women; both are reminiscent of the medieval European hennin. They also wear an *aghlila* (short-sleeved vest) under a *djubba* (ankle-length gown). Several members of the family hold fans shaped like flags, a fashion in Europe during the 16th and 17th centuries, and popular in Persia and Mughal India.

REFERENCES: N. Armstrong, *Fans: A Collector's Guide*, 1984, London and Canada, Souvenir Press, 1990, p. 66; Rubens, *Costume*, 1973, fig. no. 79; Rubens, *Iconography*, 1981, no. 2350.

510 ÉCOLE JUIVE (Jewish school)
[and] SYNAGOGUE JUIVE

(Jewish synagogue)*

France, 1845. L'Illustration, Journal Universal, p. 189. Engraving. Page: 14¾ x 10⅜ in.; images: 4½ x 5½ in., 5¾ x 8¼ in. Moldovan Family Collection, New York.

The article accompanying these prints discusses the emancipation of the Jews of Algeria as a result of the French conquest of Algiers in 1830, and the organization of the synagogues and Jewish schools of Morocco by the French in 1845.

508

511 MARCHAND JUIF
(Jewish merchant)

Paris, 1850–1863. Musée Cosmopolite. Algérie no. 6. Artist: François-Claudius Compte-Calix (1813–1880). Engraver: Ernst Monnin. Colored engraving. 8 x 6 in. Moldovan Family Collection, New York.

François-Claudius Compte-Calix was a watercolorist, and painted costume illustrations for *Les Modes Parisiennes*. The merchant, a dashing fellow whose appearance and non-chalant pose would appeal to the romantic taste of the time in Europe, leans on the edge of a table bearing colorful wares.

REFERENCE: Rubens, *Iconography*, 1981, no. 57.

512 ENFANS JUIFS
(Jewish children)

Paris, 1850–1863. Musée Cosmopolite. Algérie no. 11. Engraver: A. Portier. Colored engraving. 7½ x 5½ in. Moldovan Family Collection, New York.

These Algerian children wear Ottoman-style clothing, somewhat different from that of their parents. The boy's *chéchia* (hat) with pompon resembles the headgear worn by Muslim children. He wears a *ghlîla* (short-sleeved vest) under a *bed'iya* (jacket), a wide sash, and voluminous breeches, stockings and *cobbât* (shoes without heels). The girl wears a chemise; its long sleeves extend beyond the short sleeves of the patterned *ghlîla* which she wears beneath the *djubba* (long outer dress), tied with a sash. Her hat is velvet, decorated with gold coins.

REFERENCES: Rubens, *Iconography*, 1981, no. 59; Rubens, *Costume*, p. 70 and fig. no. 90.

513   MARCHAND DE LIVRES
(Bookseller)

Paris, 1850–1863. Musée Cosmopolite. Algérie no. 52. Musée de Costumes, no. 433. Colored engraving. 9½ x 6 in. Moldovan Family Collection, New York.

The bookseller has laid out his wares, several protected from the ground by a cloth, others in a basket, much as any sidewalk vendor today.

REFERENCE: Rubens, *Iconography*, 1981, no. 64.

514   THE MOORISH SPANISH WAR IN AFRICA

Origin unknown, ca. 1860. Colored engraving. 5½ x 10½ in. Moldovan Family Collection, New York.

Encampment of Moroccan Jewish refugees, many of them destitute women and children, during the Spanish-Moroccan war of 1860.

Sir William Codrington, governor of Gibraltar, permitted the Jews to camp on the Brigade Parade Ground, and provided them with tents as well as daily bread rations.

Moroccans were enraged by European interference in their internal affairs, ostensibly in aid of Jews but motivated by economic concerns. The execution of a Jewish consular agent was one of the incidents that triggered the 1860 war.

515

510

516 DANS L'ECHOOPE D'UN JUIF D'ALGER

(In the stall of a Jew of Algeria)

France, February, 1888. H. Hiriat. Magasin Pittoresque, Tome VI. Engraving. Moldovan Family Collection, New York.

Engraving after a photograph of an old Jewish man spinning wool. The text describes the pathos of the man's being forced to spin in a corner of the shop that once was his but is now owned by his children, since he can no longer do the famous delicate embroidery. The author speaks of the long history of textile embroidery among Jews dating back to Egyptian times, and mentions the recent discoveries of "strange" (Coptic) textiles in Egypt by Maspero.

515 A JEWISH CONCERT: TLEMCEN*

France, 1870. Tour du Monde. Artist(?): M.D. Engraver(?): Hildebrand. Engraving. 19¼ x 12½ in. Moldovan Family Collection, New York.

Informal entertainment in the doorway of a home; the instruments are: the tambourine (*tar*), *ud* (lute), *rebab* (a violin played with a bow), and the *kanun* (zither).

Jews played a role in the transmission of Arab music, Andalusian plainsong, and 15th-century Spanish folk songs. The scale, rhythm and instruments of Jewish music in North Africa are Arabic, held in common with their Muslim neighbors, another example of the cultural symbiosis of Sephardic Jews.

517 JEWISH WOMAN FROM TETUAN

Origin unknown, 19th–20th century. Postcard: engraved. 5¾ x 3¼ in. Moldovan Family Collection, New York.

This postcard may have been printed in Germany; the caption is written in Russian, Hebrew and German. The woman is dressed in Moroccan Jewish ceremonial dress, the *keswa el kbira* (see cat. nos. 381–382), complete with *soualef ez-zohar* (tiara sewn with pearls and jewels; see cat. no. 384), to which graceful, though massive, pendants are attached. Her jewelry is probably gold (or silver washed with gold) and includes a *chouka et teyr* (bird brooch), necklaces and bracelets.

518 NOCES JUIVES
(Jewish wedding)

Origin unknown, 19th–20th century. Color post-card. Einhorn Collection, Tel Aviv.

Scene depicting a Jewish wedding in Tunis. The veiled bride is seated on a raised platform. The women and girls wear the *kufia* (pointed conical headdress), short tunic tops and tight leggings characteristic of northern Tunisia. The *kufia* ceased to be worn after World War I. The men wear clothes more typical of North Africa as a whole rather than specific to Tunisia (red fez or turban, capes, loose-fitting tops, wide sashes, baggy pants and leather slippers).

519 RABBI EFRAIM ENKAOUA AT TLEMCEN*

North Africa, 19th–20th century. Postcard: engraved. 5⅛ x 4⅜ in. Collection of Dr. and Mrs. Henry Toledano, New York.

519

517

R. Ephraim ben Israel Ankawa (Alnucavi, Ankava, Ankoa, Anqawa, known as "Rabbi" in North Africa) was a rabbi, scholar and physician, and the founder of the Jewish community of Tlemçen. According to legend, Rabbi Ankawa arrived in Tlemçen riding on a lion, using a serpent as a bridle. He died in Tlemçen in 1442 and was buried there.

520 RABBI AMRAM DIOUANE

Morocco, 20th century. Postcard: engraved. 5¹⁵⁄₁₆ x 4¼ in. Collection of Dr. and Mrs. Henry Toledano, New York.

An exhibited mezuzah cover (cat. no. 446) invokes Divine protection in the merit of this rabbi.

521 MOORISH HATRED OF THE JEW: CUSTOMS OFFICERS ABUSING HEBREWS AT THE GATE OF CASA BLANCA*

New York, August 31, 1907. The Illustrated London News, Vol. 41, no. 1060, cover. Engraving. 15⅜ x 11¾ in. Moldovan Family Collection, New York.

The caption states that even in times of peace, customs officers mistreat Jews: they beat Jewish men and search the baggage of Jews for plunder, regardless of whether they damage the belongings of the travelers in the process.

521

522

PHOTOGRAPHS

522 ISRAÉLITES REFUGIÉS DANS LA COUR DES MÉNAGERIES DU SULTAN

(Jewish refugees in the court of the Sultan's zoological gardens)*

Morocco(?), ca. 1912–1915. Niddam and Assuline. Photographic postcard. 3½ x 5¼ in. Einhorn Collection, Tel Aviv.

Depiction of Balkan war refugees in Fez, April 17–19, 1912.

523 PORTRAIT OF A MAN*

Morocco, late 19th century. Photograph: lacquered; metal stand. H: 6 in. Collection of Juliette Halioua, New York.

Portrait of a cousin who left Morocco for Eretz Israel via Marseilles.

524 CORDONNIER JUIF

(Jewish shoemaker)*

Paris, early 20th century. Photographic postcard. Lév and Neurdein. 3½ x 5¼ in. Einhorn Collection, Tel Aviv.

This photographic postcard shows an old man making shoes in the manner traditional in Morocco.

REFERENCE: IM, *Maroc*, p. 308.

523

524

525 THE BEN OLIEL FAMILY

Tangier, ca. 1940s. Colored photograph. 11¼ x 9⅛ in. Collection of Mrs. Esther Ben Oliel Ifrah, Buffalo, New York.

Miriam Cohen Ben-Oliel, her husband Moshe and their children Samuel and Estrella posed for this photograph in their most festive clothes: the mother in the *keswa el kbira* (grand costume; see cat. nos. 381–382) with gold bracelets and necklaces; the father in a robe; and the children in stylish European outfits. *(Plate 13)*

526 TOMB OF RABBI MEIR AMRAM BEN DIOUANE

Morocco, 1941. Black and white photograph. 2¼ x 3¼ in. Collection of Coty Nussbaum, New York.

The tomb during a *hillula* (see cat. no. 528).

527 BAR MITZVAH CELEBRATION OF ELIEZER TOLEDANO*

Meknes, Morocco, ca. 1950. Black and white photographs. 3½ x 4⅝ in.; 3³⁄₁₆ x 5¾ in. Collection of Dr. and Mrs. Henry Toledano, New York.

527A

527B

529

Various stages in the bar mitzvah celebration, including the triumphal procession in which the bar mitzvah boy is carried through the streets of the city on the shoulders of the rejoicing members of his family. This custom is widely practiced today in Israel, at bar mitzvah celebrations at the Western Wall (*Kotel ha-Maaravi*).

528 PHOTOGRAPH OF HILLULA

Ouzen, Morocco, ca. 1950. Black and white photograph. 3½ x 4⅝ in. Collection of Dr. and Mrs. Henry Toledano, New York.

Tents have been set up to celebrate the *hillula* of Lag ba-Omer, the traditional pilgrimage marking the anniversary of the death of Rabbi Shimon bar Yohai, regarded as the author of

the Zohar, the classic work of Kabbalah (Jewish mysticism).

Tombs of saints were venerated by Jews in Morocco. In addition to annual pilgrimages, a *zyara* (visit to a tomb) could be made to request a cure or other favor, or to fulfill a vow. On the *hillula*, Jews visit the tombs and recite psalms. At night, a fire is lit in which some believe the image of the saint appears.

REFERENCE: IM, *Maroc*, p. 124.

529 WEDDING GUEST*

Morocco, ca. 1956. Black and white photograph. 6½ x 4¾ in. Collection of Coty Nussbaum, New York.

Moroccan teenager dressed in the *keswa el kbira* (see cat. nos. 381–382) for her cousin's wedding.

Seder Hamisha Taaniot, Amsterdam, 1723/26. Editor: Shlomo Yehuda Leåo Templo;
Printer: Yitzhak ben Shlomo Rafael. Cat. no. 587.

WESTERN EUROPE

AUSTRIA · ENGLAND · FRANCE · GERMANY
HOLLAND · ITALY

"Seek not acquaintance with the ruling power"

ETHICS OF THE FATHERS 1:9

"And these words are truly exact, and I too will testify that all my days I was raised in the courts of kings and in their palaces, and woe to those who know them and become close to them, and happy is he who keeps a distance from them and from their honor, and does not become close, except to the Supreme King of kings, Blessed be He, as the Psalmist says 'as for me, nearness to God is good' (Ps. 73:28)"

DON YITZHAK ABRABANEL (1437–1508)

530

WESTERN EUROPE

SYNAGOGUE AND COMMUNITY

530 MODEL OF THE PORTUGUESE SYNAGOGUE*

Amsterdam, Holland, 1671–1675. Architect: Elias Bouman (1636–1686). 47½ x 23¼ x 41 in. Collection of Yeshiva University Museum, New York, endowed by Erica and Ludwig Jesselson, 89.89.

In 17th-century Europe, Holland was a haven for the Jews expelled from Spain and Portugal. The anti-Spanish, anti-Catholic attitude of the Dutch attracted great numbers of Marranos who reverted to Judaism. By 1620 there were three Sephardic congregations in Amsterdam, each with its own synagogue.

In 1639 these congregations merged and in 1675 consecrated what was then one of the grandest synagogues in the world. The importance of this edifice lies not merely in its splendor but in the numerous liturgical and stylistic precedents which it codified and which were adopted by many Sephardic houses of worship in the centuries that followed.

The significant interior plan of the building was inspired by the Protestant meeting houses popular in Holland. The synagogue adopted a seating plan modeled on the council chambers of these meeting houses. The central space remained empty. Seating was limited to the *banco*, or *seat*, for the *Parnas Presidente* and to benches that lined the walls. In order to adhere to this plan the Ark and *bimah* (reader's platform) were placed at opposite ends of the central axis, thereby creating a sense of spiritual unity throughout the hall. The women's galleries on the upper level were modeled on similar galleries found in the meeting houses.

The enormous space (125' x 95'), which could accommodate 2,000 seats, is illuminated by 72 windows, one for each of the appellations of God, and numerous brass chandeliers which hold a total of 613 tapers, one for each of the 613 *mitzvot* (commandments) of the Torah. The Ark and *bimah* are made of Brazilian jacaranda wood, the gift of Moshe ben Yaakov Curiel (d. 1697), financial agent to the King of Portugal in Amsterdam. The Tablets of the Law on the Ark are the first dated examples of their kind.

THE PORTUGUESE SYNAGOGUE OF AMSTERDAM

Amsterdam's Sephardic community was established by 1607. In 1639 three congregations united to form the K. K. Talmud Torah, the community now known in Dutch as the *Portugees-Israëlietische Gemeente*. The community flourished as an intellectual and cultural hub and became a center for the return of *conversos* to Judaism. The members of the community prospered in the 17th century due to the Dutch involvement in modern capitalist foreign trade, industry and finance. This prosperity made possible the construction of the community's famed synagogue and the commissioning of outstanding Torah ornaments and other ritual silver and textiles. Amsterdam's synagogue architecture and ceremonial objects were emulated by Sephardic communities throughout Europe and America.

The precious silver and textiles belonging to the congregation were hidden by members of the community during the Nazi occupation. They were placed beneath the synagogue's wooden ceiling cornice and were recovered after the war. The exhibited objects from the *Portugees-Israëlietische Gemeente* have never before been shown outside of Amsterdam (cat. nos. 531–533, 536, 538, and 542–544).

531 TORAH MANTLE

Amsterdam, late 17th century. Silk velvet and brocade: embroidered with silver and gold threads; gold fringe; satin lining. 12 x 37 in. Collection of the Portugees-Israëlietische Gemeente, Amsterdam, KK 85.

This mantle is typical of West European Sephardic mantles. It is unusual because of the inclusion of Biblical scenes in roundels on the mantle's side panels. The portrayals of the binding of Isaac and of Jacob's dream, both scenes which relate to the covenant between God and the Jewish people, are appropriate imagery for the covering of the Torah, the embodiment of that covenant. *(figs. 40, 41)*

532 TORAH MANTLE

Amsterdam, 17th century. Silk velvet and brocade: embroidered with silver and gold threads; gold fringe; satin lining. 13½ x 39½ in. Collection of the Portugees-Israëlietische Gemeente, Amsterdam, KK 84.

This mantle, like most examples from the Amsterdam congregation, is constructed of vertical panels, with alternate panels ornamented with embroidery. It features a soft top and an opening in the back. Lavish amounts of gold and silver thread and fringe add to the overall richness of the mantle. The textiles ued in the Amsterdam mantles come from a variety of sources. The brocades are primarily from Lyons, France, then the weaving center for sumptuous fabrics of this type. Italy was the center for most velvet production. This mantle is ornamented with a coat of arms, possibly that of the Teixeira de Mattos family, the probable donors. *(fig. 51)*

533 TORAH SHIELD

Amsterdam, 1606. Silver: engraved, pierced and cast. Silversmith: Leendert Claesz. Hebrew inscriptions: Crown of the Torah; For New Moons; Yaakov Tirado Rahel Tirado. 10 x 8½ in. Collection of the Portugees-Israëlietische Gemeente, Amsterdam, KK 231.

This is the earliest known extant Torah shield. In the late 16th century a group of *converso* families from Spain and Portugal moved to Emden, where they were encouraged by Moshe Uri son of Yosef ha-Levi, a native of Emden, to move to Amsterdam and to return to Judaism. It is probable that Yaakov Tirado, the donor of this shield, sought to emulate the practices of Emden Jewry and thus commissioned this shield from Claesz, a craftsman who had recently arrived in Amsterdam from Emden and who might have been familiar with Jewish ceremonial silver used there. In about 1608, Tirado along with Shmuel Palache and Yaakov Yisrael Belmonte founded *Beit Yaakov*, the first Sephardic congregation in Amsterdam, the predecessor of the *Portugees-Israëlietische Gemeente*. Tirado moved to Jerusalem sometime before 1616, when he is known to have distributed funds collected by the Amsterdam community to the poor of the Holy Land. *(fig. 40)*

534 TORAH SHIELD

Turin, Italy, after 1832. Silversmith: Pacifico Levi (active after 1818). Silver: repoussé and engraved. 14⅛ x 10⅝ in. Gross Family Collection, Tel Aviv, 51.1.15.

Pacifico Levi, one of twelve Jews nominated for membership in the Turin silversmiths' guild, used as his mark a hand holding a pouring pitcher, a symbol of his Levite lineage. *(fig. 31)*

REFERENCE: NYJM, *Gardens*, cat. no. 217.

535 RIMMON (Torah finial)

Amsterdam, ca. 1650–1680. Silver: repoussé, chased and pierced. Hebrew inscription: Donation of the women which they brought to the House of G[od] on the occasion of the 40th anniversary. Collection of the Jewish Museum, New York, F4320.

536 RIMMONIM (Torah finials)*

Amsterdam, ca. 1690–1715. Silver: pierced and chased. 11 x 4¼ in. Collection of the Portugees-Israëlietische Gemeente, Amsterdam, KK 34.

These finials are placed on the Torah staves for *levantar* (*hagbaha*), the raising of the Torah scroll. The finials are pierced with acanthus foliage and with beaded scroll brackets for bells. The shafts are chased with overlapping leaves. (*fig. 51*)

Cf. Barnett, cat. no. 106.

537 RIMMONIM (Torah finials)

Amsterdam, 1703/4. Silver: parcel-gilt. Collection of the Jewish Museum, New York, F5642a,b.

Finials of this shape were placed on the Torah for *levantar* (*hagbaha*), the raising of the Torah before it is read. (*fig. 50*)

538 RIMMONIM (Torah finials)

Amsterdam, 1770. Silver: repoussé, chased and cast. 17 x 4¾ in. Collection of the Portugees-Israëlietische Gemeente, Amsterdam, KK 17.

These finials are a typical multistoreyed form used in The Netherlands and in Spanish and Portuguese congregations in other centers such as London and New York. Finials of this type are modeled after Amsterdam buildings with majestic towers. These finials resemble the tower of the *Westerkerk* (West Church). (*fig. 40*)

Cf. Amsterdam, Joods historisch museum, *Guide to the Jewish Historical Museum*, 1988, no. 21.

539 RIMMONIM (Torah finials)

Holland, 18th century. Silver: repoussé, parcel-gilt and cast. 14 x 4¼ in. Collection of Mr. and Mrs. Abraham Halpern, New York.

Rimmonim of this shape were frequently crafted in 18th-century Holland. The shaft and lower tier of this pair have been replaced, probably due to wear caused by the great weight of the upper tiers. The use of cast dolphins as ornament on this pair is unusual. (*fig. 48*)

REFERENCE: Weinstein, fig. no. 90.

540 RIMMONIM (Torah finials)

Holland, 18th century. Silver: filigree, parcel-gilt and cast. Hebrew inscription: Crown of the Torah. 15¼ x 5½ in. Collection of Mr. and Mrs. Abraham Halpern, New York.

Torah finials made of silver filigree were traditionally used in Amsterdam's Portuguese Synagogue only on Rosh Hashanah and Yom Kippur. (*fig. 49*)

REFERENCE: Weinstein, fig. no. 91. *Cf.* M. Kaniel, *Judaism*, Poole, Dorset, 1979, after p. 106.

541 PAROKHET (Ark curtain)

Vienna, 1887. Silk: embroidered with silk and metallic threads. Hebrew inscriptions: These are the names of the family of the brothers Matity[ahu] and Yisrael Russo that are listed on this side and the other side the embroiderers that donated their spirit to bring this curtain as a donation with effort and care for . . . Devorah of Matity[ahu] Russo b[lessed] a[mong women within the] t[ent] on the day of the dedication of the synagogue in honor of the One Who dwells on high by her son Moshe Matity[ahu] Russo the leader of the Sephardic congregation Bnei Yisrael (Children of Israel) may he be forever happy the year "take pity on Zion" (Ps. 102:14) [Chronogram = (5)648] here in the p[raised] city of Vienna b[uild] t[he city of] G[od]; Rena of Yitzhak Russo; Miriam of Aharon Yisrael Russo; Mazal-Tov of Shmuel Yisrael Russo; Henrietti of Avraham Hayyim Russo; Rivka of Shmuel Menahem Russo; Sultana of Yaakov Shmuel Russo; Buena of Yaakov Yitzhak Russo; Esther of Moshe Matitiyah[u] Russo; Irmoza of Yisrael Matitiyah[u] Russo; Rivka of Menahem Yisrael Russo; Leah of Matityahu Moshe Russo; Gamila of Yisrael Hayyim Russo; Esther of Yaakov Menahem Russo; Rahel of Yisrael Yitzhak Russo. 137 x 89⅛ in. Collection of Mr. and Mrs. Abraham Halpern, New York.

This masterfully embroidered curtain was donated for the dedication of the new Moorish-style Sephardic synagogue in Vienna's *Zirkusgasse* on September 17, 1887. It is remarkable for its great size and magnificent multicolor decoration. The elaborate inscription is arranged to heighten the beauty of the curtain's composition. The inscriptions list 14 women of the Russo family, who embroidered the curtain. The curtain combines elements of Ottoman influence, such as the overall composition of a portal with Alhambra-shape hanging lamp, also found in Islamic prayer rugs, with stylized Art Nouveau proto-Vienna Secessionist ornament. Vienna's Sephardic community was predominantly of Turkish origin, due to the close contacts between the Ottoman and Habsburg empires, and the synagogue was popularly known as the *Türkentempel*. The *Türkentempel* was destroyed on *Kristallnacht* in 1938. *(cover)*

542 LAVER USED BY KOHANIM BEFORE PRIESTLY BLESSING

Lisbon, second half of the 16th century. Silver: repoussé, embossed, punched, engraved and parcel-gilt. 18 in. diam. Hebrew inscription: Dedicated by Avraham and Sarah Kohen Herrera. Collection of the Portugees-Israëlietische Gemeente, Amsterdam, KK 203.

This basin is typical of Hispano-Moresque metalwork crafted on the Iberian peninsula and greatly resembles similarly shaped and decorated ceramics. It is probable that this plate was brought to Amsterdam by *conversos*

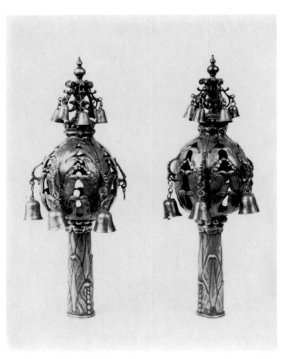

fleeing Portugal in order to return to Judaism in Amsterdam. The engraving in the central flat roundel, the Hebrew dedicatory inscription encircling hands posed for the priestly blessing, was probably added in Amsterdam, so that this basin is an embodiment of the return of Portuguese *conversos* to Judaism.

The donor, Avraham Kohen de Herrera, also known as Alonso Nunez de Herrera and Avraham Irira (1570?–1635/9), was well known as a religious philosopher and kabbalist. He was a descendant of a noble *converso* family which emigrated from Portugal to Italy. Herrera left Florence for Morocco. He was taken captive during the English conquest of Cadiz, where he had been temporarily staying. He was taken to England and freed before 1600 following a diplomatic exchange between Elizabeth I and the Sultan of Morocco. He lived as a Jew in Ragusa (Dubrovnik) in the late 1590s, and there studied Lurianic kabbalah. Herrera arrived in Holland around 1605 and probably converted to Judaism soon thereafter. His opinions strongly influenced the Amsterdam community. He was the first author to undertake a systematic philosophic interpretation of Kabbalah. Herrera's *Casa de Dios* (see cat. no. 571) was later translated into Hebrew by Isaac Aboab da Fonseca (*Beit Elohim*, Amsterdam, 1665). *(fig. 86)*

543 LAVER USED BY KOHANIM BEFORE PRIESTLY BLESSING*

Augsburg, 1693/94. Silver: repoussé, engraved, cast, parcel-gilt, rivets. Goldsmith: Johann Beckert III, 1654–1704 (Master ca. 1684). Portuguese inscription: Manuel Aleny Constancia Aleny 5454. 34 x 42½ in. Collection of the Portugees-Israëlietische Gemeente, Amsterdam, KK 205.

This exceptionally massive, lavish basin is decorated with a scene portraying the tributes presented by the Queen of Sheba and her maidservants to King Solomon (I Kings 10:10; II Chronicles 9:9). Around the border are hunting motifs. Augsburg was famed for its silversmiths, and the sophistication of the Amsterdam community is evident in their use of metalwork crafted at this German center. The dedicatory inscription is engraved on the basin's reverse. *(fig. 83)*

543

544 TAZZA

Holland, 1684. Silver: repoussé, chased and engraved. Judeo-Portuguese inscription: Fez Codes Jahacob Alenÿacat Piementel. Lúnto Jassas de Prata Aok: K:de TT. Amsterdam. A 14 de Adar Anno 5444. 4¹⁵⁄₁₆ x 5¹⁄₂ in. Collection of the Portugees-Israëlietische Gemeente, Amsterdam, KK 2.

This tazza is one of four which were dedicated on the same date. According to tradition, these pedestaled dishes were used to collect coins on Purim. This type of dish belongs to a limited group of standing dishes whose original use is not clear. Such pieces may have been purely ornamental, particularly during the late Renaissance. The tazza is decorated with fruit and floral motifs. *(fig. 62)*

Cf. YUM, *Purim,* cat. no. 40.

545 SPOON WITH THE EMBLEM OF AMSTERMDAM'S PORTUGUESE COMMUNITY

Amsterdam, 17th–18th century. Silver: stamped and engraved. 6³⁄₄ x 2¹⁄₄ in. Collection of the Reuben and Helene Dennis Museum, Beth Tzedec Synagogue, Toronto, CR 524.

The emblem of the Portuguese community of Amsterdam, a pelican biting at its breast to feed its young with its own blood, is depicted twice on this commemorative spoon. The symbol probably alludes to the self-sacrifice of the Portuguese community in remaining loyal to Judaism despite the tribulations of the forced conversions of 1497 in Portugal.

546 LORD MAYOR'S DISH

London, 1737. Silversmith: Jos. Sanders (Master 1730). Silver: engraved and cast. English inscrip-

tions: THE ARMS OF Y TRIBE OF JUDAH GIVEN THEM BY THE LORD; This Piece of Plate was presented to Sir John Barnard Kn: Lord Mayor of the City of London by the Body of Jews residing in the said City Anno 1737. 2¾ x 19⁷⁄₁₆ in. diam. Collection of the Israel Museum, Jerusalem, gift of Mr. Edward M. Warburg, New York, in memory of Audrey and Stephan Currier, 139/27.

This plate is an example of the traditional annual gift made by London's Sephardic community to the city's Lord Mayor. These gifts were presented from 1679 to 1778 and were accompanied by a purse of £50 or sweetmeats. Jews were not alone in the practice of presenting an annual *douceur* to the Lord Mayor; French and Dutch Protestant communities did the same.

The last gift of Lord Mayor's plate was made in 1778, after which Sephardic community leaders decided to write a letter to the Lord Mayor explaining that since the expense had become too great, they would be obliged to discontinue the practice.[1]

At the center of this plate is the emblem of London's Spanish and Portuguese Synagogue (Bevis Marks). The style of the uniform of the "Guardian of Israel" depicted in the synagogue seal varies according to fashion; in this example the guard's uniform resembles that of a British Grenadier early in the reign of George II. *(fig. 67)*

547   ERUV HATZEROT PLATE

Italy, 1758. Brass; iron: pierced; glass. Hebrew inscription: As a reminder for the Children of Israel that during the fifty years t[hat will come upon us] a[s a] b[lessing] beginning in the month of Adar of this year 5518 the eruv can be renewed from year to year on the basis of the enactment which was made by me Shmuel son of Moshe Gallico of b[lessed] m[emory] according to the laws of the holy Torah and happy is he who waits and will live to renew it according to the law. 15¼ in. diam. Collection of the Jewish Museum, New York, F4584.

This plate was hung in the synagogue and held matzot owned by the entire community, thereby creating the legal reality of an *eruv hatzerot*, a linking of courtyards and passageways as communal property to permit the carrying of objects in these areas on the Sabbath. Plates of this type are exceptionally rare.[1]

REFERENCE: Kayser and Schoenberger, cat. no. 203.

548   CONTAINER FOR DOWRY LOTTERY TICKETS

Amsterdam, 1781/82. Silver: cast and engraved. 11½ x 10 in. Collection of the Santa Companhia de Dotar Orphas e Donzellas, Amsterdam.

The *Santa Companhia de Dotar Orphas e Donzellas*, commonly known as Dotar, was founded by 20 members of Amsterdam's Portuguese community in 1615 in order to provide dowries for needy girls of Sephardic ancestry. In the 17th and 18th centuries over 100 organizations served the social, communal and charitable needs of Amsterdam's Portuguese community.

This container was used to hold lots for special drawings for dowries, as specified in bequests to Dotar. The society held a celebration and lottery each year on Shushan Purim, a day traditionally associated with lotteries and merriment. The lots were placed in special silver containers such as this one and were drawn by a small child. The Haham (rabbi) would then unfold the winning tickets and read aloud the lucky candidates' names. After the French occupation in 1795 the society's investments in the Dutch East India Company suffered greatly, and dowry awards were halved. The Nazi occupation saw the cessation of the society's activities, which were resumed following World War II and which today address a broad Jewish social and cultural agenda.

This vessel was probably originally intended for use as a soup tureen. *(fig. 66)*

Cf. Amsterdam, Rijksmuseum, Nederlands zilver/ Dutch silver, 1979, cat. no. 132.

1. See L. D. Barnett, *Bevis Marks Records*, Oxford, 1940, pp. 11–12; A. G. Grimwade, "Anglo-Jewish Silver," *TJHSE*, XVIII, 1953–55, 123; C. Roth, "The Lord Mayor's Salvers," *The Connoisseur*, X, 246–99.

1. *Cf.* Washington D.C., Smithsonian Institution, *The Precious Legacy: Judaic Treasures from the State Czechoslovak Collections*, D. Altschuler, ed., cat. no. 94.

SABBATH AND FESTIVALS

549 SABBATH WALL SCONCE

Holland, 18th century. Brass: hammered, punched and engraved. Collection of the Sir Isaac and Lady Edith Wolfson Museum, Hechal Shlomo, Jerusalem.

Lamps of this type were used in the home or at the synagogue. Similar lamps were used in North Africa (see cat. no. 353).

REFERENCE: Bialer, p. 100.

550 SABBATH LAMP*

Piedmont, 18th–19th century. Silver: repoussé, chased and cast. Collection of Mr. and Mrs. Paul Rava, St. Louis, Missouri.

The ornate, heavy ornament seen in this lamp is typical of Italian ceremonial silver. Lamps of this type were used in the home.

551 SPICE CONTAINER

Amsterdam, 1711/12. Silver: cast, repoussé and engraved. Hebrew inscription: "Lo, I will send the prophet Elijah to you before the coming of the [awesome and fearful] day of the Lord" (Mal. 3:23). Portuguese inscriptions: Sight, touch, hearing, taste, smell; Elias gabay Henriques [the] y[ear] 5472. 7 x 3⅛ in. Collection of the Portugees-Israëlietische Gemeente, Amsterdam, KK 308.

The overall shape of this container, a sphere atop an elongated pedestal, resembles a tree. A snake is coiled around the trunk. This alludes to the Tree of Knowledge in the Garden of Eden. The six-sided, fruit-shaped top has a hinged lid for the insertion of spices. Six scenes are depicted on the sides of this sphere. One scene depicts Adam and Eve. The association with the Creation story is appropriate for a havdalah spice container used to mark the separation between the Sabbath, which commemorates God's resting on the seventh day of Creation, and the workday week.

The other five scenes are titled with each of the five senses and depict scenes or objects

550

associated with that sense. A lit candle is represented on the sight panel; the Prophet Elijah rising to heaven in the fiery chariot (II Kings 2:1–11) for touch; an angel blowing a horn for hearing; a hand holding a cup for taste; flowers for smell. The Elijah scene relates to the Hebrew inscription, and to the association of the havdalah ceremony with the appearance of Elijah and the coming of the Messiah. The Elijah scene may also refer to the name of the donor. (*figs. 84–85*)

552   HANUKKAH LAMP

Holland, 18th century. Brass: sheet and cast. 11¹⁵/₁₆ x 10½ in. Gross Family Collection, Tel Aviv, 35.11.80.

The overall shape of this lamp is modeled after the rounded gable form which frequently tops Dutch buildings. The use of tulip motifs is characteristic of Dutch decorative arts.

553   HANUKKAH LAMP

Holland, 18th century. Brass sheet: hammered. Moldovan Family Collection, New York.

This finely crafted lamp features decorative motifs common to Dutch folk art, such as tulips and hearts. *(fig. 78)*

554   HANUKKAH LAMP*

Holland, 18th century. Brass sheet: hammered and pierced. H: 13½ in. Collection of Mr. and Mrs. Abraham Halpern, New York.

The depiction of jugs on the backplate of this lamp refers to the famed Hanukkah miracle, the single cruse of oil which burned for eight days.

REFERENCE: Weinstein, fig. 140.

555   HANUKKAH LAMP

Amsterdam, 1795. Silver: repoussé and engraved. Silversmith: Isaak van Wijk, 1733–1798 (Master 1755). Hebrew inscription: "For the commandment is a lamp, the teaching is a light" (Prov. 6:23). Judeo-Portuguese inscription: FEZ CODES EM HOME DA BM AA. HANNA DE ISHAC LORES SALZEDO 14 MENACHEM 5637. 16¾ x 12⅛ x 4 in. Collection of the Portugees-Israëlietische Gemeente, Amsterdam, KK 201.

On the backplate of this lamp is a depiction of a man dressed in typical 18th-century costume, including breeches and tricorn hat, lighting a large menorah-shaped floor lamp. The backplate is modeled on an elaborate portal arch with flanking columns and decorated with profuse rococo ornament.

Engraved on this lamp is the monogram of the de Castro family, traditionally identified as the donors of this lamp to the Portuguese Synagogue. *(fig. 80, Plate 16)*

556   HANUKKAH LAMP

Holland, 18th–19th century. Brass sheet: hammered and pierced. 12 x 9¼ in. Collection of Prof. and Mrs. Solomon Feffer, New York.

Brass lamps of this type were popular in Holland throughout the 18th and 19th centuries. The pediment form of the backplate may be based on the gabled roofs of many Dutch homes. Hanukkah lamps are frequently modeled on architectural forms; this is probably due in part to the halakhic requirement that the lit lamp be displayed in a doorway or window in order to publicize the miracle of Hanukkah.

557   HANUKKAH LAMP*

Holland, 18th–19th century. Brass sheet: hammered. 9½ x 9 in. Collection of Prof. and Mrs. Solomon Feffer, New York.

An eight-branched menorah is depicted on the backplate of this lamp.

Cf. Magnes, *Hanukkah Lamps*, cat. no. 105.

558   ESTHER SCROLL AND ROLLER

557

LIFE CYCLE

Holland, 1673. Salom d'Italia (1619–1655?). Engraving on vellum; ivory: carved. H: 8 in. Private collection.

Salom d'Italia, a Jewish artist, studied drawing and engraving in Italy before settling in Amsterdam in 1641 (see also cat. no. 621). In this scroll, he has framed the text of the Book of Esther with elaborate, baroque arched portals. The ends of the carved roller feature depictions of Ahasuerus and Esther. These carvings appear to be based on chess pieces, although they include attributes specific to the portrayed Biblical characters, such as the quill in Esther's hand, relating to Esther's writing and sending of letters (Esther 9:29). *(fig. 71)*

REFERENCES: M. Narkiss, "Salom Italia," no. 1, pp. 445–46; Detroit Institute of Arts, *Exhibition of Jewish Ceremonial Art,* 1951, cat. no. 135; New York, Parke-Bernet Galleries, Inc., *The Charles E. Feinberg Collection of Valuable Judaica,* November 30, 1967, lot no. 317; YUM, *Purim,* cat. no. 54.

559 KETUBBAH (Marriage contract)

Amsterdam, 1617. Ink, tempera and gold paint on parchment. 24 x 18⅞ in. The Stieglitz Collection was donated to the Israel Museum with the contribution of Erica and Ludwig Jesselson, New York, through the American Friends of the Israel Museum, 1987, 179/346.

Groom: David Curiel
Bride: Rahel Curiel
Witness: Rabbi Yosef Pardo
This is the earliest extant illustrated Amsterdam ketubbah. The text and Italianate decoration of this contract are essential proofs of the links between the Jewish communities of Portugal, Amsterdam and Venice.[1] In this ketub-

1. See J. M. Cohen and J. C. E. Belinfante, "The *Ponentini* and the *Portuguese,* The influence of Venetian Jewry on the Portuguese Jewry of Amsterdam" in Joods, *The Ghetto.*

bah the dowry includes vast property, in cash, jewels, and land in Portugal. Both bride and groom were members of the same wealthy family of Portuguese origin.

The contract is signed by Yosef Pardo, who served as rabbi at the *Beit-Yaakov* Sephardic synagogue of Amsterdam. Originally from Salonika, Pardo served as rabbi in Venice before coming to Amsterdam. *(fig. 18)*

REFERENCES: Sabar, "The Golden Age," pp. 89–91; IM, *Stieglitz*, cat. no. 214.

560   KETUBBAH (Marriage contract)

Amsterdam, 1663. Copperplate etching, ink on parchment. 27⅝ x 19¾ in. Gross Family Collection, Tel Aviv, 35.12.24.

Groom: Yaakov de Castro
Bride: Rahel daughter of Yitzhak Athias
The engraved border of this ketubbah was used by Sephardim for more than 200 years. Extant examples come from Sephardic communities in Holland, France, Germany, England and even colonial America. The engraving was created in Amsterdam in the 1650s. This fine example is one of the earliest ketubbot extant with this popular border. *(fig. 19)*

Cf. Sabar, "The Golden Age," pp. 96–97; Sabar, *Ketubbah*, cat. nos. 154, 157 and 169.

561   KETUBBAH (Marriage contract)

Bayonne, France, 1758. Ink and gouache on parchment. 16¾ x 12 in. Collection of Dr. and Mrs. Carl Urbont, Larchmont, New York.

Groom: David son of Avraham de Leon
Bride: Esther daughter of Yitzhak Lopes de Leon
The floral motifs which decorate this ketubbah are typical of French folk art. The vases of flowers flanking the text are copied after similar depictions in printed ketubbot (see cat. no. 560). This ketubbah was discovered and rescued by the lenders from a New York City garbage truck.

Bayonne was a center for *converso* exiles from the early 16th century. Although *conversos* had formally established a Jewish community by the mid-17th century, they were not officially granted the right to practice Judaism openly until 1723. *(fig. 20)*

562   KETUBBAH (Marriage contract)

Corfu, 1781. Ink and gouache on parchment. 27 x 18¼ in. Einhorn Collection, Tel Aviv.

Groom: Yitzhak Hayyim son of Avraham Hayyim
Bride: Celeta daughter of Shmuel Hayyim di Ozmo
In Corfu ketubbot the years are dated both from the Creation and from the Destruction of the Temple (70 C.E). The pictorial themes, based on a decorative program popular in Venetian ketubbot, include the cycle of the zodiac, allegories of the four seasons, David playing the harp, Jacob's ladder, Moses the Lawgiver and the binding of Isaac.

563   KETUBBAH (Marriage contract)

Corfu, 1830. Ink and gouache on parchment. Einhorn Collection, Tel Aviv.

Groom: Avraham Hayyim de Castro son of Yitzhak de Castro
Bride: Regina Esther daughter of Binyamin Nissim ha-Levi
The emblems of the two families are depicted in the center of the upper border: a castle for the de Castro family and a water jug for the bride, whose father is a Levite (the function of the Levites being to pour water over the *kohanim* before the latter recite the Priestly Blessing at the synagogue).

564   KETUBBAH (Marriage contract)*

Gibraltar, 1886. Ink and paint on parchment. 27½ x 23½ in. Collection of Yeshiva University Museum, New York, gift of Abraham Pinto, 81.7.

Groom: Shimon David
Bride: Ohana
The text, written in black ink with gold initials at the beginning, is framed by a wreath of flowers and ribbons, decorative motifs typical of Gibraltar ketubbot.

Cf. Sabar, *Ketubbah*.

565   WEDDING RIDDLE

Venice(?), first half of 18th century. Ink and gouache on paper. 20 x 14¼ in. Einhorn Collection, Tel Aviv.

564

Prepared for the wedding of David Shmuel son of Yaakov Pardo and Rivka daughter of Yedidiah Valencin.

Hebrew, Italian or Judeo-Italian poems were frequently composed by Italian Jews to entertain the bride, groom and guests at wedding festivities (see cat. nos. 112 and 566). The bridegroom, Rabbi David Pardo (1718–1790), was a well-known Sephardic rabbinical author and poet. He was born in Venice, but from 1760 served as rabbi of the Sephardic community in Sarajevo, now in Yugoslavia. In 1776 he went to Jerusalem, where he became one of the most important authorities and head of the *Yeshiva Hesed le-Avraham*.

566 WEDDING POEM

Italy, 19th century. Ink and gouache on paper. Einhorn Collection, Tel Aviv.

Poems were frequently recited at Italian Jewish weddings (see also cat. nos. 112 and 565). The winged, androgynous nude in the center of this sheet reflects the widespread acceptance of figural representation among Western Sephardim.

567 MARRIAGE PLATES*

London, 1681. Maker: I. Smith (active 1670–1690). Pewter: engraved. Hebrew inscriptions: "He who finds a wife has found happiness, And has won the favor of the Lord" (Prov. 18:21); Yaakov s[on of] Yosef de Almeida Iyar [5]441; Sarah Nunes De Almeida y Pereira [5]441. Aramaic inscription: In a good sign and with good luck. 2 x 18 in. diam. Collection of Dr. Norman P. Schenker, Munich, Germany.

These two plates were made to celebrate the marriage of Sarah Nunes de Almeida y Pereira and Yaakov de Almeida. The engraved Hebrew and Aramaic inscriptions are often found on ketubbot and other artifacts celebrating marriage. The central scenes, Adam and Eve and the return of the spies after surveying the Promised Land, are probably copied from popular prints or from illustrated Bibles. The depiction of Adam and Eve is appropriate, as it refers to the first union of man and woman. The plates are decorated with engraved roses and tulips and with family coats of arms.

567A

567B

568

PERSONAL JUDAICA

568 TALLIT KATAN*

Italy, 18th century. Silk: embroidered with metallic threads. Collection of Mr. and Mrs. Abraham Halpern, New York.

The lavish embroidery on a garment of this type is unusual, but many examples of elaborate Italian ceremonial textiles are known.

REFERENCE: London, Sotheby's, *Hebrew Books and Works of Art*, February 12, 1986, lot no. 537. *Cf.* Jerusalem, IM, *Paris*, cat. no. 120.

569

569 TALLIT (Prayer shawl)*

Italy, 18th century. Silk: embroidered with silk threads. Collection of Mr. and Mrs. Abraham Halpern, New York.

This tallit formerly belonged to a member of the De Senis family of Florence.

REFERENCE: New York, Sotheby's, *Fine Judaica: Printed Books, Manuscripts, and Works of Art*, June 2–3, 1982, lot no. 330.

570 TALLIT (Prayer shawl)

Italy, 19th–20th century. Silk. Collection of Mr. and Mrs. Max Eis, Berkeley, California.

This tallit features woven decoration: the appropriate blessing in a cartouche.

MANUSCRIPTS

571 LIBRO PRIMERO DE LA CASA DE LA DIVINIDAD

(First Book of the House of Divinity)

Avraham Kohen de Herrera. Amsterdam, 18th century. Ink on paper. Collection of the Jewish National and University Library, Jerusalem.

Alonso Nunez de Herrera (1570?–1635/9), known in Hebrew as Avraham Kohen de Herrera, was a philosopher and kabbalist of Marrano origin. His most important works on Kabbalah were written in Spanish: *Puerta del Cielo* (translated into Hebrew as *Shaar ha-Shamayim*, Amsterdam, 1655), and *Casa de Dios*, of which our manuscript is an example (here the title is modified). The two titles were taken from Genesis 28:17—"This is none other than the abode of God, and that is the gateway to heaven." This codex deals with theories about angels (names appear in Hebrew) and spiritual phenomena.

Herrera donated to Amsterdam's Portuguese synagogue a basin for washing the hands of the Kohanim before they recite the Priestly Blessing (see cat. no. 542).

REFERENCE: G. Scholem, *Avraham Kohen Herrera: Baal "Shaar ha-Rahamim," Hayyav, Yetzirato ve-hashpaatah*, 1977/8, pp. 28–29.

572 PREVENCIONES DIVINAS CONTRA LA IDOLATRIA DE LAS GENTES

(Divine Protection Against the Idolatry of the Gentiles)

Isaac Orobio de Castro. Scribe: Abraham Machorro. Amsterdam, 1704. Collection of the Ets Haim Library, Amsterdam.

Isaac or Balthazar Orobio de Castro (1620–1687) was a Marrano philosopher and physician who was born in Portugal and became a renowned professor of metaphysics at the University of Salamanca, where he was arrested and tortured by the Inquisition. He subsequently fled to France and in 1662 settled in Amsterdam. This manuscript is one of his most important polemical works. It attempts to refute the ideas and principles of Christianity from a Jewish point of view. The title page, apparently the work of Jacob Guedelha, depicts various Biblical scenes. A copy of this manuscript from the collection of the Bibliotheca Rosenthaliana is in this exhibition (see cat. no. 573). This text was later translated into English by Grace Aguilar (see cat. no. 643) and was published as *Israel Defended* in 1842.

573 PREVENCIONES DIVINAS CONTRA LA IDOLATRIA DE LAS GENTES

(Divine Protection Against the Idolatry of the Gentiles)*

Isaac Orobio de Castro. Artist: David Lopez Quiros. Amsterdam, 1712. Collection of the Bibliotheca Rosenthaliana, Amsterdam.

This text is a polemical work in defense of Judaism against Christianity. A copy of this manuscript from the Ets Haim collection is in this exhibition (see cat. no. 572).

This manuscript contains six separate title pages by David Lopez Quiros. Each title page is decorated differently.

574   KETER SHEM TOV

(Crown of a Good Name)

Register of circumcisions performed by Shlomo ben Yitzhak Curiel Abaz. Amsterdam, 1724–1761. Ink on paper. Collection of the Ets Haim Library, Amsterdam, HS.EH.48D18.

The attractive title page of this manuscript is dedicated to the author and his profession. Since his name was Shlomo, he selected verses and episodes that describe the merits of King Solomon. At top center, two semi-nude heraldic nymphs flank the meaningful inscription: "Thus the kingdom was secured in Solomon's hands" (I Kings 2:46). A parallel episode at center bottom depicts Solomon's Judgment, flanked by a scene showing the birth of the Biblical King (left) and a contemporary circumcision (right). The two side niches symbolically represent the altar of Solomon (left) and the covenant between God and Israel. *(fig. 16)*

REFERENCES: Fuks and Fuks-Mansfeld, no. 378; JNUL, *Ets Haim*, cat. no. 30.

575   SEFER HESHEK SHLOMO

(Book of Solomon's Delight)

Shlomo son of Yitzhak Saruco. The Hague, 1767–1773. Ink on paper. Collection of the Ets Haim Library, Amsterdam, HS.EH.47A20.

According to the title page, this manuscript contains "commentaries on the prayers recited throughout the year, explanations of the festivals and of popular customs . . . tables setting out the weekly readings from the Torah and the haftarot, and information on the chronology of the festivals and New Moons." The author, who wrote the manuscript himself, was cantor and teacher of the *Honen Dal* Congregation in The Hague. *(fig. 15)*

REFERENCES: Fuks and Fuks-Mansfeld, no. 439; JNUL, *Ets Haim*, cat. no. 57.

576   PASSOVER HAGGADAH

Bordeaux, France, 1813. Scribe: Isaac Zoreph. Illustrator: Jacob Zoreph. 12¾ x 9⅜ in. Moldovan Family Collection, New York.

Isaac and Jacob Zoreph were sons of Salomon and Rebecca (Peigne) Zoreph, a Bordeaux merchant family of Portuguese descent. Two other manuscripts by Jacob Zoreph are known.

The advent of printing did not end the production of illuminated manuscripts; on occasion, printed books were specially illustrated for a wealthy patron. The court Jews of Europe were among those who commissioned luxury manuscripts, usually liturgical works such as Haggadot and prayer books.

This manuscript, known as the Bordeaux Haggadah, copies some of the illustrations and initial letters of the 1712 edition of the Amsterdam Haggadah. It is not a slavish copy; there are a number of original compositions. The Haggadah includes a French translation (the first printed French translation is the Metz version of 1819), instructions in Ladino; translations of Hebrew into Aramaic; three maps (map of Eretz Israel; map of Jerusalem; map of the wandering of the Jews in the wilderness after the Exodus from Egypt); blessings for various holidays; and the *sheva berakhot*, the seven blessings used in the marriage ceremony. Napoleon's coat of arms appears before the *Hallel*, perhaps as evidence of respect for the French Emperor who convened the "Great Sanhedrin" in 1807 to establish the status of Jews in his empire. *(fig. 17)*

REFERENCE: Alfred Moldovan (introduction), *La Haggada de Bordeaux*, facsimile, Paris, 1987.

577   PRAYER BOOK

Terceira Island, Azores, 1875. Scribe (?): Maimon son of Avraham Abuhbut. Collection of the Bibliotheca Rosenthaliana, Amsterdam.

Large numbers of Moroccan Sephardim settled in Portugal and its islands in the late 19th century. Names of important Moroccan rabbis appear in this manuscript. In the colophon, the scribe explains that he wrote this manuscript with his left hand because he was ill; apparently his right side was paralyzed. The use of pasted cutouts as decoration was common in many Sephardic communities, particularly in Turkey (see cat. nos. 83, 85, 131 and 277).

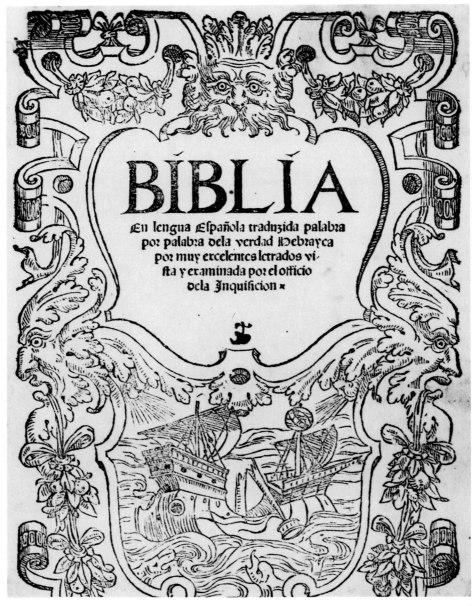

BÍBLIA

En lengua Española traduzida palabra
por palabra dela verdad Hebrayca
por muy excelentes letrados vi-
sta y examinada por el officio
dela Inquisicion ×

PRINTED BOOKS
AND BINDINGS

578 BIBLIA (Bible)*

Ferrara, 1552. Printer: Duarte Pinel (Avraham ibn Usque) for Jeronimo de Vargas (Yom-Tov ben Levi Athias). Ink on paper. 11½ x 7¾ in. Collection of Dr. Viviane A. Ryan and Tomás L. Ryan, New York.

This text is the earliest printed Spanish translation of the Hebrew Bible. It was printed in two distinct editions. One, intended for Spanish Jews, was dedicated to Dona Gracia Nasi (see cat. no. 611) and featured a colophon with a Hebrew date and the printers' Hebrew names. It also included a schedule of haftarot, weekly readings from the Prophets. The edition intended for a Christian audience was dedicated to Duke Ercole d'Este, the enlightened ruler under whose leadership Ferrara became a center of Jewish banking. It bears a colophon dated March 1, 1553, which lists Pinel and Vargas as printer and publisher, respectively. In the Christian edition the translation of Isa. 7:14 allowed for a Christological interpretation of the text by using the term *virgen*, a common error of Christian translators. The Jewish edition used the Spanish term for young woman, *moca*, or, for fear of the Inquisition's censure, a transliteration of the Hebrew *almah*.

The dual nature of this publication reflects the double lives led by the printer and publisher. Duarte Pinel and Jeronimo de Vargas lived as Christians in their respective homelands, Portugal and Spain. After their emigration to Ferrara they reverted to their families' original Jewish faith and began to use the names Avraham ibn Usque and Yom-Tov ben Levi Athias. Athais recognized the need for the publication of Jewish texts in the vernacular in order to facilitate the return of *conversos* to Judaism.

The galleon with shattered crow's-nest sailing in a storm-tossed sea depicted on the frontispiece symbolizes the steadfastness of 16th-century Spanish Jewry despite the hardships of the Expulsion and persecution by the Inquisition. The logo of this exhibition was adapted from this frontispiece.

REFERENCE: NYJM, *Gardens*, cat. no. 69.

579 HAGGADAH ZEVAH PESAH

With commentary by Don Yitzhak Abrabanel (1437–1508). Cremona, 1557. Printer: Vincenzo Conti. Ink on blue paper. Moldovan Family Collection, New York.

Don Yitzhak Abrabanel was born in Lisbon and served as treasurer to King Alfonso V of Portugal. Forced to flee Portugal after Alfonso's death, he moved to Castile, where he entered the service of King Ferdinand and Queen Isabella.

As one of the leading financiers of the royal treasury, Don Yitzhak provided major support for Spain's victory over the Moors. On the eve of the 1492 Expulsion, Ferdinand and Isabella ordered the royal treasury to settle his account. He was paid 1½ million maravedis, and granted royal permission to take a large amount of gold and silver with him into exile. Following the Expulsion, Abrabanel was one of many Jews who settled in Italy. Don Yitzhak was subsequently employed in the service of Ferrante I, King of Naples, and his heir Alfonso II.

Abrabanel was an extremely prolific writer throughout his many travels, despite his numerous responsibilities as a statesman. He is greatly renowned for his Biblical exegesis and philosophy.

REFERENCE: Yaari, *Haggadot*, no. 17.

580 HAGGADAH — LADINO EDITION

Venice, 1609. Printer: Giovanni da Gara. Ink on vellum. 11⅛ x 7⅝ in. Moldovan Family Collection, New York.

This Haggadah was published in three editions (Judeo-Italian, Judeo-Spanish and Judeo-German), in order to meet the linguistic needs of the Italian, Sephardic and Ashkenazic members of the Venetian Jewish community. The illustrations were highly innovative and served as models for many later editions. This includes the first use of a composition combining depictions of the Ten Plagues, and of a page devoted to an arrangement of 13 scenes portraying various stages of the Passover seder. (*fig. 5*)

Cf. Yaari, *Haggadot*, no. 37; NYJM, *Gardens*, cat. no. 77.

581   A RELATION OF A JOURNEY BEGUN AN: DOM: 1610

London, 1621. George Sandys (1578–1644). Printed. Collection of Yeshiva University Museum, New York, gift of Herbert M. Honig, 87.54a.

George Sandys, a cultivated Englishman of the early 17th century, made a grand tour of the Middle East in 1610 and published this profusely illustrated record of his travels. The book provides interesting insights into the prejudices against Jews held by Englishmen of that time.

In one section, Sandys singles out a woman named "Hester" for special mention as in influential figure at the court of the Sultan. She was probably Esther Chiera/Kiera (ca. 1520–1593). Generally, the women who handled affairs for the Sultan's wives in the royal harem were Jewish; their official title was Kiera. One such Jewish woman is depicted in the print, *Femme Juive Courtière* (cat. no. 213).

582   SERMÕES QUE PREGARÃO OS DOCTOS INGENIOS DO K.K. DE TALMUD TORAH DESTA CIDADE DE AMSTERDAM

(Sermons Presented by the Learned Doctors of the H[oly] C[ongregation] Talmud Torah in this City of Amsterdam)

Amsterdam, 1675. Printer: David Castro Tartaz. Engraver: Romeyn de Hooghe. Gross Family Collection, Tel Aviv.

This book contains sermons delivered during the week of celebrations for the dedication of the magnificent new Portuguese Synagogue in Amsterdam in 1675. It opens with a series of engravings honoring the event which depict in detail the exterior and interior of the building and emphasize its new and costly furnishings.

David Castro Tartaz was also the printer of the *Gazeta de Amsterdam* (1675), a Spanish-language paper dealing with economic and commercial matters. *(fig. 14)*

REFERENCE: JNUL, *Ets Haim*, cat. no. 5.

583   SEDER TEFILLOT KE-MINHAG K' K' SEPHARDIM

(Order of Prayers According to the Custom of the H[oly] C[ongregation] of Sephardim)

Amsterdam, 1708/9. Printer: Immanuel Athias. Ink on paper; leather binding with gold tooling and cast silver clasps (clasps: Amsterdam, 1700, maker: HOF). 3 x 2½ x 1 in. Collection of the Reuben and Helene Dennis Museum, Beth Tzedec Synagogue, Toronto, CR 378.

The last four pages of this beautifully bound miniature prayer book contain a special Hebrew and Ladino hymn composed for the dedication of the Portuguese Synagogue in Amsterdam in 1675.

584   PRAYER BOOK AND COVER

Amsterdam, 1709. Ink on paper; printed; tortoiseshell; silver mounts. Collection of the Jewish Museum, New York, 1986-166.

The increase in international trade encouraged the importation of new luxury goods. Tortoiseshell was much in demand in the 18th and 19th centuries, and was used for personal objects, such as combs and amulets, and for book bindings.

585   THESOURO DOS DINIM

(Treasury of Laws)

Amsterdam, 1710. Menasseh ben Israel. Printer: Immanuel Athias. Binding: vellum. 7¼ x 4¾ in. Collection of Yeshiva University Museum, New York, gift of Herbert M. Honig, 88.241.

This edition of the 613 commandments is written in Portuguese. The five sections were printed individually from 1645 to 1647. The last section is dedicated to the patrons, Abraham and Isaac Israel Pereyra. An engraved portrait of the author by Rembrandt is included in this exhibition (cat. no. 620).

586   ESPEJO FIEL DE VIDA QUE LAS PSALMOS DE DAVID EN VERSO

(Faithful Mirror of Life in the Psalms of David in Verse)

London, 1720. Daniel Israel Lopez Laguna (ca. 1653–ca. 1730). Ex Libris: Haham Rabbi Abraham Haim Rodrigues. 9⅝ x 8⅞ in. Collection of Yeshiva University Museum, New York, gift of Herbert M. Honig in memory of Alexander and Esther Honig, 87.56.

This book contains a Spanish paraphrase of the Book of Psalms, and descriptions of Laguna's imprisonment by the Inquisition in Spain. Planned in prison, it represents 23 years of labor on the author's part.

Daniel Israel Lopez Laguna was born in Portugal of a Marrano family and studied in Spain, where he was arrested by the Inquisition. After his release, he settled in Jamaica where he professed Judaism. In 1720, he went to London, where Mordecai Nunes de Almeyda helped him publish this book.

587 SEDER HAMISHA
TAANIOT (Liturgy for Five Fast Days)

Amsterdam, 1725/26. Editor: Shlomo Yehuda Leão Templo (d. ca. 1733). Printer: Yitzhak ben Shlomo Rafael. Ink on paper. Collection of Dr. Viviane A. Ryan and Tomás L. Ryan, New York.

This book contains the liturgy for various fast days. The beautiful engraving on the upper portion of the first page depicts the destruction of the Temple in Jerusalem, an appropriate subject for the text. Shlomo Yehuda Leão Templo was the son of Yaakov Yehudah (Aryeh) Leon Templo (1603–1675; see cat. no. 621), whose famed depiction of Solomon's Temple can be seen in the lower portion of the page. (See illustration on p. 324)

588 ORDEN DE LAS
ORACIONES QUOTIDIANAS
(Order of Daily Prayers)

The Hague, 1733/34. Printer: C. Hoffeling. Ink on paper; leather binding; gold tooled. Moldovan Family Collection, New York.

Miniature prayer books were printed for use while traveling and for children.

589 ORDEN DE ORACIONES
COTIDIANAS (Daily Prayer Book)

Amsterdam, 1735. Printer: J. Lobedanus. 3¼ x 2¼ in. Collection of Yeshiva University Museum, New York, gift of Herbert M. Honig in memory of Alexander and Esther Honig, 87.57.

This miniature daily prayer book is written in Spanish with Hebrew transliteration of important prayers. It is perhaps the earliest Sephardic prayer book to include the Benedicion del Rey (Prayer for the King). Previous books only refer to the recitation of this prayer. Printed by order of Haham Aharon Mendes.

590 SIDDUR TAANIOT
(Prayer Book for Fast Days)

Venice, 1736. Publisher: Isaac Foa. 6⅞ x 4¾ in. Collection of Yeshiva University Museum, New York, gift of Herbert M. Honig in memory of Alexander and Esther Honig, 87.53.

This is the earliest edition of the Sephardic prayer book to include two kinnot (elegies) on the Expulsion, to be recited on Tisha be-Av.

REFERENCE: H. P. Salamon, "Two Elegies on the Expulsion of the Jews from Spain," The Sephardic Scholar, series 3, 1977–78, pp. 37–47.

591 ORDEN DE ORACIONES
(Order of Prayers)

Amsterdam, 1755/56. Ink on paper; tortoiseshell binding; silver mounts. Moldovan Family Collection, New York.

Cf. cat. no. 584.

592 SEFER BRIT YITZHAK
(Book of the Covenant of Isaac)

Amsterdam, 1768. Printer: Gerard Johan Jansen. Ink on paper. Gross Family Collection, Tel Aviv.

This is a circumcision book according to the Sephardic rite. Its most interesting feature is the printed list, at the end, of all the certified Sephardic mohelim (circumcisers) in the communities of Amsterdam, The Hague and Naarden in Holland, as well as those in London, Hamburg, Bayonne, Curaçao and Suriname.

593 MAHZOR LE-YAMIM NORAIM
(Prayer Book for the High Holy Days)
AND COVER

Venice, 1786/87. Printer: Yitzhak Foa. Ink on paper: printed; silver: repoussé and chased. Inscriptions: AL; GK. Collection of Mr. and Mrs. Paul Rava, St. Louis, Missouri.

This prayer book is according to the rite of Jews from the Ottoman empire. The Sephardic community of Venice was divided into two groups: *Ponentini* Jews from Western Europe, most usually *conversos* who returned to Judaism in Italy after fleeing from Spain and Portugal, and *Levantini*, Ottoman Jews. The monograms on either side of the cover suggest that this book and decorative binding were presented as a betrothal or wedding gift. In Italy and in the Ottoman empire, book bindings were frequently presented as gifts to bridegrooms (see cat. nos. 596, 136, and 137).

594 MAHZOR LE-EREV YOM KIPPUR (Prayer Book for Yom Kippur Eve)

Livorno, 1821. L. E. Ottolenghi. Printer: Sadahun Molco. Collection of Yeshiva University Museum, New York, gift of Herbert M. Honig, 88.242.

A Sephardic prayer book with Italian translation, including a prayer for Ferdinand III, Grand Duke of Tuscany (1769–1824). This Habsburg prince, who ruled from 1791 to 1801 and from 1814 to 1824, retained elements of the Napoleonic reforms which gave equal citizenship rights to Jews. The Jews were not always so fortunate in the period of reaction that followed the fall of Napoleon and the restoration of former regimes in territories he lost.

595 HEBREEUWSCH SPEL-EN LEESBOEKJE
(Hebrew Speller and Reader)

Amsterdam, 1881. Jacob Lopes Cardozo. Ink on paper: printed. 7 x 4½ in. Collection of Rev. and Mrs. Abraham Lopes Cardozo, New York.

The author and publisher were both members of the Cardozo family (see cat. nos. 645 and 648–650).

596 BOOK BINDING

Venice (?), Italy, 18th century. Silver: engraved and parcel-gilt. Hebrew inscription: This is my name and this is my memorial. Gross Family Collection, Tel Aviv.

This book binding is decorated with a coat of arms similar to that of the Lusena family of Livorno.

597 SERMON BOOK COVER

London, early 19th century. Velvet; silver: engraved. Inscription: Meldola. Collection of Haham Dr. Solomon Gaon, New York.

This cover held a sermon by Reverend Raphael Meldola (1754–1828). A native of Livorno, Italy, Meldola was elected Haham of the Spanish and Portuguese Jews of London in 1804/5 (see also cat. no. 641).

PERSONAL ARTIFACTS

598 DRAWSTRING PURSE

Italy, 16th century. Silk: embroidered with silk and metallic thread. 5½ x 4½ in. Collection of Gloria Abrams, New York.

Family tradition referred to this object as a bridal purse. Until approximately 1650, women's clothes did not have pockets inserted in skirt seams, and a purse such as this one often formed part of a woman's costume.

599 AMULET AND AMULET CASE BEARING THE ABRABANEL COAT OF ARMS

Italy, 19th century. Ink on parchment; silver: cast and engraved. 3⅜ x 1¹³⁄₁₆ x ⅛ in. Collection of the Jewish Museum, New York, F2083.

The bottom of this case pulls out for the insertion of the amuletic manuscript, a folded text of selections from Psalm 72. On one side of this case is a six-pointed star with a Divine name in its center and a hexagram, a magical inscription of six letters arranged one in each point of the star. On the opposite side is a cartouche containing a rampant lion flanking a tower beneath a star, the shield of the Abrabanel family (see cat. no. 579).

The use of coats of arms by Italian Jews was prevalent by the seventeenth century, and may have had its roots in heraldic devices adopted by Jews in medieval Spain. Coats of arms may also have been used by *conversos* living as Christians in Spain and Portugal after the expulsions. The use of such shields may have been continued by these families even after their emigration.

REFERENCE: NYJM, *Gardens*, cat. no. 227.

602

600 LETTER TO ABRAHAM CORCOS

London, July 31. Sir Moses Montefiore (1784–1885). Ink on paper. 6¾ x 8½ in. Collection of Ernest and Maisie Corcos, Casablanca, Morocco.

Sir Moses Montefiore (see also cat. nos. 311, 601–603, 644 and 646) wrote this letter of thanks to Abraham Corcos. In it, Montefiore expresses the hope that the Temple in Jerusalem will be speedily rebuilt.

601 LETTER TO HENRY SOLOMON

Ramsgate, England, May 30, 1875. Sir Moses Montefiore (1784–1885). Ink on paper. 7¼ x 8¾ in. Collection of Mr. and Mrs. David Goldman, Fort Lee, New Jersey.

This letter from Sir Moses Montefiore thanks Henry Solomon (1826–1904) for raising money in Savannah, Georgia, on behalf of Jews in Eretz Israel.

REFERENCE: B. W. Korn, "The Jews of the Confederacy," *American Jewish Archives*, Vol. XIII, April, 1961, pp. 73–75.

602 KIDDUSH CUP PRESENTED TO SIR MOSES MONTEFIORE*

England, 1884. Silver: cast; engraved. English inscription: With Respect and gratitude presented to Sir Moses Montefiore Bart F.R.S., on his hundredth birthday by the Board of Governors. 8¼ x 3¾ in. Collection of Cantor and Mrs. Jacob Rosenbaum, Monsey, New York.

This elegant stemmed cup shows the influence of the Gothic ornament on English style at this time.

603 POTPOURRI CONTAINER

England, late 19th century. Wood: carved. Inscriptions: MM; 1873. 4½ x 5½ x 3⅛ in. Collection of Cantor and Mrs. Jacob Rosenbaum, Monsey, New York.

Used as a spice container for havdalah by Sir Moses Montefiore, this box, decorated with vine scrolls, reflects late Victorian taste.

604 MEERSCHAUM PIPE WITH BOWL IN THE SHAPE OF BENJAMIN DISRAELI'S HEAD

British empire, late 19th century. Meerschaum: silver. Hallmarks: MF. 5 x 6½ x 1½ in. Einhorn Collection, Tel Aviv.

Meerschaum (magnesium silicate) is a soft white mineral used chiefly in pipe bowls because it allows the tobacco to burn coolly. A much-used meerschaum pipe takes on an ivory-yellow coloration. The bowls of meerschaum pipes are usually carved to represent faces or animals. This one bears the features of Benjamin Disraeli (1804–1881; see also cat. no. 647), Earl of Beaconsfield, Prime Minister of England (1868 and 1874–1880) during the reign of Queen Victoria.

605 BRAZIER*

Holland, ca. 1700. Brass: hammered, chased, pierced, punched and engraved. Hebrew inscription: H; N; Y; S. 6 x 8⅜ x 8¼ in. Collection of Mr. and Mrs. Abraham Halpern, New York.

This octagonal brazier is constructed so that three sides hinge open for the insertion of heated coals. The use of fruit and flower motifs is typical of the decoration of Dutch household wares; however, the inclusion of Hebrew on an object of this type and date is very rare.

REFERENCE: New York, Sotheby Parke Bernet, Inc., *Good Judaica and Related Works of Art*, May 13, 1981, lot no. 104.

605

606 AMBRON FAMILY PRIVILEGE

Rome, October 30, 1756. Watercolor and ink on parchment. 22¼ x 17¼ in. Einhorn Collection, Tel Aviv.

On October 30, 1756, Girolamo Cardinal Colonna issued this privilege in Rome to Gabriel, Leone and Sabato Ambron, and to Gabriel's son Ezekia, confirming a former privilege previously issued by the Reverend Monsignor Nicolo Casoni, Secretary of Defense for Pope Benedict XIV.

On March 28, 1752, Gabriel and his son Ezekia, who lived in Rome, and Alessandro Rossi and Abram De La Vida from Ferrara, had been given the privilege to make uniforms and to rent beds for the soldiers of the Ferrara guard. The aforementioned were also exempt from the obligation to wear distinctive clothing identifying them as Jews, and were given permission to travel throughout the papal state. The present document orders all public officials, wherever they may be in the papal state, including Bologna, Ferrara and Urbino, not to interfere with their business or travel, or risk sanction of a fine of 1,000 scudi, plus jail and other bodily penalties, "especially because they are not wearing black hats with the usual sign," which Jews are ordinarily obligated to wear at all times wherever they go at home and outside, and because they are carrying weapons which are allowed to them because they hold official positions.

This is one of many known lavishly decorated examples of privileges issued to the Ambron family, the earliest dated 1687.[1] It was customary in Italy to decorate private documents, and Italian Jews frequently commissioned the decoration of religious certificates, most frequently marriage contracts, and of secular documents such as university diplomas and priviliges.

Hezekia Ambron is known to have donated Torah finials to Rome's Catalan Synagogue ca. 1767.[2] He is probably identical with Ezekia son of Gabriel specified in this privilege. *(See illustration on p. 364)*

(See illustration on p. 364)

1. NYJM, *Gardens*, cat. no. 106.
2. NYJM, *Gardens*, cat. no. 196.

607

607 SAMPLER*

Livorno, 1827. Artist: Esther Sahadun. Cotton: embroidered with silk thread. 13 x 9½ in. Collection of the Judah L. Magnes Museum, Berkeley, California, 75.183.307.

In addition to the Latin alphabet, the young artist included in her embroidery charming figures, animals, flowers and ships. Usually, Italian samplers have cut, unhemmed edges, and a characteristic form of cross stitch that forms a pattern of double parallel lines on the reverse. The fine stitches on this sampler are indicative of the high quality of workmanship mastered by Sephardic women in Italy. Young girls worked samplers to practice stitches they would require for household sewing, including mending and creating decorative pieces.

608 MINIATURE CUP

Thuringia (Central Germany), ca. 1880. Maker: Meissen (?). Porcelain; overglaze decoration. H: 1½ in. Hebrew inscription: May you merit many years. Collection of Prof. and Mrs. Solomon Feffer, New York.

The handpainted inscription on this cup is a common Sephardic expression used as a greeting on Rosh Hashanah. This cup may have been used to celebrate the New Year. However, its small size and the inscription suggest that it was probably presented as a gift for a newborn child. Since it was crafted in Germany, it may have been used in the large Sephardic communities of Hamburg and Altona.

609 ROSE WATER SPRINKLER

Italy, late 19th century. Silver: cast, engraved. Hebrew inscription: Cant. 1:13–14, 2:16, 4:10. 9½ x 3¼ in. Collection of Selma and Stanley I. Batkin, J.152.

610 DECANTER AND GOBLET WITH BELILIOS FAMILY COAT OF ARMS

London, early 20th century. Glass: engraved. 11⅞ x 4¼ in. diam.; 4¾ x 2¼ in. diam. Einhorn Collection, Tel Aviv.

Permission to use a coat of arms was granted by Queen Victoria to Emanuel Raphael Belilios in 1901. Belilios came to London from Calcutta, India, where his father had gone from Venice. This family was apparently a branch of the family of Rabbi Daniel Belilios, a known writer and poet in Amsterdam during the second half of the 17th century and the son-in-law of Rabbi Isaac Aboab da Fonseca. The coat of arms includes the menorah supported by two rampant lions.

611

NUMISMATICS

611 PORTRAIT OF GRACIA NASI THE YOUNGER*

Ferrara, 1558. Artist: Pastorino di Giovan Michele de'Pastorini (ca. 1508–1592). Bronze, cast. Hebrew inscription: Gracia Nasi; Latin inscription: [In her] Eighteenth Year. D: 2½ in. Collection of Manfred Anson, Bergenfield, New Jersey.

Gracia Nasi was the name taken on her return to Judaism by Beatrice de Luna (ca. 1510–1569), who fled Portugal with her family following the death of her Marrano husband, Francisco Mendes, eventually settling in Venice in 1546. Gracia the Younger, the subject of this portrait, was the daughter of Gracia Nasi's sister Brianda. She married her cousin Joseph Nasi (formerly Joao Micas/Miques/Miguez) in 1554. They settled in Istanbul, where Joseph was given the title of Duke of Naxos by Sultan Selim II in 1566.

REFERENCES: NYJM, *Tale,* cat. no. 144; NYJM, *Gardens,* cat. no. 169; Friedenberg, *Medals,* pp. 44–46, 128; Roth, *Doña Gracia.*

612 MEDAL COMMEMORATING THE BIRTH OF A SON

Amsterdam, 1665. Gold: cast, chased and soldered. Hebrew inscriptions: Obverse—Born on the 5th day of Tammuz in the year "And the Lord said, Rise and anoint him, for this is the one." (I Sam. 16:12) [Chronogram = (5)425); Reverse— "David whirled with all his might before the Lord; David was girt with a linen ephod." (II Sam. 6:14). 3⅛ in. diam. Collection of the Israel Museum, Jerusalem, gift of Mr. Moshe Oved.

The Biblical verse on the obverse refers to the future King David. At the center Samuel is depicted holding a horn and anointing David. On the floor, beside the kneeling David, there is a harp and a rod or cane. A group of his followers and warriors are watching the ceremony. In the background are buildings and pillars, a chair partly covered by a curtain decorated with an embroidered design of a warrior and a running lion(?).

On the reverse David is shown playing the harp and dancing before the Ark, which is carried by four priests. Behind him are other kohanim blowing shofarot. Above, David's wife Michal, the daughter of Saul, looks out from the palace window. In the background are towers and buildings. Since the scenes represented on the obverse and the reverse of the medal depict David, it appears that the medal celebrates the birth of a boy who was given the name David. *(figs. 81–82)*

REFERENCES: *Catalogue of Anglo-Jewish Historical Exhibition,* London, 1887, no. 2619; Friedenberg, *Medals,* pp. 65–67, 136.

613 HALF PENNY WITH PORTRAIT OF DANIEL MENDOZA

England, 1790. Copper: cast. English inscriptions: obverse—D. Mendoza; Reverse—Fashionable Amusement. 1⅛ in. diam. Collection of Manfred Anson, Bergenfield, New Jersey.

Daniel Mendoza (1764–1836), the middleweight English boxer who became the favorite of the then Prince of Wales, formulated ways to fight heavier opponents, opened his own boxing academy, and toured the British Isles giving exhibition matches. He proudly billed himself as "Mendoza the Jew." Author of *The Art of Boxing* (London, 1789) and *Memoirs of the Life of Daniel Mendoza* (London,

1816), Mendoza was among the first elected to America's Boxing Hall of Fame in 1954.

REFERENCE: Friedenberg, *Medals*, pp. 133–34.

614 PORTRAIT OF DANIEL MENDOZA

England, 1790. Bronze: cast. 1⅛ in. diam. Collection of Manfred Anson, Bergenfield, New Jersey.

Boxing was a popular spectator sport, and the features of the preeminent boxers were reproduced in prints and on tokens and souvenirs such as pottery jugs (see cat. no. 613).

615 MEDAL COMMEMORATING THE RETURN OF SIR MOSES MONTEFIORE FROM EGYPT

England, 1841. Bronze: cast, gilt. 1¹¹/₁₆ in. diam. Collection of Manfred Anson, Bergenfield, New Jersey.

Among Montefiore's concerns during this trip was the accusation of ritual murder brought against the Jews of Damascus in 1840, commonly known as the "Damascus Affair." When Sir Moses Montefiore and his wife Judith began their trip, Syria was under Egyptian jurisdiction, but Turkey regained control of Syria and Eretz Israel, and the Montefiores went to Istanbul to meet with Sultan Abdülmecid I (1839–1861).

REFERENCE: S. W. Massil and R. Winston-Fox, *Sir Moses Montefiore 1784–1885*, Enfield, England, 1984.

616 MEDAL OF SIR MOSES AND LADY JUDITH MONTEFIORE

England, 1864. C. H. Weiner. Bronze: cast. 2⅝ in. diam. Collection of Manfred Anson, Bergenfield, New Jersey.

Judith Barent Cohen (1784–1862) married Moses Montefiore in 1812. A diarist like many women of her time, she has left a record of her visits to Eretz Israel in 1827 and 1838. She also was the author or co-author of the *Jewish Manual*, the first Anglo-Jewish cookbook, whose author is given as "A Lady" (1846).

617 LODGE MEDAL

England, 1958. Bronze; ribbon. English inscription: Lodge Montefiore. 1½ x 1¼ in. Collection of Manfred Anson, Bergenfield, New Jersey.

Following Montefiore's death in 1885, many Jewish institutions and organizations were named or renamed after him.

PRINTS

618 DOR. EPHRAIM BONUS, MEDICUS HEBRAEUS*

Amsterdam, 17th century. Artist: Jan Lievens (1607–1674). Engraver: Clement de Johghe. Etching. 18¼ x 22 in. Moldovan Family Collection, New York.

Ephraim Bueno (Bonus; d. 1665) was of Marrano descent. He studied medicine at Bordeaux (1642), was active as an author and editor of Spanish poetry, supported publishing, edited Yosef Caro's *Shulhan Arukh*, and helped found the Or Torah Academy (1656), which engaged not only in Torah studies but also in the study of literature.

Lievens brings the sitter to the foreground, emphasizing his rich, elegant attire which somewhat detracts from his features, in the manner of contemporary portraitists including Van Dyck.

REFERENCES: Landsberger, p. 49; Rubens, *Iconography*, 1981, no. 152; Morgenstein and Levine, p. 33.

619 DOCTISSIMO Y CLARISSIMO SENOR H. H. REBY YAHACOB SAPORTAS RABINO DEL K. K. DE AMSTERDAM*

Amsterdam, 17th–early 18th century. Artist: Pieter van Gunst (1659–ca. 1724). Engraving. 13⅛ x 9⅜ in. Moldovan Family Collection, New York.

R. Yaakov Sasportas (ca. 1610–1698) was a fierce opponent of the Sabbatean movement (followers of the pseudo-Messiah Shabbetai Zevi). Born in North Africa, Sasportas was appointed rabbi of Tlemçen, Algeria. After his dismissal by the government in 1647, he

619

traveled through Europe. His lifelong ambition—to be appointed rabbi of Amsterdam—was realized in 1693 when he was 83 years of age. Sasportas' son Abraham published his responsa collection, *Ohel Yaakov*, in Amsterdam (1737).

The engraver, Pieter Stevens van Gunst, frequently engraved portraits after paintings by Van Dyck.

REFERENCES: Rubens, *Iconography*, 1981, no. 2212; Morgenstein and Levine, fig. 34.

620 MENASSEH BEN ISRAEL*

Amsterdam, 1636. Attributed to Rembrandt van Rijn (1606–1669). Etching. 4⅛ x 4 in. Einhorn Collection, Tel Aviv.

A fine, delicate etching showing the artist's mastery of the engraving medium. Although it is not inscribed, the portrait is believed to be that of Menasseh ben Israel, executed by Rem-

brandt. Menasseh lived near Rembrandt in Amsterdam's *Breestraat*. In 1655, Rembrandt illustrated Menasseh ben Israel's *Piedra Gloriosa*.

If this is indeed a portrait of Menasseh ben Israel, it was not his favorite, for he chose the Salom d'Italia portrait of himself as frontispiece for his publication of *Hope of Israel* in 1650.

REFERENCES: Morgenstein and Levine, p. 33; Wischnitzer, "Menasseh Ben Israel," pp. 125–29.

621 JACOB YEHUDAE LEONIS HEBRAEI*

Amsterdam, 1641. Artist: Salom d'Italia (1619–ca. 1655). Engraving. Moldovan Family Collection, New York.

Born to a Marrano family, Yaakov Yehudah (Aryeh) Leon (1603–1675) served as Haham at Middleburgh, Holland. There he published

his work on the Temple, *Retrato del Templo de Selomoh* (1642), from which he derived his nickname Templo (see also cat. no. 587). He later taught in Amsterdam's Ets Haim Seminary and worked at Menasseh ben Israel's press on the 1646 edition of the Mishnah. In 1643, Templo presented Queen Henrietta Maria of England with models of the Temple and Tabernacle he had constructed in connection with his learned treatises.

Salom d'Italia is best known for his engravings decorating megillot (cat. no. 558) and marriage certificates; he produced engravings for Templo's books as well. Born in Mantua, Italia is first heard of in Amsterdam in 1641.

REFERENCES: Gans, *Memorbook*, p. 37; Rubens, *Iconography*, 1981, no. 1733; M. Narkiss, "Salom Italia."

622 DER JOODEN TEMPEL OF SINAGOGE*

Amsterdam, 1664. Artist: I. Veenhuijsen. Tobias Domselaar, *Beschrijving van Amsterdam*, 1664, pl. 25. Engraving. Imprint: 4½ x 5⅜ in. Moldovan Family Collection, New York.

This print shows the interior of an early Sephardic synagogue in Amsterdam. This print was an illustration in one of the many popular historical/topographical descriptions of Amsterdam.

REFERENCES: Rubens, *Iconography*, 1981, no. 1582; Gans, *Memorbook*, p. 47; Morgenstein and Levine, p. 30, fig. no. 4.

623 BEGRAEF-PLAETS DER JODEN, BUYTEN AMSTELDAM
(Burial Ground of the Jews near Amsterdam)

Amsterdam, 1670. Artist: Jacob van Ruisdael (1628/29–1682). Engraver: Abraham Blotelingh. Engraving. 7½ x 11 in. Moldovan Family Collection, New York.

Jacob van Ruisdael was a nature painter; his best-known works on a Jewish subject are his paintings (Detroit Institute of Art and Dresden State Picture Gallery) of the Oudekerk cemetery, the burial place of Amsterdam's Sephardic community.

REFERENCE: Rubens, *Iconography*, 1981, no. 1577.

624 BEGRAEF-PLAETS DER JODEN, BUYTEN AMSTELDAM
(Burial Ground of the Jews near Amsterdam)*

622

624

Amsterdam, 1670. Artist: Jacob van Ruisdael (1628/9–1682). Engraver: Abraham Blotelingh (1640–1690). Engraving. 7½ x 11 in. Moldovan Family Collection.

Oudekerk cemetery, the burial place of Amsterdam's Sephardic community, contains elaborate, carved tombstones in the Italianate style. Located on the Amstel River, several miles from Amsterdam, the cemetery was reached by barge. Neither this nor the other etching of the same subject by Jacob van Ruisdael (see cat. no. 623) is exactly the same as his

haunting painting, now in Detroit and Dresden, of the cemetery.

REFERENCES: Rubens, *Iconography*, 1981, no. 1576; Morgenstein and Levine, p. 29, fig. no. 19.

625 CÉRÉMONIE NUPTIALE DES JUIFS PORTUGAIS

(Wedding Ceremony of the Portuguese Jews)*

Amsterdam, 1723. Artist: Bernard Picart (1673–1733). Cérémonies et coutumes religieuses de tous les peuples du monde, Vol. I. Colored etching. 5½ x 8 in. Private collection.

In the tradition of Dutch genre interior scenes and earlier illustrated anthologies of Jewish customs, Bernard Picart created a series of depictions of Jewish ceremonies (see cat. nos. 625–630 and 632–638). This series was very popular, and was published in several editions.

This may be the oldest picture in which a Sephardic bride is shown wearing a veil, a custom that may stem from the story of Rebecca modestly covering her face at her first meeting with Isaac (Gen. 24:65). The bride sits on a canopied dais between her mother and mother-in-law while the groom stamps

625

626

on a glass placed on a silver tray (rather than breaking it against a wall or a *traustein* as did some Ashkenazim). Although the practice of breaking a glass was not known among medieval Sephardim, it had become customary in Holland and England by the 18th century.

REFERENCES: Gans, *Memorbook*, p. 154; J. Gutmann, *The Jewish Life Cycle*, Leiden, 1987, p. 17; Rubens, *Iconography*, 1981, pp. xii–xvi, no. 454.

626 LA CIRCONCISION DES JUIFS PORTUGAIS

(Circumcision of the Portuguese Jews)*

Amsterdam, 1723. Artist: Bernard Picart (1673–1733). Cérémonies et coutumes religieuses de tous les peuples du monde, Vol. I. Colored etching. 5⅝ x 7⅞ in. *Private collection.*

The inset at right, resembling a painting hanging on the wall, may represent the mother of the child since women did not attend the ceremony. The scene resembles contemporary paintings depicting a lady of fashion receiving visitors from her bed. The woman wearing a cross is presumably a curious gentile servant.

Circumcision is performed on the eighth day after the birth of a male child in accordance with Gen. 17:11–13.

REFERENCES: Gans, *Memorbook*, p. 156; Rubens, *Iconography*, 1981, no. 452.

627 ROSH HASHANAH

Amsterdam, 1723. Artist: Bernard Picart (1673–1733). Cérémonies et coutumes religieuses de tous les peuples du monde. Vol. I. Colored etching. Private collection.

The Chief Rabbi, Haham Shlomo ben Yaakov Ayllon (see cat. no. 631), stands at the bench before the railing.

REFERENCES: Gans, *Memorbook*, p. 149; Rubens, *Iconography*, 1981, no. 443.

628 SIMHAT TORAH*

Amsterdam, 1723. Artist: Bernard Picart (1673–1733). Cérémonies et coutumes religieuses de tous les peuples du monde. Vol. I. Colored etching. Private collection.

REFERENCES: Gans, *Memorbook*, p. 152; Rubens, *Iconography*, 1981, no. 449.

629 DURING THE PRIESTLY BLESSING*

Amsterdam, 1723. Artist: Bernard Picart (1673–1733). Cérémonies et coutumes religieuses de tous les peuples du monde. Vol. I. Colored etching. Private collection.

The Ark and railing depicted were donated to the Portuguese Synagogue by Don Antonio (Isaac) Lopes Suasso of The Hague, Baron of Avernas de Gras in Brabant, and treasurer of *Honen Dal* (Support of the Poor), the official Portuguese congregation founded in 1709 in

628

The Hague. The Sephardim of The Hague paid to have the stone bridges across the canal surrounding The Hague demolished, and wooden drawbridges constructed instead, so that the city could be a closed city within which, according to Jewish law, it was permissible to carry objects outdoors on the Sabbath. This alteration is noted in a responsum of R. Yaakov Sasportas (see cat. no. 619).

The silver basin depicted in this scene was used to catch the water poured over the hands of the Kohanim (priests). For a similar basin see cat. no. 542.

REFERENCES: Gans, *Memorbook*, p. 232; Rubens, *Iconography*, 1981, no. 441.

630   SUKKOT

Amsterdam, 1723. Artist: Bernard Picart (1673–1733). Cérémonies et coutumes religieuses de tous les peuples du monde. Vol. I. Colored etching. Private Collection.

REFERENCES: Gans, *Memorbook*, p. 151; Rubens, *Iconography*, 1981, no. 447.

631   DOCTISSIMUS PERITISSI-MUSQUE THEOLOGUS D. D. SALOMON AELYON MAXIMUS AMSTAELODAMENSIS RABINUS

Amsterdam, 1728. Artist: J. Houbraken. Engraving. 14 x 9 in. Moldovan Family Collection, New York.

Despite his early Sabbatean leanings, R. Shlomo ben Yaakov Ayllon (1664–1728), a native of Salonika, was appointed rabbi of the Portuguese community in Amsterdam in 1700, holding that position until his death.

REFERENCES: Gans, *Memorbook*, p. 148; Rubens, *Iconography*, no. 96.

632   LE RACHAT DU PREMIER NÉ (Redemption of the First-born)

London(?), 1733(?). Artist: Bernard Picart (1673–1733). The Ceremonies and Religious Customs of the Various Nations of the Known World, Vol. I. Colored etching. 5¾ x 8 in. Private collection.

This depiction of the ceremony shows that Jews imitated many of the social habits of their gentile neighbors. The redemption of the first-born (*pidyon ha-ben*) is based on the Biblical injunction (Ex. 13:11–16) that every firstborn male belongs to the Lord and must therefore be "redeemed." The redemption consists in the payment of five shekels, or its equivalent in local currency, to a kohen (descendant of Aaron the high priest) 30 days after the baby's birth.

Here, an African page, a popular servant in many 18th-century homes in England and Holland, holds a plate on which rests the money to be used for the "redemption" of the first-born son. The close relationship between Sephardic Jewish masters and their servants was evident from the fact that when the latter died they were taken by canal to be buried next to the Oudekerk cemetery, the burial ground of the Sephardim. This plate reverses the original Picart plate, and is from a later edition.

REFERENCES: Gans, *Memorbook*, p. 158; Rubens, *Iconography*, 1981, no. 453.

633 THE SPOUSES OF THE LAW BEING CONDUCTED HOME/MANIERE DE CONDUIRE LES EPOUX DE LA LOY CHEZ EUX

London(?), 1733(?). Artist: Bernard Picart (1673–1733). The Ceremonies and Religious Customs of the Various Nations of the Known World, Vol. I. Colored etching. 5¾ x 7⅞ in. Private collection.

This vivid night scene shows the readers of the last and first portions of the Torah, the *Hatan Torah* and the *Hatan Bereshit* ("Bridegroom of the Torah" and "Bridegroom of Genesis" respectively) being escorted home from the synagogue on *Simhat Torah*, the holiday on which the Torah scroll readings are completed with the closing verses of Deuteronomy and

immediately begun again with the opening verses of Genesis. The men given these honors were expected to give sweets to the children in the congregation, and to give a reception for the entire congregation. The original scene is reversed here.

REFERENCES: Gans, *Memorbook*, p. 152; Rubens, *Iconography*, 1981, no. 450.

634 MANIERE D'EXPOSER LA LOY AU PEUPLE AVANT QUE DE COMMENCE À LA LIRE

(The Manner of Showing the Law [Torah] to the Congregation before Beginning to Read from It)

London(?), 1733(?). Artist: Bernard Picart (1673–1733). The Ceremonies and Religious Customs of the Various Nations of the Known World, Vol. I. Colored etching. 5¾ x 7⅞ in. Private collection.

The interior of the Portuguese Synagogue at The Hague. This plate reverses the format of Picart's original publication, and is from a later edition.

REFERENCE: Rubens, *Iconography*, 1981, no. 442.

637

638

635 SEARCH FOR LEAVEN/ L'EXAMEN DU LEVAIN

London, 1733. Artist: Bernard Picart (1673–1733). The Ceremonies and Religious Customs of the Various Nations of the Known World, Vol. I. Colored etching. 5¾ x 7¾ in. Private collection.

There must be no *hametz* (leaven) in a Jewish home during Passover (Ex. 12:15). The caption, in English and French, describes the ritual *bedikat hametz*: after the home has been completely cleaned of leaven, the mistress of the house places several symbolic crumbs of bread into each room of the house on the night before Passover (on the 13th day of Nisan, unless the 13th is Friday, in which case she does it on the 12th day of Nisan). The master of the house must then search for these crumbs and gather them up to demonstrate that the house is now indeed clean of leaven. They will be burned the following day. This later edition reverses Picart's plate.

REFERENCE: Rubens, *Iconography*, 1981, no. 445.

636 JEWISH ENTERTAINMENT DURING THE FEAST OF TABERNACLES/REPAS DES JUIFS PENDANT LA FÊTE DES TENTES

London, 1733. Artist: Bernard Picart (1673–1733). Engraver: C. du Bosc. The Ceremonies and Religious Customs of the Various Nations of the Known World, Vol. I. Colored etching. Private collection.

The scene in the foreground shows a well-to-do Jewish family eating in the sukkah (booth) in compliance with the Biblical injunction to dwell in booths for seven days (Lev. 23:42) during the festival of Sukkot to recall the sojourn of the Children of Israel in booths as they traveled through the wilderness on their way to the Promised Land.

Claude du Bosc re-engraved Picart's 1723 engraving for the second English edition of *The Ceremonies and Religious Customs of the Various Nations of the Known World* (London, 1733). His engravings show the Picart scenes in reverse.

REFERENCE: Rubens, *Iconography*, 1981, no. 448.

637 PASSOVER OF THE PORTUGUESE JEWS/LE REPAS DE PÂQUES CHEZ LES JUIFS PORTUGAIS*

London, 1733. Artist: Bernard Picart (1673–1733). Engraver: C. Du Bosc. The Ceremonies and Religious Customs of the Various Nations of the Known World, Vol. I. Colored etching. 5¾ x 7⅞ in. Private collection.

A Passover seder celebrated in a fashionable Dutch Jewish home in the early 18th century. Picart (the hatless man before the fire) himself participates, as he did while studying Jewish customs for his plates. Du Bosc reversed this and the other Picart scenes he engraved for this edition.

REFERENCE: Rubens, *Iconography*, 1981, p. xvi, no. 446.

638 THE ASSISTANTS CASTING EARTH ON THE BODY/LES ASSISTANTS JETTANT DE LA TERRE SUR LE CORPS*

London, 1733. Artist: Bernard Picart (1673–1733). Engraver: C. Du Bosc. The Ceremonies and Religious Customs of the Various Nations of the Known World, Vol. I. Colored etching. Private collection.

Jewish tradition requires the mourners to remain during this poignant part of the funeral, thus bringing home the separation caused by death.

REFERENCE: Rubens, *Iconography*, 1981, no. 457.

639 MOSES GOMEZ DE MESQUITA

London, 1751. Artist: S. Da Silva. Engraver: J. Faber. Engraving. Einhorn Collection, Tel Aviv.

Rabbi Moses Gomez de Mesquita (1688–1751) was the *Haham* of London's Spanish and Portuguese community from 1744 until his death.

REFERENCE: Rubens, *Iconography*, 1981, no. 1871.

640

640 GEZICHT VAN DE POR-TUGEESCHE JOODEN-KERK, VAN DE BREESTRAAT TE ZIEN, TOT AMSTERDAM/VUE DE LA SYNAGOGUE DES JUIFS PORTUGAIS, A AMSTERDAM

(View of the Synagogue of the Portuguese Jews on Breestraat in Amsterdam)*

Amsterdam, 1764–71. Artist: P. Fouqet junior. Afbeeldingen van de Wyd-Vermaarde Koopstad Amsterdam. Colored etching. 19¹⁵⁄₁₆ x 22⅛ in. Collection of Derek Content, Houlton, Maine.

This bright scene brings to life the locale of the Amsterdam Portuguese Synagogue in the late 18th century.

REFERENCE: Rubens, *Iconography*, 1981, no. 1592.

641 REVD. DR. RAPHAEL MELDOLA, CHIEF RABBI OF LONDON

England, 19th century. Artist: E. B. Barlin. Engraver: J. C. Anderson. 5⅜ x 3¾ in. Engraving. Collection of the Sephardic Studies Department, Yeshiva University, New York.

A native of Livorno, Italy, Raphael Meldola (1754–1828) was appointed Haham of the Spanish and Portuguese Jews of Great Britain in 1804/5 after the office had been vacant since 1784. Meldola was responsible for various educational reforms. His writings include *Huppat Hatanim* (1797), a handbook on marriage, and sermons and poems (see also cat.

no. 597). He was the great-grandfather of Rabbi Henry Pereira Mendes (1852–1937), rabbi and *hazzan* of New York's Spanish and Portuguese congregation Shearith Israel from 1877 to 1923 and a leader of Orthodox Judaism in the United States.

642 REVD. DR. M. EDREHI*

London, 1836. Engraver: J. C. Hunter. Copperplate engraving. Einhorn Collection, Tel Aviv.

Rabbi Moshe ben Yitzhak Edrehi (ca. 1774–1842) was a Moroccan itinerant preacher. He studied, lectured and wrote in London and Amsterdam, finally settling in Eretz Israel. Edrehi wrote many books, including a collection of tales of the Ten Tribes which was published in English during his lifetime (1834).

REFERENCE: Rubens, *Iconography*, 1981, no. 754.

643 GRACE AGUILAR

London, mid 19th century. Engraver: J. Cochran. Engraving. 8 x 5½ in. Einhorn Collection, Tel Aviv.

Descendant of a Portuguese Marrano family, Grace Aguilar (1816–1847), who lived in England, was a prolific author but did not live to see most of her books published. The novel which made her famous, set in medieval Scotland, *The Days of Bruce*, and her best-known Jewish novel, *The Vale of Cedars*, were published in 1852 and 1850, respectively.

She wrote about the significance of women's role in Judaism and the family, and defended Judaism against Christian missionaries. Her works were important in America at a time when many Jews lacked a traditional Jewish upbringing. The 1842 edition of her *Spirit of Judaism* had notes by Isaac Leeser (1806–1868; see cat. no. 655), rabbi and pioneer of traditional Judaism in the United States.

REFERENCES: Rubens, *Iconography*, 1981, no. 35; D. Ashton, "Grace Aguilar's Popular Theology and the Female Response to Evangelists," *Jewish Folklore and Ethnology Review*, 12, 1990, p. 22; P. Weinberger, *The Social and Religious Thought of Grace Aguilar*, unpub. PhD diss., New York University, 1970.

644 SIR MOSES MONTEFIORE, BART.*

February 18, 1865. Illustrated London News, p. 153. Page: 18¹¹/₁₆ x 10¾ in.; Image: 6¾ x 5⅞ in. Moldovan Family Collection, New York.

This portrait of Sir Moses Montefiore (1784–1885; see also cat. nos. 311, 600–603, 615–617 and 646) was done from a photograph by J. S. Twyman of Ramsgate. The article, in which Montefiore is described as a merchant, philanthropist and leader of the Jewish community, was published to commemorate the vote of thanks awarded Montefiore at the meeting of the Common Council at the Guildhall of London on October 6, 1864, for Montefiore's ". . . missions to various countries in relief of communities oppressed for religious convictions . . ." both Jewish and Christian. At least from his first visit to Eretz Israel until the end of his life, Montefiore was a strictly observant Jew.

645 LE SERMON DE DAÏAN CARDOZO: SYNAGOGUE D'AMSTERDAM*

Paris, 1867. Artist: H. Brandon. Engraver: Philippe Fortune Durand (1798–1876). Printer: A. Salmon. Gazette des Beaux-Arts, Vol. 23, Bk. 2, Aug. 1867, pp. 100–1. 5¼ x 11⅞ in. Moldovan Family Collection, New York.

David de Jahacob (ben Jacob) Cardozo (see cat. no. 648) delivers an address in the Amster-

642

THE ILLUSTRATED LONDON NEWS ...

SIR MOSES MONTEFIORE, BART.

644

LE SERMON DE DAIAN CARDOZO
Synagogue d'Amsterdam

645

dam Synagogue on July 22, 1866. He had been made a *dayan* (rabbinical judge) in the absence of a chief rabbi for the Portuguese community. H. Brandon was also Sephardic.

This engraving is found in the middle of an article on the 15th-century French painter Jean Fouquet, to which it bears no relation. Several other engravings in this volume of the French art periodical are similary unrelated to the text; they were presumably included for their ethnographic or artistic interest.

REFERENCES: Gans, *Memorbook*, p. 363; Rubens, *Iconography*, 1981, no. 1603.

646 SERVICE AT THE JEWISH SYNAGOGUE, BEVIS MARKS, TO COMMEMORATE THE ONE HUNDREDTH YEAR OF SIR MOSES MONTEFIORE

England, 1884. Engraving. Image: 13⅞ x 18⅞ in. Moldovan Family Collection, New York.

The 100th birthday of the great philanthropist, Sir Moses Montefiore (1784–1885; see also cat. nos. 311, 600–603, 615–617 and 644), was celebrated by Jewish communities the world over.

PHOTOGRAPHS

647 PORTRAIT OF BENJAMIN DISRAELI

England, mid 19th century. Black and white photograph. 3¹⁵⁄₁₆ x 2⅜ in. Collection of Manfred Anson, Bergenfield, New Jersey.

Benjamin Disraeli (1804–1881; see also cat. no. 604), British author and statesman, came from a Sephardic family but was converted to Christianity in adolescence. His political life began in 1837 with his election to the British Parliament, and in 1868 he became Prime Minister, holding that office again from 1874 to 1880. Queen Victoria made him Earl of Beaconsfield in 1876 following her proclamation as Empress of India, which he made possible.

During a trip to the Middle East (1828–1831), Disraeli conceived an admiration for the Ottoman empire, in which Jews were treated with tolerance. Many of his books have Jewish heroes (e.g. *Alroy*) or themes, or plead for the recognition of Jewish contributions to British law and society and to Christianity.

648

649

648 R. DAVID DE JAHACOB (BEN JACOB) LOPES CARDOZO*

Amsterdam, ca. 1880. Black and white photograph. 4 x 2½ in. Collection of Rev. and Mrs. Abraham Lopes Cardozo, New York.

Haham David Lopes Cardozo (1808–1890; see also cat. nos. 649 and 722), a native of Amsterdam, was the last spiritual leader of Amsterdam's Portuguese community to preach in Portuguese. He is the Cardozo represented in the print, *The Sermon of Daïan Cardozo* (cat. no. 645).

649 CLARA ISRAEL RICARDO*

Amsterdam, ca. 1880. Black and white photograph. 4 x 2½ in. Collection of Rev. and Mrs. Abraham Lopes Cardozo, New York.

Clara Israel Ricardo (1811–1893) was the wife of Haham David Lopes Cardozo (see cat. nos. 645, 648 and 722). The Ricardo family probably migrated from Italy to Amsterdam at the beginning of the 18th century.

650 JACOB LOPES CARDOZO

Amsterdam, late 19th century. Black and white photograph. Collection of Rev. and Mrs. Abraham Lopes Cardozo, New York.

Ambron Family Privilege, Rome, October 30, 1756. Cat. no. 606.

THE NEW WORLD

"your sect by it's sufferings has furnished a remarkable proof of the universal spirit of religious intolerance . . . our laws have applied the only antidote to this vice, protecting our religious, as they do our civil rights by putting all on an equal footing. but more remains to be done. for altho' we are free by the law, we are not so in practice. public opinion erects itself into an Inquisition, and exercises it's office with as much fanaticism as fans the flames of an Auto da fé."

THOMAS JEFFERSON (1743–1826) to
Mordecai-Manuel Noah (1785–1851),
May 28, 1818

THE NEW WORLD

SYNAGOGUE AND COMMUNITY

651 TOURO SYNAGOGUE MODEL*

Newport, Rhode Island, ca. 1763. Architect: Peter Harrison. 22 x 37 x 44 in. Collection of Yeshiva University Museum, New York, endowed by Erica and Ludwig Jesselson, 89.90.

The Touro synagogue has the unique distinction of being the oldest existing synagogue in the United States and one of this country's outstanding examples of religious architecture. Commissioned by Jeshuat Israel, a Sephardic congregation which dates back to the 17th century, it bears the name of the group's renowned benefactor, Rabbi Isaac Touro and his family.

Peter Harrison, the eminent American architect, offered to design the building. He created a truly noteworthy Georgian colonial exterior and a neoclassical white interior whose symmetry, refinement of detail and delicate proportions have continued to merit acclaim. The exquisitely classical motifs of the Ark and the delicate balustrades of the *bimah* remain outstanding testaments to Harrison's talent.

Harrison's building carefully acknowledged its Sephardic legacy. The original seating plan called only for wainscotted benches along the interior walls of the main hall and an upstairs gallery for women congregants. Twelve Ionic columns representing the Twelve Tribes of Israel were designed to support the upper women's gallery. On the upper level twelve Corinthian columns supported the domed ceiling.

Beneath the *bimah* is a trap door which according to legend led to a hiding place used by runaway slaves. This is a plausible explanation, since the Touro Synagogue also occupied a unique place in American history. Between 1781 and 1784 it served as a meeting place for the General Assembly and the Supreme Court of Rhode Island. In 1781 George Washington attended a town meeting there. His now famous statement on religious tolerance: "The Government of the United States gives to bigotry no sanction, to persecution no assistance . . ." was addressed to the Touro congregation.

In 1946 the United States Department of the Interior designated the Touro synagogue a Historic Shrine, making it the first and only Jewish National Shrine in the United States. With the decline of Newport's commercial importance, many of the original members of the congregation left the city.

652 RIMMONIM (Torah finials)

New York, ca. 1772. Silversmith: Myer Myers (1723–1795). Marks: "Myers" script in shaped cartouche. Silver: cast, parcel-gilt. H: 13¼ in. Collection of Congregation K.K. Mikveh Israel, Philadelphia.

Some neoclassical influences, characteristic of 18th-century American silver, are evident in these *rimmonim* as well as in other work by Myers.

Myer Myers was a silversmith who served as president of the New York Gold and Silversmiths' Society in 1786. He was active in Jewish communal life and served three terms as president of Congregation Shearith Israel in New York, for whom he produced ceremonial pieces that are still used at congregational services. His work was popular with both Jews and non-Jews; he created tableware (see cat. no. 714) and other household objects for such prominent families as the Schuylers, and the Murrays of Murray Hill. Myers was one of seven children born in New York to parents who had emigrated from Holland. He is buried in the St. James Place–Chatham Square Cemetery in New York City. *(fig. 52)*

REFERENCES: Rosenbaum, *Myer Myers*, pl. 2; p. 66, no. 5; Schoenberger, "Myer Myers," pp. 1–9.

653   YAD (Torah pointer)

America, 18th century. Silver: cast. L: 13 in. Collection of Congregation K.K. Mikveh Israel, Philadelphia.

Gift from Congregation Shearith Israel in New York City, the oldest congregation in America (founded in 1654), to Congregation K.K. Mikveh Israel in Philadelphia, the second oldest (founded in 1740). In 1990, on the occasion of the 250th anniversary of the founding of Congregation Mikveh Israel, Congregation Shearith Israel of New York presented the former with a second *yad*.

REFERENCE: NMAJH, cat. no. 8.

654   CEREMONIAL EWER

England, early 19th century. Silver: cast; engraved. Hebrew inscription: K.K. Mikveh Israel, Philadelphia. H: 14 in. Collection of Congregation K.K. Mikveh Israel, Philadelphia.

This elegant ewer in the neoclassical style, decorated with satyr masks, is still in use.

655   CEREMONIAL EWER AND SALVER

Ewer: Philadelphia, 1851. Silver, repoussé, engraved. English inscription: The Revd. Isaac Leeser from his friends as a testimonial of his Zeal and Devotion in the cause of Judaism in America. Phila. Adar 5611. 17½ x 6½ in. Salver: America, 19th century. Silver, repoussé, engraved. C. Bart & Son. English inscription: To the Revd. Isaac Leeser from his friends as a TESTIMONIAL of his Zeal and Devotion in the cause of Judaism in America. Phil. Adar 5611. Collection of Congregation K.K. Mikveh Israel, Philadelphia.

Congregation K.K. Mikveh Israel of Philadelphia owns a set of two ewers and salvers bearing dedications to Isaac Leeser (1806–1868), *hazzan* of Congregation Mikveh Israel of Philadelphia from 1829 to 1850. Leeser was not a Sephardi but of German birth and originally came to the United States to enter business. An essay he wrote in defense of Judaism first attracted the attention of Congregation Mikveh Israel. A strong advocate of traditional Judaism, Leeser in 1838 published the first Hebrew primer for children, in 1843 founded a monthly, *The Occident*, and in 1848

published the first Sephardic prayer book with a complete English translation. In 1849 he founded the first Hebrew high school, and in 1867 Maimonides College, the first American rabbinical school. His major literary achievement was the first American translation of the Bible, which appeared in 1845.

REFERENCE: NMAJH, cat. no. 28.

656   REGISTER BOOK OF CONGREGATION SHEARITH ISRAEL

New York, 1759–1946. Ink on paper. 13 x 9 x 2 in. Collection of Congregation Shearith Israel in the City of New York, The Spanish and Portuguese Synagogue.

This register contains the records of all major events of the Shearith Israel community, such as births, marriages and deaths. Included in this register is an added list of events which occurred during the Revolutionary War, when fighting and political turmoil prevented the keeping of exact records.

657   CONTRACT FOR HAZZAN SEIXAS

New York, 1795. Ink on paper. 9½ x 15 in. Collection of Congregation Shearith Israel in the City of New York, The Spanish and Portuguese Synagogue.

Gershom Mendes Seixas served as the leader of the congregation throughout much of the 18th century (see also cat. nos. 683, 685–686, 688 and 713). Included in the provisions of this contract is the requirement that Seixas check the accuracy of the Torah scroll text each week before the Sabbath. The *hazzan* was rewarded for each error in the *parsha* found and repaired before the Sabbath, and was fined for every error found during services.

658   DIAGRAM FOR A SHOHET*

New York, early 19th century. Jacob da Silva Solis (1780–1829). Ink on paper. 13 x 14⅞ in. Hays Collection, Collection of the Westchester Historical Society, 1092.

As stated in the caption, "This Draft is to Give

a Faire Explanation of the Lights, as they are found in the Breast which makes them Cosher or Trafa." Written by Jacob da Silva Solis (1780–1829; for biographical information, see cat. no. 732) for his brother-in-law, Benjamin Etting Hays (1779–1858). Hays, whose family had emigrated from Holland to America in the early 18th century, was a farmer in what is now New York's Westchester County. He was an observant Jew, and was held in esteem by his Christian neighbors, who referred to him as "Uncle Ben, the best Christian in Westchester County". Hays was the great-grandfather of Arthur Hays Sulzberger (1891–1968), publisher of the *New York Times*.

This diagram shows how to position the knife in relation to the vertebrae. The term "lights" was used in early 19th-century America to denote the lungs of an animal eaten for food.

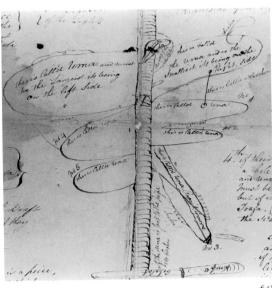

658

659 CERTIFICATE AUTHORIZING A SHOHET*

Mount Pleasant, New York, November 11, 1813. Jacob da Silva Solis (1780–1829). Ink on paper. 12⅞ x 7¾ in. Hays Collection, Collection of the Westchester Historical Society, 1091.

Certificate authorizing Benjamin Etting Hays (see cat. nos. 659 and 732–734) to function as a *shohet* (ritual slaughterer) "for Killing, and Sheaching of Beast and Fowls." Jacob Solis (see cat. nos. 659 and 732–734) attests that he has examined Benjamin Etting Hays (his brother-in-law) and "Finding that his Knowledge, of the (*Shacheta*) of the (*Cuts*) and the (*Badecan*) for the Searching According to the Denim of them, is so much to my Satisfaction, that, I do Give him Leave to Kill, and that all the (*House of Israel*,) may Eat of his Killing. . . ." Jacob da Silva Solis himself had been certified by Jacob Abrams, the *shohet* of Congregation Shearith Israel in New York City.

660 LETTER OF DONATION

New York, 1817. Ink on paper. 9½ x 7¾ in. Collection of Congregation Shearith Israel in the City of New York, The Spanish and Portuguese Synagogue.

In 1768, the first synagogue in Canada was founded in Montreal by former members of New York's Congregation Shearith Israel. This letter documents a donation to the New York congregation by members of the Montreal community.

661 LETTER OF DONATION

Curaçao, 1818. Ink on paper. 15¾ x 12¾ in. Collection of Congregation Shearith Israel in the City of New York, The Spanish and Portuguese Synagogue.

The Sephardic community of Curaçao was founded at the same time as the community in New Amsterdam, following the Portuguese reconquest of Brazil in 1654. At that time Jewish immigrants from The Netherlands left Brazil and settled in Dutch colonies in North and South America.

662 LETTER FROM THOMAS JEFFERSON TO MORDECAI MANUEL NOAH

Monticello, May 28, 1818. Ink on paper. 9¾ x 7¾ in. Collection of Yeshiva University Museum, New York, gift of Erica and Ludwig Jesselson, 86.59.

In the spring of 1818, several days before Passover, New York's first Jewish congregation, Shearith Israel (known as The Spanish and Portuguese Synagogue) consecrated a new synagogue building and invited Mordecai Manuel Noah (1785–1851) to be the guest speaker.

In keeping with his political alertness, Noah sent a copy of his consecration speech to Thomas Jefferson (1743–1826), who had retired from the Presidency nine years earlier.

Jefferson was so impressed with Noah's speech that he wrote him this remarkable letter. The letter discusses the importance of America's codification of religious freedom, and the dangers of anti-Jewish prejudice.

Noah, a native of Philadelphia, eventually entered United States politics, wrote plays and, in 1825, helped buy a tract of land on Grand Island in the Niagara River in Buffalo, New York, which he named Ararat and visualized as a Jewish colony. When this project failed, Noah became more interested in the idea of Eretz Israel as a national home for the Jews.

REFERENCE: YUM, *Noah*, pp. 26–27.

663   RABBINIC CONTRACT OF SABATO MORAIS

Philadelphia, 1851. Ink on parchment, wax seals. 12¼ x 15⅜ in. Collection of Congregation K.K. Mikveh Israel, Philadelphia.

Sabato Morais (1823–1897) was descended from a Portuguese family that settled in Livorno, Italy, after the Expulsion. He studied Hebrew with Rabbis Funaro, Cureat and Peperno, and in 1845 became the assistant *hazzan* at the Spanish and Portuguese Congregation in London.

In 1850, when Isaac Leeser (see cat. no. 655) left the pulpit of Congregation Mikveh Israel in Philadelphia, Morais was elected *hazzan*. A firm defender of traditional Judaism, he was one of the founders, in 1886, of the Jewish Theological Seminary of America in New York. He was also the first Jew to receive an honorary doctorate from the University of Pennsylvania.

REFERENCE: NMAJH, cat. no. 30.

664   LETTER AND ENVELOPE

Washington, DC, May 13, 1862. Abraham Lincoln (1809–1865). Ink on paper. 9¾ x 7¾ in. Collection of Congregation K.K. Mikveh Israel, Philadelphia.

President Lincoln wrote this letter of thanks on an unknown occasion to Abraham Hart, *Parnas* (President) of Congregation Mikveh Israel in Philadelphia. The congregation has a long history of correspondence with Presidents of the United States from George Washington to the present.

REFERENCE: NMAJH, cat. no. 35.

665   SCHEDULE OF YOM KIPPUR SERVICES

Philadelphia, 1877. Collection of the Sephardic Reference Room, Yeshiva University, New York.

This handwritten schedule lists the times for various components of the Yom Kippur services at Congregation Mikveh Israel, Philadelphia.

666   EXCERTS FROM BARBADOS NEWSPAPERS DESCRIBING THE CONSECRATION OF THE SYNAGOGUE

Barbados, 20th century. Ink on paper: printed. Collection of the Sephardic Reference Room, Yeshiva University, New York.

667   CLUB RIBBON

America, 1919. Metal; silk. English inscription: Alba Sephardic Club 1919. 7 x 2½ in. Collection of Manfred Anson, Bergenfield, New Jersey.

Ribbon worn by a member of a Sephardic society.

668   LA VARA SUBSCRIPTION CARD*

New York, ca. 1930. Ink on paper: printed. 3¼ x 5½ in. Collection of the Sephardic Reference Room, Yeshiva University, New York.

La Vara was the leading Ladino newspaper in 20th-century New York.

669 POSTER ADVERTISING A BALL

New York, 1933. Ink on cardboard: printed. 22 x 14 in. Collection of Yeshiva University Museum, New York, 91.97a.

This poster announces the second annual ball given by Congregation *Ahavat Ahim*, with music supplied by Peter and his Pennsylvanians, whose photograph is included on the poster. The price of admission was 75 cents.

670 NOTICE OF RELIGIOUS SERVICES*

Bronx, New York, 1937. Ink on cardboard: printed. 22 x 14 in. Collection of Yeshiva University Museum, New York, 91.97g.

Rosh Hashanah and Yom Kippur services were organized by Sha-Re Rahamim, Inc., Jewish Ladies Day Nursery of The Bronx. Admission was one dollar for men (*hombres*), 50 cents for women (*damas*).

671 FUNDRAISING POSTER*

New York, 1938. Ink on cardboard: printed. 22 x 14 in. Collection of Yeshiva University Museum, New York, 91.97f.

This poster advertises an entertainment and dance at the Audubon Ballrooms in Washington Heights. It was offered by the Ez Ahaim Society, and featured Joseph Bruno and his Orchestra, and Radio Headliners.

672 MOHEL DIPLOMA*

Amsterdam, 1939. Ink on paper: printed with handwritten additions. 9¼ x 12½ in. Collection of Rev. and Mrs. Abraham Lopes Cardozo, New York.

671

This diploma certifies that Rev. Abraham Lopes Cardozo was properly trained as a *mohel* (ritual circumciser). In 1939, he moved from Holland to Suriname. Many Dutch Jews early realized the danger posed by Nazi Germany, and moved to long established Sephardic communities in the New World, such as Suriname, where Dutch Jews had settled in the 17th century.

673 BICENTENNIAL CONGRATULATIONS

Hyde Park, New York, 1940. Franklin Delano Roosevelt (1882–1945). Typed, ink on paper, hand-signed. 10¼ x 8 in. Collection of Congregation K.K. Mikveh Israel, Philadelphia.

President Roosevelt congratulates Congregation Mikveh Israel on its 200th anniversary. He mentions the great history of the congregation since its founding 36 years prior to the signing of the Declaration of Independence, and its illustrious members (including Haym Solomon) and friends (including George Washington and Benjamin Franklin).

REFERENCE: NMAJH, cat. no. 56.

668

DIPLOMA · תעודה

672

674 MEMBERSHIP BOOK AND CALENDAR — EZ ACHAIM SOCIETY

New York, 1942/43. Ink on paper: printed. 6 x 4¼ in. Collection of the Sephardic Reference Room, Yeshiva University, New York.

675 MEMBERSHIP CARD IN UNITED DAUGHTERS OF THE CONFEDERACY

Savannah, 1953. Printed. 2⅛ x 3½ in. Collection of Mr. and Mrs. David Goldman, Fort Lee, New Jersey.

This is Mrs. I. H. Friedman's membership card in the United Daughters of the Confederacy, Savannah, Georgia. Mrs. Friedman, née Sara Solomon, was a descendant of Henry Solomon. Surviving correspondence indicates that Henry Solomon, like many of his fellow Southern Jews, was an ardent son of the Confederacy and deplored the toll the Civil War took on the land and its people.

REFERENCE: B. W. Korn, "The Jews of the Confederacy," American Jewish Archives, Vol. XIII, April, 1961, no. 1, pp. 3–90.

676 SET OF COMMEMORATIVE PLATES

New York, 1954. Porcelain: transfer printed and handpainted. Esther H. Oppenheim. 10 in. diam. (75.40–75.45); 13 in. diam. (75.46). Collection of Yeshiva University Museum, New York, gift of the artist, 75.40–46.

This set of seven plates was issued by the Sisterhood of the Congregation Shearith Israel, Spanish and Portuguese Synagogue in honor of the congregation's tercentenary (1654–1954):

The Mill Street Synagogue, home of the Spanish and Portuguese synagogue (1730–1817), was the first synagogue building erected in New York.

The second synagogue building of Shearith Israel was located on what is now 20–26 South

William Street. It was home to the congregation from 1818 to 1833. Mordecai Manuel Noah (1785–1851) spoke at the dedication in 1818 (see cat. no. 662).

56 Crosby Street was the third home of Congregation Shearith Israel. Mordecai Manuel Noah delivered the address at the dedication of the new building in 1834, even as he had been guest speaker at the consecration of the building on Mill Street in 1818.

The fourth home of Shearith Israel was located at 3 West 19th Street in New York City from 1860 to 1896.

The fifth and current home of Congregation Shearith Israel, on Central Park West and 70th Street, was dedicated in 1897 by the Rev. Dr. Henry Pereira Mendes (1852–1937; see cat. 641), descendant of one of the founders of the congregation.

The seal of Congregation Shearith Israel, adopted in 1797, represents the world resting on truth, righteousness and justice, with the motto, "I will take unto me faithful witnesses." (Is. 8:2).

The Touro Synagogue, Newport, Rhode Island, the oldest surviving synagogue building in the United States, was dedicated in 1763 and designated a national shrine in 1946 (see cat. no. 651).

677 COMMEMORATIVE PLATES, CONGREGATION SHEARITH ISRAEL

New York, 1954. Porcelain: transfer printed and handpainted. Esther H. Oppenheim. 10½ in. diam. Private collection.

These plates depict the Mill Street synagogue used by Congregation Shearith Israel from 1730 to 1817, and the current home of the congregation on Central Park West.

678 FIRST SYNAGOGUE IN AMERICA, MILL STREET 1730–1817

Jerusalem, 1975. Maker: Vida Corcos Simons (b. New York, 1928). Cotton: embroidered with silk. Collection of Vida and Fred Simons, Jerusalem.

Modeled after the plate by Esther Oppenheim (cat. no. 676).

679 SYNAGOGUE (1818– 1833)

Jerusalem, 1975. Maker: Vida Corcos Simons (b. New York, 1928). Cotton: embroidered with silk. Collection of Vida and Fred Simons, Jerusalem.

Modeled after the plate by Esther Oppenheim (cat. no. 676).

680 TOURO SYNAGOGUE FIRST DAY COVER

Newport, Rhode Island, 1982. Bernard Goldberg, no. 62/90. Ink and gouache on paper. 3⅝ x 6½ in. Collection of Manfred Anson, Bergenfield, New Jersey.

A special edition of the first day issue Touro Synagogue stamp in handpainted envelope.

681 DEPICTION OF THE TOURO SYNAGOGUE

America, 1987. Cotton: embroidered with cotton thread. 13⅛ x 19¼ in. Collection of Manfred Anson, Bergenfield, New Jersey.

FESTIVALS

682 SUKKOT PLATE AND FOOTED FRUIT DISH*

Philadelphia, 1910. Katherine Myrtilla Cohen (1859–1914). Earthenware: handpainted overglaze. Dish: Greenwood China, Trenton, New Jersey. 4¾ x 8½ in. Plate: Johnson Brothers, England. 9 in. diam. Hebrew inscription (both): Congregation K.K. Mikveh Israel Philadelphia 1910. Collection of Congregation K.K. Mikveh Israel, Philadelphia.

Artistic young ladies in the 19th and early 20th centuries frequently painted decorations on specially produced white china as personal gifts to friends or relatives. Katherine Cohen painted a set of plates and fruit dishes with *lulav* and *etrog*, and donated it to Congregation Mikveh Israel for the sukkah, where it is still used today.

REFERENCE: NMAJH, cat. no. 45.

682

683   HANUKKAH LAMP*

America, 18th century. Pewter: sheet and cast. 10⅝ x 9⁹⁄₁₆ x 2⅞ in. Collection of Abigail Kursheedt Hoffman.

Family tradition attributes ownership of this piece to Gershom Mendes Seixas (1746–1816; see also cat. nos. 657, 685–686 and 688), a *mohel* and *shohet*, who served as the first *hazzan* of Congregation Shearith Israel in New York from 1768. He and his family fled from New York City during the American Revolution. While in Philadelphia (1780–1784), Seixas was active in Congregation Mikveh Israel.

683

LIFE CYCLE

684   MOHEL SET

Amsterdam, ca. 1939. Stainless steel; glass; gauze. Collection of Rev. and Mrs. Abraham Lopes Cardozo, New York.

These implements were used by Abraham Lopes Cardozo to perform circumcisions in Amsterdam and in Suriname (see cat. no. 672).

685   KETUBBAH (Marriage contract)

Philadelphia, 1773. Ink on parchment. Collection of Yeshiva University Museum, New York, gift of the Sephardic Studies Department.

Groom: Yehiel son of Naftali Katz
Bride: Leah daughter of Yaakov
Yehiel and Leah were married in Philadelphia on the 29th day of Av, 5533 (1773). Their ketubbah was written by Rev. Gershom Mendes Seixas, the minister of Congregation Shearith Israel, New York (see cat. nos. 657, 683, 686 and 688). One of the witnesses was Mathias Bush, a Philadelphia merchant who joined the Revolutionaries and was one of those who signed the Non-Importation Act against Britain. Bush's son, Solomon (1753–1795), who fought in the Revolutionary War, was made a lieutenant colonel, the highest rank held by a Jew in the Revolutionary Army.

686   KETUBBAH (Marriage contract)

New York, 1789. Ink on parchment. 8 x 7⅛ in. Private collection.

Groom: Jacob Deleon
Bride: Hannah daughter of Uri
Gershom Mendes Seixas (see cat. nos. 657, 683, 685 and 688) acted as a witness to this marriage; his signature in Hebrew and English can be seen on the contract.

PRINTED BOOKS

687 EMET VE- EMUNAH— REASON AND FAITH, OR PHILOSOPHICAL ABSURDITIES AND THE NECESSITY OF REVELATION INTENDED TO PROMOTE FAITH AMONG INFIDELS

Philadelphia, 1791. Ink on paper: printed. Collection of the Sephardic Reference Room, Yeshiva University, New York.

688 A SERMON . . . ON THE OCCASION OF THE DEATH OF THE REV. GERSHOM MENDES SEIXAS

Philadelphia, July, 1816. Ink on paper: printed. Private collection.

See cat. nos. 657, 683, 685–686.

689 BY-LAWS OF SAAR SHAMAIM CONGREGATION

Kingston, Jamaica, 1833. Ink on paper: printed. Private collection.

A Sephardic community existed in Jamaica at the time of the British conquest in 1655.

690 SIDDUR SIFTEI TZADIKIM—THE FORM OF PRAYERS ACCORDING TO THE CUSTOM OF THE SPANISH AND PORTUGUESE JEWS, VOL. I, DAILY PRAYERS

Philadelphia, 1837. Ed. Isaac Leeser. Ink on paper: printed. Private collection.

See cat. no. 655.

691 THE CONSTANCY OF ISRAEL, A DISCOURSE

Charleston, South Carolina, 1850. Rev. M. J. Raphall. Collection of the Sephardic Reference Room, Yeshiva University, New York.

692 INCIDENTS OF TRAVEL AND ADVENTURE IN THE FAR WEST

New York, 1857. Solomon Nunes Carvalho (1815–1897). 7⁹/₁₆ x 5¼ in. Collection of Joan Sturhahn, Sarasota, Florida.

The first Jewish photographer in America, Carvalho (see also cat. no. 737) was also a pioneer of the daguerreotype in the field work he did with General John Charles Frémont. Carvalho served as official photographer of the 1853–1854 expedition led by General Frémont to survey a route for a transcontinental railway. This book is the only eyewitness account of the expedition, and may have been written during Frémont's campaign for nomination as the first Republican candidate for the presidency of the United States (1855–1856).

Only one of the daguerreotypes taken by Carvalho during the trip is known to survive; it is the earliest documented record showing a Native American village. Among the stories recounted by Carvalho in this book is a section on the Mormons, with whom Carvalho stayed while recuperating from the rigors of the trip across the Rockies. During this time Carvalho records painting two portraits of Brigham Young.

REFERENCES: S. N. Carvalho, *Incidents of Travel and Adventure in the Far West*, int. B. W. Korn, Philadelphia, 1954, pp. 33–35; B. P. Fishman, "Solomon Nunes Carvalho: Photographer," *Solomon Nunes Carvalho: Painter, Photographer, and Prophet in Nineteenth Century America*, The Jewish Historical Society of Maryland, 1989, pp. 25–32.

693 A SYNOPSIS OF THE HISTORY OF THE JEWS OF CURAÇAO FROM THE DAY OF THEIR SETTLEMENT TO THE PRESENT TIME

Curaçao, 1897. Rev. Joseph M. Corcos. Collection of Vida and Fred Simons, Jerusalem.

694 NIETO'S JEWISH ALMANAC FOR ONE HUNDRED YEARS FROM NEW YEAR 1902 TO 2002

New York, 1902. Ink on paper: printed. Rev. Abraham H. Nieto. Private collection.

695 MARRIAGE NOTICES FROM THE NEWSPAPER PRESS OF SOUTH CAROLINA (1776–1906)

New York, 1917. Barnett A. Elzas. Ink on paper: printed. Private collection.

COSTUME

696 NAVY FROCK COAT

United States, ca. 1862. Wool: brass buttons. L: 29¾ in. Collection of the Civil War Library and Museum, Philadelphia, Pennsylvania.

This regulation naval frock coat belonged to Jacob da Silva Solis-Cohen (1838–1927), a grandson of Jacob da Silva Solis (see cat. no. 732). He was a surgeon in the Union navy during the Civil War. The official buttons show the displayed eagle over fouled anchor.

Jacob da Silva Solis-Cohen's career is unusual in that he served as a medical officer (assistant surgeon) in the United States Navy from 1862 to 1864, and after his honorable discharge, enlisted in the army where he headed a Philadelphia army hospital during the last year of the Civil War.

Cf. Illustrated Catalog of Civil War Military Goods by Schuyler, Hartley & Graham, 1864, New York, 1985.

697 LACE FROM BRIDAL GOWN

United States, ca. 1912. Battenberg lace. Private collection.

According to family tradition, this lace is from the wedding dress of Henrietta Schulhofer (1870–1964), who married Ralph Benjamin Oppenheim (1868–1940) in Selma, Alabama, on February 9, 1892. The current form with puffed sleeves, high waist, and a fullness above the waist was the height of fashion around 1912.

Battenberg or tape lace could be purchased in the shape of an overblouse and lace panels which could be made into an afternoon or promenade dress. Such dresses looked well on everyone, young or old, and were available as expensive couturier creations as well as inexpensive mass-produced versions using machine-made lace.

698 JACKET

America, ca. 1870. Silk lace. L: 30 in. Collection of Abigail Kursheedt Hoffman.

699 TODDLER'S DRESS AND PURSE

Suriname, 19th–20th century. Cotton: crocheted. Collection of the Judah L. Magnes Museum, Berkeley, California, 86.48.6a,b.

The crocheted pattern creates a bold effect in this garment.

Cf. Rose, pp. 73–89.

700 OVERDRESS

America, early 20th century. Silk gauze: sequins. Collection of Regina Slovin, New York.

This is the semi-transparent tunic worn in the wedding photograph (cat. no. 747). Such overdresses became popular after World War I.

701 WEDDING SLIPPERS

New York, early 19th century. Leather: silk. 9¾ x 2½ x 3¼ in. Label: Reuben Bunn Ladies Shoe Maker No. 60, William Street Formerly No. 22 Smith Street Between Wall Street and Maiden Lane. Collection of Congregation K.K. Mikveh Israel, Philadelphia.

Family tradition attributes these fashionable dainty shoes to Belle Simon (1755–1832/33), sister of Miriam Simon (1749–1808), the mother of Rebecca Gratz (1781–1869). Gratz was a philanthropist and Jewish communal worker who helped found the first Jewish Sunday School in the United States. She is believed to be Sir Walter Scott's model for the character Rebecca in *Ivanhoe.* Although not Sephardim, Miss Gratz's father, Michael (1740–1811), and his brother Barnard (1738–1801) were founders, officers and supporters of K.K. Mikveh Israel, which was the first synagogue in Philadelphia.

702 HANDKERCHIEF

France, early 20th century. Cotton: drawn work; lace. Private collection.

For other objects from this American Sephardic family see cat nos. 715–719.

703 KIPPAH

Jerusalem, 1980s. Maker: Vida Corcos Simons (b. New York, 1928). Cotton: appliquéd and embroidered with cotton threads. 6 in. diam. Collection of Vida and Fred Simons, Jerusalem.

Vida Corcos Simons has interpreted the traditionally shaped Sephardic Dutch *kippah*. She has stressed its origin by decorating it with a running frieze of typical Amsterdam buildings, a form echoed in the architectural forms of Dutch Hanukkah lamps (see cat. no. 556), and with the symbol of Amsterdam's Portuguese community, a pelican biting at its breast to feed its young (see cat. no. 545).

Vida Corcos Simons combines her Sephardic heritage with contemporary concerns as seen in a series of *kippot* of this form. Other examples are designed for use as women's headcoverings or are inscribed in Amharic for recently arrived Ethiopian Jewish immigrants. The brightly colored embroidery of this *kippah* is typical of North African textiles and manuscripts, but deviates from the more restrained works typical of Amsterdam. The vivid colors indicate the melding of the Sephardic world in the artist's own family, as seen in the Corcos family tree (cat. no. 758), and in contemporary Israeli society.

PERSONAL ARTIFACTS

704 FAN

America, 19th century. Ivory; silk gauze; metal sequins. 8½ x 15 in. Collection of Abigail Kursheedt Hoffman.

A delicate fan of the type sometimes referred to as a dance fan. Fans formed an important part of a lady's fashionable ensemble during the 19th century, and survived as an evening accessory into the 20th century.

705 FAN

America, 19th century. Mother-of-pearl; wood; painted silk. Private collection.

The romantic landscape painted on this fan depicts a shepherdess; it was inspired by 18th-century pastoral paintings by Watteau and Nattier.

706 FAN

America, 19th century. Teak; painted silk. Private collection.

707 EMBROIDERY THREADS

China(?), 19th century. Silk; paper wrapper with Chinese stamps in ink. 16¾ x 25 in. (open). Collection of Abigail Kursheedt Hoffman.

Abigail Judah (1816–1898), the owner of this packet of silks, was the granddaughter of Gershom Mendes Seixas (1746–1816; see cat. nos. 657, 683, 685–686 and 688). Abigail married her cousin, Asher Kursheedt, grandson of Gershom Mendes Seixas by his first wife. Their sons owned the Kursheedt Manufacturing Company on 18th Street in New York, which made the first brocade curtain for the Metropolitan Opera Company.

708 THREE BOOKMARKS*

New York or Philadelphia, 19th century. Silk: embroidered, embroidery card. 1½ x 11 in. (each). Hebrew inscriptions: "I the Lord in My grace, have summoned you. And I have grasped you by the hand. I created you and appointed you a covenant people, a light of nations" (Is. 42:6); "O Lord of hosts, happy is the man who trusts in You" (Ps. 84:13); "Your people come forth willingly on your day of battle" (Ps. 110:3). Collection of the Sephardic Reference Room, Yeshiva University, New York.

Bookmarks were among the personal items made by Victorian women and girls as gifts for friends and relatives.

709 COMB

America, 19th–20th century. Tortoise shell (?); gilt metal; coral (?). 3⅛ x 4 in. Collection of Abigail Kursheedt Hoffman.

Combs were often worn as fashion accessories during the Victorian period. Cameos (gems carved in relief), such as the two decorating this comb, became popular in the wake of antiquarian discoveries including Pompeii.

710 PURSE

Paris, 20th century. Silk damask; velvet; silk lining. 4¾ x 7⅛ in. Collection of Abigail Kursheedt Hoffman.

This fashionable purse opens to reveal a mirror as well as a pocket for change.

711 CALLING CARD CASE

Probably Jamaica, 19th century. Silver: engraved. Collection of Vida and Fred Simons, Jerusalem.

Personal calling cards, like business cards today, were indispensable elements of a lady's social life. She would carry a card case with her, or wear it suspended on a chain or ribbon. This case is engraved with the name "Angelita," and belonged to Angelita Cohen Henriques.

712 ÉTUI

Holland, 19th century. Silver. Collection of Rev. and Mrs. Abraham Lopes Cardozo, New York.

Small, decorative cases such as this were popular ladies' accessories and usually were used to hold needles.

DOMESTIC OBJECTS

713 FLAGON

New York, 1763. Silver: repoussé and cast. 10½ x 7 in. Private collection.

This large covered tankard was presented by Congregation Shearith Israel to Gershom Mendes Seixas (1746–1816; see cat. nos. 657, 683, 685–686 and 688).

714 TABLESPOON

New York, ca. 1775. Silversmith: Myer Myers (1723–1795). Marks: MM (block letters cojoined) in rectangle twice. Silver: cast, engraved. Inscription: IAB. L: 7⅞ in. Private collection.

Simple tablespoon formed with an elliptical bowl with rounded top stem. Larger than a dessert spoon, the type (and term) was developed in the early 18th century. Myer Myers (1723–1795) was a highly skilled and versatile craftsman, who created the first American examples of Jewish ceremonial objects, including silver *rimmonim* for the synagogues of New York, Newport and Philadelphia (see cat. no. 652), as well as executing alms basins and baptismal bowls for churches.

REFERENCES: New York, Sotheby Parke Bernet, Dec. 12, 1988, lot no. 319. *Cf.* Rosenbaum, *Myer Myers*, pl. 24C and p. 122; Schoenberger, "Myer Myers," pp. 1–9.

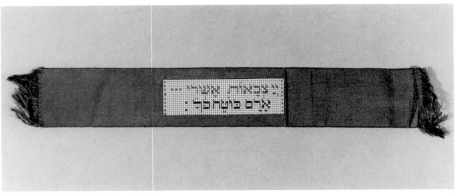

The objects described below (cat. nos. 715–719) come from a private collection belonging to a descendant of a Spanish-Portuguese family that arrived in New York during the 17th century. Although its members intermarried with Ashkenazim, the family has maintained its Sephardic identity to this day.

715 MANTLE CLOCK

American, 19th century. Pewter. 15½ x 8½ x 4¼ in. Private collection.

This was a wedding gift of Henrietta Schulhofer (1870–1964), the bride who wore the Battenberg lace (cat. no. 697 and 723).

716 ARMCHAIR

Charleston, South Carolina, 19th century. Oak: carved. 37 x 23½ x 22 in. Private collection.

This chair was made on the southern plantation Great Oaks, in North Charleston, owned by Isaiah Moses (1772–1857) and his wife Rebecca Phillips Moses (1792–1872); the couple were married on November 11, 1807.

717 TEA TABLE

Charleston, South Carolina, 19th century. Oak: marble top. 28 x 31 x 34 in. Private collection.

This table was the property of Sarah Ann Goldsmith.

718 UNION FLAG

America, 1860s. Silk. 24 x 35 in. Private collection.

This 37-star flag is from the Phillips family home in New York, and belonged to Elward Jonas Phillips (1883–1967).

719 EASEL

New York, ca. 1890. Gertrude Illoway. Oak. 81 x 24 x 23½ in. Private collection.

Gertrude Illoway, a talented member of Congregation Shearith Israel and an ancestor of the lender, hand carved this easel.

720 BELL PULL

New York, 19th century. Petit point. 73 x 7 in. Collection of Prof. and Mrs. Solomon Feffer, New York.

From the time they were very young, women kept busy with needlework, and their homes were filled with both decorative and utilitarian pieces they created. This bell pull for summoning servants was made by a member of the Phillips family, who gave it to the lenders. Jonas Phillips (1736–1803), the founder of the family in America, was a native of Germany but came to the United States as an indentured servant of Moses Lindo, a member of a British Sephardic family who settled in America. Phillips first engaged in business in New York but during the Revolutionary War settled in Philadelphia. He served as president of Philadelphia's Congregation Mikveh Israel.

721 CAKE SERVER*

Europe, 19th century. Silver: cast, repoussé. L: 9¼ in. Collection of Vida and Fred Simons, Jerusalem.

721

722

Saide Da Costa presented this cake server to the lender's mother on her marriage to Mr. Da Costa. The cake server originally belonged to Dr. Bambino, the lender's dentist. *Bambino* is the Italian for "baby." The motif of the swaddled infant with arms outstretched was popularized by the roundels that decorated the famous *Ospedale degli Innocenti* (Foundling Hospital), in the *Piazza della SS. Annunziata* in Florence. Designed by Filippo Brunelleschi (1377–1446), it was begun in 1419 and completed by the middle of the century.

In the 19th century a revival of interest in the Middle Ages brought with it a new popularity for genealogy and heraldry, and family coats of arms, real or assumed, were prominently displayed on possessions.

REFERENCES: W. Leaf, S. Purcell, *Heraldic Symbols: Islamic Insignia and Western Heraldry*, London, 1986, p. 114; F. Hartt, *History of Italian Renaissance Art*, New York, n.d., pp. 115–6.

722 CHOCOLATE SERVICE*

Amsterdam, ca. 1890. Porcelain: overglazed and gilt. Marks: A.C. Legrand, Rokine 171, Amsterdam. Dutch inscriptions: Forget-us-not; Forget-me-not. Collection of Rev. and Mrs. Abraham Lopes Cardozo, New York.

This service was presented by members of the Lopes Cardozo family to relatives before their emigration to America. The pieces are decorated with the floral motif of the forget-me-not, and monogrammed with the initials of many family members, including Haham David Lopes Cardozo and Clara Israel Ricardo

(see cat. nos. 648–649). The Lopes Cardozo family moved to Charleston, South Carolina, a center of Sephardic culture established in the 18th century.

723 COFFEE/CHOCOLATE SERVICE

France, 1890s. Limoges. Porcelain: overglazed and gilt. Private collection.

This set includes a coffeepot, four cups and saucers, a creamer, a sugar bowl and a biscuit tray. It was a wedding gift of Henrietta Schulhofer (1878–1964; see cat. nos. 697 and 715).

724 TWO BUTTER DISHES

Probably Curaçao, 19th–20th century. Silver: cast; engraved. ½ x 3¼ in. (each). Collection of Vida and Fred Simons, Jerusalem.

Butter dishes such as these and nut dishes were popular wedding favors in Curaçao.

725 TWO NUT DISHES

Probably Curaçao, 19th–20th century. Silver: cast. ½ x 3¼ in. (each). Collection of Vida and Fred Simons, Jerusalem.

Cf. cat. no. 724.

726 AMULET

Jerusalem, 1980s. Maker: Vida Corcos Simons (b. New York, 1928). Cotton: embroidered with cotton and metallic threads; sequins; metal hooks. Collection of Vida and Fred Simons, Jerusalem.

Fish made of stuffed and embroidered textiles were frequently displayed in North African homes as fertility symbols (see cat. no. 455). Vida Corcos Simons, a contemporary Jerusalem textile artist, has interpreted this traditional symbol. The use of the metal closure as the fish's eye stems from the common use of found objects in both traditional North African Judaica, as seen in Hanukkah lamps (see cat. nos. 264 and 371), and in contemporary assemblage. The Corcos family's roots in Spain, Morocco, Holland and other Sephardic centers can be seen in the Corcos family tree (cat. no. 758).

NUMISMATICS

727 CONFEDERATE CURRENCY; TWO-DOLLAR BILLS

Confederate States of America, 1862. Printed: ink on paper. 109882. 43436. 3⅛ x 7⅛ in; 2¾ x 6⅛ in. Collection of Manfred Anson, Bergenfield, New Jersey.

Judah Philip Benjamin (1811–1884), whose portrait is depicted on these bills, was a descendant of the Mendes family expelled from Spain in 1492. Born in St. Croix, British West Indies, his family moved to Charleston, South Carolina, while he was a young boy. Charleston was the first community in the New World to grant Jews the right to vote. He was sent to the school of the Hebrew Orphan Society. His intelligence and talent attracted the attention of Moses Lopez, a rich Charleston merchant, who offered to pay for Judah's education and to send him to Yale University to study law. After two years at Yale, Benjamin moved to New Orleans, where he was admitted to the bar in 1832.

In 1852, Benjamin was the first Jew to be elected to the United States Senate. He led the Southern politicians who favored secession from the Union, and briefly served as the first attorney general of the Confederacy (1861). President Jefferson Davis appointed Benjamin Secretary of War in September, 1861, and Secretary of State in 1862 despite anti-Semitic attacks and charges of incompetence. After the defeat of the Confederacy in 1865, Benjamin moved to England, where he enjoyed a successful career as a barrister until his retirement in 1882. Benjamin is the only Jew depicted on United States currency.

728 BOND COUPON*

Confederate States of America, 1861. Printed: ink on paper. Collection of Yeshiva University Museum, New York, gift of Manfred Anson, 91.08.

This Confederate bond coupon (no. 848) for $500 at eight percent was due to mature January 1, 1875. Four coupons have been clipped— mute testimony to the tragedy of the secession. Like the two-dollar bills (cat. no. 727), the bond coupon bears the portrait of Judah P. Benjamin.

729 MEDAL COMMEMORATING THE 250TH ANNIVERSARY OF JEWISH SETTLEMENT IN AMERICA

America, 1905. Bronze. Isidore Konti. 3 in. diam. Collection of Yeshiva University Museum, New York, gift of Louis Werner, 81.24.

Dutch New Amsterdam (New York) had Jewish settlers as early as 1654. Most of the settlers were Sephardim, and they long remained the leaders of the Jewish community. Ashkenazim frequently joined Sephardic congregations such as Shearith Israel in New York and, like Mordecai Manuel Noah (1785–1851; see cat. no. 662), emphasized the Sephardim among their ancestors for the status this conveyed.

On the obverse of this medal is depicted the triumph of Liberty and Justice over Intolerance; the reverse shows History with an American eagle.

Cf. YUM, *Noah*, p. 9.

730 MEDAL OF THE TOURO SYNAGOGUE

Newport, Rhode Island, 1963. Silver: struck. 1¾ in. diam. Collection of Yeshiva University Museum, New York, gift of Erica and Ludwig Jesselson, 80.18.

Medal commemorating the 200th anniversary of the dedication of the Touro Synagogue.

728

731 THREE MARDI-GRAS TOKENS

New Orleans, late 20th century. Metal: stamped. 1½ in. diam. Collection of Yeshiva University Museum, New York, gift of Manfred Anson, 91.08.

These tokens are characteristic of ephemera distributed during Mardi-Gras celebration. They depict Belle Chasse, the home of Judah P. Benjamin (see cat. no. 727), a showplace of the South.

PORTRAITS AND PAINTINGS

732 SILHOUETTE OF JACOB DA SILVA SOLIS

New York, early 19th century. Silhouette on paper. 3½ x 2¹³/₁₆ in. Hays Collection, Collection of the Westchester Historical Society, gift of Joan Sturhahn, 1181.

734

Jacob da Silva Solis (1780–1829), a native of London, settled in New York in 1808 and married Charity Hays, sister of Benjamin Etting Hays (see cat. no. 659). On a business visit to New Orleans in 1826, noting that the city had neither a synagogue nor a matzoh factory, Solis began work to organize both. The synagogue became known as "the Shaarai Chasset [i.e. *Shaarei Hessed*] Congregation."

The popularity of Greek and Etruscan vase painting as well as other forms of classical art during the 18th century contributed to a vogue for profile silhouettes. The craft was also known as skiagraphy and shadowgraphy, and was popular in Russia as well as in Europe and America. Considered by some as the most accurate rendition of an individual's features, it was an inexpensive method of portraiture whose appeal lasted through the advent of photography. It is fascinating to note how much of a sitter's character can be portrayed in a profile silhouette, and to compare this silhouette with the painted portrait of Solis (cat. no. 734).

733/734 PORTRAITS OF CHARITY HAYS SOLIS AND HER HUSBAND JACOB DA SILVA SOLIS*

America, early 19th century. Watercolor on ivory. 3⅝ x 3⅛ in. Collection of Joan Sturhahn, Sarasota, Florida.

Jacob (1780–1829; for biographical details see cat. no. 732) and Charity (1782–1839) were the parents of Sarah Miriam Solis, the wife of Solomon Nunes Carvalho (1815–1879; see cat. no. 737).

The anonymous artist has used rich colors and small, vibrant brushstrokes which impart a sense of movement and immediacy, and are especially effective in the depiction of the foaming lace in the portrait of Charity Hays Solis.

Miniature portrait painting is often regarded as a separate category of painting. Presumed to descend from portraits in Flemish medieval manuscripts, separate small portraits painted on vellum existed by the 16th century in England; among the notable practitioners at this time were Holbein and Hilliard. The use of ivory as a support was an innovation dating to around 1700. Portrait miniatures were usually ovals, worn as jewelry or carried. In the early 19th century a fashion arose among artists for painting square miniatures, and a method developed for cutting and flattening large sheets of ivory. The taste for miniature portraits spread from England to her colonies. *(Plate 18)*

REFERENCES: Sturhahn, *Carvalho*, p. 38; R. Bolton-Smith and D. T. Johnson, "Tokens of Affection: The Portrait Miniature in America," exhibition catalogue, New York and Washington, DC, The Metropolitan Museum of Art and the National Museum of American Art Smithsonian Institution, 1990.

735 PORTRAIT OF DAVID SEIXAS

New York or Philadelphia(?), 19th century. Watercolor on ivory. 3¼ x 2¼ in. Collection of Abigail Kursheedt Hoffman.

David Seixas (1788–1865), a son of Gershom Mendes Seixas (the first *hazzan* of the Sephardic Congregation Mikveh Israel in Philadelphia), established a noted pottery factory in Philadelphia in 1816. He produced creamware (also known as Queensware), developed by Josiah Wedgwood in 1767 in England and already popular in America by 1771. Seixas also founded the Philadelphia Deaf and Dumb Institute.

REFERENCE: *The Complete Encyclopedia of Antiques*, ed. L.G.G. Ramsey, 1962, New York, 1968, p. 868.

736 PORTRAIT OF JOAQUIN DE HEREDIA Y SARMIENTO

Mexico City, ca. 1810. Oil on canvas. 21½ x 16¾ in. Collection of Dr. Viviane A. Ryan and Tomás Ryan, New York.

The son of José de Heredia y Velarde y Alianzas.

737 BATTLE OF THE AMALEKITES

America, ca. 1848–1852. Solomon Nunes Carvalho (1815–1879). Oil on board. 16 x 20 in. Collection of William Loewy, Monsey, New York.

Carvalho, artist, daguerreotypist and portrait painter, a native of Charleston, South Carolina, later resided variously in Barbados, Philadelphia, Baltimore and finally New York. He helped establish a Sephardic congregation, Beit Israel, in Baltimore, which, however, did not survive the departure of the Carvalho family from the city. Both of Solomon Nunes Carvalho's parents were Sephardim. His mother, Sarah D'Azevedo, came from a family which included Moses Cohen D'Azevedo, Haham of London (1720–1784).

Reverend Isaac Leeser (1806–1868), *hazzan* of Congregation K.K. Mikveh Israel in Philadelphia, was a friend of the artist. He performed the marriage of Carvalho and Sarah Miriam Solis (1824–1894) in 1845. She was the daughter of Jacob da Silva Solis and Charity Hays Solis (see cat. nos. 733–734).

Solomon Carvalho was keenly interested in Jewish life and concerned about religious reform. He wrote several articles in Isaac Leeser's journal, *The Occident*. Carvalho corresponded with Leeser for many years, especially during 1851–1852, on issues including Jewish belief, survival and assimilation, and the subject of prayer in English rather than Hebrew. He was also a member of the Hebrew Young Men's Literary Association of Baltimore, and participated in its debates. Sarah Carvalho was founder and President of the Baltimore Hebrew Sunday School Association. After moving to New York City, Carvalho was active in Shearith Israel and later Temple Israel in Harlem, where he and his wife founded and taught in the school.

This is one of two known narrative Biblical subjects painted by this artist, and the only one still extant. It is also the earliest Biblical painting by an American Jewish artist. The placement of monumental figures in the foreground with the background far in the distance is similar to works by contemporary Europeans, but there is no direct prototype for this painting. It depicts Aaron and Hur supporting Moses' arms so that Israel would prevail in the battle with Amalek (Ex. 17:12).

The painting can be viewed as an expression of Carvalho's adherence to traditional Judaism. It also epitomizes the faith and prayer that sustained the crypto-Jews under the Inquisition, and in the various countries in which they built new Jewish lives after fleeing from Spain. *(cover)*

REFERENCES: Gutmann, "Visual Arts"; I. Leeser, "Native Jewish Talent," *The Occident and American Jewish Advocate*, Vol. X, 1853, pp. 500–5; S. N. Carvalho, *Incidents of Travel and Adventure in the Far West*, int. B. W. Korn, Philadelphia, 1954, pp. 13–52, 29, 70; Berman, "Carvalho," cat. no. 16; p. 22; Sturhahn, *Carvalho*; B. W. Korn, "Some Additional Notes on the Life and Work of Solomon Nunes Carvalho," *The Seventy-Fifth Anniversary Volume of the Jewish Quarterly Review*, Philadelphia, 1967, pp. 361–68.

738 PORTRAITS OF TWO CONFEDERATE SOLDIERS: MIKELL MEARS GOLDSMITH (1847–1864) AND ISAAC PHILLIPS GOLDSMITH (D. AGE 22)

Confederate States of America, 1860s. Pastel on canvas. 25½ x 21¼ in. Private collection.

Gentlemen of Sephardic descent proudly fought on both sides in the Civil War. Both brothers in these paintings gave their lives for the Confederacy.

PHOTOGRAPHS AND PRINTS

739 PORTRAIT OF A WOMAN OF THE DE HEREDIA FAMILY

Mexico City, ca. 1860. Daguerreotype. 2 x 1½ in. Collection of Dr. Viviane A. Ryan and Tomás L. Ryan, New York.

This woman, mother of the young boy in the pendant portrait (cat. no. 740), wears a stylish dress with a white collar.

A daguerreotype, named for its inventor, the artist Louis J. M. Daguerre (d. 1851), is an early photograph—a positive image on thin, polished copper coated with silver. The image is developed with heated mercury vapor and then "fixed." Daguerreotypes were popular from around 1840 to 1860. They were usually protected in hinged cases with leather coverings (as were their more expensive prototypes,

miniature portraits on ivory); often the case contained two images, one at each side. These are elaborate cases, with stamped leather on the outside, and velvet facing and protecting the image, which is behind glass.

REFERENCES: Kelbaugh, pp. 33–36; J. M. Reilly, *Care and Identification of 19th Century Photographic Prints*, 1986.

740 PORTRAIT OF A SON OF THE DE HEREDIA FAMILY

Mexico City, ca. 1860. Daguerreotype. 2 x 1½ in. Collection of Dr. Viviane A. Ryan and Tomás L. Ryan, New York.

Marranos came to Mexico as early as the time of Cortés (1521). The earliest auto-da-fé in Mexico took place in 1528; they decreased during the 17th century. The Jewish population grew during the 19th century. Jews engaged in all aspects of professional life.

741 MR. AND MRS. MOSES CORCOS

Kingston, Jamaica, mid-19th century. Black and white photograph (copy). 3¾ x 2½ in. Collection of Vida and Fred Simons, Jerusalem.

Julia Brandon Rodrigues and Moses Corcos, parents of Rabbi Joseph Corcos, posed for this photograph.

742 FOUR GENERATIONS

Kingston, Jamaica, ca. 1900. Black and white photograph (copy). 12 x 4⅛ in. Collection of Vida and Fred Simons, Jerusalem.

Matilda Levine Henriques with daughter Sara Henriques Abrahams, granddaughter Amelia Abrahams Corcos (see cat. no. 743) and great-granddaughter Julia Corcos. The Henriques family's progenitor was Moses Henriques of Kingston, Jamaica, who married Abigail Quixanoi in 1768.

743 FAMILY AT HOME

Kingston, Jamaica, ca. 1900. Black and white photograph (copy). 8⅛ x 5¾ in. Collection of Vida and Fred Simons, Jerusalem.

Amelia Abrahams Corcos with her husband Rev. Joseph Corcos and his sister Ada Corcos. This picture gives us a rare glimpse of a domestic interior. It was taken when Rev. Corcos was Minister of the Kingston Spanish and Portuguese Congregation (1893–1903). Later, he was connected with Congregation Shearith Israel (Spanish and Portuguese Synagogue) in New York. In 1922 he became Rabbi of the Spanish and Portuguese Synagogue in Montreal.

744 PURIM PARTY

Kingston, Jamaica, early 20th century. Black and white photograph (copy). 7¹/₂ x 9¹/₄ in. Collection of Vida and Fred Simons, Jerusalem.

The guests at René and Eric Davis' party included Stella Corcos, her sisters Julia and Lucille and their first cousin, Gloria Lyons. Stella (1857–1948), a native of New York and wife of Moses Corcos (d. 1903), settled in Mogador, Morocco, where she founded a Jewish free school, fought the influence of Protestant missionaries and represented the Anglo-Jewish Association.

745 PHOTOGRAPH ALBUM*

Suriname, ca. 1910–50. Black and white photographs. 12¹/₂ x 10¹/₂ in.; 21¹/₄ in. open. Collection of Rev. and Mrs. Abraham Lopes Cardozo, New York.

The album contains family portraits of an anniversary celebration ca. 1915.

746 PORTRAIT OF SAM GORMASAN AND SISTER

New York, ca. 1920. Black and white photograph. 6³/₄ x 4¹/₄ in. Collection of the Sephardic Reference Room, Yeshiva University, New York.

747 WEDDING PHOTOGRAPH OF SIGNORA (CHANA) SIMHA AND ISAAC S. COHEN

New York, ca. 1920. Black and white photograph. 16¹/₂ x 12 in. Collection of Regina Slovin, New York.

The bride is wearing the fashionable long slim look of the early 1920s, de-emphasizing bust and hips, with short hair curling softly at the sides of her face. Her overdress is a delicate tunic (cat. no. 700).

748 MOISE GADOL

New York, ca. 1920. Black and white photograph, Franco's Photo Studios. 6¹/₂ x 4¹/₂ in. Collection of the Sephardic Reference Room, Yeshiva University, New York.

Gadol was the publisher of *La America*, a Ladino-language newspaper published in New York for immigrants from Ottoman countries.

749 MARDI GRAS

Peru, 1926. Black and white photograph. 5 x 8¹/₂ in. Collection of Fortuna Calvo Roth, New York.

According to the lender, Rafael Calvo, depicted here with local celebrants, was the only Jew these Peruvians had ever met, and they expected him to have horns.

750 LAYING THE CORNER-STONE OF THE SEPHARDIC SYNAGOGUE

Lima, Peru, ca. 1928. Black and white photograph. 6³/₄ x 9 in. Collection of Fortuna Calvo Roth, New York.

Among those attending the ceremony were the lender's uncle Rafael Calvo (at left; see also cat. no. 749), her father Isaac Calvo (second from left), Rabbi Eskenazi (third from left) and Benjamin Alhalel. Alhalel, now a doctor, was recently decorated by the Peruvian government. The synagogue was opened in 1932.

751 AUTOGRAPHED PORTRAIT OF JUSTICE BENJAMIN NATHAN CARDOZO

New York, ca. 1930. Black and white photograph, Times Wide World Studios. English inscription: Faithfully yours, Benjamin N. Cardozo. 9 x 7 in. Collection of the Sephardic Reference Room, Yeshiva University, New York.

Benjamin Nathan Cardozo (1870–1938) was the descendant of a prominent American Sephardic family founded by Aaron Nunez Cardozo (d. 1800) around 1750, and a member of Congregation Shearith Israel in New York.

President Herbert Hoover appointed Cardozo, a graduate of Columbia Law School, to the United States Supreme Court in 1932, after he had served on the Supreme Court of New York (1913), and as Chief Judge of the New York Court of Appeals (1927–1932). Cardozo backed such Franklin D. Roosevelt "New Deal" social reforms as Social Security and old age pensions.

Yeshiva University's law school, established in 1975, is named for him.

752 HEBREW SCHOOL CLASS

Peru, ca. 1930s. Black and white photograph. 4½ x 7 in. Collection of Fortuna Calvo Roth, New York.

753 PURIM PLAY*

New York City, 1936. Black and white photograph. 9 x 11⅞ in. Collection of Yeshiva University Museum, New York, gift of Mrs. Adatto Schlesinger, 79.21.

This is a presentation photograph showing the cast of a Sephardic community's Purim play presented on June 26, 1936, signed by eleven members of the cast.

754 SYNAGOGUE INTERIOR

Paramaribo, Suriname, ca. 1950. Black and white photograph. 7¾ x 9½ in. Collection of Rev. and Mrs. Abraham Lopes Cardozo, New York.

755 HIGH SCHOOL DIPLOMA

Philadelphia, Pennsylvania, 1854. Ink on paper: printed with handwritten additions; silk ribbon; wax seal. Collection of The Temple Judea Museum of Kenesseth Israel, Elkins Park, Pennsylvania.

This is the diploma of Jacob da Silva Solis–Cohen (see cat. no. 696 for further biographical details) from Central High School, Philadelphia.

756 MEDICAL SCHOOL DIPLOMA

Philadelphia, Pennsylvania, 1860. Ink on paper: printed with handwritten additions; silk ribbon; wax seal. Collection of The Temple Judea Museum of Kenesseth Israel, Elkins Park, Pennsylvania.

Jacob da Silva Solis–Cohen (see also cat. no. 696) was awarded this diploma by the University of Pennsylvania Medical School.

757 BILL OF LADING

Newport, Rhode Island, May 31, 1771. Nathaniel Hathaway. Printed and handwritten on paper. 6½ x 8¾ in. Collection of Dr. and Mrs. Manfred Lehmann, Miami Beach, Florida

This is a receipt for supplies taken aboard the brig Charlotte in Newport, Rhode Island. It was issued by the Captain, Nathaniel Hathaway, for items shipped for Aaron Lopez for delivery in Suriname. Lopez was a Sephardic merchant, who George Washington called a patriot, ". . . a friend of the liberties and independence of the United States."

The cargo transported for Lopez on the Charlotte included ". . . Ninety-four kegs of Jew Beef, One Quarter Barrel Cashier Neats [beef] Tongues, Four Kegs Cashier Fatt, One Cask Cashier Smoked Beef . . ." and non-kosher foods as well.

Suriname in Dutch Guiana, had Jewish settlers as early as 1639. The community remained Sephardic into the early 19th century. Many Jews established sugarcane plantations, and the Jews were granted full enjoyment and free exercise of their religion in 1665, freedoms that were reinforced after the Dutch gained control of Suriname in 1667.

758 CORCOS FAMILY TREE

Jerusalem, ca. 1980. Compiled by David and Sidney Corcos. Ink on paper: printed. 39½ x 27½ in. Collection of Yeshiva University Museum, New York, gift of Vida and Fred Simons.

This family tree traces the genealogy of the Corcos family back to 13th-century Tortosa, Spain, and through the many communities of the Sephardic diaspora.

745

753

Some of the thousands of visitors, adults and children, who have toured the exhibition.

CHRONOLOGY

PREPARED BY GERTRUDE HIRSCHLER

412–711: Visigoths Rule in Spain

586 King Reccared, originally an Arian Christian, adopts Catholicism. Persecution of Jews begins.

613 King Sisebut, in agreement with the Church, decrees that Jews must accept baptism or leave the country. Thousands of Jews emigrate; others remain and officially convert to Christianity, but many of them later return to Judaism.

682 Practice of Judaism officially forbidden; converts are closely watched and excluded from positions of authority.

711–c.1085: The Muslim Era

711 Muslims conquer Spain and are welcomed as saviors by secret Jews. Many Jews who left Spain return from North Africa. Muslims offer opportunities to Jews, sometimes entrust them with garrisoning of various towns.

c.755–c.1031 Umayyad caliphate with Cordoba as capital. Jews active in many occupations, including medicine, agriculture, commerce and crafts. Beginning of "Golden Age" in the history of Spanish Jewry that reaches its climax in 11th and 12th centuries.

Early 11th century Decline of Muslim caliphate in Spain. The country is split into many smaller kingdoms and principalities. Christians in the north begin campaign of *reconquista* (re-conquest) of Muslim Spain.

c.1020 Shlomo ibn Gabirol, poet and philosopher, is born in Malaga.

c.1085–1479: The Era of Transition

1085 Toledo is conquered by Christians.

1135 R. Moshe ben Maimon (Maimonides) is born in Cordoba.

1148 Cordoba is conquered by Almohades, a militant Muslim sect from Africa. They and the Almoravids fight to keep Spain in the Muslim fold and to convert Jews. Many Jews flee to northern Spain, which is in Christian hands.

1212 Almohades suffer a crucial defeat by Christian ruler Alfonso VIII of Castile in the battle of Navas de Tolosa.

1250 Pope Innocent IV refuses permission to Jews of Cordoba to build a new synagogue.

1263 Jewish-Christian disputation of Barcelona opens. The Christian spokesman is Pablo Christiani, a convert from Judaism. The Jews are represented by R.

Moshe ben Nahman (Nahmanides), who is subsequently exiled and settles in Jerusalem.

R. Yonah ben Avraham Gerondi, Talmudist and moralist, dies.

1327   R. Asher ben Yehiel (ROSH), outstanding Talmudist and codifier, dies in Toledo.

1348   Massacres of Jews begin as a mass reaction to Black Death epidemic.

1391   Anti-Jewish riots break out in Seville. This begins a wave of violence that spreads rapidly through the Iberian peninsula and claims 50,000 victims before the year ends. The riots give rise to the marranos, who are able to escape with their lives at the price of conversion. The Jewish communities of Valencia and Barcelona are destroyed.

1413   Jewish-Christian disputation of Tortosa opens. The Christian spokesman is Geronimo de Santa Fé, a convert from Judaism. The Jews are represented by the philosopher Joseph Albo and Don Vidal Benveniste (the latter chosen as spokesman because of his familiarity with Latin). The disputation resulted in issuance of a papal bull forbidding Jews to study the Talmud.

1424   Don Alfonso V of Aragon grants Barcelona the right to exclude Jews for all time.

1435   Massacres and conversions of Jews in Majorca.

1473   Massacre of marranos in Cordoba and Valladolid.

1474   Massacre of marranos in Segovia.

1479   Kingdoms of Aragon and Castile unite under King Ferdinand and Queen Isabella, who seek to establish Catholicism as the only permissible faith in their country.

1479–1497: Expulsion

c.1480   The Inquisition is established in Spain, Tomás de Torquemada is appointed Inquisitor-General of Spain three years later.

1490   La Guardia blood libel

1492   *January 2:* Ferdinand and Isabella make triumphant entry into Granada.
March 30: Ferdinand and Isabella sign decree expelling the Jews from Spain; the decree is made public the following day.
August 2 (Tishah be-Av): Period of expulsion of the Jews from Spain begins. Many exiles flee to the Ottoman empire, which opens its gates to Jewish exiles from Spain.

1496   King Manuel of Portugal orders expulsion of all Jews from his country.

1497   The Jews are expelled from Portugal.

1497–1794: A Second Diaspora

1506   Massacre of marranos in Lisbon.

1508 Don Yitzhak Abrabanel, head of Spanish Jewry and former confidant of Spanish monarchs, dies.

1536 The Inquisition is established in Portugal to watch over loyalty of "New Christians," resulting in the large-scale flight of "New Christians" from Portugal; "New Christians" set up "Portuguese" communities in western Europe and eventually in the New World.

1577 Portuguese marranos are granted permission to settle in Brazil.

1593 First Jewish settlers—Sephardim—arrive in Amsterdam.

1597 Beit Yaakov, first synagogue in Amsterdam, is dedicated.

1629 Dutch West India Company grants religious freedom to Jewish settlers in Dutch West Indies.

c.1642 First Jewish settlers arrive in Brazil.

1654 Recife, Brazil, falls to Portugal, ending the legal existence of a prosperous Jewish community there. On September 7, a party of 23 Jewish refugees from Recife arrives in New Amsterdam.

1656 Petition of R. Menasseh ben Israel for official permission to practice Judaism in England is granted.
Elders of the Jewish community of Amsterdam excommunicate Baruch (Benedict) Spinoza.

1675 Portuguese Synagogue of Amsterdam is dedicated.

1699 Construction of Bevis Marks Synagogue, London's oldest Jewish house of worship, begins.

1730 Congregation Shearith Israel (organized in 1654) dedicates its first synagogue on Mill Street in lower Manhattan.

1763 Congregation Yeshuat Israel of Newport, R.I. (organized in 1677) dedicates its synagogue ("Touro Synagogue").

1782 Congregation Mikveh Israel of Philadelphia, Pa. (organized in 1745) dedicates its first synagogue.

1794 Congregation Beth Elohim of Charleston, S.C. (organized in 1749) builds its first synagogue.

Mid-18th Century–Present: Reconciliation

Mid-18th century Some Jewish individuals, mostly from Gibraltar, practice Jewish rites privately in Portugal under British protection.

1813 A congregation is formally founded in Lisbon under the auspices of R. Abraham Dabella.

1869 Spanish constitution grants religious tolerance to all residents of Spain, thus removing barrier to legal residence of Jews in the country.

Late 19th century Jews are allowed to live in Spain as individuals but not as an organized community.

1902 A new synagogue is built in Lisbon but is not allowed to bear external signs of a house of worship.

1910 Revolution in Portugal is followed by the establishment of freedom of religion.

1914–18 During World War I Madrid gives asylum to a number of Jewish refugees and exiles, including the Zionist leader Max Nordau and the Orientalist Abraham Shalom (A.S.) Yahuda.

1917 The first synagogue is dedicated in Madrid since the Expulsion after the Spanish *cortes* (parliament), under Alfonso XIII, annuls the prohibition against synagogues in Spain.

c.1939 Portugal has a small Jewish community headed by the scholar and economist Moses Bensabat Amzalek, a friend of Portugal's Premier Antonio de Oliveira Salazar.

1939–45 Modest Jewish influx into Spain as a result of World War II and Nazi persecution; thousands of other Jewish refugees pass through Spain.
Many thousands of Jewish refugees pass through Portugal, particularly Lisbon, on their way to the free world.

1941 The Arias Montano Institute for Jewish Studies is founded in Madrid and a department of Jewish studies is organized within the University of Madrid.

1949 A public synagogue, the second since the Expulsion, is dedicated in Madrid. It is relocated and rededicated in 1959.

1965 *January 20:* In the first meeting between Jews and the head of a Spanish government since the Expulsion, Generalissimo Francisco Franco confers with Jewish representatives to discuss the legal status of Spain's Jewish community. Legal recognition is granted to the Jewish community for the first time since the Expulsion.

1967 *June 26:* The *cortes* passes a law on "The Exercise of the Civil Right to Religious Freedom," giving Jews and Protestants the right of public worship for the first time since Ferdinand and Isabella proclaimed Catholicism as Spain's only legitimate religion. Under this law, Jews are permitted, for the first time, to mark their places of worship and to advertise their religious services.

1968 *December 16:* The first new synagogue built in Spain in 600 years is dedicated in Madrid. On the same day, the Spanish government annuls the decree of expulsion signed by Ferdinand and Isabella.

1990 The Prince of Asturias Concord Prize is awarded by the Principe des Asturias Foundation to the Sephardic community of the world. Sephardic spiritual leader Haham Dr. Solomon Gaon travels to Spain to accept the award on behalf of the world's Sephardim from Crown Prince Felipe.

CONTRIBUTORS

DR. MARC D. ANGEL, an historian, is the Rabbi of Congregation Shearith Israel, The Spanish and Portuguese Synagogue, New York. He is the author of many works on Sephardic life, including the recent *Voices in Exile: A Study in Sephardic Intellectual History.*

PROF. HAIM BEINART, Bernard Cherrick Professor of the History of the Jewish People, Hebrew University, Jerusalem, was the recipient of the 1991 Israel Prize. Prof. Beinart is the preeminent scholar of medieval Iberian Jewry and has published extensively on this topic. His works in English include *Records of the Trials of the Spanish Inquisition in Ciudad Real* and *Conversos on Trial: The Inquisition in Ciudad Real.*

CHAYA BENJAMIN, Judaica Department, The Israel Museum, Jerusalem, is an art historian specializing in Jewish ceremonial art. She is the author of *The Stieglitz Collection: Masterpieces of Jewish Art.*

HAHAM DR. SOLOMON GAON, Director of the Jacob E. Safra Institute for Sephardic Studies, Yeshiva University, New York, is Haham of the World Sephardi Federation and the former Chief Sephardic Rabbi of the British Commonwealth. Haham Gaon received the Asturias Prize on behalf of the world Sephardic community in 1990 and is the author of *Minhath Shelomo, a commentary on the Book of Prayer of the Spanish and Portuguese Jews.*

GERTRUDE HIRSCHLER has translated and edited many Jewish texts. In 1986, she edited the Yeshiva University Museum exhibition catalogue *Ashkenaz: The German Jewish Heritage.* She is probably best known for her translation of *T'rumath Z'vi,* the Pentateuch and excerpted commentary of R. Samson Raphael Hirsch.

PROF. YOSEF KAPLAN, Netherlands Institute for Advanced Study in the Humanities and Social Sciences, The Hague, is an historian specializing in the Sephardic communities of Western Europe. He is the author of *From Christianity to Judaism: The Story of Isaac Orobio de Castro.*

DR. SHALOM SABAR, Center for Jewish Art and Department of Art History, Hebrew University, Jerusalem, is the leading authority on illuminated Jewish marriage contracts. He is the author of *Ketubbah,* the catalogue of marriage contracts from the Skirball Museum and the Hebrew Union College Klau Library.

MATILDA COHEN SARANO has been compiling Judeo-Spanish folklore and folktales for the past ten years. In 1986, her book *Kuentos — Stories of the Judeo-Spanish Family Folklore* was published in Jerusalem.

SYLVIA A. HERSKOWITZ, Director, Yeshiva University Museum, New York.

GABRIEL M. GOLDSTEIN, Assistant Curator, Yeshiva University Museum, New York City.

BONNI-DARA MICHAELS, Assistant Curator, Yeshiva University Museum, New York City.

Children participating in the puppets and crafts workshops created for the exhibition.

SELECTED BIBLIOGRAPHY

Abbreviated references for frequently cited works are listed next to their respective complete bibliographical entries.

I. ART AND MATERIAL CULTURE

Allan, James, and Julian Raby, "Metalwork." In *Tulips, Arabesques & Turbans*, ed., Yanni Petsopoulos, 17–71. New York, 1982.
ALLAN, "METALWORK"

Amsterdam, Joods-Historisch Museum, *Guide to the Jewish Historical Museum*, 1988.

——, Joods-Historisch Museum, *The Ghetto in Venice: Ponentini, Levantini e Tedeschi 1516–1797*, exhibition catalogue, 1990.
JOODS, THE GHETTO

Amsterdam, Rijksmuseum, *Nederlands zilver/Dutch silver*, 1979.

Anderson, Ruth Matilda, *Hispanic Costume 1480–1530*, New York, 1979.
ANDERSON

Armstrong, Nancy, *Fans: A Collector's Guide*, 1984, London and Canada, 1990.

Avery, Charles, "Giuseppe de Levis of Verona, Bronze Founder and Sculptor." In *Studies in European Sculpture*, 45–78, London, 1981.

Avrin, Leila, "The Box Binding in the Klau Library Hebrew Union College," *Studies in Bibliography and Booklore*, 17 (1989): 27–35.

——, "The Sephardi Box Binding," *Scripta Hierosolymitana* 29 (1989): 27–43.

Baltimore, Maryland, The Jewish Historical Society, *Solomon Nunes Carvalho: Painter, Photographer, and Prophet in Nineteenth Century America*, exhibition catalogue, Elizabeth Berman, 1989.
BERMAN, CARVALHO

Barnett, R. D., *Catalogue of the Permanent and Loan Collections of the Jewish Museum, London*, London, 1974.
BARNETT

Belgrade, Jevrejski Istorijsk Muzej, *Vezene Tkanne iz Jevrejskin Zbirki u Jugoslavij*, exhibition catalogue, 1978.
VEZENE

Belinfante, Judith C. E., et al., *The Esnoga a monument to Portuguese-Jewish Culture*, Amsterdam, 1991.

Benjamin, Jonathan, "Ketubah Ornamentation in Nineteenth Century Eretz-Israel," *Israel Museum News*, 12, (1977): 129–137.
BENJAMIN, "KETUBAH ORNAMENTATION"

Berkeley, California, The Judah L. Magnes Museum, *Embellished Lives: Customs and Costumes of the Jewish Communities of Turkey*, exhibition catalogue, 1989.
MAGNES, EMBELLISHED

——, *Hanukkah Lamps of the Judah L. Magnes Museum*, Ruth Eis, 1977.
MAGNES, HANUKKAH LAMPS

——, *Ornamented Bags for Tallit and Tefillin*, Ruth Eis, 1984.
MAGNES, ORNAMENTED BAGS

——, The Judah L. Magnes Museum, *Threads of Time*, exhibition catalogue, Ruth Eis, 1978.
MAGNES, THREADS

Berman, Elizabeth Kessin, "Transcendentalism and Tradition: The Art of Solomon Nunes Carvalho," *JA*, 16/17 (1990/91): 64–81.

Berry, Burton Yost, "Old Turkish Towels —I, II," *The Art Bulletin*, 14 (1932): 344–358; 20 (1938): 251–265.
BERRY, "TOWELS I"; BERRY, "TOWELS II"

Besancenot, Jean, *Bijoux Arabes et Berberes du Maroc*, Casablanca, 1953.
BESANCENOT, BIJOUX

——, *Costumes of Morocco*, trans. Caroline Stone, 1988, London and New York, 1990.
BESANCENOT, COSTUMES

Beyer, R., *Die Königin von Saba, Engel un Damon Der Mythos einer Frau*, Cologne, 1978.

Bialer, Yehuda L., *Jewish Life in Art and Tradition*, New York, 1976.
BIALER

Biesboer, Pieter, "'Tulipa Turcarum' Über die 'Tulipomania' in Europa." In *Europa und der Orient 800–1900*, exhibition catalogue, Gereon Sievernich and Hendrik Budde, Berlin, 1989, 288–293.

Blum, Stella, ed., *Victorian Fashions & Costumes from "Harper's Bazaar": 1867–1898*, New York, 1974.
BLUM

Brilling, B., "Die Estehung der jüdischen Gemeinde in Emden (1570–1613)," *Westfallen Hefte für Geschichte, Kunst, und Volkskunde*, 51. Band, Heft 1–4 (1973).

Bryk, Nancy Villa, ed., *American Dress Pattern Catalogs, 1873–1909: Four Complete Reprints*, New York, 1988.
BRYK, PATTERNS

Carvalho, Solomon N., *Incidents of Travel and Adventure in the Far West*, int. Bertram Wallace Korn, Philadelphia, 1954.

Casanowicz, I. M., *Collections of Objects of Religious Ceremonial in the United States National Museum*, Smithsonian Institution United States National Museum Bulletin, 148; Washington, D.C., 1929.
CASANOWICZ

Castro, D. de, *Keur van Graafsteenen op de nederl.— Portug. Israel Begraafsplaats te Ouderkerk aan den Amstel*, Leiden, 1883.

Champault, Dominique, "Notes sur les Bijoux Tunisiens." In IM, *Jewellery*, 125–129.
CHAMPAULT, "BIJOUX"

Champault, D., and A. R. Verbrugge, *La main ses figurations au Maghreb et au Levant*, Paris, 1965.

Cotterel, H. H., A. Riff, and R. M. Vetter, *National Types of Old Pewter*, New York, 1972.

Cunnington, C. Willett, *English Women's Clothing in the Nineteenth Century*, 1937, New York, 1990.
CUNNINGTON

Dancheva-Blagoeva, Snezhana and Maria Veleva, *Bulgarian National Costumes and Folk Jewelry*, trans. Marguerite Alexieva, Sofia, n.d.
DANCHEVA-BLAGOEVA

Detroit, Institute of Arts, *Exhibition of Jewish Ceremonial Art*, 1951.

Ferrara, Palazzo dei Diamanti, Palazzo Paradisio, *Arte e Cultura Ebraiche in Emilia-Romagna*, exhibition catalogue, 1988–89.

Frankel, Giza, *Migzeirot Niyyar*, Givataim, 1983.

Friedenberg, Daniel M., *Jewish Medals from the Renaissance to the Fall of Napoleon (1503–1815)*, New York, 1970.
FRIEDENBERG, MEDALS

Fuks, L., and R. G. Fuks-Mansfeld, *Hebrew Typography in the Northern Netherlands 1585–1815*, I–II, Leyden, 1984–1987.
FUKS AND FUKS-MANSFELD

Furman, Jacobo, "A Glass Synagogue Lamp from Damascus," *JA* 12–13 (1986–87): 279–284.

Gargouri-Sethom, Samira, *Le bijoux traditionnel en Tunisie*, Aix-en-Provence, 1986.
GARGOURI-SETHOM

Garassimov, T. *Metal Work, Wrought Iron, Weapons and Pewter Vessels*, Sofia, 1983 (Bulgarian, with Russian and English summaries).

Gibbs-Smith, Charles H., *The Fashionable Lady in the 19th Century*, London, 1960.

Gotzman, Andreas, "Some Characteristics of Moroccan Jewish Jewelry," *JA*, 17 (1990/91): 12–19.
GOTZMANN, "JEWELRY"

Graham-Brown, Sarah, *Images of Women*, New York, 1988.

Grimwade, A. G., et al., *Treasures of a London Temple*, London, 1951.
GRIMWADE

Grossman, Cissy, "The Real Meaning of Eugène Delacroix's *Noce Juive Au Maroc*", *JA*, 14 (1988): 64–73.
GROSSMAN, "DELACROIX"

——, *A Temple Treasury: The Judaica Collection of Congregation Emanu-El of the City of New York*, New York, 1989.
GROSSMAN, TEMPLE

——, "'Womanly Arts' A Study of Italian Torah Binders in the New York Jewish Museum Collection," *JA*, 7 (1980): 35–43.

Grunwald, M., *Portugiesengräber auf Deutscher Erde, Beiträge zur Kultur und Kunstgeschichte*, Hamburg, 1902.

Gutmann, Joseph, "Jewish Participation in the Visual Arts of Eighteenth- and Nineteenth-Century America," *American Jewish Archives*, April, 1963: 21–57.
GUTMANN, "VISUAL ARTS"

——, "The Illuminated Medieval Passover Haggadah—Investigations and Research Problems," *Studies in Bibliography and Booklore*, VII (1965): 3–24.

——, *The Jewish Life Cycle*, Leiden, 1987

La Haggada de Bordeaux, facsimile, int. Alfred Moldovan, Paris, 1987.

Hartt, Frederick, *History of Italian Renaissance Art*, New York, n.d.

Hasson, Rachel, *Later Islamic Jewellery*, Jerusalem, 1987.
HASSON, JEWELLERY

Hayward, J., *Virtuoso Goldsmiths, 1540–1629*, London, 1976.

Held, Robert, *Inquisition: A bilingual Guide to the exhibition of Torture Instruments from the Middle Ages to the Industrial Era presented in various European cities*, New York, 1987.
HELD, INQUISITION

Hernmarck, C., *The Art of the European Silversmith, 1430–1830*, London, 1977.

Hildburgh, W. L., "Images of the Human Hand as Amulets in Spain," *The Warburg and Courtauld Institutes Journal*, 18 (1955): 67–89.

Jerusalem, The Israel Museum, *Amanut ve-Omanut be-Eretz Yisrael be-Meah ha-19*, exhibition catalogue, 1979.
IM, AMANUT

——, *Architecture in the Hanukkah Lamp*, exhibition catalogue, Suzanne Landau, 1978.
IM, ARCHITECTURE

——, *Jewish Tradition in Art: The Feuchtwanger Collection of Judaica*, Jerusalem, 1971.
IM, FEUCHTWANGER

——, *Jewellery and Goldsmithing in the Islamic World*, International Symposium, 1987, ed., Na'ama Brosh, Jerusalem, 1991.
IM, JEWELLERY

——, *Jewish Treasures from Paris, From the Collection of the Cluny Museum and the Consistoire*, exhibition catalogue, 1982.
IM, PARIS

——, *Sephardi Jews in The Ottoman Empire*, exhibition catalogue, Esther Juhasz, ed., 1990.
IM, OTTOMAN

——, *La vie juive au Maroc*, exhibition catalogue, Aviva Müller-Lancet and Dominique Champault, eds., 1986.
IM, MAROC

——, *From the Secular to the Sacred*, exhibition catalogue, 1985.
IM, SECULAR

——, *The Stieglitz Collection. Masterpieces of Jewish Art*. Chaya Benjamin, exhibition catalogue, 1987.
IM, STIEGLITZ

Jerusalem, The Jewish National and University Library, *Treasures from the Ets Haim/Livraria Montezinos of the Portugees Israëlietisch Seminarium Ets Haim, Amsterdam*, exhibition catalogue, 1980.
JNUL, ETS HAIM

Jacobs, Joseph and Lucien Wolf, *The Catalogue of the Anglo-Jewish Historical Exhibition*, London, 1887.

Jewish Art, formerly the *Journal of Jewish Art*,
JA; JJA

Johnstone, Pauline, *Turkish Embroidery*, London, 1985.
JOHNSTONE

Juhasz, Esther, "Costume," in IM, *Ottoman*, 120–171.
JUHASZ, "COSTUME"

——, "The Custom of Serving Sweets among the Jews of Izmir," trans. R. Grafman, *The Israel Museum News*, 15 (1979): 72–79.
JUHASZ, "SWEETS"

——, "Marriage," in IM, *Ottoman*, 196–217.
JUHASZ, "MARRIAGE"

——, "Textiles for the Home and Synagogue," in IM, *Ottoman*, 64–119.
JUHASZ, "TEXTILES"

Les Juifs de Tunisie, Paris: Editions du Scribe, 1989.

Kaniel, Michael, *Judaism*, Dorset, 1979.

Kayser, Stephen S., and Guido Schoenberger, eds., *Jewish Ceremonial Art*, rev. ed., Philadelphia, 1959.
KAYSER AND SCHOENBERGER

Keen, Michael E., *Jewish Ritual Art in the Victoria & Albert Museum*, London, 1991.

Kelbaugh, Ross, "A Visit to Carvalho's Gallery of Fine Arts." In Berman, *Carvalho*, 33–36.
KELBAUGH

Kirin, Vladimir, *Narodni Plesovi Jugoslavije*, costume plates, Costume Institute, The Metropolitan Museum, 1965.

Klagsbald, Victor, *Catalogue raisonné de la collection juive de la musée de Cluny*, Paris, 1981.

——, "Un plaque de Torah antique," *JA*, 6 (1979): 127–132.

Korn, Bertram Wallace, "Some Additional Notes on the Life and Work of Solomon Nunes Carvalho," *The Seventy-Fifth Anniversary Volume of the Jewish Quarterly Review*, Philadelphia, 1967.

Krinsky, Carol Herselle, *Synagogues of Europe*, New York, 1985.
KRINSKY

Kühnel, Ernst, *The Minor Arts of Islam*, trans. Katherine Watson, 1963, New York, 1970.
KÜHNEL

Kybalová, Ludmilla, Olga Herbenová, and Milena Lamarová, *The Pictorial Encyclopedia of Fashion*, trans. Claudia Rosoux, New York, 1968.
KYBALOVÁ, HERBENOVÁ AND LAMAROVÁ

Landsberger, Franz, *Rembrandt, The Jews and the Bible*, trans. Felix N. Gerson, Philadelphia, 1972.
LANDSBERGER

Leaf, William, and Sally Purcell, *Heraldic Symbols: Islamic Insignia and Western Heraldry*, London, 1986.

Leeser, Isaac, "Native Jewish Talent," *The Occident and American Jewish Advocate*, 10 (1853): 500–505.

Lewis, Raphaela, *Everyday Life in Ottoman Turkey*, New York, 1971.
LEWIS

Mackie, Louise W., "Rugs and Textiles." In *Turkish Art*, ed. Esin Atil, 298–373. Washington D.C. and New York, 1980.
MACKIE

Maslin, Judith B., *An Analysis of Jewish Ceremonial Objects of Congregation Mikve Israel-Emanuel, Curaçao, Netherlands Antilles; Dutch Silver: 1700–1800*, Master's thesis, University of Chicago, 1980.

Massil, S. W., and Ruth Winston-Fox, *Sir Moses Montefiore 1784–1885*, Enfield, England, 1984.

Micklewright, Nancy, "Late Nineteenth-Century Ottoman Wedding Costumes as Indicators of Social Change," *Muqarnas*, 6 (1989): 161–174.
MICKLEWRIGHT, "COSTUMES"

——, "Tracing the Transformations in Women's Dress in Nineteenth Century Istanbul," *Dress*, 13 (1987): 33–43.
MICKLEWRIGHT, "TRANSFORMATIONS"

Montreal, Canada, The Jewish Public Library, *Planets, Potions and Parchments*, exhibition catalogue, Barry Levy, 1990.

Morgenstein, Susan W., and Ruth E. Levine, *The Jews in the age of Rembrandt*, Rockville, Maryland, 1981.
MORGENSTEIN AND LEVINE

Muller, Priscilla E., *Jewels in Spain 1500–1800*, New York, 1972.
MULLER

Müller-Jürgens, G., *Vasa Sacra: Altargeräte in Ostfriesland*, Aurich, 1960.

Müller-Lancet, Aviva, "Elements in Costume and Jewellery Specific to the Jews of Morocco," *The Israel Museum News*, 11 (1976): 47–66.

MÜLLER-LANCET, "COSTUME AND JEWELLERY"

——, "Some Motifs in Moroccan Jewellery." In IM, *Jewellery*, 113–124.

MÜLLER-LANCET, "MOTIFS"

Narkiss, Bezalel, "The Gerona Hanukkah Lamp—Fact and Fiction," *JA*, 14 (1988): 6–15.

——, "Oriental Esther Scroll Cases," *Sefer Hamoadim*, VI, Tel Aviv, 1956 (Hebrew).

Narkiss, Bezalel, Bracha Yaniv and Yael Zirlin, *Gross Family Collection*, Index of Jewish Art, ed., Joe Lockard, Jerusalem, 1985 (2 volumes).

IJA, GROSS

Narkiss, Mordecai, *The Hanukkah Lamp*, Jerusalem, 1939 (Hebrew, English summary).

——, "Yetzirato shel Salom B'KMR Italia (1619–1655?)", *Tarbiz* 25 (1956): 441–451; 26 (1957): 87–101.

M. NARKISS, "SALOM ITALIA"

New York, Fraunces Tavern Museum, *The Jewish Community in Early New York 1654–1800*, exhibition brochure, Ellin Burke, 1979.

New York, The Jewish Museum, *Le-Hayyim—To Life! Cups of Sanctification and Celebration*, exhibition brochure, Susan L. Braunstein, 1984.

NYJM, CUPS

——, *Fabric Of Jewish Life. Textiles from the Jewish Museum Collection.*, exhibition catalogue, Barbara Kirshenblatt-Gimblett and Cissy Grossman, 1977.

NYJM, FABRIC

——, *Gardens and Ghettos: The Art of Jewish Life in Italy*, exhibition catalogue, Vivian B. Mann, ed., 1989.

NYJM, GARDENS

——, *The Mamluk Revival: Metalwork for Religious and Domestic Use*, exhibition brochure, Estelle Whelan, 1981.

NYJM, MAMLUK

——, *Personal Vision: The Furman Collection of Jewish Ceremonial Art*, exhibition catalogue, Susan L. Braunstein, 1985.

——, *A Tale of Two Cities: Jewish Life in Frankfurt and Istanbul 1750–1870*, exhibition catalogue, Vivian B. Mann, 1982.

NYJM, TALE

——, *Treasures of The Jewish Museum*, exhibition catalogue, Vivian B. Mann and Norman L. Kleeblatt, 1986.

NYJM, TREASURES

New York, The Metropolitan Museum of Art, *In Style. Celebrating Fifty Years of the Costume Institute*, The Metropolitan Museum of Art Bulletin, Jean L. Drusedow, Fall 1987.

IN STYLE

New York, Metropolitan Museum of Art and Washington D.C., National Museum of American Art Smithsonian Institution, *Tokens of Affection: The Portrait Miniature in America*, exhibition brochure, Robin Bolton-Smith and Dale T. Johnson, 1990.

New York, Pierpont Morgan Library, *Hebraica from the Valmadonna Trust*, exhibition catalogue, Brad Sabin Hill, 1989.

New York, Yeshiva University Museum, *Ashkenaz: The German Jewish Heritage*, exhibition catalogue, Gertrude Hirschler, ed., 1988.

YUM, ASHKENAZ

——, *The Jewish Wedding*, exhibition catalogue, Shlomo Pappenheim, 1977.

YUM, WEDDING

——, *Mordecai Manuel Noah: First American Jew*, exhibition catalogue, Abraham J. Karp, New York, 1987.

YUM, NOAH

——, *Purim: The Face and The Mask*, exhibition catalogue, Shifra Epstein, 1979.

YUM, PURIM

Oman, C., *The Golden Age of Hispanic Silver, 1400–1665*, London, 1968.

Palotay, Gertrude von, "Turkish Embroideries," *Ciba Review*, 102 (1954): 3658–3683.

VON PALOTAY

——, "Embroidery on velvet, silk and leather," *Ciba Review*, 102 (1954): 3677–3680.

——, "Turkish Linen Embroidery," *Ciba Review*, 102 (1954): 3658–3664.

——, "Motives and Composition," *Ciba Review*, 102 (1954): 3665–3672.

Pape, Maria Elisabeth, "Turquerie Im 18. Jahrhundert und der 'Recueil Ferriol'." In *Europa und der Orient 800–1900*, 305–323, exhibition catalogue, Gereon Sievernich and Hendrik Budde, Berlin, 1989.

Petsopoulos, Yanni, ed., *Tulips, Arabesques & Turbans*, New York, 1982.

Philadelphia, National Museum of American Jewish History, *Kahal Kadosh Mikveh Israel: Congregation and Community*, exhibition catalogue, 1984.

NMAJH

Radojkovic, B., *Phylaktarien Enamluks Patrontaschen*, Belgrade, 1947 (Serbian, German summary).

——, "Srpsko zlatarstvo XVI:XVII veka." (Serbian Goldsmith's Art in the 16th and 17th centuries) In *Matica Srpska Odelnje za Likorne umethnati (Studije za istorijie srpske umetnosti.3.*

(Studies in Serbian Art History). Novi Sad, 1966 (in Serbian).

Ramsy, L.G.G., ed., *The Complete Encyclopedia of Antiques*, 1962, New York, 1968.

Reilly, James M., *Care and Identification of 19th Century Photographic Prints*, USA, 1986.

Rose, Clare, *Children's Clothes Since 1750*, New York, London, 1989.
ROSE

Rosen-Ayalon, Myriam, "The Islamic Jewellery from Ashkelon." In IM, *Jewellery*, 9–19.
ROSEN-AYALON, "ASHKELON"

Rosenbaum, J. W., *Myer Myers, Goldsmith*, Philadelphia, 1954.
ROSENBAUM, MYER MYERS

Roth, Cecil, "Judah Abenzara's Map of the Mediterranean World, 1500," *Studies in Bibliography and Booklore*, 9 (1970): 2–3.

——, ed., *The Casale Pilgrim, a Sixteenth-Century Illustrated Guide to the Holy Places*, facsimile, London, 1929.

——, "The Lord Mayor's Salvers," *The Connoisseur*, 96 (1935): 246–299.

Rouach, David, *Bijoux berbères au maroc dans la tradition Judéo-Arabe*, Corbevoie, 1989.
ROUACH

Rubens, Alfred, *A History of Jewish Costume*, New York, 1967.
RUBENS, COSTUME, 1967

——, *A History of Jewish Costume*, New York, rev. ed. 1973.
RUBENS, COSTUME, 1973

——, *A Jewish Iconography*, London, rev. ed. 1981.
RUBENS, ICONOGRAPHY, 1981

Russo-Katz, Miriam, "Childbirth," in IM, *Ottoman*, 254–280.
RUSSO-KATZ, "CHILDBIRTH"

Sabar, Shalom, "The Beginnings of *Ketubbah* Decoration in Italy: Venice in the Late Sixteenth to the Early Seventeenth Centuries," *JA*, 12/13 (1986–87): 96–110.

——, "Decorated *Ketubbot*," in IM, *Ottoman*, 218–237.
SABAR, "DECORATED *KETUBBOT*"

——, "The Golden Age of *Ketubah* Decoration in Venice and Amsterdam." In Joods, *The Ghetto*.
SABAR, "THE GOLDEN AGE"

——, *Ketubbah. Jewish Marriage Contracts of the Hebrew Union College Skirball Museum and Klau Library*, Philadelphia, New York, 1990.
SABAR, KETUBBAH

——, "The Use and Meaning of Christian Motifs in Illustrations of Jewish Marriage Contracts in Italy," *JJA*, 10 (1984): 47–63.

Scarce, Jennifer, *Women's Costume of the Near and Middle East*, London, Sydney, 1987.
SCARCE

Schliemann, E., *Die Goldschmiede Hamburgs*, Hamburg, 1985.

Schoenberger, Guido, "The Ritual Silver Made by Myer Myers," *American Jewish Historical Society*, 43 (1953): 1–9.
SCHOENBERGER, "MYER MYERS"

Shadur, Yehudit and Joseph, "Three Papercuts from Jerusalem," *JA* 16/17 (1990/91): 6–11.

Shinar, Pessah, "Magic and Symbolism in North-African Jewellery and Personal Adornment." In IM, *Jewellery*, 131–146.
SHINAR, "MAGIC"

Sieberg, "Stadt Emden," *Die Kunstdenkmäler der Provinc Hannover* VI, no. 1,2, Hanover, 1927.

Sijelmassi, Dr. Mohamed, *Lew Arts Traditionnels au Maroc*, Paris, 1986.
SIJELMASSI

Stavroulakis, Nicolas, "Preziosi's Jews," *The Jewish Museum of Greece Newsletter*, 24, Spring 1988: 5.

——, *Sephardi & Romaniot Jewish Costumes in Greece & Turkey*, Athens: The Jewish Museum of Greece, 1988.
STAVROULAKIS

Stillman, Yedida K., "The Costume of the Jewish Women in Morocco," *Studies in Jewish Folklore*, Frank Talmage, ed., Cambridge, Mass., 1980.
STILLMAN, "COSTUME"

——, "Hashpaat Sephardit al ha-tarbut ha-homrit shel Yehudei Maroco." In *Moreshet Yehudei Sepharad ve-ha-Mizrah Mehkarim*, 361–366, I. Ben Ami, ed., Jerusalem, 1982.
STILLMAN, "HASHPAAT"

Sturhahn, Joan, *Carvalho: Potrait of a Forgotten American*, New York, 1976.

Tezcan, Hülye, and Selma Delibas, *The Topkapi Saray Museum: Costumes, Embroideries and other Textiles*, trans. J. M. Rogers, Boston, 1986.
TEZCAN AND DELIBAS

Thornton, Lynne, "Frauenbilder zur Malerei der 'Orientalisten'." In *Europa und der Orient 800–1900*, exhibition catalogue, Gereon Sievernich and Hendrik Budde, Berlin, 1989, 342–367.

Turin, Archivi de arte e cultura Piemontesi, *Ebrei a Torino: Ricerche per il centenario della sinagoge, 1884–1984*, 1984.

Veleva, Maria, and Snezhana Dancheva-Blagoeva, *Bulgarian National Costumes and Folk Jewellery*, trans. Marguerite Alexieva, Sofia, n.d.

Voet, E., *Merken van Amsterdamsche Goud- en Zilversmeden*, The Hague, 1912 (Dutch).

Washington, D.C., Library of Congress, *From the Ends of the Earth: Judaic Treasures of the Library of*

Congress, exhibition catalogue, Abraham J. Karp, 1991.

Weinstein, Jay, *A Collectors' Guide to Judaica*, New York, 1985.
WEINSTEIN

Weinstein, Rochelle, *Sepulchral Monuments of the Jews of Amsterdam in the Seventeenth and Eighteenth Centuries*, Ph.D. diss., New York University, 1979.

Wilcox, R. Turner, *The Dictionary of Costume*, New York, 1969.
WILCOX

Wischnitzer, Rachel, "Ezra Stiles and the Portrait of Menasseh Ben Israel," *From Dura to Rembrandt: Studies in the History of Art*, Jerusalem, 1990, 125–129.
WISCHNITZER, "MENASSEH BEN ISRAEL"

Yaari, A., *Bibliographia shel haggadot Pesah*, Jerusalem, 1960.
YAARI, HAGGADOT

Yaniv, Bracha, "The Origin of the 'Two-Column Motif' in European *Parokhot*," *JA* 15 (1989): 26–43.

Yarwood, Doreen, *The Encyclopedia of World Costume*, 1978, New York, 1986.
YARWOOD

Zagreb, Muzejski prostor, *Jews in Yugoslavia*, exhibition catalogue, 1989.

Zagreb, Muzejski prostor, *Zidovi na tlu Jugoslavije*, 1988.
JUGOSLAVIJE

II. HISTORY AND LITERATURE

Alkalay, A., *Dichos i refranes sefaradies*, Jerusalem, 1984.

Andrada, J.A.P.M., *A Record of the Jews in Jamaica from the English Conquest to the Present Time*, Kingston, 1941.

Angel, Marc D., "The Planting of Sephardic Culture in North America." In *The Sephardim: A Cultural Journey from Spain to the Pacific Coast*, Portland, Oregon, 1987.

——, *The Rhythms of Jewish Living: A Sephardic Approach*, New York, 1986.

——, *Voices in Exile: A Study in Sephardic Intellectual History*, Hoboken, 1991.

Ashton, Dianne, "Grace Aguilar's Popular Theology and the Female Response to Evangelists," *Jewish Folklore and Ethnology Review*, 12 (1990): 22.

Azulai, H.Y.D., *Avodat da-Kodesh*, Warsaw, 1879.

Balleti, A., *Gli Ebrei e gli Estensi*, rev. ed., Bologna, 1969.

Barnai, J., "Jewish Guilds in Turkey in the Sixteenth to Nineteenth Centuries." In *Jews in Economic Life: Collected Essays in Memory of Arkadius Kahan (1920–1982)*, ed., N. Gross, Jerusalem, 1985 (Hebrew).

Barnett, R. D., *Bevis Marks Records*, I, Oxford, 1940.

Barnett, R. D., and W. M. Schwab, eds., *The Sephardi Heritage*, Grendon, Northants, 1989.

Beinart, Haim, "The Jews in the Canary Islands: a Reevaluation," *TJHSE*, 25 (1977): 48–86.

——, "Sephardi Settlement in Savoy," In *Scritti in Memori di Leone Carpi*, D. Carpi et al., eds., Jerusalem, 1967, 72–118 (Hebrew).

Benazeraf, R., *Refranero, Recueil de Proverbs Judeo-Espagnols du Maroc*, Paris, 1975.

Benayahu, M., "The Great Fires in Izmir and Adrianople," *Reshumot* 2 n. s. (1946): 144–154 (Hebrew).

——, *Rabbi H.Y.D. Azulai*, Jerusalem, 1959.

Bentov, Hayyim, "Shitat Limud ha-Talmud be-Yeshivot Saloniki ve-Turkiah," *Sefunot*, 13 (1970/71): 5–102.

Benvenisti, D., *Hebrew Words in Judeo-Spanish*, Jerusalem, 1984 (Hebrew).

Berg, J. van den, *Juden en Christenen in Nederland gedurende de zeventiende eeuw*, Kampen, 1962.

Cahen, A., "Les Juifs de la Martinique au xviiè siècle," *Revue des Études Juives* 3 (1983): 93–122.

Cantera, F., and J. M. Millas, *Las inscripciones hebraicas de Espana*, Madrid, 1956.

Cassuto, M. D., *The Jews of Florence in the Renaissance*, Jerusalem, 1967 (Hebrew).

——, "Die portugiesischen Juden in Glückstadt," *Jahrbuch der jüdisch-literarischen Gesellschaft* 21 (1930): 287–317.

Chouraqui, A. N., *Between East and West: A History of the Jews in North Africa*, New York, 1973.

Cirot, G., *Recherches sur les Juifs espagnols et portugais à Bordeaux*, Part I, Bordeaux, 1908.

Cohen, R., *The Jewish Nation in Surinam — Historical Essays*, Amsterdam, 1982.

Confanton, Yitzhak, *Darkhei ha-Talmud*, Jerusalem, 1980/81.

Cooperman, B. D., *Trade and Settlement: The Establishment and Early Development of the Jewish Communities in Leghorn and Pisa (1591–1626)*, Ph.D. diss., Harvard University, 1976.

Croutier, Alev Lytle, *Harem: The World Behind the Veil*, New York, 1989.
CROUTIER

Dan, Joseph, *Jewish Mysticism and Jewish Ethics*, Seattle, 1985.

Diamond, A. S., "The Community of the Resettlement, 1656–1684; A Social Survey," *TJHSE* 24 (1974): 134–150.

Dobrinsky, Herbert C., *A Treasury of Sephardic Customs*, Hoboken, 1988.
DOBRINSKY

Emmanuel, I. S., *Precious Stones of the Jews of Curaçao: Curaçaoan Jewry 1656–1975*, New York, 1975.

Emmanuel, I. S. and S. A., *History of the Netherlands Antilles*, I–II, Cincinnati, 1970.

Encyclopaedia Judaica, Jerusalem, 1971.

    EJ

Federation of Jewish Communities in Yugoslavia, *Proverbs and Sayings of the Sephardi Jews of Bosnia and Herzegovina*, Belgrade, 1976.

Galimir, M., *Proverbios*, USA, 1951.

Gans, Mozes Heiman, *Memorbook. History of Dutch Jewry from the Renaissance to 1940*, trans. Arnold J. Pomerans, Baarn, Netherlands, 1977.

    GANS, MEMORBOOK

Gaon, M. D., *Spices from Spain*, Jerusalem, 1989 (Hebrew).

Gaon, S., *Minhath Shelomo: A Commentary on the Book of Prayer of the Spanish and Portuguese Jews*, New York, 1990.

Hacker, Yosef, "Lidmutam ha-Ruhanit shel Yehudei Sefarad be-Sof ha-Meah he-Hamesh Esre," *Sefunot* 17 (1972/73): 47ff.

Hyamson, A. M., *The Sephardim of England*, London, 1951.

Ibn Migash, Abraham, *Kevod Elohim*, Jerusalem, 1976/77.

Israel, J. I., "The Economic Contribution of Dutch Sephardi Jewry to Holland's Golden Age, 1595–1713," *Tijdschrift voor Geschiedenis* 96 (1983): 505–535.

——, "Menasseh Ben Israel and the Dutch Sephardic Colonization Movement of the Mid-Seventeenth Century (1645–1657)." In *Menasseh Ben Israel and his World*, ed., Y. Kaplan et al., Leyden, 1989, 139–163.

——, "Sephardic Immigration into the Dutch Republic," *Studia Rosenthaliana*, special issue published together with volume 23, (1989).

——, "Spain and the Dutch Sephardim, 1609–1660," *Studia Rosenthaliana* 12 (1978): 1–61.

Kaplan, Y., *From Christianity to Judaism. The Story of Isaac Orobio de Castro*, Oxford, 1989.

——, "The Portuguese Community in Amsterdam in the Seventeenth Century, between Tradition and Change," *Proceedings of the Israel Academy of Science and Humanities*, Vol. 7 (1988): 161–181 (Hebrew).

——, et al., ed., *Menasseh Ben Israel and his World*, Leyden, 1989.

Katz, D. S., "The Abendana Brothers and the Christian Hebraists of Seventeenth Century England," *Journal of Ecclesiastical History* 40 (1989): 28–52.

——, *Philo-Semitism and the Readmission of the Jews to England 1603–1655*, Oxford, 1982.

Katz, D. S., and J. I. Israel, eds., *Sceptics, Millenarians and Jews*, Leiden, 1990.

Kayserling, M., *Biblioteca Española Portugueza Judaica*, Strasbourg, 1890.

Kellenbenz, H., *Sephardim an der unteren Elbe*, Wiesbaden, 1958.

Koen, E. M., "The Earliest Sources Relating to the Portuguese Jews in the Municipal Archives of Amsterdam up to 1620," *Studia Rosenthaliana* 5 (1970): 25–42.

Kolonomós, Z., *Proverbs, Sayings and Tales of the Sephardi Jews of Macedonia*, Belgrade, 1978.

Léon, H., *Histoire des Juifs de Bayonne* (Paris, 1893), Marseilles, 1975.

Leoni, A. Di-Leone, "Gli ebrei sefarditi a Ferrara da Ercole I a Ercole II; nuove ricerche e interpretazione," *La Rassegna Mensile di Israel* 52 (1986): 406–43.

Levy, I. J., *The Study of the Refranero Sefardi*, New York, 1969.

Malvézin, T., *Histoire de Juifs à Bordeaux*, rev. ed., Marseilles, 1967.

Marwedel, G., *Die Privilegien der Juden in Altona*, Hamburg, 1976.

Méchoulan, H., *Hispanidad y Judaismo en Tiempos de Espinoza. Edición de 'La Certeza del Cemino' de Abraham Pereyra*, Salamanca, 1987.

Michman, J., ed., *Dutch Jewish History* II, Jerusalem, 1989.

Modona, L., "Les exilés d'Espagne à Ferrare en 1493," *Revue des Études Juives* 15 (1887): 117–21.

Molho, M., *Usos y costumbres de los Sephardies de Salonica*, Madrid, 1950.

Moscona, I., *Phiné Sfarad*, Tel-Aviv, 1981.

Nahon, G., *Les "Nations" juifs portugaises du Sud-Ouest de la France (1648–1791), Documents*, Paris, 1981.

——, "The Sephardim of France." In *The Sephardi Heritage*, Vol. II, R. D. Barnett and W. M. Schwab, eds., Grendon, Northants, 1989, 46–74.

Oppenheim, S., "The Early History of the Jews in New York, 1654–1664. Some New Matter on the Subject," *Proceedings of the American Jewish Historical Society* 18 (1909): 1–91.

——, "An Early Jewish Colony in Western Guiana, 1658–1666, and its Relation to the Jews in Surinam, Cayenne and Tobago," *Proceedings of the American Jewish Historical Society* 16 (1907): 95–186; 17 (1908): 53–70.

Pick, Christopher, ed., *Embassy to Constantinople. The Travels of Lady Mary Wortley Montagu*, London, 1988.

    PICK

Pieterse, W. C., *350 jaar Dotar, Santa Companhia de Dotar Orphas e Donzellas*, Amsterdam, 1965 (Dutch, English summary).

Pohl, H., *Die Portugiesen in Antwerpen (1567–1648). Zur Geschichte einer Minderheit*, Wiesbaden, 1977.

Popkin, R. H., "Menasseh ben Israel and Isaac La Peyr," *Studia Rosenthaliana* 8 (1964): 59–63.

Pullan, B., *The Jews of Europe and the Inquisition of Venice, 1550–1670*, Oxford, 1983.

Ravid, B., *Economics and Toleration in Seventeenth-Century Venice*, Jerusalem, 1978.

——, "The First Charter of the Jewish Merchants of Venice, 1589," *American Jewish Studies Review* 1 (1976): 187–222.

——, "The Religious, Economic and Social Background and Context of the Establishment of the Ghetti of Venice," in *Gli Ebrei a Venezia secoli xiv–xvii*, Milan, 1987, 727–770.

Remedios, M. dos, *Os Judeus Portugueses em Amsterdam*, Coimbra, 1911.

Revah, I. S., "Les marranes," *Revue des Études Juives* 118 (1959–1960): 29–77.

——, *Spinoza et le Dr. Juan de Prado*, Paris and The Hague, 1959.

Rophe, Yitzhak, "Benevolent Society of the Boat-Owners in Constantinople," *Sefunot* 10 (1966): 621–632 (Hebrew).

Silva Rosa, J. S. da, *Geschiedenis der Portugeesche Joden te Amsterdam 1593–1925*, Amsterdam, 1925.

——, *Die Spanischen und Portugiesischen Gedruckten Judaica in der Bibliothek des Jud. Portug. Seminars 'Ets Haim' in Amsterdam*, Amsterdam, 1933.

Roth, Cecil. *A History of the Marranos*, Philadelphia, 1932.

——, *The Jews in the Renaissance*, New York, 1959.

——, *The History of the Jews in Venice*, rev. ed., New York, 1975.

Salomon, H. P., *Os primeiros portugueses de Amsterdao*, Braga, 1982.

——, *Saul Levi Mortera en zijn "Traktaat betreffende de Waarheid van de Wet van Mozes,"* Braga, 1988.

——, "Two Elegies on the Expulsion of the Jews from Spain." *The Sephardic Scholar*, series 3, 1977–78: 37–47.

Samuel, E. R., "The First Fifty Years." In *Three Centuries of Anglo-Jewish History*, V. D. Lipman, ed., Cambridge, 1961, 27–44.

Samuel, W. S., "The First London Synagogue of the Re-Settlement," *TJHSE* 10 (1924): 1–147.

——, "A Review of the Jewish Colonists in Barbados in the Year 1680," *TJHSE* 13 (1932–35): i–iii.

Saperstein, M., "Martyrs, Merchants and Rabbis: Jewish Communal Conflict as Reflected in the Responsa on the Boycott of Ancona," *Jewish Social Studies* 43 (1981): 215–28.

Saporta y Beja, Enrique, *Refranes de los Judios Sefardis*, Barcelona, 1978.

Schechter, Solomon, "Safed in the 16th Century," *Studies in Judaism*, second series, Philadelphia, 1908.

Scholem, G., *Abraham Koen Herrera's "Puerta del Cielo," His Life, His Work, and Its Influence*, Tel Aviv, 1974 (Hebrew).

Schwarzfuchs, S., ed., *Le Registre des Délibérations de la Nation Juive Portugaise de Bordeaux (1711–1787)*, Paris, 1981.

Segre, R., "Nuovi documenti sui marrani d'Ancona (1555–1559)," *Michael* 9 (1985): 130–233.

Serels, Mitchell, *A History of the Jews in Tangier in the 19th and 20th Centuries*. New York, 1991.

Sola, D. A. de, *The Ancient Melodies of the Liturgy of the Spanish and Portuguese Jews*, London, 1867.

Sonne, I., "Une source nouvelle pour l'histoire des martyrs d'Ancone," *Revue des Études Juives* 89 (1930): 360–80.

Swetschinski, D. M., *The Portuguese Jewish Merchants of Seventeenth-Century Amsterdam: A Social Profile*, Ph.D. diss., Brandeis University, 1979.

Toaff, A., "Cenni storici sulla communitá ebraica e sulla sinagoga di Livorno," *La Rassegna Mensile di Israel* 21 (1955): 345–59.

——, "L'Universitas Hebraeorum Portugallensium' di Ancona del Cinquecento; Interessi economici e ambiguita religiosa." In *Mercati, Mercanti denaro nelle Marche (secoli xiv–xix), Atti e Memorie della Deputazione di Storia Patira per le Marche* 87 (1982): 115–45.

——, "Nuova luce sui' Marrani di Ancona (1556)." In *Studi sull'Ebraismo Italiano in memoria de Cecil Roth*, Rome, 1974, 261–80.

——, "Statuti e Leggi della 'Nazione Ebrea' di Livorno—I. Gli Statuti del 1655," *La Rassegna Mensile di Israel* 34 (1968): suppl.: 1–51.

——, "II. La Legislazione dal 1655 al 1677," *La Rassegna Mensile di Israel* 38 (1972) suppl.: 1–68.

Transactions of the Jewish Historical Society of England. TJHSE

Weinberger, Philip, *The Social and Religious Thought of Grace Aguilar*, Ph.D. diss., New York University, 1970.

Wiznitzer, A., "The Exodus from Brazil and Arrival in New Amsterdam of the Jewish Pilgrim Fathers 1654," *Proceedings of the American Jewish Historical Society* 10 (1954–55): 80–97.

——, *Jews in Colonial Brazil*, New York, 1960.

——, *The Records of the Earliest Jewish Community in the New World*, New York, 1954.

Wolf, L., "Crypto-Jews under the Common-wealth," *TJHSE* 1 (1893–94): 55–99.

———, "The First English Jew," *TJHSE* 2 (1894–95): 14–46.

———, "The Problems of the First Jewish Settlers in New Amsterdam 1654," *Studia Rosenthaliana* 15 (1981): 169–77.

Yerushalmi, Yosef Hayyim, *From Spanish Court to Italian Ghetto: Isaac Cardoso, a Study in Seventeenth-Century Marranism and Jewish Apologetics*, New York and London, 1971.

Zimmels, H. J., "The Contribution of the Sephardim to the Responsa Literature Till the Beginning of the 16th Century." In *The Sephardi Heritage*, ed., Richard Barnett, New York, 1971.

"Dressing up" in the Sephardic costume workshop.

INDEX

PHOTO CREDITS

THE SEPHARDIC JOURNEY: 1492–1992
has been typeset, printed and bound by
The Stinehour Press in Lunenburg, Vermont.
The typefaces are Sistina and Bembo.
The paper is Warren Lustro Dull 80 pound text.
Production supervision by Marlene Polson.
Design by Jerry Kelly.

YESHIVA
UNIVERSITY
MUSEUM